HISTORIC PEMBROKESHIRE HOMES AND THEIR FAMILIES

EXTENDED EDITION

Previous publications by Francis Jones

HISTORY OF THE 172 FIELD REGIMENT
HISTORY OF THE SURREY YEOMANRY QMR
THE HOLY WELLS OF WALES
THE PRINCIPALITY AND PRINCES OF WALES
GOD BLESS THE PRINCE OF WALES
AN APPROACH TO WELSH GENEALOGY
AN APPROACH TO WELSH HERALDRY
HISTORIC CARMARTHENSHIRE HOMES AND THEIR FAMILIES
HISTORIC HOUSES OF PEMBROKESHIRE AND THEIR FAMILIES
TREASURY OF HISTORIC PEMBROKESHIRE
HISTORIC CARDIGANSHIRE HOMES AND THEIR FAMILIES

PENBROKSHYRE described AND THE SITTUATIONS both of PENBROKE and St DAVIDS shewed in due form as they were taken by John Speed
PART OF CARDIGAN
PART OF CARMARDEN SHIRE
SAINT DAVIDS
Cardigan
Keven Bryn
Capel Laughrid
Tyvy flud
Kennarth
Kilgarren Cast.
Manerdue
Capel Kiluaure
Brydelthe
Llanyhangle penbedo
Capel Colman
KILLGARRAN HUND.
Penrith
Eglosserron
Malenay
Nantgwin
Capel Kestellan
Kilryden
Cledye
Whitchurch
Kilgwyn
HUNDRED
Wrenny vair hill
Llanunnach
Clethy flud
Monachlogdee
Llangludwen
Llangolman
Maencloghay
Kilymanelloyd
Lannakeuen
Bletherston
Llanfilio
Castle Deram
Egremond
Llandewye
Llanbeder Velfray
Llanhaddon
Bobeston
Creno
Clethy flud
Narbarth cast.
Narbarth
Cast Meherye hill
Redcastle
Templeton
Newton
Crunuejer
Dynnaston
Earware
NERBERTH
Amrath
Redmalston
Begely
St Issels
Jeffrayston
Williamston chap
HUND
Redhart
Carow Cast.
Tenbye
St Florence
Trelloyne
Pennalye
Caldey Island
Northard
Iameston
Ludsop
Ludsop poynt
Fresh Water
Stackpoole
The Scale of Pases
Jodocus Hondius caelavit

Dedicated to the memory of

Francis Jones and his wife Ethel

Major Francis Jones, Wales Herald at Arms and his wife, Ethel.
Preparations for the Knights of the Garter ceremony at Windsor Castle.

THE FRANCIS JONES

HISTORIC PEMBROKESHIRE HOMES

AND THEIR FAMILIES

EXTENDED EDITION

From the Archives, articles, manuscripts and researches of the
LATE MAJOR FRANCIS JONES,
C.V.O.,T.D., F.S.A., M.A., K.ST.J.,
WALES HERALD AT ARMS

Editor CAROLINE CHARLES-JONES

Additional Editorial HUGH CHARLES-JONES

Published by
BRAWDY BOOKS
2001

Published by
Brawdy Books, Plas yr Wregin, Dinas, Newport
Pembrokeshire, SA42 0YH
Telephone: 01348 811450
PlasWregin@aol.com

Web sites
www.brawdybooks.com
www.westwalesgenealogy.co.uk
info@brawdybooks.com

ISBN 0 9528 344 56

Illustrations
The National Library of Wales
National Museums of Wales
Leon Olin, Sylvia Gainsford
Thomas Lloyd
Mr & Mrs Morris
David Brunel White

Book Jacket Design
H. Charles-Jones

Design and Make-up
ARTdesigns
Telephone: 01267 290670
artdesigns@hotmail.com

Printed and Bound by
Bath Press
Midsomer Norton

CONTENTS

Acknowledgements ix

Editorial Foreword x

Preface by Francis Jones xii

List of Patron Subscribers xxiii

Parish Map xxvii

Index to Parish Map listing Houses in each Parish xxviii

Glossary of useful terms xxxii

Bibliographical Abbreviations xxxiii

Historic Houses 1-341

Francis Jones (1908-1994) 343

Strange Sequels 364

Bibliography 365

Index 370

The Francis Jones Archives 394

Welsh Historical Societies 398

ACKNOWLEDGEMENTS

Firstly our most sincere thanks to the ever growing number of Patron Subscribers; their support for Francis Jones's work has given us a global network of friends. Without them none of Francis Jones's work would have been published since his death.

Many others have contributed to our book publications. Notably Andy Taylor whose consistent dedication to the intricate technicalities of computer publishing is remarkable.

For illustrations we are grateful to artists, Leon Olin and Sylvia Gainsford, David Brunel White, The National Library of Wales. Thomas Lloyd for his generous permission to use images from his *Lost Houses of Wales*, his private collection and his collection of coats of arms. Robert Innes-Smith for his advice on heraldry, and Mr. & Mrs. E. Morris for their kind permission to use their painting of Castle Villa, their old family home.

Mrs. Pamela Davies of Argoed again made an outstanding contribution, somehow she managed to find time to proof read this book. Also our thanks for the kind assistance of David Ellis of Poyston for his help. Indexers are often the unsung hero's of publishing, so it gives us great pleasure to thank Mrs. Mary Madden who so capably coped with the indexing of this complex book. Other stalwart friends are the secretaries of the many historical societies whose kind assistance also proved invaluable. The Garnon Peters in Canada, Bettye Kirkwood in Australia, Juan Peel in Argentina and so many others who are a source of help and support to us and to the cause of Welsh genealogy and family history.

Many thanks to Major Francis Jones's kinsman, Anthony Henniker-Gotley, for valuable family information and Trevor Woolner (of the notable old Batin family), is another subscriber who has become a valued friend.

Finally our thanks to the Bath Press for producing books worthy of the high standards set by Francis Jones.

HUGH CHARLES-JONES

November 2001

EDITORIAL FOREWORD

I remember seeing my father-in-law, Francis Jones sitting at his desk in his study in Carmarthen, working at his papers. As he courteously explained his files and showed me his archive neither of us could ever have thought that one day I would be studying them myself. He usually kept his archive meticulously tidy, but after his death, my husband Hugh, his eldest son and I, returned to find them in total disorder. We decided that they should be catalogued and brought them home. Eventually a girl friend and I spent a winter sorting them into families, categories and counties and finally into alphabetical order. Even after eight years of cataloguing and documenting my father-in-law's massive literary legacy we have still by no means completed the undertaking.

The Archives fill a small room; those viewing them are awestruck by the sheer volume and depth of his research. How did he have time to enjoy life, to fight in a world war, to marry, to raise a family? He started young, making collections of church records, memorials, registers of births and deaths. We have essays written when he was twelve years old. He left endless notebooks filled with Welsh interests, with legends, records, holy well information, family genealogy. Dipping into just one file can consume hours of reading; the files contain hundreds of slips of paper, notes written on the torn up reverse sides of papers of Minutes of the National Trust or the National Museum of Wales, every space covered with Quarter Sessions records, leases, fragments of genealogy, all correctly filed over the 70 years from the early 1920s to the late 1980s. He wrote between lines, and along the margins of paper already covered with other essays or printed matter. There must have been so much more information lodged in his memory; now sadly lost to us forever. How inadequate I feel as I struggle to read his handwriting and to transcribe the material left to us.

You must forgive me, as I hope he would, if there are errors, or omissions because I have done my best to put before you all I can, which is just a fraction of the content of his Archives. Francis used every Welsh spelling he came across according to the century about which he wrote, or because he thought it the correct one; (see his comment on Treyarched), and he felt the same about Tresissyllt now spelt Treseissillt or Treseissyllt. He thought any building 19th century or later to be 'modern' so the records often end around 1800. Only if exceptionally interesting to him do they continue until the 20th century. These are the records of one man, and of what interested him personally; that is Welsh families and their homes. He may not have recorded every family although it often seems that no one escaped his eagle eye.

So I have worked to give you some of the extra information that has come to light. Wherever possible I have used material verbatim from his essays. The references are included to enable readers to research further. All the material used comes from referenced sources; the Public Record Office in Haverfordwest which Francis started; the National Library of Wales where he worked for many years; The College of Heralds where he catalogued the Welsh material; the endless private houses and their archives which he visited, referenced and researched; Picton Castle (Philipps), Trewern, (Protheroe-Beynon Papers),

Treyarched (Williams Deeds), Eaton Evans Deeds, the Morgan-Richardson Deeds, the Wagner Papers, the Bronwydd Deeds, the Golden Grove Manuscripts, the Llangwarren (Mathias) records and of course the Francis Jones Archives where he detailed the information he had gathered at first hand.

We have over 400 essays, many unpublished, full of detailed genealogy. There is an index on our website, www.brawdybooks.com of the family history and pedigree files we hold.

Visitors are welcome to call and research these files for a small fee. My father-in-law's greatest wish was that his life's work be recorded and chronicled as his legacy to his much loved Pembrokeshire.

NOTA BENE

Regarding the contentious matter of Welsh place-name spellings, we have referred to those listed by the University of Wales Press in *A Gazetteer of Welsh Place-Names*. However, where this could lead to confusion or an inability to find the village or house on modern OS maps, we have used popular spellings. In the spelling of place-names in deeds and documents of past centuries, we have used the spellings current at that time where possible so that readers can follow the evolution of Welsh spelling through the centuries.

PREFACE

Old Pembrokeshire Houses

An introduction by Major Francis Jones
Being the transcript of a Talk given by him in 1986

A word that has become fashionable during the last few years is 'Environment'. Indeed, so much so, that a government department has been established – Department of Environment – with a Minister of the Crown at its head. Suddenly, we have become aware of the importance of our surroundings, and of the enemies within our gates, such as pollution, an unhappy concomitant of industrialisation which now threatens not only to blunt our aesthetic sense, but also to destroy plant and animal life, and in some areas even to endanger human life. The worm has entered the national woodwork, but with the new awareness of the problem it becomes possible to arrest its progress, if not to eliminate it completely.

To those of us living in southwest Wales, the word environment means landscape. This is largely a rural area, a land of hills and vales, woodlands, villages, hamlets, scattered farms, cottages, and country houses, necklaced by coastal scenery, rock-bound ramparts punctuated with innumerable coves and stretches of sand. The fact that several preservation societies, planning authorities, the Countryside Commission, National Park, and the National Trust, have been established, indicates our awakened sense of not only the importance but the necessity of these amenities, at the same time providing an indictment of the lack of public responsibility towards these varied features of our environment in bygone days.

My introduction concerns a particular aspect of the Pembrokeshire environment, namely domestic architecture. It includes a variety of buildings that fall into different categories but I propose to confine my remarks to one class of domestic architecture, namely the country houses of Pembrokeshire.

During the past, emphasis has been placed on castles and churches, most of which have been discussed at length in the various learned journals devoted to antiquities. But our historic houses have been mostly ignored, and those who are familiar with the Report of the Ancient Monuments Commission on Pembrokeshire, published in 1925, will be painfully aware of the inadequate and peripheral treatment accorded to such architecture by its compilers. Even lists of houses of architectural interest compiled by the local Authority in post-war days, however laudable the intention, falls woefully short of what an interested person has a right to expect. Nevertheless, it is a step in the right direction, and with the support of the present Ancient Monuments Commission, the Historic Buildings Council for Wales, and the Welsh Office [now National Assembly], it is hoped that a complete list of these buildings will yet be compiled accompanied by competent descriptions and informed comment.

Very little of our environment has been untouched by the hand of man. Certain areas along the sea coast, and the higher and more unproductive parts of our hills and moorlands may be considered as virgin products of nature, and yet some of these have been intruded by wireless masts or mechanical "daleks" conveying electrical power across the face of the land and worse still, by a Sargasso of fir trees, a green plague that might well have made Pharaoh blink. Indeed most of our landscape has been created by man – fields, hedges, buildings, bridges, roads – while certain natural features such as streams have been culverted, courses of rivers have been changed, artificial lakes and reservoirs have been created, swamps have been reclaimed, great forests deliberately planted; and, on the other hand industrial activity has resulted in large functional buildings, waste from industries creates hideous artificial hills, fumes and smoke pollute not only the atmosphere, but the natural products of the earth necessary for human sustenance.

Of the more agreeable contributions made by man to the landscape, are the habitations raised to protect him from the weather, and, in primitive times, from his enemies also. Rarely have these disfigured the landscape, while their ruins often produce a picturesque quality that gives an added attraction to the landscape, such as ruins of Celtic hill forts, Roman villas, Norman castles. These were primarily military in purpose. The habitations of peace, such as country mansions, farmhouses, cottages, churches and chapels, have survived longer, although often changed or improved during the centuries of their existence. Many have survived to our own time, and might well outlive the present century were it not for new hazards hatched from the minds of men more devoted to domestic requirements and profitability than to historical appreciation. Foremost among the new threats are Local Authority financial grants for the improvement of homes and other buildings; such changes are usually necessary and are to be welcomed, but often are achieved by the destruction of architectural details of a bygone age, which might well have been preserved had a more careful plan been evolved. Pharaoh had a plague of frogs to contend with, we have Planning Officers. Another enemy is the demolition order, applied to ruinous or affected structures – which in some cases have been deliberately allowed to deteriorate – even when listed as protected buildings of historical interest. At the lowest scale in popularity are the speculators and property developers, often totally insensitive to local traditions but wholly wedded to the profits likely to accrue from their environmental invasions. There is a new and sinister music in the air – the thud of the hammer, the roar of the bulldozer, and the crash of falling masonry.

The unhappy aspect of such activity is that much historical evidence of our vernacular architecture, some of it unique, is often swept away without a record having been made of it – photographs, drawings, plans should be preserved among our archives. However, examples do occur that help to restore our faith in human nature by illustrating that the appreciation of Pembrokeshire's past still exists, and can be combined with judicious improvements, so that practical innovations harmonise with traditional outlines. Thus a year or two ago, an Englishman bought a small country residence near the Pembrokeshire-Carmarthenshire border, and as a good deal of internal re-arrangements were necessary, employed a Haverfordwest architect, to conduct matters. Before doing anything they invited me to look over the house, to tell them what I could about the past ownership, and to indicate such vernacular features worthy of being integrated into the renovated parts. Another example concerns an old residence in the parish of Nash. This had been an old country seat of a family called Davies who had produced a High Sheriff in 1737, and whose coat-of-arms is on the chancel wall of the church nearby. The house had become a farmhouse in course of time so that some of its earlier features had become less evident with the passing years. Accordingly I arranged for an inspector of the Ancient Monuments Commission, one of the greatest experts in Wales on historical architecture, to make a detailed survey and to report on characteristic features worthy of retention.

On another occasion I was invited to see a quite remarkable house at Vaynor in Llawhaden, which belonged to the early seventeenth century. It had a well-preserved stone pillared entrance with a coat of arms above it; the home of the ancient Skyrme family, and despite the fact that it had been used by farmers for the last 150 years still retained its earlier character. Here again we were able to obtain expert guidance from the inspector of Ancient Monuments.

These were cases of "look before you alter" and I would commend such an attitude. Sometimes significant features come to light during alterations, which have been long concealed. Not so long ago a Carmarthenshire farmer uncovered two large plaques under several layers of whitewash on an outer wall of an old farmhouse, which from Tudor times until 1870 had been the seat of an important county family. On these plaques there were the outlines of a shield. Fortunately his wife was a member of the W.I. and she remembered that on one occasion I had given them a talk on heraldry, and decided to ask me to visit the house in order to examine the plaques. On doing so I found the coat-of-arms of the ancient family in excellent state of preservation, and what is more one of the plaques bore the initials of one of the family and the date on which it had been inset in the walls. This provided useful evidence relating to the history of the fabric.

Occasionally changes are made which obscure architectural features and destroy significant evidence. Thus, one of the oldest residences in the county is that of Brawdy, originally a large building built in the form of a hollow square with a courtyard in the centre. Although it remained the possession of the original owners until 1919, it had been tenanted by a farmer from 1796, and in 1826 a large portion of it had been taken down, so that from that time onwards it conveyed very little idea of its earlier construction, and looked to be a house of two storeys. However, on the uppermost part of its southern gable end were the clear outlines of two large windows that had been blocked up in 1825, which, with other evidence, proved that it had been a three-storeyed structure before its mutilation. After the last world war (1939-45), the gable end has been efficiently cemented, so that now all traces of the architectural evidence of its third storey have been completely obliterated. Fortunately, I took some excellent photographs of it in 1934 which clearly show the lost windows. Another slightly different example, which concerns the intrusion of a feature apparently in harmony with the earlier structure is found at the old Tudor mansion of Trewern in Nevern. I took photographs of the house in 1935, accompanied by the late Mr. Martin Phillips of Hermons Hill, which show the characteristic Tudor porch with one window above it. Since the last war, a second window has been inserted, and although it does not mar the general effect, is nevertheless an interloper.

Here, I would like to indicate a method whereby a great deal of important architectural material may be preserved. It is hardly necessary for me to emphasise the importance of photography, of sketches or paintings of these houses, and where possible of ground plans, and plans of interior arrangements. It would be a considerable boon to historians if a well-directed campaign could be carried out to photograph the historic houses of the county, not only the larger and better preserved residences but also of those which have been converted into farmhouses. This project could be directed by the County Museum, the County Record Office, or by both in partnership so that a permanent visual archive could be produced of these historic buildings. These could be supplemented by the numerous old Sale Catalogues some of which were lavishly illustrated, which still lie mouldering in the offices of auctioneers and solicitors, many of which have been of the greatest help to me. Then, the County Library could make a list of all photos or drawings of these houses that have appeared in printed books – such as Bradley's *South Wales*, or old numbers of Archaeologia Cambrensis for example – so that the attention of students of such architecture could be directed without delay to sources of information. As an admirer of the work of the Women's Institutes who have been responsible for collecting and preserving various facets of county history, I feel that they might be invited to co-operate in this worthwhile operation. I make this suggestion – I think it both practical and sensible in the hope that it will be considered by those in a position to implement it.

I would like to mention the work of a Mr. Allen, a photographer of Tenby, who was active in the latter half of the last century. He photographed nearly all of the more important country houses in Pembrokeshire, Carmarthenshire, and Cardiganshire, which he bound in large volumes and sold to the owners of the houses. Fortunately several of these volumes have survived, covering the period 1865-1900, and as the majority of the houses are now used for other purposes, such as hospitals, Old People's homes, hotels and so on, and as many changes have been made to them, these photographs are of prime importance.

Occasionally the more artistic members of families made paintings and sketches of their homes. An interesting watercolour hangs in the hall of the mansion of Clynfyw in Manordeifi. The first family at Clynfyw was called Lloyd, and eventually in the late eighteenth century the property passed to the Lewis-Bowen family. In the first half of the last century, the family built a new mansion, about a hundred yards from the original house, part of which remains in use as an outbuilding. However, before it was abandoned a very fine watercolour was made of it, which enables us to see what the earlier mansion looked like before being abandoned.

Information regarding interior arrangements is less easily come by. Where plans have been made, interpretation presents no problems. But few of the older plans have survived, and even fewer engravings or drawings, so that we have to turn to other sources. Foremost among these are inventories of the goods of a deceased owner, and a considerable number of them describe the contents of each room, so that we are able at least to learn the approximate number of rooms in a house. An example of what an Inventory can produce is provided by those of the Ap Rhys family of Rickeston in Brawdy parish taken in 1650 and 1673, which shows that the house contained the following rooms:

Ground Floor; Bedrooms; The Hall; The Great Chamber; Wool loft; Parlour; My Master's Chamber; Ploughmen's chamber; Dining Room; The Gentlewomen's Chamber; Room over the Kennel; Kitchen; The Children's Chamber; Cart house; Upper Kitchen; Maids Chamber; Ox house; Dairy, Chamber near Maids Chamber; Stable; Larder houses; White Chamber; Storehouse; Little Larder; Yellow Chamber; Meal loft; Chamber over the buttery; Little Chamber over the stairs; Cellar; Chamber over the hall door; Cockloft; Rye loft.

Of course these do not inform us of the size of the house, or of the rooms. In 1670 it was taxed for five hearths, which means that it was a biggish house. I have deliberately chosen Rickeston, for about the year 1740 the old mansion was demolished, so that today not a single stone remains to indicate the site – it has disappeared off the face of the earth, and only the cellars are left to show where it stood. After it had been taken down, a new commodious farmhouse was built about 50 yards away, now called Rickeston Hall, a well-known farm. A stone bearing the Ap Rhys coat-of-arms, a chevron between 3 ravens, was built into the cart house wall, which I saw and easily deciphered over 40 years ago, but today it is so weathered that the shield is almost obliterated.

Another interesting example is provided by Landshipping in Martletwy, once the largest mansion in Pembrokeshire, bigger than Picton Castle, Orielton or Stackpole Court. In 1670 it contained 20 hearths, which indicates its enormous size. Unfortunately I have been unable to unearth an Inventory, but in 1789 the residence required extensive repairs, and a contractor was sent to report on its condition. This document has survived and the following rooms are mentioned:

Hall; Blue Room; Lime House; Drawing Room; Plaid Room; Malt House; Best Parlour; Lady Owen's Room; Coach House; Common Parlour; Dressing Room; Carpenter's Workshop; Butler's Pantry; Closet; Stable 22 x 18; Housekeeper's Room; Yellow Room; Steward's Hall; Red Room; Servants' Hall; Sir Hugh's Closet; Kitchen; Nursery; Scullery; The Gallery. A wing 100 ft. long by 20 ft. broad on the east side of the house containing Kitchen, Larder, Dairy, Brewhouse, with bedchamber over it.

Not all the rooms are included in this report, so that in fact the house would have contained more. Alas, the Owens ceased to live there, preferring Orielton, so that Landshipping mouldered and decayed, and by 1811 Richard Fenton described it as "formerly a very respectable mansion now unroofed and in ruins".

The historian will find his task considerably lightened by the Hearth Tax List of 1670. In that year a tax was levied on every fireplace in each house throughout the county, and from their number we are able to form an idea of the size of the house, particularly as we are able to compare them with each other, and also to study the inventories relating to their owners. I must enter one caveat. The assessments were kept as low as possible, and there is little doubt that the numbers, in some cases are below the true figure, and I do not think that we should be mistaken in believing that many of them contained more hearths than shown in the Tax List. In any case it is an excellent yardstick for our purpose.

Fortunately the labours of the late Mr. Francis Green of St. Davids have rendered these lists, (kept in the Public Record Office) available for historians. He laboriously copied out the Pembrokeshire list which he published in the West Wales Historical Records, thereby placing us in his debt. Perhaps I may be allowed to draw your attention to the contents of this list.

6	Houses with	11 to 20	hearths
7	"	10	"
3	"	9	"
8	"	8	"
16	"	7	"
17	"	6	"
37	"	5	"
42	"	4	"
30	"	3	"
13	"	2	"

To date, I have listed over 500 homes and more than 310 of these are gentry residences in Pembrokeshire, and it is likely that there are others that have escaped my net. I must emphasise that all these houses are not contemporaneous, and when one disappeared another rose somewhere else, nevertheless, they were very numerous. The distribution indicates the difference between the Welsh gentry and their English counterparts. In England, the gentry were fewer, but much richer, usually not more than one squire to a parish, with large imposing houses, and extensive estates. In Wales, the gentry were far more numerous, their estates smaller (sometimes as few as five or six farms), and the houses less ambitious architecturally. One of the main differences was that the Welsh gentry laid far greater emphasis on their lineage, and it was the pedigree as much as their worldly possessions that determined their social standing. I have listed the Pembrokeshire mansions by parishes, which gives an idea of the special nature of their distribution. Here are some of the parishes containing a high number of these houses: five in each of the parishes of Carew, Castlemartin, Llanfihangel Penbedw, Llanstadwell, Mathry, Meline, St. Davids, St. Ishmaels, Steynton; six in each of the parishes of Brawdy, Camrose, Llanddewi Velfrey, Llanrhian, Marloes; seven in each of the parishes of Cilgerran, Llawhaden, Narberth, St. Dogmaels, St. Mary and St. Michael Pembroke, Eglwyswrw; eight in each of the parishes of Clydey, Manordeifi, Roch, and, believe it or not, more than 20 in the parish of Nevern. Very few parishes are without one house of interest, and large numbers contain from two to five.

Apart from the northern most part of the county, there is no particular pattern in the siting of the houses. Probably most of them started as farmsteads, and with increasing prosperity developed into more ambitious buildings. A large number of the older houses are built on hill-slopes, very often at right angles to the slope: others are on low ground, in river valleys, or near the coast. Doubtless they were originally wholly utilitarian, and it was in much later times, in the seventeenth century, and especially from the eighteenth century onwards, that sites were consciously selected for the views afforded from them. Even then many of the older houses continued, while the adjacent areas were landscaped by experts, special parks, gardens, and walks, including herds of deer or white cattle, introduced.

The distribution in the northernmost parts reflects the early structure of Welsh society, where a family group was more or less anchored in its patrimonial area. Most of these houses belonged to the descendants of the kinglet of Cemaes, Gwynfardd Dyfed. The younger sons and cousins of the main stems established themselves at homesteads within the area, and spread like a network of Incas throughout Cemaes, all being cousins within some degree, tracing their lineage to Gwynfardd. In this way they resembled a Scottish clan. When newcomers settled among them, like the families of Peverill, Cantington, Picton, and Cole for example, they intermarried with the Gwynfardd stock, and some of them went so far as to relinquish their Norman or English names, and to adopt the *ap* nomenclature of the native born. This explains the concentration of the families and their country houses in this area. One of their most remarkable attributes has been their power of survival, chief amongst them being the Bowen's of Llwyngwair, which maintained their position from the twelfth century until about twenty years ago, when Air Commodore J. B. Bowen was Lord Lieutenant of this county. It is one of the most remarkable examples known of the persistence of an old stock for so long a time without any "decline and fall" attending it. The tenacity of these families, particularly in Nevern and adjoining parishes, is unparalleled elsewhere in Wales.

A knowledge of genealogy in this connection is important, and the help afforded by that science enabled me to identify many houses.

Very few of the older residences have survived, and even these have been altered from time to time to such a degree that their original form has been obscured. Among the three older residences that have come down to us with recognisable medieval features are Eastington in Rhoscrowther, Haroldston St. Issells near Haverfordwest, Scotsborough near Tenby, and possibly the older part of Sandyhaven. Eastington was the home of the families of Perrot, Philipps, and Meares, in that order; and probably dates from the early 1400s: it has a plain vaulted undercroft (not to be confused with cellars) which is typical of medieval structures of this type, with access to the upper apartments by an exterior flight of stone steps, another characteristic of the period. There are indications that it had been a fortified dwelling. From 1768 extensive repairs were necessary for the house, particularly the roofs; these were carried out; but deterioration continued and by 1790 it was described as "fallen to decay and unfit for habitation", and the owner John Meares left and settled at an estate he bought at Kingston on Thames. Eastington was then let to farmers and part of the house adapted for farming purposes. It is now a farmhouse but retains many of its early features.

Haroldston was the original home of the family of Harold, whose heiress subsequently brought the property to her husband Peter Perrot (died 1378), in whose descendants it remained for many centuries. Fortunately we have several descriptions and some drawings and paintings of the old house, which shows that some of its thirteenth century section had survived to the last century. A strongly built square house with a tower of three storeys, and the usual vaulting below it, it was assessed at 10 hearths in 1670. The land around it had been acquired from the nearby Priory, and into its groves, according to George Owen of Henllys, Sir John Perrot introduced pheasants from Ireland, said to have been the first appearance of that species in this county. Among its distinguished visitors was the poet Addison. Its fate was not unlike that of some of our historic houses today. In 1767 a visitor wrote of the two chief mansions near Haverfordwest – "here are two old houses now in ruins, Prendergast and Harriston lately belonging to the Packingtons, but now sold to a man who has pulled down all the materials which were saleable": he added that around the house he noticed the rare plant *Origanium Onite* growing. It was bought by Sir John Philipps of Picton Castle before 1764, and the tower part of the house was inhabited by tenants well into the nineteenth century.

It is interesting that the next house, Scotsborough, was also a Perrot residence, and afterwards of the Ap Rice family whose beautiful heraldic tomb is in St Mary's Church, Tenby. It was a very large structure, and traces of defensive features survived. Although it ceased to be inhabited by a county family in the eighteenth century, it was afterwards inhabited by farmers and finally labourers, but had become a total ruin by the nineteenth century. The ruins are impressive, and fortunately several engravings and sketches were made of it in 1810, 1851, and 1870 so that we are able to learn what this large double-pile house looked like while it was still covered by a roof.

Part of Sandyhaven in St. Ishmaels, is in an excellent state of preservation, it is probably medieval, with a 17th century wing added to it.

First the home of the family of Rhys, it passed to Admiral Button, and from him to Richard Philipps a cadet of the Picton Castle family. It was fortunate to have a succession of respectable farming tenants from the mid-eighteenth century, with the result that so far as its outward appearance is concerned it is unspoilt, although parts of the interior arrangements have been modified. It was assessed at 7 hearths in 1670.

Also medieval in origin and still inhabited – indeed they have never ceased to be inhabited since the middle ages – are Picton Castle and Upton Castle, but as they come into another category of architecture I do not propose to dwell on them here. Three other ancient castles, having been ivied ruins for centuries, which have been restored in the present century are Newport Castle, Roch Castle, and Benton Castle.

I would like to mention one matter which is of particular importance to students of vernacular architecture. As I have already indicated most of the houses have been altered in part, some pretty extensively, so that only the sites they stand on are ancient and historic. However, there are several cases where the older houses have been abandoned or dismantled, and a completely new house erected some distance away. Unless one knows their history, wholly misleading conclusions may well be drawn by antiquaries, and it may be of some advantage if I were to describe some of my own experiences in this field.

Last year I called at a most interesting house called Llandre in the small parish of Egremont. This parish is part of the administrative county of Carmarthen, but territorially it is in Pembrokeshire into which it thrusts like a vagrant appendix. It is one of those topographical lunacies spawned by blinkered government servants. It is an early three-storeyed house of the 18th century, and over the main entrance is the coat-of-arms, crest, and motto of John Protheroe, High Sheriff of Pembrokeshire in 1784, who built the mansion in 1788, which date is carved on the heraldic plaque. The farmer's wife, Mrs. Thomas, was herself most interested in the history of the house and gave me all the information she could. One thing puzzled me enormously. About ten yards in front of the house was a fine well-preserved dovecote, unusual in shape, in that it was square. I could not understand why it had been built so near to the residence, for usually dovecotes are some distance away. When I mentioned this to Mrs Thomas, she said, "Oh there was a much older mansion, part of which is still standing over there, which we use as an out-house for cattle". "Over there" was about 100 yards away, and when I walked over, I could see a strongly built building, at right-angles to the slope, and here was the original mansion of Llandre – and so in relation to it the location of the dovecote became entirely logical.

Manorowen near Goodwick provides another example. The earliest family there from Elizabethan days was that of Williams, and about 1650 the estate was bought by one John Lewis of Henllanowen, a descendant of Gwynfardd Dyfed. The mansion of Manorowen stands in a grove on a little eminence, and below it runs the main road. Now, across that road and near the church, is a large old walled garden belonging to the mansion. Logically, we could expect the garden to be near, alongside or in rear of the mansion, rather than in an inconvenient spot cut off from the mansion by the main road.

Fortunately a clue is provided by Samuel Lewis the topographer. He tells us in 1835: "The ancient seat and residence of John Lewis Esq, a magistrate, in the reign of James II, is now deserted and in ruins." This was the original mansion for which John Lewis was assessed at 5 hearths in 1670. Lewis goes on to say, "the estate is the property of his descendant Richard Bowen, Esq., who has erected a handsome mansion a little higher up the hill". Now, there can be no doubt that the original mansion was just below the garden near the church, and this explains the location of the walled garden. The words "higher up the hill" are significant, and the mansion built there by Richard Bowen, is still there, now used as outhouses. But there was yet another change; about 1840 a third mansion was built by Dr. Moses Griffith, J.P., a retired army doctor, who had bought the estate, immediately in front of Bowen's mansion. And so, in this instance, we have three mansions whose history we have to trace.

Boulston provides another example. No detective work is needed to locate this. The ruins of the old mansion, which had 13 hearths in 1670, still stand near the riverside, and photographs of the house provide us with an idea of the home of the Wogans. The present mansion, built early in the nineteenth century stands on higher ground a little distance away. Ffynnone (originally called Ffynnonau Bychan), Pentre (originally called Pentre Ifan, and not to be confused with the seat of the same name in Nevern), Park y Pratt in St. Dogmaels parish, Cresselly, Blaiddbwll in Llanfyrnach, Trefloyne near Penally, all were built some distance away from the original sites.

I should like to mention Castle Malgwyn in Manordeifi, home of the ancient family of Mortimer. This stood on a knoll above a steep slope, and was undoubtedly fortified in earlier days; the present structure is a farmhouse and probably some of the old mansion is incorporated in it. However, in the 1790s, a brand-new mansion was built on the banks of the Tivy below Llechryd by the wealthy iron-master Sir Thomas Hammett, and was bought in the early part of the last century by the Gower family, and as this is called Castle Malgwyn many people have concluded that it was the home of the Mortimers.

Another circumstance that has led to difficulties is the change in place-names that has occurred, and as this is not always generally known, errors are apt to arise. Thus in the seventeenth and eighteenth centuries, there was a residence in Eglwyswen parish known as Gwern Ffulbro, home of the family of Bowen who owned a large estate in the county. However, between 1760 and 1800, the name Gwern Ffulbro ceased to be used, and today the mansion, a short distance south east of the church is known as Plas Eglwyswen, now a large farmhouse.

Early documents show that a land owning family of Lewis was seated at Bwlch y Clawdd near Maenclochog. However in the late eighteenth century it was bought by a man called Bulkeley who took down the old house, and built an entirely new one from a plan by John Nash, to which the name Temple Druid was given. However, the older inhabitants still refer to it as Bwlch y Clawdd. The name of Rhosygilwen was changed in the last century to Morgenau by which name it was called for some years, until the owners reverted to the original name. The name of Colby Lodge near Amroth was Rhydlangoeg and that is the form given in old deeds and documents. In the parish of Burton stood an ancient mansion with the delicious name of Dumpledale, home of the Jordan family since the days of Henry VII, but about 1840 it became the property of one of the Lort-Phillips family who rebuilt it in modern style and changed the name to Ashdale.

Care must be taken in cases where mansions have disappeared entirely, and people are apt to believe that a surviving farmhouse of the same name represents that of the original residence. For instance the old historic mansions of Prendergast at Haverfordwest, Fletherhill (Rudbaxton parish), Cilast (Manordeifi), Morfil, Llanreithan, Rickeston (Brawdy), Martel (Puncheston), Dolau Llannerch (Clydey), Trellewelyn (Manorowen), Henllan (Llanddewi Velfrey), have completely disappeared leaving hardly a trace, and the farmhouses bearing the same names have no architectural relation to them. Sometimes the farmhouse is commodious and old, and people may be forgiven for believing them to have been the original mansion. Take for example Llanreithan. The farmhouse of Llanreithan, a genuinely old structure, contains 13 rooms on the ground floor and an equal number on the upper floor. However the old mansion stood near the river bank below the house, alongside the walled garden – still intact – although not a single stone remains to mark the mansion's site, and only masses of garden flowers run wild growing in profusion in spring and summer indicate that this part of the land was other than a pasture field at a former time. Some of these vanished mansions were large and imposing, and their ruins are sufficient to indicate their extent. I have already named some, to which I will add Cresswell and Bangeston (Angle).

A large number of these residences have survived as farmhouses, some of which retain features of their earlier status. A delightful example is Tredefaid in Llantood, home of the family of Lewes, standing on the lip of a deep ravine, others are Trewern, Penybenglog, Plas y Meibion in Llangolman, Cilciffeth, and Lochmeyler. Some, although used as farmhouses, have retained their architectural appearance practically unchanged, among which we find Jordanston in Dewsland, Trevaccoon in Llanrhian, Cwmgloyn, Llether, Llanunwas, Longridge in Bletherston and Court near Llanychaer.

Quite a number have been sold in the present century, and have been adapted to various purposes, such as St. Bride's (holiday apartments), and Sealyham (activity holidays), Haylett and Begelly (private schools), Holyland, Castle Malgwyn, and Llwyngwair (hotels), St. Botolphs, (club), Bush (offices), Orielton (Field Study centre) Amroth Castle (holiday camp),

Langton (Old People's Home), and Scolton as a county museum. Most of these have preserved their exteriors largely unchanged, but the interiors have been largely, in some cases drastically, rearranged. Some remain empty and are bound to deteriorate very rapidly unless some use is made of them, such as Butter Hill for example which is in a sad state of dereliction.

Of the 310 Pembrokeshire mansions, only a handful remain today as residences Picton Castle, Slebech, Cresselly, Cottesmore, Manorowen, Tregwynt, Llangwarren, Pentypark, Angle Hall, Welston Court, Clynfyw, Upton Castle, Stone Hall, and a few more.

Although my subject is country houses, there are some interesting houses in certain towns, once homes of older families, Foley House and Hermons Hill in Haverfordwest, the home of the Elliots in Narberth for example. I would especially mention the premises in the High Street, Haverfordwest, once occupied by Messrs W. H. Smith, once an imposing town house of George Owen with a perfectly preserved heraldic fireplace of Elizabethan days.

In the space at my disposal it is not possible to attempt more than a general survey of the subject, and to indicate its more important aspects and to direct attention to the architectural treasures that once gave added interest and dignity to our environment. I would like to list some of the points that should be looked for by those carrying out a survey of Pembrokeshire houses:

1. Location on high or low ground.

Exterior

2. Plan of the house — H, E, T in shape or cube, or double pile. Tudor -Jacobean – Georgian – Regency – neo-gothic and imitation by Victorians.
3. Number of storeys – ground floor, 1st, 2nd floors etc. Attics, cellars, undercrofts, pitch of roof, value of rafters as evidence. Chimneys.
4. Number of windows in a range – are there dormer windows. Shape of windows-gothic, arched, square headed, mullioned, bow windows.
5. Entrances – Porch – pillars – courtyard. Use of stone, brick, verandahs.
6. External decorations – coats of arms - insets with initials and dates.
7. Measurements – length and breadth of house, estimated height.

Interior

8. Style of main staircase – nature of woodwork.
9. The Hall, pillars, screens.
10. Number and shape of rooms. Corridors. Gallery.
11. Interior decorations – fireplaces – overmantles (e.g. Llether farm) heraldic, alcoves.

Environs

12. Is there a walled garden – location.
13. Is there a dovecot (e.g. Great Nash).
14. What outbuildings are there.
15. Lawns, shrubberies, and parklands. Sundials, croquet and tennis lawns, bowling green.
16. Drives and Gateways – ironwork, pillars, Jambs.
17. Lodges. These are a subject in themselves, and there are numerous little gems throughout the county.

General

18. General state of building, and present use.

The best method of studying these houses is to visit them, and an examination will reveal the essential features. This can be supplemented by references to deeds and documents, estate accounts, letters, bills, descriptions by tourists and so on. A fruitful source of information is contained in old newspaper files containing advertisements of sales, and these often describe a house room by room, in some cases giving the dimensions. The files of *The Cambrian* newspaper, the *Milford Haven Telegraph, The Western Telegraph*, the *West Wales Guardian*, etc, are useful quarries for the researcher. Sale catalogues prepared by auctioneers are also extremely useful, and many of these contain both exterior and interior photographs or engravings. The works of George Owen of Henllys, Fenton, Laws and others contain additional information. Although not strictly architectural, it is important to collect any legends relating to the house. There are tales of underground passages, innumerable ghosts, "Henry Tudor slept here", "Cromwell slept here", tales of elopements, smuggling, and so on. All contribute to the atmosphere of a house, and some, even if they are inventions or exaggerations, may provide a clue to a far-off event.

Such legends are associated with the house, so long as the house stands they will be remembered if only vaguely. But as soon as the house is demolished the visual reminder is removed, and thus legends and even the names of former possessors tend to pass from the memory of man.

LIST OF PATRON SUBSCRIBERS

W. Anderson, Kilmacomb, Scotland

Mrs. J. M. Archer, Hundleton, Pembs.
Mr. D. Ayers, Pill, Milford Haven
Mr G. & Mrs. S. Bailey, Llangrannog, Ceredigion
Mr. G. Barrett, Bethlehem, Pembs.
Mr. S. R. Beesley, Haverfordwest
Mr & Mrs. S. Beresford-Davies, Wells-next-the-Sea
Mr. F. Bevan, Ferryside, Carms.
Mrs. M. Beynon-Isaac, Swansea
Miss J. Bird, Freshwater East, Pembs.
Mrs. J. H. Bland, Lochturffin, Mathry
C. P. F. Blundell, Mynachlogddu, Pembs.
Mrs. G. M. Bowen, Blaenffos, Pembs.
Mrs. P. M. Bowen, Penffordd, Pembs.
Mr. A ap I. Bowen-Jenkins, Queensway, Haverfordwest
Mr. L. Brantinham, Texas, USA
The Rev. R. L. Brown, Welshpool, Powys,
Mr. J. P. O. Bushell, New Moat, Pembs.
M. & R. Butler, Coldstream, Berwick,

Lord Carbery, Wimbledon, London
Mrs. S. J. Castle, Llandeloy, Pembs.
The Rev. D. St. John Chadwick, Glasgow
Mr. A. Charles, Eltham, London
Mr. & Mrs. G. Charles-Jones, Bridstow, Devon
Mr. & Mrs. J. Charles-Jones, Ampney St. Peter, Glos.
Mr. & Mrs. R. Charles-Jones, Oddington, Glos.
Dr. W.E. Church, Bethersden, Kent
Prof. D. Cohn-Sherbok, Bwlchllan, Ceredigion
M. M. Cohoe, Kingston, Ontario, Canada
Anne & Stephen Coker, Clarbeston Road, Pembs.
Miss J. Coleman, Abergwili, Carms.
Mrs. P. M. Collinson, St. Florence, Pembs.
Mr. A. G. Cook, Musselwick, Pembs.
Mrs. E. M. Cowley, Llangeitho, West Wales

Major & Mrs. R. Davies, Hinchley Wood, Sy.
Mr & Mrs. M. Davies, Argoed, Nevern, Pembs.
Mr. R. K. Davies, Eglwyswrw, Pembs.
Mr. C. L. Davies, Molleston, Narberth
Mr. D. V. W. Davies, Betton Strange, Shrewsbury
Mr. Glan Davies, Nantgaredig, Carms.
Mr. J. Davies, Withington, Manchester
Mr. M. Davies, Yelverton, Devon
Mr. P. H. C. Davies, Stow Hill, Newport
Mr. R. Davies, Little Newcastle, Pembs.
Mr. S. J. Davies, Buckspool Farm, Bosherston, Pembs.
Mr. T. & Mrs. E. K. Davies, Llanybydder
Mrs. C. A. Davies, Little Dumpledale Farm, Sardis
Dr. J. Davies-Humphreys, Flookersbrook, Chester
Mr. P. E. Davis, Aberarth, Ceredigion
Mr. R. de Wilde, Chiswick, London
Mr. H. G. G. & Mrs. A. Devonald, St. Lawrence, Fishguard
Mr. J. Devonald, East Morton, W. Yorks.
Mr. & Mrs. R. Dixon, Boarstall Tower, Oxford

Mr. D. Ellis, Poyston Hall, Pembs.
Mr. & Mrs. S. E. M. Evans, Dinas, Pembs.
Mr. A. R. Evans, Trecadwgan, Solva, Pembs.
Mr. P. L. Evans, Mount Pleasant, Carmarthen
Mrs. E. D. Evans, Ffrwdgrech House, Brecon
Mrs. E. Evans, Llandaf, Caerdydd
Mrs. J. M. Evans, Solva, Pembs.
Mrs. R. Evans, Llanychaer, Pembs.
Mrs. S. Evans, St. Fagans, Cardiff

Mr. J. W. A. Fackrell, Caerleon, Newport
Mr. D. Fielding, *Pembrokeshire Life Magazine*
Mrs. G. E. Fitch, Hamilton, Bermuda
Mr. M. Ford, Yateley, Hants.
Miss H. A. Formby, Ysceifiog, Holywell
Mr. R. Francis, Putney, London
Mrs. S. Francis, Penbanc, Fishguard
Mrs. S. C. Fraser-Hungrecker, London SW6
Mr. & Mrs. Fullagar, North Carolina, USA
Mrs. I. O'C. Fullard, Cwmann, Lampeter
Mrs. E. J. Fuller, Sarratt, Rickmansworth

Mrs. N. Gainsford, Rhos y Caerau, Pembs.
Mr. & Mrs. R. Garnon-Peters, Victoria, BC, Canada
Mrs. C. M. George, Milton, Tenby
Mr. J. D. Gibbon, Great Vaynor, Clynderwen
Col. R. H. Gilbertson, Lampeter Velfrey, Pembs.
Mrs. G. A. Gill, Fieldale, Sardis, Pembs.
Mr. C. Gladitz, Somerset
Capt. & Mrs. J. Goddard, Rencombe, Glos.
Mr. E. O. C. Goddard, Merlins Bridge, Haverfordwest
Mr. C. Goodman, London, W9
Mr. D. R. Gorman, Hoghton, Preston
Mr. R. Goswell, Plas Glyn-y-Mel, Fishguard
Mrs. P. Grantham, Barkston Gardens, London
Mrs. M. Gray, Boone, N. Carolina, USA
Mrs. L. Greenberg, London
Mr. & Mrs. R. J. Griffiths, New Road, Haverfordwest
Mrs. M. A. Griffiths, St. Clears, Carms.

A. R. Harries, Gustard Wood, Herts.
Dr. N. S. Harries, R.A.F
Mr. & Mrs. E. D. Harries, Maleny, Queensland, Aust.
Mr. E. G. S. Harries, Llandysilio, Pembs.
Mrs. R. B. Hartard, Begelly House, Pembs.
Mr. A. Hayward, Berry Hill House, Nevern, Pembs.
Mr. A. R. Henniker-Gotley, Great Bedwyn, Marlborough
Mrs. S. Henry, Johnston, Pembs.
Mr. D. Herring, Waterford, Ireland
Mrs. W. E. Hilling, Berkhamsted, Herts.
Miss. J. A. Hoare, Bricket Wood, Herts.
Mrs. J. Hobbs, Twyford, Shaftsbury, Dorset
Mr. & Mrs. J. Hogg, Lords Meadow Farm, Pembroke
Mrs. E. Horne, Millais, Jersey
Mr. & Mrs. P. & E. Houseman, Letterston, Pembs.
Mr. D. M. Howell, Morvil, Clynderwen
Mr. R. Howells, Amroth, Pembs.
Dr. P. Howell-Williams, Llanfair Road, Rhulhun
Mrs. V. Hurford & G. R. Hurford, Llanelli, Carms.
Mrs. A. Hurst, English Bicknor, Glos.

Mr. R. Innes-Smith, Derby

Mrs. S. J. Jackson, Weymouth
B. Ll. James, Birchgrove, Cardiff
Mr. A. C. J. James, Gowerton, Swansea
Mr. R. J. James, Farthings Hook Farm, Haverfordwest
P. F. James, Swallowcliffe, Wilts.
Mr. I. H. Jenkins, Poynton, Cheshire
Mr. P. K. Jenkins, Llandeilo, Carms.
Mrs. M. B. Jenkins, Trearched Farm, Croesgoch
Miss A. L. Jones, Carmarthen
Mr. D. R. L. Jones, Garsdon, Wilts.
Mr. J. D. Jones, Fountain Hill, Crymych
Mr. W. A. Jones, Thatcham, Berks.
Mrs. E. V. Jones, Pentyrch, Cardiff
Mrs. M. Jones, Stradey Hill, Llanelli

Mrs. B. J. Kirkwood, St. Ives, NSW, Aust.
H. Koster, Warwick

Mr. & Mrs. J. Lane-Fox, Chedworth, Glos.
G. T. Lewis, The Forty, Cholsey
Mr. A. Lewis, Llansaint, Kidwelly
Mr. J. B. Lewis, Westminster Park, Chester
Mrs. D. Llewellyn, Pentyrch, Cardiff
Mr. D. Lloyd, Cardiff
Mr. T. Lloyd, Freestone Hall, Cresselly
Joanna Lloyd-Davies, Market St., Aberaeron, Ceredigion
Mr. P. Lloyd Harvey, Aberaeron, Ceredigion
Llyfrgell, Ceredigion, Aberystwyth
The Hon. & Mrs. J. Long, Highworth, Wilts.
The Viscount Long, Newquay, Cornwall
Mrs. K. M. Lynch, North Lambton, NSW, Aust.
Mrs. J. F. Lyne, Beulah, Newcastle Emlyn

Mr. & Mrs. P. Maddison, Lagos, Portugal
Dr. I. Manoli, Athens
Mr. A. G. Marriner, Dorridge, Solihull
Mrs. M. Martin, Johnston, Pembs.
Mr. & Mrs. C. Mason-Watts, Noyadd Trefawr, Ceredigion
Mr. C. Mathias, Carew, Tenby
Mrs. R. May, Epsom, Surrey
Mrs. E. McAteer, Tredefaid, Pembs.
Miss C. McCann, Llansaint, Kidwelly
Capt. E. D. Mellon, Bare, Morecambe
Viscountess Melville, Far Oakridge, Glos.
Mrs. M. Mitchell, nèe Bowen, Beaconsfield
Dr. M. Mohindar, Hong Kong
A. Moon, Trewern, Whitland
Miss J. Morgan, Cambridge
Mr. H. P. G. Morgan, Ynystawe, Clydach
Mr. T. L. Morgan, The Grove, Ickenham
Mr. & Mrs. R. Morris, Romara, Fishguard

Mrs. E. S. R. Morris, Parc-y-nole, Mathry
Mr. B. J. Munt, Haverfordwest

M. O'Donnell, Bristol
Mrs. A. Owen Taylor, Creigiau, Cardiff
Mr. & Mrs. D. Owen, Natal, S. Africa,
Mr. A. Owen, Lerwick, Shetland

Mr. M. S. Palmer, Little Shelford, Cambridge
Mr. & Mrs. J. Pearce, Carrow Hill, Caldicot, Mons.
Mr. E. Peel, Madrid, Spain
Mr. E. H. Perkins, Bethesda, Pembs.
Mr. R. Phillips, Brisbane, Aust.
H. V. Phythian-Adams, Leamington Spa
Mr. T. Picton-Devonald, Pontardawe, Swansea
Mr. & Mrs. P. Pocock, Vallee du Lot, France
Mr. C. Poole, Bainswood, Yorks.
Mr. J. S. Powell, Penmaen, Swansea
Mr. G. D. Pratten, Alsager, Stoke-on-Trent

Mrs. A. Reed, Pencraig, Trefin
Dr. R. G. Rees, Penygroes, Crymych
Mr. G. B. Rees, Dinas, Pembs.
Mr. & Mrs. W. Rees, Llanelli
Mrs. B. Rees, Llanelli, Carms.
Mr. J. S. Richard, Taplow, Berks.
Mr. A. D. Richardson, Cothill House, Abingdon
Mr. & Mrs. G. V. Robinson, Green Castle, Carmarthen
Mr. & Mrs. M. H. B. Ryder, Tiers Cross, Haverfordwest

Mrs. S. E. Savage, Hull, E. Yorks.
Mr. T. Scarrott, Grondre, Clynderwen, Pembs.
Mr. G. Scoles, Nottinghamshire
Mr. R. W. Scott, Kiln Parc, Burton Ferry
Dr. E. Scourfield, Sully, Penarth
Mrs. K. Silcox-Butt, Franks Hall, Kent
Mr. I. F. Skyrm, Broadheath, Worcs.
Mr. C. Stringer, Burbage, Leics.
Capt. & Mrs. G. J. Thomas, Newport, Pembs.
Mr. A. R. W. Taylor, Felingwm, Carms.
Mr. E. R. Thomas, Leominster, Hereford
Mr. J. E. Thomas, Bridgend, Mid. Glam,
Mr. R. B. Thomas, Cinnamon Grove, Haverfordwest
Mr. M. Tree, Llanrwst
Mrs. G. M. Truslove, Boncath, Pembs.

M. Uptain, Wyoming, USA,
Mrs. A. Usher, Edinburgh, Scotland

Mr. J. C. Van Bylevelt, Coast & Country Estates, Pembs.
Mr. D. A. J. Vaughan, Builth Wells, Powys
Mr. A. Vaughan-Harries, Hayston Bridge, Pembs.

Mr. & Mrs. I. Walters, Torrevieja, Spain
Mrs. C. Ward, Longbridge Deverill, Wiltshire
Mrs. E. F. E. Warlow, Dale, Pembs.
His Honour D. Watkin Powell, Morknnedd
Mrs. M. Watson, Stone Hall, Welsh Hook
Mr. K. West, Winchester
Mrs. J. M. White, Milford Haven, Pembs.
Mrs. E. H. Whittle, Usk, Mons.
C. R. Williams-Ellis, London, N14
Mr. G. H. C. Wilmot, Langland Bay, Swansea
Wilson Museum, Narberth, Pembs.
Mr. T. J. Woolner, Long Compton, Warks.

PARISH MAP INDEX WITH HOUSES LISTED BY PARISH WITH MAJOR ISLANDS

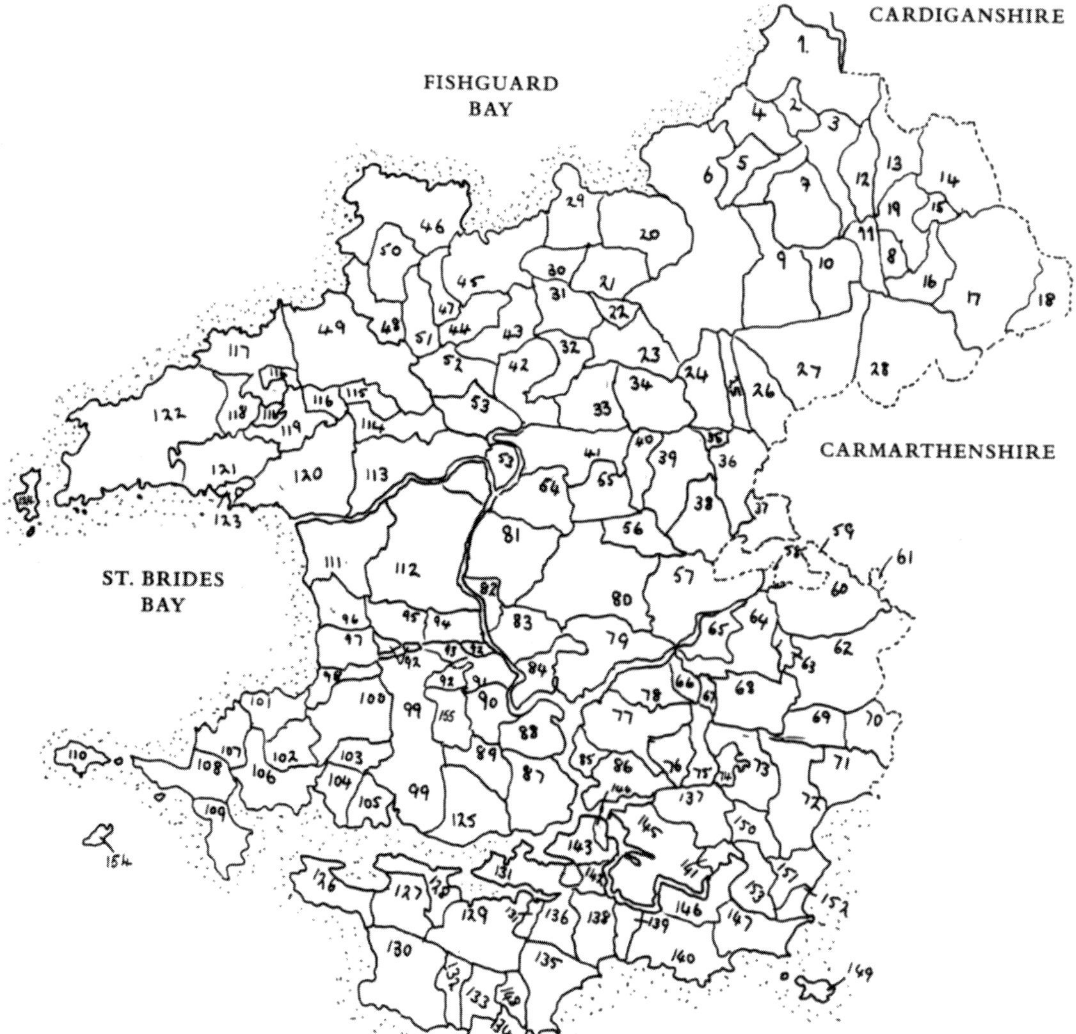

Ambleston 41
Hook
Rinaston
Scollock
Woodstock

Amroth 71
Amroth Castle
Coed Rath
Colby Lodge
Eastlake
Merrixton
Rhydlangoeg

Angle 126
Angle, The Hall
Bangeston

Bayvil 5

Begelly 73
Begelly House

Bletherston 38
Bletherston
Longridge
Posty
Tregendeg

Bosherston 134
Buckspool

Boulston 84
Boulston

Brawdy 120
Asheston (Trefasser)
Brawdy-Breudeth
Castle Villa
Eweston (Trewen)
Grinston
Llether
Lochvane (Lochfaen)
Newgale
Pointz Castle
Rickeston
Tancredston

Bridell 12
Bridell, (Plâs)
Cwmbettws
Ffynnon Coranau
Tŷ Gwyn

Burton 87
Ashdale/Dumpledale
Benton Castle
Milton
Williamston

Caldey Island 149
Caldey Island

Camrose 112
Camrose North
Camrose House
Cleddau Lodge
Dudwell
Keyston (Keeston)
Leweston
Roblinston
Wolfsdale

Capel Colman 15
Cilwendeg
Llwynbedw

Carew 145
Carew Castle
Carew Rectory
Ford
Freestone Hall
Milton House
Welston

Castellan 8

Castlebythe 33
Castlebythe (Casfuwch)
Longhook

Castlemartin 130
Bowood
Brownslade
Bulliber
Flimston
Linney
Moor

Cilgerran 13
Castle Malgwyn (New)
Forest
Glandovan
Glynhenllan
Morgenau
Penallt Cadwgan
Penralltrheiny
Rhosygilwen

Cilrhedyn 18
Dyffryn Pibyll

Clarbeston 56

Clydey 17
Blaenbylan
Coedllwyd
Dolau Llanerch
Drysgol Goch
Glog
formerly Glog-y-fran
Lancych
Nantylladron
Penalltcych
Werngoy

Coedcanlas 85
Coedcanlas

Cosheston 143
Cosheston Hall
Paskeston

Crinow 63
Park Glas

Crunwear 70
Llanteg/Llanteague
Trenewydd

Dale 109
Allenbrook
Broomhill
Dale (Castle)

Dinas 29

East Williamston 150
Morgans

Eglwyswrw 7
Berllan
Carn Huan
Court (Cwrt)
Esgair Wilym
Frochest
Henllan Owen
Pencelli (Capel)
Pencelli Fawr
Pencelli Fychan
or Fawr
Pencelli Forest
Treclyn
Trewilym

Fishguard 45
Fishguard
Cefnydre (Cynheidre)
Cronllwyn
Fishguard
Glyn-y-mel
Pentour (Pentower)
Tregroes
Trewrach

Freystrop 90
Clareston
Little Milford

Granston 48
Llangloffan
Tregwynt
Treseissyllt

Grondre 58
Glanrhyd
Grondre

Gumfreston 153
Gumfreston
Wedlock

Haroldston, St Issells 91
Fern Hill
Haroldston
Haylett

Haroldston West 97
Haroldston Hall

Hasguard 102
Hasguard

Haverfordwest, St Martin's 94
Foley House
Glenover
Haverfordwest
Hermons Hill
Slade/Anastaslade
Sutton Lodge

Haverfordwest, St Thomas 92
Avellanau
Cinnamon Grove

Hayscastle 113
Brimaston
Hayscastle (Caslai)
Treindeg
alias Rhindaston

Henry's Moat 34
Barnards Well
Farthings Hook
(Clynffyrddin)

Herbrandston 104
Neeston

Hodgeston 139

Hubberston 105
Gelliswick

Hundleton 156
Orielton

Jeffreston 137
Cresselly
Jeffreston House

Johnston 155
Johnston (Hall)
Popehill

Jordanston 51
Clegyr
Jordanston (Hall)
Llangwarren

Lambston 95
Honey Hook

Lampeter Velfrey 62
Cilrhiw
Dyffryn
Lampeter Velfrey
Llanmarlais
Penlan
Treffgarne
Trewern
Tygwyn
Waungron

Lamphey 138
Lamphey Court
Lamphey Palace
Lamphey Park
North Down
Portclew
Trewent Hall

Lawrenny 86
Cresswell
Lawrenny

Letterston 52
Heathfield

Little Newcastle 42
Colston
Ffynnone
Summerton

Llanddewi Velfrey 60
Byrn
Caerau
Caermaenau Fawr
Fron
Henllan
Panteg (Panteague)
Penblewyn
Plâs Crwn

Llandeilo 25
Llandeilo

Llandeloy 119
Caerwen
Hendre
Lochmeyler
Llandinog
Trenichol

Llandissilio West 37
Byrnaeron
Brydysil
Castell Gwyn

Llanfairnantgwyn 11
Pantyderi
Pistyll Meigan
Trefach

Llanfairnantygof 43
Cilgelynen (Cilglynen)
Nantybugail
Trecwn

Llanfallteg West 59

**Llanfihangel
Penbedw 19**
Dolau Llwyd (ion)
Bachendre
Cilgadfarch
Cilrhiwe
Ffynnone Gleision
Gilfachwrnell
Penbedw
Plâs Iwerill (y werill)
Werddofn

Llanfyrnach 28
Blaiddbwll
Blaen Tâf
Graig
Pontygafel
Trefawr
Trehenry

Llangwm 88
East Hook
Hook
Nash, Great

Llangwm West 61

Llangolman 26
Clynsaithman
Cwm Cerwyn
Llangolman
Plâs y Meibion/Meibon
Pencraig

Llanhowel 118
Cerbyd
Lecha
Trefeugan
Treglemais

Llanllawer 30
Cwrt
Trellwyn
Trenewydd

Llanreithan 116
Llaney
Llanreithan

Llanrhian 117
Cartlett
Henllys
Park Court
Porthiddy Fawr *or* Fach
Torbant
Trefin
Trenewydd Fawr
Trevaccoon
Treyarched
Ynys Barry

Llanstadwell 125
Hayston
Honeyborough
Jordanston
Newton

Llanstinan 44
Cilau Wen
Llanstinan

Llantood 3
Fagwr Goch
Rhydgarnwen
Tredefaid

Llanwnda 46
Carne Coch
Dyffryn Wdig
Felindre
Goodwick (Wdig),
Llanwnwr
Penrhiw
Penysgwarn(e)
Trehowel
Trenewydd Manor

Llanycefn 36
Llandre

Llanychaer 31
Cilciffeth
Y Garn

Llanychllwydog 21
Mynyddmelyn
Tredafydd

Llawhaden 57
Llawhaden
Ridgeway
St. Kennox
Talybont
Vaynor
Vaynor, Great

Llysyfran 40
Felindre
Southfield

Lubston 75

Ludchurch 69
Hill
Westerton

Maenclochog 24
Bwlch y Clawdd
alias Temple Druid
Cotty
Vorlan

Manorbier 140
East Moor
Lydstep Palace
Manorbier Castle
Norchard
Sunny Hill

Manordeifi 14
Blaen Mwrw
Castle Malgwyn, Old
Cilast Ucha
Cilfowyr
Cilrhiwe Fach
Clynfyw
Ffynnonau Bychan, *later* Ffynnone
Parc Cynhaethw (Y)
Penalltyllyn
Penlan Cych
Pentre
Plâs y Berllan
Vaynor

Manorowen 47
Brwynant
Langton
Manorowen
Scleddau
Trebrithin
Trellewelyn

Marloes 108
Crabhole
Fobston
Hook
Marloes Court
Musselwick (Muslick)
Philbeach (Filberch)
Winterton

Martletwy 77
Landshipping
Landshipping Ferry
Landshipping House
Landshipping Quay
Martletwy House

Mathry 49
Carnachenwen
Castle Cenlas
Castle Morris
Lochturffin
Longhouse
Llwyn-y-gorras
Mabws Fawr
Pencnwc
Priskilly
Rhoslanog Fawr
Rhyd yr Harding
Trefellyn
Trewallter Lwyd
Waunberry

Meline 9
Blaen y Groes/Gors
Bryanog
Glanduad
Hafod Tydfil
Helygnant
Hendre
Merianog
Penpedwast
Penybenglog
Pontgynon
Rhosdwarch
Rhosmaen

Minwear 78
Minwear

Monington 2
Pantsaeson
Trefigin

Monkton 129
Castleton
Crickmarren
Fleet
Monkton Old Hall

Morfil 23
Morfil

Mounton 67
Mounton

Moylgrove 4
Fagwr Eynon Fawr
Hafod Grove
Trefaes
Treprisk (Tre-prysg)

Mynachlogddu 27
Dolemaen
Dyffryn Ffilbro
Pentre Ithel

Narberth North 64, South 68
Blackaldern
Eastwood
Greenway
Grove
Molleston
Narberth Plâs
Rushacre
Sodston House

Nash 142
Nash, Lower

Nevern 6
Argoed
Berry Hill/Bury
Cilgwyn
Cilrydd, Cilryth
Coedwynog
Crugiau Cemaes
Cwmeog
Cymgloyn
Frongoch
Gellifor
Glastir (Glasdir)
Henllys
Llwyngoras
Llwyngwair
Llwynihirion
Llystyn
Nevern (Nanhyfer)
Nevern Castle
Pentre Ifan/Evan
Penyrallt
Tredrissi
Trefach
Tregamman
Trehaidd
Trellyffaint
Trerickert
Trewern
Trewrdan
Wenallt

New Moat 39
Ffynnon Gain
The Mote (Moat)

Newport 20
Brithdir
Holmws
Llannerch (y Bleddiau)
Newport Castle

Newton North 66
New House (Red Castle)

Nolton 96
Druidston
Nolton

Pembroke, St Mary's 131
Bangeston
Bush
Golden
Llanion
Paterchurch
Pembroke Castle
Pennar

Pembroke St Michael 136
Alleston
Biers Pool
Grove
Holyland
Kingston
Underdown

Penally 147
Carswell
Penally Abbey
Penally Court
Tarr
Trefloyne
Whitewell

Penrith 16
Dolpwll

Pontfaen 22
Pontfaen

Prendergast 82
Cottesmore
Prendergast
Scotchwell

Puncheston 32
Martel

Pwllcrochan 128
Greenhill

Ramsey Island 124
Ramsey Island (Ynys Dewi)

Redberth 141

Reynoldston 74

Rhoscrowther 127
Eastington
Henllan

Robeston Wathan 65
Canaston, Great
Robeston Wathan House

Robeston West 103
Rickeston Hall
Robeston Hall

Roch 111
Cuffern
Ferny Glen
Folkeston
Hilton
Roch
Simpston
Summer Hill
Trefran (Trevrane)

Rosemarket 89
Moor
Rosemarket
Westfield

Rudbaxton 81
Fletherhill
Kilbarth
Newton
Poyston Hall
Rudbaxton, Great
Withybush

Skokholm Island 154

Skomer Island 110

Slebech 79
Arnoldshill
Picton Castle
Slebech

Spittal 54
Haythog
Scolton Manor

St Brides 107
Orlandon
Pierston
St Brides

St Davids 122
Clegyr
Clegyr Boia
Cruglas
Cwmwdig
Hendre Eynon
Llandigige Fach
Llandigige Fawr
Penarthur
Penberry
Port Clais
Trefinert
Treginnis Issa
Treginnis Ucha
Treleddyn
Tretio Fawr
Trewellwell
Warpool Court

St Dogmaels 1
Esgair
Glanpwllafon
Hendre
Pantirion
Penyrallt
Rhosmoeled
St Dogmaels
Trerees

St Dogwells 53
Sealyham
Trefgarne, Little
Welsh Hook
Wolfscastle

St Edrins 115
Parselle
Treddiog
Trehale (Trehal)
Trewallterwen

St Elvis 123
St Elvis

St Florence 146
East Jordanston
Ivy Tower

St Ishmaels 106
Bicton
Butterhill
Hoaten
Mullock
Sandyhaven
Trewarren

St Issells 72
Bonville's Court
Hean Castle
Kilgetty
Kilvelgy (Cilvelgy)
Netherwood

St Lawrence 114
Stone Hall
Trerhos
Trewilym

St Mary out Liberty 151
Cornish Down

St Nicholas 50
Trefayog

St Mary's Petrox 148
Stackpole Court

St Twynells 133
Lacerry
Loveston
Thorne

Stackpole Eldior 135

Steynton 99
Annikell
Barret's Hill
Bolton Hill
Bunker's Hill
Castle Hall
Denant
Harmeston
Hill
St Botolphs
Scovaston
Studda
Thornton House

Talbenny 101
Howelston
Talbenny Hall

Tenby (St Mary) 132
Croft House
Scotsborough
Sion House
Waterwinch

Turzey Park and Portfield 93

Upton 144
Upton Castle

Uzmaston 83
Cartlett
Good Hook

Vorlan 35

Walton East 55
Pentypark

Walton West 98

Walwyn's Castle 100
Capeston
Moor
Rosemoor
Rosepool
Walwyn's Castle

Warren 132
Merrion Court

Whitchurch in Cemaes 121
Clyn Meredith
Gwern Fullbrook
Rhydydrissi
Whitchurch

Whitchurch 10
Caerforiog
Hendre Riffith
Llanunwas
Trecadwgan

Wiston 80
Colby
Wiston

Yerbeston 76

N Pembs. site unknown
Llether Wogan
Winterton

Miscellaneous
Bishop's Palaces

GLOSSARY OF USEFUL TERMS

* : New house entry.

BOVATE: Area an ox can plough in a season.

CARUCATE: See PLOUGHLAND.

COCKROAD: Clear cut road through a wood across which a net is hung from opposite trees to catch woodcock. Cockshoot time is dusk when birds are most likely to fly into the nets.

COUPLES: The pairs of 'A' frames which hold up a roof.

CULM: the slack of anthracite coal, mixed with beaten clay and water and made into 'balls', and used on the fire it burned very slowly and the fire could be kept in all night.

DEMESNE: Land retained by the lord of the manor for his own use and upon which tenants give free labour as part of their obligations in return for their holdings.

FOREST: Originally used to describe an open area with trees and pasture, moorland and mountain reserved for hunters.

GAVELKIND: Equal succession to land of all heirs.

HUSBAND: Tenant farmer

INTIA ALIA: Among others.

KNIGHT'S FEE: Land held by a knight in return for military service being roughly 640 acres (10 ploughlands).
20 knight's fees held of the King make a Barony.
5 knight's fees held of Earldom of Pembroke make a Barony.

MESNE: Subordinate

MESSUAGE: Dwelling house with outbuildings and land assigned to its use.

OUTSHUTE: Lean-to room attached to the house and an integral part of the design.

PLOUGHLAND: The amount of land that could be ploughed in a year.
Varying from 60-180 acres from place to place.

PROTONOTARY: Chief clerk or registrar in a law court.

STANG: Measure of land, a quarter of a Welsh acre.

SUIT OF COURT: Obligation to attend the lord's court.

TOWNRED: Township or cluster of homesteads.

IURE UXOIS: In right of his wife.

VIDE: See

Ref: G. Owen, *Elizabethan Pembrokeshire.* Ed Brian Howells, 1973. Pembs. Record Office.

BIBLIOGRAPHICAL ABBREVIATIONS

Anc. Mon. Pembs.:	Ancient Monuments Commissioners Pembrokeshire.
Arch. Cam.:	*Archaeologia Cambrensis.*
B. G. Charles, *NCPN*:	*Non Celtic Place Names,* Dr. B. G. Charles, 1938, Ldn. Medieval Studies.
Burke, *LG,* 1850:	Burke's Landed Gentry, 1850 edn.
C of A:	College of Arms, London.
Carms. RO:	Carmarthenshire Records Office.
Carms. Studies, 1974.:	Carmarthenshire Studies, presented to Major Francis Jones, ed. T. Barnes and N. Yates, Carmarthen, published 1974.
Chancery Proc.:	Chancery Proceedings Ser. 11420/40.
DNB:	Dictionary of National Biography, 63 vols., Ldri. 1885-1900, reprinted Oxford 1921-22.
DWB:	Dictionary of Welsh Biography down to 1940 - London 1959.
Dwnn:	Heraldic Visitations see Meyrick, Samuel Rush.
Fenton *Tour Pembs.*:	An Historical Tour through Pembrokeshire, Richard Fenton. 1811.
fo.:	Folio.
GGMS:	Golden Grove Manuscripts.
ibid.:	See last reference.
JBAA:	Journal of British Architectural Association.
LT:	Land Tax lists.
Laws, *Little England:*	Laws, *Little England Beyond Wales,* edn. 1888.
Lewis, *TDW*:	Lewis Samuel, *A Topographical Dictionary of Wales.* Vols. 1 & 2, London 1833, 4th Edn.
MS/MSS:	Manuscript/s.
NLW:	National Library of Wales.
PRO:	Public Record Office.
Papers of GS:	Papers of Great Sessions.
Pembs. RO:	Pembrokeshire Records Office.
Pembs. Arch. Svy.:	Pembrokeshire Archaeological Survey.
Pembs. Hist.:	The Pembrokeshire Historian.
Protheroe:	Protheroe Beynon Collection.
R. Comm. on Land in Wales:	Royal Commission on Land in Wales.
RCAM:	Royal Commission for Ancient and Historical Monuments in Wales, An Inventory of the Ancient Monuments in Wales and Monmouthshire, London 1917.
Rees, *Beauties* of *S. Wales:*	Rees Thomas, The Beauties of England and Wales, South Wales, Vol. XVIII, London 1815.
SC (JF) 1988.:	John Francis Sale Catalogues.
Steegman, *Portraits*:	*A Survey of Portraits in Welsh Houses,* Vol. 11, J. Steegman, Cardiff 1962.
Taylor's *Cussion*:	George Owen, the Taylor's *Cussion,* London.
Timmins, *Nooks Pembs.*:	*Nooks & Corners of Pembrokeshire* 1895. Timmins.
Trans. Cymmrodor.:	*Transactions of the Honourable Society of Cymmrodorion.*
VL:	Voter's Lists.
WWHR:	West Wales Historical Records.

ALLENBROOK, *Dale*
An interesting 19th century residence in attractive grounds. One part of it was the former vicarage which, with attached houses, has been transformed into a commodious dwelling. It contains a portrait, said to be by Gainsborough, of John Hook Campbell of Bangeston, Lord Lyon King of Arms. Home of Lt. Col. G. B. A. Rind, High Sheriff in 1935, and of his son B. H. G. Rind, High Sheriff in 1966. Lt. Col. George Burnet Abercrombie Rind was the son of W. B. Rind. George Rind married Gwladys Mary, daughter of Thomas Cairns of Delston Hall, Northumberland. Their arms: ermine a cross.

ALLESTON, *St. Michael's Pembroke*
In 1382 it was known as Aylwardiston, which developed into the present form. During the first half of the 17th century it was the home of the Webb family. The original owner was Sir John Carew of Crowcombe Court, Somerset, and in 1605 Edward Webb agreed to surrender a lease on the property to Sir John, but with the right to occupy it till 1608, to preserve deer in the park, to kill two bucks, and to leave '400 sheep with 40 other cattle' to Sir John. In 1609 Edward Webb of Alleston gent. was sued by Margaret Elliott alias Shepherd, widow, for taking some of her cattle from 'le roughe parke in Carew'. Edward Webb married an unknown Margaret, whose will was proved 2 August 1632. They had three sons, the eldest, Thomas Webb was of Alleston in 1637, the other sons were Richard and Alexander viv. 1624. Alderman Francis Davies of Pembroke, the third son of Henry Davies of Bangeston, whose will was proved 16 October 1706, married an unknown Mary and they had a sole heir Francis Davies who was of Alleston. He married Elinor, daughter of Barrett Bowen of Neston, by Rebecca Allen of Gelliswick and they had three daughters, Margaret who married Rev. Willliam Williams of Nash parish; Elizabeth of whom nothing is known and Judith baptized 1698, who married Rev. Rowland Gwynne and who had two daughters both of whom died unmarried. Judith's will was proved 1740. Thomas Poyer of Alleston, was the second husband of Anne, widow of Thomas Warren of Pembroke by whom she had had one son and two daughters. Anne was the daughter of Richard Jordan of Dumpledale and Elenor Morgan of Muddlescomb.

Alleston was owned in 1904 by the Owens of Withybush, and let to farming tenants.

Refs: BM Egerton 2586, fo. 385; B. G. Charles, *NCPN,* p. 24; Rees, Map of 14th century Pembs.; LT 1786, and subsequent VL.

ALLT-Y-RHEINY,
see **PENRALLTRHEINY**

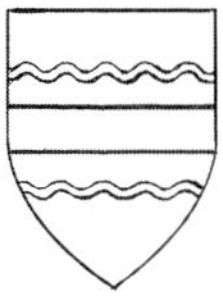
Elliot

AMROTH CASTLE/ EARWERE, *Amroth*
On a low meadow near the seashore. The original name Earwere may be derived from a Scandinavian word 'eyrr' denoting a sand or gravel bank. Although superseded about 1800 by the name Amroth Castle, the older name is still used locally, pronounced 'eah-weah'. Seat of the Elliots, from about 1445 it continued in that family for nearly three and a half centuries. They also had residences at Plâs (Narberth), Westerton and Kiffig, the estate lying in the parishes of Amroth, St. Issells, Crunwere, Robeston, Ludchurch and Narberth. In 1597 the herald Dwnn recorded the family pedigree and arms, *argent* a fess *gules,* two bars wavy *azure*. In 1670 Earwere contained five hearths. They provided the county with High Sheriffs in 1585, 1609 and 1754. The last of the family, Alexander Elliot, died at Earwere of the gout in 1756. By his wife Elizabeth (widow of Joseph Walter of Rosemarket and Roch, and daughter of John Barlow of Lawrenny) he had no issue. Elizabeth died before 1780, and

Earwere became the property of her sister, Mrs. Catherine Owen who was still living at the mansion in 1791. Before 1798 it had been sold to James Acland who built a castellated residence at Earwere, to be named Amroth Castle – which is, substantially, still standing.

Fanny Price Gwynne in *Sketches of Tenby* described a building hardly recognisable today. 'The entrance is from a lodge-gate, under an avenue, to the principal door on the same side, with a sloping lawn in front, ornamented by clumps of young trees, and a richly wooded hill opposite. The principal sitting rooms open to the sea on the other front. The drawing room is of most noble and lofty dimensions, and lit by a large bay window, of itself almost a room. This projecting turret is carried two storeys in height from the garden beneath, and forms a sort of balcony to the room above the drawing room. The gardens are very extensive with high walls. There are numerous sleeping and sitting rooms, with a broad easy staircase; the lower rooms are of great extent and variety with numerous kitchens, offices etc.' Fenton tells us that although the garden walls 'are literally washed by the ocean surge, yet by means of their height and frequent intersecting shelter he has plenty of fruit etc., the conservatory and grapery, entered by handsome glass doors, are so contrived that you can walk out of the dining parlour into them . . . This noble room, as now converted into a dining-parlour was a vault–roofed ale cellar in the time of the former proprietors; and by the strength, gloominess and massiveness of its ancient portal, Captain Ackland is inclined to think, that in the feudal times it was the castle prison'. Francis Jones gives the complete history and pedigree of the Elliotts of Earwere in his essay of that name.

Ownership changed a few times during the 19th century, and by 1852 had been converted into a Lunatic Asylum by Dr. Norton, the then owner. In 1897 Amroth Castle was advertised for sale and was bought by Sir Owen Cosby Philipps (created Lord Kylsant in 1923). It remained in the ownership of his descendants until quite recently.

Refs: Dwnn, i, pp. 122, 154, 204: Fenton, *Tour Pembs.*, 1811; Lewis, *TDW,* 1840; F. P. Gwynne, *Sketches,* edn. 1852; B. G. Charles *NCPN*, p. 91; NLW, Probate Wills; *RCAM Pembs.* 1925; Carms. RO Llanstephan docs. Sale 1897. illust: Roscoe Howells, *Old Saundersfoot*, 1977, Cat. illust; Pembs. RO, Deeds D/LJ, 598 and also Carmarthen Deeds in Pembs. RO.

ANASTASLADE (SLADE),

St. Martins, Haverfordwest

The farm lies on the northern outskirts of Haverfordwest, just off the St. Davids road. In old deeds it is given as Aunsellsland, Ancellislade, Anastaslade, from 1324 to the 17th century, and according to Dr. Charles it was originally 'Ansel's slade' named after the occupier. Colby's Map of 1831 shows three farms named Slade and a fourth named Lower Slade, in the area where Slade farm still survives. It was the home of the gentry family of Morgan, the first being Anthony Morgan of Answerslad, who was followed there by his son Rees Morgan, Esquire, who had married, before 1556, Thomasin Sutton of Haverfordwest. Their son Harry Morgan was living at Hoaton in Roose in 1578. One of the farms was occupied in 1578 by Roger Marcroft described as 'of Ansterslade, gentleman alias mercer.' In 1610-1613 James ap Rice (Price) gentleman, lived there, being followed in 1621 by his son Thomas Price of Anteslade, gentlemen.

In the next century 'Slade otherwise Little Slade otherwise Anastaslade' became the property of Daniel Evans of Peterwell (Cards), and in 1722 was given to his daughter Sarah who had married Marmaduke Gwynne of Garth (Brec). A deed of 1754 mentions the messuage called Great Slade. By 1774-85 Slade land was owned by Lord Milford. Slade messuage and lands formerly the property of Joseph Fortune, given by his widow, Hannah to her son, William 30 June 1803. A Report on new Hunt kennels (Slade Farm) made to Lord Milford 1899. Valuation Book Picton estate, 1911-12 shows Slade and other properties owned by Elizabeth Phillips – tenanted D. Morris. Slade House and land, owner, C. E. G. Philipps, tenant R. Wade and Sons. At a sale of part of Picton Estate 25 July 1928 Slade dwelling house, outbuildings and 12 acres. Sold to T. Wade for £2,160. Sold in 1968 to Mr. W. & H. Goodridge. Mr & Mrs M. Goodridge, now farm there. In the 16th century Slade belonged to the Crown and Henry VIII gave the revenues to Ann Boleyn.

Refs: Pembs. Public Records, Vols. I and II; *RCAM Pembs.*, 309; Slebech Deeds; Picton Castle Deeds: NLW, Papers of Great Sessions, Pembs.; Partition of the Peterwell estate 1722, document loaned to me by the late Major H. Lloyd-Johns; Mr. & Mrs. M. Goodridge.

Mirehouse

ANGLE, The Hall of,
just SE of Angle village

Fenton recorded a local legend that three co-heiresses decided each to build a residence at Angle: one built a castle, the other 'a very handsome building' in the village, and the third built 'a mansion a little way out of the village to the southeast called the Hall which appears in its day to have been very respectable and belonged till of late years to a family of the name of Kinnar, a name that still exists in the village.' (A similar tale is told of Trefloyne, *vide infra.*) The Kinners were engaged in trade and farming at Angle and Haverfordwest, and intermarried with families like the Voyles and Walter of Roch.

In 1587 Sir John Perrot was lord of 'the manor of Hall place in Nangle'. The herald, Dwnn, in 1613 recorded the pedigree of 'William Kiner off the Hawl off Angel'. The family continued at the hall for nearly two more centuries; John Kinner was assessed at four hearths at the Hall in 1670; and William Kinner was mayor of Pembroke in 1703. The house is described in 1739 as 'The Hall alias Court House in Angle'. In 1786 William Kinner was owner-occupier of Hall lands while John Hook Campbell owned a part of the same lands. Early in the 19th century the Hall was purchased by John Mirehouse of Brownslade, and became the main seat of that family. Notably an 'improving landlord' and an enterprising farmer, the new owner was also a J.P., and in 1810, High Sheriff. He improved the Hall as a residence which his descendants still occupy. The Tithe Schedule 1841 describes John Mirehouse as owner of 'Hall Manor', with George Thomas as farming tenant there, one of the fields being known as 'Kiners meadow'.

Lewis tells us that 'near the church is a mansion called the Hall, the property of John Mirehouse, Esq. of Brownslade, to whom the whole parish belongs, and now in the occupation of a tenant. John Mirehouse was at Cambridge at the same time as John Campbell, later Lord Cawdor, and came to Pembrokeshire as his agent, (see *Treasury of Historic Pembrokeshire pp.* 120-137), and lived at Brownslade where a new mansion was built c. 1800. He was a notable farmer and lived finally at Angle dying there in 1823. He was the son of Rev. Thomas Mirehouse, Canon of Peterborough, Rector of Elton and of Welford, and descended from the Marquis of Cumberland. John Mirehouse married in 1788 Mary, sister of Sir John Edwards, Bt. of Garth who died 30 November 1856 aged 91. Their son, also John, had one son, John (1826-64), and two daughters, Elizabeth and Mary. Elizabeth married Richard Byrd Lovett of Staffordshire and it was their son, Richard who assumed the name of Mirehouse and lived at Angle. He was High Sheriff in 1886 and married Mary Beatrice Entwhistle who died in 1941. They had three daughters, one of them Gwladys married Col. Norton Symons Allen who took the name of Allen-Mirehouse.

Refs: Dwnn, i, 109; Taylor's *Cussion,* fo. 98; Picton Castle Deeds; Cawdor Muniments; *Arch. Cam.* 1868, 75; ibid. 1877, 311; ibid. 1880, 342 (illust); *Anc. Mon. Pembs.,* 9-10; Steegman, *Portraits of South Wales,* 175.

ANNIKEL (ANNIKELL), *Steynton*

A short distance northeast from Tiers Cross, and near the road leading to Merlins Bridge and Haverfordwest, now a farmhouse. There are references to the place as early as 1326, but little is known about it, and by the 17th century it formed part of the Picton Castle estate. Lawrence Hore, husbandman, was living at Annikell in 1628. It was later tenanted by the Stokes family. There was a spring on the land, but in 1664 Nicholas Stokes husbandman failed to clear and scour the ditch so the water did not have a free passage to Necell, which led to his appearance in the Court of Great Sessions. By 1670 the Elliots came there and later had a lease from Picton Castle, but this was surrendered to Sir Richard Philipps in the 1760s, and the family moved to St. Botolphs. Annikell was later held by farming tenants.

Refs: Picton Castle Deeds; NLW, Probate Wills.

ARGOED, *Nevern*

Now a farmstead, between Wenallt and Pentre Ifan. These are the words of George Owen of Henllys, written in 1603 , 'Argoed, the mansion house of John Bowen ychan, gentleman, beinge a house of long contynuance . . . this and much other landes was the portion of Owen vychan sonne to Llewelyn ap Owen [of Pentre Ifan], who had yssue Howell ap Owen ychan, which Howell had two sonnes, Thomas and Llewelyn, between whom he parted his inheritaunce, leaving Argoed and diverse landes with the same to Thomas; and to Llewelyn he gave Trefcoyged and diverse other tenementes neere hande. Thomas of Argoed had yssue James Thomas ap Howell, father to Rees, Gruffith, and Mathias. Rees sould Argoed to Mathias his younger brother, who, by his will devysed the same to John Bowen ychan who now enjoyeth it . . . the armes of the said John Bowen ychan are those of Pentre Ievan with the difference of a fowrthe brother descended of a third. The arms of the yssue of the said Owen vychan is also that of Pentre Ievan.'

Robert Bowen of Argoed was fined £40 'for unlawfully entering into the bedchamber of Thomas Lloyd, Esq. deceased of Cilciffith in the night-tyme presently after his decesse, locking the doore thereof, at such tyme the chests, trunks and coffers were opened.' Robert Bowen was the son of Owen and great-grandson of Sir James Bowen. Robert married Anne Birt relict of William Bowen his first cousin, son of James Bowen. They had two daughters, Elenor and Anne.

Over two centuries later, Richard Fenton of Glyn-y-mel reflected, 'Nevern Argoed now sunk to a farm-house, but once the residence of one of the four sons of Llewhellin ap Owen, a wide-spreading branch of the Gwynfardd tree, but long since decayed.' John Bowen ychan who inherited Argoed from Mathias James, married Elizabeth daughter of Owen ap Rhys of Towyn (in Ferwig) but had no issue. He died in 1605, his wife *circa* 1614. His brother Morgan Bowen followed him but the line petered out. In 1634 Elizabeth, daughter of William Bowen of Argoed and widow of George Lloyd of Cwm-gloyn lived there and by 1642 Rees Young, gentleman, lived at Argoed, and by 1652 it was in the hands of Elizabeth Jones, widow. Thereafter it became a farmstead.

Refs: George Owen, *2nd Book,* 1603-4, p. 275; Fenton *Tour Pembs.,* 1811; LT 1786; GGMS Gwynfardd; College of Arms, Protheroe MS IV; NLW, Pembs. Plea Rolls, Bronwydd Deeds; *Dwnn,* i, 166, 169, 170; BM Egerton MS. 2586; Harl. MS 4220; Fines of Court of Cl. of the Marches 1616-37.

ARNOLDSHILL, *Slebech*

A farmstead some four miles east of Haverford-west between Deep Lake and Slebech (new) church.

It once comprised various holdings. From 1331 onwards it was described as Arnolds Hill, doubtless preserving the name of the first or early owner. In 1419 Sir John Wogan owned 1¼ carucates 'in Arnoldshille'; in 1472 it belonged to Philip Alexander, and by 1501 was owned by Rogers of Pentypark, and Stephens. In 1526 Philip Stephen leased 'the manor of Arnoldshill in the barony of Dungleddy' and other properties to Hugh Mansel gentleman and his wife Jane (Wogan) for 60 years.

Philip Stephen of Arnoldshill was heir of his brother, John viv. 1501. They were the sons of Thomas Stephen (Stephyn), by Alice, daughter of John Rogers of Pentypark. The Rogers family of Pentypark owned considerable lands in Arnolds Hill. On 11 September 1501 John Roger, senior, of Bentebergh, gave a grant for life to Matilda Butler of three messuages and two carucates at Arnoldshill and a burgage at Slebech, with reversion to John Stephyn, son of Thomas Stephyn of Arnoldshill and Alice his wife (which Alice was daughter of said John Rogers), and their heirs. Bridget Tooley and Margaret Warner of Slebech were before a jury in 1619 'for absenting from their parish church for 15 months past'. In 1648 John Tooley was compounded for delinquency: his will was proved 26 July 1655. Margaret Tooley also dated her will in that year, and Catherine Tooley in 1668.

By 1532 John Husband was in possession, and in that year he mortgaged 'the capital messuage' to the Wogans; seven years later John Wogan of Wiston granted 'the capital messuage of Arnoldeshyle' to his son and heir Richard Wogan and his wife Elizabeth, and in 1577 sold that property and seven other farms to John Barlow of Slebech for £600. Thereafter Arnolds Hill formed part of the Slebech estate whose owners leased it to a series of yeomen – John Tooley from 1619 to 1658. John Bell who had settled there was assessed for seven hearths in 1670 which shows Arnoldshill to have been commodious. Walter Thornborough, an attorney, tenanted it in 1705, but by 1715 it was leased to a yeoman, George Barzey, whose descendants were granted renewable leases. The Barzeys had lived from 1692 to 1810 at Lecha in Dewsland (vide infra), the last male of the family, Richard, son of Thomas Barzey of Arnoldshill, died there suddenly on 12 February 1814. Afterwards various tenants held the property. Eventually it became property of the de Rutzen family and is still owned by descendants.

In 1921 Arnolds Hill farm comprised 265 acres, the dwelling house contained parlour, dining room, two kitchens, larder, pantry, dairy, seven bedrooms, two attics, cellar and outbuildings. I visited the house in 1976: it was a cross-passage house of two storeys and an attic storey: a square house, large chimney at each end, a 'simne fawr' has been closed in: a short wing extends at one end now arranged as dairy and store-room; below the whole is an arched cellar or undercroft built above a rocky outcrop: an extension, 'catslide', now houses a kitchen and dining-room, with a porch entrance: there are some stone corbels supporting oak beams: the main entrance door leads into a hallway: the parlour has an ornamental frieze, probably an 18th century decoration: fine old range of outbuildings and a coach-house with the date 1832 carved on a stone above the entrance: in the farmyard is a well with remains of a cupola, the whole walled: remains of a walled garden and orchards: remains of an avenue of trees and a drive from the house to main road: the house stands on high land, with a good southward view.

Refs: NLW, Slebech Deeds; Carms. RO. Sale Cat. No. 460; WWHR, vi; Owen Pembs. vols II and III.

Jordan

ASHDALE,
formerly **Dumpledale,** *Burton*

An ancient mansion, renamed Ashdale in the period 1845-50 by the then owner-occupier George Lort-Phillips, later of Lawrenny. The property is at the northern end of the parish, about half a mile from Llangwm on the Eastern Cleddau. From the reign of Henry VII it was the home of the Jordan family, also settled at Jordanston (in Llanstadwell), Honeyborough, Hayston, Neeston, Barrett's Hill, Berllan (in Cemaes), and Haverfordwest. John Jordan of Dumpledale was assessed at four hearths in 1670. The family arms were; *Argent* a chevron between 3 greyhounds courant *gules.* The last of the male line at Dumpledale was the Rev. John Jordan, M.A. (Jesus College, Oxon.), J.P., who died without issue on 27 April 1808 at the age of 59.

Francis Jones gives an account of the unfortunate family of Jordan of Dumpledale: The first of the Jordans there, was Leonard Jordan who married the daughter of John of 'Doomple Dale': he was followed by his son, John Jordan who married a daughter of Jenkin Lloyd of Cemais; and was followed by his son, also John Jordan the elder who was slain at Banbury with Sir Henry Wogan. His wife was Elizabeth Shermyn; John Jordan the younger, was aged eight or nine years when his father

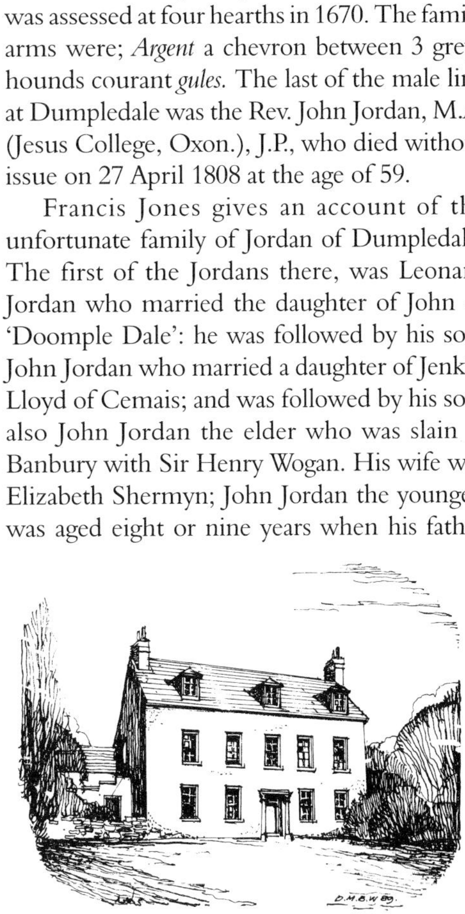

was killed, he married Anne Elliot and went with his master, the Duke of Buckingham against the King, and was beheaded in Haverfordwest Castle: his son, William Jordan was four years old when his father was beheaded. He married Margaret Fychan of Cilgerran and went with Sir John Wogan as captain to Terwin and Turney, and there was slain; Richard Jordan his son, was nine years old when his father was killed, married Eleanor Morgan of Muddlescomb and had issue. "During these minorytyes som of theire kinsmen entryd into the Jordans land in Kemes and kept yet ever sins". This would appear a family unable to keep their heads about them.

Later in the 19th century Dumpledale was sold to George Lort-Phillips, who made alterations to the house, described in 1840 by Lewis (*TDW*) as 'a handsome modern mansion'.

It changed hands several times after the Lort-Phillips occupation and was bought in 1973 by Mr. William Rees of Haverfordwest who repaired and improved the house. A sale catalogue of 1983 describes Ashdale as of two storeys with range of five windows, and an attic storey with three (modern) dormer windows, six bedrooms, three reception rooms, kitchen: the present courtyard at the rear was formerly part of the domestic quarters, and was once a north wing which accommodated the principal rooms. Today called Ashdale, but the old name is perpetuated in the name of an adjoining farm, Little Dumple Dale.

Refs: Dwnn, i, 157; Carms RO, SC 607 (1907); G.D. in Egerton 2586; NLW, Slebech Deeds, No. 11422, Morgan-Richardson Deeds, i, GS; Pembs Plea Rolls.

ASHESTON (TREFASSER),
A large farm in Brawdy parish
Mentioned in 1326 as Assepiston (Asseriston). From Elizabethan days until the late 18th century it formed part of the estate of the Laugharne family. Described as Treffasser in 1580, as Asheston alias Trevasser in 1632. Among the tenants were Edward Philpin (1630), John Bateman, Thomas Evan and John Charles in 1842. The owner, John Philipps Laugharne of Orlandon, mortgaged Asheston in £600 to Henry John, gentlemen, of Caerwen in 1787; in 1795 the said John Philipps Laugharne and Lettice, widow of the said Henry John, conveyed Asheston to Thomas Raymond, gentleman and in the following year Raymond leased Asheston to Thomas Evan, farmer, and in 1845 he conveyed Asheston to Henry and Anne Harries and William Rees. It was later sold to the Perkins family. The original dwelling house now forms part of the farm outbuildings, and the present dwelling house is of 19th century construction.

AVELLANAU, *St. Thomas, Haverfordwest*
A large, attractive, residence with a pillared porch built in 1845 by William Evans, solicitor of Haverfordwest, represented today by Mr. James Eaton Evans, the fifth of successive solicitors of the family. William Evans, of Narberth, gent. viv. 1797 married Mary daughter of James Eaton, prenuptial settlement dated 1 October 1787 and had by her four sons, the youngest of whom was William Evans solicitor. He married Cecil, daughter of William Warlow by whom he had two sons; Eaton Evans, great-grandfather of James Eaton Evans, and R. W. P. Evans of Treforgan, near Cardigan whose daughter Edith married Grismond Philipps of Cwmgwili.

Later in the 20th century it became the property of the County Council and until recently was a children's home. The *Western Telegraph*, 13 April 1988, has photographs of the house in 1870/71 and 1949.

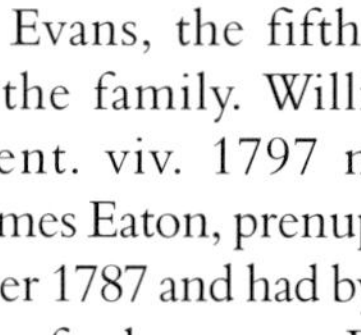

BACHENDRE,

in the chapelry of Capel Colman in the parish of Llanfihangel Penbedw

Philip Morris, settled at Bachendre in 1650, is said to have been descended from Jenkin Llwyd 'o Cemaes'. John Morris of Bachendre made his will in 1774, and died not long after, leaving an only son Thomas Morris and three daughters, Mary who had married Griffith Jenkins of Cilbronnau (Cards), Elizabeth who had married William Harries of Castlebythe, and Anne Morris, spinster. Anne his widow was living in 1786. The son Thomas bought Trefigin in Monington parish about 1802 and went to live there. Thereafter Bachendre was let to farmers, and later sold.

Refs: NLW Pembs. GF, GS; Carms. RO, J. Francis Colln. Deeds; Parish Tithe Map and Schedule 1849; Pembs. RO LT 1786.

Dawes

BANGESTON, *Angle*

The mansion stood about a mile to the east of the village (NB. There are three other places bearing this name – a residence north of Pembroke town, and two farms – one southwest of Cheriton and one northeast of Kilgetty). It was named after an early owner 'Benger's tun', and families named Beneger are recorded in South Pembrokeshire between 1272 and 1342. The earliest known family at Bangeston is that of Dawes (first found in the county in 1437), who held the property for six generations. Dwnn called there in 1591 and recorded the family pedigree. Griffith Dawes died in 1592 leaving four children. One, Griffith Dawes, was High Sheriff in 1665, Mayor of Pembroke in 1672 and in 1689, died in 1694 and was buried in Angle church where his memorial is decorated by his coat of arms, *or:* a fesse dansette *ermine* between 3 daws proper. His only child and heiress, Phoebe, married Griffith White of Henllan, and had an only daughter, Elizabeth, last descendant of the family to live at Bangeston. She married four times – Thomas Lort of Eastmoor (died 1687), Richard, Viscount Bulkeley of Anglesey (died 1704), Brigadier Thomas Ferrers (died 1722), and John Hooke. Elizabeth died in 1736, aged 76, and the Bangeston estate passed to her fourth husband who died in 1757, leaving his wife's estate to John Campbell, a younger son of Stackpole Court, Lord Lyon King of Arms, on condition that he took the name and arms of Hooke. The legatee did so and for a time was called John Campbell Hooke, which he later changed to Hooke-Campbell. In 1786 the Lord Lyon sold the Bangeston estate for £52,318 to his nephew John Campbell (later created Lord Cawdor), who sold Bangeston and other properties to his agent John Mirehouse of Brownslade, and it remained in possession of that family down to our times. The old mansion had been improved prior to 1720 by the heiress Elizabeth and her husband Thomas Ferrers, but before the end of the 18th century had been abandoned and became ruinous. Fenton described it in 1810 as a 'mere shell of a mansion lately remembered as the seat of hospitality, and one of the first of note in Pembrokeshire'. *Timmins* in 1895 wrote, 'Bangeston House proves to be nothing more than the gaunt, dismantled walls of a vast group of buildings'. It is also described by Mrs. M. B. Mirehouse of the Hall of Angle in her book published in 1910.

Refs: Dwnn, i, 128, 130: Fenton, *Tour Pembs.*, 1811; Timmins, *Nooks Pembs.,* 1895; RCAM 1925; M. B. Mirehouse, *South Pembs.,* 1910; Carms. RO, Cawdor Collection; Tithe Map and Schedule 1841.

BANGESTON, *St. Mary Pembroke*

The three-storeyed mansion stands to the north of Pembroke town. An 18th century residence, used today as a home for the aged, and, according to the matron, is haunted, and in 1982 she cited some lively occurrences. Described as a yeoman, the first dweller at Bangeston was Morgan Ap Powell (descended from Gwynfardd Dyfed) who had emigrated from north Pembrokeshire where a local plague had broken out. He was living at Bangeston in 1520/21, from where he moved to the town of Pembroke. His descendants continued to live at Bangeston. Lewis Powell and his son Morgan were there in 1578, and the latter moved to nearby Greenhill. It was later owned by the Laugharne family and in 1684 Thomas

Laugharne lived there. By 1722 it had been purchased by the Colby family, and in that year was occupied by Lawrence Colby, High Sheriff, and three years later Mayor of Pembroke. The Stokes family were there from 1699 to 1708, when it reverted to the Colbys. By 1786 it had been sold to Sir Hugh Owen of Orielton. In 1873 the owner was Thomas Meyrick of Bush who lived here after Bush burnt down in 1866. On 20th century maps it is called Bangeston Hall.

Refs: NLW Bronwydd Deeds, Cwrtmawr Deeds; Pembs. RO, LT 1786; *Western Telegraph,* 22 July 1982 (illust.)

BARNARDS WELL, *Henry's Moat*
Now a farm about a mile to the east of the village, on the southern slope of Barnards Well Mountain. The name is said to derive from Brynach. Nearby is Barnards Well, close by the ruins of an old chapel dedicated to St. Brynach. Among the early owners of the property were the Warlows, and in 1290 it was the home of David Warlagh, who may have been an ancestor of Janet Warlow who married David Gwilym Rees of Llanfairnantygof *circa* 1450.

In 1595 George Owen Lord of Cemaes confirmed the right of Owen Jones of Trecwn to 'a capital messuage called Burnaghswill in Harryesmote' parish', and it remained with Owen Jones' descendants to the beginning of the 20th century. The property was divided into two farms, *Ucha* and *Issa.* A rental of the Trecwn estate in 1839 includes Barnardswell-Ucha (230 acres) and Issa (193 acres). From the Joneses of Trecwn, the estate passed through successive heiresses to the families of Vaughan and Barham.

Refs: PRO, AD, D4057; NLW Bronwydd Deeds; *RCAM Pembs.* 1925; BM Egerton MS. 2586; Francis Jones, *Holy Wells of Wales,* 1954, p. 203.

BARRET'S HILL, *Steynton**
This house lies half a mile northeast of the parish church of Steynton and is marked on Colby's Map of 1831. In 1654 Hugh Butler of Scovaston mortgaged Barrett's Hill to Henry Bateman who died in 1679 in £100. In 1704 it was the home of Elizabeth Jordan, widow; and in 1748 Dorothy Warren of Longridge, widow, William Warren of same, Esq. and Jane, uxor. gave a lease to Thomas Battin(e) of Walwyn's Castle, yeoman of Barrets Hill for lives of lessee, William Battin eldest son of lessee by Elizabeth uxor. and Margaret, (born 17 Oct. 1767), third daughter of lessee at a rent of £37 10s. 0d. per annum; to keep a dog and a cock for said William Warren and Jane. In 1766 the lease was assigned from Thomas Battine who had moved to Steynton to his only son, William. By 1797 Barrattshill was owned by Lord Kensington with William Battine, tenant paying £2 16s. 2d. in Land Tax. The will of Morgan Jones of Cilwendeg, dated 6 December 1837 mentions William Battine formerly of Barret's Hill, Esq. and now a Colonel in the East India Army. Barret's Hill was being farmed by William Parsell the younger in 1834; the Voters' List of 1894 shows the Thomas family farming there.

Refs: Eaton Evans and Williams Deeds; Mathry PR; NLW, W & W (H'west). 16918; LT 1797; VL 1894.

Child

BEGELLY HOUSE, *Begelly*
On high ground above Begelly church. Home of a number of yeomen in the 16th century, the house was remodelled later to suit more affluent days. It is now a guest house. The history of the Child family illustrates the rise of yeomen, finally to become leading county landowners. The first member of the family at Begelly, Owen Child, lived there during the years 1540-69. In the following century they were described as gentlemen, and in 1670 their Begelly home was assessed at four hearths. In 1725 John Child was High Sheriff, thereafter his descendants were described as esquires, and it was during the 18th century that the house assumed its present form. The last of the family, who had been there for some 340 years, was James Mark Philipps Child, Captain in the Royal Pembrokeshire Rifle Corps who died without issue in 1877.

John Child of Begelly was High Sheriff in 1725 and died in office. In 1745 his son, James Child married Margaret, daughter of the Rev. Theophilus Rice, vicar of Talbenny. Their eldest son, James Child, the first of the family to

become a J.P., married about 1775 Maria Philippa Artemesia, daughter of Bulkeley Philipps of Pembroke and of Abercover, Carms., younger son of the 4th Baronet of Picton Castle, and uncle of the 7th Baronet who was created Baron Milford in 1776. By her he had two sons who died young and a daughter. Mrs. Child died in 1786, and the widower married in 1791, Sarah, (with a fortune of £4,000), daughter of Mark Davies of Bristol, and by her had a son, James Mark Child, Captain in the Royal Pembrokeshire Rifle Corps (Militia), J.P., D.L, and M.F.H. who died in 1870 leaving a son, James Mark Philipps Child who died without issue at Pope Hill, Steynton in 1877. James Child's only surviving child by his first wife, named after her mother, Maria Phillipa Artemisia married John Grant, eldest son of the Rev. Moses Grant, vicar of Nolton and had an only child, Richard Bulkeley Grant. When Lord Milford died in 1823, without issue, his peerage dignity became extinct, but his inherited baronetcy passed to the nearest of kin, who proved to be the above Richard Bulkeley Grant, who then assumed the additional surname of Philipps.

In 1765 Abraham Leach, a rich businessman of Pembroke, loaned £3,000 to James Child Esq. of Begelly; by April 1780 the debt had become nearly £5,000, and Leach foreclosed, and with the mortgage in his possession took over Child's estate in the parishes of Begelly, St. Ishmaels and Llanstadwell. He received rents from this estate for the years 1780-91 and perhaps later. Abraham Leach died 1811, aged 82 and was buried at Loveston.

Thereafter the property had several owners and after World War II the house was used as a preparatory school until its closure in 1969 when it was converted into flats.

The Childs family bore arms: *gules* a chevron *ermine* between three eagles proper, with crest of an eagle, wings expanded, a snake wrapped around its neck. The present mansion, built in the first quarter of the 19th century, is a large square building of three storeys, a basement – and attics, but retains older features at the back.

Refs: NLW, Papers of GS; PRO, Lay Subsidies 1543 *et seq;* GGMS; Picton Castle Deeds; *Arch. Cam.,* Ser. 2, vol. iv, p. 115; Burke, *Commoners,* iii, p. 692 and *Landed Gentry,* 1852; *Western Mail,* 16 August 1986 illust.

BENTON CASTLE, *Burton*

On a steep cliff above the western banks of the Cleddau. A small medieval castle which has been ruinous and deserted for many centuries. Little of its history is known. Like many such buildings it had its ghost as shown by the letter written on 22 December 1693 from Nicholas Roberts of St. Davids to Edward Llwyd – 'Benton Castle, formerly said to be haunted, upon which account seldom visited, where they say the Devil would often appear in the shape of a black mastiff dog and sometimes lie by the fire, but mostly in a vault or cellar, to guard some hidden treasure there.'

The author, R. M. Lockley in *Pembrokeshire,* 1977, p. 121, informs us that the castle 'was uninhabited from the time of its reduction by Cromwell until about 1930 when its reconstruction was undertaken by a genial hermit Ernest Pegge, who with his own hands lovingly rebuilt it, using the rock tumbled from its walls by time and Cromwellian cannons, and oak beams from the shipbreakers' yards at Milford Haven. Many a happy hour have I spent with Ernest Pegge, a surprising but sane man and contented as he worked in and about his castle in the lovely wooded estuary. He placed his own

mark in concrete over the entrance to the renovated castle'. After World War II it was the home of the late Colonel J. A. Sulivan, High Sheriff of Dyfed in 1974.

Refs: RCAM Pembs. 1925, illust; *Arch. Cam.* 1865, p. 82.

BERLLAN, *Eglwyswrw*
On the north side of Pencelly woodland, not far from Eglwysswrw village. A large well-preserved three-storeyed house of double-pile type. Behind it is a much older house (once attached to the larger by a wide passage) doubtless the original Berllan now occupied by a farmer. A number of families lived there in medieval days like the Jordans, but were comparatively short-lived. In the 16th century it became the home of William Owen, a natural son of William Owen of Henllys (d. 1574) who had bought the Lordship of Cemaes in 1543. William married Alison daughter of Morgan Bowen of Trerickert, and had issue; six generations of the family dwelt there, the last being John Owen, High Sheriff in 1751. The Land Tax for 1786 names the owners as Mrs. Hay and Mrs. Price. Not long afterwards it became the residence of the Rev. David Griffith who had married Anne Bowen of Llwyngwair in 1781. He died in 1834, and his son George David Bowen Griffith succeeded as owner-occupier, being so described in 1838. It was later owned by the Lloyds of Bronwydd and is now owned by Mrs. Hawkesworth, a descendant of Bronwydd.

Refs: WWHR, ii, 90-1; NLW, Vaerdre Book, Bronwydd Deeds, Cwrtmawr Deeds, Morgan-Richardson Deeds; Carms. RO, GGMS; Pembs. RO, Deeds.

BERRY HILL/BURY, *Nevern*
On a slope, northwest of Llwyngwair, overlooking the Nevern estuary, Newport, Carn Ingli, and the Preseli foothills. The commodious residence consists of two parts – the main portion is an early 19th century edifice, and to the rear extends a much older wing now used as a farmhouse. In the period 1198-1230 part of the land was granted to the Knights Hospitallers of St. John. The name occurs as Bury during the next three centuries. The tract of Bury formed the demesne of Newport Castle, and in 1523 John Tuckett, Lord of Audley, and Lord of Cemaes, leased part of the land to two yeomen.

An early lease dated 7 October 1577 may be of interest; '1. George Owen of Henllys, gt. 2. David Meredydd of Newport, yeoman. Lease for 21 years of a parcel of ground called the Burge sometime being the demesne of the castle of Newport as amounts to the value of an old mark, being the 12th part of the said Burie according to the ancient division and partition thereof. Rent 33s. 4d., a hen at Shrovetide, an able man with two horses to load dung, a day's harrowing, a horse to fetch a horse-load of lime, a horse to fetch salt or coals yearly, also to render a heriot and "ymado" when due according to the custom of the country, to grind all corn at mill of lessor at Newport and paying customary tolls therefore; lessor to enjoy such quarries of stone as are on the premises. If the fair now held at Sainte Meigan's be removed to the said Bury the lessor shall have as much ground there as shall be necessary to serve the said fair together with all such profits and commodities of that fair to lessor's use'.

By 1631 Berry (so called) was the home of George Owen, (son of Alban Owen of Henllys, Lord of Cemaes) whose daughter Bridget married Alexander Ford. Their son, Owen Ford of Berry who was assessed at three hearths in 1670, married Anne Barlow of Minwere, and died in 1704 leaving two daughters, co-heiresses, Joan who married William Lloyd of Henllys and Penpedwast and Bridget who married William Gower of Glandovan. In 1731 William Lloyd leased land at Berry 'with a warren and a salmon weir' there, to Evan Rees yeoman and Thomas Lewis gentleman.

In 1786 Berry was owned by George Bowen Esq. of Llwyngwair, described as owner-occupier. He was followed by his son-in-law, the Rev. David Griffith of Berllan, Vicar of Nevern, who died in 1834 leaving the property to his son George David Griffiths Esq. who was still living there in 1854. Mr. Griffith wrote to his daughter Eliza Ann on 10 March 1810 that 'Berry Hill is about to be completed', referring to the main block then being erected. After 1854 the property was alienated.

Refs: NLW, Bronwydd Deeds, Poyston Deeds, Llwyngwair Colln., Slebech Deeds; Pembs. RO LT 1786; Fenton, *Tour Pembs.*, 1811; *Pembs. Arch. Svy* Map 1896; *Country Quest,* June 1967, contains a photograph of Berry Hill; NLW Bronwydd Deeds No. 1257.

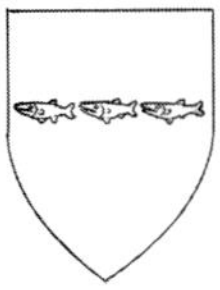

Picton

BICTON, *St. Ishmaels*
Now a farm between St. Ishmael's village and Sandy Haven. Described as 'terra de Biketunia' in 1242, and 'Birkton in Ros' in 1421, John Picton Esq. in 1422 granted to Thomas Perrot and Alice his wife (daughter of grantor) all his messuages, lands, and rents in Bikton at a yearly rent of two greyhounds; the deed has a beautiful seal showing the canting arms of Picton – three fishes (pikes) in fesse. The first owner of whom I have knowledge is Thomas Lloyd, Esq. of Cilgilynen, who leased for 21 years a messuage and fields of Bicton, to a yeoman, John Roch, who assigned the lease to his son John in 1631. Afterwards the father bought the property and on his death in 1663 left it to his son William. William Roch died in 1689 and left Bicton to his son Nicholas Roch, a draper of Haverfordwest. In 1694 William Allen of Gelliswick brought a Chancery suit to oust Nicholas Roch from Bicton. Seemingly he succeeded, for in the Land tax of 1786 Joshua Allen Esq. is shown as owner of Bicton, with Mr. John Morgans as tenant, and it remained part of the Allen estate down to the 20th century. In 1915 William Bird Allen of Bicton, grandson of Joshua Julian Allen of Bicton, was High Sheriff, and the same office was filled by Herbert Charles Gordon Allen of Bicton, and of Cwm, Saundersfoot. It is now a farmhouse.

Refs: Burke, *LG,* 1850 contains a pedigree of the Allens; PRO, AO, iii 1723; Eaton Evans and Williams Deeds; VL 1834 *et seq.*

BIERS POOL, *Pembroke St. Michael*
On the west banks of Llanion Pill, and just north of Llanion farm – Colby Map 1831. 'At Bierspool another farmstead, dating back to a very early period, stands intact', according to an ancient map this district was in bygone times known as Bayard's Pool. In the grounds of the farm, still to be seen is an old ruined dovecote or pigeon-loft built of limestone, a piece of ancient masonry, but how far back it dates is not known. The earliest occupants within living memory of the old farmhouse were called Dawkins, and were near relations of the late Mr. William Dawkins of Albion House'.

Refs: Mrs. Stuart Peters, *History of Pembroke Dock,* 1905, p. 4.

BISHOPS' PALACES
Former residences of the Bishops of St. Davids in medieval times, namely St. Davids, Trevine, Lamphey and Llawhaden (castle). Most were built in Norman and later times, but by today they are all in ruins. Numerous references occur to them in manuscript and printed records, and on maps such as Speed. They feature in many 18th and early 19th century engravings such as those by Sandby, Gastineau, Sheppard, Wallis, etc.

BLACKALDERN,
about half a mile southeast of Narberth
Formerly a farmhouse at a place where alder trees grew. In deeds of 1609 it is described as Black Alderne and Black Aldren. It formed part of the estate of the Barlows of Slebech in 1705, but in 1786 its owner was Lord Kensington. During the 19th century a residence was raised near the farmhouse which was tenanted by farmers. In 1858 it was the home of William Gwynne Esq. and afterwards was the seat of a branch of the family of Allen of Cresselly.

Refs: NLW Bronwydd Deeds; Pembs. RO, Deeds DX/148, No. 36; Eaton Evans and Williams Deeds.

BLAENBYLAN, *Clydey*
In the northern part of the parish about one and a quarter miles southwest of Ffynnonau. Blaenbylan was part of an estate in northwest Pembrokeshire, and the home of the Morgan family from Elizabethan days to 1768 when it was sold and ceased to be a gentry residence having become ruinous. The first of the family to settle at Blaenbylan was Morgan ap Howel descended from Ednyfed Fychan of Gwynedd whose arms the family bore. Morgan died before 1597. The eighth in descent, Maurice Morgan, was the last of the line to own the property, and in 1768 it was sold. Maurice Morgan inherited it from his elder brother, William who died unmarried some years before 1768. Maurice Morgan became private secretary to Lord Shelburne, and later an under Secretary of State, and in 1783 was Secretary to the embassy for peace with America. He wrote several pamphlets on political and social subjects and a work entitled 'Essay on the Dramatic Character of Sir John Falstaff'(1777). He died at Knightsbridge in 1802. The family is now represented, through the female line by Lieut. Col. J. Lewis-Bowen of Clynfyw in Manordeifi, parish.

The house, already ruinous, deteriorated, was finally dismantled, and today no trace of it remains. Fenton wrote in 1810 – 'Blaenbylan, the inhabited residence within these 60 or 70 years of a most respectable family of the name of Morgan whose possessions in this county were very extensive. The House situated in the most objectionable part of the demesne, was meanly and irregularly built as to its exterior and within consisted of several small, low and dismally dark rooms, the whole quite dispro portionate to the fortune and rank of the former inhabitants and the style of architecture even in those days . . . The last two of the name, sons of that house, William Morgan and Maurice Morgan, Esquires, I had the pleasure of being well acquainted with . . . ' When I called there in December 1974 I found that the site and environment in no way justified Fenton's strictures. The farmhouse, built in the 18th century, consisted of a structure of two storeys, with a range of five windows, and on the ground floor an entrance leading to the 'best' part of the house, and another leading to the kitchen and domestic offices. It comprises some 195 acres.

Refs: For a detailed account see Francis Jones's essay in *Ceredigion,* 1976, pp. 307-331; Fenton, *Tour Pembs.,* 1811; Rees, *Beauties of South Wales,* 1815; DNB; Francis Jones Archives.

BLAEN Y GROES/GORS*
Thought to be Blaen-gors in Meline parish
There was a Blaen y Gorse in Meline parish mentioned in deeds from 1572 contained in the Bronwydd Deeds amongst others. Francis Jones gives a predigree of the family who resided there at that time. Llewelyn Jenkin of Blaenygroes had by an unknown wife two known sons and a daughter and is thought to have had four other children. The eldest son, Morris Llewellyn had a son, Lewis Morris and grandson, Morgan Lewis. The second son, Gitto Llewelyn had a son, Thomas Gitto and grandson, Lewis Thomas who married Katherine, daughter of Lewis Philipps of Pentre Evan and had by her two sons. Lewis Thomas was 'kill'd by a gret mischaunce with a gunne'. The daughter of Llewelyn Jenkin, Lleceu, married Howell ap Owen David Evan and had a son, Lewis Powell of Pembroke, B.A. and a daughter, Anne who married Rees ap Thomas ap Rees of Esger Wilim. Anne died in 1590 leaving a sole heiress, Elizabeth, who married William Griffith of Penybenglog. Elizabeth died in 1620/1 and William Griffith in 1618.

Refs: GGMS Gwynfardd; Protheroe IV.fo.144; Llanst. 101 fo. 66-7 (GWG); WWHR ii, 74. Ex. Info. Dr. B. G. Charles.

BLAEN MWRW, *Manordeifi*
A farm east of Newchapel and south of Pentre. Home of Thomas Jones, illegitimate son of John Morgan of Blaenbylan. He married Elizabeth, daughter of John Harry Lloyd, a descendant of Gwynfardd Dyfed. She was a widow when she made her will on 10 February 1714/15. The son Samuel Jones inherited Blaenmwrw where he was still living in 1727 with his wife Margaret John of Brongwyn, Cards. He had three sisters, but it is not known whether he had any issue.

Refs: GGMS vol. iv (Ednyfed Fychan); Carms. RO, J. Francis Deeds.

BLAEN TÂF, *Llanfyrnach*

This ancient mansion has disappeared without trace. It is marked as Blaen Tâf on the O.S. maps of Mudge (1819) and Colby (1831), and on the Tithe map (1838) as 'Old Blaentaf Cottage', part of Nantydd Ucha farm. It stood on the slope of a small dingle on the south bank of the upper waters of Afon Tâf. Home of a younger son of the Philipps family of Cilsant, and his descendants from 1540 to 1690. Their names appear in six Lay Subsidy Lists between 1543 and 1670, several being Justices of the Peace. By the end of the 17th century the family had slid down the scale, and by 1670 when John Philipps lived at Blaen Tâf, his brother David Philipps farmed at Penrhiw (in 1685) and his sisters Ursula and Margaret, respectively had married James John a fiddler, and John Thomas James of Lletty ffwlbert, farmer. After this, Blaen Tâf was let to farmers, and became part of the estate of the Lloyds of Cilrhiw and Bronwydd. In 1750 Rees David of 'Blantafe' was churchwarden and overseer of the parish, and in 1776 Martha Phillips of Blaen Tâf was a petty constable of the parish, a somewhat formidable lady. In time the acreage of Blaen Tâf was reduced and became absorbed into the neighbouring farms, chiefly nearby Nantydd Ucha. The old house was later destroyed. In 1904 only a cottage remained. The Whitland-Cardigan railway passed close to it. Local tradition states that beneath the garden soil 'the ground is paved like a courtyard'.

Refs: Dwnn, i, 171; NLW, Bronwydd Deeds and MSS, Vaerdre Book, *Extent of Cemaes,* Carms. RO GGMS; George Owen, *2nd Book,* p. 282.

BLAIDDBWLL, *(e.p. Bribwll), Llanfyrnach*

The property is in the eastern part of the parish, bordered by Afon Tâf. The earliest residence, among trees below the farmyard was replaced in 1898 by a modern farmhouse erected to the north of the original buildings. Some remains of the older house have survived. During the Middle Ages it was home of the eminent landowner, Jenkin Lloyd of Cemaes, descended from Gwynfardd Dyfed, who bore the arms *azure* a lion rampant within an orle of roses *or.* A later descendant at Blaidbwll changed the colour of the roses from *or* to *argent* to denote his adherence to the House of York. The last male of this family, John ap Owen, died a few years before 1570, leaving an only child, Joan heiress of Blaiddbwll, and as she had no issue she left the property to her third cousin, Robert Morris, whose son Philip Robert Morris sold it to Eynon Philipps of Cardigan shortly before 1589. That worthy's grandson, Thomas Philipps, sold Blaiddbwll, then comprising six farms, four tofts, two mills, and 354 acres, to Reynald Morris a local landowner, whose descendants bore the surname Reynolds. The house was assessed for three hearths in 1670. The last male of the family, John Reynolds, died unmarried in 1741 leaving Blaiddbwll to John Parr, son of deceased's sister Sarah Reynolds who had married Thomas Parr of Haverfordwest. John Parr died without issue in 1811, aged 88. In that year Fenton wrote 'I pass by an ancient place called erroneously Bribwll a very powerful man of his time Jenkin Lloyd of Cemaes; though long deserted as a residence of a man of fortune, all the remains of ancient consequence from the venerable growth that surrounds it, amongst which I observed two or three remarkably large, sweet chestnuts, always a distinguishing appendage of a great man's residence, it being a tree not commonly cultivated. The demesne appears to be very extensive, and to consist of land of the best quality.' John Parr (died 1811) devised Blaiddbwll to his sister's great-grandson, the Hon. William Henry Yelverton, son of Viscount Avonmore. It remained in that family until 1888 when W. H. M. Yelverton of Whitland Abbey sold the property then consisting of the farms of Blaiddbwll, Blaiddbwll Mill, Troyan, Bryneithin, Penlanfach Ucha, Pantybigny, Plâs y bailey alias Fron Lebon, and a rent charge payable by the Whitland and Cardigan Railway, to John Nicholas, gentleman, of Graig, for £12,400. It is still owned and occupied by John Nicholas's descendants, the Harries family (of Fron).

Refs: Dwnn, i, 217; NLW MSS 12045, 12356; George Owen, *2nd Book,* 1603-4, p. 282; Tithe Map Llanfyrnach 1838; BM Egerton MS 2586; Fenton, *Tour Pembs.,* 1811; Carms. RO, Trant/Yelverton Deeds; Francis Jones 'The Families of Blaiddbwll'; *NLW Journal*, Summer 1981, and refs. there.

BLETHERSTON, *Bletherston*
A large farmstead on the outskirts of the village of Bletherston in the southwest of the parish. The name derives from Bletheri, Blethery, or Bledri, and is known locally as Trefelen, and is described in 1700 as 'Bledheston or Trevelen'. The earliest family there were the Colbys, who owned it from 1597 to 1786 (and later). In 16th and 17th century deeds they are described as yeomen, later as gentlemen and in the 18th century blossomed forth as esquires. Younger branches were established at Grondre, Bangeston near Pembroke and finally Rhosygilwen, Ffynnone and Pantyderi. The farmstead was described as 'the capital messuage called ye Great House' in 1681 and 1707. It was assessed at three hearths in 1670. In 1786 John Colby, Esquire, was the owner-occupier. Several Colbys held public offices – High Constables of Dungleddy Hundred in 1617, 1623, 1664 and High Sheriffs of the county in 1722, 1770, 1807, 1838 and 1891. The last in the male line, Major John Vaughan Colby of Ffynnone and the Grenadier Guards, was killed in action in October 1914.

Refs: B. G. Charles, *NCPN;* NLW, Owen and Colby Estate Deeds, St. David's Episcopal Records, Poyston Deeds, Eaton Evans and Williams Deeds; Carms. RO; GGMS.

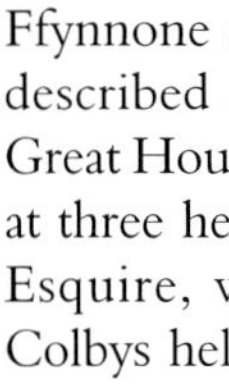
Bolton

BOLTON HILL, *Steynton*
To the northwest of Johnston village. Described as Bolton 1380, Bulton Hill 1515, Bulton 1556, Bowlton Hall 1597, and Boulton Hill 1665. Malkin in 1804 called the house 'an agreeable residence'. In the 18th century, this large property was divided into four farms, all called Bolton Hill. The family of Bolton were in the district in 1324. Philip de Bolton held courts as Steward in Haverfordwest in 1376-78. His son Philip de Bolton junior, was outlawed in 1385 for the manslaughter of Howel ap Griffiths of Llandissilio.

Thomas Bolton (1515-38) was succeeded by his son David Bolton to whom Sir Gilbert Dethick, Garter King at Arms, granted the following arms on 1 July 1556: *argent* on a bend *gules* 3 leopard faces *argent,* between 2 fleurs de lys *azure;* crest, a fawn's head and neck parted per pale indented *argent* and *azure,* in its mouth a broad arrow or feather *argent,* point downwards.

In 1670 John Bolton of Bolton Hill was assessed at five hearths. Nine generations of the family lived there until 1740, after which the family became extinct, and the property was sold. In 1760 Essex Devereux Jones, apothecary, is described as of Bolton Hill. In 1786 the four farms called Bolton Hill, and Bolton Hill Mill, were owned by Lord Kensington. An episode in the family history was recorded by S. Lewis in 1840 as follows – 'Bolton Hill an ancient seat formerly belonging to a family of that name, is situated in the northern part of the parish, near an abrupt and lofty eminence called Bolton Beacon. While Cromwell lay at Haverfordwest, two of his soldiers entered this mansion with the intention of plundering it, and Bolton, who had concealed himself, was denied by his wife to the soldiers, who nevertheless, suspecting that he was in the house, one of them took up his child and pretended to throw it on the fire, on which the father rushed from his concealment, and killed the ruffian on the spot; his comrade escaped, and Bolton on reflection deemed it prudent to inform Cromwell of all that had occurred, observing to that General, that the man he had killed had only one eye; the latter replied 'the fellow was a great rascal and you have saved me the trouble of having him executed.'

Refs: Dwnn, i, 121, 133; Pembs. Plea Rolls, 1625, 1665, 1691, 1705; Picton Castle Deeds; NLW, Crosswood Pedigrees 139A; PRO Anc. Deeds, Nos. 1079, 4659; Harl. MS 1359; Oxford, Queen's College MS 39.

BONVILLE'S COURT, *St. Issells*
The old historic residence stood a short distance northwest of Saundersfoot, in what became a coal-mining area; about 600 yards from the above, a modern house, also called Bonvilles's Court, was erected in the 19th century on high ground near the roadway. Both residences are marked on Colby's Map, 1831. The name is derived from the surname Bonville, known in south Pembrokeshire since 1274.

The earliest known owner of the mansion was William ap David who was living there in the 16th century; his eldest son, John Williams, married Ann Bowen of Trefloyne, Penally, by whom he had five daughters, co-heiresses. We are told by a contemporary that the eldest co-heiress, Eleanor Williams 'hadd all the Landes assryd her by her father, and the other [sisters] hadd money', and when she married William Jones from Brynygroes near Llanelli, he came to live at his wife's home, Bonville's Court. Both parents and their nine children were living in 1591 when the herald Dwnn called there and recorded the family pedigree which William Jones duly signed. He bore the coat-of-arms of one of his ancestors, Gwynfardd Dyfed. Assessed at seven hearths in 1670, the family remained at Bonville's Court for over a hundred years more, the last being William Jones who died without issue in July 1690. His widow, Lettice Barlow from Cresswell, was so deeply grieved, that in the following year she cut her throat with a knife and so died. Bonville's Court then passed to William Jones's sister Catherine who had married James Philipps of Pentypark. She died in 1724, her husband in 1735 aged 90. Later, Bonville's Court became the property of James Child, described as owner in 1786, and by 1835 it was the residence of Hugh Bowen Mendes.

In 1791 James Child formerly of Begelly, now of Tenby, Esq. owned Bonville's Court which formed part of his estate then mortgaged in £6,000. On 5 November 1835 James Mark Child of Begelly House and William Bowen of Narberth gent, mortgagee conveyed lands in St. Issells parish to Saundersfoot Railway and Harbour Co. 'which lands had been mortgaged in £105 which sum has not been paid by J. M. Child to Hugh Bowen Mendes of Bonville's Court and Charles Poyer Callen of Lamphey Court, esquires, trustees'.

The mining activities encompassed the house which became dilapidated and parts of it were used as a workshop and the remains of the old house, situated in what is now called Crow's Meadow were buried under the coal tip, and a new house built.

Fenton wrote in 1810 that the red mansion retained 'some small remains of a baronial appearance'; by 1861 it had become a 'fragment' with a ruined tower that gives its name to the colliery beside it; in 1868 it was 'in a vaery neglected condition – the walls however are in tolerable sound condition'; and by 1895 only 'a single dilapidated tower and stair-turret remains'.

Refs: BM Egerton MS 2586; *Dwnn,* i, 122-3; GGMS; NLW, Papers of GS, 1691; Crosswood Pedigrees No. 139; Picton Castle Deeds; *Arch. Cam.* 1868, illust; *Pembs. Arch. Svy,* 1896-1907; Peter Smith, *Carms. Studies,* 1974; WWHR, ii, 76; Lewis of Henllan Schedule pp. 187a, 191.

Wogan

BOULSTON, *Boulston*

An ancient mansion (now a ruin) on the north bank of the Cleddau some three miles below Haverfordwest. Former residence of the Wogans an old Welsh family descended from Gwgan ap Bleddyn of Breconshire whose name became the permanent patronymic of his Pembrokeshire descendants who settled in the county during the 12th century. The first known occupant of Boulston was Henry Wogan, a younger son of Wiston, who settled there after his marriage to the daughter of Wilcocks Dyer of that place in the 1450s. The Wogans remained there until 1715, having filled the office of High Sheriff on nine occasions, providing a Member of Parliament, besides holding numerous local appointments. The estate was particularly extensive. Among illustrious visitors was the Duke of Beaufort and his retinue in 1684, on their return to Haverfordwest by boat from Picton Castle, 'in the cool of the evening having been well collationed on the way by (Lewis) Wogan Esquire, att the seat of Bolston.' The last of the line at Boulston was Anne Wogan (wife of John Laugharne of St. Brides) who died

without issue in 1715 when the property passed to kinsfolk, Wogan of Gawdy Hall, Norfolk. Boulston was then abandoned as a residence.

In 1786 the owner was Elinor Wogan, the mansion being tenanted by Benjamin Phelps, and the home farm by George Morse. In 1797 it was sold by Admiral Sir Charles Cotton, Bart., to Major Dudley Acland, and as the mansion was then in ruins, he built a new residence on high ground to the north, which was named Boulston Manor (now the home of the Llewellin family). The old mansion was a large residence and in 1670 contained 13 hearths. Part of it was of three storeys, and had large cellars as shown by the surviving ruins. Memorials of the Wogans remain in Boulston church which show the family arms as *or,* on a chief *sable,* three martlets *or,* with a crest of a cockatrice *gules* jalloped *sable,* crowned *or* (to commemorate an exploit by a Wogan who is said to have slain the creature near Boulston). The surname persisted county down to the present century.

Refs: Francis Green in *Y Cymmrodor* 1902, pp. 100-149, illust; RCAM, 1925, illust; College of Arms MS Fellowes, 1530, Banners (1510-25) and Protheroe MS XII; Laws, *Little England Beyond Wales,* 1888, p. 374 and sketch of ruins of Boulston.

BOWOOD, *Castlemartin*
Name and site lost. A pedigree shows descendants of John Warren of Trewern (1485-86) living at Bristol and at 'Bowood in Castlemartin', and were still at both places in 1638, Matthew Warren at the former and John Warren at the latter.

Refs: College of Arms MS, Wagner MS 3 and 12 (in hand of George Owen, York Herald).

Brawdy Church

Jones

BRAWDY-BREUDETH, *Brawdy*
Home of the family of Jones the old mansion, a four-fronted edifice, stood on a slope immediately below the parish church, about a mile inland from the hamlet of Penycwm above St. Brides Bay. In the same parish also stood the early mansions of Castle Villa, Eweston, Llether, Newgale, and Rickeston. Brawdy was the house of landowning families from medieval days. In 1670 it contained four hearths and an inventory of 1704 mentions The White Chamber, Porch Chamber, Dark Chamber, Dining Room, Parlour, The Hall and kitchen. Two closed-in early windows in the southern gable showed that it had been a three-storeyed building, the upper storey having been removed about 1825. One room, now the parlour, retains its original oak panelling. An ancient arch connected the rear part of the house to the walled garden, the walls continuing in good state of preservation. One of the outbuildings bears the date 1740.

In 1796 Brawdy was let to a George Gwyther whose family bought the freehold in 1919 and whose descendant, Richard Gwyther, still farms there. About 1825 a large part of the dwelling-house was pulled down and the remainder adapted to farming usages. In 1921 a corn-drying kiln collapsed, formerly connected with the house by a gallery leading from a window on the first storey. One of the mansion walls is hollow, said to have been used to hold smuggled wines borne from the cove of Cwm Mawr, along the hidden dingle below Llether.

Brawdy remained in the blood of one family for 17 generations, covering some 530 years. The first known member of the family was David of Brawdy whose son Philip ap David was living there in the years 1400-37, whose grandson Henry ap David ap Phillip had an only child, Alice sole heiress of Brawdy who, about 1510, married Richard Jones a younger son of John ap Thomas of Treowen, Mon., and from the Treowen family the family of Herbert Earls of Pembroke descended. By this marriage, Brawdy passed to Richard Jones who died in 1546/7. His descendants improved the estate by marriage with daughters of landowning families – Warren of Trewern, Bowen of Upton Castle, Philipps of Woodstock, Stokes of Cuffern, Reynish of Camrose, Protheroe of Nantyrhebog and Lloyd of Wenallt (both in Carms.). By 1600 the Brawdy estate consisted of 30 farms and 1,344 acres, an acreage maintained until 1800.

Dwnn recorded the family pedigree in 1613, duly signed by John Jones. The family filled numerous public offices – commissioners of Acts of Parliament, officers of Train Bands, Grand Jurors, High Constables of Dewsland, Justices of the Peace, a coroner, and two High Sheriffs. William Jones was Standard Bearer to Henry VIII. Cadet branches settled at Llether, Eweston, Grinston, Penbiri, Cruglas, Llangungar Fawr and Ludlow (Salop). Brawdy, Pointz Castle, and Trenewydd formed an episcopal manor of the Bishop of St. Davids, and Joneses of Brawdy were lords of the lay manor of Trefinert (*St. Davids*). The family bore the well-known arms, per pale *azure,* and *gules,* 3 lions rampant, *argent,* with crest, a woman's head and breast affrontee; Motto *Asgre lan diogle ei pherchen.*

John Jones (1727-1787) H.S. and his wife Thomazine Stokes (1728-1781) of Brawdy left two daughters, co-heiresses, Jane Maria Jones (1765-1829) married Thomas Mathias (d. 1796) in 1790 and her only child, a daughter, died young, leaving her share of the Brawdy estate to her sister and eventual owner, Mary Brand Jones (1771-1849). Mary Brand Leach left her Brawdy estate to her eldest son William Henry Leach (1803-1889), who, on his mother's death took the name of Jones by Royal Licence in June 1849.

Refs: Dwnn, i, 196; PRO Anc. Deeds E210, MSS 5173 and 9238; *RCAM Pembs.*; Deeds and family papers, penes me; R. J. H. Lloyd, *Trans. Cymmr.* 1956; A. Henniker-Gotby.

Editor's Note: Francis Jones was a direct descendant of the Joneses of Brawdy. His earliest memories were of his grandparents and parents telling him of the family's lineage and history. This kindled his lifelong love of antiquity and genealogy.

BRIDELL (PLÂS), *Bridell*

A mile and a quarter southwest of Cilgerran village, and standing just northeast of Bridell parish church. Very little is known of the old farmhouse called Bridell which became known as Plâs y Bridell in the 19th century. In 1786 the owner-occupier was Mary George, widow. On Colby's Map of 1831 it is marked as Plâs y Bridell. It became the home of James W. Bowen Q.C. whose estate comprised 1,416 acres in 1873. About that time he completely rebuilt the Plâs which has survived to the present day. In the early years of the 20th century it was the residence of Walter Francis Roch, Liberal Member of Parliament for the county from 1908 to 1918. Later it became a Carmelite Convent which closed in 1975.

Refs: For plans of the present residence see NLW Clynfyw Deeds; a photograph of it occurs in C. S. Allen's *Photographs in South Wales,* 1871.

BRIMASTON (TREOWMAN), *Hayscastle**

In early times the name of this large property (now two farms called Brimaston Hall and Grange) was variously rendered Bremerston (1326) Bromaneston (1373), Bromandston (1568). To Welsh speakers it is Treowman. In 1739 a Circulating Charity School (25 pupils) was held in 'Trefowman alias Brimeston'. In 1292 and 1326 it was an Episcopal manor of the Bishop of St. Davids, and in the latter year was leased to Peter Russell. During the time of that family it became a lay manor. John Russell,

last of the male line left an only child, the heiress Elizabeth Russell who brought Brimaston to her husband Richard Laugharne of St. Brides. During the 18th century it became the property of Ford of Stone Hall in the neighbouring parish of St. Lawrence. The last member in the main line of that family, Miss Mary Ford of Brimaston, died in 1798. The two substantial farms were farmed by tenants and leaseholders, finally freeholders – Watts 1624, 1770-1862 Harries of Brimaston Hall, Morse 1748-1834 and in late 19th and 20th centuries by Jenkins and Lloyd of Brimaston Hall, and Morris of Brimaston Grange. A Methodist chapel stands in the hamlet. A pedigree of the Harries family is given; Essex Harries viv. 1774 of Brimaston married an unknown Elinor and by her had a son, Thomas Harries who married an Elizabeth Harries of Llwyngorras, prenuptial settlement dated 24 November 1774. They had four sons, James, John, a third unnamed son, Essex and a daughter Elizabeth. Thomas died 17 April 1793 predeceasing his wife who was still alive in 1814. James Harries the heir viv. 1851, married in 1815 Margaret, daughter of Diana Furlong, widow and had three sons, Thomas, Harry and John, who married Susan Phillips on 29 March 1860 at Ebenezer Chapel, Haverfordwest and came to live at Brimaston. John died in 1862 and his widow was living at Slade, Haverfordwest in 1864. Elizabeth one of the two daughters of James and Margaret Harries, married Stephen Lewis, 'Minister of God' who died 1861. The youngest daughter Dinah, marriage settlement dated 13 November 1854, married Thomas Williams, druggist of Market Street, Haverfordwest and had a son, James who was 21 on 4 July 1877 and a daughter Sophia Margaret who died 29 January 1882.

Refs: PRO Anc. Deeds E210. No. 24, 709; Pembs RO, LT 1786; *Black Book of St. Davids*, 1326; NLW Poyston Deeds; Sir A. Wagner, Coll. of Arms, Geo. Owen MS; Francis Jones, *Hist. Journal of the Church in Wales*, 1969.

BRITHDIR, *Newport*

Now a farmstead on the lower eastern slope of Carn Ingli and overlooking the valley of Afon Clydach. In 1540-74 Thomas ap Howell ap Jenkin lived at Brithdir.

In 1584 William Warren of Trewern sold part of the land of Brythtyr to Melchior ap Ieuan ap Newport, yeoman. In the early 17th century it became the residence of Thomas Jones, younger son of John Griffiths Philip Evan ap Clydey. Thomas was also of Pentre Ithel and his younger brother Stephen Jones was of Rhosygilwen. Thomas Jones was buried in Newport church on 9 June 1654, leaving a son Morris Jones who married Lettice Owen heiress of nearby Wenallt and settled at her home, and had two daughters, Mary who married John Protheroe of Dolwilym, and Elizabeth who married David Morris of Whitchurch. Morris's cousin, Thomas Jones lived at Brithdir in 1670 and was the last of the family there.

For a short time the Ford family lived there, and John Ford of Brithdir died in 1711. Later the property became two farms. In 1786 George Bowen of Llwyngwair owned Brithdir Mawr, tenanted by James Griffiths, and Thomas Nicholas owned Brithdir Bach, tenanted by Benjamin David. In 1834-41 it was occupied by Thomas Rees, farmer. In 1873 the owner-occupier of Brithdir Mawr was the Rev. David George, and the farm then comprised 362 acres. In 1894 Mary George was owner-occupier of Brithdir Mawr, and Thomas Lewis owner-occupier of Brithdir Bach.

Refs: NLW, Morgan-Richardson Deeds; Pembs. Papers of GS; Carms. RO, GGMS vol. 1, p. 36.

BROOMHILL, *Dale*

Now a farmstead south of Dale village. The earliest-known owners were the Paynters. In 1599 David Paynter was described as merchant. The family owned Broomhill until early in the 19th century. In 1669 Richard and Bridget Walter sold the manor of Dale to David Paynter, and in 1699 he sold the said manor to his son-in-law William Allen of Gelliswick. Evangelism attracted some of the family, like George Paynter of Broomhill who married Eleanor Musgrave of Llanina (Cards.), and later emigrated to Haverford, Pennsylvania. In 1743 David Paynter was High Sheriff of the county. Broomhill had been leased to Dr. George Harries of Haverfordwest who held that property in 1786. The last of the family in the male line was David Runwa Paynter, owner of Broomhill in 1823, and three years later lived in Haverfordwest.

Refs: Pembs. RO, LT 1786; Burke, *LG,* 1850, i, 333.

Holcombe

BROWNSLADE,

Castlemartin

About half a mile south of Castlemartin village, and westwards from the mansion we follow Frains lake (the latter being an old Pembrokeshire word meaning stream) to reach the sea coast at Frainslake Sands. The mansion was set in attractive grounds, and adjoining the grounds is Brownslade Farm, and it would seem that the farmstead was the original dwelling house, for we are informed by Malkin (1804) that 'we find the newly-formed residence of Mr. Mirehouse. The ground now occupied by the house and lawn was a field twenty years ago [c.1784]. Mr. Mirehouse began in the same year with Mr. Johnes; and the present state of the premises evinces the judgment with which his operations have been conducted', and Malkin later states that the new mansion was built about 1800. Plans and illustrations of the proposed house were made in 1783 by William Thomas, architect and surveyor. The property formed part of the estate of Lort of Stackpole Court, which passed to Alexander Campbell by marriage to the Lort heiress. The old house was a commodious building and in 1670 contained eight hearths, the occupier being John Leach. Leach died in 1675, and in 1709 Lady Campbell granted a lease of Brownslade for 21 years, to his son Abraham Leach, yeoman. The family remained until the death of John Leach soon after 1774, and his widow Elizabeth (Prout) surrendered the existing lease to John Campbell of Stackpole Court in 1789 for £3,500. It is clear that another family lived at Brownslade at the same time as that of Leach, which suggests that there may have been two houses there. This was the family of Holcombe.

The will of William Holcombe of Brownslade, dated 1653, was proved in 1662: he was followed by three generations all being described as of Brownslade, and who intermarried with Meares of Eastington, Meyrick of Bush, and Corbett of Nash. The last of the family to live there was Admiral Essex Holcombe, R.N., who died in 1769/70. Not long after this, the Mirehouse family arrived, descended from Mirehouse of Miresdyke, Westmoreland. John Mirehouse, born in 1753, had been at Cambridge University with John Campbell (later created Baron Cawdor), and became his land agent in Pembrokeshire. In 1786 John Mirehouse, Esq. was tenant of Brownslade, and it was he who built the mansion house and later bought the freehold. He was High Sheriff in 1810. A progressive farmer and planter of trees, he converted a morass of 2,674 neighbouring acres into productive land, for which he received the gold medal of the Society for Encouragement of Arts, Manufacture and Commerce in 1800. His estate, including Brownslade, eventually passed to R. B. Levett who had married a Mirehouse daughter, and his son R. W. B. Mirehouse, C.M.G., J.P., D.L. of The Hall of Angle, took that surname in 1864. His descendants are still at The Hall.

On 23 August 1902 King Edward VII and Queen Alexandra lunched at Brownslade on their visit to Pembroke Dock, then the residence of Col. and Lady Lambton. After lunch the King expressed a wish to see some Castlemartin Black cattle. About 30 cattle belonging to Mr. Thomas of Bulliber were driven in front of Their Majesties.

After the Second World War, Brownslade became a guest-house. Later the area became part of an artillery training range and the house and farm became ruinous. The old ruined house has been demolished.

Refs: Pembs. RO, HDX, No. 527, Report on Brownslade Mansion made by Mr. A. J. Parkinson in 1976; W. Thomas, *Original Designs in Architecture,* 1783, with illust. of the proposed mansions at Brownslade: *NLW Journal,* 1980, xxi, No. 4; R. G. Thorne, 'History of Leach family', *Pembs. Historian,* 1981; Malkin, *South Wales,* 1804; Stuart Peters, *History of Pembroke Dock,* 1905; *RCAM Pembs.*, 1925; *Come to Pembrokeshire, Guide,* c. 1936, good illust. of house; Mrs. R. B. Mirehouse, *South Pembs.,* 1910; T. Lloyd, *Lost Houses of Wales,* 1986, p. 70, illust. of the ruined mansion; Stuart Peters, *History of Pembroke Dock,* 1905, p. 148.

BRWYNANT, *Manorowen*
Now a small-holding, it belonged for some time to the Manorowen estate, but was sold after the Second World War by Captain T. G. V. Johns, D.L. It is an interesting small L-shaped house with a wing extending to the front. In earlier times it enjoyed a more august status. In 1326 it was a Knight's fee (Welsh tenure). During the 16th century it was owned by Harry David, a younger son of David Thomas, squire of Cilgelynen. He had four daughters, the eldest of whom Jane, married David ap Ieuan Gwallter, who came to live at his wife's home. By this time it had become a farmhouse, and in 1670 its owner, Owen Griffith of Brwn-y-nant,was assessed at two hearths. Later it became a small farm, finally a smallholding.

Refs: BM Egerton MS. 2586; *Dwnn,* i, 174; *Black Book of St. Davids,* 1326.

BRYANOG, *Meline*
There exists a grant dated 10 May 1412 from Phillip ap Howel ap Jenkyn to Owen ap Gwilym dduy, of a messuage at Brenanog Vawr and four acres at Henllys Morgan with the wood there, an exchange of a messuage at Bwlch Seys of fee of Diffrintaffle and of a messuage at Penkelly Vechan (Bronwydd Deeds No. 1283).

In the 1630s James Thomas, his brother and sisters were in possession, children of Thomas Rees of Merianog Issa and his wife Alice, daughter of James Bowen (of Pontgynon) ap Rees ap Rhydderch ap Jenkin ap Rees ap Gwilym, descendants of Hal Freda.

Twyning

BRYN, *Llanddewi Velfrey*
Marked on Mudge Map 1819, and on Colby's Map 1831 where the farms of Brynhafod and Brynglâs are shown to the south-east of Bryn Mawr. In 1692 Bryn was the house of Philip Mathias, gent. By 1760 it had become property of the Twyning family who settled there, the occupier in that year being Mr. Daniel Twyning and the Rev. Benjamin Twyning, vicar of Henllan-amgoed (Carms.), both being Parliamentary voters. In 1786 it was still owned by the Rev. Benjamin Twyning, while another parson of the family, the Rev. Griffith Twyning owned part of Caermaenau Fach in the same parish. In 1820 it was the home of William Twyning, Esq. J.P., and the family still owned it in 1870, when William Henry Twyning Esq. J.P. lived there, and bore arms: *sable,* two bars between two stars of six points *or;* with canting crest, the twin brothers Castor and Pollux in their infancy (the stars in the shield represent them after death), and motto, *Stellis aspirate genellis.*

Refs: NLW, Llwyngwair Deeds, Pembs. GF; Burke, *General Armoury,* 1885.

BRYNAERON, *Llandissilio West*
An attractive house to the southeast of the parish church, and near the banks of Afon Rhydy-bennau. In 1769 John Gwynne and the Rev. Morgan Gwynne, clerk, were Tax Commissioners for the county. In 1786 it was owned and occupied by the Rev. John Gwynne, clerk, and in 1788 John Gwynne, J.P., lived there. By 1809 it had passed to David Morgan, J.P. Later it was home of the Rev. Henry Thomas and Mary his wife (they had previously lived at Tŷ Hen and Bryn). Mary died there in 1843 and three years later was followed by her husband who had been a Baptist member for 73 years. Their son was the Rev. Theophilus Evan Thomas of Trehale, Baptist minister of Blaen-llyn and Newton. In 1904 Brynaeron was owned by Abel Thomas, Q.C., a son of Trehale.

Refs: NLW, Pembs. Papers of GS; *Seren Gomer,* 1846, p. 191; Pembs. RO. VL, 1894 and 1904.

BRYNDYSIL, *Llandissilio West*
A large house near the parish church at the north end of Llandissilio village, marked as Bryndissil on Colby's Map 1831. In 1847 it was the home of Rev. Edward Harries. In 1862 it was the home of the Rev. Thomas Harries, clerk, who is said to have built Bryndysil as his residence, and it contains some remnants of ancient stone work taken from Llandissilio church. It is now owned by Mr. Skeel Harries, who has sold Bryndysil house, but retains the land which he farms.

Refs: RCAM, 1925, p. 160.

Adams

BUCKSPOOL, Bosheston
Now a farmhouse, half a mile south of the parish church. Fenton writes (1810) 'I pass Buck's Pool so called from a small piece of water close to the house . . . formerly a residence of a branch of the respectable family of Adams . . . It has now no remains of ancient grandeur or of any thing above the condition of a Castle Martin farmhouse; all its importance if, as is probable, it possessed any, having left it with its ancient possessors when they migrated to a more desireable situation [Paterchurch] on the banks of Milford Haven.' The family of Adams had been in south Pembrokeshire since the 13th century and had lived at Buckspool until Henry VI (1422-3) when John Adams married Elen, daughter and heiress of David de Paterchurch, and then moved to his wife's home near Pembroke Dock, where his descendants remained until early in the 18th century when they moved to Holyland near Pembroke.

Buckspool remained part of the estate and became a farmstead. By 1786 it had been sold to John Campbell, and became part of the Stackpole estate. Henry Dawkins was tenant in 1786, Henry Hitchings in 1834 and George Hitchings in 1894. The arms of the Adams family were *sable* a martlet *argent*, and, as crest, a *martlet* as in the arms.

Refs: Fenton, *Tour Pembs.,* 1811; *Dwnn,* i, 130-1, 172; WWHR ii, 76.

BULLIBER, *Castlemartin*
A large farm about half a mile south of Brownslade, formerly part of the Stackpole Court estate, is now within an artillery range. When John Leach of Slade, yeoman, died in 1675, his eldest son Richard Leach had a lease of Bulliber where he died in 1732 and as he had no sons, he left the lease to his wife Elizabeth. On her death the lease passed to her late husband's nephew, Abraham Leach who remained there until 1776. Abraham was followed by his son Nicholas Leach who died in 1811 without issue. In 1834 John Bowling held a lease of Bulliber. Thereafter it was tenanted by farmers. About 300 yards to the southwest of Bulliber are the remains of an ancient promontory fort.

Refs: RCAM Pembs., 1925; Pembs. RO, LT 1786.

BUNKER'S HILL, *Steynton*
An attractive small residence, near Milford Haven. It was named after its first owner who probably built the house. Uriah Bunker was living at Bunker's Hill in 1786, and was still living there in 1834. It is marked on Colby's map 1831. Early in the present century it was the home of George Griffith, J.P. In the years 1930-40, R. A.Wheatley, Clerk of the Peace for the county, lived there.

Refs: Pembs. RO, LT 1786; VL; *Contemporary Biographies of South Wales and Monmouth*, 1907, p. 101, photo of the interior of the house.

Meyrick

BUSH, *St. Mary's Pembroke*
A large mansion, across the river to the northwest of Pembroke town. Home of the Meyrick family originally from North Wales. Founding ancestor, Cadefael Lord of Cydywain in Powys, and 8th in descent from him was Llewelyn ap Heylin who fought under Henry Tudor at Bosworth, and was followed by his son Meurig ap Llewelyn, appointed by Henry VIII, Yeoman (later Captain) of the Guard. He was succeeded at Bodwrgan (Anglesey) by his eldest son Richard Meyrick, while his younger son, Rowland Meyrick became Bishop of Bangor. This generation was the first to use the permanent surname, Meyrick. The Bishop

(died 1568) married Catherine, daughter of Owen Barrett of Gelliswick, near Milford Haven, and their four sons all settled in Pembrokeshire, one being Sir Francis Meyrick (died 1663) of Fleet, Monkton, from whom the Meyricks of Bush descended.

The family held numerous public offices, Members of Parliament, High Sheriffs, and Justices of the Peace, while one became a Judge. Seventh in descent from Sir Francis was Sophia Jane, only child and heiress of Thomas Meyrick of Bush. She died in 1837, having married in 1820 St. John Chiverton Charlton of Apsley Castle, Salop, and their son, Thomas Charlton took the surname Meyrick by R.L. on 31 March 1880, and was created a Baronet on 5 May following, the family being now represented by Sir David John Charlton Meyrick, 4th Baronet, of Great Wedlock, Gumfreston.

Fenton writes in 1810 'Bush is a mansion most charmingly situated in a grove . . . The house and grounds occupy the summit of a gentle acclivity to the north of Pembroke, the pleasure grounds are planned with taste, its gardens unrivalled in their produce . . .' On 8 January 1866 the mansion was burnt down, through a beam in a chimney taking fire, but many valuables and portraits were saved. The mansion was largely rebuilt in 1906, with Tudor-style windows. It was said to be haunted by one of its former owners, Judge John Meyrick (d. 1732). After the departure of the family the house became a Grammar School and later formed part of Bush Comprehensive School. The house is now a residential home for the elderly.

Refs: Dwnn, i, 136-7, 154, 156, 178, 185; WWHR II, 87-8; DNB and DWB; Mrs. Stuart Peters, *History of Pembroke Dock;* Burke, *Peerage and Baronetage;* Steegman, *South Wales,* vol. II, 1962, pp. 198-200.

Roch

BUTTERHILL,

St. Ishmaels

About a mile and a quarter north of the village. The earliest family at Butterhill was that of Allen. In 1581 Howell Allen of Butterhill, husbandman, maligned Thomas Bowen, gentleman who brought an action against him in the Great Sessions of the county. He seems to have survived, and in 1604 Howell Allen and William Wolfe, yeoman, were both living at Butterhill. Some three years later, Thomas Roch of Butterhill married Lettice Voyle of Filbeach in the neighbouring parish of Marloes, and their marriage settlement included 'Butterhill alias the Grange of Butterhill'.

The property had been a grange of the Priory of Pill, later of the Priory of Haverfordwest, which owned it until the Dissolution. In 1633 a lease of Butterhill was granted to the then tenant of Sivers Hill for the lives of his sons, John, William and Morris, and the freehold was later acquired by the Roch family, whose descendants owned it until 1906. The family had married several daughters of Dewsland squires – Wilkin of Trefin, Jones of Llether, Laugharne of Llanunwa, Protheroe of Stone Hall. Four held the office of High Sheriff in the period 1760-1901, while the last of the family, Walter Francis Roch, barrister was for some time Liberal M.P. for Pembrokeshire and died without issue in 1963. When sold in 1906, Butterhill was described as follows: basement, five cellars and larder; ground floor, hall, drawing room, dining room, study, two kitchens, servants' hall, scullery, butler's pantry; first floor, three double bedrooms with dressing rooms,

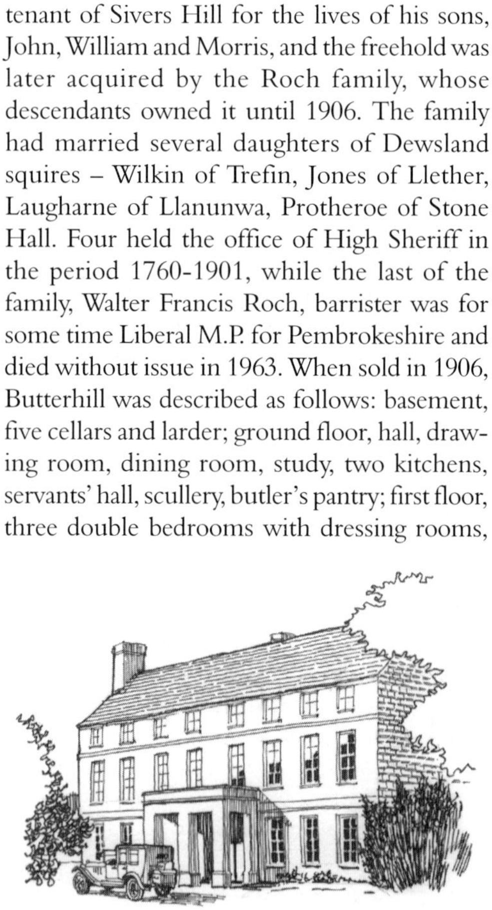

two single bedrooms; second floor ten bedrooms; a main staircase and two back-staircases; numerous outbuildings and an old pigeon house. When I visited Butterhill in 1975, it was empty, becoming dilapidated, a large 3-storeyed double-pile house, with ranges of eight windows in each floor, and a porch-entrance; the fine ornamental ceiling in the drawing room was badly damaged. Miss Lawrence of Tenby in 1950 owned a some-what unusual relic, namely an early Victorian dolls' house being a replica of the old mansion of Butterhill. The Roch family of Butterhill bore arms: *azure* semee of roses *or*, a lion rampant *or.*

Refs: Fenton, *Tour Pembs.*, pp. 98-9; Burke, *LG,* 1898, ii, 1267; *Welsh Furniture,* p. 28; *Western Telegraph,* 14 Nov. 1984, contains two excellent photographs of Butterhill in 1895 and 1984.

BWLCH Y CLAWDD, *Maenclochog*

To the east of the village, close to the border of Llandeilo parish, and now represented by a few cottages near Temple Druid. Home of a yeoman family in the 15th century, and in the later half of the century, the occupier was Griffith Llewelin whose daughter Ellin married Evan Mortimer, a younger son of Richard Mortimer of Coedmore, of Cardigan in 1480. In 1498 Griffith, Howel and David, sons of Howel ap David ap Griffith, granted 'on account of great necesesity and poverty' all their lands in Llangolman, and at Bulgh Clawth in Maenclochog, held by Welsh tenure, to Lewis ap David ap Griffith Fychan of Llangolman, Yeoman.

In February 1503/4, Ieun ap Morgan Gwyn of Bulgh y Clawth owned five plots and 100 acres there, three farms in Cemaes, and five properties in Maenclochog, and his sons John, Morgan, and Owen, all being 23 years old and more. Later, Eva verch Peres Broghton, relict of the said Ieuan held properties for her life at Clenesaithman in Llangolman, Bulghepant, in the lordship of Maenclochog, a farm in the lordship of Cemaes, and Pont Kenan (Pont Gynon) in the demesne of Eglwyswrw. For a period in the years 1543-74, William Griffith ap Howel Fychan was in ward for Bulch y Clawth to William Owen, lord of Cemaes.

Later in that century the occupier was Lewis Dedwydd, followed by his son William Lewis Dedwydd, and he by his son William Lewis William Dedwydd, who married Morfydd daughter of John Rees ap Howel of Penybenglog, and had a son, Lewis William, who lived at Bwlch y Clawdd in 1658. He was followed by his son Arthur Lewis who married Mary Beddoe, and had a son Lewis (William) who married Elen Vaughan of Farthingshook. Lewis William, gentleman, was living at Bwlch y Clawdd for which he was assessed at four hearths in 1670.

In 1731 Roger Lewis of Narberth owned 'the capital messuage called Bwlch y Clawdd', and in 1734/5 his brother William Lewis, gentleman, was living there. Roger Lewis of Bwlch y Clawdd supported the Picton Castle candidate in the 1760 election, and in 1786 Thomas Lewis, Esquire, of the same place was owner-occupier. Shortly after this the property was sold and a new mansion was built and called Temple Druid. The name Bwlch y Clawdd ceased to be used but still survives locally.

Lewis Morris, the antiquary, wrote, 'in 1743 a stone 6 feet long on the roadside by Mr. William Lewis's house called Bwlch y Clawdd in ye parish of Maenclochog was found marked *Curcagni fili Andagelli*. The stone has been removed to the churchyard at Cenarth'.

This was one of several houses in South Wales designed by John Nash (1752-1835), one of George IV's architects. It was rebuilt in the 1790s for Henry Bulkeley, (1760-1821), as a hunting box. His arms: a Chevron between three fox masks; crest a fox mask, motto *Nec temere nec timide*. When Bulkeley died, the property was put up for sale. It had eight principal bedrooms and some fine reception rooms 'fitted up with statuary, marble chimney pieces and correspondingly finished' as the sales particulars described it. The house was drastically altered so that little of Nash's work remains and its name was changed to Temple Druid. Nearby was a prehistoric cromlech said to have been a druids' temple. This no longer exists, only the house's name reminds us of the fact.

The Temple Druid estate became part of the Trecwn (Barham) estate between 1819-39. In the 1839 Trecwn rental we have Temple Druid, with Rev. J. Davies, tenant, Temple Druid farm, Ebenezer Meyler, tenant, and Temple Druid cottage, W. Rees, Tenant. There were several owners over the years and there was even a rumour that the place had been bought on behalf of Nelson as a retreat for himself and Lady Hamilton. Among other owners were a Mr. Pryce who had made his fortune in India, Leo Walmsley, the author, who lived there during the last war and recently it was the home of Mr. and Mrs. Harry Furmstone who lived there for over 20 years. In 1989 Temple Druid was put up for sale with 88 acres of woodland, pasture, a lake and a trout stream.

Francis Jones tells us that in the mid-18th century one of the descendants of the old family of Bwlch y Clawdd went to London and entered the service of the Bank of England and established a fortune. One of the descendants of the family was R. A. Butler, the Statesman.

Refs: Francis Jones, *The Hand of Nash in West Wales; Cambrian Travellers Guide,* 1840 edn. p. 289; Pembs. GS 1792; VL 1894, 1834; *RCAM Pembs.,* 1925, p. 207; Fenton *Tour Pembs.* pp. 192-5; *Anc. Mon. Pembs;* Prof. David Williams, *Aberystwyth,* 1976; Deeds, Baronia de Kemes, Trenewydd Deeds; Carms. RO, GGMS vols. II and III; *Arch. Camb.* 1896; Pembs. RO, HDX/695/No. 1.

CAERAU, *Llanddewi Velfrey**

This was the first home in the 18th century of Lewis of Henllan. Roger Lewis of Caerau had two co-heiresses, Elizabeth baptised on 29 November 1735, and Martha, baptised 5 June 1733.

On 4 March 1662/3 Sir Erasmus Philipps of Picton Castle granted a lease to 'Jenking a Bevan of Llandewy Wellfrey, of the Keyri in parish of Landewy W. rent £7 10s., two couple of fat hens, a couple of capons, a bushel of great oats, two horses to carry coals for one day annually, and a heriot'. By 1684 there was a new lease in favour of Roger ap Evan, husbandman for 21 years at a rent of £8 10s. a bushel of oats, a couple of hens, a couple of capons, and one day's harvest work at Picton annually. By 1786 Lord Milford owned Caerau with William Evan the occupier assessed at £1 6s. 4d. in tax.

Refs: Picton Castle Deeds. LT 1786.

CAERFORIOG, *Whitchurch*

Now a farmstead in the north of the parish near the banks of Afon Solfach. Near the buildings are the remains of a moat and a pool called Llyn yr Alarch, while a dovecot stood nearby, but there are no relics of it now. All these were associated with the ancient mansion of Caerforiog. About 30 yards southwards stood a chapel, several parts of which survived as late as 1925. According to Fenton (1811) parts of the chapel remnant were incorporated in an outbuilding; remains of the dovehouse were to be seen in 1856, but were practically destroyed in 1898. Adam Houghton, Bishop of St. Davids 1361-89 is said to have been born here.

The names of previous owners are preserved in a field-name near Caerforiog, Parc Tir Perrot, and in the name of a cottage near Solva, Pant y Perrot. The earliest known owners were the Perrots of Haroldston who owned lands in Dewsland. By his will dated 1491, Henry desired to be buried in 'the parish church (of Whitchurch) before the image of the blessed Christopher the Martyr', and left all his property to his wife Isabella for life, then to William Perrot of Haroldston and his heirs for ever. In 1498 Isabella granted all the land to the said William Perrot. In 1502 Sir William Perrot made a partition of properties in Dewsland 'whiche sumtyme was Harry Perrotte late of Caerveriocke esquyer'. About 1524 Jenkin Perrot lived at Caerforiog. The 'capital messuage' of Caerforiog was held by Sir James Perrot as of the manor of Trecadwgan, near Solva, in 1613. During the reign of James I (1603-25) David Gwyn, gentleman, described as of Caervoriog, brought an action against Francis Parry of Trecadwgan, gentleman, for forcible entry on Caerforiog. Towards the end of the 17th century it was home of Thomas Williams gentleman, trustee of Dr. Jones's Charity in 1698. In 1718 Rees Price of Tenby, gentleman, and his wife Jane owned Caerforiog, and by his will in 1724 left the property to Jane, who by her will dated 1733 bequeathed it to Anne Wogan of Minwere. The owner in 1740 was

John Laugharne of Pontfaen, who in that year sold the property to Samuel Harries of Cruglas, and it passed to his son John Harries who owned it in 1786, the then tenant being John James.

In 1838 Mary Harries is described as owner (188 acres), with William Meyler as tenant. Thenceforward it continued to be owned by farmers. It has been extensively modernised.

Refs: PRO, AD III; NLW, Poyston Deeds; College of Arms, Wagner MS No. 2 (AD 1610); *Pembs. Arch. Svy,* 1896-1908; Fenton, *Tour Pembs.,* 1811; Jones and Freeman, *St. Davids,* 1856; WWHR, vols. 3 and 8; *RCAM Pembs.* 1925.

CAERMAENAU FAWR, *Llanddewi Velfrey*

On a gentle slope, a quarter of a mile north of Penblewin crossroads. In early documents the name is spelled variously as Cremina, Cremine and Creminah. In the 17th century the Jones family (descended from Sir Rhys ap Thomas) lived firstly at Vaynor, Llawhaden, but had moved to Caermaenau by 1687 when John Jones lived there. He was followed by his son William Jones, appointed a Justice of the Peace in 1707, who often served as a Grand Juror, and sealed deeds with the chevron and ravens of his ancestor. He died shortly after making his will in 1738. The estate, which continued to include Vaynor, was substantial, and the family intermarried with landowners like Colby of Rhosygilwen, Garnons of Cilgerran, and Adams of Whitland. The last of the family at Caermaenau was Thomas Jones, living there in 1783.

By 1786 the property belonged to John Dunn, with Edward James as tenant. Later it was let to yeomen. It is still an attractive homestead built in the vernacular style. An inventory of Caermaenau made in 1751 names the following rooms: The Blue Room, Dining Room, Study, White Room, Porch Room, Kitchen, Servants' Hall and domestic offices.

After the Second World War it became the seat of Mr. R. W. A. P. Lewis (of Henllan) and Mrs. Lewis, who improved the old house and environs, happily without disturbing traditional features. A tablet on an outbuilding is inscribed 'W. Jones Esq. 1721', and another, 'J. 1744'. Mr. Lewis, a J.P. and D.L., served as High Sheriff in 1972.

Refs: NLW, Pembs. Papers of GS, Coleman Deeds; Pembs. RO, LT 1786; Lewis, *Efailwen to Whitland,* 1978, illust.

CAERWEN, *Llandeloy*

A farm in the western end of Llandeloy parish. In 1512 William Vychan 'of Gaere Wen' also owned lands at Hendre Fach and Tyre Eva (both in Llandeloy parish) Porthiddy Vawr and Trebedw (in Llanrhian parish), which he mortgaged to Howel David Howel Gwilym, for 4 marks. In July 1565, the owner of Caerwen was John Lewys Perkin gentleman, who lived there with his wife Agnes and summoned Thomas Scourfield for £11 due on a bond.

He died in that year leaving sundry debts which involved his widow, Agnes Lewys and sons, William, Thomas, Meyler, John and daughter, Margaret, in court appearances.

The next owner mentioned was David Howell of Caerwen who had died before 1580 when the Caerwen estate was partitioned between his two daughters, co-heirs, Nest and Margaret, the former married David Johnes, husbandman, and was living at Caerwen in 1587, and the latter married Henry James of Treglemais, living there in 1587. In the following year John ap Rees, esquire, of Rickeston agreed to buy a messuage and two tofts, and 74 acres in Caerwen and Llandeloy from David ap John and Nesta his wife, and in 1613 his son, Thomas ap Rees, bought further lands at Caerwen. The family continued to possess the estate until 8 October 1706 when James ap Rhys (Rice) sold it to John Rickson of Pembroke, merchant, and included 'the capital messuage of Caerwen' among other properties in Dewsland.

In 1714 Mrs. Jane Rickson widow, and her son Joseph granted a lease of Caerwen to Francis John, Dorothy his wife and Henry their son, for their lives, at a yearly rent of £15. On 11 May 1754 Henry John of Caerwen bought the farm for £575 from Anne Rickson, and her son William Rickson. Henry John, a Parliamentary voter in 1760, died in 1794, aged 82, and Caerwen passed to his son, Francis John. It remained in the possession of the John family till the death of Thomas John in 1877. In 1878 his trustees sold Caerwen and Gwindy for £6,345 to the second cousin of Thomas John, Mrs. Mary Thomas of Trehale, so that it continued in the family. Mrs. Thomas, wife of Rev. T. E. Thomas, Baptist Minister, died in 1901, aged 83 and was buried with her husband at Blaenclyn chapel.

Thereafter Caerwen continued to be owned by Henry John's descendants until sold in 1913. Later it was sold several times, finally to Pembrokeshire County Council who divided it into two farms.

The Sale Catalogue of 1913 showed the farm to be of 210 acres in the parish of Llandeloy and Whitchurch, consisting of a farmhouse, three cottages and gardens, then held by David Howells at a rent of £185 p.a.

It had been in the possession of the John family as tenants from 1713, owners from 1754. Francis Jones visited the house in 1976 and found it 'well maintained'.

Refs: Pembs. Plea Rolls Nos. 23, 26, 96; Eaton Evans and Williams Deeds; VL 1894; Sale Cat. 625 Carms. RO; LT 1786; Maesgwynne Deeds 15; Fines in Pembs. GS.

CALDEY ISLAND, *off the coast of Tenby*

Although an island, Caldey nevertheless forms an intimate part of the life of Pembrokeshire. During medieval times it maintained a monastery which ended by the Dissolution in 1535/36, afterwards to be inhabited by various farmers and fishermen, and in the 19th century by a landowner who erected a residence attached to the old monastic building. The *Reminiscenses of Colonel Morgan-Clifford, M.P.,* published in London in 1893 tell us that 'Caldey Island is the property of a gentleman who has built on it and made a comfortable residence; and farms the land, about six hundred acres, in a very superior manner. The Island having no population of its own, he brings from the mainland a number of labourers. They come over on the Monday and return to their homes on Saturday evenings'. This was Cabot Kynaston, Esq. The Rev. W. Done Bushill wrote in 1931 that 'The Bradshawes held it until 1612 when it was sold by the great-grandson of the above, John Bradshaw to Walter Philpin, Mayor of Tenby and his son Griffith. In 1653 it was sold by the Philpin family to Reeve Williams of Llandridion, Glam. and Robert Williams of Loughor. In 1786 John Williams, a great-grandson of above Reeve Williams, sold it to George Greville, Earl Brooke and Earl of Warwick, who in 1798 sold it to Thomas Kynaston of Pembroke. It remained with the Kynaston family until 1867 when it was sold to James Wilson Hawksley, and was sold in 1894 to Thomas Dick Smith-Cuninghame. From Mr. Smith-Cuninghame it passed in 1897 to Rev. W. Done Bushell, FSA who sold it in 1906 to Rev. Father Aelred OSB. The mansion was later demolished, being in a ruinous condition. The wheel had turned its full circle by 1906 when it once more became a religious centre in the possession of the Roman Catholic church and continues to flourish as such.

Refs: Rev. W. Bushell, *An Island of the Saints,* 1931; and especially Roscoe Howell's well illustrated *Caldey,* 1984, and references there.

CAMROSE HOUSE, *Camrose*

To the south of Camrose church, across a little stream, and close to an ancient earthwork, stands the Georgian mansion, a square three-storeyed structure, with ranges of fine windows. Home of the Owen, Webb-Bowen and Penn families. The longest lasting of these was that of Bowen, a branch of the Lochmeyler family, who had settled in Camrose parish in the early 14th century, and also lived at Roblinston (about half a mile northwest of Camrose church) and Wolfsdale. Camrose House was their final home.

Fenton wrote in 1811 'I come to the next mansion of my friend Hugh Webb-Bowen, Esq. on whom the property of the last surviving Bowen of this house of Roblinston has dwelt, a mansion enbosomed in wood, in a situation pleasingly retired, and supplying all the elegant comforts of life, which the hospitable possessor has a heart to enjoy.' Almost in front of the house stands an immense tumulus. A deed dated 1722 describes it as 'a capital messuage called Castle, containing six ploughlands.' About thirty years after Fenton, the topographer S. Lewis wrote, 'Camrhos House, the seat of Hugh Webb Bowen, Esq. is the only residence within the parish which is entitled to notice.' Hugh Webb Bowen, who had been High Sheriff in 1806, died in 1833, and his descendants continued at Camrose House until after the Second World War. It was later converted, and in 1970 used as a club for a while. It is still owned and occupied by the family.

Refs: Fenton, *Tour Pembs.;* J. R. P. Penn and Green, 'Bowen of Roblinston and Camrose', WWHR 1926, pp. 37-62; *RCAM Pembs.,* 1925; NLW, Morgan-Richardson Deeds; *Coastal Cottages of Pembrokeshire,* 1987 illust.

CAMROSE NORTH, *Camrose*

The earliest known resident in North Camrose was the Reynish family, descended from Flemings who had settled in the Hundred of Rhos. In 1623 the property called North Camrose was owned by Charles, Prince of Wales, and a Survey made in that year consisted of (1) North Camrose, 72 acres with Jenkin Renish tenant; the house consisted of a hall, five couples and outshute, and two couples, an inner room with loft over it, four couples, a room below the hall door and three couples; all being on a ground floor, and thatched. (2) 24 acres (3) 38 acres (4) 56 acres (5) and several others of very small acreage. John Estmond was tenant of Nos. 2-4. All were described as North Camrose. Jenkin Reynish was a yeoman and was succeeded by his son William. When William Reynish's only son and heir Thomas Reynish married Jane daughter of William Jones of Brawdy, gentleman, in 1651 all the Reynish messuages of North Camrose were settled on them.

In 1690 Thomas and Jane settled two messuages, six cottages and 700 acres being the extent of their North Camrose estate. They left two sons, Jenkin and William Reynish. In 1786 messuages and lands in North Camrose owned by John Crowther Reynish, gentleman, consisted of Wolfsdale (occupied by the said owner) Camrose (by William Reynish) and Mountain Cott (by Thomas John). In 1796 messuages and lands in North Camrose were in occupation of David Reynish. In 1808 he had a lease of Eweston in Brawdy, and was followed there by his son Jenkin Reynish who married Sarah Bennett of Camrose in 1812, and left issue.

Refs: Jones of Brawdy Deeds; *NLW Journal,* 1980, XXI No. 4; Pembs. RO, LT 1786.

CANASTON, GREAT, *Robeston Wathen*

This residence is believed to have stood where the farmstead of Great Canaston is today. Canaston Bridge, over the highway from Narberth to Haverfordwest, is a short distance northwards. Home of the medieval family of Canaston, whose heiress, Mabel Caneston 'Ladie of Caneston', brought the property to her husband Peter Perrot. According to deeds in the Slebech collection, it was formerly a manor. Marked as Canyston on William Rees' 14th century map. Towards the end of the 17th century the Poyers lived there and in 1688 was occupied by John Poyer, a wealthy tanner, who founded the fortunes of his family. It was later acquired by the Foleys, and in 1786 was owned by Herbert Foley of Ridgeway, tenanted by Mr. Griffith Gwynne. An estate map of Great Canaston was made by Charles Hassall in 1794.

Refs: NLW, Slebech Deeds, Nos. 652, 809.

CAPESTON, *Walwyn's Castle*

In the southern part of the parish and named after one of its medieval owners, is 'Caprich's tun' which developed into its present form. In 1373 Peter Caprich son and heir of Robert Caprich, granted to Thomas de Hoton, Joan his wife, and Thomas their son, the lands he had inherited from his father at Capriston and Ricordeston in the lordship of Haverford, and dated the deed on 4 August 1373 at Capston. By 1608 it was the home of Francis Noote. On 26 June 1738 Nicholas Roch, Esq. of nearby Rickeston, made his will whereby he stipulated that 'the message called Capeston lately purchased by me from Hugh Fowler, esq., (is) to be sold and the proceeds to be paid to my three younger children when 21 years of age.' From deeds of the period 1753-84 we find William Cozens living at Capestone; he died in 1784, and his sons William and John A. Cozens settled at Sandyhaven and Rosepool.

The next at Capeston was William Davies (will dated 1808), whose eldest son Evan Davies became an Indian Army cavalry Lieut.-Colonel, known as 'Tiger' Davies for his exploits in hunting that animal, and who was killed in 1827 by disaffected troops of his regiment; and whose younger son Lewis Davies became a naval officer, commanded the sloop *Rose* at Navarion, being thereafter known as 'Navarion' Davies, rose to the rank of Captain R.N., and was appointed C.B. In the latter half of the 19th century, and up to 1950, the family of Scale of Capeston enjoyed the reputation of being progressive farmers.

Refs: PRO, Anc. Deeds, Nos. 2590 and D6091; NLW, Pembs. Plea Rolls, 92; Carms. RO, J. Francis Colln.; Pembs. RO, LT 1786.

CAREW CASTLE, *Carew*

For architectural details of the castle, with illustrations or plan, *see* RCAM 1925. The interior arrangements, windows, etc. were made early in the 16th century by Sir Rhys ap Thomas (d. 1526). A description of a tournament held by Sir Rhys is contained in Cambrian Register, 1795. Leland, writing about 1538 says 'I saw the castel of Carew repaired or magnificently builded by Syr Reese ap Thomas. It stondith by a creke of Milford Haven' (*Tour*, p. 115). Sir Rhys ap Thomas had inherited the Dynevor estates and was an intimate of Henry Tudor who stayed there on his way to Bosworth. Rees fought beside HenryVII as he became, and was knighted on Bosworth field. Sir Rhys (d. 1526), held the last great Welsh tournament there in 1507 lasting five days. Rhys's grandson forfeited the estate to Sir John Perrot who was reputed to be an illegitimate son of Henry VIII. It was he who built the magnificent river front of the castle with its Elizabethan windows. However he was not to enjoy it long, being condemned to death for treason against Elizabeth. He died in 1592 and the castle and demesne was leased to Edward

Webb who assigned it to Sir John Carew, both of whom resided there. Sir John Carew conveyed it to Sir John Philipps of Picton. A note of the decays in the castle was taken on 3 April 1610 and later Sir Richard Philipps restored it. For the Carew family pedigree see Burke's *Landed Gentry,* 1850. Sir John Carew was High Sheriff in 1623 and George Carew in 1640. The castle descended from the Carews to G. H. Warrington, Esq. In 1873 Captain Carew of Carew Castle Court held 1217 acres with a value of £1,393 per annum.

There is in the archives, the details of the food provided for a Public Feast by 'John Perrot of Carew Castle Knight' in 1552, the year he was High Sheriff: 7 stone of beef at 14lb to the stone, 5 geese, 1 hind quarter of Veal, 1 fore quarter ditto, 1 breast and 'coast' of mutton, 1 tine mutton and shoulder of veal, 6 brace of partridges, 3 couple of hares, 6 couple of rabbits, 4 dozen eggs, 2 barrels double beer, 2 ditto small beer, 18 loaves white bread, 20 ditto wheaten bread, 3 bushels of flour, 3 turbot. The spelling has been modernised.

The castle, damaged by the Roundheads in the civil war in 1644, now a ruin, is open to the public. When I visited in the early 1980s the rooms in the base of the tower were being used for lambing ewes. – Ed.

Refs: Dwnn, i, 78; Carlisle, *TDW,* 1811; Spurrell, *History of Carew;* Laws, *Little England;* WWHR ii, 71; Pedigree in BLG 1850; *Arch. Cam.,* 1886, p. 27.

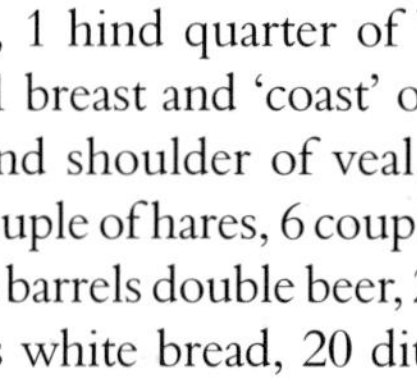

CAREW RECTORY, *Carew*

Called The Old Rectory, situated within 100 yards of the parish church. It is possible that it may have been first built when Sir Rhys ap Thomas was modernising the castle. In 1811 Fenton describes it as 'of a singular appearance, having a square tower on one side through an arched opening, in which, now stopped up, was once the principal residence. It is an irregular building, a great part of considerable antiquity, unroofed, and in ruins.' The low square tower with its corbel table and newel staircase, and also a portion of the sunbathed wall that surrounded the house, have survived. Timmins informs us in 1895, from Carew church 'we make our way to a curious-looking structure known as The Old Rectory.

Though now a mere farmhouse the place bears traces of considerable antiquity, and appears to have been built with an eye to defence. The massive walls are corbelled out beneath the eaves of the roof, which is pitched at a steep angle, giving the old structure a picturesque appearance. The house has apparently been formerly enclosed within a walled precinct, and a fast-fading tradition tells of 'the soldiers' having been quartered here in the turbulent days of old.' I visited the house when Mr. Michael Whitlock dwelt there, and who had 'restored' in excellent manner, both internally and externally. He sold the property in 1977.

Refs: Fenton, *Tour Pembs.,* 1811; *Arch. Cam.* 1877, P. 312; and 1881, P. 238, illust; Timmins, *Nooks Pembs.*, 1895, illust; Laws, *Little England,* 1888, illust; *RCAM Pembs.,* 1925, illust.

CARNACHEN WEN, *Mathry*

An ancient homestead on a gentle slope facing northwards, about a mile inland from Penmorfa and about half a mile northwest of Mathry parish church. During the Middle Ages there were several holdings in the district, and between 1326 and 1630 were variously known as Knachan, Knachan Dawkin, Knachan Thomas Brown, Knachan Castell, Knachan Jenkin, Knachan Tregwynt, Knachan Walter, and from 1630 the form used is Carnachen Wen, alias Carnachan Brown, and only as Carnachen Wen thereafter. In those days Carnachen Wen is also described as a manor. All the other holdings had been absorbed into local farms and their earlier names discontinued.

The first known family there was that of Brown, descended from Fromand the Fleming, one of whose descendants took the name Perkin. By the early 16th century the family had adopted the Welsh form of nomenclature, so that those living at Tregwynt became known as Harries, and those of Carnachenwen as Perkin. In 1503 David Philip Perkin was lord of the manor of Carnachenwen, and his son Lewis David Perkin occurs in the taxation lists of the 1540s. In 1657 William Tucker of Sealyham bought 'Carnachen wen otherwise called Carnachan Browne', from Owen Perkin who died there about 1668. Thereafter the property formed part of the Sealyham estate and remained in the hands of the Tucker-Edwardes family till the end of the 19th century, during which period Carnachenwen was leased to several gentlemen farmers. In 1740 it was held by the Rogers family from Goodwick, once noted for their successful enterprise as smugglers. The last of the family to hold the lease was Blanche Maria who married David Davies,

banker, of Aberystwyth, and their son David Davies of Carnachenwen was High Sheriff in 1832. Blanche Maria was a devout Methodist and the house became the abode of several ministers, and Sunday Schools were held there. Blanche Maria was the last leaseholder and when she died without heirs in 1846, Carnachenwen reverted to the Sealyham family. Thereafter it was held by several yeomen, and finally sold. It was bought later by the Morgan family of Trewallterlwyd, and is now owned by Miss Jill Morgan who has modernised the old homestead without disturbing its traditional features. The Rogers family had also improved it and the house and buildings have initials and dates engraved on them – 1743, 1754, 1758, 1776 and 1784 and the glass label to a wine bottle is inscribed 'W. Rogers 1762'.

Refs: Dwnn, i, 111 (1613 AD); PRO AD, 2781, 4714, 11066; College of Arms, Wagner MS. No. 2, Protheroe MS XII, 34; Pembs. RO, Deeds; WWHR, viii, p. 194; NLW, Deeds, Morgan-Richardson, Cwrtmawr, Sealyham, Lucas, Bronwydd, Eaton Evans and Williams; Pembs. Plea Rolls, GF, and Fines; Francis Jones, 'The Lay Manor of Carnachenwen', *Journal of Historical Society of the Church in Wales.*

CARN HUAN, *Eglwyswrw**

Lying about threequarters of a mile southwest of Eglwyswrw, a short distance northeast of Pontygynon. On 23 May 1646 a settlement was agreed between Gwilym Myles of Eglosserew, clerk, and Jane Warcoppe alias Miles his wife, of two messuages and land called Carn Hyan ycha, and two messuages and land called Carn Hyan issa in the parish of Elwyswrw, after death of said Jane, to revert to Henry Myles junior of Eglwyswrw, eldest son of Gwilym Miles junior of Llanfairnantgwyn, gent. and his heirs, and failing heirs to the said Henry, then to revert to Nathaniel Myles, grantor's son, and to his heirs. In the land tax records of 1786 Henry John was owner with David Evans, tenant, and in the Voters lists of 1894 Griffith Lewis was of Carnhuan, land and tenet.

Refs: Bronwydd Deeds No. 1902.

CARNE COCH, *Llanwnda*

On a slope overlooking Goodwick Bay, and near Ffynnondruidion farm. It was described as a Knight's fee in 1326. In the late 16th century it was the home of William Griffith, gentleman, who also owned Trefayog farm. He married, as his second wife, in November 1610 Ursula, daughter of William Warren of Trewern, Nevern. In 1630 in the Great Sessions he claimed 'Ffynnon y grib parcel of the capital messuage called Carney coch' as his property, and he was ordered by arbitrators to build a stone wall at least 4 foot high, and a headstone along the boundary. By 1640 Carne Coch formed part of the Trellewelyn estate (Phillips). Martha Phillips who married Sparks Martin of Withybush inherited part of that estate, including Carne Coch, after his wife's death. He died in 1787. After this it was held by various yeomen, and in 1978 its owner was Mr. R. V. Johns, a younger son of Manorowen.

Refs: Black Book of St. Davids; NLW, Pembs. Plea Rolls, Spence Colby Deeds; LT 1786.

CARSWELL, *Penally*

About half a mile eastwards of St. Florence village. Carswell is mentioned in 1348. William Whyte of that place witnessed a deed re Trefloyne in 1397; and Phyllypp Nicoll, husbandman, lived at Carswell in 1543. In 1586 Richard Merydith of Pembroke town, yeomen, left to his fellow townsman, Peter Williams, merchant, the portion of Carswell with the messuage and garden on the hillside; in 1601 the Mayor and Burgesses of Tenby leased their land at Carswell to the Bowens of Trefloyne, for life. The Tenby church wardens received £6 from William Lewis for rent of Carswell in 1659/60; the Mayor and Burgesses leased Carswell in 1686 to Owen Williams of Tenby, butcher, and in the same year, Griffith Dawes of Bangeston, Angle and others, representatives of Abra Bowen, spinster, of Gloucester, who had bought a messuage and land at Carswell.

Part of Carswell was owned by Tenby Corporation, and occupied by Frances Ankern in 1786. In 1834 John Keys obtained the lease of the farm of Carswell, with William Llewellin as tenant.

Laws writes – 'Carswell consists of two distinct buildings standing about thirty yards apart; they are not quite in line, but very nearly, and are much of a size. The house to the north consists of a lower chamber vaulted, and an upper one with a curiously high pitched roof. At least the roof was high pitched some twenty years ago, only the gable ends now remain . . . At the north end is a huge square chimney. To begin with the lower room, one end is almost taken up with the fireplace, in the right side of which is a large recess, larger than would be required for an oven; a man can well stand up in it. On the left hand of the fireplace is a block of masonry; this Mr. Barnwell suggests, 'was a stone seat, which might also have served for a table' (*Arch. Cam.* July 1867, illust.). There is a square window over the table which is an evident insertion. Another apartment has been built on to the east side, which, as it is not bonded . . . may safely be put down as later; the doorway faces the fireplace, and is too mutilated to serve as evidence. The upper chamber is reached by an outside stair; here is a fire-place and two small deeply splayed windows; three others have been closed. The second building consists of three storeys. There is no sign of an original chimney, this building has been used as a cottage, and a chimney has been cut in the wall for the first floor; this is clearly recent. The lower chamber is vaulted, lighted by two splayed windows. The vaulting has been cut through for a door, the original of which now leads into another vaulted apartment which blocks the windows. The first floor is reached by an outer stair and lighted by one small splayed window and a modern square one. The attic storey is approached from the same outside steps; these enter the first floor apartment about halfway to the ceiling, from whence I suppose a ladder reached into the roof. In later days the farm seems to have always been divided between two proprietors. Nearer our day we find Carswell farm, 87 acres three roods 14 perches, advertised to be sold on 19 June 1920; the dwelling house, 'recently erected' contains parlour, kitchen, back-kitchen, five bedrooms and outbuildings: 17/28ths of the farms belong to 'The Tenby Charities (vendors) and 11/28ths belong to The Church Charities Tenby'.

Refs: Laws, *Little England,* 1888, pp. 189-193, three illusts, and p. 190; *Arch. Camb.* p. 867, illust.; *RCAM,* 1925; NLW Picton Castle Deeds; Peter Smith, *Houses of the Welsh Countryside,* fig. 8 (133), and also *Land of Dyfed,* p. 31; Carms. RO, SC No. 457.

CARTLETT (1), *Llanrhian*

In the village of Trefin. A large commodious house, known to the local folk as Gallod. In the 19th century house of the Thomas and Morgan families. Still inhabited and well cared for. William Arthur Morgan died at Cartlett 23 July 1897. He was a great Methodist and was buried at Llanrhian. His wife, Elizabeth died at Cartlett 16 January 1894.

Gibbon

CARTLETT (2), *Uzmaston*

Now a suburb of Haverfordwest. Also called Carthlett. Perhaps this is the property later called The Great House. Home of the 14th century family of Gibbon whose seal to a deed of 1342 shows a lion passant guardant. In 1786 five properties called Cartlett were owned by Lord Milford, and a similar number by John Campbell Esq. Lord Milford leased the messuage called The Great House in the village of Cartlett, to John Attwood of St. Mary, Haverfordwest, limner, for the lives of lessee Martha Attwood and Thomas Mathewman Attwood, which seems to have been afterwards sold to John Attwood, who, on 29 September 1784 released the messuage called The Great House to Francis Edwardes of Haverfordwest, Esq. On 1 November 1801 the said Francis Edwardes leased it to Cecile Picton, widow, at a yearly rent of £16 16s. 0d.

Refs: LT 1786; Carms. RO, Trant Deeds.

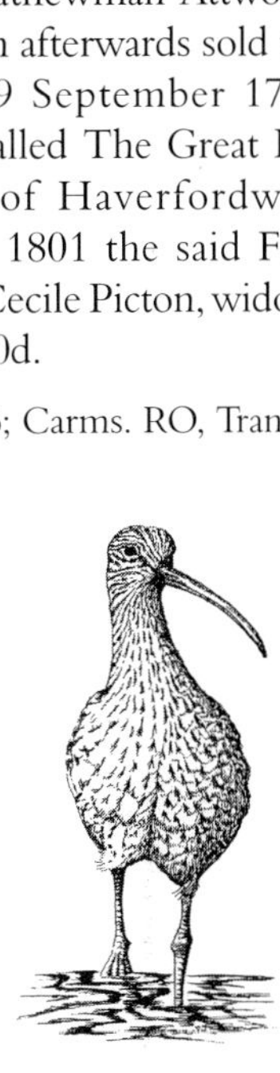

CASTLE CENLAS, *Mathry*

In a grove on a hill-top 1¼ miles southwest of Mathry village, a commodious attractive house, the front portion of which was built in the late 19th century: the outbuildings to the rear are large. In 1326 it is described as a knight's fee, and in 1342 John ap Robert Goch of Preskilly transferred half a carucate of arable land at 'Berry in the fee of Castle Kynlas' to Philip Cadwgan of Trecadwgan near Solva. By 1566 Castle Cenlas was a manor, and in 1622-25 consisted of the manor and farm of Castlecenlas, and the farms of Castell Rhedyn, Penywern, Mabws Fach and Lochturffin, in all comprising over 587 acres.

Its early owners were the Wyrriots of Orielton, and from them passed by marriage to the Owens of Orielton, from them to the Laugharne family, and from them back to the Owens. On 14 January 1790 Miss Elizabeth Owen granted a lease of Castle Cenlas to the Rev. John Mathias, J.P. of Lochmeyler, and on 15th June of the same year she sold Castle Cenlas, Castle Rhedyn and Mabws Fach to the same buyer for £840. And so the descendants of the old manorial lords departed. The manorial rights had long ceased.

By his will of 1806 the reverend gentleman left Castle Cenlas to his son Richard Mathias who spent the remainder of his days there. Richard Mathias died in 1846, leaving an only child and heir, Letitia Mathias. She had created a bit of a stir by eloping with the Rev. James Jones, vicar of Mathry, by whom she had four children. In 1859 she leased Castle Cenlas to Henry Tibbetts, and in 1875 to James Griffith. She died on 27 September 1888. As none of her children had married, Castle Cenlas was sold early in the present century to the Rees family of Carnachenlwyd (cousins of my mother), who then settled there, and finally, in 1973 the property was sold.

Refs: Black Book of St. Davids; NLW, Slebech Deeds, No. 169; Poyston Deeds, No. 240; Pembs. RO, Land Tax 1786; Tithe Schedule 1842; WWHR IX, p. 153; see Francis Jones on lay manors in *Journal of Hist. Soc. of the Church in Wales,* 1969 and refs. there.

CASTLE HALL, *Steynton*

Just east of Milford marked on Colby's Map 1831. This residence was built in the 1770s by J. Zephoniah Holwell, sometime Governor of Bengal, who escaped from the Black Hole of Calcutta. He was at Castle Hall in 1786 and soon afterwards moved to Somerset and sold it to Robert Farquhar, purser of HMS *Hyena*. In 1797 Robert Robertson, gentleman, was owner-occupier. In 1799 the property was bought by John Warlow, wine merchant, of Haverfordwest, but by 1804 he had become bankrupt, and Castle Hall was conveyed to Benjamin Rotch, a Quaker merchant from Nantucket. He was also a whaler and general trader, and his son, Francis Rotch, established a private bank in Milford. Fenton (*Tour Pembs.*) in 1811 calls it 'a beautiful villa' then owned by 'Mr. Rotch (who) enlarged and beautified the house, grounds and gardens, and raised very extensive hot-houses, conservatories and other necessary appendages of fashionable luxury and taste', and the same author writes further in *Tour in Quest of Genealogies* 'Castle Hall, the pretty villa of Mr. Rotch . . . The house is not large, but commodiously elegant, . . . the demesne (has) a summer-house most judiciously placed. This charming spot once belonged to the former Governor Holwell (but) after the Governor left, it continued long untenanted, but about seven years ago was purchased by a wine-merchant of Haverfordwest . . . on his failure it was sold to the present proprietor (Mr. Rotch)'.

In 1819 Rotch left Milford, and sold Castle Hall to Robert Greville, who died in 1824 and left it to his son Robert Fulke Murray Greville. Owing to financial difficulties Greville left the county but returned to Castle Hall in the 1850s and was High Sheriff in 1854. He built Black Bridge, a wooden structure across the Pill. About 1857 he employed W. H. Lindsay of

Bloomsbury to improve the mansion and he reproduced it in appearance of an Italian Renaissance villa. Greville died in 1867. A London builder and contractor, Sam Lake, came there next, but became bankrupt in 1883.

By 1911 Castle Hall was occupied by Benedictine nuns. They left in 1917, and the next owner was Sir Hugh Thomas, estate agent and landowner of Haverfordwest, who built a new bridge across Castle Pill in 1922. He was High Sheriff in 1924, but died shortly after and in 1925 Castle Hall was advertised for sale. It became deserted, and during the mid-1930s was demolished and the area became a permanent mine depot. This is a tale of woe for house and families, though in the last few years a new interest has been taken in the gardens.

Refs: Fenton works cited; Pembs. RO, LT 1786; Carms. RO, Sale Catalogue 1925; Photo in T. Lloyd, *Lost Houses of Wales,* 1986, pp. 68-9; H. E. Busteed, *Echoes from Old Calentha,* 1908 with portrait of J. F. Holwell.

Gower

CASTLE MALGWYN (Old), *Manordeifi*

This house stood on a high wooded bluff. Today it is a farmhouse with no apparent features to indicate its former status. Originally, a fortified stronghold of the Prince Maelgwn, son of Rhys ap Griffith ruler of Deheubarth, and from him derived its name – Castell Malgwyn. Throughout the succeeding centuries a series of different families lived there. About the year 1400 the owner was Ieuan Fychan, (descended from Cadifor Fawr of Blaen Cych), whose son Owen followed him at Castle Malgwyn. Owen ap Ieuan Fychan left two daughters co-heiresses, Eleanor, who married James ap Griffith ap Howell who settled at Castell Maelgwyn, and Angharad, who married Rhys Fychan of Dyffryn Hoffnant in Penbryn (Cards.). James ap Griffith ap Howell, living in the years 1529 to 1555 described in contemporary records as 'domino de Castell Maelgorn in Wallia', has a most remarkable history which I have related elsewhere. On his death Castle Maelgwyn passed to Morgan Jones of Towyn (Cards), grandson of Angharad the other coheiress.

In 1584 Morgan Jones of Towyn, gentleman, granted a lease for 32 years to David Mortimer (who had been living at Castle Malgwyn since 1576) gentleman of the capital mansion house called Castle Malgwyn, and a meadow called Dolgamlyn in Llangoedmore, paying a yearly rent of £4, lessor reserving rights of the mill on the Teyvy near Lleghrid bridge 'now in decay'. He was a younger son of Coedmore, and was followed by his son Thomas Mortimer who died in 1613, and was succeeded by his son Edmund who moved to Cilfowyr.

By 1630 the property had passed into the ownership of David Thomas Parry of Noyadd Trefawr (Cards), and in 1634 had passed to his grandson David Parry who in that year mortgaged Castle Malgwyn to David Jenkins. The Parrys disposed of the property before 1647, and 1680 the 'messuage called Castle Molegwin formed part of the estate of William Jenkins of Blaenpant (Cards). By about 1740 it had ceased to be a residence, and became occupied by tenant-farmers. By 1766 it had been sold to the Symmons family of Llanstinan, and twenty years later 'Castell Malgwyn' was owned by the Pen-y-Gored Company, with Daniel Davies as tenant. In 1792 it was owned by (Sir) Benjamin Hammett (who built the *new* Castle Malgwyn on the banks of the Teifi) and in 1806 his son sold the old farmstead and lands to A. A. Gower, esq. of Glandovan. It formed part of the Gower estate for over a century. When I called there in the late 1960s it had been bought by Count Munster and farmed by tenants.

Mr. Phythian-Adams has written to say that he finds 'it is stated that the house passed to

Morgan Jones of Towyn, "grandson of Angharad" the wife of Rhys Fychan of Penbryn. In fact her grandson, Morgan Jones of Dyffryn Hoffnant was a different man and not of Towyn. See GGMS Gwynfardd p. 27 where it can be seen that Morgan of Towyn's father, John married Elizabeth, heir of the James Griffith ap Howell of Castle Malgwyn. This is clearly how Morgan John of Towyn inherited Castle Malgwyn, for his grandmother was a Bowen of Pentre Evan. See also Chetham MS p. 440 No. 78. GGMS Gwynfardd p. 28'. – *Ed.*

Refs: Dwnn, i, p. 55; GGMS vol. 2 (Cadifor Fawr) fo. 33; LT 1786; NLW, Muddlescombe Deeds, Noyadd Trefawr Deeds, Eaton Evans and Williams Deeds; WWHR, XIV, p. 231; *RCAM,* 1925; Francis Jones, 'Trail of the Fugitive', *Treasury of Historic Pembrokeshire & Historic Cardiganshire Homes and their Families.*

CASTLE MALGWYN (New), *Cilgerran*
At the western end of the parish on the banks of the Teifi, close to Manordeifi parish boundary, and about threequarters of a mile from the old Castle Malgwyn which is in the last-named parish. On or near the site stood the farmhouse of Penygored where an ironworks had been erected, and owned by the Penygored Company in 1786. The Company was bought about 1792 by Sir Benjamin Hammett who, some six years later built the present residence, known locally at that time as 'Ty mawr y gwaith', and named by the builder, Castle Malgwyn. In 1806 the works ceased to operate, and Hammett's son sold the property to Abel Anthony Gower of Glandovan, and it remained the seat of that family until sold after the Second World War. It is now a country hotel and outwardly retains its original form. Described in 1797 by Warner as follows: 'We attended Sir Benjamin Hammett to his house, Castle-Malkwn, a commodious mansion in the immediate neighbourhood of the works . . .'; described by Fenton in 1811 as 'an elegant modern building, affording a suite of handsome apartments and most commodious offices'; and by Rees in 1815 as 'a neat modern edifice'. A photograph by Allen of Tenby in 1917 has survived. The mansion is a large square edifice of three storeys each with a range of five windows, with extensions to the rear, renovated in 1978-79.

Refs: NLW, Coedmore Deeds; Tours by Warner Lipscombe, 1797, 1802; Fenton, *Tour Pembs.,* 1811; Rees 1815; Photograph of house, *Western Mail,* 8 June 1979; C. Allen, *The Tivyside Photographic Souvenir,* Tenby, 1871.

CASTLE MORRIS, *Mathry*
Locally called Casmorris. A small hamlet to the east of Mathry, clustered around a crossroads on the north side of which on a wooded hillock are the remains of an early fortification, the caput of an episcopal manor, known in medieval times as Le Bailey House, and later as Pencnwc, 'a farmstead which now occupies the site of the destroyed mount of Castell Morris. Within living memory the mound seems to have been fairly intact and to have borne some stone foundations. When removing it from the farmyard, the skeleton of a man was found'. (*RCAM Pembs.,* 1925, p. 224). The home and lands were held by the Bishop's leaseholders. The first family that is known at Le Bailey (Pencnwc) was that of Jones. In 1545 William John (later Jones) contributed to a lay subsidy, and in 1571 and again in 1573 William Jones of Castle Morris, gentleman, was High Constable of Dewsland. His coat-of-arms was *argent* an eagle *sable,* armed and langued *gules*. The family ceased to hold the property in the early 17th century. During the years 1654-56 John Mathias Esq. of Llangwarren was Steward of Dewsland for the Bishop, and in 1661 he had a lease 'of the manor house called Le Bailey, a fair tenement', and was still holding it when he died about 1683. The next-known holder of the property was a minor squire, John Mathias (with no connection with the Llangwarran family), who had married, prior to 1697, Lettice, daughter of John Ford of Stone Hall and Mary Wogan his wife. The Bishop granted him a lease of 'the manor house called Le Bayle' in Castle Morris in 1746, in 1749 granted a similar lease

to Bernard Baine. In 1766 a lease of the manor was granted to Henry Leach of Loveston, and in the following year of the house and land only. The Mathiases continued at Pencnwc (otherwise Le Bailey) until the mid-20th century, and today it is owned and occupied by a descendant, Mr. Johns. The manorial rights had long reverted to the Bishop of the See.

Refs: Dwnn, i, 110; Egerton MS 2586; Chetham MS; and College of Arms, Protheroe IV; Francis Jones, 'Episcopal Manors', *Journal of the Historical Society of the Church in Wales,* 1967; Carms. RO, Terrier of the Bishop's Lands 1817; GGMS Adv. Pembs.

Morris

CASTLE VILLA (CASWILIA), *Brawdy*

Now a farmhouse in the northern-most corner of the parish, and close to the remains of an ancient castell of the Iron Age, which gives its name Castell Wilia to the spot, a name still used locally in preference to the anglicized version, Castle Villa. From 1400 until the middle of the present century, a period of about five and a half centuries, it was held by various owners.

Henry Morris who was the first owner of this extensive estate, held a high position in the community and bore as his coat-of-arms *argent* three towers *azure.* His descendants took their wives from the families of Laugharne, Bowen of Pentre Evan and Wogan.

Last of the line, Anne Morris, sixth in descent from David Morris, married William Scourfield of New Moat about 1550 and was followed by his son John Scourfield, and he in turn by his son Thomas Scourfield. The last named became involved in financial difficulties, and in 1615 sold the Castle Villa estate to his elder brother William Scourfield of New Moat. The canting arms of the family were – *gules* three greyhounds courant *argent,* with crest of a greyhound *argent,* in his mouth a scroll bearing the Welsh word 'Ffyddlon' (Faithful). The Scourfields never lived at Castle Villa afterwards, and that property was thereafter let to yeomen tenants. Among these yeomen were the following – Bowen from 1621 who left about 1630, Owen there until about 1650, John Protheroe there in 1670 who died in 1697,

Courtesy of Mr. & Mrs. Morris

about 1700 came the Davies family who remained there for four generations, and after Phoebe Davies married Joseph Harries of Trenichol in 1814, that family became tenants of Castle Villa, and their grand-daughter Pheobe Davies Harries married Walter Morris of Chapel Farm, Pembroke in 1894. She died in 1897.

After the Second World War Colonel Davies-Scourfield, whose family had owned Castle Villa for some 400 years, sold that property to a Mr. Pettijohn, who after a brief period sold it to a business firm. And so the Pembrokeshire squires and yeomen bid their farewells to their ancient acres. All that is now left of bygone days is the apparition of a medieval owner who, mounted on a spirited horse, gaily clears the entrance gate of Castle Villa in the gloaming. See *Treasury of Historic Pembrokeshire*, pp. 181-192.

Refs: Dwnn, i, 175; GGMS, I; College of Arms MSS; Protheroe MS V, 155; Wagner MS 2 (Geo Owen 1610); NLW, Records of the Church in Wales; Francis Jones, 'Castle Villa', *Treasury of Historic Pembrokeshire*; PRO, AD, E210, D5173; *RCAM Pembs.* 1925; BM, Egerton MS 2586.

CASTLEBYTHE (CASFUWCH),
Castlebythe

On the lower slope of Mynydd Casfuwch, clustered around an early Celtic fortification, is a small hamlet consisting of two farmsteads, and until it was recently demolished, the parish church, sheltered by a well grown grove. Both farmsteads are called Castlebythe (Casfuwch). The one at the northern entrance to the hamlet is the ancient home of the former gentry families. It consists of a two storey, stone built structure with entrance porch, entrance hall, lounge with attractive chimney corner, dining room, kitchen, utility room, W.C. four bedrooms and bathrooms, outbuildings, and farmyard.

The earliest known family at this farm was that of Philipps, a branch of Picton Castle. During the second half of the 16th century William Philipps, son of Morgan Philipps of Picton, married Elinor daughter of Thomas Lloyd of Cilciffeth, and settled at Castlebythe, and their descendants remained there till towards the end of the 17th century, the last being James Philipps, gentleman, who paid two hearth taxes in 1670. In the 16th century James Lloyd, son of William Lloyd of Cilciffeth came to the lower farm, and was followed there by his son Owen Lloyd who does not seem to have had issue. During the 18th century there were four farms at Castle Bythe, and in 1786 William Wheeler Bowen esquire, owned two; (Eliz. Lewis and Griffith Evan tenants), Caesar Mathias esquire, owned the third (William Harris, tenant), and the fourth was owned and occupied by John Harries, gentleman. After this there were several successive owners and tenants, the longest-lasting being the Harries family who continued there till the 20th century.

Refs: BM Egerton MS 25486, fo. 2909; College of Arms, Wagner MS No. 2; Land Tax 1786; *RCAM Pembs.* 1925; *Western Telegraph,* 8 Feb. 1984, illust.

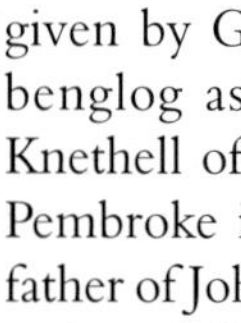

Castlemartin

CASTLETON, *Monkton*
Named after the Castle family. The seal of Philip Castlemartin to a deed of 1314 shows: a fesse between three castles. Dwnn describes the arms as *gules* three castles *argent,* and this is also given by George William Griffith of Penybenglog as Castle or Castletowne. Philip Knethell of Castleton in Monkton, Bailiff of Pembroke in 1546, died in 1587/88 and was father of John Knethell, heir to his grandfather, and aged 23 years in 1587/88. In 1786 Francis Meyrick Esq. owned Upper Castleton, Mrs. Price tenant; in 1834 Evan Evans held a lease of the same property. Both Upper and Lower Castleton are marked on Colby's Map of 1831.

CASTELL GWYN, *Llandissilio (West)**
Lying to the southwest of Llandissilio church about half way between it and Egremont church so it is shown on Colby's map 1831. There were two farms both called Castell Gwyn; Upper Castle Gwyn was owned in 1786 by John Purser and Sam Parry, tenanted by Philip Lewis, and Lower Castle Gwyn was owned by Mrs. Edwards, widow and tenanted by George Henton, both were assessed at 7s. By 1894 the lands were held jointly by Morris Lewis, John Lewis, Daniel Owens and John Thomas.

CEFNYDRE (CYNHEIDRE), *Fishguard*
This homestead stands 1¼ miles to the south of the town of Fishguard, on a slope above Criney Brook. The original farm of the name was Cynheidre, but from the early 19th century it took the form Cefnydre, this local pronounciation of which still contains an echo of the earlier form. In 1512 William Dyer of Fishguard, gentleman, owned the property and neighbouring properties like Trefbover, Llanest, and Le Escaer (today Esgyrn). John ap Rees ap Owen, gentleman, owned Kynhedre in 1545, and in 1558 Walter Dyer of Fishguard, granted Trefbover, Llanest, and Escaer to him. In 1590 Owen ap Rees of Kinhaydref, gentleman, and Margaret Davies his wife were paid the mortgage that they and others had on lands in the township, vill, and fields of Llangloffan in Dewsland. In 1593 Thomas Revell, Esq. and John Garnons, gentleman, were concerned with Owen ap Rees and Margaret his wife and a fine of 13 messuages, 2 tofts and 720 acres in Kynheidrey, Fishguard and in five other parishes. Kynhaydre and other properties were granted to Thomas Lloyd of Cilciffeth.

By 1637/8 a new name appears when John Owen Jenkin of Trefgroys yeoman, Grace his wife, and Luce Jenkin otherwise Thomas of Kynhaydre widow, mortgaged in £50 on 226 acres in Trefgroys, Treboeth and Clyn-vinocke, all in Fishguard parish to Thomas Wogan of Llanstinan, gentleman. By 1705 Kevenhydre and Hottypace in Fishguard formed part of the estate of Sir George Barlow of Slebech. The property was again to change owners, when John Vaughan of Trecwn, (died 1735), bought Kevenhydre from John Barlow.

Later in the century, the Vaughans sold Kevenhydre to Hugh Harries of Henry's Moat, and in 1786 he was the owner of 'Cinhidre' with David Davies as tenant there. From that time onwards it continued in Harries's descendants.

The pedigree of the Harries family is given: Daniel Harries, gent., born c. 1680-1700 and who died after 1759, had a son, Hugh Harries of Cefnydre and Henrys Moat, who married Mary, daughter of John James of Fagwr Goch, Morfil, the marriage settlement being dated 10 February 1759. Their son, Thomas, (1768-1832), married Martha, (1769-1848), daughter of John Philipps of Felindre by Mary, daughter of William Philipps of Southfield, both tracing to Philipps of Picton Castle. They had a son, Thomas Harries of Henry's Moat, born 1803 who married Martha Llewellin of Martel, Puncheston. Their son, Hugh Llwyd Harries of Cefnydre (1843-86), married Martha, daughter of Levi James of Llysyronnen. They had a daughter, Martha Philipps Harries (1875-1956), who married Walter Levi Williams, solicitor of Fishguard, later of Cefnydre (1867-1953). Martha and Walter Williams had a son, Hugh whose younger son, Huw Walter Hillary Williams was of Cefnydre in 1986; and a daughter Philippa whose descendants still reside in the county.

Huw Llwyd Williams is the owner-occupier today.

Refs: NLW, Bronwydd Deeds, Slebech Deeds, Pembs. Plea Rolls, Fines in GS, Eaton Evans and Williams Deeds; LT 1786; Tithe Schedule, Fishguard, 1939; College of Arms MSS, Protheroe MSS IV and V.

CERBYD, *Llanhowel*

A farmstead about a quarter of a mile east of the parish church and about the same distance from Afon Solfach. For many centuries home of yeoman families. In a deed dated at Castro Vilia in 1406, Ieuan ap Ieuan ap David ap Philip Thomas de Kerbyt granted land in Castro Vilia and Penryn to John, son of Henry Morris of Castrovilia (see Castle Villa). We next hear of Cerbyd in Tudor times when Rees ap Owen (Bowen) of Lochmeyler (died 1563) owned, inter alia, two tenements in Kerbit and Trec-

lemes. William Scourfield of New Moat married Katherine, daughter and heiress of the said Rees ap Owen, and in 1622 Scourfield owned two messuages and half a carucate in Kerbett and Treglemes held of Sir John Wogan as of his manor of Treglemes otherwise Carn Fawr. In 1786 Henry Scourfield and Thomas Evans were co-owners of Cerbyd, the last-named being also occupier. Not long afterwards Scourfield sold his share of the property to Mr. Evans.

About 1600 Robert John occupied the farm and after his death in 1625 it passed to his daughter Elizabeth who had married Rees ap John, (will proved 1650), whose children took the permanent surname of Rees, and whose descendants remained until 1728 when Anne Rees married Thomas Evans who came to live at Cerbyd, and their grand-daughter Anne Evans married William Meyler who came to live there. William died in 1847, and was followed at Cerbyd by his son Thomas Meyler who died in 1861. A branch of the original Rees family bought Cerbyd towards the end of the 19th century. John Rees of Cerbyd was followed by his son John Lewis Davies Rees (died 1952) and Cerbyd passed to his only son Leonard John Rees who has converted the homestead and outbuildings into a holiday centre. Mr. Rees now (1987) lives in Cerbyd which he continues to own and administer.

Refs: College of Arms MSS, Wagner MS 2; NLW Eaton Evans and Williams Deeds, Cwrtmawr Deeds; LT 1786; WWHR ix, 153.

CILAST UCHA, *Manordeifi*

To the north of Boncath lay a tract of land called Gwestfa Cilast, consisting of the farmsteads of Cilast Uchaf, Cilast Isaf, Penalltyfelin and Wendros. Cilast Uchaf stood in a field about 1¼ miles from Boncath, and is marked on Colby's Map of 1831. Since that time the old farmstead was abandoned and no traces of it remain today, and a new farmstead, also called Cilast Ucha, was built near the roadside about 500 yards to the east of the former building. The name Gwestfa Cilast persisted; a gwestfa was an area whose freemen paid dues to a King.

In the area, too, was Cilast Fawr, but this, or its remains, have not been located. The first known family at Cilast Ucha, descended from the princeling Gwynfardd Dyfed, was Rees ap Howel, followed by his son Thomas ap Rees. Thomas's son, James Thomas became an attorney in the Great Sessions and he was followed at Cilast Ucha by his son David James who married in 1625 Janet, daughter of Thomas Lloyd of Cilciffeth one of the most powerful landowners in the county. His son, Thomas James, gentleman, married Bridget, daughter of Ieuan Lloyd of Faerdre, Cards. His children left the area – John James was a mercer at Newcastle Emlyn in 1685, and Mary James married John Havard, son of an ale house keeper in the same village. After this, only a few references occur to the property. In 1663 Llewelyn David of Llangolman Penbedw mortgaged a messuage called 'Plâs Kilast' to Thomas Jones of Brithdir.

In 1676 Francis Jones was owner of Cilast. In 1727 Eynon George of 'Cilast Fawr' was churchwarden, and in 1742 David Rees of Cilast Ucha; while in 1743 David William of Cilast Fawr and John Alban of Cilast Issa were church wardens. After this only Cilast Ucha and Issa are named. For some time the Saunders-Davies family of Pentre owned this property. The highly respected family of George lived at Cilast Ucha and were still there in the first half of the 20th century. It was later bought by another family of George, from South Pembrokeshire, who held Cilast Ucha until 1980 when they sold the property.

Refs: NLW, Papers of GS, Owen and Colby Deeds, S Deeds; Pembs. RO, LT, 1786; Carms. RO, GGMS Gwynfardd; Francis Jones, *Historic Cardiganshire Homes and their Families.*

CILAU WEN, *Llanstinan**

Home of the Griffith and Evans families. Owned by John Symmons of Llanstinan, Esq. in 1759 and leased to David Griffith of Cilewen, yeoman whose will was proved in 1799. 'To my sister Elizabeth Rees of Cilgwyn, Manordeifi for her life, then to her son John Rees in tail with rents to John Evans of Reynaston, Ambleston, farmer. Bequests – to my nephew, James Rees, to my sister Mary Griffiths, to my niece Anne, wife of John Bowen of Trevwrgy, Llanwnda parish, my sister Sarah Griffiths, my niece Elizabeth, wife of John Thomas of Hendrewen, my sister Sarah Griffith to be residuary legatee and sole executrix.' The son of Elizabeth and Evan Rees, John Evans (d. 1816), was of Cilau wen and Rinaston having married Phoebe, daughter of David Morse of Rinaston. Their son, David Evans (1777-1831), was of Treffgarn Hall, and married in 1814 Bridget, daughter of James Higgon of Spittal. The Evans family continued to hold Cilau Wen with Miss Margaret Evans farming 358 acres at a rent of £309 p.a. in 1873 and still there in 1894. By 1899 Cilau Wen had passed from the Evans family and was the home of Frederick Richardson, son of the late Canon Richardson, M.A., vicar of Northop.

Cilau Wen was sold in 1913 then comprising 331 acres, the catalogue describes the house 'Lot 1. Residence or mansion house, drawing and dining rooms, library, vestibule, conservatory, eight bedrooms, large kitchen, servants hall, pantry, large dairy and other offices. Surrounded by a charming old world garden and plantations of rare and flourishing trees and shrubs, approached by a carriage drive, a quarter of a mile long. Lodge at entrance to drive, outbuildings, coach house and stabling for four horses'. There were two other farms offered, Cilau Forge Farm with 60 acres, Penrhiw Farm with 17 acres and Troedyrhiw farmhouse with 7 acres.

Refs.: F. Green Deeds No. 408 NLW; LT 1786; VL 1894; Landowners Return 1873; Pembs. RO Saunders-Davies Papers; Pembs. RO D/LJ/125.

CILCIFFETH, *Llanychaer*

To the southeast of Fishguard, on high ground overlooking the Gwaun valley and the Pontfaen district, stands the old house of Cilciffeth, now a farmstead within a copse, and further sheltered by the heights of Mynydd Cilciffeth crowned by two cairns. Below the house, within an enclosure of 1½ acres, are the remains of an early fortification called Castell. Although the old mansion has been much reduced it continues to retain relics of earlier days, such as a vaulted basement, and a long window that lit up the staircase. The original name was Cilceithed, which became standardised as Cilciffeth. Fenton wrote in 1811, 'Cilyceithed, the ancient residence of David Ddu, or the Black (whose descendants for centuries were the first men in that county), falling among three co-heiresses in the time of Charles I, was deserted for the seats of the gentlemen on whom they had bestowed their lands and fortune.

'The possessors of this house were the kings of the mountains and stretched their sway far and wide. Their mansion, as the tradition is, was every way commensurate with their extensive property, command and hospitality; and though at the removal of the heiresses, the fabric was suffered to be dilapidated; amongst the ruins, from time to time, have been discovered much cut stone, vaults, and other relics indicatory of a style of magnificence not common in this country at that period. This part of the estate fell to the share of the daughter who married at Slebech, and came to the late Sir William Hamilton by his first lady Miss Barlow, and is now the property of his nephew, the Hon. Robert Greville.'

David Ddu, the first of his family at Cilciffeth, was descended from Gwynfardd Dyfed. His son, Ieuan Llwyd gave his name to his descendants. Sixth in descent was Thomas Llwyd, born in 1535, the founder of the Haverfordwest Grammar School, High Sheriff in 1596 and 1613. A patron of the bards, who were frequent callers at his hospitable house, and owner of a large estate situated in 41 Pembrokeshire parishes. He died at Cilciffeth in 1615, aged 80. His grandson David Lloyd was the last of the male line at Cilciffeth where he died in 1631, leaving three co-heiresses, one of whom Joan, (b. 1630), had Cilciffeth as part of her share of the 96 properties owned by her father. She married George Barlow of Slebech on whom she settled Cilciffeth.

The Hon. Charles Greville, who inherited the estate from his uncle, Sir William Hamilton, died unmarried in 1809, leaving Cilciffeth to his brother Robert whose son, Robert Fulke Greville, in 1856 sold the house and its demesne to John Meyler, yeoman, who advertised it for sale in 1880, then comprising 781 acres. Some of the previous tenants, such as the Thomases who came there in 1700 held it under leases, being followed by the Gwynnes who left Cilciffeth in 1847. It is still a large farm, occupied today by the owner.

Refs: Dwnn, i, 167-8: NLW, Tynewydd Deeds, Slebech Deeds; *RCAM Pembs.*, 1925; Peter Smith, *Houses of the Welsh Countryside,* 1975, map 7, p. 373; Francis Jones, 'Lloyd of Cilciffeth, *Pembs. Historian,* 1975, Burke, *Peerage.*

CILFOWYR (CILFOWIR), *Manordeifi*

On high ground, near Carregwen, about a mile due south of Llechryd. A medieval chapel stood here, marked on Rees's 14th century map, and near it is the farmstead of Cilfowir, also called Capel Cilfowir, and Chapelry of Cilfowir. A Baptist chapel of more modern times stands nearby. In 1493 Thomas ap Griffith ap Howel, a younger son of Castell Malgwyn, was Warden of the chapelry of Cilfowyr. In 1543 Philip ap Ieuan ap Meredydd lived there; in 1593 James ab Eynon of Cilvowyr, gentleman, died, leaving his wife Agnes and his brothers Gruffydd and Morris to inherit a farm in Clydey, and half a close at Cilvowyr. Before 1613 Thomas Mortimer of Castle Malgwyn owned Cilfowir, and was succeeded by his son Edmund Mortimer. Edmund died at Cruglas in Dewsland, (will dated 1666), and his daughter Lettice became the ultimate heir of Cilvowir.

Francis Jones leaves a detailed note which may be of interest: In 1668 Lettice Morgan, Cilfowyr submitted to laying on of hands. She was Lettice Mortimer, heiress of Cilfowyr. She married pre May 1668, Edward James Morgan, who had four sons and daughters by a previous marriage, and all came from England and settled at Cilfowyr. Lettice was apparently without issue. Cilfowyr was settled on his son, James who returned to England, became a lawyer, and later a minister. In 1689 Edward and Lettice Morgan and his son, Phillip Morgan were members at Rhydwilym. Ultimately James Morgan came to Cilfowyr, was a strong Baptist and gave land to build the chapel at Cilfowyr, and gave a lease of [sic] 'White Water Runs'. He had two daughters, one was Mrs. Rees of Cilfowyr, a great Baptist, who died in 1774: his other daughter, Elizabeth married at Newcastle Emlyn, firstly Thomas Morgan, and secondly, William Melchior. She died without issue. Her heiress was another daughter of James Morgan who married Griffith Thomas, afterwards minister at Newcastle Emlyn. She died without issue, a Baptist 1697.

The last of the Morgan family there was Mary Morgan grand-daughter and heir of James Morgan from whom she inherited Cilfowyr in 1736. By 1747 she had married one Julian Courtin, and after mortgaging the property, they ceased to live in the area. By 1762, Cilfowyr had been bought by Francis Skyrme of Llawhaden in 1762, and in 1807 was bought by Morgan Jones of Cilwendeg, esquire, and thereafter occupied by tenant farmers.

Refs: NLW, Papers of GS, Bronwydd Deeds, Spence-Colby Deeds, Owen and Colby Estate Records, Eaton Evans and Williams Deeds, Morgan-Richardson Deeds; Pembs. RO, Saunders-Davies Deeds; Carms. RO, GGMS, II; D. Jones, *Hanes Bedyddwyr,* 1839 p. 226.

CILGADFARCH, *Llanfihangel Penbedw*

This homestead stood on the north-eastern slopes of Frenni Fawr, near Wernddofn farm, and about 1¾ miles south of Llanfihangel Penbedw church. From medieval times, when it was called 'Plâs Ynghil Gatfarch', to the mid-16th century it was the home of a gentry family, then for over two centuries, was occupied by farmers and divided into two farms, Cilgadfarch Ucha and Issa. In 1792 both were incorporated into Wernddofn, that estate being then owned by David Morgan, gentleman. The old property was marked on Colby's Map 1831. The Tithe Map and Schedule includes 'Cilgedfach cottage' among fields belonging to Wernddofn. The Voters' List for 1894 lists 'Gilgedfach Farm' (David Evans, tenant), and in 1904 there were two farms of that name, held jointly by Thomas James and Daniel Phillips. According to the local County Councillor, Mr. Thomas George, all that is left today (1981) are some ruins.

Among early owners was Howel ap Llywelin ap Griffith, whose grandson lived at Cilyfforest, Cilrhedyn parish, Carms., who signed for Dwnn in 1591. Another early family was that of Ieuan ap Gwilym, descended from Cadifor Fawr of Blaen Cych, whose grandson Ieuan Llwyd of Gilgadfarch and whose daughter and co-heiress Nest married Rees ap John, descended from the Cardiganshire magnate, Rhys Chwith, Esquire of the Body to Edward I, and their descendants lived at Cilrhiwe.

Refs: Dwnn, i, 103-4148; Dale Castle Pedigrees; WWHR i, 32-3, s. Crygbychan; College of Arms, Wagner MS 2; Carms. R.O. GGMS (Gwyddno), II (Cadifor Fawr), John Francis Deeds; Francis Jones, *Historic Cardiganshire Homes and their Families.*

CILGELYNEN (CILGLYNEN),
Llanfairnantygof

In the east end of the parish, bordering that of Llanychaer. The homestead stands on high ground overlooking Cronllwyn and the cwm of Esgyru. The earliest forms of the place-name were Cilygolynen and Cilglynen, the latter being the accepted name today.

The first known owner was Thomas ap Lewis ap William, grandson of the said William, a blind landowner who lived at Trehros in St. Lawrence. Thomas was followed at Cilgelynen by his son David ap Thomas, who was succeeded by his son Hugh ap David living there in 1591. His son, known as David ap Hugh, and as David Davies, married Elizabeth, daughter of Sir John Wogan of Wiston. Their only child, the heiress, Charity, married in 1609 Thomas Lloyd, son of David Lloyd of nearby Morfil, who came to Cilgelynen where he was living in 1616.

In 1620 David Hugh of Cilgelynen conveyed that estate consisting of the manor of Llanstinan and 27 farms to his son-in-law. The son-in-law, who also held Morfil, died on 2 May 1635, leaving issue to inherit the property and who still owned it in 1705. Thomas Lloyd of Cilgelynen and Morfil was High Sheriff in 1669. It passed to the Owens of Orielton, and in 1786 was owned by Sir Hugh Owen, with

John Raymond as tenant at Cilglynen as it was then called, and was still owned by the Owens in 1838. Afterwards it passed through several hands and the residence became a farmhouse.

Refs: Dwnn, i, 174; College of Arms MS, Protheore VI; Pembs. RO, HDX.661, No. 2; Tithe Map and Schedule, Llanfairnantygof, 1838; NLW, Papers of GS, Pembs. Plea Rolls, No. 154.

CILGWYN, *Nevern*
In the western part of the parish, above the valley of the Clydach and near Carnedd Meibion Owen. There were two farms, Cilgwyn and Cilgwyn Mawr. The area was a chapelry with its own chapel for local folk, and a small Victorian chapel exists there today but is now closed. Several families dwelt within the chapelry but it is not always clear whether they lived at Cilgwyn or at Cilgwyn Mawr. Among these was Howell ap Rhys ap Llewelyn who left a house and land in the tenement of Cilgwyn to Harry Bowen, a younger son of Llwyngwair, who was followed by a son and grandson in the period 1600-18; Thomas James, (died 1614) followed by his son Griffith James living in 1636, and left two sons, Robert and Thomas James. In 1734 Cilgwyn Mawr was owned by the Warrens of Trewern whose descendants still owned it in 1788, while the Vaughan family was also there in the 18th century. Cilgwyn farm still exists.

Refs: NLW, Bronwydd Deeds; College of Arms, Wagner MS No. 6 Protheroe MS IV; RCAM 1925, B. G. Charles, *George Owen of Henllys*, 1973, pp. 46, 53.

CILRHIW, *Lampeter Velfrey*
A Georgian residence sheltered by a copse about four miles east of Narberth, situated between Princes Gate and Treffgarne; marked as Cilrhiw (residence) and nearby Cilrhiw farm, on Slebech estate, and in 1738 John Barlow gave a lease for three lives of this property to William Lewis, yeoman. The property had become part of the possessions of William Knox of Slebech by 1786 with Evan Rogers as tenant. In 1834 it was owned by Lancelot Bough Allen, the tenant being Morgan David who enjoyed a lease for 21 years. With the advent of the Allens the house was greatly improved and thereafter was the home of esquires of that family. In 1852 it was described as 'Cil Rhu, lately residence of Launcelot Bough Allan, and passed to his son Gough Bough Allen. The present resident tenant is R. Spranger, Esq.' It continued in the Allen family and in 1948 Bertram Wedgwood Allen of Cilrhiw was High Sheriff and it was occupied by him and Gladice Joyce Allen in 1950. Some time later it was sold.

Refs: DWB p. 5; Burke *LG,* for Allen pedigree; NLW, Slebech Deeds; Pembs. RO, LT 1786; F. P. Gwynne, *Sketches of Tenby* etc., edn. 1852, p. 67; *Western Mail,* 2 April 1988, illust.

Davies-Lloyd

CILRHIWE,
Llanfihangel Penbedw
This homestead stands about threequarters of a mile west of the parish church (the northern transcept being still 'the Kilrhiw'), and the same distance south of Rhosygilwen. Marked on Kitchin's Map (1749-70) as 'Killrhua, Lloyd Esq.', and on Colby's Map 1831. I visited Cilrhiwe in 1975 and again in 1983. Built in the 17th century as a double-pile two storey house with an attic storey, and a range of five windows, it has lasted in a fair state of preservation to our time. That it contained eight hearths in 1670 indicates it was commodious. The interior contains a broad Jacobean staircase with balustrades and finials, rising from the hall to the upper storeys; the old parlour is fully panelled as is also one side of the hall. A wing extending to the rear was added in later times and is now used for farming purposes. The attached 275 acres are farmed by Mr. W. D. R. Davies, whose maternal grandfather bought the property from Sir Marteine O. M. Lloyd of Bronwydd in 1911. The drive is sheltered by an avenue of beech trees, and opposite the entrance is a large fishpond.

The mansion, a fine example of the vernacular style of former days, faces northeast, with a view over green pasture fields now used for grazing. The garden was a little distance away, below the outbuildings. The first known family there, descended from the Cardiganshire magnate Rhys Chwith (or Chwitt), Esquire of the Body to Edward I, and came into the area by the marriage of John ap Meredith to Nest, daughter and co-heiress of Ieuan Lloyd of Cilgadfarch. The great-grandson of the marriage, Owen Phillip, was living at Cilrhiwe in 1567, and also when he signed his pedigree for Dwnn on 22 August 1591. He had two children, David Phillip who died without legitimate issue, and Elizabeth who married Nicholas Bowen of Crugbychan, Verwig, near Cardigan. The family then left Cilrhiwe.

The next family there, Lloyd, came from Montgomeryshire (descended from Bleddyn ap Cynfyn), the first member to come southwards being the Rev. Henry Lloyd, rector of Cilrhedyn. He had two sons, both of whom settled at Cilrhiwe. The elder, John Lloyd, married Cissie, daughter of Hector Philipps of Cardigan Priory, and died at Cilrhiwe on 11 July 1657 in his 36th year, having had no issue. His brother, James Lloyd then succeeded and married Bridget, sister of the said Cissie. In 1661 he was High Sheriff and in 1670 paid tax for eight hearths at Cilrhiwe, died in July 1707 aged 83 and was buried in Cilgerran church. Cilrhiwe passed to his only child Anne who married Lewis Wogan of Wiston. She died in 1703, her husband having predeceased her in 1694. They had one son, Lloyd Wogan who died unmarried, and their mother's estate then passed between three daughters. The eldest daughter Anne Wogan inherited Cilrhiwe mansion and married Thomas Lloyd of Bronwydd (died 1737). His descendants continued to live there from time to time until it was sold in 1910.

In 1752 James Lloyd of Cilrhiwe was concerned in mine works at Llandre in Llanfyrnach and the family took an active part in the silver lead industry there until it closed in 1890. When Sir Marteine Lloyd advertised for sale 'The Kilrhwe Estate' in July 1911, it consisted of the residence of Cilrhiwe (172 acres), and 40 other portions in north Pembrokeshire. The south transept of the parish church is known as 'Cilrhiwe chapel'.

Refs: Dwnn, i, 158, 217; Dale Castle Pedigrees, p. 25; WWHR, ii, p. 95; NLW, Bronwydd, Noyadd Trefawr and Deri Ormond Deeds; Pembs. RO, James of Narberth Deeds, Saunders-Davies Colln. Box 10, Sale Catalogue No. 642; I and II Bleddyn ap Cynfyn fo. 32; *RCAM Pembs.*, 1925.

CILRHIWE FACH, *Manordeifi*

Now a farm, situated between Pentre and Newchapel: marked on Colby's Map 1831 as Cilrhiwe fach. The first known family there descended from Cadifor Fawr of Blaen Cych, who were living at Rhosychen (Carms.). A later member of that family, Griffith ap Ieuan married Margaret daughter of Sir James Bowen of Pentre Evan, and their son, Morris married Lucy, (living 1613), daughter and heiress of James, (living 1539), ap Ieuan Lloyd ap Gwilym ap Philip 'o Gilriweun' which she brought to her husband. Their son David ap Morris settled at Cilrhiwe Fach and was living in 1613. This David married a daughter of Howel ap Morris of Gellydywyll (Carms.), the last-known of the family at Cilrhiwe Fach being their great-grandson John David Thomas. In 1786 it was owned by one Captain Haye, with David Beynon as tenant. In 1894 Sarah Lewis lived there and in 1950 Alwyn and Florrie Lewis.

Refs: Dwnn, i, 217 S.A. 'Manordeifi Kilrywenn'; GGMS; LT 1786; subsequent VL (Pembs.).

CILRYDD, CILRYTH,

Also called Coed Cilrydd, Nevern

This house stood in the woodland of Cilrydd, close to the residence of Pentre Ifan (q.v.). During medieval times it was a seat of the family of Cyhylyn ap Gwynfardd, ancestor of the Bowens of Pentre Ifan, Warren of Trewen, etc. When Pentre Ifan was built it became the main residence, and Coed eventually became a farm. The name is now lost and no trace of Coed remains. One of the first of the family to live there was Eynon ap Gwilym ap Gwrwared, known as 'Eynon Fawr o'r Coed', or 'of Coed Cilrydd'. He was living in 1278-1281, and was followed by his son Owen ap Eynon Fawr, living at Coed about 1302. A descendant, Thomas Bowen of Pentre Ifan, at his death in 1586 owned 'the manor or capital tenement of Pentreyvan and Kilyryth'.

In 1614 William Owen, natural son of William Owen of Henllys, lived at Coed, but his two sons John and George Owen after a few years left Coed and settled at Berllan and at Torbant (Llanrhian) respectively. In 1638 Elizabeth Bowen, widow of Pentre Ifan, died, owning (inter alia) 'the capital messuage called

Pentyre Ievan and 200 acres, and a tenement and 20 acres called Place y Coed'. Both these properties became part of the estate of Warren of Trewern, (also descended from Cyhylyn ap Gwynfardd). In 1786 the farm of Coed was owned by Mrs. Jones of Llanina (Cards.) and Trewern, with John Thomas as tenant. Mrs. Jones (née Catherine Warren, heiress of the Trewern estate, married Philip Jones of Llanina) and her will was proved in 1793. Coed is not marked on Colby's Map 1831.

Refs: GGMS Gwynfardd; Francis Jones, 'Warren of Trewern', *Pembs. Historian,* 1974, p. 115 and 'Bowen of Pentre Ifan and Llwyngwair, ibid., 1979, pp. 27-30, 36.

CILWENDEG, *Capel Colman*

Situated about half a mile east of Capel Colman parish church, and one and a quarter miles to the northeast of Boncath. The first owner of Cilwendeg was Llewelyn ap Howel, descended from Edwyfed Fychan of Gwynedd, Seneschal of Prince Llewelyn the Great. Llewelyn was at Cilwendeg in the early 16th century, and was followed by his son David Llewelyn, and he by his son Llewelyn David. The last named was followed by his son David Llewelyn living in 1646, and in 1670 paid for two hearth taxes, which suggests that it was a small house at that time. On 17 September 1687 he conveyed the capital messuage of Cilwendeg to his son and heir apparent Jonathan Llewelyn, who in the same year mortgaged the property to one David John, and on 13 January 1698/9 Jonathan assigned the equity of redemption of Place Kilwendeg, Wenros Ucha and Isha, to Miss Mary Skyrme, daughter of William Skyrme of Llawhaden Esq. The mortgage of 1687 held by David John passed to his widow and son who assigned it to Jacob Morgan of Vaynor, Manordeifi, attorney-at-law, who afterwards acquired the freehold of Cilwendeg and came there to live.

Jacob died in 1732/33, leaving three daughters and the property eventually passed to the youngest daughter, Margaret Morgan who married John Jones of Llanbadarn, Cards., who then settled at his wife's house. Their descendants succeeded to Cilwendeg; Morgan Jones was High Sheriff in 1801 and his nephew

of the same name in 1831. The family left Cilwendeg in the second half of the 19th century and were settled at Llwynbedw, Penylan in the Tivyside, and at Llanmilo near Pendine. Morgan Jones of Llanmilo was High Sheriff of Carmarthenshire in 1909. Fenton in his *Tour Pembs.* of 1811 writes 'another handsome mansion of modern growth, Cylywendeg, bursts upon the eye, built by the gentleman who now inhabits it, Morgan Jones Esq. owner of the Skerry Lighthouse off the north coast of Anglesey, a property from which he derives a large income.'

Writing in 1840, Lewis says 'Cilwendeg the seat of Morgan Jones Esquire, is an elegant mansion, erected within the last fifty years by the uncle of the present proprietor, ornamented with a handsome receding portico in good taste, and occupies the centre of an extensive demesne beautifully laid out in plantations and pleasure grounds to which are entrances by two handsome lodges, recently added by the present properietor.' A good photograph of the mansion was taken by Allen in 1871. Cilwendeg was advertised for sale in 1931, described as 'a handsome modern mansion' of three storeys, with, on the ground floor, hall, inner hall, double drawing room, dining room, morning room, library, billiard room, two conservatories, domestic offices; on the first floor, twelve bed and dressing rooms and offices; on the second floor, six rooms. It is now used as an old people's home. There is no trace of the earlier residence.

Refs: Carms. RO, GGMS (Cadifor Fawr, Gwyddno, Edwyfed Fychan), John Francis Deeds; NLW, Morgan-Richardson Deeds, Penally Deeds; Pembs. R.O). Saunders-Davies Deeds.

CILVELGY, *see* **KILVELGY**

CINNAMON GROVE,
St. Thomas (Haverfordwest)
Marked on Mudge (1819) and Colby's (1831) Maps, two miles southwest of Haverfordwest, above Merlins Brook. Very little has been found about this residence. Cinnamon Hill is mentioned in a deed of 1745, and Robert Prust J.P., senior, of Cinnamon Hill in a deed of 1785. Cinnamon Grove was the residence of Joshua Roch, Esq. in 1795, a kinsman of Hugh Allen of Rickeston. Joshua made his will in 1801. It is recorded that Sparks Martin Walker, aged 13, eldest son of Thomas Walker of Cinnamon Grove, died in 1826. To Malkin, author of *Tour in South Wales,* Cinnamon Grove is 'an agreeable residence'. Now a farm. For photograph of house and description see *Western Telegraph* 10 September 1986.

CLARESTON, *Freystrop*
Some half a mile south of Freystrop Cross. Fenton (1811) writes 'Clareston, the seat of George Roch Esq. approached by a handsome avenue extending to the road, in midst of a modern but thriving plantation, raised by thick planting, though in an exposed situation and an unfavourable soil;' and S. Lewis (1840) observes, 'Clareston, an elegant modernized mansion, seat of George Clayton Roch, Esq. which was originally the residence of the family of Powell, and came by marriage to the ancestors of the present proprietor; it is pleasantly situated, and the grounds are well laid out'. George Roch, first of his family at Clareston where he was living in 1738, was the son of Nicholas Roch (d. 1745) of Rickeston. By his wife Martha Allen of Gelleswick, George Roch had a son, George Roch who left two sons George Roch of Clareston, High Sheriff 1789, died unmarried in 1820, and Joshua who followed his brother at Clareston where he died in 1827, leaving an only son, George Clayton Roch, High Sheriff 1830, who was burnt to death in his bed on 17 April 1833. He was the last of the line at Clareston.

Later, Clareston was purchased by Thomas Henry Davies, son of Henry Davies of Mullock and Trewarren; he was High Sheriff in 1865, and later sold Clareston to William Ballinger of Swansea who was living at Clareston in 1873, whose family was still there in 1907. A relic of the Roch occupation is an erect stone standing in the grounds, inscribed 'G.R. 1755'. I recall visiting Clareston in the early 1930s when it was the seat of Sir Charles Price, M.P.

Refs: Contemporary Biographies of South Wales and Monmouth, 1907, illust; *RCAM Pembs.*, 1925; D. Miles, *Pembrokeshire Sheriffs,* 1974.

CLEDDAU LODGE, *Camrose**
In the early part of the 19th century the sisters Mary and Catherine Tucker lived there. The latter married, in 1777 John Owen Edwardes of Llanmilo. Mary Tucker spinster was resident in 1833. Robert Dudley Ackland who married Elizabeth Mary Lloyd was of Cleddau Lodge in 1853. they had a daughter Jane, baptised at Camrose 7 May 1853. William Henry Adley was at 'Cleddy' Lodge in 1894.

Trefgarne of Cleddau

CLEGYR, *St. Davids**
Lying 1¼ miles east of St. Davids and occupied in 1618 by Walter John of St. Davids, yeoman, on a 21 year lease at a rent of 21s. per annum. Clegyr was owned by Rice Hargest. By the late 17th century the Harry or Harries family was farming Clegyr, David Harry and his wife, Grace being in possession in 1658. In 1668 Henry David, David Harry and his wife Grace gave a bond in £20 to William Loveling of St. Martins parish Haverfordwest, gent. 'For the peaceable possession by William Loveling of a moiety of the messuage in townred and fields of Clegyr Tylerwr and Tyrrooman'. The Release was granted the same day.

In 1702 'Phillip Harry and his eldest son, Thomas Harry made a bargain and sale and release for ever to the Rev. William Loveling of Castlemartin, parish, clerk of a moiety of a messuage in the townred and fields of Clegyr

Tylerwr and Tyrrooman formerly in the possession of Hugh David and now in tenure of John Rees, and also the other moiety of the same in possession of said John Rees'. In 1735 Henry Hitchings of the parish of St. Mary Pembroke, and Anne his wife, one of the daughters of William Loveling, late of Castlemartin, granted for ever to Samuel Harries of Crigglas, all the messuage of Clegyr Tylerwr and Tyrrooman in recognizance of Henry Rees, yeoman which had formerly been granted to said William Loveling by Phillip Harry and Thomas Harry.

Refs: Trant Deeds; Pembs. Plea Rolls Nos. 110, 112.

CLEGYR (N), *Jordanston in Dewsland*
Known as 'Clegyr Mawr otherwise Clegyr Meidrim', and finally just as Clegyr. Today it is locally called Clegyrn and spelled thus on modern OS maps. On the maps of Mudge (1819) and Colby (1831) it is given as Clegyr Mawr. In 1567 William ap John ap Ieuan lived at 'Clegir Meyderym otherwise Clegir Mawr'. Early in the 16th century its owner was William Davids of Dyffryn Wdig, and in 1640, having mortgaged Clegir Mawr otherwise Meidrim he conveyed that property to Ursula Williams widow of Jordanston. In 1697 Thomas Davids of Dyffryn Wdig married Elizabeth daughter and co-heiress of Richard Williams of Clegir Mawr, and so that property returned to the family of the previous owner. Finally, Jane Davids, co-heiress of Dyffryn Wdig married Stephen Colby of Ffynnone, and brought Clegyr Mawr to her husband. In 1784 Jane Colby, then a widow, leased Clegyr Mawr to John Dedwith gentleman, then tenant there. Dedwith, in 1800, married Mary Mathias, daughter of the Squire of Llangwarran. It continued to be owned by the Colbys to the second half of the 19th century. Today it is a farmhouse.

Refs: NLW, Pembs. Plea Rolls, Morgan-Richardson Deeds, Spence-Colby Deeds; Carms. R.O., GGMS Gwynfardd; Pembs. RO, LT 1786.

CLEGYR BOIA, *St. Davids**
About a quarter of a mile east of Clegyr Boia is a Castell about 180 feet above the right bank of the river Alun, and marked on Colby's Map 1831 as 'camp'; Leland says of this 'camp': 'Ther remayne tokins of Cairboias Castel standing by Alen ryveret about a quarter of a myle lower than St. David on the same ryveret'. Leland erred in calling it Cairboias Castel. This was the home of the Chieftain Boya, see St. Davids *vitae*. It was a capitular manor, and later sold to become a lay manor. A grant made on 2 November 1462 by William Perrot, son and heir of Thomas Perrot, Esquire to Isabella, late wife of said Thomas, for her life of all his messuages and lands in St. Davids, viz . . . drigiff, Thlegerboya and Harnglo, all in Pebidiog lordship.

In 1535/6, the Prebendary of Llanstinan held the manor of Clegyr Foya or Boia, and one tenement called Crukcluse, worth 73s. 4d. yearly. In 1587/8 Cleger Viva manor was held by the archdeacon of Carmarthen, held by the Prebendary of Llanstinan. This manor seems to have been alienated at a later date, for in the period 1784-91 the lord of the manors of Clegyr Voya and Porthlisky, namely Thomas Williams of Treleddyd, (Treleddyn) Esq. appointed Nathaniel Bland, gent. to be gamekeeper for the said manors.

Refs: Anc. Deeds PRO iii, D665; *Anc. Mon. Pembs.*, 1925, pp. 64, 325; Val. Eccles IV, p. 383; Taylor's *Cussion* fo. 97; Pembs. QS. Order Book.

CLYN MEREDITH,
Eglwyswen (Whitchurch in Cemaes)
A large farmhouse half a mile southwest of the parish church. Home of yeomen from medieval times. On 8 October 1418 Griffith ap David ap Gwilym ap Rhys granted to Perkyn ap Gwallter ap Rhys ap Rhydderch a messuage, 14 acres, mill and a meadow, and his part of the advowson of the church there, at Clyn Mereduth in the fee of Whitchurch, the messuage and land being near the water of Nevern. In 1507 it was recorded that Gwilym ap Perkyn had died leaving his lands, among them Clene Meredyth at 'Egloyswen'. Before 1574 Morris Lewis ap Ieuan ap Ieuan was in ward to William Owen, Lord of Cemaes, for Clyn Meredyth in Whit-

church, and about 1600 James William Lewis was in ward to George Owen, Lord of Cemaes, for only half a year, for Clyn Meredyth. Melchior ap Ieuan ap Howel ap Newport, gentleman, died in 1590, and left Clyn Meredith and eight other properties to his son William Melchior (High Constable of Cemaes in 1611). In 1760 Mr. Owen Thomas was tenant of the farm. In the period 1772-82 it was owned by John Symmons of Slebech, with William Davies as tenant-farmer.

In 1786 it was owned by Owen Thomas, gentleman, with William Davies as tenant. In 1839 Mr. Thomas was tenant, the farm then being 90 acres in extent. Later in the century Margaret Thomas of Clyn Meredith (died 1900, aged 65) married George Harries of Castle Villa (died 1908, aged 82) in Dewsland, and their only child Pheobe Davies Harries married Walter Morris of Chapel Farm, Castlemartin.

Refs: NLW, Bronwydd Deeds, Foley of Ridgeway Deeds; Pembs. LT 1786.

CLYNFYW, *Manordeifi*

On a slope to the west of Afon Cych, between Abercych village and the mansion of Pentre. The ancestor of the first known family at Clynfyw was the Yorkist Jenkin Lloyd of Blaiddbwll, whose great-grandson also named Jenkin Lloyd was living at Clynfyw in 1500. He was followed there by six further generations. The last owner was David Lloyd of Clement's Inn, London, whose uncle, Griffith Lloyd lived at the mansion. David Lloyd remained in London and on 10 March 1684/5 sold Clynfyw to David Llewelin, gentleman, of Penalltcych, Clydey.

About 1712 the old mansion of the Lloyds was pulled down, and a new one built. David was followed by his son Leoline alias Llewelin Davies who died on 10 April 1747, aged 80, and was succeeded at Clynfyw by his son Owen Davies. Owen's interesting career was spent far from his early home. On 31 October 1729 he was appointed receiver-general of Westminster Abbey, and was also connected with the Augmentation Office. He and his wife Mary lived in the Little Cloisters until their deaths, Owen on 24 April 1759 in his 60th year, his wife in May 1778, both were buried within the Abbey.

Recorded in the Westminster Abbey Register by Harleian Society: 'Buried in Westminster Abbey 1 May 1759. Owen Davies, Esq. Receiver-General of this church: in the north cloister. Only son of Leoline Davies of Clunfyw, parish Manordeifi, Pem. Gt. By Anne his wife, who after a union of about 52 years, both died in April 1747, she on 13th and he on 10th, each aged about 80 years, and were buried in the parish church where he erected a M.I. to them. He was appointed Receiver-General of the Abbey 31 October 1729, and is said by the journals of the day, to have been also converted with the Augmentation Office. He died 24 April in his 60th year. His will dated 27 January 1756 proved 21 May 1759 by his relict, Mary, (buried 11 May 1778). He bequeathed £1,000 to his eldest daughter, Anne, (bapt. 14 September 1736 – buried 2 April 1791 at Westminster Abbey), and his second daughter Mary, (bapt. 13 January 1739/40 – buried 6 February 1786), and if both shall die without issue, then his three sisters, Esther Harries, Lettice Bowen and Sarah Thomas then or lately living at Clunfyw were each to have £500. Residue of estate to his wife.'

Their two children, Anne and Mary died in 1791 and 1786, also buried in the Abbey. Davies was the last of the family to own Clynfyw.

In 1750 he ordered a valuation to be made of Clynfyw so that a sale could be effected. Accordingly the valuation was made in that year. In 1751 a description of the properties was made, which included Clynfyw and properties at Penybont, messuages called Tyr-y-wern ddu alias Tyr-y-ty-hên, three pieces of land at Llwyn-y-Gore called Llain-yn-nhyr-y-Kilgwyn, message called Plâs-gwern-Aaron with three pieces at Kilgwyn, a piece in Gwestra Kilast at a place called Kil-valgen, a piece between lands of William Lloyd Esq. and James Davies, and a piece bounded with a little brook called Gwern Aaron on the west, with lands of Samuel Jones on the north side, with a path from Blaen Morrow to Aberchen on the east side. In 1752 a further valuation was made of the Clynfyw estate and the timber thereon, including some 'hollow trees about the mansion house,' the said Mansion or Capital House well built in stone in or about the year 1712, and covered with slate, and having good orchards and springs of water near thereunto'. Clynfyw was bought in 1753 by Thomas Lewis of Llwyngrawys, Cards, and in 1760 Thomas Lewis Esq. is described as living at Clynfyw.

The Lewis family came from the Narberth area, and were successful businessmen. Thomas Lewis first worked at the Blackpool Iron Forge near Canaston Bridge, and then moved to the Tivyside; in 1714 was living at Llwyngrawys, and was associated with the Coedmore Forge near Llechryd, and in 1719 he bought the tools and equipment of that forge. In 1749 he took a lease of the corn mill Melin Abercych, which he converted into an iron-forge. Thomas Lewis was the first at Clynfyw which has remained in the hands of his descendants, the Lewis-Bowens, to this day. During the first half of the 19th century a new mansion of three storeys was erected about 100 yards from the one that had been built in 1712. In 1840 Lewis says 'Clynview the seat of T. Lewis Esq. is a handsome residence pleasingly situated.' The old mansion still survives as an outbuilding, and two delightful watercolours of it painted in its prime in 1845 may be seen in the present residence.

Refs: NLW, Noyadd-Trefawr Deeds; Pembs. RO, Deeds D/JP; Carms. RO, John Francis Deeds, Coedmor Deeds, WWHR, ii, pp. 40-1; GGMS Gwynfardd; Deeds and papers still at Clynfyw (Lewis-Bowen); C. S. Allen, *Photographs in South Wales,* 1871; Francis Jones, 'Families of Blaiddbwll', *NLW Journal,* Summer 1981; Phillips, *Llofruddiaeth Shadrach Lewis,* 1986, illust. opp. p. 84 of Clynfyw as it was in 1840.

CLYNSAITHMAN, *Llangolman*

A mile and a quarter southeast of the peak of Moel Cwm Cerwyn, and three-quarters of a mile west of Pentrithel. An old farmstead, alas demolished during military excercises of World War II. Home of the yeoman family of Morris. Griffith Morris of Clynsaithman paid tax for three hearths in 1670. He died in 1684 and was followed by his son Griffith Morris, who married in 1693 as his first wife, Elizabeth Howell of Rushacre and then moved to the farm of Cwm Cerwyn (*vide infra*) where he was living in 1694; by her he had three children. He became a member of Rhydwilym Baptist Chapel in 1689 and religious meetings were often held at Clynsaithman. His second wife was Dorothy, by whom he had ten children. His will was proved in 1734, and he was followed by his son Stephen Morris. In 1786 Griffith Morris was owner-occupier of Clynsaithman.

Refs: Pembs. RO, LT 1786; *RCAM Pembs.,* 1925.

COED RATH, *Amroth**

Coedrath Forest was between Amroth and St. Issells parish. William Istans of Coedrath married Janet Phillips, daughter of Philip Gl(y)n of Stone Hall by Jane, daughter of Philip Elliot of Earwear. She married secondly William Thomas Vaughan of Llanboidy parish and by him had Thomas and Mary. By William Istans Janet bore 16 children. Philip, the second son, married Jenet Lawrence and by him had two sons, Philip Istance who married 'an Irish-woman'; David who died with issue, and two daughters; Avice who married Richard Eynon who was iure uxoris of Coedrath; and Katherine of whom nothing is known. No dates are given.

Refs: BM Egerton MS 2586 ff. 363, 368.

COEDCANLAS, *Coedcanlas*

In the southernpart of the parish, near the waters of the Cleddau. The name means the woodland of Cenlas or Cynlas, and the name occurs as Castle Cenlas (Mathry) and Coed Canlas (Eglywswen in Cemaes). The farmhouse, a commodious edifice of three stories, retains a number of its earlier features. It is built over a vaulted undercroft, now used as a basement storey, has a large chimney at one gable end, and corbelling at the other gable end, and there

are two mullioned windows that have been filled in. Steps lead from the road level to the basement, and there is an exterior flight of stairs from ground level to the first floor. The walls of the house are nine feet thick. Behind the house is a large courtyard, beyond which are farm outbuildings. It was excellently preserved when I visited it on 17 April 1974, the owner-occupiers being the Merriman family who farmed the land.

Coedcanlas was one of Sir John Carew's Knight's fees in 1362, and was then held by John Perceval. The Percevals remained at Coedcanlas until the latter half of the 15th century, when the heiress Elizabeth, daughter of Philip Perceval married John Butler, a younger son of the family of Dunn. John Butler, described as Lord of Coedcanlas in 1495/6, was succeeded at the mansion by six generations of his descendants. John Butler was a strong supporter of Sir Rhys ap Thomas. Arnold Butler was High Sheriff in 1558, and Member of Parliament in 1554/5. Another John was High Sheriff in 1608, and died in 1629 when he was followed by his namesake who was the last of the family at the old home. John Butler sold Coedcanlas to the Owens of Orielton, and died in 1655. Sir Hugh Owen paid tax for ten hearths in Coedcanlas which shows that it was a large residence. The land had been divided into two messuages in Butler days, mentioned in 1637 as 'Koedkenlas parva, and Magna Koedkanlas'. The Free Chapelry of Coedcanlas had belonged to the Percevals, the Butlers, and finally the Owens. The edifice was 'in decaye' in 1535, restored by the Butlers, fell again into decay about 1660, but in 1718 it was rebuilt on the old foundation and endowed by Sir Arthur Owen, Bt. By 1912 it was again a total ruin.

Refs: Dwnn, i, 76; WWHR ii, p. 72; O. Pembs, i, 309, ii, 338; *RCAM Pembs.*; NLW, Pembs. GS, Pembs. Plea Rolls; Fenton, *Tour Pembs.,* 1811.

COEDLLWYD, *Clydey*

On 20 August 1977 I visited Coedllwyd, a 240 acre farm owned by Mrs. Jenkins and her two sons. They told me that the former mansion, 'Rhen Goedllwyd' (old Coedllwyd), had stood in the valley below the farmhouse, on the left bank of a little stream below Penybanc, not far from Star. Old ruined walls and other remains of the Plâs were still visible until 1958 when the Jenkins' bulldozer levelled the site and removed the remains. The site was in fields marked on the parish Tithe Map of 1841 as 1317, and 1326 by the west side of the stream, about half a mile from the hamlet of Star, and a mile southwest of Clydey church.

The gentry family traced to Edwyfed Fychan of Gwynedd. Two of his descendants, the brothers David ap Morgan and Morris ap Morgan were the first to settle in Pembrokeshire, David at Blaenbylan, the last of whom died in 1802, and Morris at Coedllwyd who married Margaret, daughter of John Thomas Lloyd of Clynfyw. Morris Morgan whose will was proved in 1656, left two children – Susan who married her first cousin Morris Morgan of Blaenbylan, and their son David Morgan succeeded to Coedllwyd. David was High Sheriff in 1662, and died, leaving a son David Morgan of Coedllwyd, and Elizabeth who married Edwardes of Rhydygors near Carmarthen.

David Morgan was High Sheriff in 1685, paid for four hearths in 1670, and died without issue in 1688, leaving Coedllwyd to his sister Elizabeth Edwardes. She died without issue, and Coedllwyd passed to her aunts, Susan of Blaenbylan (died 1707) and Mrs. Mary Lewes of Pantyrodin (Cards.). Coedllwyd mansion was afterwards owned by the Blaenbylan family until 16 May 1751 when it was sold to William Thomas of Castell Gorfod, and from him passed to the Bowens of Llwyngwair who were the owners in 1786. In 1830 the Bowens sold Coedllwyd and several other properties in Clydey to Thomas Lewis of Clynfyw, and about 1910 Mr. Lewis-Bowen sold it to Mr. Jenkins, whose descendants entertained me when I called. The farmhouse of Coedllwyd is on high ground, over a quarter mile from the site of the old plâs.

Refs: Francis Jones, 'Blaenbylan', *Ceredigion,* 1976; Carms. RO, John Francis Deeds, Trant/Yelverton Deeds; NLW, Tithe Map and Schedule, Clydey Parish 1841; Pembs. RO, LT 1786.

COEDWYNOG, *Nevern and Bayvil*

About midway between the parish churches of Nevern and Bayvil. A few medieval references occur. Thus, in 1331 Jevan elder son of Howe ap Martin granted all his messuages at Coedwinog to his daughter Joan for her life, with reversion to Philip ap Gwilym Lloyd and his heirs; in 1409/10 David ap Philip ap Gwilim Lloyd released lands at Coedwynnocke, (held by Joan Verch Howell, their mother, for life) to his brother Perkin ap Phillip ap Gwillim Lloyd; in 1427/8 Wilcoke ap David ap Howell (his mother was Eva Lloyd) granted to his brother David ap David ap Howell a messuage and lands within a carucate at Coyt Wynog on the south of the river Gwithwch; and in 1491 Howel ap Jenkyn ap Howel of Nevern and Morgan Dayfor granted to James ap Owen [of Pentre Evan] their messuages and lands in the two carucates of Coed Wynog in the fee of Bayvil.

In 1516 David ap Gwillim ap Perkin and Jeuan ap David ap Perkin arbitrators in a dispute relating to a messuage lying within the two carucates of Coydewynoke, ordained that 'Thomas ap David ap Perkin and Agnes his wife shall pay 10 shillings to Llewelyn ap Philip ap Oweyn and Isabel his wife before the next Feast of the Saints and Martyrs Civic, and Jubita his mother, and that the said Llewelyn and Isabel shall withdraw their claim to the property in dispute'. In 1547 Agnes verch David Vychan of Nevern, widow, released a tenement in Koedewnioc to James ap Owen Lloyd. In 1549 'William ap Rees David ap Hoell of Meline parish, gent, and Thomas ap Lewis Yonge gent, of Nyverne,' were arbitrators in a dispute between Jevan ap David ap Eynon, husbandman, and James ap Owen Lloyd merchant, both of Nyvern, relating to a third part of a house called Coydwynocke and an acre on the west side of the house. In 1565 Owen William of Nevarne, husbandman, granted a messuage called Place Koed y Wynock to Jane verch Mathias of Bayvil, spinster, for her life, then to her heirs, and in default to revert to the heirs of grantor. In 1586 George Owen of Henllys bought Coed-wynog and lands there from the Pentre Evan family and others, and in the following year he leased it to Chancellor Richard Edwardes and Mirabella his wife at an annual rent of £4 6s. 0d.

The *Extent of Kemes* for 1 May 1594 recorded 'Coed y Winog. Richard Edwardes, clerk, Chancellor of St. Davids and Mirabella his wife, hold by lease for their lives a chief mansion at Coedywinog to the south of the stream of Gwythwch, in which they live, and also another tenement on the other side of the Gwythwch.' George Owen of Henllys wrote as follows in 1603/4, 'Coedwynok was the mansion house of Mr. Richard Edwardes, Chancellor of St. Davids, deceased, and by him built and about 16 yeares past much beautified, being the first man that caused the place to be acompted or spoken of allthoughe there was some prettie buildings there before his tyme yett nothing to that which he left behind him. This man for his discreete behaviour, Curteouse and liberall Intertaynment in his house, his grave and well advised Counsell to men of all sortes, and for his natural Inclynation, his facyll method in peace makinge, ys not a lyttle myssed in his Countrie; his valye noted fault in his liffe tyme was too much leuytaie in not bearing himselfe as his places and Calling required. This goodman hath made this his house to be in accompt as saith Cicero, *Non doemus dominum* and *domino domum exornat.*'

David James, gentleman lived at Koedwinock in 1610/11, and Mathew Bowen, gentleman, in 1632. It was owned by George Owen a descendant of Thomas Lloyd esquire of Bronwydd, Cards., in 1786, with David Evans as tenant, and later was owned by Rev. David Griffith of Berllan, clerk, who on 5 July 1831 granted a lease for life of Coedwinog Fawr and Fach to Thomas Davis at an annual rent of £120.

Refs: BM Egerton MS 2586: College of Arms, Protheroe MS N; NLW, Bronwydd Deeds, Morgan- Richardson Deeds; George Owen, *2nd Book,* B. G. Charles, *NLWJ,* Winter 1948, p. 271.

COLBY, *Wiston*

Now a farmstead with very large outbuildings 1¼ miles southeast of Wiston village. About half a mile to the north of Colby farm, is the farm called Colby Moor, both being marked on Colby's Map 1831. The first known owner is Sir John Wogan of Wiston who held a quarter of a Knight's fee in Colby at the time of his death in 1410. Colby and adjacent lands continued in Wogan hands until towards the mid-17th century when John Vongler was described as of Colby, yeoman, in 1649. In 1670 John Vongler was assessed at five hearths, which shows it to have been a substantial house. A few years later he sold Colby to George Owen, D.D., who came there to live. He was described in 1690 as Professor of Theology. In his will dated 1 July 1690, proved 29 January 1690/1, he bequeathed 'Colby which I purchased from John and William Vongler, and the mill belonging thereto' to my wife Mary, with remainder to their eldest son George Owen, who succeeded to the property. George Owen the son was a barrister, a Justice of the Peace, and in 1708 a Land Tax Commissioner for the county. Shortly after on 21 February 1708/9 he sold Colby for £2,300 to John Barlow (of the Slebech family) who came to live at the house. A note made by the Registrar who accompanied Bishop Adam Ottley (1713-1723) on his Visitations in the diocese, records that they called on Mr. John Barlow at Colby, where 'we were entertained there in a London way, everything little but neat, and perfect in the kind; a new house, well seated, garden, etc.' This suggests that John Barlow erected the 'new house' soon after he acquired it. It remained in that family until 1758 when the heiress Catherine Barlow married (Sir) William Hamilton, and when he died without issue he left the Slebech and Colby estates to his nephew Charles Greville. The residence at Colby had become ruinous, and in 1768 certain improvements were made to it, and Hamilton was warned that the repairs would 'incur considerable expense'. In 1786 the tenant of Colby was one Daniel Roberts. Fenton observed in 1811, 'The ancient mansion has long since been taken down to make room for a farm-house, and its name alone is retained'. In 1838 the owner was Capt. Robert Fulke Greville, and the tenant was Elizabeth Parry.

Refs: NLW, Slebech Deeds, Pembs. GS, Pembs. Plea Rolls, The Ottley Papers, Bronwydd Deeds, Eaton Evans and Williams Deeds; Pembs. RO, Deeds D/RTP/P/C, LT 1786; College of Arms, Wagner MS 2; BM Egerton MS 2586; WWWR iii and vi.

COLBY LODGE, *Amroth*

Now an attractive residence in a dell, about half a mile to the west of the parish church. The earliest name of the property was Rhydlangoeg. A farmhouse in the 18th century belonging to the Skyrmes of Vaynor (Llawhaden). In the Land Tax of 1786 it is not specifically named, but as 'New house' owned by Thomas Skyrme, Esq. with Mrs. Brock as tenant. In a description of the Skyrme estate in 1787 it is called 'Rerdlangwig' (13 acres) which was held on a lease of lives by Mrs. Brock (55), Mrs. Bamfield (51) and Miss Thomas (48). On 13 September 1794 the marriage settlement of Jane Bamfield of 'Rhydlangwyg' and James Lewis, mercer, of Carmarthen was executed. The Skyrmes were encountering financial difficulties, and in 1779 parts of the estate were sold by order of Chancery to clear Skyrme debts. Among the properties was the messuage called 'Red Land Wig', which was purchased by John Colby of Ffynnone. Nearby was the 'Redlangoige Colliery' worked by the Colbys in 1806-7. Shortly after, in 1803, a large residence was built, and named after the then owners, Colby Lodge, the building of which was supervised by John Nash's Clerk of the Works. Nash was also concerned with changes to Ffynnone House. In 1834 Lewis wrote 'Colby Lodge, an elegant mansion, seat of Captain Protheroe [later of Dolwilym], is beautifully situated in a romantic dell opening at one extremity towards the sea, of which it commands a fine and interesting view'.

In 1839 Cordelia Maria Colby, widow, granted the 'dwelling house called Rhydlangoeg' to her son John Colby. In 1852 'Mr. Thomas Evans the present resident has lately opened an Hydropathic Establishment at Colby Lodge, the first of its kind in South Wales' – so wrote Miss F. P. Gwynne. The 'freehold mansion and estates called Rhydlangoeg otherwise called Colby Lodge' was advertised for sale in 1855. In 1873 Samuel Kay and David Thomas lived at Colby Lodge and Rhydlangoed respectively. Samuel Kay, J.P., was living at Colby Lodge in 1914 when his daughter Gladys married Lt.-Col. J. C. H. Crosland, who, after the 1914-18 war, came to live at his wife's home, and was there in 1925 when he served as High Sheriff for the county. It was finally sold by Miss E. F. Dixon Mason to the late Mr. I. O. Chance of Christie's, London, in 1965.

The Colby Lodge estate, (less the mansion and its 20 acres), comprising 870 acres, was bequeathed to the National Trust by Miss Mason (Miss Crosland's niece). Mr. & Mrs. Chance reduced the house to two storeys, modernised it, and beautified the garden and grounds. In 1980 they made a gift of the property to the National Trust. Alas, Mrs. Chance died in 1981, and her husband at the end of 1984. Mr. and Mrs. A. Scourfield-Lewis, who hold a 99-year lease on the house, have extensively renovated and improved the property.

Refs: NLW, Owen and Colby Estate Records; Pembs. RO, LT 1786; Lewis, *Top. Dict. Wales,* 1834 edn.; Fanny Price Gwynne, *Sketches of Tenby* etc., 1852 edn.; *Western Mail,* 5 Oct. and 23 Nov. 1985, illust. of the mansion: Nola D. Davies, *The Story of Amroth, The Church and the Parish,* 1980; Mr. & Mrs. A. Scourfield Lewis.

COLSTON, *Little Newcastle*

Marked as Colston south of Martel farm on Kitchin's Map 1764, and as Old Coldstone on Colby's Map 1831. Home of the Voyle family in early Tudor days. George Owen in *The Second Book* (p. 273) 1603, notes that 'Lewis Yongue [of Glastir, Nevern] the eldest son married Gwenllyan Voel of Colston a gentlewoman and heyre of dyverse landes', and had issue.

In 1500 Jenkyn Voel of Colston granted lands and tenements in Dyffryn Gwayne in the

fee of Nantgwyn to John ap Owen ap Rees. The next family there was one Symmons, and in 1670 John Symmons of Colston was assessed at three hearths. A pedigree of the Symmons family of Colston is given from the archives: Thomas 'Symins' of Colston married Margaret, daughter of John Tucker of Sealyham, (his will dated 1654), and by her had a son, John Symmons. John (will proved 1709), paid tax on three hearths in 1670, had a son and heir John Symmons, gent.,(will proved 24 April 1728), who married Anne, daughter of James Rowland, marriage settlement dated 21 October 1713 and they had five children; Thomas (will dated 1807), Anne, Mary who married William Lloyd of Martel; Martha who married in 1752; Elizabeth who married William Bennett of Camrose, and another natural son, Morris. The will of John Symmons proved in 1728 devised £20 to each of his four daughters and to his natural son, Morris, a cow and six sheep.

Mary and William Lloyd had four sons, William, Thomas who was later of Colston, George and James. Evan Symmons of Colston, husbandman whose will was dated 15 July 1753 and whose relationship to the above is not defined, had a son, William Symmons who died on HMS *Duke of Acquitaine* in the East Indies c. 1763/4. He left the settlement of all claims under the will of his father to Anne Symmons, step-daughter and executor of Evans Symmons's estate. In her will, dated 24 November 1797 and proved in 1805, Anne Symmons, spinster, devised her messuages called Skyber, and Finnone to her trustees, left many money bequests and Thomas Symmons her brother to be executor.

The family remained at Colston until 1800. The Land Tax 1786 lists four farms called Coulstone owned by William Knox of Llanstinan. The Voters' Lists for 1894 names two farms so-called, while that of 1904 lists the freehold farms of Old Coldstone, New Coldstone and Martel Mill.

Refs: WWHR ii, p. 41; BM, Egerton MS 2586; NLW, Bronwydd Deeds; Pembs RO, HDX/562, pp. 34, 35, 36, 37.

CORNISH DOWN,
St. Mary out Liberty Tenby★
This was the home of John Perrot, son of William Perrot of Scotsborough viv. 1494/5 who married Anne, daughter of Thomas Wyrriot. John Perrot married Jane, daughter of John Lloyd of Tenby and they had an heiress, Catherine who married John ap Rice viv. 1574/5. Nothing further is known until William Thomas is shown as owner, David Llewhellin, tenant in the Land Tax records of 1786. In the Voters lists of 1904 Charles William Rees Stokes of Warwick House, Tenby owned Cornish Down and Knighton farms.

Refs: GGMS (Adv. Pem.).

CORSTON, *Monkton*
A mansion to the northeast of Castlemartin village. Marked as Causon on Kitchin's Map 1763/4, as Corston House on Mudge's Map 1819, and as Corsiton on Colby's Map 1831. Home of the Meares family from 1665 to 1770; Francis Meares of Corston was High Sheriff in 1695. An inventory of his possessions in 1720 gives some particulars about the house at that time; the ground floor contained the hall, parlour, kitchen, pantry and an inner cellar; on the upper floor were the large chamber, middle chamber, chamber over the kitchen, two lodging rooms, and 'closet of conveniency'; the garrets contained a number of rooms, store-rooms, and the maid's chambers; the 'outer rooms' consisted of outer store room, dairy, outer cellar, brewhouse, cooling house, stables, ox-house, cart house, and other outhouses; and nearby was the haggard. In the Hearth Tax of 1670 Francis Meares is assessed at 3 and 4 hearths, which suggests it was then of moderate size as indicated by the inventory of 1720.

Francis Meares was described in 1665 as a mariner; he died in 1695. Francis Meares junior was described in his marriage settlement to Anne Elliot as being 'of Jamaica'. William Meares a witness to the settlement was 'late of Corston, now of The Six Clerk's Office, London Gent'.

In the prenuptial settlement of Francis Meares junior and Anne Elliot of Pembroke, dated 1726, he settled 'the capital messuage called Corston' to the uses of the marriage. The last of the family, William Meares, sold Corston in 1770 to John Prout a yeoman of Moor, and after his death about 1780, Corston passed by purchase to Abraham Leach of Pembroke, and it remained the seat of that family until the death without issue of Brig. Gen. H. E. Burleigh Leach, C.B., C.M.G., C.V.O. on 16 August 1936. His widow married Captain Lionel Green and went to live in Herefordshire. In 1940 the mansion was requisitioned by the R.A.F., and afterwards by the County War Agricultural Committee who used it as a Land Girls' Hostel. In 1946 Mrs. Green sold the house. The Leach family produced High Sheriffs in 1797, 1852, 1855 and 1933.

Refs: Pembs. RO, Deeds 1665-1885; NLW, Morgan-Richardson Deeds; R. G. Thorne, 'History of the Leach Family', *Pembs. Hist.,* 1981.

COSHESTON (HALL), *Cosheston*
On 26 August 1556 Gelly Barrett, gentlemen, of Gellyswick and his wife Mary sold 'a tenement called the Hall of Cosheston' to John Rossant of Nash, husbandman, and Isabel his wife, and it remained in the ownership of the Rossant family for several generations. In 1659 the will of John Rossant of Cosheston, yeoman, mentions the 'house called the Hall of Cosheston'. His son, Francis, was assessed at two hearths in 1670. In 1786 the Hall was owned and occupied by Mr. Abraham Leach. Just north of Cosheston village there was a farm called Snailton owned and occupied by Reverend William Holcombe. For a time the Allen family were in occupation including Seymour Phillips Allen (High Sheriff 1850) and his wife Lady Catherine, daughter of the 4th Earl of Portsmouth (*Vide* Burke's *Landed Gentry* 1969 under Evans of Cresselly). Later, the name was

changed to Woodfield and in 1894 it was occupied by George Stepney Gulston, and shortly afterwards bought by Major Ivor, afterwards Major-General Sir Ivor Philipps, K.C.B., D.S.O., who enlarged the house and gave it the name Cosheston Hall. The General died in 1940, and afterwards it was the seat of his daughter, Mrs. Basil Ramsden, and her son, Major Ivor Ramsden, M.B.E. (High Sheriff 1967) now one of H.M. Gentlemen at Arms, is the present owner-occupier, and is a D.L. The Hall was entirely rebuilt in the mid-19th century.

Refs: BM Egerton MS 2586; *RCAM Pembs.*, 1925; Pembs. RO, D/LLC, No. 1; For portraits at Cosheston (Mrs. Ramsden) see Steegman,. *S. Wales,* vol. II, 1962.

COTTESMORE, *Prendergast*

A mansion about a mile north of Prendergast church. The first house there was a farmstead known as Cotts. William Williams was living there in 1731 and his descendants owned the property until 23 December 1801 when it was sold by Francis Williams to Louis Devandes of Cotts, and Mary (Stokes) his wife. In 1814 the new owners assigned Cotts to the Peel family. In 1826 J. H. Peel of Cotts was High Sheriff and described in 1834 as owner of freehold land there. In 1835 his only daughter Helen married Edward Taylor Massy and in 1839 he bought Cotts from his father-in-law, and in that year commenced building a residence very close to the original house which was completed in 1841, and given the name Cottesmore. In 1873 E. T. Massy is described in the Landowners' Return as of Cottesmore 231 acres. One of the last of the family at Cottesmore was Lieutenant-General H. R. S. Massy, High Sheriff in 1946. Some years later Cottesmore was purchased by Colonel G. T. Kelway, High Sheriff in 1958 who died in 1990.

Refs: Cottesmore (Massy) Deeds; Landowners' Return 1873; Nicholas, *County Families,* 1870, illust.

COTTY, *Maenclochog*

Today a farm between Maenclochog village and Rosebush and known as Gotty. During the Tudor era, it was known as Cotty Whiaid. The earliest known family there was that of Dedwydd, sometimes spelled as Dedwyth. Lewis Dedwydd had two sons, the elder, Griffith Lewis Dedwydd succeeded to 'Cotty Whyad', had an only child, Elizabeth who married James ap John Rees David Howel (of the Penybenglog family, descended from Gwynfardd Dyfed), and their son Anthony James settled in Meline where he was living in 1628; the younger son William Lewis Dedwydd had a son, Lewis William of Bwlch y Clawdd near Maenclochog who married Morfydd, sister of the above named James ap John, and had issue (*vide* Bwlch y Clawdd *supra*). In 1786 Cotty was owned by Lord Milford, with William Howell as tenant.

Refs: GGMS Gwynfardd; College of Arms, Protheroe MS IV fo. 50, and XII fo. 44; LT 1786.

COURT (CWRT), *Eglwyswrw*

Now a farmstead just over half a mile north of Eglwyswrw. The first family there was that of Cantington. William Cantington, of Eglwyswrw lived at Court in 1199, and died in 1227. His descendants lived there throughout the middle ages and during the Tudor period adopted the Welsh form of nomenclature. Court became part of the Owen of Henllys estate. We are informed in 1594 – 'Coorte Hall the manor house [of the manor of Eglwyswrw]; there was in ould tyme an ancient manor howse or castell called Coorte Hall, nowe commonly called the Coorte, which was seated upon a faire plaine within a square mote standing very commodiously for woodde, water, and other comodities. The howse is now utterly decayed, and the lords kepeth the demeynes in his owne handes.' In 1603 George Owen, Lord of Cemaes wrote, 'The Coorte being this manor house of His lordshipp in tymes past (and as is reported, the mansion house of Bishopp David

Martin, bushopp of St. Davids, being lorde of the said manor) seemeth to have been a house both of accompt and strengthe, for I have seene within the moate there hugh walles and roomes of great breadeth all envyroned within a stronge and deepe mote digged out of the mayne rock fadd with a freshe springe ryshing in the same, and all the greenes there about growen with camamyll.' In 1925, the RCAM reported that 'nothing except the moat remains of the manorhouse of the lordship of Eglwyswrw, the mansion house of Bishop David Martin [1293-1328].

The site, now part of the modern farmhouse of Court, is about 30 yards by 20 yards; it is surrounded on its north, east and west sides by the remains of a moat 15 feet wide, which, on the east, is cut through rock; here it is seen at its best, the remaining parts being overgrown and largely filled in with soil.' In September 1597 George Owen settled the Court estate on his son Alban Owen who then came to the new house probably built on the site of the old one. Some time after 1615, Alban moved to Henllys. Afterwards it was occupied by several families, the most important being that of Ford, and on their departure at the end of the 17th century, was occupied by farming tenants.

The present edifice was never large, and in 1670 Alexander Ford of Court was assessed at three hearths only. The yeoman family of Devonald held it from 1764, and the last two members, Anne and Martha Devonald died some years before 1845.

Refs: Extent of Cemaes 1594, pp. 59, 63; George Owen, *2nd Book,* 1603-4, p. 278; *RCAM Pembs.,* 1925, p. 93; Fenton, *Tour Pembs.,* 1811, p. 292; George Owen's *Elizabethan Pembs.* in Pembs. Record Series No. 2, 1973, pp. 32-7, 97-8; NLW, Bronwydd Deeds; Pembs. RO, Davies-Scourfield Papers; GGMS II (Adv. Pembs.); College of Arms, Protheroe MS IV (GWG), p. 143; B. G. Charles, *George Owen of Henllys,* 1973.

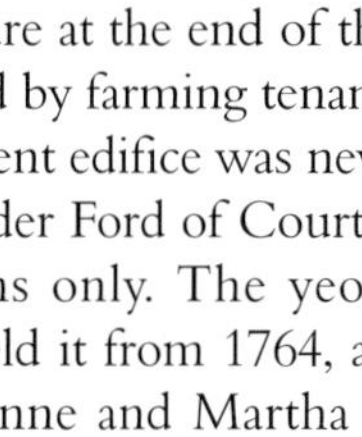

COURT (CWRT), *Llanllawer*

Originally a farm, until 1800 when the present large mansion was erected. Fenton's description shortly after the mansion had appeared reads as follows: 'Opposite to Cronllwyn on the other side of the river Gwayn, placed on high ground, though well-sheltered from the north, stands Court, a handsome modern mansion belonging to my friend John Gwyn Esq. in the midst of a well-managed demesne, finely sloping to the sun, and commanding pleasing views of the vale where the hospitable genius long exiled from so many deserted houses, and a wanderer, still delighting to hover around the scenes she loved and had once enlivened, has at last found an asylum.'

The old house has a long history. In 1594 Owen Johns, gent., of Brecon held land called Y Coort in Llanllawer, in occupation of Thomas ap Howel ap Gronow and Harry Hugh; and a memorial roll of Cemaes for 9 May 1650 records that among farms on the estate of Owen of Trecwn was Trellwyn and Tir y Court in Llanllawer. Towards the end of the 17th century those two properties became part of the estate of Warren of Trewern. On 1754 an estate map made by John Butcher defines Trellwyn Ucha and Court.

On 14 November 1770 Thomas Williams Esq. of Pope Hill and Haverfordwest, and his wife Anne (née Warren, co-heiress) made a lease of Court to Griffith Gwynne of Cilciffeth, gent. and in 1784 Griffith assigned the lease to his third brother William Gwynne. The Land Tax of 1786 shows 'Esquire Williams' as owner of 'Curt' in Llanllawer. The property changed hands on 5 October 1799 when the said Thomas and Anne Williams sold Court to John Gwynne of Haverfordwest, Attorney-at-Law and a martyr to the gout. The new owner immediately set about building a mansion on the site of the older house, and it still stands today. In 1847 a detailed map of Court, Trellwynfawr and Ty Cam was made by the Gwynnes. In 1874 and 1875, the last of the Gwynnes, Anne and Martha died unmarried, and Court passed to the next heir, the Revd. Thomas Gwynne Mortimer, whose mother was a Gwynne. During a visit to the Holy Land, he brought back some fig cuttings which were

planted in the walled garden at Court where they flourished mightily. He lived the remainder of his life at Court, was Rector of Castlebythe and Rural Dean of Fishguard, and died in 1903 leaving Court to his kinsman, Mortimer Thomas. It continued in that family until 1956 when it was sold to a local farmer who still owns it. There are plans to restore the mansion and grounds.

Refs: NLW, Vairdre Book, *Extent of Cemaes* 1594; Bronwydd Deeds, Trenewydd Deeds; information from the late Mrs. Catherine Royston Brown (née Mortimer Thomas) of Trenewydd, Pencaer; Francis Jones, 'A Pembrokeshire Squarson', *Pembs. Hist.*, 1974.

CRABHOLE,. *Marloes*

A farmstead close to an inlet, about six miles north of Dale. Home of a medieval family who bore the name of the property. In the years 1384-1405 Philip Crabhole lived there, one of whose daughters and co-heirs married a Laugharne (late of St. Brides) who later alienated the property. During the 1500s the family of Loughor owned it, and were still there in 1666 when Thomas Loughor of Crabhole, gentleman, is mentioned in legal records. Loughor was probably a tenant, for in 1637 it belonged to Sir John Wogan of Boulston. The Wogans continued to own it, and in 1773 John Wogan of Boulston was the owner of Crabhole (309 acres) with Cornelius Davies (aged 60) as a leaseholder. He was the son of Gilbert Davies (will proved 1739) member of successful yeomen stock, who also owned Mullock and Broomhill, and a descendant, Warren-Davis, was owner of Trewarren, a mansion in the neighbouring parish of St. Ishmael's. Crabhole continued in the hands of successful farmers.

Gilbert Davies of Crabhole, married, c. 1691 an unknown Margaret by whom he had three sons, and one daughter, Alice who married Richard Runwa(y) of Hook who died in 1766 aged 69. Gilbert and Margaret's eldest son, Cornelius born 1713 and still alive in 1773, married Anne thought to be a daughter of Allen of Fobston. She died 22 June 1776 aged 72 having had a son, John. In 1768 John Davies and his father Cornelius made a division of the Crabhole estate between them.

John Davies viv. 1768 had a lease of Broomhill from the owner Benjamin Runwa(y) in 1790. John Davies married Lettice Mathias of Lochmeyler, she died in 1829 in her 84th year. John and Lettice's son and heir, Thomas Mathias Davies of Broomhill succeeded his father in 1805, he had 12 children, all deeply religious, by his wife, Emily Alicia Palmer who died 18 March 1862 aged 60. Thomas was commissioned as 1st Lieutenant Loyal Haverfordwest Fusilier Volunteers in 1799. Their eldest son, was Vaughan Palmer Davies who married in Bombay Cathedral, January 1858, Ellen, daughter of Edward Robinson. Vaughan Davies farmed Skomer Island from 1861 to 1891, was appointed on the barque, *Worcester* 1844, became Mate, finally Master, traded in India and the Far East, and engaged in the opium trade. Edward Robinson later took a lease of Skomer Island and lived there. Cornelius Davies the second son of Thomas and Emily drowned at Calcutta in 1842 aged 24. The other children listed are Emily, Myra, Charles, Henry and Richard; the remaining children have not been detailed.

When I visited it on 6 September 1977, I found a large old farmhouse. It once had a gable-end chimney, but this was removed by the present owner-occupiers, Mr. and Mrs. James, who kindly received and assisted me. A walled garden stretched in front of the house, with another, but smaller, walled garden at the side of the house. Mr. and Mrs. Rind now of Allenbrook House, Dale, who once lived at Crabhole have an excellent photograph of the house showing the old gable-end chimney.

Refs: NLW, GS, Pembs. Plea Rolls, Maesgwynne Deeds; Sale Catalogue of the estates of John Wogan, 1773; Fenton, *Tour Pembs.,* 1811, p. 171; Pembs. LT 1786; Francis Green, 'Wogan of Boulston', *Y Cymmrodor,* 1902; Tablets in Marloes parish church.

Allen

CRESSELLY, *Jeffreston*

About a mile and a half to the west of the parish church. The original house stood in the middle of a colliery in the valley below the present mansion. For many generations Cresselly was the home of a yeoman family. The earliest known member was Peter Bartlett, yeoman living at Cresselly in 1564. He was followed by John Bartlett who died just before 1672, leaving his property to his son John Bartlett, junior. On the death of the last named in 1629, he was succeeded by his son David Bartlett who married Elizabeth Phelps of Carew.

On David's death in 1652, he was succeeded by his son John Bartlett, yeoman, who became agent for John Barlow of Lawrenny. The yeoman's house at this time was a modest one judging from the fact that it was assessed at but two hearths in 1670. His eldest son died unmarried in 1728 leaving Cresselly to his niece Joan, daughter of his brother John Bartlett of Cresswell. In 1729 Joan Bartlett married John Allen of Goodhook, who became the first of that family to settle at Cresselly which from that time has remained in the hands of his descendants who continue to live there.

In 1732 John Allen became High Sheriff of the county, and died in 1752. In 1770 another John Allen pulled down the orginal house which stood on low ground near the coal mines, and erected a new mansion at the present site on the higher ground. It was enlarged in 1869, and still stands today, being the home of the son of the late Mrs. Auriol Evans (née Allen) heiress of Cresselly. Malkin wrote in 1803, 'Cresselly, with its luxurious plantation of firs, seems to possess a comfortable establishment, but my attention was not directed to anything worth describing'.

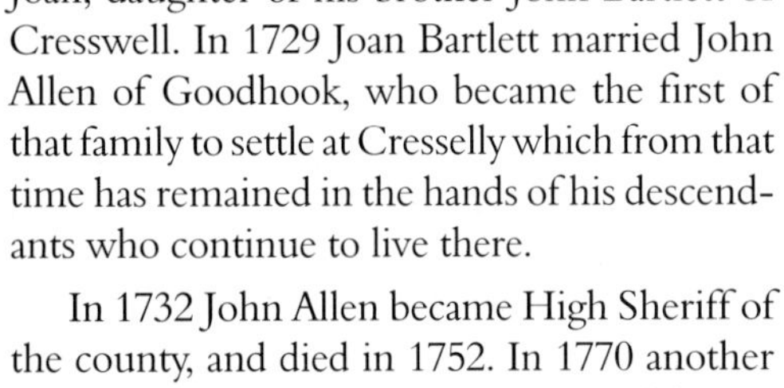

Fenton, in 1811, noted 'Cresselly the elegant seat of John Allen Esq. lately my brother circuiteer [barrister, M.P. Pembr. Bor. 1818-26] stands in the midst of a colliery, judiciously planted woods screened those dingy volcanoes from its windows.' Five of the Allens of Cresselly were High Sheriffs.

Refs: Pembs. RO, Deeds DH/99, No. 8; NLW, Picton Castle Deeds, Eaton Evans and Williams Deeds; E. Inglis-Jones, 'A Pembrokeshire County Family in the 18th century' (the Allens of Cresselly), *NLWJ,* vol. 17, 1971-2 Col. F. S. Allen; Family records of the Allens of Cresselly and some family letters, etc., priv. printed, 1905; Malkin, *Tour, S. Wales;* Fenton, *Tour Pembs.,* 1811; *Contemporary Biographies, South Wales and Mon.,* 1907, p. 106, illust.of exterior of Cresselly; T. Nicholas, *County Families,* 1875; C. S. Allen, *Tenby,* Photos of Pembs. Mansions, 1871.

CRESSWELL, *Lawrenny*

The ruins of this former mansion are engulfed in undergrowth so that it is difficult to examine it. The RCAM found a similar difficulty when they visited the site in March 1923, but managed to produce a fair description, which may be summarised as follows. The mansion is rectangular in form, 30 ft. by 40 ft., and has a turret at each angle some 16ft. high. Two, perhaps three of the turrets were vaulted, and one had been used as a dovecot; the courtyard is 15ft. by 20ft., and there are remains of a fine porch and doorway on the east front, with a short, broad walk to the banks of the Cresswell river. Beyond the north wall stretched the garden, an almost square enclosure, with a river frontage; there are stables and outbuildings to the east of the house; and about 300 yards west of the house are remains of the domestic chapel; to the northeast of the mansion is Cresswell farm. The mansion was assessed at nine hearths which shows it to have been a commodious building.

The Barlows of Slebech bought numerous lands from the Crown, and it is likely that Cresswell and the chapel was among them for they were owned by John Barlow of Slebech (d. 1600). His younger son William Barlow settled at Cresswell, and married Elizabeth ap

Rhys of Rickeston, Brawdy parish. William was High Sheriff in 1612, and died in 1636. His son Lewis Barlow paid taxes for nine hearths at Cresswell in 1670, and is described as of that place in 1679. He was High Sheriff in 1641 and 1668. He also inherited Lawrenny, and died in 1681. His son John Barlow lived for a time at Cresswell, but moved after his father's death to Lawrenny, where he died in 1700-1. The property remained in Barlow ownership. In 1786 Sir William Hamilton, (who had married a Barlow), was described as owner of Cresswell, with Mrs. Elizabeth Barlow as occupier. Elizabeth also owned Cresswell Mill. It seems that it was about this time that the mansion was abandoned.

Refs: RCAM Pembs., 1925, p. 144; WWHR, iii, p. 137; NLW, Slebech Deeds, Spence-Colby Deeds; Pembs. RO, Lawrenny Deeds; LT 1786; T. Nicholas, *County Families,* 1875 edn. p. 909.

CRICKMARREN, *Monkton**

Home of the Dwnn family. Thomas Dwnn owned lands at Crickmarren in 1620. Nicholas Dwnn, will proved 1773, mentions that he inherited 'my home at Brownslade' (this was not the mansion), from his uncle Nicholas Dwnn, will proved 1734. The 1786 land tax records show Crickmarren owned by Sir Hugh Owen tenanted by Nicholas Dwnn. Members of the family also lived at Tarr, Welston and Westmoor House.

CROFT HOUSE, *Tenby St. Mary**

Home of the Richards family. Jacob Richards made a fortune in India. He settled in Tenby towards end of 18th century. He was Mayor of Tenby in 1812, 1817, 1822, 1829 and 1831. He had two known sons, William Richards who was High Sheriff in 1850, Mayor of Tenby in 1836, 1837, 1838, 1839 and numerous times after that. He and his father were buried in the Scotsborough vault under the northeast corner of the church but have no memorial. The second son was Lt. Colonel Henry Richards of the Indian army. He had a son, William Henry Richards, J.P., born in 1844 who married Florence Antonia Emilia, daughter of Lt. Col. Antony Bowen Owen Stokes of St. Botolphs. He was High Sheriff in 1878 and Mayor of Tenby from 1880-86 and in 1894. He died suddenly in November 1895 and is buried in Tenby cemetery. Jacob's daughter Mary Anne married George Lloyd, Captain RN of The Green, Haverfordwest. She died 31 December 1849 and is buried in St. Mary's Tenby.

CRONLLWYN, *Fishguard*

Now a farmstead in the Gwaun Valley, about half a mile on high ground to the south of Bont Llanychaer, and near to another old mansion, Cilgelynen. Fenton wrote in 1811, Cronllwyn 'a favourite spot of Sir William Martin as I find it the property of my great-grandfather (John Lewis) of Manorowen soon after his marriage with a daughter of Mortville (Morfil) probably part of his wife's dowry.'

During the 16th and 17th centuries Cronllwyn was the house of local gentry. In 1573 John ap Rees, gent, gave seizin of a tenement and 100 acres at Place y Crwnlloyn and Dolwen, to Griffith John Llewelin, and a few years later we learn that Owain ap Gruffydd ap Llewelin o' Grynllwyn o Abergwn (of Plâs Abergwaun) was married to Marged daughter of John Bateman (of Mynydd Melin), and had two children, Sion ap Owen and Ann, who were living in 1591 when Dwnn called there. The father, Owen (ap) Griffith of Cronllwyn witnessed the will of Lewis Nash of Fishguard on 20 April 1608. The son John Owen was still living at Cronllwyn in 1657. Thomas Owen of Cronloyne was alive in 1637, and married to a daughter of David Lloyd of Morfil. By the next century Cronllwyn was held by farming tenants. In 1786 it was owned by Thomas Bowen Parry Esq. of Manorowen, with John Williams as tenant, and since then has always been a farm held by local folk.

Refs: Fenton, *Tour Pembs.,* 1811; NLW, Cemais Court Rolls (Bronwydd colln.), Papers of GS, Pembs. Plea Rolls; Carms. RO, GGMS; *Dwnn,* i, 173.

CRUGIAU, *in Nevern and Bayvil*

The six Crugiau Cemmaes tumuli occupy the eastern end of Bayvil parish where it meets those of Nevern and Moylgrove. These sepulchral cairns (or twmps) and the relics found in some have been noted in Gibson's edition of Camden's *Britannia,* 1695 which quotes the views of Edward Lloyd. George

Owen of Henllys, *Pembs.* vol. 1, 108, see also *Second Book* (ed. B. G. Charles), describes the tumuli as 'four little tumps of earth, and yet to been seen 40 miles off, viz from Plynlimmon.' The whole area, some 600 feet high occupies a commanding position, and slopes gently westwards. The boundary between Bayvil and Nevern runs through the area along a roadway. North of that road, and in Bayvil, are the tumuli, one of which, just over the further boundary, is in Moylgrove parish, and there are several farms and holdings at Pantgwyn, Trecernydd, Pengwndwn, and Pencrugiau on the road boundary.

South of the boundary and in Nevern, is the main farmstead of Crugiau, also called Crugiau Cemmaes, and the farms of Rhydymaen, Cwmeog, and Samaria, the cottages of Penuel Cemaes and Post-coch, and due south, across Nant Duad, is historic Coed Pencelli. In earlier days there were several other tenements whose names and locations are now lost – Cwm bychan, Pistsyll y Blaidd, 'the vill of Ryowe Crugie', Caereglwys Mawr, Pantygroes, Crugie yr elyrch (all mentioned 1517), Crugie Ucha (1469) Crugie Issa (1550), and Tir yr Esker in Crugie Ucha (1594). All the above south of the road boundary occupied 'the Crugie Quarter' of Nevern parish, and in 1786 'Crugie' farm was owned by John Protheroe, and tenanted by widow Thomas. In 1840 Crigie (171 acres) was owned by James Propert, tenanted by Eynon Havard; in 1894, Eynon, William, Walter and Ellen Havard held the land and farmlands of Crugiau, jointly; in 1909 Crigie farm in Nevern and Bayvril, comprising 213 acres, part of Cwmgloyn estate, tenanted by Eynon and Walter Havard, was advertised for sale. This was the capital messuage of the area, and formerly belonged to Rhys ap Rhydderch, descended from Gwynfardd Dyfed; fifth in descent from Rhys, was Lewis ab Owen 'who dyverse yeares past pawned the said house and lands of Crigie (Ycha) to Thomas Young of Tredrissy father to Phillip Younge father to John Phillip Young who now dwelleth there' – thus George Owen, *Second Book,* (1603-4), p. 271.

Part, if not all of Crugiau Ucha once belonged to Thomas ap David ap Ievan of Court, Eglwyswrw, descended from the Cantingtons; Thomas was followed by son Owen, who married Avis, daughter of Llewelyn Tew of Cilgwyn, whose only child Avis married James ap Rees a younger son of Penybenglog. Avis's only child and heiress married Thomas Jones of Brawdy, and they, in 1582, broke the entail on a messuage and 26 acres in 'Criggie Ycha in Nevarne'.

Crugiau had been purchased by William Owen of Henllys between 1493 and 1508: his son, George Owen, in 1585 bought a further 16 pieces of land from a yeoman, John Lewys Llywelyn who then lived at Crigiau. In 1594 Philip John Howel held lands at Crugiau Ucha lately owned by John Lewis Llewelin, while John Philip Younge held a tenement at Crugiau Issa. In the succeeding years Crugiau changed hands several times, before it was sold with the Cwmgloyn estate in 1909.

Refs: NLW, Bronwydd Deeds, Cemais Court Rolls, Roll of Wards, George Owen, *2nd Book*; B. G. Charles, *George Owen*; Cambrian Register, 1796, ii, 491; Additional Morris Letters, p. 109; Carms. RO, GGMS; WWHR ii, p. 91; BM Egerton MS, 1586.

CRUGLAS, *St. Davids*

Now a farmstead, south of Cwmwdig, on rising ground overlooking Spite Moor, and Pont Cruglas on the main road from St. Davids to Fishguard. For long, home of farming families. In the years 1546-49, William John, husbandman, lived there and in 1562 Maurice ap John ap Ieuan, husbandman. In 1595 the Reverend Walter Thomas, clerk, and Arnold Johnes, gentleman, brought an action in the court of Great Sessions against John Woolcock for trespassing with animals 'at a place called Kriggles' and depasturing there. David John Woolcock of Crickglase, yeoman, made his will on 10 March 1612, in which his three children inherited. Before 1637 it was held by William Jones, younger son of Thomas Jones of Brawdy, on a tenancy granted by the See of St. Davids which owned the property. It later became the home of George Harry, a younger son of David Harry the elder of Llanrhian parish, yeoman. When he made his will on 13 November 1650, George Harry held a lease of Crikeglas farm, and his descendants held renewal leases for six generations, until the death of John Harding Harries (High Sherriff 1846) in 1869.

The family whose surname was extended to Harries, were strong Nonconformists. 'Mrs. Harries, Criglas' was a communicant at Trefgarn Owen chapel while 'Mr. John Harries of Kirkglace' and his wife became members of Albany chapel at Haverfordwest. The family gradually added to their possessions and became members of the landed gentry, and left Cruglas in order to live at the nearby mansion of Trevaccoon. The old farmstead of Cruglas was improved, and shortly after 1797 the east front was added to the building. The property has been sold by the See of St. Davids (owner of the freehold), and today is the home of the Evans family, formerly of Trenewydd, Brawdy.

Refs: 'History of Harries of Cruglas and Trevaccoon' by Francis Green, WWHR, VIII a work containing several errors; Albany Chapel Records, and Records of Trefgarn Owen Chapel; NLW, Records of GS; Carms. RO, Trant Deeds; Pembs. RO, LT 1786.

CUFFERN, *Roch*

A mansion, some two miles from Roch Gate on the St. Davids-Haverfordwest main road, immediately north of the mansion in the high land called Cuffern mountain, Coffrwm by the Welsh. From early days Cuffern consisted of several farms which continued until modern times. During the years 1150-70 the 'manor of Cuffern' (2 carucates) was granted by Robert fitz Richard fitz Tancred to the Hospitallers of St. John of Slebech.

In 1392 we find that John Bateman and Margaret his wife occupied lands at Wyddinston and Coffron, held of the manor of Roch, and in the following century Coffron formed part of the possessions of the Knights Hospitallers. The Barrett family owned lands there which were finally inherited by two co-heiresses – Jennet Barrett wife of Nicholas Hurde whose descendants were living in 1592, and Joan Barrett wife of William Roblin whose daughter married John ab Owen of Lochmeyler, from whom descended the Bowens of Roblinston. The will of John Roblin 'of Cuffern' is dated 1434. In 1566 William Yonge 'of Coffrone' yeoman, lived there, and in 1577 John Tankard of East Dudwell and Thomas Bowen of Roblinston held, as assignees of Griffith White, 'a carucate of ploughland' on Goffremont alias

Cofferun', being 'but heath grounds, and good for neither pasture nor corn' – this, clearly, being Cuffern mountain.

By 1608 one William David Perkin lived 'at Koffrwm'. In 1623 James Young and Francis Stephen lived there. In 1639 Laugharne Young (son of James Young and his wife Maud, née Reynish) died owning lands 'in Cuffern,' and in 1671 Anthony Stokes, gent., claimed a messuage and 190 acres 'in Coffrom'. By will of 1716 James Young of Dale parish bequeathed 'Cyffran alias Cyffrwn', being two ploughlands, in Roch, to his daughter Jane, wife of Constant Stokes. Anne Young, the other co-heiress married James Harries, and owned part of Cuffern in 1736, and their son, Francis Harries, by will of 1760 left Cuffern to his wife Elizabeth for life, with remainder to John Rees, son of testator's sister Mrs. Anne Rees. This John Rees had adopted the name John Rees Stokes by 1775 when he married Frances Warren of Trewern. Cuffern was still divided into two parts, and in 1786 one was owned by John Rees Stokes, the other by John Jones Esq. of Brawdy. The present mansion at Cuffern was built about 1770 by the said J. R. Stokes, whose descendants remained in possession thereafter. In 1837 his son, John Stokes Stokes owned Cuffern and demesne (240 acres), Cuffern farm (Thos Reynish, tenant) 94 acres, Cuffern Mountain 114 acres, and Start 95 acres. The present mansion is large and commodious, of four storeys, with ranges of seven windows each storey, a pillared Georgian entrance, and gable-end chimneys. Fenton, who was entertained by John Rees Stokes in 1811, states 'Kyffern, the seat of its present proprietor, a handsome modern mansion, well placed with a rising ground to the north . . . here under this hospitable roof I lose the fatigues of the day, and next morning pursue my route'. In 1986 a hotel and in 1988 renovated and made into a nursing home and a home for the elderly, now closed. Recently sold and being restored.

Refs: Fenton, *Tour Pembs.*, 1811; WWHR XI; W. Rees, *History of St. John,* 1947; Pembs RO, Deeds D/EE/2 and Saunders-Davis Colln.; GGMS; BM Egerton MS 2586; NLW, Pembs. Papers of GS; Good photo of mansion in *Western Telegraph* 20 October 1977, and see also 10 August 1988.

CWM CERWYN,

Llangolman and Mynachlogddu parishes

This farmstead stood in Mynachlogddu parish, above the eastern banks of Afon Wern which forms the boundary of that parish with Llangolman. It is on high ground due east of Moel Cwm Cerwyn (Precelly Top). Marked on Rees' 14th century map. This district is mentioned in the Mabinogi, (Olwen and Culchurch), when Arthur and his retinue hunted the Twrch Trwyth. Land in this area had been granted to St. Dogmaels Abbey and is mentioned in deeds of 1344/45. After the Dissolution the tenement called 'Come Kerwyn', part of the dissolved monastery of St. Dogmaels, was leased for 99 years to David ap Rhys ap Owen, on 12 October 1535, and later assigned to John Bradshaw and his heirs at an annual rent of 10s.

During the years 1538-44 John ap Ieuan ap Morgan Gwyn of Cwm Kerwyn brought an action in Chancery against David ap Ieuan ap Jenkyn and Isabel his wife, and William David John and Alison his wife, the said females living daughters and administrators of Ieuan ap Morgan Gwyn and his wife Eva Broughton to properties called Cwmkerwyn, Havod Madog alias Portisepant berth duy, and Tref Loyn, in Kemes. Isabel had a son Piers David (married a daughter of Owen Lloyd of Cwmgloyn) and Alison, had a son Thomas David; this lawsuit involved the custom of gavelkind.

Towards the end of the 17th century, it became the home of Griffith Morris, gent. son of Griffith Morris of Clynsaethmaen, just south of Cwm Cerwyn. Griffith was a Baptist and member of Rhydwilym Chapel, and in 1693 married Elizabeth, daughter of Griffith Howel of Rushacre, Narberth. After the marriage he went to live at Cwm Cerwyn and is described in 1694 as Griffith Morris 'of Cwmckerwyn, gent.' He died between 1732 and 1734, and his son, Griffith Morris, junior, gent. followed him 'at Cwmkerwyn Isha'. In 1726 Griffith Thomas and John Griffith, yeomen, of Mynachlogddu, held a lease of Cwm Kerwyn and adjacent lands, all part of the former monastery of St. Dogmaels.

In 1786 James Bowen Esq. owned Cwm Carun, with John Griffith as tenant. On 5 April 1817 Daniel Owen of Cwmcerwyn was baptized, and on 30 January 1833 ordained Baptist minister of Pope Hill, south of Haverfordwest. Cwm Cerwyn became part of the Cwmgloyn estate, and in 1909, described as a farm of 296 acres, rented by Morris Thomas, was advertised for sale.

Refs: BM Egerton MS, 2586, fo. 352; Lewis, *Early Chancery Proceedings conc. Wales,* 1937, p. 67; Pritchard, *Hist. of St. Dogmaels Abbey,* pp. 28, 45, 64, 109, 121; Pembs RO, Deeds DB/13/98; NLW, Morgan-Richardson Deeds, No. 2918.

CWMBETTWS, *Bridell*

Now a large old farmhouse, south of Bridell church, and 1¾ miles northeast of Eglwyswrw. Home of the Williams family who later succeeded to the Cwmgloyn estate (q.v.). In 1786 William Williams, Esq. was owner, with John Phillips as tenant.

CWMEOG, *Nevern*

Now a farmstead some two miles to the north-east of Nevern church; to the west of Pencelli wood, and due north from Henllys. At one time it was divided into two messuages called Cwmeog-fawr and -fach, and Cwmeog-ucha and -issa. It eventually became one farm as it now is. The properties were acquired by the Owens of Henllys, and later by their descendants the Lloyds of Bronwydd. In 1470 Owen ap Ieuan ap Oweyn mortgaged a messuage at Cwmhyok in the fee of Bayvil (which Owen's father had of the gift of David ap Ieuan ap Llewelin Vechan), to Thomas ap Howel ap Gwilym ap Phillip: in 1493 Ieuan ap Philip Lloyd mortgaged all his lands at Cwmyok within the ploughland of Tre Vorgan in the fee of Bayvil; in 1503 the messuage in Komeyok was in mortgage from Howel ap Ieuan ap Rees the elder, to Sir Ieuan ap Owen, Knight [of

Pentre Evan] and on 2 June 1503 John ap Howel ap Ieuan ap Rees of Henllys gent., covenanted not to sell any of the properties to anyone except his brother Henry ap Howel when required. In 1542 James ap Howel ap Ieuan ap Rees (descended from Gwynfardd), was owner-occupier of Cwmeog, which he sold in 1548 to William Owen of Henllys. Afterwards it passed to William's son, George Owen of Henllys, and in 1612 he granted Cwmeog Issa to his sons Rees, Thomas, and William, and Cwmeog Ucha to his sons Rees, George, William and Thomas, all to hold the properties at an annual rent; in 1665 Cwmeog was held by George Owen's illegitimate son William Owen of Cwmeog (living 1673) from whom it passed to his son Thomas Owen, barrister, of Grays Inn (will proved 1708) who left three sons, Caleb, Thomas and Richard Owen. Caleb was still living there in 1767.

In 1740 the two farms, Cwmeog fawr and fach were sold to Thomas Lloyd of Bronwydd and Anna his wife, and in 1786 it was owned by the said Thomas Lloyd, with David William, tenant. Later the farms were sold, and changed hands several times. When I visited Cwmeog on 4 October 1978, it was owned by Mr. D. Douglas-Osborn. The old farmhouse has been heavily modernised but still retains features of its former days, one of which is its two 'simne fawr' with massive beams over them, one of the beams being forked, a most unusual feature: a small garden bounded one gable end. The owner runs riding-stables there mainly for visitors.

Refs: NLW, Bronwydd Deeds, Papers of GS, Pembs. Plea Rolls; G. Owen, *Extent of Cemais,* 1594; BM Egerton MS, 2586 fo. 311a; GGMS III (Bradwen); Bloome's List, 1673; LT 1786; B. G. Charles, *George Owen of Henllys,* pp. 5, 18-19, 36, 45.

CWMWDIG, *St. Davids*

A farmstead on a long slope above Porthreiddy and Abereiddy, about threequarters of a mile from the latter, with a view over the coast from Ynys y Barri towards Penbiri and Penmaendewi. It is an L-shaped building, compact, with small extensions at either end, with dormer windows fronting northeastwards. The earliest known proprietors were Philip ap David and his wife Joan (née Sutton) of Brawdy, who owned in 1448 two messuages and an acre in Eglewscomydik, in tenure of Philip Nicholl, Ieuan ap Rees Menyth, and David ap Philip ap Walter. The name makes it clear that there was a medieval chapel in this remote part of Dewsland. It may have stood within the farmyard below the house near to the holy well, still there, and just below these was a field called Parc y Fynwent, described in Elizabethan deeds as ' Hen Fwnwen' and 'Tir yr hen fynwent'.

Ownership passed from the Brawdy family to that of Voyle of Haverfordwest, and from them to Thomas Canon. In 1607 Thomas Canon sold the two messuages at Cwmwdig, and other properties, to the sitting tenant, William James Harry, who held them in mortgage from Morgan Voyle. The new owner was the son of James Harry, son of Harry Hooper, yeoman, living at Ynys y Barry in 1543. William James Harry made a good marriage, his wife Katherine being daughter of Thomas Jones gent., of Brawdy. He died in 1619 leaving ten children. His eldest son, Thomas William James, married in 1632 Alice Tucker of Sealyham, by whom he had an only child, Joan, who inherited Cwmwdig in 1672. The heiress married a yeoman, William Williams of Caerforiog, who came to live at his wife's home. Joan died without issue in 1700, and Cwmwdig passed to her husband's family. The last Williams to own Cwmwdig was Thomas Williams of Pope Hill (d. 1810), and Cwmwdig was inherited by his daughter and co-heiress, Mary, who married Samuel Harries of Trevaccoon near Croesgoch. Thereafter Cwmwdig was let to farming tenants until its sale in the 20th century.

Refs: Pembs. RO, Land Tax 1786, Sale Cat. AD 1919; NLW, Morgan-Richardson Deeds, Eaton Evans and Williams Deeds; *Dwnn,* i, 113, 193; WWHR, vi, p. 32; Browne Willis, *Survey of St. Davids,* 1717; Fenton, *Tour Pembs.,* 1811; *RCAM Pembs.,* 1925.

CWMGLOYN, *Nevern and Bayvil*

Now a farmstead about threequarters of a mile north of Felindre (which is on Afon Nyfer). From Felindre a wooded vale (called Coch Cwmgloyn) runs northwards as far as Cwmgloyn, through which the drive ran from the now ruined lodge along the western bank of the Gloyn to the old mansion. Fenton states in

1811, 'Cwmgloyne the only mansion of the many in its neighbourhood which is not in ruins or has not been metamorphosed into a farm-house and stripped of its surrounding woods. The principal residence of the Lloyds, a slip of the prolific stock of Gwynfardd prior to its being planted here, was Hendre near St. Dogmaels . . . The late possessor of this place (Cwmgloyn) and the last of his name, in whom his family became extinct, Thomas Lloyd Esq. was a most valuable country gentleman, highly esteemed, deservedly popular, leading a useful life among his neighbours and tenants, and to a taste for general literature added a profound knowledge of the language and antiquities of Wales. Dying a bachelor, he left his estate by will to Maurice Williams, Esq. the present proprietor'.

The earliest known owner of the property was Rhys ap Rhydderch (also descended from Gwynfardd). Fifth in descent from him was Jane, daughter and co-heiress of David ap Gwilym ap Perkin of Cwmgloyn, who brought that home and estate to her husband Owen Lloyd a younger son of Hendre, who settled at his wife's home. The marriage took place towards the middle of the 16th century. Cwmgloyn remained in Lloyd ownership for seven succeeding generations until the death of the bachelor squire Thomas Lloyd, J.P. (High Sheriff in 1771). Numerous poems of praise to him, as well as his elegy, are contained in *Blodau Dyfed*, 1824. Although the male line became extinct with his death, the property remained in descendants of the Lloyds. Thomas bequeathed Cwmgloyn to his kinsman, Morris Williams of Trellyffant whose grandmother was Frances Lloyd, daughter of Evan Lloyd of Cwmgloyn. It was a commodious house in 1670 when it was assessed at five hearths and has been enlarged since, as its present condition indicates. Morris Williams was followed by his nephew Owen Owen, son of his sister who had married a Mr. Owen. From Owen Owen, Cwmgloyn passed to his son Morris Williams Lloyd Owen, who died without issue in 1908, and in the following year the property was sold.

From Cwmgloyn came five High Sheriffs, and numerous magistrates. After this the property changed hands several times, and an interesting account of its condition in 1940 is given by the author, R. M. Lockley, as follows: 'Cwmgloyn was a noble building even in 1940 when I first saw it as the farmhouse of a derelict farm which I subsequently rented for a song on condition that I would restore the farm. All the land here is up hill or down dale, wild, and near to the bone of the slate rock; not fertile, yet kind to the eye of the naturalist. On each stone pillar of the entrance gate to Cwmgloyn used to be an ancient gargoylish stone face, one of which was lately smashed by a passing lorry. The old house had a great kitchen and cellars under a panelled hall. During my occupation of this house I pulled away a modern stove which had blocked the entrance to a vast hearth in the kitchen. This revealed an old wall-baking oven in which I found books, nearly 150 years old; Marshall's *Agriculture* and a farm account book of 1750 with many entries curious to a modern farmer. In the huge chimney (*simne fawr*) could be discerned, above lintel height, a walled-in doorway with, if I remember aright, a pointed arch. We called this the priest's chamber, according to local hearsay it was used as such during the Reformation, as hideouts in several local manors and churches were said to be. The clear spring issuing from the rocks at Cwmgloyn flows through a steep wooded ravine containing a beautiful drive from lodge gates in the hamlet of Velindre, but the woods have lately been felled and the lodge become roofless, and in the general levelling of human society, Cwmgloyn, like many another late medieval manor, is now an ordinary farm.' (Lockley, *Pembrokeshire,* 1957, edn 1977. p. 99). Fenton, thou art fortunate not to be here today! On 4 October 1978 I visited Cwmgloyn and was kindly shown around by Mr. Hugh Thomas, eldest son of the former-owner. It is an excellent example of the vernacular mansions popular in this area, and is now L-shaped, the other wing having been removed, nevertheless still an impressive building. There is a carved medieval head said to represent that of a bishop.

Refs: RCAM Pembs., 1925; *Dwnn,* i, pp. 246-7; Carms. RO, John Francis Colln.; NLW, Bronwydd Deeds; George Owen, *2nd Book,* p. 271; Francis Jones, 'Lloyd of Hendre and Cwmgloyn', *NLWJ,* 1984.

DALE (CASTLE), *Dale*

The ancient residence now called Dale Castle, stands on the western fringe of the village of Dale, at the entry into the haven of Milford. The family of de Vale, which suggests that such was the original form of the place-name, held the manor of Dale and several appointments in West Wales during the period 1131-1364. One obtained a royal grant for a weekly market and an annual fair in 1293. The last of the male line died about 1300 and the estate and manor was divided between daughters, co-heiresses. One of these, Ellen de Vale, married Llywelyn ap Owen, a sprig of Welsh royalty, and from that marriage descended the Tudor dynasty, and Owain Glyndwr no less. Nearly two centuries later we find one Richard Walter of Dale owning property there which his widow Isabel sold in 1504. The Walter family, later of Haverfordwest, Roch Castle, Rosemarket, and Cwmgigfran (Carms.) continued to hold Dale in the 17th century, until 1669 when Richard Walter Esq. sold his interest in the manor of Dale to David Paynter. This family lived at nearby Broomhill farm and acquired wealth. David Paynter's daughter Elizabeth married William Allen of Gelliswick, and in 1705 he granted Dale Castle and the manor to his son-in-law.

A descendant, John Allen of Dale Castle married Mary Stepney, and had an only child, Elinor. On her father's death in 1767 Elinor inherited Dale Castle, manor, and lands, and married in 1776 a Cardiganshire squire, John Llwyd of Ffosybleiddiaid, Mabws, and Ystrad Teilo, and from them descended the Lloyd-Philipps family who continue to hold Dale Castle to this day. Extensive additions were made to the old residence which was given the official name of Dale Castle. *The Pembrokeshire Archaeological Survey* (1896-1907), states, 'The South Wing of Dale Castle is part, if not the whole, of the original building. The lower part is vaulted: the floor above the vaulting is used as a stable, and the floor above as a corn loft and manservants' room. Probably the original building was a small oblong block of buildings. The North Wing was built by the late Mr. Lloyd-Philipps.'

An interesting feature is that during the Walter family ownership, a portrait of the sprightly Lucy Walter hung on the wall of the mansion, which came with possession of the succeeding owners, the Paynters, who, after selling Dale to the Allens, moved the portrait to Portclew (q.v.) where it still remained in the years 1896-1907.

Refs: RCAM Pembs., 1925; WWHR VI, pp. 174-5; *Dwnn,* i, p. 71; BM Egerton MS 1586, fo. 371; H. Owen, *Old Pembroke Families,* 1902; Francis Green, 'Walter of Roch Castle', WWHR V; Francis Jones 'Gelliswick and its Famillies', *Arch. Cam.,* 1980; Pembs RO, Deeds D/LP; Lewis, *TDW*, 1840.

DENANT, *Steynton*

A pleasant, well-preserved residence, with a farmhouse and outbuildings nearby. Some 300 yards eastwards from the house is Denant Rath, an ancient hill fort on a tree-clad mount. In 1392 William Malefant held three carucates at Denant by Knight's fee in service and suit of court. In 1535 it was owned by John Wogan; in 1580 the occupier was Richard Browne, yeoman; in 1613 the owner was John Barlow, of 'namely one carucate then held by Sir James Perrott and Thomas Butler, gent.' By 1658 it was the home of Patrick Couzens, gent. (brother of Thos. Couzens of Robeston Hall) and Alice his wife.

For some time in the 18th century the Packingtons of Westwood (Worcs.) owned the property, and in 1786 John Meyrick, Esq. owned Denant with F. Owens, and T. Miller as tenants; the Owens were there at the end of the century, one of whom, Mary Owen, married the Rev. Benjamin Davies, Baptist Minister of Molleston, who came to live at his wife's home at Denant; in 1833 Thomas Batine held Denant (525 acres) on a lease of lives; and a yearly rent of £240; by 1844 it had been bought by John Howarth Peel, who was followed by his son Xavier Peel; then came Herbert Fisher and John Thomas Fisher who held Denant jointly in 1894-1904. It is now owned and occupied by Mr. David George and his son.

Refs: Glam. RO, Deeds (late Cardiff Free Library); Val. Eccles; Picton Castle Deeds; Pembs RO, LT 1786; *RCAM Pembs.*, 1925.

DOLAU LLANERCH, *Clydey*

Now a farmhouse about a mile southwest of Clydey Church, near the hamlet of Star. Of the original mansion, said to have been built in the castellated style, nothing is now visible; it stood immediately south of the present farmhouse, near the present entrance. The old mansion is marked on Colby's Map 1831 as Dolau Llanerch, and also buildings where the present farmhouse stands, so that it appears that some remains were still there in 1831.

Fenton in 1811 says that 'not a vestige of the old mansion is left, a near farm-house having of later years sprung from its ruins.' Home of the Lloyds, said to descend from Cadifor Fawr of Blaen Cych, from *tempus* Henry VII until the late 17th century. Seventh in descent was Bridget Lloyd, heiress, who married Hugh Lloyd of Ffoshelig, Cards. Their eldest son Morgan Lloyd succeeded to Ffoshelig, and the younger son, Thomas Lloyd, to Dolau Llanerch. Thomas Lloyd was living there in 1738, and died about 1760 when his will was proved. The property eventually passed to Sarah Griffiths (grand-daughter of Hugh and Bridget Lloyd of Ffoshelig), and from them to kinsfolk, Jones, whose descendants Jones Lloyd of Lancych were the last owners of Dolau Llanerch, being still owned by Mr. Owen Jones Lloyd, D.L. of Abercych in 1972, Dolau Llanerch being then let to a farmer. In 1972 I examined the site of the old mansion of which no traces now remain.

Refs: GGMS; WWHR ii, p. 76; Chetham MS; Fenton, *Tour Pembs.*, 1811; NLW, Derwydd Deeds, No. 705, and Lancych Deeds.

DOLAU LLWYD(ION),
Llanfihangel Penbedw

Marked as 'Dolellwyddon' just south of Rhyd Howel and to the west of Wern ddofn (Penrith parish) on Colby's Map 1831. The first known owner was David Lloyd of Dole Llwyd, descended from the family of Cilgadfarch (vide supra) who traced to Cadifor Fawr. He had five sons and four daughters. The eldest son, Thomas Lloyd had an only son, Morgan Thomas. In the Clynfyw Deeds, (NLW), Dolau Llwyd traces back to 1589 when it appears as Place y ddol y Llwyd. In 1786 Dolellwydon was owned by Thomas Lewis Esq. with Sarah Lewis as tenant.

Refs: GGMS II Cadifor Fawr; Tithe Schedule and Map 1837; Ex Inf. Dr. D. B. Charles.

DOLEMAEN, *Mynachlogddu*

An ancient farmhouse, once centre of a small estate, northeast of Mynachlogddu village, and southwest of Pentre-galar, about half-way between them. It is high in the Preseli mountains, bounded on the east by Afon Cleddau, and on the north by Waun Cleddau. Little has been found about its early history. In 1786 the owner-occupier was Thomas John, gentleman. By 1840 he had died leaving his estate (655 acres) in the hands of trustees, with his widow Elizabeth John as tenant. By the beginning of the 20th century, the property was owned by Arthur Owen Evans and was advertised for sale on 25 June 1907 as 'the Dolemaen Estate' comprising nine farms, a slate quarry, about 630 acres, and rights of pasture over 2000 acres, all in Mynachlogddu parish, as follows – 1. Dolemaen farm (220 acres), 2. Portis-tô (89 acres), 3. Pwll y Crychydd (cottage and outbuildings, 9 acres), 4. Penddafedd farm (53 acres), 5. Llwyndrain farm (65 acres), 6. Pistyll têg (38 acres), 7. Mountain farm called Foel (64 acres), 8. Llwyneithin (25 acres), 9. Dolemaen Newydd, south of and adjoining Dolemaen (115 acres). It was a small but compact estate close to the main messuage which the sale map shows as a farmstead with six outbuildings, sheltered on the south side by trees, and to the north was a large pond.

Refs: Pembs. RO, LT 1786; Carms. RO, SC 633; NLW, Tithe Map 1840.

DOLPWLL, *Penrith*

A farmstead on the high slopes on the north of Frenni Fawr, and south of Penrith church. Marked on the maps of Mudge (1819) and Colby (1831). The home of Morris Morgan who died there in 1739. By his wife Frances Lewis (1666-1719) he had two children – Morris Morgan (1682-1763) who moved to Wernddofn, married, and had issue and Bridget Morgan (1689-1763) who married Richard Howell of Ffynnonfelen, Carms. whose grandson was Dr. John Howell M.D. of Tegafynyd in Llanfallteg parish in 1840. In 1786

'Dole Pooll' was owned by Rachel Morgan, with Hannah Thomas as tenant. In 1837 it was owned by Thomas Brightwell Esq. with Rachel Lewis as tenant, then comprising 235 acres. In 1894-1904 it was farmed by James Sandbrook, who had married Margaret daughter of John Griffith George of Cilast, she died in 1899, aged 70.

Refs: NLW, Croydon Deeds, Tithe Map 1837, LT 1786.

DRUIDSTON, *Nolton*

About a mile south of the village, on high ground above Druidston Haven: near the sea stands the 19th century residence of Druidston Villa. The name is derived from the surname Drue found in Pembrokeshire in the middle ages. In 1392 Walter Symond is described as 'of Drewyston'. George Roch, Esq. owner-occupier of 'Druson' in 1786 also owned four other tenements called West, South, North and East Druson. In 1859 Druidston Villa was advertised for sale, described as comprising, on the ground floor – dining and drawing rooms, and three best bedrooms, and on the upper floor six bedrooms; butler's pantry, W.C., kitchen, servants' hall, dairy and cellars, flower and kitchen walled gardens, pleasure grounds, stables, coach house and outbuildings, with a total of 101 acres. Lord Kensington used it as a residence.

Refs: PRO, Deeds, D, 2503, 2692; Sale Catalogue June 1859; LT 1786.

DRYSGOL GOCH, *Clydey*

A farmstead near Llwynydrain and the Pedran, a tributary of the Cych. Home of a minor gentry family in earlier days. Thomas ap David ap Howel of 'Trustlegoch' in Clydey, married Eve, daughter of John Mendes and had a daughter and heiress Elen who married John Thomas Lloyd of Clynfyw, descended from Jenkin Lloyd of Cemais. Their daughter Margaret married Morris Morgan of Coedllwyd. In 1786 the owner-occupier of Drisgol goch was George Bowen, gent.; in 1834 Zephaniah Bowen owned and occupied the property; in 1841 Daniel Bowen and in 1873 the owner-occupier was Thomas Bowen.

Refs: GGMS; College of Arms MS; Protheroe XII fo. 84; Manorowen MS. fo. 149; WWHR ii, p. 40; Colby Map 1831.

Tankard

DUDWELL, *Camrose*

A small cluster of farmsteads south of Dudwell Mountain; the most important being East and West Dudwell. A few references occur in medieval times; at his death in 1324 Aymer de Valence, Earl of Pembroke, owned lands in Dodowell; in 1419 a messuage and two carucates at West Dodewall was part of the manor of West Trangar (Trefgarn). The most important family here was that of Tancred who were at Dudwall in 1451, and by 1503 the family also owned Leweston.

The main pedigree of the Tancred family is recorded on page 128 of Dwnn's *Heraldic Visitations,* with subsidiary entries on pages 50, 194 and 195. It begins with William 'Tangard' Esq. of Dudwall and Lewelston, who was father of the David 'Tangred' who married Annes (Agnes) daughter and co-heiress of John Wolf of Leweston. David's holdings were increased on 22 January 1452 when one David John released to him a messuage, garden and three stangs in the township and fields of 'Luelleston; on 9 November 1468 when John Willy of Haverford granted him a messuage and half a carucate in 'Leweliston'. In these deeds he is described as David Tankard of Leweliston.

A deed in the National Library of Wales suggests that David Tancred had a sister, for we learn that on 21 March 1504, Philip Elliot of Bletherston in the barony of Llawhaden, granted lands in Bletherston to William Howell of Trawgarn Owen, (*'fabr'* – smith) and his wife Johanne daughter of William Tanckard, and the heirs of their body, and in default of issue, to Phillip Tanckard of Dodwell and Walter Tanckard of Lowelliston, and their heirs.

David Tancred predeceased his wife Annes (Wolfe). She died on 23 January 1502/03. David and Agnes were followed by their sons Phillip Tancred of Dudwell and Walter Tancred, heir of his mother, whose son John died apparently without issue.

Phillip Tancred of Dudwell married Annes (or Agnes) daughter and co-heiress of Peter Barrett of Filbeach in Marloes. Apparently

Dwnn was not wholly sure for he commented, 'I think Philip Tancred mared Anes dotyr off Peter Baret off Ffulbech'. But, as we shall see, Dwnn later included the arms of Barrett in the Tancred heraldic achievement, to which Agnes was entitled as co-heiress, and to which the Tancreds would not have become entitled unless they had a lineal descent from her.

Phillip Tancred was followed by his son Watkin who married Joan, daughter and co-heiress of Piers Elliott of Hook (perhaps the place of that name in Ambleston or else in Freystrop). Watkin had two children, John Tancred, and Margery who married William Phillips of Stone Hall.

John Tancred married Jane daughter of John Philipps of Picton Castle by a concubine. According to Dwnn (i, p. 128) she was one Agnes Moel, while Chetham MS calls her Jane daughter of John de Langridge.

In 1554 John Tankard and his son Owen, both described as of Lueston were engaged in an transaction, probably relating to a lease, with one William Thomas Phillip of Mountain Cott in Camrose parish. Not long after this, the Dudwell property reverted to the Leweston branch, doubtless due to the death without issue of Walter Tancred's son John. John Tancred and Jane his wife had four children: Owen; Richard, dead by 1591; Maud – married Harry Price 'of Gyldewell', and also was dead by 1591; Anne – dead by 1591.

In October 1565 Owen Tanckard sued Marcus ap Owen (Bowen) of Camrose for uttering the fully false and scandalous words, 'Owen Tanckard is a noughtie person, a thyffe, and a robber of men's houses', (Pembs. Plea Rolls). Owen Tancred married Maud daughter of Henry Scourfield of The Moat in the parish of New Moat by his wife Etheldred Butler of Trecadwgan near Solva, the marriage had taken place before 1553. However, he never succeeded to the paternal estate for he died during his father's lifetime. Owen and Maud had the following issue: William, Phillip – married Elen daughter of John Bolton, son of Bolton of Harmeston in Steynton. He is not included in Dwnn's pedigree, but both he and his wife appear in the *GGMS;* Anne – married Ieuan ab Ieuan ap David; Anne – the younger, living in 1591; Janet – married Rees Jenkin, vicar of Llawhaden. Dwnn enters her as *daughter* not sister of *William* Tancred.

William Tancred succeeded his grandfather to the Leweston and Dudwell estates. According to a survey of the lordship of Haverford, taken in 1577, William Tancred held the capital messuage of Lewelston and 3½ carucates of land of the said lordship by services and a yearly rent of 6 pence payable at Michaelmas. He married Elen Batho, daughter of John Batho, son of David Batho, by Joan daughter of John Alein. The marriage took place before 1581, for in that year William Tankard of Dudwal and Luelston, and Elen his wife, sold lands in Luelston to Morris Canon of Haverfordwest.

On 18 November 1591 Lewis Dwnn called on William who provided genealogical information to enable his family tree to be recorded, and paid the deputy herald three shillings for the work. Dwnn recorded his client's heraldic achievements, as a shield of four quarters – 1. '*Yr hen Tangard yw*' (it is the old Tankard *(gules* a chevron between three escallops on *argent*); 2. '3 *weff kochion*' (3 wolves *gules*); 3. Eliot on *argent* a fess *gules* between four barulets wavy on *azure;* 4. This would be as 1.

The name William Tankard, gentleman of Camrose parish (or his son of that name), appears in the Muster Roll for 1613.

William Tancred had the following children: Griffith – alive in 1591, who died evidently without issue in his father's lifetime; William, Morgan – of Camrose parish, who is listed in the Muster Roll of 1613; Harry and Jane Tankard – both living in 1591.

William Tankard, the second son, succeeded to the estate. By this time Leweston had been sold, for hereafter the family is described as of Dudwell. He married Elizabeth elder daughter of Thomas Jones of Harmeston, by Elinor Wogan of Wiston, descended from a younger brother of Sir Rhys ap Thomas K.G. Thomas Jones had served as High Sheriff of the county of Pembrokeshire in 1589. William died before 1657, for in that year the widow was sued in the Court of the Great Sessions for an unpaid bill by a Haverfordwest mercer. The will of Elizabeth Tankard of Dudwell, widow, dated 8 July 1661, was proved at Carmarthen, the inventory of her goods being compiled on 25 September following. She desired to be buried in Camrose Church.

William and Elizabeth had six children: Griffith, John, Hugh, Frances and another unknown child. Mary, married before 1661, to a Mr. Morgan; and secondly, Walter Warlow of Dudwell, and had seven sons and one daughter. The husband's will was proved in 1689.

Griffith Tankard married his second cousin Mary, daughter of Thomas Haward of Fletherhill by Cecilia Butler his wife. The prenuptial settlement made on 1 January 1652/53, included among the lands settled Harmeston and Harmeston mill which his widowed mother settled on him.

Mrs. Mary Tankard's aunt, Frances Haward, had married Robert Birt of Llwyndyrus, Cardiganshire, by whom she had a son, Richard Birt. Mary took an interest in her little cousin and suggested to Mrs. Birt, that he be sent to be educated at the house of the Rev. John Price, vicar of Fishguard, who enjoyed a high reputation for scholarship. On 25 November 1649, Mary (being then unmarried), entered into an arrangement with the vicar for boarding, lodging and educating the boy, at a fee of £6 a year. After he had been there for two years and a half, the vicar wrote pointing out that the agreed fees had not been paid, and asked her to remit the sum of £15. By this time Mary had married, so that her husband had now become responsible for her liabilities. As no payment was forthcoming, the vicar had no option but to sue Mary and Griffith Tankard for the amount.

Griffith Tankard seems to have been unlucky or improvident, for far from being unable or unwilling to pay his wife's debts, he could barely cope with his own. He was being constantly sued for sums of money in the Great Sessions. Griffith Tancred was clearly on the downward path. In order to provide for his son James, he entered into an arrangement with his brother-in-law James Haward, who later had difficulty in enforcing the agreed terms. On 5 December 1654 Griffith mortgaged Easter Dudwell in the sum of £60 to Thomas Phillips of Trelewelyn, and on 23 July 1663 encumbered that property with a further mortgage in £150. The mortgage remained on the property. Matters worsened, and finally Griffith Tancred fled to Ireland to evade creditors who were baying at his heels.

On 22 April 1687, the mortgage on Easter Dudwell was assigned by John and James Tankard, to Rees Jones of St. Paul's, Covent Garden, merchant tailor. By 1691 Susanna Bowen of St. Andrew's, Holborn, spinster, had acquired a right of £100 on the property and this she assigned on 14 November of that year to Sir William Wogan, Sergeant at law.

James Tankard, only child of the defaulting Griffith, does not appear to have redeemed the encumbered estate to which he was heir, and some time after 1685 he left London and settled in Haverfordwest. His wife's name was Mary Taunton, probably a daughter of Robert Taunton of Haverfordwest.

In 1698 James Tankard died intestate at Haverfordwest, and on September 27 of that year, administration of his goods was granted to his widow. James Tancred and Mary had an only child, John Tankard of whom nothing further is known.

A sister of Griffith Tancred the galloping debtor, married a yeoman, Walter Warlow who came to live at Dudwall and was assessed at two hearths in 1670. His will, dated 1689, shows that he held a lease of Wester Dydwall which he left to his son Walter Warlow, who died intestate in 1700. The Tancred arms were *gules* a chevron *argent* between three escallop shells of the second. Another family there in late medieval days was that of Barrett who were there for four generations, the last being Peter Barrett who left two daughters, co-heiresses, one of whom, Anne, married Philip Tancred, gent., 'of Dowdwell'. In the 18th century several changes took place. In 1786 East Dudwall was owned by the Haverfordwest Corporation, with James Harries as tenant, and two messuages both called West Dudwall were owned and occupied by John Morse, gent., and Miss Mary Davies. In later times the properties were sold to local farmers.

Refs: Dwnn, i, pp. 71, 128; Pembs RO, Deeds DG/ 13, No. 95, LT 1786; Francis Jones essay, 'Tancred of Dudwell and Leweston'.

DUMPLEDALE *see* ASHDALE

DYFFRYN, *Lampeter Velfrey*★

This was the home of the Thomas and Philipps families. In the Will of William Thomas of Dyffryn, Lampeter Velfrey, gent. dated 26 December 1734 and proved at Carmarthen on 12 August 1738, he left Dyffryn and Cwm Llan 'to my friend Miss Lettice Rees who now lives with me and who is grand-daughter of my last wife, for one year. Then to my godson, John Philipps, youngest son of my cousin, Thomas Philipps of Lampeter Velfrey, and also all my realty in Lampeter Velfrey and Llanddewi Velfrey. Grace Philipps of Tenby, widow by her will proved 21 February 1798 left £10 to 'my friend Mrs. Jane Philipps of Dyffryn for mourning'. In 1779 Rev. Edward Philipps, rector of Lampter Velfrey, and Catherine his wife, mortgaged Dyffryn to John Mathias of Llangwarren for £400 which they increased to £600 in 1780. In 1798 Thomas Philipps, gent, of Dyffryn sold part of his estate to Nathaniel Phillips of Slebech for £1,000, and in 1805 the remainder of the estate in Lampeter Velfrey was sold to Slebech for £4000. The Voters Lists for 1894 show Catherine and Anne Thomas as tenants of Dyffryn. The house was put up for sale in 1913 but no details are given.

Refs: SC 453, Carms RO; Slebech Deeds 440, 443.

DYFFRYN FFILBRO, *Mynachlogddu*

An abandoned farmstead southwest from Mynachlogddu village; in a little grove on the edge of a windswept moorland; below the homestead flows a tributary of the Glandy brook. It was untenanted when I visited in in 1976. Marked on Eman. Bowen's map 1760, as 'Duffrin Fwlbrocke, Lewis Esq.'; on Kitchin's map 1763 as 'Dyffryn Fwlbrook Lewis, Esq.', as 'Dyffrynfullbrook' on Mudge's Map 1819, and as 'Dyffryn Filbro' on Colby's Map 1831. In 1786 the owner-occupier was Stephen Griffith, and also Edward Price, gent. owner, and John Griffith tenant. In 1783 the owner of 'Dyffryn Fulbrook otherwise called Tredwdwr' was Griffith Gwynne, gent. of Cilciffeth. In his will dated 1823, the Revd. John Foley, Vicar of Maenclochog, bequeathed the farm of 'Blaendyffryn Fullbrook alias Tredwdwr' to his five younger children. In 1834 the owner was Nathaniel Rowland of Parke, Henllan Amgoed, Carms. with Edward Owen as tenant.

Refs: NLW, Tithe Schedule 1840, shows a cruciform farmhouse, Trenewydd Deeds, No. 173.

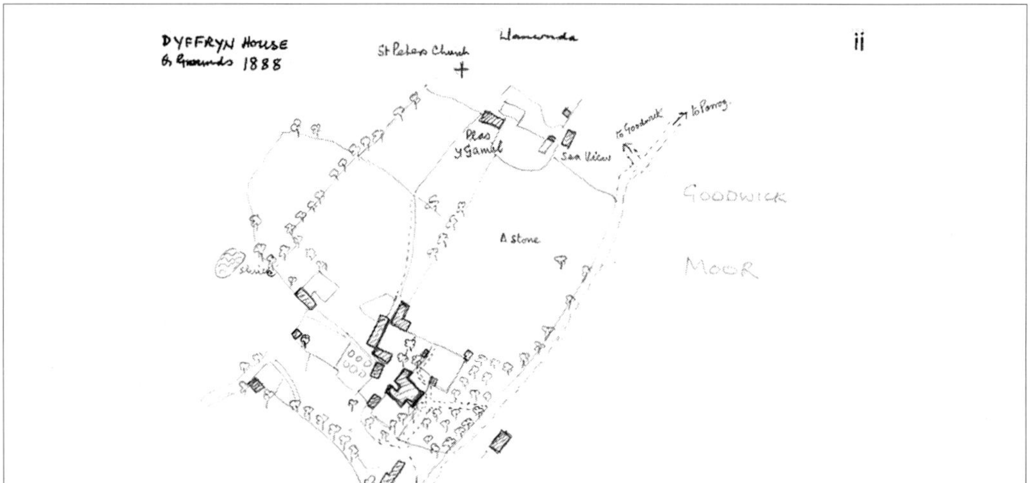

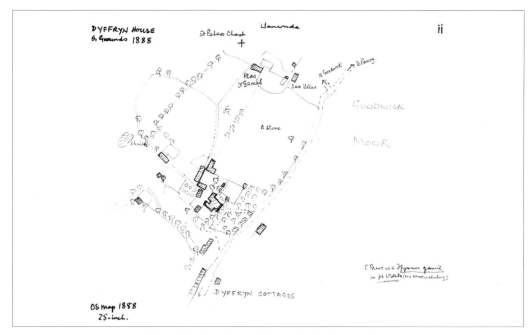

Map of Dyffryn House, Llanwnda, by Francis Jones

DYFFRYN PIBYLL, *Cilrhedyn**

In 1728 Dyffryn Pibith figures in the transfer of a mortgage by David Edwardes of Rhydygarn to Erasmus Lewis of Abercastle. In 1780 Rev. Benjamin Evans, vicar of Cilrhedyn, devised Dyffryn Pibyll to the use of his nephew, John Lewis, son of Philip Lewis of Trehendre, Pembs. and his heirs. The Revd. Benjamin Lewis, MA., J.P., vicar of Cilrhedyn from 1824 until his death in 1855, was the son of this John Lewis. In the Tithe Schedule of 1841, the Rev. Benjamin Lewis owned and occupied Dyffryn Pibyll and Llancwm; when he died he was described as of Wyke House, Brentford, Essex, late of Dyffryn. John Lewis was owner-occupier assessed at £1 13s. 10d. in Land Tax in 1786. In 1894 Benjamin Davies lived there, and by 1904 Howell Evans owned the freehold house and land. Francis Jones visited the house in 1968 and described it as 'an interesting old gentry house, some English folk then living there'.

DYFFRYN WDIG, *Llanwnda*

Now in the township of Goodwick (Wdig). Much of the old mansion has survived despite the fact that it had been used as a farmhouse. The 25 inch OS map made in 1888 shows a large house set among trees and orchards with an uninterrupted view of the sea over large sloping meadows; the outbuildings stood a little northwards, and are today mostly ruinous. About 1900 with the coming of the Great Western Railway, and the transformation of the coastal strip into Fishguard Harbour, the modern Goodwick came into being and the pleasant seaward meadows were built over by modern houses such as Plâs y Gamil Road and St. Davids Place, while a railway line was built through the orchard close to the house. Nevertheless, Dyffryn House as it is now called, is still pleasantly situated in well-tended grounds, although its seaward view has been disrupted by the modern buildings.

During my younger days I spoke to numerous people who remembered it before 1900. My younger brother having married the coheiress, lived in the house till his death in 1990. For several centuries the capital messuage of Dyffryn Wdig and its estate remained in one family. This was that of the Davies family who

were there in 1624 and who intermarried with local gentry families. In 1715 Thomas Davies J.P. was High Sheriff, and not only was he the first to hold that office, but he is the only man in the parish ever to have held it. The last male member of the house, Thomas Davies, J.P. died without issue in 1747, and the estate, consisting of 24 properties and 1010 acres, passed to his sisters, two of whom married sons of the Colby family who became owners of Dyffryn Wdig and most of the estate. The main seat of the Colbys was at Ffynnone, and Dyffryn Wdig was let to a succession of farming tenants, and finally sold in the late 19th century.

Refs: Pembs RO, LT 1786, Deeds, No. D/RT; NLW, Spence-Colby Deeds, Cwrtmawr Deeds, Papers of GS.

EAREWERE,
Amroth, vide Amroth Castle *supra*

EAST HOOK, *Llangwm*

There are three farms in the north of the parish, near the banks of the western Cleddau, viz. East-, West-, and Lower-Hook, all being houses of minor gentry, the most important being East Hook. In 1548 Richard Eynon is described as 'of East Hook, yeoman'; in 1599 Owen Jordan, gent., lived there, and in 1614 his executor Richard Hicks, yeoman, who in 1634 was concerned in sharing one-half of East Hook with John Hicks, gent. By 1656 Richard Eynon, gent., was owner-occupier, and in 1669 it was held by John Jones of East Hook gent. Mary, daughter of Owen Hicks, married the said John Jones who was a son of William Jones, a wealthy landowner of Bonville's Court, near

Saundersfoot. During the 18th century the owner-occupier was Richard Knethell, Esq. who was there in 1786.

Refs: Haverfordwest Corpn. Deeds; NLW, Papers of GS, Pembs Plea Rolls; GGMS I Gwynfardd, fo. 15.

EAST JORDANSTON, *St. Florence*

About half a mile northwest of St. Florence village, while another farm called West Jordanston is a little farther to the west. I visited this interesting old house on 22 September 1977, being then empty and owned by the Dyfed County Council who were advertising it for sale. It consisted of two storeys and an attic storey, with large rooms, and at the rear of the house – opposite the entrance – is a projection containing a staircase rising to attic height; there was also a wing to the rear. The entrance porch with stone arch consisted of two storeys. Inside the house were several corbels which had once supported the ceiling beams. The style suggests it to have been either Elizabethan or Jacobean in origin. Dr. Charles cites reference to it in 1331, 1376, 1480 etc. In the 17th century it formed part of the Barlow estate. Anne Barlow, daughter of John Barlow, married firstly Nicholas Lewis of Hean Castle, who died without issue, and secondly, in 1663, Lewis Wogan of Wiston. The marriage settlement made on 1 September 1663, mentions 'the manor, mansion, and lanes called Jordanston in the parish of St. Florence'. In 1786 both East and West Jordanston were owned by John Campbell Hooke (of the Stackpole family). About the year 1820, East Jordanston was bought by the tenant George Locke, and in 1873 another of the family, George Locke owned the property and its 244 acres. Afterwards it was bought by Benjamin J. Edwards who sold it to the Pembrokeshire County Council in 1918. It is still used as a farmhouse but the land, some 200 acres, was divided into three smallholdings. The farmhouse was described in 1977 as follows; porch, hall, four reception rooms, two kitchens, dairy, store-room, seven bedrooms, two attic rooms, with stone built outbuildings.

Refs: WWHR vi, p. 219; LT 1786; Landowners' Returns 1873; B. G. Charles, *NCPN,* p. 21, see *Western Mail* 17 and 27 September 1977, illusts.

EAST MOOR, *Manorbier*

To the west of Manorbier village, near the coast, above Swanlake Bay. East Moor was the home of the Lorts in the 17th century; near it is another farmstead called West Moor. Sampson Lort, second son of Henry Lort of Stackpole Court, established himself at East Moor. Like his father he served on both sides during the Civil War. His first wife Olive was a daughter of Sir John Philipps of Picton. She died in 1637, and four years later Sampson married Lettice, daughter of Thomas ap Rhys of Rickeston (Brawdy) and Scotsborough. He was High Sheriff in 1650, and died in 1667. His only son, Thomas Lort succeeded to East Moor; he married Elizabeth White of Henllan, but died without issue. A few references have been found to East Moor. In 1670 Thomas Lort was assessed at seven hearths, indicating it to have been a commodious residence.

An inventory of the possessions of Thomas, compiled in 1687 mentions the following rooms in East Moor – hall, the little room within the hall, the little parlour, chamber over the outward kitchen, 'another little room', closet, little room over the entry, chamber over the kitchen, closed within the said chamber, buttery, kitchen, outer kitchen, larder, dairy, and outhouses.

Over a hundred years later, Fenton wrote in 1811 – 'Turn to the left to see Moor, one of the chief mansions of this district about two hundred years ago, of a very irregular form with many ruinous and extensive outbuildings, once entered by a gateway now stopped up, leading to a porter's lodge. With very few exceptions, this may serve as a model of the style of building their houses among the great of that era in this country which invariably appears to have been surrounded by a high court-wall having a large arched gateway, and essentially differing from the form of the principal houses of the same date, in the upper part of the country . . . '.

Commissioners of Ancient Monuments who visited the site in 1923 state that in the farmyard to the West of the modern house, were the ruins of a small E-shaped two-storeyed dwelling house 'of no architectural importance'; in its original state it may have consisted of a hall, with North and South wings, and central porch, but most of the features had disappeared leaving only the hall which had been altered almost out of recognition. After the departure of the Lorts the house changed ownership several times. The Land Tax of 1786 names four messuages, each called East Moor, as follows: (1) Sir Hugh Owen, owner, Peter Gwyther tenant, assessed at £3 18s. 0d.; (2) Peter Gwyther, owner-occupier, assessed at 7s. 5d; (3) Thomas Voyle, owner, Peter Gwyther tenant, assessed at 14s.; (4) George Leach, owner, Peter Gwyther, tenant, assessed at 14s. 6d. From this it seems that the dwelling of the Lorts was No. 1. The *Pembrokeshire Archaeological Survey* (1896-1907) states that in the farmyard of East Moor is an ancient house now used for farm buildings, probably the dwelling of Sampson Lort.

Refs: Fenton, *Tour Pembs,* 1811; *RCAM Pembs.*,1925; LT 1786; Francis Jones essay, 'Lort of Eastmoor'.

Meares

EASTINGTON,

Rhoscrowther

Just over a quarter of a mile northwest of Rhoscrowther village, near the shores of Angle Bay. Today it is bounded by the extensive installations of Texaco Oil Company who also own the buildings and land of Eastington. During medieval times it was a home of the powerful family of Perrot who owned it till the end of the 16th century. In the 17th century, for a brief time, home of Hugh Philipps (d. 1652) younger son of Sir John Philipps of Picton Castle by Anne daughter of Sir John Perrot of Haroldston, and was followed at Eastington by William Meares who was assessed at five hearths in 1670. William, High Sheriff in 1673, died in 1687 and was followed by five generations of his descendants. Finally, John Meares tells us that Eastington had 'fallen to decay and was unfit for habitation', so he bought the Bank Farm estate, Kingston-on-Thames where he died in 1814; his son, John Meares inherited Plâs Llanstephan in 1833, and in 1842 he sold Eastington to Common Serjeant Mirehouse of Angle. It was then let to various tenants.

The later stage in the house's history is depressing. T. F. Holwell had an interest in the place, and on 12 April 1769 he wrote to the

attorney, Richard Knethell of Haverfordwest, as follows – 'Sir. I have been to view the premises at Eastington and find them in such a ruinous state that no tenant can possibly enter them in the condition they are, nor engage to keep them in tenantable repair, unless they are previously put into that necessary state. Therefore I beg leave to point out to you what must be absolutely done to make it habitable. The breach in the garden wall of the orchard and the fence of the south court to be made good. The roof of the house which leaks in one place to be tiled and secured; a large breach in the ceiling of what they call the lumber room, another in the ceiling of the back-kitchen, and another through the floor of the south-west bedchamber, two pairs of stairs where a plank is wanting, and a hole in the ceiling under it to be repaired. The panels in the wainscotting of the dining room are in general loose and falling out, as well as some in the parlour, and both these rooms ought to have at least one coat of paint as well the windows, and the panels secured, and as we are content to become tenants a quarter before the premises are in shape habitable, I will not doubt but you will be so obliging as to order the above absolutely necessary repairs to be done forthwith, as I expect my friend and his lady down the latter end of next week.'

Knethell acted immediately, and on 13th April a mason and two carpenters examined the edifice, and reported that the great part of rafters and laths in the north side of the roof were decayed and ruinous; all other parts of the roof required being pointed with lime mortar; to put this in order would cost £25. They also reported that several beams, the rafters and joints in the roof, and lofts in some of the bed-chambers were ruinous and in danger of tumbling down unless speedily repaired: also, the wooden railing before the court was quite rotten and fallen, and must be entirely new-built; this would cost £45. By November 1769 the repairs had been effected.

The next part of the tale is given by Fenton in 1811 – 'Jestington or as it is commonly called Iseston, for many years the residence of the family of Meares, now property of John Meares Esq . . . It seems to have been once castellated, though very little of the original building exists, but that little clearly proves it to have been of a form to entitle it to the name of Castle. The Perrots for some centuries continued to inhabit it till their union with Haroldston, near Haverfordwest, when they appear to have abandoned this venerable residence on the haven.' A detailed description of the house appears in *Arch. Cam.* 1868, pp. 79-80, where it is dated 'temp Edward II', adding that 'The modern house of the Meares, recently removed, abutted on the western wall of the main building, and a farmhouse stands at present on the other side.'

H. Thornhill Timmins describes it more explicitly in 1895 – 'This quaint old homestead of Eastington . . . is honeycombed with curious nooks and corners . . . crooked passages, and crumbling stairways. The long south front with its homely porch and small paned windows, is flanked at its western end by a massive medieval structure whose rough, lichen-clad walls are pierced with narrow, deep-set windows, and topped by ruinous battlements . . . By a rude steep flight of grass-grown steps we mount to a clumsy door . . . we push our way into the interior . . . a large and lofty chamber, whose solid concrete floor is prettily marked with lines traced in simple geometrical patterns. Rudely-arched windows admit light at either end, one of them having cusped openings; while a ruined fireplace yawns in the centre of the opposite wall. A small vaulted cell opens from one end of this room, and a narrow stair which has a gangway all around and is pierced with loopholes for defence. The dark vaulted basement of this ancient fabric forms a capital dairy . . .' The *RCAM Pembs.*, 1925, describes it as a small ruined manor house of the peel-tower type, probably of the 15th century, now used as a farmhouse; it has a plain vaulted undercroft with two apartments above, to which access is by an exterior flight of steps. From the longer of the two rooms, a short newel stairway leads to the summit of a low lantern or beacon tower; around the roof runs a corbel table and parapet; the windows have been modernized . . . '.

Refs: Fenton, *Tour Pembs.,* 1811, pp. 218-220; *Arch. Camb.,* 1868, pp. 79-80, illust., June 1977, p. 175; Laws, *Little England*, 1888, p. 207, illust;. Timmins, *Nooks Pembs.,* 1895, pp. 85-6, illust.; *Pembs. Arch. Survey* 1897-1907; M. B. Mirehouse, South Pembs. 1910, p. 47; H. Owen, *Old Pembroke Families,* 1902, p. 52; *RCAM Pembs.*, 1925; *Journal Brit. Arch. Assn.* XLI, p. 82; *Dwnn,* i, p. 89; *Pembrokeshire Magazine,* March 1983, illust.; *Western Mail* 16 and 28 April 1983, illust.; *Carms. Studies,* 1974, p. 50, fig. 6; P. Smith, *Houses of the Welsh Countryside,* 1975, pp. 30, 31, 339, 373; Mr. T. Strickland (descended from the Meares family).

Howell

EASTLAKE, *Amroth*

Now a farmstead to the northeast of Amroth Castle. It is called locally, Islick. During the 17th-18th centuries it was the home of the Howell family whose arms were: *sable* a lion rampant regardant *argent.* John Howell of Eastlake died in 1688 leaving his wife *enciente;* the posthumous child, John Howell Esq. lived there till he died in his 91st year in 1778. The next owner was Edmund Probin, Esq. who let the property to Zacharias Rogers.

EASTWOOD,

one mile south of the town of Narberth

Home of the Hassall family, land agents, built towards the end of the 18th century. The house was advertised for sale in 1810 and described as comprising two parlours, vestibule, three principal bed chambers with dressing room and store room, two garret bed chambers, two other garret bed chambers, three lodging rooms for servants, two kitchens, butler's pantry, larder, water closet, cellars, granary, stable for five horses, gardens and grounds. Charles Hassall of Eastwood died in 1814, aged 60. It then became the home of Sir Henry Mannix, Bt., who died at his seat, Eastwood, in 1822, aged 83. The house is marked on the maps of Mudge, 1819 and Colby, 1831.

ESGAIR, *St. Dogmaels*

Also called Esgyrn. A farm near Ceippyn, northwest of Hendre. Home of a branch of Lloyd of Trefigin (an offshoot of Lloyd of Hendre). George Lloyd of Esgair died some time before 1714 and he was followed by his younger son Evan Lloyd who was living at Esgair in 1733. By 1786 Esgair was owned by William Rowlands, gent. with Lettice Llewelin as tenant. The property was divided into two farms. In 1834 John and Thomas Llewellyn were owner-occupiers of the farms of Esgyrn-fawr and-fach: in 1894 George Llewelyn lived at Esgyrn fawr, and Levi George at Esgyrn fach.

ESGAIR WILYM, *Eglwyswrw*

Thomas ap Rees of Esgair Wilym was followed there by his son Rees ap Thomas who married Anne daughter of Howell ap Owen of Court (descended from the Cantingtons). Rees died in 1560, his wife Anne in 1590. Their daughter and co-heiress Elizabeth (d. 1621) married William Griffith of Penybenglog, Meline (died 1618), whose son and heir was the antiquary George William Griffith. Between 1579 and 1597 George Owen of Henllys bought lands at Esker and in 1594 the following free tenants held land at Esker Wilêm – Rhydderch Jenkin ap Rees, William Griffith of Penybenglog, gent. and Llewellin Morris. In 1786 there were three farms there – Ysgarwilim Issa owned by Thomas Lloyd Esq. (of Henllys and Bronwydd), Ysgarwilim Ucha by William Jones Esq. (of Llether, Brawdy) and Ysgar Ganol by John Lloyd, gent. (of Fagwrgoch in Llantood).

Refs: College of Arms MSS, Wagner MS 12, and Protheroe MS XII (both by G. W. Griffith; NLW, Llanstephan MS 101B, fo. 66-7; GGMS; Bronwydd Deeds.

EWESTON (TREWEN), *Brawdy*

About threequarters of a mile to the east of Brawdy church, are two adjoining farms of this name, neither retaining any early architectural features. Eweston is marked as a knight's fee on Rees' 14th century map. Several references occur to the manorial lords who either held the manor in its entirety or in part. In 1287 William Hu of Owenynstonne granted four messuages, two carucates and half a carucate at Oweynstonne, and a messuage and two bovates in nearby Knareston, to John Howel of Woodstock, absolutely. Some time later John Cole was lord of the manor. In 1326 William de Rufe held half of the fee, and in 1517 Sir John Wogan of Wiston owned one fourth of certain messuages in Owenston; and in 1581 the manor of 'Owenstone alias Routhditch' was held by the following lords, – Corbett, Henry Longueville, and Morris Wogan of Stone Hall, and the family of Wogan of Stone Hall continued to own part of the manor of Yeweston in 1631. The ownership of the manor of 'Yeweston alias Rowditch' in Brawdy parish, passed by marriage from the Wogans to the family of Ford who settled at Stone Hall and were the owners in the years 1689-1712. The manorial status seems to have lapsed afterwards, and in 1786 the two properties at Eweston were owned by John Laugharne, with William Hooper and John Thomas as tenants. A doctor, John Thomas J.P., lived at Eweston, apparently having an aversion to paying taxes, for when Levi Griffith the Collector and Receiver of Taxes for the parish, called at Eweston on 8 August 1816, 'Mr. Thomas did beat, wound, and illtreat him so that his life was greatly despaired of'. In 1845 both the Eweston farms were owned by a less belligerent person, Mr. George Roch of Llether, the tenants being Stephen Hooper and James Phillips.

Refs: Journal Hist. Soc. of Church in Wales, 1969, pp. 25-7, and refs. there; Tithe Map Brawdy parish, 1845.

FAGWR EYNON FAWR, *Moylgrove*★

Home to the Phillips family. William Phillips (d. 1744), of Fagwr Eynon Fawr, gent., post nuptial settlement dated May 1738, married Anne, daughter of William Garnon of Cilgerran, parish and later of Trerees. This William Phillips was later of Penralltreiny (q.v.). Anne his wife married secondly, John Devonald gent. of Moylgrove some time before 1752. Mrs. Devonald was owner of Fagwr Eynon with Jane Philip, tenant assessed at 7s 8d in the Land Tax of 1786.

William and Anne Phillips had issue, William Phillips of Penralltreiny their son, in his will dated in 1802 left Vagwr Einon to his son, John Phillips.

FAGWR GOCH, *Llantood*★

Situated one mile northwest of Llantood church near the border with Monington just north of Glanrhyd. Home of the Lloyd family from the 16th to the 19th centuries. In 1760 John Lloyd of Vagwr goch was a Parliamentary voter. He was still alive in 1785/6 when he was assessed at 7s. 9d. in land tax, and had, by an unknown wife, a daughter Joan who married John Lloyd of Trefigin, a cadet line of Cwmgloyn. They had three children, William of Trefigin, gent. imprisoned in Haverfordwest goal in 1801 for debt, John of Fagwrgoch viv. in 1801 and a daughter, Frances.

In 1586 Owen Lloyd of Fagwrgoch, gent. had sued David ap Rees of Trefriffeth for trespass and depasturing in Moelgrove manorial court on lands at Keven Llech y drybedd and Pwll y Kregin and Keven Treryffith. This may have been the Owen Lloyd shown on an undated pedigree as the son of Thomas Lloyd and Jane, daughter of Owen Picton by Janet, verch Rees David Howel who traced to Jenkin Lloyd of Cemais. Owen Lloyd married 'Barnel' Powell of Cardigan.

The 1894 Voters' Lists show William Edwards of Fagwrgoch.

Refs: Pembs. Plea Rolls No. 70; Egerton MS 2586, fo. 323.

FARTHING'S HOOK (CLYNFFYRDDIN), *Henry's Moat*

A farmstead about half a mile southeast of Henry's Moat, and near Afon Syfanwy which enters the northern end of Llysyfran Reservoir. In 1462 the Rev. John Elliot granted lands in Verthinge Shoke, Woodstock and Scollock to John Perrot, son of Sir Thomas Perrot. In 1485 Verthyngeshoke was the home of Thomas Yryss and Margaret his wife, as tenants. The property remained in Perrot hands until 1548 when Rees Perrot granted Farthinshock to Morgan ap William Lloyd of Llanstinan, yeoman. From 1590 to 1607 it was home of Edward ap John 'of Klynffyrdhin' who had married Margaret daughter of Henry David of Llanstinan. By 1621 it was owned by William Scourfield of New Moat who also owned the fulling and corn mills attached to the property. About 1627 he sold Farthingshook, its land and mills to Thomas Vaughan, a son of Pontfaen, who then settled there. In 1670 it was assessed at four hearths.

It remained in Thomas Vaughan's direct descendants who were there until 1696 when John Vaughan inherited Trecwn estate from his cousins and went to live at the mansion of Trecwn, and let Farthingshook to the Harding family in 1708. They then consisted of three brothers; John Harding, an attorney whose will was proved 25 January 1727/8 who had been a tenant since c.1700; and had married Mary, an unknown wife by whom he had four daughters, Grace, Elizabeth, Jane who married Lewis Protheroe of Egremont, and Mary who married William Jones of Llether. The second brother, David was viv. 1733 and the third brother was Richard Harding who was of Trevaccoon (q.v.) by 1728 and married Grace, the daughter of William Propert.

The Vaughans continued at Trecwn until the death of Admiral John Vaughan. It continued in the Barham descendants until 1939 when the estate was advertised for sale, including Farthingshook, then a farm of 293 acres. The property had continued in Vaughans and their descendants for over 300 years.

Refs: NLW, Coleman Deeds, Poyston Deeds, Bronwydd Deeds; WWHR, ii, pp. 93, 152; GGMS; PRO Anc. Deeds; Francis Jones, 'Trecwn' (unpubl. essay).

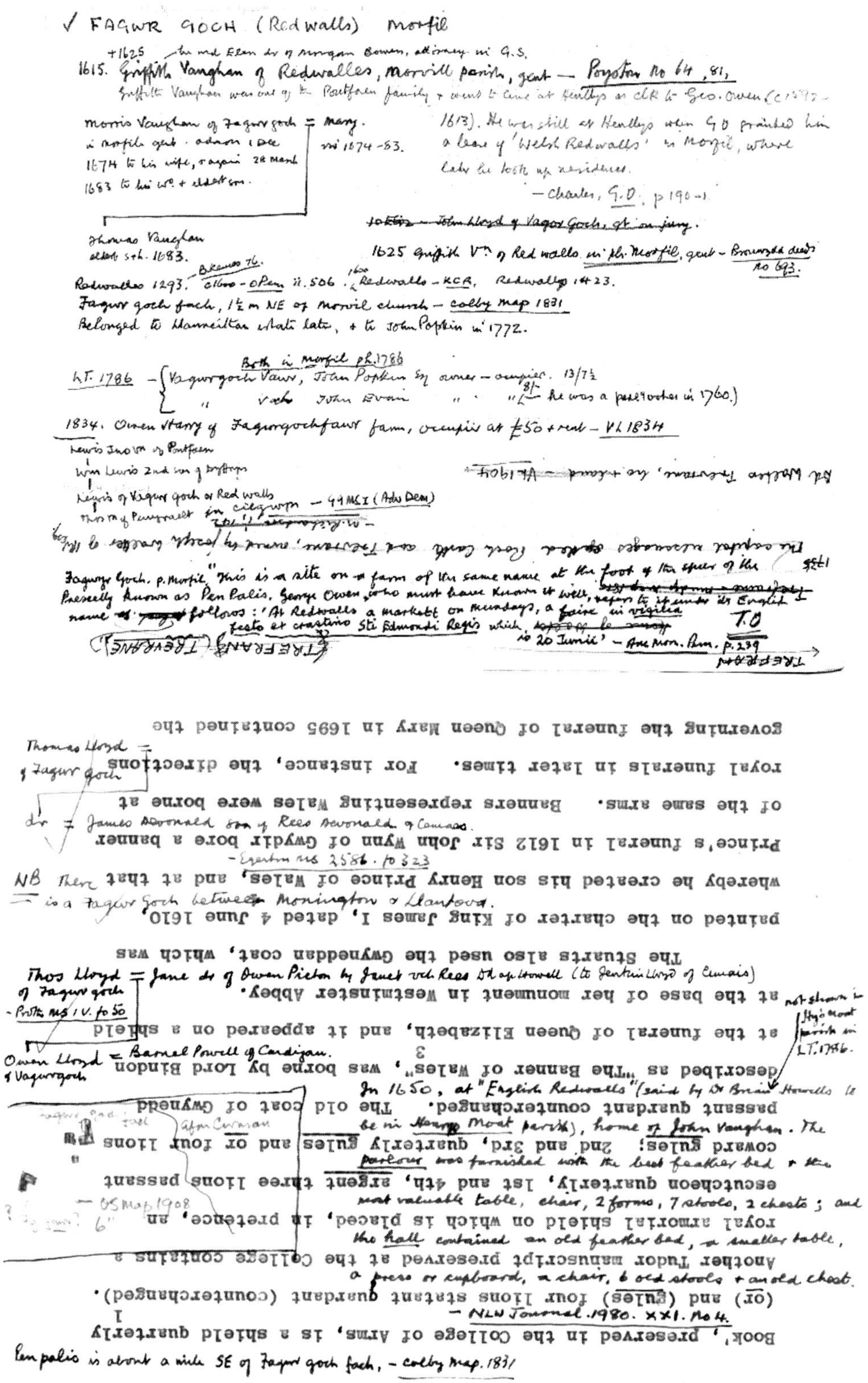
✓ FAGWR GOCH (Redwalls) Morfil

1615. Griffith Vaughan of Redwalles, Morvill parish, gent — Poyston No 64, 81,

1625 Griffith V[n] of Red walls in ph. Morfil, gent — Bronwydd deeds No 693.

Fagwr goch fach, 1½ m NE of Morvil church — Colby map 1831

Belonged to Llanreithan estate later, & to John Popkin in 1772.

1834. Owen Harry of Fagwrgochfawr farm, occupier at £50 + rent — VL 1834

NB There is a Fagwr Goch between Monington & Llantood.

Pen palis is about a mile SE of Fagwr goch fach, — Colby Map. 1831

Original notes made by Francis Jones when researching Fagwr Goch

FELINDRE, *Llanwnda**

Felindre was a Knight's fee (Welsh) in 1326. The Bishop of St. Davids estates included some fields at Felindre, one of which was called Park Vair Edward. In 1318 Gruffydd ap Ieuan mortgaged land in the holding of Llanwaran and Melyndreve at Penkayr in 8 marks for eight years, and later, in 1549 John Butler of Cokekendlas, gent. leased five acres of arable at Lyndre for 60 years at 2s. p.a. to Morris Thomas of Treffvarchoke in Dewisland. By 1623 Felindre was in the possession of Hugh Lewis and Agnes his wife and in 1630 he mortgaged for £200 to Jenkin Gwyn of Jordanston, 'the capital messuage formerly distinct messuages, called Velindre in the parishes of Llanwnda and St. Nicholas and other landes in these parishes'. In 1638 Thomas Hughes of Velindre was suing William Griffith for stealing 'a red horse'. Again in 1702 there were legal tussles over land when William John of Velindre was involved with others in court battles with Sir William Wogan over land. William John, husbandman, whose will was proved 11 February 1715, had married an unknown Margaret by whom he had five sons, Thomas, William, Edward, David and John and a daughter, Lettice. Felindre was part of the estate of Tucker of Sealyham in 1752; the Voters' Lists of 1894 show Levi Hughes living there.

Refs: PRO AD iii, D556; Slebech Deeds J. H. Davies Deeds NLW; Pembs. Plea Rolls Nos. 150, 271; *Black Book of St. Davids,* 1326; PRO Anc. Deeds D2967; Fines in Pembs. QS; Terrier of Bishopric estates 1817. Carms RO; Spence Colby Deeds No. 154.

FELINDRE, *Llysyfran*

A farmstead on high ground above the east bank of Llysyfran Reservoir, and to the west of New Moat village.

Home of a cadet of Philipps of Pentypark who was a cadet of Picton Castle. By his will dated 26 March 1695 John Philipps of Pentypark bequeathed 'Velindre' to his son Rowland Philipps. Rowland was succeeded at Felindre by seven generations, the last being William Rowland Philipps who was owner-occupier in 1904. Several descendants through marriages with daughters of Felindre still survive in the county.

Refs: Family wills; Pembs. RO, LT 1786; MSS of Sir Evan Jones, Bt., of Fishguard.

Mathias

FERN HILL,
Haroldston St. Issells

A modern residence in grounds and trees above a bend of the river Cleddau; Lewis *TDW* 1840 described it as 'pleasantly situated on the bank of the Cleddau and surrounded by living plantations.' Its most important owner-occupier was Sir Henry Mathias (son of Caesar Mathias of Hook, Freystrop, High Sheriff 1774). He was Mayor of Haverfordwest in 1806, and ten years later was High Sheriff. During his shreivalty he presented an address to the Prince Regent, and was knighted. He was the last Protonotary of the Great Sessions for the Carmarthen circuit. His wife Katherine was the daughter of Philip Jones of Llanina, Cards, by Katherine Warren of Trewern. He died in 1832 aged 75, and his wife in 1848 aged 83. He bore as arms: *or* between three lions couchant a chevron engrailed *sable* thereon five ermine spots *argent;* crest: a boy's head couped at the shoulders, a snake entwined round his neck. Motto *Spero meliora.*

Refs: Colby Map 1831; Sir Henry's first cousin, Rev. Caesar Morgan of Ely, married Mrs. Mary Morgan, author of *Tour to Milford Haven,* 1791.

FERNY GLEN, *also* **FERNY SLADE, FURZEY SLADE** et al., *Roch**

Seat of Edward Hugh Hannon Massy born 1836 eldest son and heir of Edward Taylor Massy of Cottesmore and Mary his wife. Called variously Furzy Slade, Ferny Slade and other variations. It featured in a lease in 1774 for three lives to Thomas Wade of Ferny Slade, yeoman from Francis Harris of Great Ormond Street, London. Excluded from the lease was the piece of land called the Castle or Old Roman Escarpment and the ditch around it. Edward and Mary Massy were still there in 1894.

Refs: Pembs. RO D/EE/2

FFYNNON CORANAU, *Bridell*

A farmstead about half a mile to the southeast of Bridell church, marked as Ffynnon Coranau on Colby's Map of 1831. The name was anglicised as Crowns Well. In 1642 David Jenkins of Hensol, Glam, Esq. leased the capital messuage called Crownes Well to James Lewis of Cardigan, Esq. and John Parry; in 1746 Margaret, eldest daughter of Jenkin Gwyn of Ffynnon Coranau married John Turner of Crugmor near Cardigan; in 1786 Samuel Lloyd, gent. owned Crownshall, with John George a tenant; in 1792 John Colby of Ffynnonau Esq. leased a property in Cilgerran parish to John George of Crownswell, yeoman.

Refs: Carms RO, John Francis Deeds; LT 1786.

FFYNNON GAIN, *New Moat*

Now a farmstead to the south of New Moat village, on a steep slope to the north of Bletherston village. In 1326 it was described as a Knight's fee divisible according to Welsh tenure; it was held by Philip Brown who owned Fonnon Keyng and Castel Kymer, being two carucates held of the fee of New Moat. On Rees's 14th century map it is marked as a Welsh knight's fee. It later passed to the Philipps family, a branch of Pentypark. In 1638 John Philipps of Ffynnongain served as High Sheriff. He was inordinately attached to his money which he carried around in a red bag which earned him the nickname *'Shon bwtsh goch'* (John of the red pouch). He also owned Haythog, and his son William of that place was High Sheriff in 1646. Ffynnongain was acquired by the Scourfields of New Moat, and Henry Scourfield was owner in 1786. By 1873 the owner of Ffynnongain (132 acres) was W. G. Purser. Some 600 yards from the house was a holy well believed to possess healing qualities.

Colby

FFYNNONAU BYCHAN, *later* **FFYNNONE,** *Manordeifi*

A mansion at the southern extremity of the parish, on high ground above Nant Dulas which joins the river Cych near the residence of Lancych. The mansion was consistently known as Ffynnone Buchan down to 1763 when it became known as Ffynnonau (Ffynnone). It has been a country residence of three successive families from the early 16th century to 1927.

The first to settle there was Griffith ab Evan, a descendant of Cadifor Fawr of Blaen Cych, and the family (who took the surname Morris) were there for six generations. In 1670 David Morris was assessed at four hearths, so that it was then a commodious residence. The last of the male line, Morris Morris, was High Sheriff in 1710-11, and died without issue, and by will, proved 1730, bequeathed Ffynnonau Bychan to his sister Margaret who married William Morgan of Blaenbylan. They had an only son, Morris Morgan, who had two sons, William and David. The elder son, William, gave the property to his brother David in 1746. David died, unmarried about 1750, and Ffynnone reverted to his said brother William, who clearly did not relish the ownership, and in 1752 sold it to Captain Stephen Colby, R.N. The captain died without issue circa 1779, and left the property to his cousin John Colby. He was interested in Ffynnone and decided to build a larger and grander residence there, employing Nash as architect. Accounts, vouchers, etc. of Nash's work have been preserved for the period 1792-99. Very little is known of the older house, and Nicholas tells us in 1875 that the new mansion stood 'a little distance from the site of the old house'; and we learn that on 1 October 1798 John Colby agreed with two masons to build a wall around a fishpond being made in the meadow and grove on the west of 'the old house at Fynone.'

When completed, the mansion consisted of a square block with pediments on each facade, with an east wing of kitchens and domestic quarters which ended in a stable courtyard. Colby also planted many thousands of trees which added to the beauty of the locality.

Further work was carried out on the house in the 1820s when it was re-roofed, and in 1827 pillared. A 'Great Doric' portico was added to the main entrance. Further extensions and modellings were made in 1904 by the architect Inigo Thomas, with the result that much of Nash's work was removed, although some of Nash's detail still survives within the mansion. The accounts for the rebuilding in 1904-8 have survived.

The estate remained in Colby possession until the death of John Vaughan Colby without surviving male issue in 1919, Ffynnone then passed to his daughter Aline Margaret who married C. J. H. Spence-Jones C.M.G., D.S.O., who took the name of Colby by Royal Licence in 1920. Ffynnone was sold in 1927 to a Glamorganshire business man, Daniel Daniel, High Sheriff of Pembs. 1939, who died unmarried in 1952. For some years the mansion was the home of his sister Mrs. Bickerton Edwards, and on her death it reverted to her nephew W. H. C. Daniel, who sold the property. When I visited it on 4 February 1980 I found the mansion in excellent order, owned by a Swansea business man, Mr. Phillips, who sold the property in 1988 to Earl Lloyd George, who greatly improved the house and the environs. It is today the Earl's main residence in Wales.

Refs: Carms RO, John Francis Deeds, Trant/Yelverton Deeds; NLW,Owen and Colby Estate Accounts, Llwyngwair and Bronwydd Deeds; Nicholas, *County Families,* 1875 edn.; Fenton, *Tour Pembs.,* 1811; Lewis, *TDW,* 1840; C. Allen, *Tivyside Photographic Souvenier,* 1871, illust.; *Country Quest,* Apr. 1966, illust.; J. Hilling, *History of Architecture in Wales,* 1976; illust.; D. L. Baker-Jones, Ffynnone, 'Notes on a Country House and its Occupants', *Trans. Cymmr.,* 1965, Part I, illust.; Francis Jones, 'The Hand of Nash in West Wales', *Trans. Carms. Antiq. Soc.,* 1939, and 'Chronical of Blaenbylan,' *Journal Ceredigion Antiq. Soc.,* 1976.

FFYNNONE, *Little Newcastle*
A farmstead south of Little Newcastle village, and near Garn Twrne. Home of yeoman families. The first known family there, that of Symmons whose ancestors were living at nearby Colston in 1670. They continued at Ffynnone until the first part of the 19th century. When Anne Symmons' will was proved in 1805, the property passed to her brother Thomas Symmons. By 1813 there were two properties there – Old Ffynnone, the original house, and New Ffynnone. By 1840 Old Ffynnone was owned by George Williams of Treyarched, and in 1843 he went to live there. He died in 1849, and left the property to his son, R. M. G. Williams, surgeon, who died at Newport Pembs. in 1910.

Refs: Pembs. RO Deeds HDX/562, No. 36; Wills of Symmons family; LT 1786.

FFYN(N)ONE GLEISION,
*Llanfihangel Penbedw**
David Jones the elder of Ffynone Gleision, gent. viv. 1774 married Elizabeth, daughter of John Phillips of Tŷr y Pantgwyn, Llandyfriog, Cardiganshire, gent. whose will was dated 12 August 1766. David and Elizabeth had two sons, one of whom nothing is known, and the younger, David, was of Ffynone Gleision in 1775. In the Tithe schedule for the parish in 1837, Ffynone Gleision was an estate of 213 acres belonging to Thomas Lloyd, tenanted by David Evans. By 1894 David Thomas was living there and still there in 1904.

Refs: John Francis Deeds.

Dyer

FISHGUARD, *Fishguard*
The site of the home of the Dyer family is not known. Records refer to the Dyer family as being 'of Fishguard', but whether their home was in the town or elsewhere in the parish is not clear. The two brothers, Walter and William Dyer, both 'of Fishguard', Pembs. were sons of Philip Dyer of Newport, Pembs. In 1558 Walter Dyer of Fishguard, gent. granted to John ap Owen of Kynheidre, lands in the vill and fields of Trebover, in Llanust, and Le Escaer, rendering 8s. yearly to the heirs of William Dyer of

Haverford who granted the said lands to Walter Dyer in 1512. Janet Dyer of Fishguard, widow, was living in 1552. These facts are entered here in the hope that further research will indicate the site of the Dyer home. The arms of Dyer of Fishguard were *gules* an eagle displayed *argent* beaked and armed *or.*

Refs: GGMS Adv. Pembs. I, 26: NLW, Bronwydd Deeds No. 999; .Plea Rolls; G. Owen in BM Egerton MS 2586.

FLEET, *Monkton*

Home of the Meyrick family in the late 16th century. Dwnn recorded the pedigree of Sir Francis Meyrick of 'Fleet House in Moncton'. Dwnn mentions Sir Francis Meyrick of 'Muncaton', c. 1608. In the Land Tax of 1786 John Francis Meyrick is recorded as owner of Upper Fleet (Wm. Powell, tenant) and Lower Fleet (Jas. Bedford, tenant) in Monkton parish.

Refs: Dwnn, i, p. 137; G. Owen, Pembs., iii; Pembs RO, LT 1786.

Hayward

FLETHERHILL, *Rudbaxton*

The scant remains of the old mansion are some distance to the northeast of the present farmstead of Fletherhill, and near the banks of a tributary of the Western Cleddau. Above it is rising land. The old mansion is marked on Colby's Map 1831. It was assessed at four hearths in 1670. The name is derived from the Welsh word *llether* (slope) and late 16th century legal records describe the property as 'Fletherill alias Letherhill' (1584).

From early times Fletherhill was a manor and is described as such down to the 18th century. The manor was held prior to 1349 by Guy de Brisau; in 1592 by Sir John Perrot of Haroldston; in 1606 it was held on a lease by (Sir) John Philipps of Picton Castle, thereafter by four successive generations of the Hayward family. The first known owners of Fletherhill were the Goddard family, descended from the Goddards of Glossop, Derbyshire. Two sons were parsons – Henry, rector of Rudbaxton from 1556 to 1563, Edward, vicar of Amroth in 1591; their only sister Alice married William Hayward who settled at Fletherhill. The Haywards intermarried with wealthy landowning families like Llwyd, Morfil and Perrot of Haroldston and amassed a considerable estate in Pembrokeshire and in England. By his will dated 6 November 1646 James Hayward, barrister, younger son of John and Mathilda Hayward of Fletherhill, charged his property in Surrey with an annuity of £20 for the revenue of the 'Hospital of Haverfordwest in St. Martins parish to be paid to the poor chosen and admitted to the Hospital,' and in 1687 the Town Council had trouble in getting the money, and threatened to prosecute Lady Hamilton, daughter and heiress of the said James Hayward, barrister, if she did not pay the £20 annuity regularly.

In 1659/60 George Hayward served as High Sheriff, and in 1681 Thomas Hayward was returned as M.P. for Haverfordwest, but William Wogan petitioned against the return. The last male member of the family, Thomas Hayward died (unmarried) as the result of a duel, on 9 July 1682, bequeathing the Fletherhill estate to his only sister Mary Hayward. He had mort-gaged parts of the estate, but these after redemption, would revert to Mary. She married George Tasker of Castle Pill, Steynton but he died without issue not long after the wedding, and was buried at Steynton on 28 July 1684. The widowed Mary Tasker made her will on 2 August 1684, and left all her estate, including the manors of Fletherhill, Rudbaxton and St. Ishmaels, the capital messuage of Fletherhill, the rectory of Spittal, and lands in the parishes of Rudbaxton, St. Ishmaels, Bletherston, Camrose, Llandissilio, Llanycefn, and houses in the town and county of Haverfordwest, to the Mayor and Corporation of Haverfordwest in trust, to erect and build an alms house in that town 'for the breeding (*sic*) and maintenance of poor children of both sexes', and for other charitable uses. And thus was founded the famous Tasker's School that served Haverfordwest and district for many generations, and still flourishes under the name Tasker-Milward School.

A local tale relates that Mary Tasker had long narrow strips of cloth placed on the road so that she should not soil her shoes when she walked from Fletherhill to Rudbaxton church. These strips were of blue cloth edged with scarlet – colours later used in the early school uniform of the school she had founded. The Haywards bore: *or* three lions rampant *gules* over all a bendlet *sable*. Crest: a lion issuant *gules*.

Refs: Fenton, *Tour Pembs.*, 1811; GGMS; *Dwnn*, i, p. 179; Taylor's *Cussion*, fo. 96b; *Pembs. Magazine*, Feb. 1984; *Arch. Cam.*, 1888, p. 132, ibid. 1889, p. 27;: NLW Pembs. GS, Eaton Evans and Williams Deeds, No. 3446; Lord Hampton Deeds.

FLIMSTON, *Castlemartin*

A farmstead near the coast, due north of Eligug Stacks. According to Dr. B. G. Charles the name is found in ancient documents of the period 1324-31 as variants of Flemisston, i.e. home of a Fleming many of whom settled in the south of the county. From 1600 onwards the form Flimston is usually found, and is thus spelt on Colby's Map of 1831. Near the house stood an ancient chapel, and on the land is an early earth fortification. Flimston was a long, commodious dwelling, an early vaulted house, with a hall above the undercroft, and a tall round chimney at the main gable end. Many similar houses occur in south Pembrokeshire. In 1786 Flemiston was owned by John Hook Campbell, with Robert Jones as tenant.

Refs: RCAM Pembs., 1925; B. C. Charles, *NCPN*, 1938; P. Smith, *Houses of the Welsh Countryside*, 1925, Maps Nos. 7, 8, 28; T. Lloyd, *Lost Houses of Wales*, 1986, illust.; Gerald Oliver, *Medieval Buildings*, 1987, illust.

FOBSTON, *Marloes*

Now a farmstead south of St. Bride's Hill. Formerly home of a cadet branch of Allen of Gelliswick. David Allen was at Fobston in 1702, and his descendants continued there for a further three generations.

On 12 March 1760 the estate was mortgaged to John Wogan of Wiston in £425 and on 13 April 1762 he assigned the mortgage to Sarah Crowther, widow. On 29 June 1769 the estate was partitioned between Mrs. Barbara Williams, Mrs. Mary Laugharne Allen and Mrs. Margaret Allen, daughters of William Allen of Fobston. On 15 June 1770 the said Mrs. Mary Laugharne Allen mortgaged Fobston in £200 to Miss Mary Roch of Ripperston, St. Brides and on 18 September 1770 Miss Roch assigned it to George Parry, attorney, Haverfordwest charged with an additional £425. On 26 March 1782 the mortgages were assigned to Rebecca Bowling, widow, enhanced by £100 arrears of interest, and she, being a cousin of the Allens of Fobston, reinstated David Allen, (son and heir of Mrs. Mary Larne Allen), in the property. On 6 October 1787 the said David Allen mortgaged it in £300 to Captain Richard Teale to whom he surrendered the deeds as security on 13 January 1792 after raising a fresh mortgage in £400 on 28 December 1791. David Allen died an alcoholic in 1797 leaving the encumbered estate to his mentor and beneficiary, John Gwynne, attorney of Haverfordwest of the Cwrt, Llanllawer family.

John Gwynne, Esq. is described as owner of the Fobston estate in 1802, with John Stewart as tenant. It was afterwards farmed by yeomen, and became part of the St. Brides estate. A sale catalogue of that estate in 1920 describes Fobston as a good stone cement-faced house of eight bedrooms, three sitting rooms, kitchen, back kitchen, dairy, cellar, with substantial farm buildings.

Refs: NLW, Eaton Evans and Williams Deeds, Brawdy Deeds, Poyston Deeds; M.I. in Marloes church; Pembs. RO Deeds D/LP, LT 1786; *see also* S.C. (J.F.) 1988, for illust., description and plans.

FOLEY HOUSE, *Haverfordwest*

A large town house built in Goat Street in 1794 by Nash, for Admiral Thomas Foley of Ridgeway. It consisted of three storeys and a basement. The ground floor comprised an entrance hall, drawing room with large bay windows, dining room, smoking room, cloak room; on the first floor, four large bedrooms, dressing room, and two bedrooms in a wing, and bathroom: on the second floor, a large bedroom, two servants bedrooms, bathroom: in the basement, a large kitchen, scullery, storeroom, wine cellar, pantries, and larders.

From 1921-47 it was home of the well-known family of George. The property was sold to the County Council in 1947.

Refs: Francis Jones, 'The Hand of Nash in West Wales', *Trans. Carms. Antiq. Soc.* 1939, pp. 93-96.

FOLKESTON, *Roch*

A farmstead one mile southwest of Roch, above Nolton Haven. In 1392 Peter Mossylwyke and Agnes his wife held two carucates at Folkerston by Knight's service held of the manor of Roch; from about 1413 to 1520 the family of Reynbot held Folkeston. The Perrots were claiming rights to the property, and in 1441 Thomas Perrot of Eastington held some parts of Folkeston which he had from Walter Reynbot of that place, and in 1507 Owen Perrot sued John Reynbot for three messuages in Folkeston. Much later, on 24 February 1664/5 James Philipps of Tregibby, near Cardigan, Esq. granted a lease of Folcaston with creeks, quays, quarries, coal and culm in the townred and fields of Folcaston to Anthony Stokes of Roch parish, gent, for lives. By 1716 Folcaston belonged to Rowland Philipps of St. Brides who gave a lease for lives of that property to Tobias Codd, which lease was surrendered on 14 September 1769 by Dorothy widow of David Codd, (grandson) of the said Tobias, to Rowland Philipps Laugharne of Orlandon who held, in 1786, three messuages at Folcaston (let to tenants) and still owned them in 1801. The Tithe Schedule of 1837, shows James Higgon as owner-occupier of Folcaston (279 acres). By 1904 William Stancomb of Bradford, Devizes, Wilts., owned the Folcaston and Southward estates.

Refs: PRO, Anc. Deeds; NLW, Pembs. Plea Rolls, Morgan-Richardson Deeds, Poyston Deeds.

FORD, *Carew*

A farmstead on Ford Pill between Carew Castle and Paskeston. In the 17th and early 18th centuries it belonged to the Philipps family, a branch of Picton Castle. John Philipps of Goodhook (q.v.), agent to his cousin Sir John Philipps, built the residence at Ford. He was agent in 1650 and was still acting as such in 1699. Sir John wrote a 'memorandum of what Privilege my cozen John Philipps had with me from Picton since 1650', and included among them are the following : 'I gave him as much timber as did build two parts of his house at Ford, and the use of my tenants to carry his slates from Llangolman to Picton Key, and my lighyter to carry them from there to Ford, and to carry his limestone from Williamston Park to Goodhook during the time he lived there, and to carry his corn and household stuff from Goodhook to Ford.'

The Philipps family continued to own Ford for most of the first half of the 18th century. Edward Philipps of Ford died leaving a son and four daughters. John Philipps, the son, matriculated at Jesus College, Oxford, in 1722, and in 1735 was High Sheriff of Pembrokeshire. He died without issue, and the Ford estate passed to his sisters, co-heiresses; Elizabeth, married John Smith of Jeffreston, Anne married John Relly of Pembroke, Mary married Reverend James Higgon of Haverfordwest, and Katherine married David Rice of London, apothecary. In 1786 John Smith Esq. is described as owner of Ford.

Ref: Picton Castle Documents; Haverfordwest Deeds.

Pher

FOREST, *Cilgerran*

Also called 'Y Plâs ynghefn y drum' (the mansion behind the ridge – a fair topographical description). About threequarters of a mile northwest of Cilgerran, on high ground above the river Teifi. Phillips wrote in 1867 – 'the old house of Forest stood a little to the north-west of the present dwelling house; and a part of the same exists now incorporated with the outbuildings. From the remains of some ornamental freestone mouldings found among the debris it is presumed that it was an elegant structure. According to the *Pembs. Arch. Survey* (1896-1907) 'of which residence not a vestige is left.' The present building is a farmstead.

In its earlier days Forest was the home of the Revell family who had been mercers and corvisors in Haverfordwest during the early 16th century. Thomas Revell, merchant, of Haverfordwest, married Janet Bowen of Lochmeyler, and was the first of the family to settle at Forest. His son John Revell died in 1546, leaving issue, and his widow Anne (née Walter of Carmarthen) married the eminent Dr. Thomas Phaer (1510-60) who came to live at Forest and was M.P. for Cardigan Borough (1555-59) and for Carmarthen Borough (1547), and was a physician and literateur of merit. He was a Roman Catholic, the author of several books and translated Virgil's *Aeneid* into English verse. He was also a poet. He was educated at Oxford, Inns of Court, a lawyer and was appointed Constable of Cilgerran Castle 1548, Steward and Forester of the Lordship of Cilgerran, Solicitor to the King and Queen in the Council of Wales and the Marches. Appointed Searcher of the Port of Milford and of all ports between Swansea and the river Dyfi in 1556 and held it until 1559 when he was promoted to Collector of the Great and Petty Customs of Tonnage and Poundage in the Port of Milford. He died as the result of an accident in 1560. The arms of Phaer: *argent* on two bars *gules* six cinquefoils pierced, a chief *or*. Crest a crab in pale reversed. *See also* DNB and DWB and Thomas Phaer M.D. of Cilgerran in *Trans. Cymmr.* 1979/1980.

Included in the notes on Forest, is the following taken from J. R. Phillips, *History of Cilgerran* 1867 pp. 96-8: 'About the time of the Civil Wars, tradition says Forest was tenanted by a man named Jones, a staunch Royalist, and [it] was taken from him by the Parliamen-tarians, where they remained during the subsequent attack on Cilgerran Castle. In the field behind the house, still called 'Bulwark', the Parliamen-tarians made an embankment or entrenchment where they had cover and could also fire their guns at the castle. Hence the tradition. This is supported by numerous human bones and cannon balls found among the present buildings and in the adjoining fields'.

John Revell's son, Thomas Revell, J.P., was High Sheriff of Pembrokeshire in 1579, and of Cardiganshire in 1582 and 1593, and M.P. for Pembrokeshire. He died without male issue, and Forest passed to his younger brother, William Revell whose great-grandson, Thomas Revell is said to have 'sold all.'

The next family at Forest was that of Parry, and in 1634 Forest formed part of the Parry of Noyadd Trefawr estate. It later passed to the family of Symmons of Llanstruan, and in 1766 John Symmons conveyed his estates (including Forest) to his son and heir, John Symmons. In 1786 John Symmons Esq. is described as owner of Forest, with John Edwards as tenant, the tax assessment being the largest in the parish. The Symmons estates were sold in 1784, and later we find the owners to be the Lloyds of Coedmore, who owned Forest down to recent times.

Refs: Dwnn, i, p. 155; Phillips, *Hist. of Cilgerran,* 1867; For Phaer *see* Dr. John Cule 'Thomas Phaer M.D. of Cilgerran', *Trans. Cymmr.,* 1880, and also DNB, and DWB, GGMS Gwynfardd; NLW, Cwrtmawr Deeds, Noyadd Trefawr Deeds, Pembs. Plea Rolls; *Pembs. Arch. Svy,* 1896, 1907.

FREESTONE HALL, *Carew*

A residence on high ground 1¼ miles northeast of Carew Castle. Lewis in 1840 comments on the site as follows – 'Freestone Hall, residence of J. Allen Esq. commanding from the grounds some of the finest views in the county . . . ' The mansion, built by Roger Allen (1734-82) second son of John Allen of Cresselly, is a three-storeyed main block with a wing stretching to the rear at one side. A good photograph was taken of the house by C. S. Allen of Tenby in 1871. James Allen (son of Roger) presented a paten and flagon 'as a New Years Gift' to the parish of Carew in 1844, and further plate was presented by Thomas Allen of Freestone Hall in 1886 in memory of his eldest son Captain Griffith Allen late of H.M. 98th Regiment. In 1910 the house was purchased by the Cresselly estate, the senior branch of the Allen family. It comprised a porch, entrance Hall, dining room, parlour, kitchen, pantry, a large back-kitchen, and dairy and outbuildings; there were seven bedrooms, 78 acres were attached. Now the home of Thomas Lloyd, eminent historian, author and genealogist who recently found a beam in the roof dated 1768 with the initials RA.

Refs: Lewis, *TDW,* edns. 1834, 1840; C. S. Allen, *Photographs in South Wales,* 1871; J. T. Evans, *Church Plate of Pembs.,* 1905; Info. T. Lloyd.

Cantington

FROCHEST, *Eglwyswrw*
A farmstead about half a mile north of Eglwyswrw, and near Court, residence of the Cantington family, lords of Eglwyswrw, a branch of which settled at Frochest in the 14th century. Later descendants adopted the Welsh form of nomenclature. Thomas David ap Evan lived at Frochest in the period 1422-61; another descendant James Morris is described by George William Griffith (1584-1665) as 'now livinge, but neere 100 yeares old.' Frochest was bought by George Owen of Henllys between 1579 – 1597. Thereafter it was let to farming tenants. The Cantington arms were*: gules* an eagle displayed *argent,* a chief chequy *argent* and *vert.* Crest: a moor's head *sable,* plumed *or.*

Refs: College of Arms, Wagner MS 12, Protheroe MS XIV; *Dwnn,* i, p. 71; GGMS.

FRON, *Llanddewi Velfrey*
A large double-pile house on the hillside of Pengawse, overlooking Whitland. It was long empty but is now inhabited again. In the 18th and early 19th centuries it was the home of the Lewis family descended from David Lewis of Fron who married Margaret daughter of Evan Protheroe, Esq. of Dolwilym. She died in 1749. Their great-grandson Evan Protheroe Lewis (b. 1792) was the last of the family at Fron, and after 1832 he moved to Narberth. By his wife, Elizabeth Lewis of Whitland (d. 1868) he had 14 children. After this, Fron was let to tenant farmers.

Refs: NLW, Griffith Owen Deeds; ibid. Morgan-Richardson Deeds.

FRONGOCH, *Nevern*
A farmstead between Nevern and Tredrissi, about three quarters of a mile north of Nevern. An Evan Robin 'de Vrongoch ar lan Nevarne' lived there in the early 16th century. The next occupant, Mathias Bowen died shortly before October 1598, and was followed at Frongoch by his son Thomas Mathias, a minor when his father died. Thomas was succeeded by his son Morgan Thomas who married Jane daughter of Mathias Bowen of Llwyngwair. He had two sons – James Morgan who moved to Tredrissi, and one with the strange name 'Sir Thomas heb achos'.

Refs: College of Arms MS, Wagner MS 5, Protheroe MSS IV and V; *Dwnn,* i, p. 162.

GARN, Y GARN, *Llanychaer*
A farmstead about 400 yards to the northeast of the parish church; an interesting old farmhouse with hall open to the rafters, and an ancient round chimney, once common in the county. I visited it in the company of Mr. Peter Smith F.S.A., of the RCAM Aberystwyth. The gentry family of Bateman, descended from the Batemans of Honeyborough near Neyland, lived for many years at houses in the Cwm Gwaun area. One of these, John Bateman of Trenewydd (Llanychaer), had an illegitimate son by Margaret, daughter of Lewis Llewelin, named Thomas Bateman, who settled at Garn, where he was living in 1603. In the second half of the 19th century, Garn formed part of the estate of Mortimer of Court, Llanychaer. The Bateman arms were *argent* a chevron between three escallops *sable.*

Bateman

Refs: College of Arms, Protheroe Ms; *Dwnn,* i, p. 173.

GELLIFOR, GELLI FAWR, *Nevern*

Now a residence on a slope above the waters of a tributary of the upper river Gwaun, and just over half a mile from Llanerch-y-bleiddiau (q.v.) marked on Colby's Map 1831 as Gellyvore, but on modern OS maps as Gelli-fawr. Locally it is still called Gellifôr, but the present proprietors use Gelli Fawr. The farmhouse consists of two parts: the original section is the kitchen area which contains the 'simme fawr' and attached to it is a section which formed the original farmhouse. At one time, the kitchen was extended to include a room. In the last century, a large extention was added, now of two storeys, and an attic storey with a dormer window. Over the outer doorway of the kitchen is a stone tablet which reads 'Rebuilt in 1860 by D. Davies, J.P., D.L., Esqr., Castle Green, Cardigan.' The property had been owned on 29 September 1860 by the said David Davies. It was advertised for sale in 1889 by David Davies, son of the said purchaser, and describes 'The Mansion House, which is newly and substantially erected, containing three reception rooms, eight bedrooms, kitchen, back kitchen, dairy, pantries, with all necessary out offices, and would make an excellent Shooting Box'; and very fine outbuildings are also described, two cottages on the property, with 241 acres.

The yeoman family of James lived there from early 18th century, for five generations, after which it was sold. The outbuildings have now been converted into holiday homes.

Refs: NLW, Morgan-Richardson Deeds, Croydon Deeds; Carms. RO Beckingale Colln.; inf. ex Mr. Dillwyn Miles.

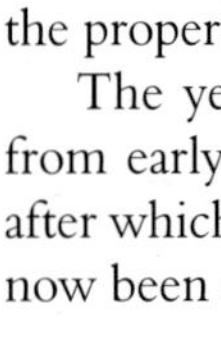

Barrett

GELLISWICK, *Hubberston*

Formerly a mansion on high ground above Gelliswick Bay, to the west of the town of Milford Haven, where it stood from Elizabethan days to the second half of the present century. The mansion, facing southeast towards the main gateway, consisted of two storeys, the entrance on the ground floor, with a range of five windows, and on the upper storey a range of seven windows. Its frontage measured 51 feet, its breadth 42 feet. The stairway rose from a room in the rear, where a wing extended. There was a chimney at each gable-end, and on the outside some corbelling. In 1670 it was assessed at five hearths. In the 1730s a companion appeared alongside its northern end. Happily, for us, in 1740 John Butcher was employed to make an estate-map-book, where he described 'The Old Building' and 'The New Building', and, what is more, made an admirable sketch of the latter. The new building faced south, and its gable-end was attached to that of the original structure so that the whole produced an L-shaped residence. The new addition was an impressive building of three storeys built over a basement storey. The entrance was in the centre of the first floor, with a semi-circular fanlight over the door; it had four windows. On the second floor there were two large bedrooms, and a bathroom and a range of five windows. The third floor had three bedrooms, with five windows in all. The projection to the rear carried the staircase, where a few of the old balustrades could be seen. The basement storey had four windows. The length of the frontage measured some 45 feet, and its breadth over 21 feet. Just to the rear (north) was a large garden of over an acre enclosed with high stone walls. These buildings remained substantially the same to our day.

The extent of the demesne and farmland in 1740 was 266 acres. Gelliswick was the home of the landowning family of Barrett from about 1550.

In the Golden Grove and the Protheroe manuscripts the arms of the Barretts of 'Gellyswyke' are blazoned as *gules* a lion rampant *argent*, and on a chief indented *argent* three escallops. Apart from saying they bore 'the Barrett arms', Lewys Dwnn (*Heraldic Visitations*, i, pp. 70, 119) does not particularise beyond recording the crest as a lion rampant holding an escallop *sable* in its forepaws, and the crest of the Dudwell branch as a thunderbolt proper.

Dwnn commences the genealogy of the Gelliswick line with a William Barrett living in the mid-15th century, who married Janet, daughter of the Pembrokeshire magnate Sir John Wogan of Wiston, and the wives of his successors were chosen from similar landowning stocks, which indicates the standing enjoyed by the family of Gelliswick. William had two sons, David who succeeded to Gelliswick, and Harry who married Elen, daughter and co-heiress of Sir Warin le Archdekne, knight.

David Barrett married Catherine, daughter of William Adams of Paterchurch near Pembroke, by Alson, daughter of Sir William Herbert of Troy, Monmouthshire. They had an only son, Owen, who inherited Gelliswick in due course and married Frances, daughter of Jenkyn Elliot who held considerable estates at Narberth and Earwere (Amroth). Owen Barrett had four children, namely, Gelly, the heir; Francis, Elizabeth and Catherine, who married Rowland Meyrick, Bishop of Bangor (died 1566), and had four sons, Sir Gelly Meyrick, executed in 1601 for his part in the Earl of Essex's rebellion, Sir Francis Meyrick, whose descendants lived at Bush near Pembroke, John and Henry Meyrick .

It seems likely that the eldest son was given the name of the family residence, generally abbreviated to the form Gelly. He married Mary, daughter of Rhys Bowen of Upton Castle near Pembroke, descended from the same family as Sir Rhys ap Thomas, K.G. of Dynevor and Carew Castle.

Some time after 1578 Gelly Barrett died, leaving seven children, John the heir; Rowland, died before 1597; Griffith, living in 1617; Francis, living in 1597; Catherine, Margaret and Mary.

The eldest son, John Barrett, succeeded to Gelliswick and married Als, daughter of Richard Meyrick of Bodorgan, Anglesey, of the same family as Rowland Meyrick, Bishop of Bangor. He served as a juror on the inquest on Sir John Perrot's possessions in 1592, and contributed to the Lay Subsidies of 1594 and 1609. He entertained Lewys Dwnn in 1597 and helped him to compile the Barrett pedigree for which he paid five shillings.

John Barrett died in 1617, and his will dated on 16 May was proved on 19 September of that year. He desired to be buried in Hubberston church 'in the sepulchre of my father', and gave 12 pence towards the fabric of St. Davids Cathedral church, 2 shillings to the poor of his native parish, £3 to his brother Gryffythe Barrett, and the remainder of his possessions to his 'wor' (wyr., grandson) Henry Bowen, whom he appointed sole executor. He 'entreats' his son-in-law, George Bowen and his wife, Margaret ('my daughter'), to have respect for the 'innocence' of testator's daughter, Mary Barrett and to treat her according to her estate.

John Barrett was the last of the male line at Gelliswick. He had five daughters: Elizabeth, died before 1597; Margaret, Elizabeth, Catherine and Mary.

Margaret Barrett, second but eldest surviving daughter and ultimate heiress, married firstly Gruffydd Davies of Neeston, son of William Davies of Greenhill in Pwllcrochan, by whom she had three daughters (all living in 1597). Gruffydd died on 29 June 1606, and Margaret afterwards married her kinsman, George Bowen, of Neeston (a younger son of Henry Bowen of Upton Castle) and had two sons, Henry Bowen who became heir of his grandfather at Gelliswick and (in due course), of his father at Neeston, and Hugh Bowen.

We do not know whether Henry Bowen the heir went to live at Gelliswick; the likelihood is that he remained at Neeston to which he succeeded after his father's death. That he was the last descendant in blood of the Barretts to own Gelliswick is clear, and it is equally clear that he had sold that property by the middle of the century to the Canon family of Haverfordwest. Henry died probably in 1658 when administration of his goods was granted at Carmarthen.

It was probably Morris Canon who purchased Gelliswick. The last in the male line, John Canon, died in 1690, leaving an only child, the heiress Elizabeth, who married Edward, eldest son of Sir Erasmus Philipps, third Baronet, of Picton Castle. Edward Philipps died during his father's lifetime, in 1694, Elizabeth in 1706, and as they had no children, the Canon possessions passed to Edward's younger brother, Sir John Philipps, whereby Gelliswick became part of the Picton Castle estate.

From the mid-17th century onwards the history of Gelliswick is intimately entwined with that of the Allens, tenants of the Canons and Philippses. Towards the middle of the 17th century, one became initially a tenant, then a leaseholder, of Gelliswick, and his descendants by diligence and application so improved their economic position, generation by generation, that they became owners of extensive estates with residences at Bicton, Blackaldern, Cilrhiw, Cresselly, Dale Castle, Fobston, Freestone Hall, Goodhook, Rickeston, and St. Bride's Hill, providing their native county with 15 high sheriffs, a Member of Parliament, a chairman of Quarter Sessions, numerous magistrates and other local functionaries, and by no means least, two eminent antiquaries and authors.

How and when William Allen, born at Newton in 1624, came to Gelliswick is not clear, but possibly through marriage with a daughter of the tenant of that property. The author of *Family Records* states 'David Allen was a good farmer (and I believe a small freeholder); he lived most of his time at Newton in Llanstadwell Parish; he married his eldest son, William Allen to Sage Hire, who lived in Gelliswick, where he came afterwards to live with his son, William, till he died. The above William Allen lived at Gelliswick all his time (he had two sons William and John), he acquired a good Estate, and was a vast great farmer; he died at Gelliswick'. But we know for a fact that the name of William's wife was Elinor, and a note by Egerton Allen, F.S.A., states that the genealogist Ridgway says, 'this Elinor was widow of Hyatt of Gelliswick'. It is possible there has been confusion as to the lady's Christian name, or maybe William had been married twice; nevertheless both versions agree that it was through marriage that he came to Gelliswick. Hire or Hyre is a surname found in several parishes in Rhos at that time, and possibly Ridgway rendered it wrongly as Hyatt.

The earliest reference I have discovered to him, at his Hubberston home, occurs in the Pembrokeshire Plea Rolls of Great Sessions for Spring 1656, where he is described as 'William Allen of Gellyswych alias of Hubberstone, yeoman'. From 1661 onwards his name often appears in Great Sessions papers, when he sued various persons for sums ranging from £7 to £1,000 due on bonds or obligations. In 1670 he was assessed at five hearths at Gelliswick which shows it to have been then a fairly large house.

As the property lay so near the coast it was inevitable that the occupiers would be concerned with maritime affairs, and the Allens used the resources of the sea as they did those of the land. But the sea took its toll, and in the days of sail the catalogue of wrecks on the Pembrokeshire coast was all too long. Early in 1677 such a shipwreck had taken place in the haven, its cargo consisting largely of casks of brandy, some of which were cast ashore in the Hubberston-St. Ishmaels area, and later in the year William Allen, gentleman, found himself charged with appropriating part of the delectable cargo to his own use. He strenuously denied the allegations, and in defence stated that, with others, he had acted as agent for Thomas Haward of Fletherhill, esquire, lord of the manor of St. Ishmaels, and 'drew off the brandy from the flotsam casks' into those he himself had provided, and afterwards conveyed to Sandyhaven mansion, home of Richard Philipps, esquire, 'but what became of it, defendant knoweth not', and received payment neither for his labour nor for the nine new barrels he had provided at his own costs. He further stated that one cask cast ashore below his house at Gelliswick, had been seized by 'poor folk', one of whom drank himself to death on the spot; and admitted that four gallons had been carried to his house, for which he was ready to account to the Vice-Admiral of South Wales or to the lord of the manor or 'whoever has jurisdiction'.

Hitherto, William Allen seems to have been a yearly tenant, but in 1681 the owner, John Canon of Kilgetty, granted a lease of the messuage and lands called Gellyswick to William Allen the elder of that place, gentleman, for the lives of lessee, his son William Allen the younger, and David Allen, eldest son of the last named.

William did not live long after obtaining the lease, and a memorial in the chancel of Hubberston church, copied by Colonel Allen, read 'Here lyeth the body of William Allen of Gelliswick, Gent. who departed this life July ye 3rd 1688. Aged 64. Elinor Allen, relict of the above William Allen, departed this life January ye 25th 1702. Aged 88'.

They had four children: William Allen the younger; John, Rebecca and Rachel. William Allen the younger succeeded to Gelliswick. In 1693 he became High Sheriff of Pembrokeshire. He took part in political affairs as a supporter of the Barlow of Slebech interest, and in the parliamentary election of 1714 cast his vote for that candidate. He married Elizabeth, daughter and heiress of David Paynter of Dale Castle and it was through this marriage that the Allens acquired Dale Castle. Through his marriage William Allen was to benefit very considerably. Intelligent and energetic, William advanced the family fortunes and made useful additions to an estate that was to be augmented yet further by his equally enterprising sons. He died on 24 March 1722, aged 64, his wife, Elizabeth, on 24 May 1724, and they were buried within the chancel of Hubberston church. Their children were: David Allen, eldest son, married Anne, daughter of Rowland Laugharne of. St. Brides and a co-heiress of her brother John. He settled at Fobston in Marloes, part of his wife's estate, died on 15 November 1712, aged 35, and was buried in Hubberston church. Anne survived him and in 1715 inherited her full share of the St. Brides estate. From them descended the Allens of Fobston, Bicton, and Cresselly.

The second son, Joseph Allen, received the Dale Castle property. He is remembered mainly as the man who, about 1714, built St. Ann's lighthouse, for long a source of revenue for his successors. He married Frances, third daughter of John Phillips of Talyfan, Monmouthshire, and by the prenuptial settlement made on 27 June 1707 the bridegroom's father settled on him the manor of Dale, the messuages called Dale Castle, Brunt, Castle Lloore, and a house called Humphrey's House. Joseph died without issue on 29 March 1722, aged 42, and was buried in Hubberston church. As he had no children, his main property, Dale Castle and its appurtenant lands, passed in due course to his next brother William. The widowed Frances later lived at Walford, Herefordshire, and in 1739 is described as wife of Kedgwin Webley (d. 1773) by whom she had a daughter and heiress, Frances (d. 1792), who married David Parry of Noyadd Trefawr, Cardiganshire. The third son of William and Elizabeth was William Allen of Gelliswick, who inherited Dale Castle from his brother Joseph. The youngest son, John Allen, matriculated at Jesus College, Oxford, on 27 March 1708, aged about 16. About 1712/13 he married Dorothy, daughter of Richard Vaughan of Torycoed, Carmarthenshire, and then lived at Carreglwyd, Llanelli. He took an active part in coal-mining in that district, and was High Sheriff of Carmarthenshire in 1724. They had no issue. The daughters of William and Elizabeth were Mary, Elizabeth, Rebecca and Martha.

The third son William Allen, succeeded to the leasehold of Gelliswick, and in 1722 to the freehold of Dale Castle under the terms of the will of his brother Joseph. In addition to managing his property, farming, shipping, and light houses, he engaged in coal-mining. He also took part in public life and was High Sheriff in 1742.

William Allen married Martha, daughter of John Fowler of Haverfordwest, merchant, by Martha, daughter of Thomas Couzens. She died in 1733 and was buried in Hubberston church. William died in 1744. His children were: William Allen, he died before 1744. The second son, John Allen, inherited the Dale Castle property. He seems to have lived at Gelliswick for part of his life as the lease had descended to him and is described as of that place in documents up to 1755, after which he is consistently described as of Dale. He married Mary, youngest daughter of Sir John Stepney, 5th Baronet, of Llanelli, the marriage bond being dated 2 June 1744 and the post-nuptial settlement 27 June 1746. She died in 1750, leaving an only child, Elinor. On 30 May 1755 John executed a deed to secure £6,000 as a marriage portion secured on the manor of Dale, Dale Castle, and other properties for his daughter and heiress. He held the profitable Government Agency for victualling vessels of the Royal Navy that put in to the haven. In 1757 he served the office of High Sheriff, and died ten years later. The heiress Elinor Allen, married on 8 July 1776 John Lloyd of Ffosybleiddied, Mabws, and Ystrad Teilo, Cardiganshire; both died in 1820 within a few months of each other, John on 16 January, Elinor on 22 May. From this union descends the Lloyd-Philipps family, now of Dale Castle. The third child of William and Martha was Hugh Allen, matriculated at Jesus College, Oxford, on 29 October 1740, aged 15, settled at Rickeston in Robeston West, and became a Justice of the Peace. He was known as 'Count Allen'. He married Tamar Dacres, and had an only child, Jemima born in 1776, who married John Lawes Waters (1765-1837), a naval lieutenant, who later served in the Battle of the Nile. Hugh Allen died on 3 June 1803 and was buried at Robeston West.

The other children were James, David, Martha and Elizabeth. The fourth son, Joseph Allen (b. 1726), remained at Gelliswick. As a younger son living in leasehold property then held by his elder brother John, his income and prospects were modest, a situation not wholly favourable to him when he sought the hand of a daughter of one of Pembrokeshire's leading county families. She was Anne, only daughter of Charles Philipps of St. Brides Hill and his wife Anne ('née' Skyrme of Vaynor). Joseph himself did not have a great deal of material advantages to offer, but happily his brother, John, came to the rescue. This example of brotherly solicitude is described in a contemporary document and preserved in the County Record Office at Haverfordwest, which reads as follows: 'An Account of Mr. Joseph Allen's Fortune, as likewise what his eldest brother propose doing for him the better to enable him to address himself to Miss Philipps of Hill. Mr. Joseph Allen, in which it appear that he is worth £1,400, which at 5% is £70. He is entitled on the death of his eldest brother to an estate given by the will of his aunt, Flaerton, to him and the issue male of his body, of yearly value of £40. Total, £110 (p.a.). His eldest brother out of the great regard he has for the young lady, and willing to do his utmost to make the proposals acceptable, will give up the Lease of Gelliswick, and all necessary furniture for the house as well as the implements of husbandry. He will resign (in favour of Joseph) his Agency under the Government for victualling his Majesties ships that touch at Milford Harbour which is a very considerable affair.'

The arrangement proving satisfactory the marriage took place in St. Brides church on 3 September 1751, and bride and bridegroom settled at Gelliswick; Joseph Allen played a prominent part in local politics as a strong supporter of the Picton Castle interest. He died at the age of 60 and was buried at Hubberston on 27 August 1786, leaving a widow and large family to mourn him. His will was proved on 15 November following. Anne, heiress apparent of her brother, William Philipps, never inherited as she predeceased him, and was buried with her husband on 16 July 1796, at the age of 66. But two years later, on 28 August 1798, William Philipps died unmarried at the age of 68, and the St. Brides estate passed to his sister's third son, Charles Allen. Joseph and Anne Allen had nine children: John Allen the eldest son and heir, born in 1752; William, Charles Allen, born on 24 May 1758. During his earlier years he served as a Royal Marine officer. On the death of his uncle William Philipps in 1798, he succeeded to the St. Brides estate and adopted the surname Allen-Philipps by Sign Manual. In 1801 he married Cecilia, daughter of the Rev. Edward Philipps, rector of Lampeter Velfrey, by whom he had issue. He was a Justice of the Peace, in 1809, High Sheriff, and died in 1827, his wife having predeceased him by ten years; James Allen, (b. 1762), became Lieut-Colonel of the 12th Foot in the HEIC Service and died before Seringapatam in 1799. Martha Allen, (b. 1753), died in 1775. Elizabeth Allen, (b. 1760), married on 10 March 1783 John Philipps-Laugharne (b. 1754) of Orlandon and Pontfaen, High Sheriff in 1788. He died in 1814, Elizabeth in 1819. They had four sons and three daughters; two of the sons succeeded, in turn, as 8th and 9th Baronets of Picton Castle, and took the surname Philipps. The daughters were Anne, Mary and Elinor.

The eldest son, John Allen, was the last of his line to live at Gelliswick which had been the main family home for five successive generations. On 26 October 1798 he married at Prendergast, near Haverfordwest, Mary (born 18 August 1777), daughter of William Bowen of Prendergast House, descended by the distaff from the interesting family of Musgrave. John Allen died suddenly on 4

December 1808 aged 56, and was laid to rest in the family vault at Hubberston. The widow remarried on 6 July 1813 James Scowcroft, Attorney at Law of Haverfordwest. For some reason, James's father, Thomas Scowcroft disapproved of the union, and on 28 June, about a week before the wedding, made a will and tried to intimidate his son by a clause naming him as a beneficiary – 'provided that he shall not intermarry with Mrs. Allen the widow of Mr. John Allen of Gellyswick, but if he does marry her, then he is to be excluded from the legacy'. Mrs. Scowcroft died at Manorowen on 2 September 1827 after falling out of a gig. She had five children by her first husband, and five by the second. The five children of John and Mary Allen were Charles, John, Hugh, George and Peregrine.

The final lease of Gelliswick, held for three lives at a yearly rent of £3, determined with the death of John Allen in December 1808, and the property reverted to the landlord, Lord Milford of Picton Castle. That a well-to-do county family should have continued as leaseholders in their main residence for so long, in this case for over 150 years, is unusual, although not wholly unique.

After the departure of the Allens, Thomas Philipps, one of the partners of the Milford Bank, came to live at Gelliswick. Born in 1776, the eldest son of the Rev. Edward Philipps of Lampeter Velfrey, Thomas Philipps read law at Gray's Inn and afterwards turned his attention to private banking in Pembrokeshire. He settled first at Neeston Hall, and later moved to Gelliswick. However, the Milford Bank failed in 1810 and Thomas Philipps was ruined. He and his family emigrated to South Africa in 1820. The next tenant, Henry Palmer, was a native of Carew who had prospered as a planter in Jamaica. So far as I know his only claim to fame was his boast that he had been cutting asparagus growing in the open at Gelliswick on Christmas Day 1818, an awe-inspiring event faithfully recorded in the *Carmarthen Journal* of 15 January 1819. In the Voters' List for 1834 he is described as leaseholder of 'Gelliswick farm and houses' at a yearly rent of £50 and upward. He died on 16 August 1849 at the age of 72. It seems that his family continued there a few years more, but by 1861 James Greenish, previously farming at Neeston, had taken over Gelliswick. He was succeeded in 1867 by his son, also named James who married Mary Elizabeth Bassett Harries of Hilton in Roch parish. He farmed the property till his death in 1899 when he was followed by his son, Robert Picton Greenish who did not remain there long. In 1910 Mr. John Belton and his sister, Cordelia, took over Gelliswick, where they continued till 1944 when the property was sold to Mr. W. J. Cowie, a Cardiff businessman. In 1947 his brother, Mr. D. K. Cowie came here, and in 1955 sold the farm to the Esso Oil Company. For information concerning the post-Allen occupiers of the farm, I am grateful to my friend Mr. R. G. Thorne, M.A., who had been brought up at Thornton in the neighbouring parish of Steynton.

The land was farmed by Mr. Reg Roberts of Haverfordwest, land agent. I visited it in 1978 and 1979, and found the 'old' and 'new' houses in good order. Alas, early in 1981 the house and buildings were razed to the ground by the Esso Oil Company who had 'no further use for it.'

Refs: Dwnn, i, pp. 70, 119, 153-4; NLW, Pembs. GS, Pembs. Plea Rolls, Map Book Picton Castle estate; Carms. RO, GGMS (Adv. Dyfed); Col. F. S. Allen, *Family Records of the Allens of Cresselly,* etc. pr. 1905; Francis Jones, 'Gelliswick and its Families', *Arch. Cam.* 1980, illust.

GILFACHWRNELL,

In the free chapelry of Llangolman Penbedw alias Llanfihangel Penbedw

Marked on Colby's Map 1831 as Gilfach to the east of Capel Colman, and in a deed of 1842 as 'Gilfach alias Kilvach Wrnell'. Home of yeomen and minor gentry. The earliest known proprietor was Thomas David Morgan of Manordeifi who owned Plâs Kilvackwrnell at the time of his death in 1655. His daughter Elizabeth married Thomas Lloyd, gent., of Clynfyn, and brought Gilfachwrnell to that family, and it was settled on their younger son Jenkin Lloyd who was living there in 1675.

David Lloyd (brother of the preceeding Jenkin) described as 'of Westminster' conveyed Gilfachwrnell in 1694 to Stephen Morris of St. Paul's, Covent Garden, who made his will in 1698. Little has been found about its later history until 1786 when David Griffiths gent. is described a owner-occupier of 'Gilfach hwrnell'. In 1798 the said David Griffiths, then of Cilau Wen, Llanstinan parish, by his will bequeathed 'Gilfach' to his sister Mrs. Elizabeth Rees of Cilgwyn, Manordeifi, widow, for her life, with remainder to her eldest son John Rees. In 1813 George Rees of Cilgwyn (eldest son of John and Elizabeth Rees both deceased) broke the entail on the messuage and land called 'Gilfach alias Kilvach Awrnell', formerly held by John Davies gent. afterwards held by David Thomas, yeoman, then by William Davies farmer, and finally by John and George Rees of Cilgwyn. George Rees mortgaged the property, being much in debt, and in his will, made in November 1842, mentions his property called Gilfach alias Kilvach Wrnell.

A plan of the property was made about 1843. The Tithe Map and Schedule of the Chapelry of Capel Colman in 1849 gives Martha Jane Jones as owner-occupier of 'Gilfach Cottage' and garden and 78 acres. The name and site are now lost.

Refs: GGMS I Gwynfardd; NLW, Bronwydd Deeds; Pembs RO Saunders-Davies papers, one of which contains the map of Gilfach and genealogical notes.

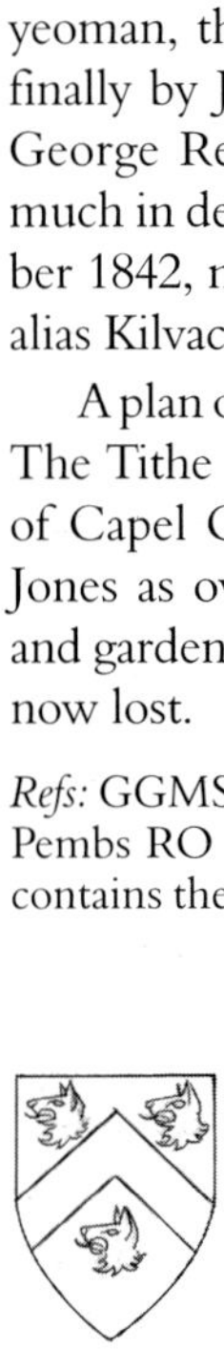

Gower

GLANDOVAN, *Cilgerran*
Originally Glendyfan, the name became generally rendered as Glandovan. The mansion stands on a wooded slope about a mile south of the town of Cilgerran. It became the home of the Vaughan family descended from the north Wales chieftain Osbwn Wyddel, whose arms, *ermine,* on a saltire *gules* a crescent *or,* they bore. The first to be associated with the parish was William Vaughan, supporter of Henry VII, appointed Constable of Cilgerran Castle, whose descendant, Robert Vaughan (living 1580) built the house of Glandovan and married Elizabeth daughter of the eminent physician and author Dr. Thomas Phaer of Forest (q.v.). In 1670 Rees Vaughan was assessed at six hearths for Glandovan, the highest assessment in the parish.

In the late 17th century the Vaughan heiress married a Stedman of Strata Florida and the Glandovan estate passed to that family. Eventually, Jane, daughter and heiress of James Stedman, married the barrister, William Gower of Boughton St. Johns, Worcs., M.P. for Ludlow for 1689, who came to live at Glandovan. There he died in 1723, his wife being sole executrix of his will. They had ten children, the third of whom, Abel Gower, succeeded to Glandovan. Six more generations succeeded, and in 1824 Robert Frederick Gower purchased Castle Malgwyn near Llechryd, which became the main residence. In 1948 Erasmus William Gower sold Castle Malgwyn. The Gower arms were *azure* a chevron between three wolf heads erased *or.*

Welsh poets of a bygone age sang the praises of some of the early owners of Glandovan, among them Tudwr Aled (fl. 1480-1526) who composed an ode of thanks to William Fychan (who had married Margaret, daughter of Sir William Perrot) for presenting him with a 'march glâs'. The house has lasted, and among its features is a fine well-stairway. When I visited it in 1976 in the company of Mr. Peter Smith, F.S.A., the owner-occupiers were Mr. and Mrs. Wetherhead, and when I called there in May 1984 it was owned by Mr. David Frost, land-agent, of Haverfordwest.

Refs: Dwnn, i, pp. 147-8; WWHR ii, 89; *Carmarthenshire Studies,* 1974, p. 71 and Plates XII, XIII; P. Smith, *Houses of the Welsh Countryside,* 1975, Plate 90; NLW, Papers of GS, Pembs Plea Rolls, Bronwydd Deeds, Noyadd Trefawr Deeds, Cwrtmawr Deeds.

GLANDUAD,
now called **GLANDUAD FAWR,** *Meline*
Also called Glanduad Fawr/Ucha, and there was another nearby farm called Glanduad Fach: in deeds of 1740 and Mudge Map 1819 given as Llandyad. A farmhouse near Afon Duad, quarter of a mile northwest of the parish church, it still possesses the vernacular style of a typical old Welsh gentry house. A large oblong house of two storeys, and an attic storey with three dormer windows. The main entrance leads into a roomy hall, at the rear of which, in a projection, is the main staircase lit by a long window (partly blocked up). On the right is the parlour with perfectly preserved oak panelling with 17th century pillars, and a plaster ceiling with traces of elaborate decoration. The dining room was

to the left, today used as a kitchen. At the rear, near the staircase, was the original kitchen with a 'simne fawr', but that and the chimney stack has been removed. An extension to the right of the front had been used as a stable, but in 1975 when I visited Glanduad, this was being converted into a dwelling for a son of the proprietors. On a pane in one of the windows of the house was inscribed 'I lost this day £5000'; on another occurred the name 'Grace Stephens', who died of consumption, and the lines

'My pain, my pleasure, no human tongue can tell
Tis heaven to have thee, without thee, hell!

In 1937 I received a letter from Mr. Joseph Thomas, then occupier, about former families, he says '. . . there was another noted old family, the Stephens, the last of whom, Grace Stephens, died a spinster, and two lines were written on a pane of glass by her lover the day she died, they are to be seen here now,' and then quotes the foregoing distich. All these inscribed panes are gone. Descendants of the chieftain Gwynfardd Dyfed, in direct descent, had lived at Glanduad for four and a quarter centuries, 1325 to 1750. The main line lived at nearby Penybenglog to which estate Glanduad belonged, and later became the seat of a cadet branch who bore Gwynfardd's arms: *azure* a lion rampant within an orle of roses *or* and adopted the surname Bowen. Fifteenth in descent, Anne Bowen the heiress, married in 1744 John Moore of Muslick, and their daughter Alice Moore married Phillip Powell of Radnorshire, from whom descends Mr. Anthony Powell, the well-known writer of our day. Glanduad afterwards passed through several hands – Lloyd (Carms.), Harries, Davies, Stephens, Colby (1869) and was afterwards owned by gentlemen-farmers.

Refs: Francis Jones 'Griffith of Penybenglog', *Trans. Cymmr,* 1939, and 'Bowen of Pentre Evan and Llwyngwair', *Pembs. Historian,* 1979; B. G. Charles, George Owen's *2nd Book, NLWJ,* Winter 1948; WWHR ii, p. 38; NLW, Bronwydd Deeds, Morgan-Richardson Deeds, F. Green Deeds and Documents; Pembs. RO DX/57/35, Sale Catalogue of Glanduad (John Colby Esq. then owner); Francis Jones, *Treasury of Historic Pembrokeshire*.

GLANPWLLAFON, *St. Dogmaels*★

Glanpwllafon lies between Forest and Pantygrwndy on Colby's Map 1831. In the Land Tax records of 1786 the property was owned by Madam Gwynn with Elliw Jenkin, tenant assessed at 10p. Thomas Williams, currier, bought Glanpwllafon, his will was proved in 1823. He had by an unknown wife, one son, Stephen, and three daughters, Mary who died in 1831, who married firstly, Thomas Edwards, and secondly Rev. William Williams, a Baptist minister. Margaret married a Thomas Williams, and Elizabeth, a Mr. Richards. In 1860 Thomas Edwardes was farming there.

Refs: Carms. RO J. Francis Colln. RO 530.

GLANRHYD, *Grondre*

A farmstead south of Clynderwen railway station, and near the road to Penblewin crossroads. The dwelling house is not striking, but there is a very fine range of splendidly built outbuildings. Home of the Griffith family in the 18th century. The first at Glanrhyd, Evan Griffiths J.P. (brother of Stephen Griffith of Llangolman) was High Sheriff of Carmarthenshire in 1766; in 1769 he was a Commissioner of Land Tax for Pembrokeshire. An inscribed tablet on an outbuilding reads 'Erected by Evan Griffiths in 1770', he subscribed to Reverend William Evans' English translation of *Cannwyll y Cymry* in 1771, and was a Grand Juror of the Pembrokeshire Great Sessions in 1783, and died not long afterwards. He was unmarried, and his property passed between his sisters Catherine, and Mary, wife of John Lewis of Henllan. In 1786 the owner of Glanrhyd was Rowland Edwardes, Esq. with the Rev. Thomas Bowen, clerk, and James Lewis as tenants. It is still a large and attractive farm.

Refs: Pembs. Papers of GS; Buckley, *Sheriffs.*

GLASTIR (GLASDIR), *Nevern*

Now a farmstead nearly one mile to the northeast of Nevern village. Writing in about 1603 George Owen tells us, 'yt was intymes past the personage howse or gleebe of the person of Nevarne before the appropriatinge thereof to the Colledge of Saint Davides [in 1377] . . . where it contynued untyll the suppressinge thereof when it was taken into the kinges handes and bought by Matheas Thomas father to Thomas Matheas' [descended from the Youngs]' men tall of person, fair of complexion and gentle of behaviour, but some now decline from the same'. Mathias Thomas was the son of Thomas Lewis who was the son of Lewis Young, eldest son of Howel ap Jenkin Young of Tredrissi. Mathias Thomas's son, Thomas Mathias of Glastir died in 1617 and from him the Mathias family of Llangwarran descend.

Mathias Thomas married Jenet, daughter of Thomas Griffith ap John Griffith of Haverfordwest and his wife, Anne daughter of Jenkin Elliot. Their son, Thomas Mathias married firstly Jane, daughter of Llewellyn Lloyd of Llanstinan, widow of John Scourfield who had received Llangwarren as her share. By her Thomas had two daughters, Margaret who married Thomas Vaughan of Penyrallt in Nevern parish, and Jenet who married Thomas Lloyd of Rhosymaen who died in 1613, his heir was his brother, David Lloyd. Thomas Mathias married secondly, Ursula, daughter of George Owen of Henllys by whom he had a son, who was of Llangwarren. Ursula married secondly, William Laugharne of Llanreithan. They all bore the Young arms: *vert* a hart trippant between 3 fleurs de lys *or*. After settling at Llangwarran c. 1600, the family ceased to use Glastir as a residence, and it was let to a series of yeomen families and in the 18th century was sold. In 1786 Thomas Keymer was the owner, in 1811 John Evans, Esq. and in 1840 Anne Evans.

Refs: B. G. Charles, George Owen's, *2nd Book*, c. 1603; Fenton, *Tour Pembs.*, 1811; NLW, Poyston Deeds, Bronwydd Deeds; GGMS (Adv. Dyfed) i, 12; College of Arms, Protheroe MS IV, ff. 148-9.

Rowland

GLENOVER,
*near Haverfordwest**

The home, built in 19th century, of the distinguished William Bowen Rowlands, born in 1836, son of T. Rowland, J.P. William was educated at Jesus College, Oxford, 1854, M.A. Headmaster of Haverfordwest Grammar School 1864, took Deacon's orders, became Curate of Narberth 1864, Student of Gray's Inn 1868, called to the bench 1871, S.W. circuit, made a Q.C. 1882, Bencher 1882, Treasurer of Gray's Inn 1889, M.P. Cardiganshire 1881-93, Recorder of Swansea from 1893. He had married in 1864, Adeline Wogan, only daughter of J. D. Brown, of Kensington House, Haverfordwest. They had four sons, and three daughters. The eldest son and heir William Thomas was of Haverfordwest, (1872-1943); Ernest became a barrister, James David was Registrar of Altringham City Council, Cyril was killed in action in World War I. The arms of William Bowen Rowland were: quarterly. 1 & 4 *or* a lion rampant *azure*. 2 & 3 *azure* a lion rampant *or* between 8 bezants: over all a shield quarterly i & iv *sable* between four cotises *argent*, 3 lions passant *azure*, ii & iii *argent* in chief *sable* 3 martlets. Crest, a fleur de lys entwined with a serpent *or*. Motto *Recte faciendo seanus*.

In the 20th century, home of Herbert John Emlyn Price, J.P., Solicitor, coroner, elder son of James Price, J.P., coroner of county of Pembrokeshire who had married Edith Mary, daughter of John Holdom of Holme Leigh, Fenny Stratford.

GLÔG (*formerly* **GLÔG-Y-FRÂN**), *Clydey*

Now a farmstead on a hill slope between Frenni Fawr and Llanfyrnach, and above the upper waters of Afon Tâf. The building consists of a central block of two storeys, weather-tiled, and a rear wing. The entrance leads to a small oak-panelled hall from which rises a flight of stairs that divides to the right and left. A door from the hall leads to the cellar. On the right of the hall is the parlour, on the left the *neuadd*, with a *simne fawr*, and a kitchen in the rear wing. There is a partly walled garden, the whole surrounded by pleasant grounds. Thus it was when I called there in 1974.

The family of Owen held the property in the 17th and 18th centuries. Thomas Owen of Glôg, gent. was assessed at four hearths in 1670, and was succeeded by his son John Owen who was a Grand Juror in 1746. John left two sons and four daughters, none of whom had issue. The eldest son, Thomas Owen gent. mortgaged the 'capital messuage called Glogue alias Gloge y vrane' and other lands to Stephen Colby of Ffynnone and W. R. H. Howell of Maesgwynne on 3 April 1767. He died in 1768. His wife Elizabeth, only daughter and heiress of

Robinson Lloyd of Vaynor, afterwards married John Ferrier. He was succeeded by his brother John Owen who settled at Nantuan in Clydey. John died without issue, and in 1786 John Ferrier was the owner-occupier of Glôg (*iure uxoris*).

Not long afterwards Glôg was sold, and in the early 19th century was owned by a gentleman-farmer, John Owen, not related to the earlier family of that name. In 1834 he was owner-occupier of Glôg, then comprising 268 acres. Five generations of this family remained at Glôg. The last male of the family, John Owen, was an innovator and introduced machinery into the local quarries whose output he greatly improved; he also took an active part in establishing the railway from Whitland to Crymych which was opened in 1875, and extended to Cardigan in 1886. This local benefactor died on 30 May 1886, aged 68, and was buried at Llwynyrhwrdd. He left two daughters, co-heiresses of Glôg, namely Anne Mary who married Mr. T. J. Rees, but died without issue; and Miss Anna Louisa Owen. It was Miss Owen and her brother-in-law who welcomed me when my wife and I called there on 10 September 1974.

Refs: Carms RO, J. Francis Deeds; NLW, Poyston Deeds, Morgan-Richardson Deeds, Pembs. Plea Rolls; Tithe Map Clydey, 1841; LT 1786; *Trans. Carms Antiq. Soc.,* 1908.

GLYNHENLLAN, *Cilgerran**

In 1867 some remains of this house could still be seen: its name has been transferred to another farm, originally called Voidir, and there are two farms called Glynhenllan Ucha and Issa. In Tudor times an ancient Welsh family lived there, and it is recorded that Margaret, daughter of Jenkin ab Owen ap John of Glynhenllan married Thomas Jenkin Lloyd of Clynfyw. During the 18th century it was occupied by the Gilbert family several of whom served as churchwardens in the period 1723-74.

In 1717 the Rev. Rice Griffith of Cardigan, clerk, granted a Lease and Release to William Hughes of Pembroke and Walter Lloyd of Cardigan Priory, gentleman, of a messuage and lands called Tŷr Place Kleen Henllan in tenure of Margaret Garnons, widow, in Cilgerran parish, and other lands in Pembrokeshire. In 1729 Abel Griffith of Pantybettws and Abel Gower of Cilgerran signed articles of Agreement for the sale of Ceynhenllan Vawr and Vach and another messuage all in Cilgerran for £610, and in 1733 Abel Gower purchased the property. In 1775 Thomas Williams of Haverfordwest, eldest son and heir of Mary Williams, widow, deceased of same and Abel Gower of Glandovan gave a lease of possession to George Worral of Carms. gent. Edward Long of Worcester, gent., and George Smith of Worcester, mercer of a capital messuage called Plas Glyn Henllan amongst others. In the Land Tax records of 1786 Mr. Worral was shown as owner of both Glynhenllan Vawr and Vach, and Thomas Francis, tenant, assessed at 6s. 9d. of the former and Peter John of the latter.

Refs: Aberglasney Colln. 2; *Dwnn*, i, p. 35; GGMS; Morgan-Richardson Deeds, ii, p. 445; Phillips, *History of Cilgerran,* 1867, p. 143; Coedmor Deeds.

Fenton

GLYN-Y-MÊL, *Fishguard*

An impressive residence of three storeys and a basement storey, on low ground overlooking Afon Gwaun near its estuary at Cwm (Lower Fishguard). About 1796-97, Richard Fenton the eminent barrister and antiquary, started clearing away the cliffs below Carn-y-Gath, where he made a large alcove for his intended mansion. It was completed by 1799, and the building has survived virtually unchanged to our day. Fenton also created a delightful environment of lawns, gardens, trees, bushes and flowers that attracted admiration; there he spent the last 20 years of his life. Historians will remember him for his *Tour through Pembrokeshire*, 1811. He was a Fellow of the Society of Antiquaries, and wrote poetry.

Fenton was a friend of Goldsmith and of antiquaries like Colt Hoare. He supported shipbuilding at the estuary. One of the family, Myfanwy Fenton was a poet of merit, while others like Ferrar Fenton, a noted antiquary. The house was sold in 1866 to satisfy the creditors of John Fenton deceased. The Action in Chancery records give the defendants as the Rev. Samuel Fenton, clerk, and Catherine

Elizabeth his wife, John Fenton and John Fenton Taylor.

Afterwards it became the home of John Worthington, a well-known philanthropist, who further developed the attractive grounds. The last of the old squires there was Miss Beatrice Chambers, J.P. active in local life. After her death the property has changed ownership several times.

Refs: NLW, Trenewydd Deeds, *Tour* 1802, No. 17508; Ferrar Fenton's family history in *Pembs. Guardian,* c.1896-1900; *Coastal cottages of Pembs.,* 1987, illust.

GOLDEN, *Pembroke St. Mary's*

Northeast of the town, across the river from the town. From 1603 to 1825 the Cuny family were associated with Golden and for short periods lived at Lamphey, Welston, and Pembroke. The Cunys came from Staffordshire, the first to come to Pembroke being Walter Cuny, whose son and heir, Richard, signed his pedigree for Dwnn in 1613.

Golden had been part of the estate of Jasper, Duke of Bedford, and eventually passed to the crown. On 28 May, 1601 the Queen gave a lease of 21 years of Golden and other lands in the Pembrokeshire area to Sir Henry Lindley of London, who on 7 February 1602/3 assigned the lease to Richard Cuny of St. Florence, Esq.

Some eight generations of the family remained in the county for two and a quarter centuries; seemingly the last in the male line was the Reverend John Powell Cuny, rector of St. Brides who died unmarried in 1820-25. On Colby's map of 1831 are marked Golden Hill and adjacent Golden Farm. The mansion has long since vanished.

Refs: Dwnn, i, p. 25; NLW, Poyston Deeds; Francis Green 'Cuny of Welston and Golden', WWHR, XII, p. 169.

GOOD HOOK, *Uzmaston*

A farmstead about two miles east of Haverfordwest. The earliest known owners of Good Hook were the family of Routh. In 1552 John Philipps of Picton Castle, in his will mentions his daughter Janet Philipps and her husband John Routh, gent. of Good Hook and their son John Routh also of Good Hook. John Routh (the younger) was living there in 1598-1600, but had died before 1629 when his widow Ann was still living there.

In the second half of the 17th century, the Rouths had sold Good Hook, and in 1670 it was owned and occupied by James Wogan, (son of John Wogan of Wiston), who had bought Good Hook from Lewis Wogan of Boulston, who was assessed at four hearths. In the late 17th century Good Hook was the home of James Allen, and a descendant, John Allen of Good Hook, married Joan Bartlett heiress of Cresselly and they settled there. John died in 1752. John Bartlett Allen owned the property in 1786, with a widow, Ann Pugh, as tenant. Another change took place in the following century, the owner in 1839 being Sir Richard Bulkeley Philipps of Picton Castle, the acreage of Good Hook then being 207 acres. Near the house stood a tumulus, still commemorated in the field names, Great, and Little Tump Park.

The residence is a good example of vernacular architecture of a modest gentry house. Dating from the 16th century it has retained characteristics of its earlier days. It is cruciform in form, of two storeys, with a chimney at each gable end. The projection in the front contains the main porchway, with a storey above rising to roof height, while the rear projection, also of two storeys, has a large cylindrical stone chimney rising from where it joins the main block. Among its interior attractions are two large alcoves, and a particularly interesting staircase, with decorated balusters. After being empty for 20 years it has been tastefully and carefully renovated by the owners, Mr. and Mrs. Lewis.

Refs: WWHR, VI, p. 212, and X, p. 50; NLW, Eaton Evans and Williams Deeds; Parish Tithe Map, 1839; *Pembrokeshire Magazine,* RO 21, 1984, illust. (interior and exterior).

GOODWICK (WDIG *also* ABER GOODICK), *Llanwnda*

This house occupied a cliff ledge, overlooking the sea not far from the present main railway station and harbour wharf. Today, the Fishguard Bay Hotel stands on the site of the original house. Fenton in 1811 states that two brothers, 'merchant adventurers from Devonshire' settled at Goodwick and added contraband trade to their legal business, and adds, 'their mansion-house, with a variety of dependent buildings, was nicked like an eagle's nest above the pier, commanding a fine view of the bay and the entrance into the port of Fishguard, and so sheltered from all winds prejudicial to the growth of trees, that it once boasted a most beautiful clothing of woods, remains of which are still visible. Perhaps as a situation for a marine villa, it is not to be equalled by any spot in the kingdom.' Fortunately, an engraving of the old mansion, made in 1814 by the brothers Daniel, has survived, and several pre-1900 photographs showing its conversion into 'Hotel Wyncliffe', and from 1906, showing its final conversion and extension when it became Fishguard Bay Hotel, which still functions.

In 1702 a lease for 99 years of the house and the quay below was granted to William Rogers of Minehead, Somerset, merchant & mariner, and remained in his descendants throughout the 18th century, until 2 February 1805 when the property and the large farm of Penrhiw was sold to David Harries of Dinas Island, husbandman, and remained in that family until the house and quay were sold to the Great Western Railway early in the present century.

Refs: For the engraving of 1814 and subsequent photographs, *see* engraving of the house and quay in Fenton, *Tour Pembs.,* 1811; Daniel's engraving 1814, *Western Telegraph,* 29 April 1982 and 21 March 1984, *The County Echo,* 6 September 1983, reproduced on p. 189 in *A Pembrokeshire Anthology,* ed. D. Miles, 1983, *The Pembrokeshire Magazine,* May-June 1984, and February 1985; For a ground outline plan of the old house and outbuildings *see* OS Map 1888; for Deeds *see* collections in Pembs. RO; for Rogers family *see* Francis Jones, 'Carnachenwen', unpublished essay. (For another Goodwick mansion see Dyffryn-Wdig.)

GRAIG, *Llanfyrnach*

A farmstead about two miles southwest of the parish church, on high ground above the west side of Nant Gafel which joins Afon Tâf near Glandwr. For some 500 years Graig was owned and occupied by the descendant of the Devonald family whose ancestor John Devonald signed his will in 1479. Fifth in descent was Thomas Devonald of Graig, gent. born on 11 August 1570, and who in March 1598 married Mary daughter of John Owen Philipps of Blaentâf, grandson of Sir Thomas Philipps of Picton Castle. His son and heir John Devonald of Graig was a member of the Pembrokeshire Train Band in 1643, and owner of property in Llanfyrnach, Moylgrove, Monington, Eglwyswrw, Nantgwyn and Clydey, and his great granddaughter Hannah Devonald married in 1761 Thomas Morse of Brimaston, Hayscastle. Her second son, John Morse, settled at Graig and in 1787 married Elizabeth daughter of Henry Skeel of Hayscastle. John died in 1818, Elizabeth in 1841. Their grand-daughter Phoebe Morse (born 1831) married John Nicholas who came to live at her home. Their daughter, Dinah Nicholas, married William Harries of Fron, whose son Mr. Lloyd Morse Harries now lives at Fron farm.

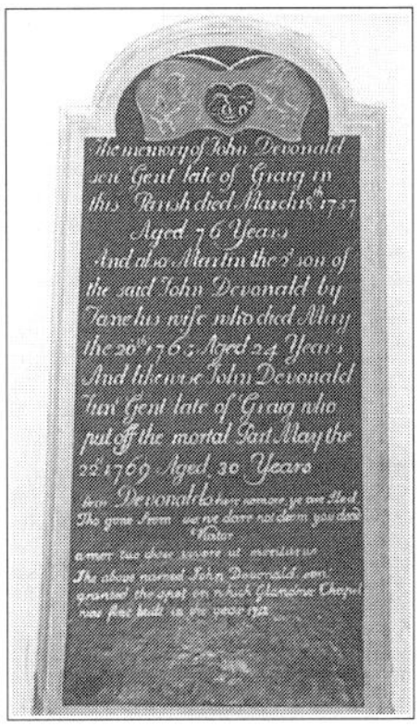

Thus 16 generations of the family had occupied Graig since 1479, and descendants continue to live in the locality. One of the ancestors, John Devonald, gent. a devout Independent, died on 18 March 1757, aged 76, and over his memorial in Glandwr chapel are his heraldic arms – a rare exhibit to be displayed in a Nonconformist chapel.

Refs: Haverfordwest Library, Francis Green MSS Vols. 19, 20; Pembs. RO, Deeds D/LJ; NLW, Pembs. Papers of GS, Bron-wydd Deeds, Maes-gwynne Deeds; BM, Egerton MS, 2586; College of Arms, Protheroe MS XIX; J. Lloyd James, *Hanes Eglwys Glandwr,* 1902; Photograph of tablet courtesy of Mr. H. Devonald.

Harcourt Powell

GREENHILL, *Pwllcrochan*
Now a farmstead on a slope half a mile south of the parish church, and about four miles west of Pembroke town. It was the residence of gentry families from Elizabethan times till the early part of the 18th century, first that of Davies whose pedigree was recorded by Dwnn in 1597, and afterwards that of Powell who came from Court near Eglwyswrw, descended from the ancient family of Cantington. The unusual circumstances leading to the settlement of this north Pembrokeshire family in the English-speaking south, has been minuted by George William Griffith, as follows: 'This Lewis ap Howell ap Owen [descended from the Cantingtons of Court] beinge a younge student in Oxford and understandinge of his father's death and of many others of his ffrendes upon depended his whole hopes, repaired home, and found of his ffrendes left (by reason of a great and infectious [sickness] then raigning in the Countrey) onely his sistere Anne livinge then a wofull widdow and great with child. And perceyvinge the ayre not to be as yet free from these infections, removed himselfe with his sistere into the remotest parte of the Countrey, right unto Pembroke about the 3 of Queen Mary [1555/6]. He married there first one Mary Lloyd, secondly Katherine Hall, one of the daughters and co-heiress of John Hall of Trewent [southeast of Pembroke], and had issue by them both. The said Mary was daughter and co-heiress to Robert Vaughan ap David Lloyd'. Lewis ap Howell was known as Lewis Powell which name was used by his descendants. They bore the Cantington arms: *gules* an eagle displayed *argent,* a chief chequy *argent* and *vert.*

From 1566 Lewis Powell was Mayor of Pembroke on seven occasions. His son, Morgan Powell was Alderman of Pembroke and Mayor in 1591 and 1603, and Morgan's son Lewis Powell of Greenhill and Lamphey, was Mayor of Pembroke in 1619 and 1622, Member of Parliament for Pembroke Borough in 1620 and 1625, for Haverfordwest Borough in 1634 which he held till his death in 1636. Thomas Powell was assessed for seven hearths at Greenhill in 1670, so that it was a large commodious house at that time. In the 18th century Greenhill became part of the Orielton estate, and in 1786 Greenhill was owned by Sir Hugh Owen and Gwynne Davies of Cwm, Carms., with Elizabeth Webb, widow of John Webb, as tenant. In 1801 Morgan Davies of Cwm sold his two-thirds share of the capital messuage of Greenhill and of Venny Lake.

Refs: GGMS II, ff. 229-30; Pembs. RO, D/Adams No. 180; NLW, Papers of GS, Pembs. Plea Rolls, Poyston Deeds; College of Arms, Wagner MS No. 12; *Dwnn*, i, p. 90; J. T. Evans, *Church Plate of Pembs.,* 1905, p. 75.

GREENWAY, *Narberth (North)*
A large residence in grounds on the eastern fringe of Narberth town. Home of the Davies family for three generations. Francis Davies, gent., was living at Greenway in the years 1654-1678. He was son of the Rev. Thomas Davies, Rector of Eglwys Cymun. The widow, Anne Davies, was assessed for five hearths in 1670. Francis was followed by his son John Davies, and he by his son, Francis Davies, sometimes called Junior, who married Hester Harries daughter and co-heiress of Vicar Harries of Cenarth. In 1708 Francis Davies is described as 'formerly of Greenway, Narberth, but now of Cenarth, Carms.', which suggests that he had gone to live in his wife's home parish. Later he seems to have had trouble concerning the ownership of Greenway, and during the years 1723-25 Francis Davies, gent., brought a suit in Chancery against John Skyrme gent. Dorothy Phillip and Jane Skyrme, re: 'the capital messuage and lands called Greenway' and two closes in Narberth parish. By 1753 Greenway formed part of the Elliot estate, and by 1786

the owner was Lord Kensington. After this it continued to pass through several hands. It is still lived in and is in an excellent state of preservation.

Refs: GGMS Gwyddno, I, p. 13; NLW, Slebech Deeds, Cilymaenllwyd Deeds, Papers of GS, Pembs Plea Rolls, Ridgway Deeds.

GRINSTON, *Brawdy*

About 1¼ miles northeast of the parish church. The manor of Grinton/Grinston was a small but compact unit composed of the following adjoining farms – Easter and Wester Grinton (now two farms called Trefgarn Owen), North Grinton (now called Grinston) the hamlet of Trefgarn Owen, Bwlch Martin, and Pengorse, a total of about 410 acres. In 1326 it was held by free tenants, and in Elizabethan times was listed as a manor belonging to the ap Rhys family of Rickeston. In 1687 James ap Rhys mortgaged the manor, and in 1706 sold it to John Rickson, a wealthy tradesman, of Pembroke, who sold it in 1754 to the widow Lettice Barlow of Rosepool, daughter of William Jones of Llether, Brawdy. In 1763 she bequeathed the manor to her nephew James Jones. When James died without issue, in 1781, it became the property of William Jones of Llether, whose daughter and heiress married George Roch of Butter Hill. The Roch owners allowed the manorial rights to lapse. The tenants of both Trefgarns, (still called Grinton in 1786), in the 17th-19th centuries were Harries, Bateman, Wilcox, and Charles. North Grinton now Grinston, is the only holding to preserve the old name. It was a small place of about 18 acres, and in 1842 was owned by Blanche Maria Davies of Carnachenwen, with William Davies as tenant. In the latter half of the century the tenant was my grandfather, John Jones, (d. 17 November 1919), and it was there that my father James Jones, (d. 22 March 1956), was brought up. After the departure of my grandmother in 1926, Grinston was bought by the owners of adjacent Villa farm, and the old dwelling house converted into an outbuilding, alas. (It still stands and continues to be owned by the Castle Villa family.)

Refs: Black Book of St. Davids, 1326; Francis Jones, 'Trefgarn Owen', *Arch. Cam.,* 1961 and 'Lordships and Manors of Dewsland', *Journal Hist. Soc. of Church in Wales,* 1969; Taylor's *Cussion*; NLW, Papers of GS, Pembs. Plea Rolls.

GRONDRE, *Grondre*★

This was the home of the Colby family in the latter half of 17th century, marked on Colby's Map 1831 just southeast of Vaynor Fawr. John Colby of Grondre in 1695 succeeded Richard Colby who paid tax on one hearth in 1670 showing it was not a commodious house at that time. Also living at Grondre was a cousin, Lawrence Colby, will proved 11 April 1700. The house belonged in 1786 to Rowland Edwardes and was tenanted by James Lewis whose memorial window in St. Anne's chapel, St. Mary's Tenby is inscribed 'In memory of James Lewis of Grondre, died 6 December 1824'. By 1843 Frances Morgan was owner-occupier farming 210 acres. Lewis tells us that 'Grondre, a hamlet in that part of Killymaenllwyd parish which is in the Hundred of Dungleddy, three miles northeast of Narberth, forms an inconsiderable and detached portion of the parish, all the rest situated in Hundred of Derllys, Carms.'

Refs: Spence-Colby Deeds; Lewis, *TDW,* 1834.

GROVE, *Narberth*

Near Molleston, a mile and a quarter southwest of Narberth town. Henry Poyer, a rich tanner of Canaston, bought Grove from Richard Hitching, and was assessed at four hearths in 1670.

The family came to south Pembrokeshire early in the 15th century and the earliest reference is to Philip Poyer, the first member of his family to own Grove, who was bailiff of Tenby in 1414. Henry Poyer in his will, dated 9 September 1677 provides some useful information about his family. He bequeathed as follows: to his grandchildren Thomas, Elinor, Jane, Hannah and Hester Child, Jane and Mary Skyrme £5 each, the money to be handed on their behalf to their fathers, John Child and William Skyrme. To his son Thomas Poyer £10, and to his grandson John Poyer £20; to his daughter Hannah Poyer £100 on her marriage; to his sister Mary Mercer £5; to his niece Alice Poyer and to his servant, Elizabeth Gwillim 40s.

each; to his son, John Poyer and his issue, freehold lands in Templeton, with remainder to his son, Henry Poyer; to his two sons, John and Daniel Poyer, lands in Lower Molleston in Narberth parish to hold for six years, Daniel to pay his brother £30. On 9 May 1678 he executed a codicil in which he stated 'I have bought The Grove in the parish of Narberth from Robert Hitchings of the parish of Easton, Pembroke, and I give the same to my son, Daniel Poyer'.

John Poyer was sued several times in the courts. In 1702/3 Dorothy Roberts of Narberth, widow told the Court of Great Sessions that when she married Michael Roberts who had £10 p.a. in his own right, he received her portion of £40, while she was to enjoy one-third share of all the realty and personalty of her husband. Roberts died about 1685, and 'being an ignorant harmless poor woman' John Poyer 'taking advantage thereof and pretending some right to all the said lands hath entered into and enjoys the said lands' refusing to pay anything to Dorothy who has become 'an object of charity'. She petitioned successfully to sue John Poyer. The result of the action is unknown.

Daniel Poyer the third son, inherited Grove, and it was there that he conducted his tannery business. He married Priscilla, daughter of William Allen of Gelliswick. He made his will on 2 November 1702, and bequeathed £300 each to his second and third sons, Richard and Thomas; £50 each to his daughters, Rebecca and Elizabeth when they became 21 years of age; £5 to his grandchild Elizabeth David; and appointed guardians of his six children who were all minors. Priscilla survived her husband and was sued by several creditors for small sums due from her late husband. One of the claimants, Thomas Jones of Newton parish, tanner, stated that he had been employed by Daniel Poyer for 20 years as his journeyman in the tanning trade at the hire of 6d. a day. Daniel had neglected to pay in full and at the time of his death owed Thomas Jones £33 13s. 8d.

John Poyer, his eldest son, who succeeded his father at Grove was killed by a fall from his horse on 20 May 1737. An account of his death occurs in a manuscript preserved in the Henllan muniments: 'his death was occasioned by a fall from his horse the day preceding that on which he dyed . . . and was taken to a neighbouring house where he continued until the following day, and about one o'clock in the afternoon he was brought in a chair to his own house at Grove, in great pain and misery, where several of his friends having heard of the accident attended and presently he desired one Mr. Eaton, an attorney, might be sent for, to whom he had before given instructions for drawing his will, which was accordingly done; but the said Eaton was not to be found, John Poyer addressed himself to his friends then about him, desiring if they would draw [write] something for the support and settlement of his children, whereupon Thomas Lewis esquire did so. He said that the estate was to be devised to his sons, John and Richard, and that the latter should also receive £100, but that he had informed his wife what he intended to do for his children, namely to give £400 to his eldest daughter Priscilla, and £300 apiece to his other daughters. However his wife, being in great agitation of mind and in distress, cried out "We will set £500 to the eldest daughter and £400 to each of the other daughters, Jane, Anne, Louisa and Mary when they are 21, and charged on Lower Chapel Hill." . . . He then died without speaking another word'.

John Poyer had a considerable personalty, stock and crop at Grove which amounted to £2,800. The deceased's friends refused to help the widow with the tanning business so she leased the management of the tan yard worth £700 or £800 yearly to Joshua Lewis for £1,000 to be paid to her within two years. The lessee who had the management of the business for about 20 years proved unfaithful and Mrs. Poyer had to proceed against him in the courts but recovered very little money. Anne Poyer spent a long widowhood and died about 1781. John and Anne Poyer left nine children. Daniel the eldest son, born about 1734 died unmarried on 23 February 1756. He was very fond of his maidservant, Elizabeth Lewis who presented him with four 'pledges of her permissiveness'. Daniel did not forget her or the children, and in his will he left her £17, (which she had lent to him), and all the wages due to her, (being £3 p.a.), 'no part of which has been paid to her since she entered my service' and also a house and garden in Templeton, a further £20, and two bedsteads in the Partridge Room in Grove House, two feather beds, two bolsters, and a pair of blankets in the Middle and North chambers of the said house, six chairs in the Blue Room, a round oaken table, and all his clothes 'to be made and fitted up for the four natural children I have had of the said Elizabeth Lewis and are now living, viz. James, George, Thomas and Robert, for whom I think it is incumbent on me to make some provision, so I give to each £6 per annum till they be 21 or out of apprenticeship, and £12 apiece to apprentice them, £50 to the said James, £40 to the said George, and £30 apiece to Thomas and Robert when 21 or out of apprenticeship'. Grove passed to his next brother, John who died without issue and so Grove passed to his sister Mrs. Anne Callen of Merrixston. She was the last surviving child of the nine children of John Poyer and the only one to have legitimate issue. She had married William Callen who died on 10 January 1793. They had two sons, Charles Poyer Callen, from whom the Lewis's of Henllan descend, and Daniel Poyer Callen from whom the Penns of Camrose descend.

Anne Poyer, ultimate heiress, died in 1808, leaving Grove to her husband William Callen of Merrixton. Fenton wrote in 1811 '. . . the respectable old house of Grove, embosomed in trees, seat of the ancient family of Poyer . . . and the property was divided by falling to heiresses, and the place has not been inhabited as a family mansion for several years'. Later, the heiress of the Callens brought the property to her husband, J. L. G. P. Lewis of Henllan (q.v.) who was also her first cousin. One of the earlier members of the family, Captain John Poyer of Grove subscribed for 16 copies of the Rev. William Evans's English translation of *Cannwyll y Cymry* in 1771.

Refs: Fenton, *Tour Pembs.,* 1811; NLW, Papers of GS, Pembs. Plea Rolls; VL 1834; Taken from an unpublished article by Francis Jones, 'Poyer of Grove'.

Morgan Davies

GROVE,
just south of Pembroke town

In the late 17th century Grove became the seat of the Lloyds, descended from the ancient family of Lloyd of Morfil, Cilciffeth and Cilgelynen. After Thomas Lloyd married Frances, daughter of Hugh Philipps of Eastington, he settled at Grove as his main seat. He was High Sheriff in 1700, and died not long afterwards, being succeeded by his son and heir, also named Thomas Lloyd. The second Thomas served as High Sheriff in 1709, and died in 1711. His widow Mary then married Morgan Davies of Cwm, Carms., and enjoyed Grove until she died in 1752, aged 70. Thomas Lloyd left daughters and co-heiresses, one of whom, Elizabeth Lloyd married in 1725 Sir William Owen, 4th Baronet of Orielton. Fenton wrote in 1811 'Grove as well as Morfil, in consequence of the late Sir William Owen becoming entitled to a share of this property by his marriage with one of the co-heiresses, and having purchased the shares of the others, forms part of the vast possessions of Orielton.'

Grove thus passed to the Owen family who abandoned it as a residence, and it became a farm. By 1786, Sir Hugh Owen, the then owner had let the property to three tenants.

Refs: Fenton, *Tour Pembs,* 1811; WWHR, ii, p. 47; LT 1786; Francis Jones, 'Lloyd of Cilciffeth', *Pembs. Historian,* 1972; Pembs. RO, Deeds D/LLW/ No. 177.

Wedlock

GUMFRESTON, *Gumfreston*

A large farmstead near the roadside in Gumfreston village, about 1¾ miles west of Tenby.

Timmins wrote in 1895, 'Most visitors to Gumfreston will notice the fine old farmhouse that rises cheek-by-jowl with the carriage-road from Tenby. If we are to believe the tradition of the countryside, this is the most ancient abode in the county. Be that as it may, the place bears traces of no mean antiquity, and is an excellent specimen of a Pembrokeshire homestead of the olden times.' The earliest known family there was that of Widlock whose members are

described as lords of Gumfreston, one of whom John Wydelock the elder, was there in 1372. They bore arms: *sable* a chevron between three lions sejant *argent*. Afterwards it was held by a Welsh family. Harry Llewelyn of Gumfreston (arms: *sable* a falcon *argent*) was followed by his son John who left an only daughter and heiress, Janet, who married Owen ap Owen of Pentre Ifan, and Gumfreston was afterwards held by his son Sir James Bowen (died beween 1518 and 1532). Sir James's son, John Bowen had a daughter and heiress, Elizabeth, who married Sir James Williams of Pant Howel (Carms.) who is described as Lord of the Manor of Gumfreston and lay patron of the parish church in 1535. Five successive generations of this family were lords of the manor, until the death of John Williams in 1693, and the manor and freeholds passed to his daughter and heiress Mary who married Judge John Meyrick of Bush who died in 1736, leaving issue. Thereafter, Gumfreston remained part of the Meyrick estate. The Land Tax of 1786 gives John Meyrick Esq. as owner of Gumfreston (farm), which passed to his descendants.

Refs: WWHR, ii, p. 89; BM Egerton MS 2586; Chetham MS, Pedigree 42; College of Arms, Protheroe MS IV; S. C. Hall, *South Wales,* 1861, p. 443, illust., and I p. 89 illust.; Timmins, *Nooks Pembs.,* p. 27; Francis Jones, 'Bowen of Pentre Evan and Llwyngwair', *Pembs. Historian,* 1979; *Come to Pembs.,* Guide, 1936, p. 21 illust.; PRO, Anc. Deeds.

GWERN FFULBROOK,
Cemaes/Whitchurch
Apart from the indisputable fact that this place was in Whitchurch parish, the location of its site is not known. It is possible that it is identical with (Plâs) Eglwyswen, or Whitchurch (q.v.). Contemporary references to Gwern Ffulbrook are as follows: In 1595, among the properties owned by George Griffith, gent., of Whitchurch, was the following: a messuage called Plâs Gwernffulbrook in occupation of the said George Griffiths. The next reference occurs in the prenuptial settlement of Thomas Bowen 'nephew and heir apparent of George Bowen of Gwernffulbrok' in Whitchurch parish, with Joyce Jones of Pantyderi, dated 11 May 1699, and among properties settled was 'the capital messuage called Gwernffulbrooke'. It occurs as 'Gwain Filbrw' on Eman. Bowen's Map of South Wales 1729, and c. 1760 edition where it is located south of Pant y Deri, between Rhos Dwarch and 'Volyanog'. Gwain Filbrw occurs in Kitchin's map of Pembrokeshire 1754 and later editions.

Information from deeds and documents among the Bronwydd and Clynfyw Deeds in the NLW, show that George Bowen of Gwernffulbrook, gent. left that property to his nephew Thomas Bowen of Gwernffulbrook who married in 1699 Joyce daughter of Thomas Jones of Pantyderi. Their son, George Bowen of Gwernffulbrook, married in 1733 Jane Warren of Trewern; he died in 1740, and Jane married secondly Richard Mathias, gent. of Whitchurch. The name no longer occurs in contemporary records, and it seems clear that it was discontinued. It is strange that the property described as a 'capital messuage' and 'plâs' could have vanished so completely. I am inclined to suspect that it is identical with Eglwyswen/Whitchurch (q.v.), a commodious family seat (now a farm) which stands nearby, once home of a family named Bowen, who also owned Gwern Ffulbrook.

Refs: NLW, Bronwydd, Owen/Colby and Clynfyw Deeds.

HAFOD GROVE, *Moylgrove*

A farmstead southeast of the village, marked as Hafod on Mudge's Map 1819, and Hafod Grove on Colby's Map 1831. At one time part of the Henllys estate. In 1725 Anne Corbett of Henllys, widow (of David Owen) granted a lease, for her life, of Henllys to William Lloyd of Pendpedwast and William Laugharne of Llanreithan (whose mothers were co-heiresses of the Henllys estate), with proviso that the tenant of Hafod Fawr, Moylgrove parish, shall retain his lease of that property.

In 1786 George Lloyd, gent. was owner-occupier of Havod (also called Hafod Glandwr in 1841), and gave a mortgage in £6,600 with power of sale to William Rees, gent. of Haverfordwest. The property is described as Hafod Glandwr alias Glandwr alias Havod Grove, in 1846. In 1852 the property was sold to Stephen Colby of Ffynnone, and afterwards let to farming tenants.

Refs: NLW, Bronwydd Deeds, Papers of GS, Pembs. GF; LT 1786.

HAFOD TYDFIL, *Meline*

A farmstead, now a complete ruin, on the northern slope of Moel Feddau, and near Bedd yr Afange. One of the earliest owners of this property was Thomas Bowen of Pentre Ifan, who died in 1586, among his possessions being 'a tenement called Hafodtydfil and eight acres'. In the following century it became the property of Lloyd of Trefach, Nevern, who leased it for lives to William Bowen gent. who was assessed for two hearths in 1670, and was still there in the 1680s. In November 1682 'the capital messuage and lands called Hafod Tidfil' were included in the post-nuptial settlement of John Lloyd of Trefach and his wife Ruth; and in September 1713 the said John Lloyd conveyed Havod Tydfil, two farms in Moylgrove, and three manors, to his only son Thomas Lloyd. In 1753 the Rev. William Laugharne of Treprisk and his wife Rebecca (daughter of John Lloyd of Trefach) mortgaged Hafod Tydfil, Treprisk, and Kilsavoi in Meline, Moylgrove, and Fishguard parishes, to Francis Skyrme, gent.

Laugharne died in January 1759, and in the following month, his widow Rebecca granted the three said properties to her nephew John Foley of Colby. In 1786 John Herbert Foley of Ridgeway owned the properties; and in 1827 Emily Mary Anne Foley, widow, granted a lease for life of Hafod Tydfil to the widow Jemima Morris. It was thereafter occupied by farming tenants. Shortly after 1945, the author, Mr. R. M. Lockley, then farming Dinas Island, bought Hafod Tydfil from the widowed Mrs. Nancy Lewis, and farmed there for several years.

Refs: NLW, Bronwydd Deeds, Foley of Ridgeway Deeds; R. M. Lockley, *The Golden Year,* 1948; Francis Jones, *Historic Cardiganshire Homes and their Families,* 2000.

HARMESTON, *Steynton*

A Tudor period farmstead, built in traditional style, a long house with a range of nine windows, and two large gable chimneys, halfway between the villages of Steynton and Johnston. Former home of gentry families. Descended from the Dynevor family, Sir Thomas Jones of Abermarlais (Carms.) and of Harmeston was the first High Sheriff of Pembrokeshire, when he served that office in 1541, and his younger brother, Morgan Jones of Harmeston was High Sheriff in 1574. Morgan married Maud daughter of Sir Thomas Philipps of Picton Castle, and was succeeded at Harmeston by his eldest son Thomas Jones, High Sheriff in 1589, who signed the family pedigree for Dwnn on 21 November 1591. He married Elinor, daughter of Sir John Wogan of Wiston, widow of Arnold Baker. In the early part of the 17th century Harmeston passed to the co-heiresses, who had married sons from the Tancred and Bolton families. William Tancred settled at his wife's home.

Elizabeth Tancred, a widow in 1652, conveyed Harmeston to her son Griffith Tancred on his marriage to Mary Howard in that year. Towards the close of the century Harmeston had been bought by a Cardiganshire squire, David Hughes of Vaenog, who was living at Harmeston in 1705. His descendants were still there in 1798, but not long afterwards the property was sold to another Cardiganshire squire, Thomas Davies of Nantgwylan, who owned it in 1827. Amongst properties settled on the marriage of Thomas Davies of Nantyddwylan (*sic*) Esq. in 1840 were East Harmeston Hall and Harmeston Mill in Steynton parish.

Refs: Dwnn, i, pp. 98-9, 189; NLW, Morgan-Richardson Deeds, Griffith Owen Collection, Bronwydd Deeds, Eaton Evans and Williams Deeds, Papers of GS, Pembs Plea Rolls; BM Egerton MS 2586; Deed in Cardiff Public Library, Basil Jones & Sons, auctioneers, Particulars of Property, 1989, illust.; Laws, *Little England Beyond Wales,* 1988, p. 72.

Perrot

HAROLDSTON,

Haroldston St. Issells

An ancient mansion, now completely ruined, due south of Haverfordwest Priory ruins, on a slope above the south bank of Merlin's Brook. Some five miles westwards overlooking St. Brides Bay is the parish of Haroldston West. The medieval family of Harold after whom Haroldston St. Issells is named, was the first known family at the mansion. An undated deed, but pre-1200, concerns William Harold of Haroldyston, and his descendants were still there in the 14th century, until Alice, daughter and heiress of Richard Harold, married Peter Perrot (d. 1378), and their descendants remained in possession of Haroldston until 1763 when it was alienated.

High Sheriffs from this house were Sir Thomas Perrot, Sir John Perrot, 1552, (an ode to him having been written by Dafydd Fynglwyd), later Lord Deputy of Ireland, died in the Tower of London in 1592. Sir Herbert Perrot was High Sheriff in 1660, was ten years later assessed for ten hearths in Haroldston, clearly a commodious mansion. Hester, sole daughter and heiress of Sir Herbert, married on 26 August 1700, Sir John Pakington, 3rd Bt. of Westwood, Worcs., and the property continued in the hands of their descendants, (see *Burke's Peerage* under Hampton).

About the years 1707-62 Addison visited Haroldston, and there at a masked ball met the Countess of Warwick whom he later married. However on 3 May 1763, Sir Herbert Perrot Pakington Bt., whose forebears had owned the property for over five and a half centuries, sold it to Sir John Philipps of Picton Castle; the conveyance describes the property as 'the manor or lordship of Haroldston, the site of the manor or mansion house called Haroldston House, the church or chapelry of Haroldston with patronages thereof, messuage, tenement and lands, consisting of a row of old houses or walls leading from the gate house of Haroldston to Haroldston Dairy, being part of the outhouses and gardens where the old dwelling house stands, fields and closes called the Old Orchard, the Grove, the Water Grove, Water Grove Park, Golf Park, Rath Park, Westfield, Upper Westfield, Oxpark (together 90 acres) and other fields (30 acres), a messuage and land called Church Park and the marsh adjoining; Coney Gare, Hill Park and the marsh adjoining, meadows, Haroldston Marsh with Furzy Hill adjoining, meadow adjoining the old hop garden – all part and parcel of the demesne lands of Haroldston, all in the parish of Haroldston St. Issells'.

An English tourist, calling at Haverfordwest, wrote in his journal in October 1767 – 'Here are two old Houses now in ruins, which have been the seats of good families, and seem built very soon after the fashion of Castles was left off; Prendergast . . . , and Harriston lately belonging to the Packingtons, but now sold to a man who has pulled down all the materials which were saleable . . .' A Picton Castle Estate Terrier made in 1773 describes Haroldston (138 acres) owned by Sir Richard Philipps, the tenant being James Lloyd, Esq. and all the fields including 'the ruins of Haroldston House with the Court and gardens' (two acres). One field called Tump Park recalls the days when a tumulus stood there. Land Tax lists for 1786-98 give Lord Milford as owner of Haroldston and lands. In 1811 the historian Fenton wrote: 'The house [Haroldston] which appears to have been a large and most incoherent aggregate of

Sir John Perrot

the building of different ages, and incapable of being traced to any regular plan, is now entirely in ruins; the widow Perrot married Sir Thomas Jones who in order to enlarge the grounds, acquired the dissolved Priory of Haverfordwest.' According to George Owen, 'the vale in which the house stands was then ornamented with groves and Sir Thomas introduced pheasants from Ireland which he placed in the grove adjoining Harredston House'. In 1834 S. Lewis wrote of Haroldston, 'the ancient mansion is now in a very dilapidated condition'.

A view of the ruins consisting of walls and a tower called the 'Stewards Tower', is given in the frontispiece to *Arch. Cam.,* 1860; this view shows a tower of three storeys (interior 11 feet by 10 feet) with a tiled saddle-back roof, a semi-detached stair rise and garderobes, and terminating in a corbel table and parapet: the lowest storey is vaulted, and the upper storeys show remains of fireplaces and garderobes, the lights are small plain loops; the tower is only a shell, but it is said in 1920 to have been inhabited within living memory. It would seem that the house was square in plan and connected with the tower by an arched doorway. J. H. Parker, in *Arch. Cam.,* 1865, assigned the date of the structure to the 13th century, and says that the hall, lit at each end by a small window of the two trefoil-headed light, occupied the entire first floor, 'the rooms below are vaulted'. The site and its straggling ruins were finally owned by the late Lt.- Col. J. H. V. Higgon of Scolton who presented it to the Town Council of Haverfordwest.

Refs: PRO Deeds (1325-1532); Picton Castle Deeds; RCAM 1925 (reproduction of Norris' sketch); Lord Hampton Deeds (Pakington) in Birmingham Ref. Library; Pembs RO, Deed D/RTP/H, 1763 sale; NLW, Penllergaer Deeds, Noyadd Trefawr Deeds and Add. MS 147C; H. Owen, *Old Pembrokeshire Families,* 1902, pp. 51, 66, and refs. there; Lewis, *TDW,* edns. 1834, 1840; *Haverfordwest and its Story,* 1882; Illustrations occur in RCAM 1925, *Arch. Cam.,* 1860; and D. James, *Sir John Perrott, 1527-1591,* printed 1962.

HAROLDSTON (HALL), *Haroldston West*

A parish, some 6 miles west of Haverfordwest, above the coast of St. Brides' Bay. It is surmised that the Perrots lived here before moving eastwards to Haroldston St. Issells, but there is no proof of this. Little of its earlier history is known. The Land Tax of 1786 gives Hugh Meares Esq. as owner of Haroldston, with John Phillips as tenant. There is a hamlet here where the parish church is located. The parish was one of the few where the rates were still being 'levied and collected by the ploughland' in 1840. On Colby's Map of 1831 a house called 'Hall' is marked to the east of the hamlet. It came into prominence in the latter half of the 19th century as the residence of William Howell Walters, son of William Walters who established a bank in Haverfordwest, and a branch at Narberth in 1863. The father was High Sheriff in 1866. The only son, William Howell Walters, born c.1857, a barrister of the Inner Temple, lived at Haroldston Hall; he was High Sheriff in 1898, knighted in 1920, and died in 1934.

Refs: Carlisle, *TDW,* 1811; Lewis, *TDW,* 1940; *Kelly's Handbook,* 1887, 1892.

Meyrick

HASGUARD, *Hasguard*

The parish lies between St. Ishmaels and Talbenny, to the west of Walwyn's Castle. There were several farms in the area of the parish church in 1786 when John Philipps Laugharne Esq. owned Hasguard Hall, and two farms called Middle Hasguard, and Francis Meyrick Esq. owned Little Hasguard and Sir William Hamilton and a Mr. Martin owned Lower Hasguard, all let to tenants.

In 1583 a grant of arms was made to Gelby Meyrick of Hasguard, viz: *gules* two porcupines in pale passant *argent,* armed *or.* In 1752 Rowland Philipps Laugharne of Pontfaen and Anne his wife, owned one half of 'Haskard otherwise called the Hall of Haskard', he also owned Middle Hasguard which he leased to John Dean of Marloes, farmer, in 1767. George Webb tenant of Hasguard Hall, died in 1792. On Colby's Map 1831, the following are marked – Hasguard Hall, Little and Middle Hasguard, and Hasguard village.

Refs: LT 1786; NLW, Poyston Deeds.

HAVERFORDWEST,
County Town of Pembrokeshire

In the town are the houses called Hermon's Hill (q.v. infra), Foley House (q.v. supra), both still in good order and inhabited. Several rich tradesmen's families lived here who enjoyed gentry status, such as Keymer, Voyle, Canon, Walter, Bateman, Davids, and Sutton. A few interesting houses have been noted – in High Street (formerly occupied by W. H. Smith's bookshop) in a rear room is a carved stone mantelpiece decorated by five coats of arms (c. 1600); 1. A boar chained to a holly tree (Owen of Henllys). 2. Royal Arms, quarterly. 3. party per pale, dexter, three escallops, sinister, on a bend three escallops. 4. On a bend three roses (or escallops). 5. A chevron between three ravens. It is likely that a descendant of the Owens of Henllys was the owner of this property. Timmins in 1895 describes a house in Quay Street '. . . we descry a low-bowed entrance opening upon the foot path, the massive nail-studded door, with its giant lion-headed knocker, being enframed by liberally moulded jambs. Passing beneath this ancient portal, we are admitted to an interior beautified by the rare old oaken stairway shown in our sketch; this stairway gives access to nicely panelled chambers whose fireplaces retain their original blue Dutch tiles painted with scenes of Biblical history. To the rear of the dwelling-house stands a flour mill driving a brisk trade in its green old age. Stepping out to the rear we find ourselves upon the riverside quay . . . '.

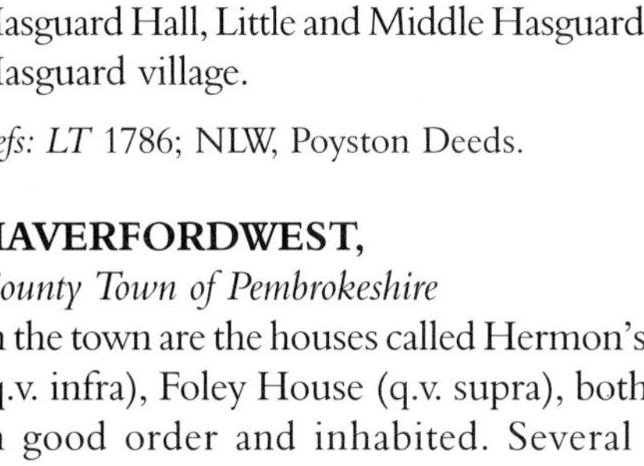

Refs: RCAM Pembs. 1925, p. 112, sketch of mantelpiece, Thornhill; Timmins, *Nooks Pembs.,* 1895, with sketch of stairway.

HAYLETT, *Haroldston St. Issells*

A residence near the road to Freystrop. A family named Haylot lived in this district in medieval times, but whether the place-name derived its name from them, or vice versa, we do not know. An undated deed, pre-1200, mentions John Heylot de Freystrop; in 1310 William Heyloht son and heir of Walter Heyloht, granted lands in Manorbier to William Harold, lord of Haroldston; and in 1774 Richard Tasker granted to William Perot, Monytharch and High Freystrop, Haroldston – iuxta – Haverford, Trechemanshill, Boydynys, and Heylot, in the lordship of Haverford. Over two centuries later on 8 January 1697/8, Miss Hesther Perrott of Haroldston, granted a lease for 29 years of (*inter alia*) Haylett, to Francis Edwardes of Haverfordwest and on 9 May 1725 Sir John Pakington, Bart. of Westwood, Worcs., and his only son Herbert Perrot Pakington, heirs of the Perrotts, granted a lease for 99 years to the said Francis Edwardes of Haylett, Esq. of messuages called Haylett and Boyden (2 ploughlands) in Haroldston

St. Issells. However, the lessee who was M.P. for Haverfordwest, did not enjoy the lease for long, for later in that year he died, his will being proved on 16 December 1725. The son, William Edwardes, was created Baron Kensington in 1776, and in the Land Tax of 1786 and 1797 is described as owner of Haylett. Little is known of it afterwards, but a publication of 1882 tells us that Lady Betty Rich resided at 'the country seat of Haylett, every trace of which has now been destroyed.' Later, a fine house was erected there, given the name of Haylett Grange, which is now (1986) a preparatory school.

Refs: PRO, Anc. Deeds, Nos. 1549, 1794; Deed in Cardiff Free Library; Pembs. RO, Deed DX/2; *Haverfordwest and its Story,* 1882, p. 16.

HAYSCASTLE (CASLAI), *Hayscastle*

Near the parish church there were once three farms, each bearing the names of the tenants in order to distinguish them. They eventually became two farms, known during my youth as 'Caslai Harries' and Caslai Nicholas'. In the vicinity are four ancient burial mounds, called Tumps locally, and the site of an earthwork fortification, which is commemorated in the name of the parish. Hayscastle is mentioned in 1286, and later became a lay manor owned during medieval days by the family of Russell, until Joan Russell, the ultimate heiress, brought the manor to her husband Richard Laugharne of St. Brides, whose descendants held it until about 1800. The farms had several owners from time to time, amongst them William Scourfield of New Moat who in 1745 gave a lease for lives of land in Hayscastle parish to Henry Skeel of Hayscastle, yeoman; in 1760 John Allen of Dale Castle gave a lease for lives of 'the West Tenement of Hayscastle' to Henry Skeel, yeoman; in 1786, one of the farms was in possession of Henry Watts, owner-occupier, and two others of Hayscastle farms, owned by John Lloyd Esq. the tenants being Henry Skeel and John Morse. The main occupiers of the three farms were the Harries family (1597-1764) Watts (1623-1842) and Skeel (1745-1847), and some of those longer than the terminal dates given above. In 1842 one farm (517 acres) was owned by John Allen Lloyd-Philipps of Dale Castle, and farmed by John Nicholas, tenant, and another farm (448 acres) owned by John Watts and tenanted by Peter Watts, while the third (69 acres) was owned by the executors of William Henry Scourfield and tenanted by Henry Skeel. Thus they were of extensive acreage. The largest was that tenanted by John Nicholas, whose descendants the Morrises, now own the farm and reside there.

Refs: Black Book of St. Davids, 1326; *RCAM Pembs.* 1925; BM Egerton MS 2586; Pembs. RO, Deeds; NLW, Pembs. Plea Rolls and GF, Morgan-Richardson Deeds; LT 1786; Tithe Map and Schedule, 1842.

HAYSTON, *Llanstadwell*

In the northern part of the parish, between Scovaston and Harmeston. There were three properties there, Hayston (Hall), Lower Hayston, and Hayston Mill, marked on Colby's Map 1831 and on modern OS maps. Hayston was the home of yeomen over the centuries. In 1550 John Mabe was living there, to be followed by his son David, living there in 1607. David Mabe does not appear to have been wholly desirable, and he was presented in the Great Sessions of 1611 as of Hayston, yeoman 'a most notorious wicked fellow, a fighter, brawler, common gamester of alehouses, sower of sedition, drunkard, ravisher, etc.' Dear me! In 1616 we learn that David Mabe sued John Philipps of Southfield, in respect of a grant he made of 'a capital messuage and land in the vill of Hayston' on 20 September 1613. Later, in 1634, Margaret Collins, widow, complained of David and John Mabe of Hayston, yeomen, for saying that she was 'an old witch' and would prove that she was just that. In the other messuage of Hayston, John Tasker, yeoman, lived in 1611.

The Mabes seemingly departed before the end of the century, for in 1699, Francis Rossant and John Tasker, gentlemen, released one third of a messuage of 22 acres in 'the townred and fields of Hayston', to Charles Jordan, gent. In 1759 John Jordan of Dumpledale, Esq. conveyed (inter alia) a messuage called Hayston, to the Rev. Owen Philipps of Haverfordwest. In 1785, Herbert Lloyd of Carmarthen and Albany Wallis of London, assignees of certain estates of Marmaduke

Gwynne, sold the lordship or manor of Hayston, the capital messuage and lands called Hayston, and a messuage with Hayston Mill, to Richard Mathias of Tierston, Steynton parish. In 1786, three properties at Hayston were owned by Richard Mathias, Reverend Dr. Phillips and Lord Kensington, all let to tenants. Shortly afterwards Richard Mathias and his family came to live there. He died before 1814, and was followed by his son, Richard, who married Justina Needham Harries of Tregwynt by whom he had children.

In 1837 appeared particulars of sale of the mansion house and land called Hayston, late residence of Richard Mathias Esq. deceased, the manor of Hayston, tithes of the whole estate, and the corn grist mill called Hayston Mill, with a newly erected house, in the parishes of Llanstadwell and Rosemarket. Thomas Henry Davies of Hayston Hall, Esq. was living there in 1877-88.

Refs: NLW, Pembs. GS; Pembs. RO Deeds, D/RTP (THD); LT 1786.

HAYTHOG, *Spittal*

About one mile southeast of Spittal parish church, marked on Colby's Map of 1831 as Upper and Lower Haythog, the latter being the old mansion. The earliest known family there was that of Barrett, one of whom John Barrett, lived there during the years 1383-1439. Later the property passed to the Sutton family, one of whom, Lewis Sutton of Haythog, was slain there on 18 July 1506. By his wife Gwenllian, natural daughter of Sir Rhys ap Thomas, he had a son, John Sutton of Haythog, and Haverfordwest, who died on 18 August 1551, leaving a daughter and heiress, Thomasin Sutton, who married Rees Morgan, gent. of Haverfordwest.

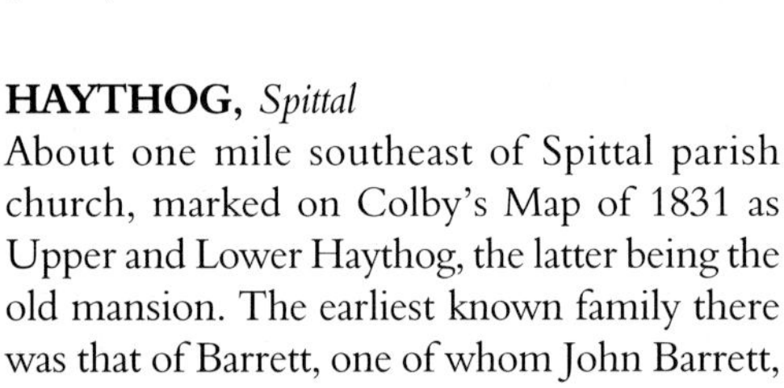

It later passed to Richard Philipps (descended from Picton Castle), whose son John Philipps, who owned Haythog and Ffynnongain, was High Sheriff in 1638. He was followed by his son William Philipps of Haythog (born c.1615), a Royalist, High Sheriff in 1645, and M.P. for Haverfordwest in 1660. He was assessed at ten hearths in 1670, which indicates that Haythog was then of considerable size. His daughter and ultimate heiress, Anne, married her kinsman Charles Philipps of Sandyhaven, and Haythog *iure uxoris.* Their son William Philipps inherited Haythog, and was High Sheriff in 1736. His granddaughter, Anne Philipps, married Joseph John Philipps Laugharne of Orlandon & Pontfaen, and Haythog passed to their descendants, one of whom, William Charles Allen Philipps of St. Brides, was owner of Haythog in 1834. After this it became the home of yeomen and farmers. There is an old rhyme:

Wiston was, Haythog is
But Pentyparc shall be
The fairest of the three.

Refs: Fenton, *Tour Pembs.*, 1811; *Pembs. Arch. Survey,* 1783; Pembs RO, Deeds; NLW, Pembs. Plea Rolls, Slebech Deeds; PRO, Anc. Deeds; BM Egerton MS 2586; Haverfordwest Corporation Deeds.

HEAN CASTLE, *St. Issells*

The original name was Hên Gastell, the Welsh for old castle, mentioned in 1295; in 1358 'Hengastel' was owned by Laurence de Hastings, Earl of Pembroke. Clearly it was an early Welsh earthen fortification, but it is doubtful whether the Normans used it for military purposes. The first known reference to it as a residence is in 1636 when its occupiers were Nicholas Lewis Esq. (from Gellydywyll, Carms.), and Katherine Vaughan, widow. It was then called Hencastle. On the death without issue of Nicholas Lewis, the property passed to his widow Anne (née Barlow of Slebech), who married Lewis Wogan of Wiston, and their son, Lewis Wogan junior, married Martha, daughter and co-heiress of David Williams (High Sheriff in 1683) who lived at Hencastle. In this period the residence was commodious, and in 1670 Nicholas Lewis was assessed at eight hearths.

It remained as one of the Wogan residences until the end of the 18th century when Thomas Wogan the last of the line died unmarried and it passed to two co-heiresses – Eleanor Wogan who married in 1793 Rev. Thomas Roberts, Methodist minister and friend of John Wesley, and Susannah Wogan who married in 1794 Thomas Stokes of Haverfordwest, a Quaker. In 1800 Susannah bought out her sister's share for £7,200 and Hean Castle passed to her husband. At this time the estate consisted of the mansion, the lordship of St. Issells and Treberth, the castle mill, and 21 farms, all in St. Issell's parish. In 1839 Thomas Stokes was owner occupier of the mansion, and the estate had 52 tenants. Later it was sold by Thomas Stokes' son (by his second wife) also named Thomas Stokes, to his brother-in-law Edward Wilson (High Sheriff in 1861).

In the 1860s Wilson sold the property to a London solicitor, C. R. Vickerman, (son of John Vicerman, a London solicitor to Lord Milford), who rebuilt the mansion in the 1870s (immediately in front of the older house) with red sandstone from Runcorn, Cheshire, brought to Saundersfoot wharf as ballast. A photograph of the original house shows a large traditional two-storeyed building. Vickerman lived at Hean Castle till his death, and in 1899 it was sold to Sir William Thomas Lewis, Bt. (created Lord Merthyr in 1911). It is now owned and occupied by the Hon. Trefor Lewis, son and heir of the second peer.

Refs: NLW, Noyadd Trefawr Deeds, Pembs. Plea Rolls, Tithe Map St. Issells, 1839; Pembs RO, LT 1786; Fenton, *Tour Pembs.,* 1811; *Contemporary Biographies of S. Wales and Mon.,* 1907, illust.; *South Wales Daily News,* 16 September 1911, illust.; Roscoe Howells, *Old Saundersfoot,* 1977, illusts. of the old and present mansions.

HEATHFIELD,
also called HEATHFIELD LODGE, *Letterston*

This Georgian residence was built at the opening of the 19th century by the Harries family of Priskilly, later of Tregwynt. In 1804 it was the home of Margaretta Theodosia Williams, widow of Thomas Williams of Treleddin, St. Davids, and sister of John Hill Harries of Priskilly, High Sheriff in 1805. By

1834 it was tenanted by William Jones, (died 1858), father of an only child Anna Jane, an extremely extravagant lady who married John Owen Tucker Edwardes of Sealyham. In 1904 it was the home of James Henry Morton who had married Suzanna Agnes daughter of the owner John Henry Harries of Tregwynt. It was later sold.

Refs: Pembs. RO, James of Narberth Deeds; Lewis *TDW,* 1840; VL 1834; Property Particulars of Heathfield, for Sale, John Francis, Halifax Property Services, 1989, illust.

HELYGNANT, *Meline*

A farmstead marked on Colby's Map 1831, as Lignant near Brynberian. The first known owner was Owen Fychan, descended from Gwynfardd Dyfed, followed by his son Howel, and he by his son Rees ap Howel who was living in 1506 when his seal to a deed shows a lion rampant within a true-love knot. It formed two or three tenements held at different times by various owners. In 1597 Thomas Griffith ap Ieuan Jenkin of Mynachlogddu, yeoman, owned Lygnant (Philip Devonald, tenant). In 1614 a tenement (15 acres) called Elygnant formed part of the estate of Thomas James of Cilgwyn, gent. lately deceased and in 1597 William Griffith of Penybenglog, gent. gave a bond in £100 to the Rev. Miles' son Thomas, parson of Meline, for the quiet enjoyment by the latter of 'Plâs Helignant'. The parson's son, the Rev. Lewis Miles, held it in 1632. In 1649 Nathaniel Miles of Meline, gent. and his mother Frances Miles, widow, sold 'Plâs Helignant' to his cousin William Miles of Llanfairnantgwyn for £50. In 1686 it was owned by Owen Miles, gent. and Janet (Bowen) his mother. There were many changes after this, and several owners. In 1737 two messuages in Helignant Issa were owned by John Warren of Trewern, in 1786 Thomas Rodger, in 1834 Thomas Lewis of Eglwyswrw.

Refs: NLW, Bronwydd Deeds, Picton Castle Deeds.

HENDRE, *Llandeloy*

At one time there were two messuages here, Hendre Ucha, and Issa, which still existed in 1865, but by 1894 they had been amalgamated to form one unit. In 1625 it was the home of Evan Harry, yeoman, probably a tenant. By 1653 it formed part of the estate of John Laugharne (later of Llanunwas) and Hendre Ucha and Issa (192 acres) continued to form part of the Laugharne estates, and still owned the farm in 1716. Later in the 18th century they were bought by Henry John of Caerwen, a successful estate agent and farmer, who owned it in 1786, the tenant being William Griffith, yeoman. The next owner was William John (Henry's younger son), followed by his only daughter Anne. She married William Scowcroft, a tradesman, of Haverfordwest. They settled at Hendre, and were followed by their daughter, Elizabeth Margaret Scowcroft who married Robert Henry Marshall Yeates. They did not remain long at Hendre, and in 1865 sold the property to a local Baptist minister, the Rev. William Reynolds of Ynys y Barry for £4,600. Mr. Reynolds died in 1908, aged 88.

Refs: NLW, Williams and Williams Deeds, Fines in GS, Bronwydd Deeds, LT 1786.

HENDRE, *Meline*

A farmstead on the east bank of Nant Brynberian, and near Crosswell. A deed, dated 6 June 1407, is a grant and confirmation from Philip ap Rudderch Cainton, gent. to Howel ap Owen ap Rees – a messuage, lands and woods in Hendref in the fee of Eglwyswrw, bounded by the river Deat, the chapel of Penkelli and the rill of Penkelli *ad magnam' viam de vado leprosoro ad villam de Penkelli.* The next reference is much later.

In 1659 Thomas Reignold of Blaiddbwll, gent. mortgaged three messuages called Hendref alias Pentref in Meline parish, to John Lewis of Henllan Owen, gent. In 1690 Hendre was the home of Sibyl Vaughan, spinster, and in 1699 of another spinster, Elizabeth Vaughan. In 1686 a Fine was suffered between Owen Miles of Llanfairnantgwyn, gent. his mother Janet Bowen, widow, and George Lewis of Meline gent. in respect of Helignant in Meline parish. In 1692 Arthur William of Meline, gent. mortgaged the messuage called Park y Meyruk to George Lewis of Hendre, gent. who was still living there in 1710, but had died by 1727, when his nephew and heir was another George Lewis. The last gentry family of note there was that of Lewis.

Refs: College of Arms MSS, Wagner MS XII; NLW Bronwydd Deeds, Eaton Evans and Williams Deeds, Ethel Jones Deeds, Penllergaer Deeds, Papers of GS, Pembs.; Carms RO, Golden Grove Books; Pembs. RO, LT 1786; B. G. Charles, *George Owen of Henllys,* 1973.

HENDRE, *St. Dogmaels*

A farmstead in the northerly part of the parish, near the coast; on the south of the cove of Pwll Grannant. The first owner-occupiers of Hendre were the Lloyds, descended from the chieftain Gwynfardd Dyfed, who held the property from 1250 down to the 19th century. George Owen of Henllys wrote of Hendre as 'the mansion house of John Lloyd, gentleman, auncientlie descended . . . the house of Hendre and manor of Granant came to him by purchase from Rees Lloyd son and heir of his uncle John Lloyd.' Owen called notice to the house as 'caput of Granant alias Hendre to his cousin-german John Lloyd of Cwmgloyn which thereafter was the chief residence of the family.

When Evan Lloyd, son and heir of John Lloyd of Hendre married Mary, daughter of George Owen of Henllys, their marriage settlement dated 1596 included the Hendre estate then consisting of eleven farms in St. Dogmael's parish, one messuage in each of the parishes of Bayvil, Moylgrove and Nevern, and four messuages in Llandygwydd parish, Cards. Hendre was then described as two messuages, -Uch and -Issa. The manorial courts of Hendre alias Granant were held at Hendre down to 1821. Emily Pritchard's work, *St. Dogmael's Abbey,* contains some useful information about the old mansion, quoting the Rev. Henry Vincent in *Arch. Cam.* 1864, as follows – 'Hendre where once was a fine mansion of the Lloyds: a part of the old house, probably an oratory, has been converted into an outhouse; a keystone of the arch of the doorway of what had been the dwelling house is inscribed "T.LL. Esq. 1744 CW"; the supposed oratory has no entrance from without, and is entered by a door on the northwest. Hendre was once owned by Major Lewis of Clynflyw, who bought the property prior to 1786; the walls are very strong, partly built of seashore pebbles embedded in the hard mortar; the walls and roof of the old chapel at Hendre are in almost perfect condition. Thomas Lloyd of Cwmgloyn (1744) turned the old chapel into a dwelling-house, and when it was later abandoned for the new farmhouse, the old building was turned into a cowhouse and stable.' Hendre is now owned by a gentleman from Herefordshire and administered by a manager; the farmhouse is comparatively modern; the outbuildings are much the same as those described by Mrs. Pritchard.

Refs: George Owen, Taylor's *Cussion,* and *2nd Book,* B. G. Charles, ed.; *Dwnn,* i, pp. 246-7; Fenton, *Tour Pembs.,* 1811; *Arch. Camb.,* Oct. 1864; *Pembs. Arch. Svy,* 1896-1907; Francis Jones 'Lloyd of Hendre and Cwmgloyn', *NLWJ,* winter 1984, and refs. there; Francis Green MSS, vol. 20, Deed dated 1516.

HENDRE EYNON, *St. Davids**

A Lay manor in 1587, now a farmhouse and called Hendre. There is a sketch of the farmhouse with a circular chimney opposite page 338 in *Ancient Monuments Pembrokeshire,* 1925. Its history as a lay manor is given in Francis Jones's article 'Lay Manors of Dewsland' in the *Journal of Historical Society of the Church in Wales,* 1969.

It was the home in the 17th century of John Propert whose will was proved in 1660. By an unknown wife, Mary he had six sons and one daughter, Margaret. Richard Propert, his eldest son, succeeded him to Hendre Eynon followed by his son, Thomas who died in 1750. Thomas had two sons, John Propert (d. 1732), of Hendre Einon who married Mary, sister and co-heiress of David Harries of Trehowell of Llanwnda by whom he had two sons, William, died 1747, Thomas died 1708, and a daughter Elizabeth (1729-93), who married firstly David Williams of Tancredston, and secondly William Mortimer of Whitchurch, a master mariner. Their marriage settlement was dated 29 December 1767. William Mortimer was shown as tenant of Hendreinon in the Land Tax records of 1786, assessed at 14s. 9d. John Harries Esq. owner.

The second son of Thomas Propert was the Rev. Richard Propert, Vicar Choral of St. Davids (1709-89) who married twice, firstly to Margaret, daughter of David Morgan by whom he had a son, Rev. David Propert also Vicar Choral of St. Davids, born 1731 and will dated 1808. Richard married secondly Elizabeth Rees of St. Davids in 1733 by whom he had issue, a great-grandson being Dr. John Propert, founder of Epsom College who died in 1867. In 1981, now called Hendre, the owner was Mr. and Mrs. Neville Davies.

Refs: Francis Jones Archives.

HENDRE RIFFITH, *Whitchurch*

A farm to the north of Solva, just beyond Gwarcoed, on the way to Felin Ganol. The earliest reference to it occurs in a deed dated 7 March 1447/8 whereby Elena Adam released a messuage and lands at 'Hendreff ap Griffith ap Oweyn', Whitchurch parish, to David Robyn, clerk. In 1786 Hendreriffith was owned by John Bateman, gent. with John Harries as tenant, paying a Land Tax of 4s. 10d. The name occurs as Hendre ruffydd in the Voters List 1904.

Refs: NLW, Eaton Evans and Williams Deeds.

HENLLAN, *Llanddewi Velfrey*

Between Llanddewi Velfrey village and the Penblewin Cross, south of the main road near an ancient earthwork called Caerau and Gaer. Originally it was a small hamlet containing several farms, and an ancient chapel of which no traces now remain. Ever since 1636 when David Lewis, gent. of Henllan, served as a Juror in the Great Sessions, the Lewis family continued as the principal landowners of the parish. In 1670 David Lewis of 'Henllan village' was assessed for two hearths. In 1786, another descendant, described as David Lewis Esquire, was owner-occupier of Upper Henllan, and also owned Lower and Middle Henllan farms, both let to tenants.

The family continued to flourish and in the 19th century produced a Bishop of Llandaff (Rt. Rev. Richard Lewis, 1883-1905) and a Judge (Sir Wilfred Lewis, Q.C.). From about 1835-54 the old mansion was untenanted, and 1854 Mr. J. L. G. P. Lewis pulled it down, and built a new mansion, two illustrations of which occur in the 1875 book, *County Families,* by Thomas Nicholas. It lasted until about 1957 when it was pulled down by the then owner of the Henllan estate, Mr. Richard Lewis, J.P., D.L., of Caermaenau Fawr which is now the main residence of the family.

Refs: LT 1786; Lewis, *TDW,* 1840; Nicholas, *County Families,* ii, p. 840, 1875 edn. illust.; C. S. Allen, *Photos in South Wales,* 1871; Francis Jones, 'A Victorian Bishop of Llandaff', *NLWJ,* 1975; Photo taken by C. S. Allen, *Tenby in 1878,* copy in NLW.

Eynon

HENLLAN/HENTLAND, *Rhoscrowther*

There were two properties here – Lower Henllan and Henllan; the former farmlands are flanked on the west and north side by oil storage tanks. The mansion once stood at Upper Henllan. The property is mentioned in a deed of 1273 between John Symon and Sir John de Castro Martin, knight, as a 'carucate in Henthlan'. The family of Eynon (descended from Gwynfardd Dyfed) and living there about the year 1400, and bore as arms *gules* a chevron *or* between three towers *or.* John Eynon of Henllan fell at the battle of Banbury in 1469. The property finally passed to a daughter, Christine Eynon who married Jenkin White, a rich burgess of Tenby where his ancestors had lived for several generations. Griffith White was living at Henllan before 1550, and died in 1590. During the Civil War in the next century, the Whites supported Parliament, and the historian Fenton quotes a letter of 28 March 1648 which describes an attack by Royalist troops – 'Henllan house was the same day beset, Mr. White, the then possessor, Mr. Roger Lort, Adjutant-General Fleming, and other commissioners meeting there, escaped on shipboard'.

In 1670 Henry White, Esq. was assessed at eight hearths for Henllan, which shows it to have been a large residence. Thomas White, last of the main male line died in 1680, and the property passed to Elizabeth White who lived mostly at Bangeston. There is a tradition that Elizabeth, widow of Griffith White of Henllan, who was married four times 'continued after death to drive in a six horsed coach from Sampson Cross Roads by Stackpole to Tenby, through Jameston, Lydstep and Penally, when the moon was full; but horses, coachman and lady had not a head between them'.

White

Henllan was abandoned and became a farmstead at the end of the 17th century. Despite her four marriages, Elizabeth the heiress died without issue in 1736, and Henllan passed to the Campbells of Stackpole Court. The Whites had provided the county with seven High Sheriffs in the period 1561-1658. They bore the following arms: *sable* a chevron *ermine* between three stags' heads caboshed *or.*

In 1786 John Hook Campbell owned Lower Hentland (John Meares, Esq. tenant) and Upper Hentland (where the old mansion stood).

In a sale catalogue of 1802, it was advertised for sale by Lord Cawdor, and then comprised of three farms held by tenants – Upper Henllan (165 acres), Lower Henllan (18 acres) and 'part of Henllan farm' (44 acres). It later became part of the Orielton estate. The Tithe Map and Schedule of Rhoscrowther parish in 1838 shows Upper and Lower Henllan as owned by Sir John Owen of Orielton, and tenanted by John Thomas and John Mirehouse. According to the *Pembs. Archaeological Survey* (1896-1907), there were remains of a large brick archway and gable-end of a building, and a place that looks as if it had been a fish-pond. An essay published in

1897 describes Henllan, 'now almost in total ruin, was a mansion of importance.' There were also traces of a walled garden.

Refs: Dwnn, i, pp. 129-30; WWHR ii, 50; GGMS; BM Egerton MS 2586; Fenton, *Tour Pembs.,* 1811; *Wales Magazine,* Aug. 1897; Timmins, *Nooks Pembs.,* 189; Francis Jones 'White of Henllan', *Pembs. Historian,* 1974; Laws & Edwards, *St. Mary the Virgin,* Tenby, 1907, p. 194.

HENLLAN OWEN, *Eglwyswrw*

A farmstead just over a mile west of Eglwyswrw, near the border with Meline. Home of a minor gentry family descended from Jenkin ap Howell of Nevern (slain at Banbury 1469). A local record of 1594 mentions 'the land of Richard James where he lives called Henllan Owen'.

In 1603/4 George Owen writes 'Henllan Owen, the mansion house of George Lewis, being his auncient patrimonie, and a brother's share of the old Howell ap Jenkin spoken of before in Nevarne. He is the son of Lewis the son of Richard the sonne of James the sonne of Jeuan ap Jenkin a younger brother of Howell ap Jenkin of Nevarne the younger for there were two of that name in Nevarne, the one grandfather to the other. He beareth the Armes of Pentre Ieuan . . . '. In 1811 Fenton writes 'At a short distance from this very memorable spot (Cefn Dianel, below Bwlchgwynt) stands the ancient mansion of Henllan Owen, once the residence of my ancestry by my grandmother, daughter of John Lewis Esq of Manorawan, which, with a considerable property that followed it, was a younger brother's portion, of the house of Howel ap Jenkin ap Ropert of Nevern . . . It is now but an ordinary farmhouse, and bears no marks of its former consequence.'

According to the GGMS, the last of the family to live there, George Lewis 'sold his inheritauncae of Henllan Owen to George Bowen of Nevarne (Llwyngwair) his cozen, for £145.' Thereafter it was farmed by tenants.

In 1717 James Bowen of Llwyngwair leased it for 21 years to Henry David, yeoman. In 1786, the Rev. James Bowen (of Llwyngwair) owned two farms at Henllan Owen (Thos. Robert, tenant), and the Rev. Mr. Lewis., D.D., owned a third farm there, tenanted by John Thomas.

Refs: Extent of Cemais, 1594; George Owen's *2nd Book,* 1603-4, B. G. Charles, ed.; GGMS Gwynfardd; College of Arms, Protheroe MS IV; BM Egerton MS 2586; NLW, Bronwydd Deeds.

HENLLYS, *Llanrhian*

A farmstead about a quarter of a mile north of Llanrhian church, on a slope above a cwm through which a rivulet runs to the sea at Porthgain. The farmlands extend to the coast and includes the islet of Ynys Fach. Henllys together with Longhouse and other properties in the parish were owned in earlier times by the Bishop of St. Davids, and formed part of the episcopal manor of Trevine (Trefin). In the *Black Book of St. Davids,* 1326, the park called Hulles' (Henllys) is named as part of the Bishop's manor of Trevine. In 1554 John David of Trevine sued seven of the parishioners for forcible entry and depasturing on his land at 'Henlles'. In 1640 the Bishop leased lands, including a ploughland called Henllys of 200 acres, to Henry Garnon of Trevine for 21 years. The said Henry Garnon was still tenant in 1660 when a survey of the Bishop's manor was made, including Henllys and a sheep-fold there. On Kitchen's Map of 1763, the farm is described as Henllisk. In the Land Tax 1786, the owner of 'Henllys Land' occurs as John Edwardes of Sealyham, Esq. with Peter Harries of neighbouring Felindre as tenant. Edwardes was probably leaseholder, for in 1817 the Bishopric of St. Davids owned Henllys, 164 acres at that time, and in 1845 still owned the farm, then comprising 194 acres, tenanted by Thomas Roch. It was later bought by the Charles family. My wife Ethel was brought up there. It is now owned by Gwilym Charles.

HENLLYS, *Nevern*

Now a farmstead on a high slope above the river Duad which joins the Nevern at the lower end of the farmlands. It was a gentry residence throughout the Middle Ages, but the Elizabethan antiquary, the celebrated George Owen, gave Henllys a foremost place among the residences of the county. It was certainly larger than any other similar seat in north Pembrokeshire judging from the 1670 Hearth Tax List, where it was assessed at ten hearths.

Originally, there were two messuages there – Henllys Uch and Issa, the former being the home of the owners. The first known owners were the family of Pentre Ifan, descended from Gwynfardd, who also owned several properties in the Henllys district. According to Dwnn, Ieuan ap Rees, a younger son, received Henllys as his share, 'a gavas Henllys', called Henllys Ucha in the Golden Grove pedigrees. His son, Howel ap Ieuan (viveus 1499-1520) started selling some of his farms to William Owen, and it was Howel's grandson, Henry Lewis, who sold Henllys Ucha and other properties to William Owen on 7 July 1543, and in 1558 Owen ap William of Cwmeog (whose father was cozen-german to Henry Lewis) sold his lands in Henllys Issa, Cwmeog, Dyffryn and Trefoes to the same William. The new owner, a successful lawyer, was descended from an old north Pembrokeshire family. His father, Rhys ap Owen Fychan was living at Henllys Issa in 1524, and by his marriage in 1487 to Jane, widow of Philip ap Gwilym of Stone Hall, he had William Owen. In addition to acquiring Henllys and other lands in the district, he bought in 1543 the lordship of Cemaes from John Touchet, Lord Audley. William died at Henllys on 29 March 1574, 'being Munday about midnight, and was buried next day at ye church of Nevarn', aged 105 years according to his son and heir, George Owen. As George had been born about 1552, he was 83 years of age when he died. The Henllys estate and the lordship of Cemaes continued in the family until 1681 when William Owen died without issue, and his possessions passed between his two sisters, co-heiresses, namely Elizabeth who married Arthur Laugharne of Llanreithan, and Ann who married Thomas Lloyd of Penpedwast, descended from the Bronwydd family, who in due course, became sole owners of the lordship and estate. After Sir Marteine Lloyd died in 1935 his daughter succeeded to the lordship and the family has descended through the female line to the present day (q.v. Newport Castle). In the early 18th century, Henllys was abandoned as a residence, thereafter inherited by farming tenants, until sold in the 20th century. The former mansion was described by George Owen in 1594 – 'The manor place or mansion house of the said manor called Henllys with all houses and buyldinges, coortlages, gardens and orchardes, ys situat in the myddest of the lordes demaine landes and ys buylded of stone, covered or tiled with slate or stone, and there is belonging a fair stable of seven bays long and a barn of 13 bays built and covered as before, with diverse chambers and necessary rooms . . . The hospitality of this house was proverbial, and its good cheer carried on upon an immense scale; if we estimate it by the accounts handed down to us of the dimensions of its oven and brewing vats.' No trace of the original structure remains in the present farmstead.

The original house of George Owen of Henllys is now currently under excavation by Professor Mytum of York University.

Refs: B. G. Charles, *George Owen of Henllys,* 1973, a definitive history and refs. there; NLW, Bronwydd Collection, George Owen's *2nd Book,* 1603-4, *Extent of Cemais,* 1594, Pembs Plea Rolls, GS; Carms. RO, GGMS; BM Egerton MS 2586; Tithe Map and Schedule, Nevern Parish, 1840; Fenton, *Tour Pembs.,* 1811; *Dwnn,* i, pp. 60, 156-8; WWHR, ii, p. 78; DWB; RCAM, 1925; Katherine H. Lloyd, *The Lords of Kemes 1087-1914,* 1930.

HERMONS HILL, *Haverfordwest*

An agreeable 18th century residence in Haverfordwest, near the boundaries of St. Mary's and St. Thomas parishes; stands on a hillside overlooking the river Cleddau and the wharves of the county town. The present structure was built in the early half of the 18th century, and was the house of the Williams family, the first of them being Dr. Perrott Williams who had practised in London before returning to settle at Hermons Hill. By his wife Hannah Skyrme of Llawhaden, he had two sons; the elder, Counsellor Williams, J.P., succeeded to Hermons Hill, was High Sheriff in 1767, and died unmarried in 1779, when the property passed to his brother William Williams, officer of the Excise. William died unmarried 1801 and Hermons Hill was bequeathed to his cousin Mrs. Jane Bassett (née Lloyd) of Neath who lived at Hermons Hill for some years. Dr. Francis Edwardes also lived there for some time.

In 1808 Mrs. Bassett, then of Neath, widow, and her kinsman, John Herbert Lloyd of Plâs Cilyhebyth (Glam.) granted a lease of Hermons Hill to Henry Rees, gent. of Haverfordwest at annual rent of £63. Mrs. Bassett died in 1828, and by her will devised Hermons Hill to Samuel Harries of Trevaccoon for life (died 1839) then to his eldest son John Harding Harries who sold Hermons Hill for £1,850 to William Owen of Haverfordwest, a successful cabinet-maker, son of William and Lettice Owen of Llanwnda parish. He continued to prosper, became a J.P. and D.L., and served as High Sheriff in 1859, then living at Poyston, which he had purchased some years previously. After this a succession of owners lived at Hermons Hill, among them Sir Charles Price, M.P.

Refs: Pembs. RO, D/EE/5, No. 19; Carms RO, Trant Deeds; G. R. Barrett, Deeds; NLW, Griffith Owen Deeds; Brawdy Papers, penes MS; James, *Haverfordwest and its Story,* 1957, opp. p. 153, illust. of Haverfordwest with a good view of Hermons Hill.

HILL, *Ludchurch*

A residence to the north of the parish church. In 1538 William, Abbot of Whitland leased lands called The Hill in the parishes of Ludchurch and Lampeter Velfrey for 99 years to Lawrence Winterhay gent. and Elizabeth his wife, and in 1593 the said lessees, described as of Hill, leased the said property to Roger Williams of Ereweare, gent. It was home of William Powell, son of Lewis Powell of Lamphey and Greenhill, descended from the medieval Cantingtons of north Pembrokeshire. By his wife Mary, daughter of Richard Vaughan of Cwrt Derllys, Carms. William Powell had a daughter Elinor who married James ap Rice, the tumultuous squire of Rickeston (Brawdy) and Scotsborough.

James died in 1692, Elinor in 1700, leaving six children. In the late 18th century it was the home of Charles Swan who was there in 1786. In the second half of the 19th century Sackville Herbert Edward Gregg Owen lived there, his son, also named Sackville, was High Sheriff in 1941. The house is still well maintained.

Refs: GGMS (Adv. Pembs), ff. 229-230; College of Arms, Gilfach MS; Picton Castle Deeds; LT 1786; Francis Jones, *Historic Carmarthenshire Homes and their Families.*

HILL, *Steynton*

Exact location unknown; the name Hill is included in nine place-names as shown in the Voters List of 1894 – Barretts Hill, Bolton Hill, Bygons Hill, Churchill, Deemshill, Dreenhill, Myrtle Hill, Hill Gate (on Denant mountain) and Sycamore Hill, and the Voters List of 1950 includes an additional seven places containing the element 'hill'. The first of the family at Hill was Rees Lewis William grandson of William ap Llewilin 'a blind man who dwelled at Trerose in St. Lawrens in Pebidiog.' Rees married Elizabeth Bateman of Honeyborough, by whom he had a son and three daughters. The son, William ap Rees gent. of Hill, married firstly Joan, sister of Owen ap Owen of Pentre Ifan, by whom he had two daughters who married north Pembrokeshire squires, and secondly Elizabeth Barrett. The prenuptial settlement was made on 10 August 1556, and he and his wife were still living at 'le Hill' in 1567. Nothing further has been found about the family.

Refs: Dwnn, i, p. 70; BM Egerton MS 2586; NLW, Bronwydd Deeds, Pembs. Plea Rolls 1559-1566.

HILTON, *Roch*

A residence, marked on Colby's Map one mile south of Roch village. Apart from their names little is known of the earlier residents of Hilton, also occasionally known as High Hilton. In 1323 it was the home of Walter de Hilton and his son and heir, William. In 1413 John Morse was there, and in the years 1436-45, lands in Hilton and Folcaston were owned by Walter Reynbot (who had received them from his father John Reynbot), who settled them on his sons John, Peter and Geoffrey Reynbot in entail. The family continued in the parish for many generations, and is still commemorated in the name of Rainbotts Hill farm.

During Elizabethan times the Harries family, from Haverfordwest, settled there. Hugh Harries died in 1566, and was followed by his son Thomas Harris gent. who owned the residence and manor of Hilton, and died some time after 1592. It passed to the Butler family of Scovaston, before 1624, in which year the manor of Hilton (200 acres) was owned by Thomas Butler, brother-in-law of the said Thomas Harries. It was later inherited by the heiress Anne Butler. She married William Mordaunt, who *iure uxoris* enjoyed the estates. They were living at Hilton in 1661, and later moved to the main Butler residence, Scovaston. Their sole surviving son, Thomas Mordaunt was living in 1723.

The Grants later lived there; in 1764 the Rev. John Grant, clerk, and in 1766, the Rev. Moses Grant, clerk, and John Grant, Esq. were living at Hilton. In 1786 the owner-occupier of Hilton was Francis Edwardes of Haverfordwest. In 1792 he married Martha Williams of Haverfordwest, and among the properties settled on her was 'the messuage and land called Hilton.' Edwardes died without issue, about 1808, and Hilton became the property of Mrs. Jane Bassett of Neath, and by her will dated 1828, the year of her death, she bequeathed Hilton to Samuel Harries of Cryglas and Trevaccoon. He died in 1839, and Hilton passed to his son George Augustus Harries, who settled there and died in 1887. G. A. Harries was followed by his son Samuel Keith Harries, the last of the line to dwell at Hilton.

Refs: PRO, Anc. Deeds; NLW, Picton Castle Deeds, Coleman Deeds, Pembs. Plea Rolls, Frances Green Deeds, Penpont (Brec.) Suppl. Deeds; WWHR VIII, (Harries of Trevaccoon).

Morgan

HOATEN, *St. Ishmaels*

In the westerly sector of the parish, near the boundary with St. Brides, were the four messuages of Great-, Little-, Middle-Hoaton, and Hoaton Hill, all marked on Colby's Map of 1831. The most important of these was Great Hoaton, home of the Morgan family in the 16th and 17th centuries. Descended from the Carmarthenshire family of Morgan of Muddlescomb, Rhys Morgan Esq. married Thomazin, daughter and heiress of John Sutton of Haverfordwest, and had a son and heir, Henry Morgan described as 'of Hoaton' in 1577. Henry is named in documents of 1592-97, 1609, and 1625. He married Janet, daughter of Griffith Wyrriot of Orielton, and had five sons and three daughters. His family arms were *argent* three bulls' heads caboshed *sable*. According to Egerton MS, Henry Morgan died in 1627, but his I.P.M. was taken on 23 January 1626, and showed that he owned extensive properties in the parish. The next reference to the family occurs in legal documents in 1650 and 1656 when John Morgan gent. dwelled at 'Hottowne' in St. Ishmael's parish.

It is not known whether Thomas Morgan of Great Hoaton in 1676 was a descendant; he died on 8 November 1715 and administration of his will was granted to his widow Dorothy. His inventory shows a value of £502, among his possessions being a one-fourth share of a barque, and a part of three other boats. By now all the Hoatens were farmed by tenants. In 1786 Great-, Middle-, and Little-, Hoaten were owned by Thomas Skyrme of Vaynor and let to farmers. On the lawn of Great Hoaten rests a huge iron anchor, said to be a relic of the Spanish Armada.

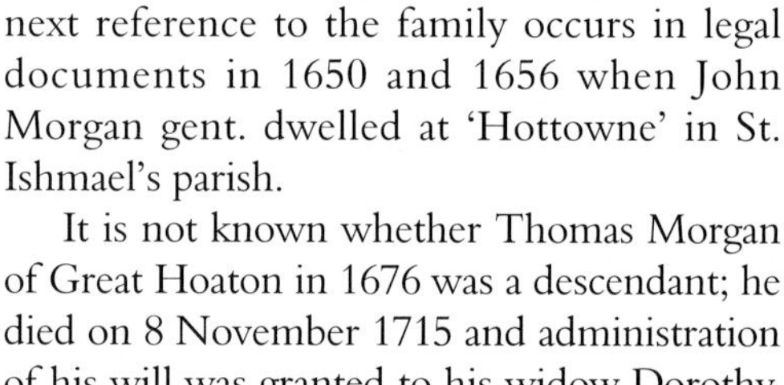

Refs: Dwnn, i, pp. 90, 218; Picton Castle Deeds; NLW, Poyston Deeds, Pembs. Plea Rolls; BM Egerton MS 2586; College of Arms, Wagner MS 2; *RCAM Pembs.*; Francis Jones, *Historic Carmarthenshire Homes and their Families.*

HOLMWS, *Newport*

A farmstead to the west of Newport near the road leading to Dinas. The name is derived from the old English 'holm', 'holmes', meaning water-meadow. It occurs in Pembrokeshire records of 1276 when Margaret, daughter of William Pecke of Newport granted a house and land at Holmes, Newport. In 1552 David Kethyn is described as of Hollmys. There were three farms there in olden time called Holmhouse-fawr, and -uchaf. In one of these lived William Bowen, son of James Bowen of Llwyngwair, in the 18th century. In 1786, the three farms of 'Rolmouse' (Yr Holmhouse) were owned by George Bowen of Llwyngwair, with Owen Bowen, Thomas Lewis and David George as tenants. By 1894 there were two farms there, Holmhouse-fawr and Holmhouse-uchaf.

Refs: PRO, Anc. Deeds; NLW, Pembs. Plea Rolls; B. G. Charles, *NCPN*, p. 52.

HOLYLAND, *St. Michael Pembroke*

A residence, today a hotel, just east of the town of Pembroke and of Golden farm. Home of the Adams family who had moved from Buckspool (q.v.) to Paterchurch (q.v.) in the early 15th century, thence to Holyland towards the end of the 16th century, where they remained till the 1940s. Writing of Paterchurch, Fenton noted in 1811 – 'a cross stood near it . . . the remaining ruins of this pious building were removed some years ago in the building of Holy Land, the seat of Joseph Adams Esq.' Holyland formed part of the Adams estate in 1629, possibly earlier, when it was let to farming tenants.

Eighteen generations of the family are known, many taking active part in local affairs, among them John Adams of Paterchurch, in 1448 lieutenant to Henry Wogan, Steward of the Earldom of Pembroke (it was this John who married Elen, daughter and heiress of David Paterchurch and settled at her home). John Adams of Paterchurch M.P. for Pembroke, 1541-44, Henry Adams, M.P. for

Pembroke 1547 and 1553, High Sheriff in 1558, Nicholas Adams, M.P. for Pembroke 1589, Mayor of Pembroke five times between 1602-1627 and a J.P. Nicholas Adams, Commissioner of Subsidies for the county in 1661, 1667 and 1669 (he paid tax for seven hearths at Holyland in 1670). Roger Adams, Commissioner of Subsidies 1692, 1695/6 and for Land Tax in 1707, Mayor of Pembroke 1695, he was the last of the family to live at Paterchurch before moving to Holyland. John Adams, J.P. High Sheriff in 1837.

The last male of the family in recent times, John Stephen Adams, was killed in action in the Second World War. Some years after the war, the family left Holyland which was afterwards sold. A curious tale concerns this part of their history. Having moved furniture, etc. orders were given to some local workers to empty what was left in the mansion and to burn it in the adjacent garden. Now, before the family had moved from Paterchurch, a young girl, Agnes Adams, died and was interred in the family burial ground. When they moved to Holyland, they dug up the remains which were placed in a sack which they took with them, and stored in the attic. After the departure from Holyland, one of the family remembered about this, went to Pembroke and asked about the remains. The workmen said that among the 'rubbish' found in the attic were some bones which they had duly consigned to the flames as ordered. And thus was little Agnes finally disposed of. The Adams bore arms: quarterly, 1 and 4 *sable* a martlet *argent* (for de Paterchurch), 1 and 3, *or* on a cross *gules* five pierced mullets *or;* crest; a martlet *argent.*

Refs: Dwnn, i, pp. 130-131, 172; NLW, Poyston Deeds; Pembs. RO, LT 1786. Adams Deeds – see 'Ancient description of Holyland', John Adams, 1836; Fenton, *Tour Pembs.,* 1811, 2nd ed., pp. 151,

198, 228, 234; Laws, *Little England,* pp. 307, 428; Burke, *Commoners,* 1837; B. G. Charles, *NCPN,* p. 23; C. Jennings, 1968.

HONEYBOROUGH, *Llanstadwell*

Just to the north of Neyland. There were several farms in the vicinity called Honeyborough, the most important being Great Honeyborough which was the caput of the manor. In 1811 Fenton wrote '. . . two mansions which formerly were of considerable rank though now nothing is left but their names, Scovaston and Honeyborough, the venerable buildings that, in the remembrance of many living, occupied the site, having being transmuted into farmhouses . . . Of the latter, Honeyborough, our ancient deeds make frequent mention, about three centuries

ago or earlier, as in the possession of the Batemans, but after that time frequently changing its possessors, till within these forty years it presented extensive ruins of very massive buildings, that to destroy required no small labour.' About 1600, it was listed as a manor, the lords having been Perrot, Bowen and Scourfield. The earliest family there, the Batemans (arms: *sable* a chevron between three escallops *argent)* were in possession during the sixteenth century, their pedigree for six generations being recorded by Dwnn and Golden Grove mss. They were still there in 1598. Later Great Honeyborough passed to the Taskers who were there till about 1810. After this it became the home of farming tenants.

Refs: Dwnn, i, p. 173; GGMS; Fenton, *Tour Pembs.,* 1811, 2nd ed.; LT 1786; Taylor's *Cussion,* fo. 98; WWHR IX, 152.

Bateman

HONEY HOOK, *Lambston*

A farmstead a mile to the west of Lambston village. For long, home of yeoman and minor gentry. In 1392 Alice Brown held two carucates at Honeyhoke and le Walles; in the years 1488-1507 Honeyhook was owned by William Popton; a deed of 1511 had the seal of Thomas Estemond of Honeyhook, son and heir of John Estemond of the same place, deceased. In the late 16th century the Bateman family, wealthy tradesmen, of Haverfordwest, whose arms were recorded in 1530 as *azure,* a chevron *or* between three escallops *argent,* with three quarterings, took an interest in Honey Hook, and on 12 March 1602/3 John Bateman of Haverfordwest bought Honey Hook and Wallis from Thomas Bowen of Trefloyne. It remained in Bateman possession for over a century, and the seal of Benjamin Bateman 'late of Haverfordwest but now of Honey Hook' is attached to a Picton Castle deed of 1733. Thereafter the property was sold, and in 1786 the owner was William Davies, with Thomas Gough as the tenant.

Refs: College of Arms Archives, Fellowe's *Visitation,* 1530; PRO, Anc. Deeds; Cardiff Free Library, Deeds; LT 1786.

HOOK, *Ambleston*

A residence one mile southwest of Ambleston village, standing on a long slope above the northern bank of Spittal Brook. Originally a farmhouse, mentioned in 1592 as 'le Hooke'. It afterwards formed part of the estate of Sir John Pakington, Bart., who sold it to David Meredith of Haverfordwest and he, in 1747, sold 'the capital messuage called Great Hook' to Admiral Thomas Tucker Esq. of Sealyham, a distinguished naval officer. He is particularly remembered for his daring capture of the

Spanish galleon *San Joseph* laden with vast treasure; in another action he killed the notorious pirate, Blackbeard who had terrorised the high seas. He died unmarried in 1766, bequeathing the property to his nephew John Tucker (High Sheriff 1763), who died in 1794 and left it to his eldest daughter and co-heiress, Catherine, who married John Owen Edwardes of Llanmilo, Carms. who came to Sealyham, and thereafter Hook remained in the Tucker-Edwardes family.

William Tucker-Edwardes was the father of Mary Tucker-Edwardes (born 1818) who became involved in the interesting 'Madam Rachel' lawsuit involving Lord Ranelagh. Mary married Colonel A. Borrodaile, and their daughter Florence Emma Anna was the last of the family to reside at Hook. She died unmarried in 1934. Some nine years earlier on 1 December 1925, Mrs. H. F. Cope had transferred the capital messuage and demesne of Hook to Thomas Charles Roberts, solicitor, of Perthyterfyn, Flint, and Richard Knight Lucas, estate agent, of Haverfordwest. It was later sold to a farmer.

In the entrance hall there once hung a banner displaying the Tucker-Edwardes crest, a silver battle-axe held in a bear's paw, with the motto *Guard the Faith.*

Hook is an excellent example of a traditional Welsh residence, and is in first-class condition. A three-storey main block, with ranges of five windows, a 'wing' in front, and another to the rear. There are eleven bedrooms, several reception rooms, a vaulted cellar, and a fine staircase lit by a long window rising to the top storey. It has been repaired and added to over the years; a massive beam that had been a *simne fawr* bears the date 1732, while a stone in the rear 'wing' has the date 1857. When I saw it in 1979 it was advertised for sale by the owner-occupier, Mrs. Griffiths, who kindly allowed me to inspect the house.

Refs: NLW, Sealyham Deeds; Pembs. RO Deeds DB/13/58; LT 1786; Francis Green on the Tucker and Edwardes families of Sealyham, WWHR VIII; *Western Mail,* 21 July, 29 September 1979, illust. and description.

HOOK, *Llangwm*

There were three properties – East Hook, West Hook, Lower Hook in the north of the parish, near to the banks of the Western Cleddau, and included on Colby's Map of 1831. East Hook: the earliest known owner was Owen Jordan, gent., and when he died Richard Hicks, yeoman of East Hook was his executor in 1614. The heiress was Mary Hicks, whose forebears 'for many generations had been owners of the capital mansion house of East Hook and of a moiety of the said tenement's land.' She married one John Jones and they had a daughter, sole heiress, Mary Jones, who married Richard Eynon gent. described in 1727 as of 'the capital messuage of East Hook.' Their daughter Elinor Eynon, married a Mr. Knethell and their eldest son, Richard Knethell, attorney, was living at 'the capital messuage of East Hook' in 1760-86. The property afterwards was acquired by the Powell family. They produced four High Sheriffs of Pembrokeshire – John Harcourt Powell, and in 1864, Thomas Harcourt Powell – all being described as of Hook and Drinkstone Park, Suffolk. The last-named was followed by his nephew John Harcourt Powell of Marsh Mills House, Henley-on-Thames, who served the office of High Sheriff for Pembrokeshire in 1910.

Refs: NLW, Pembs. Plea Rolls; LT 1786.

HOOK, *Marloes*

On Colby's Map 1831, West Hook and East Hook are marked as two adjacent farms, near the coast, on high ground between Musselwick Bay and Martins Haven, both farms being mentioned in a document dated 1307. The properties were owned from 1536 to 1802 by the family of Runwa alias Runwae alias Runway.

Ten successive generations lived at Hook, described in the earliest documents as yeomen, in the late 17th century as gentlemen, and towards the end of the 18th century as esquires. They intermarried with the Voyles of Philbeach, Davis of Crabhall, and Paynter of Dale. In 1786 the owner of both messuages was Benjamin Runwae, the tenants James Jones and John Cooker. Benjamin had a successful naval career, and in his will of 1802 he is described as 'of Hook alias East Hook, Master and Commander

R.N. (now) residing in Westbury-upon-Trim, Gloucestershire', who bequeathed the farm of Broomhill and other properties in Dale village to his 'kinsman and godson' David Runwa(e) Paynter of Pembroke town, gentleman. The properties were alienated not long afterwards, and in 1842 Lord Kensington owned East Hook, and C. A. W. Philipps owned West Hook. The family of Runwae became extinct, and few other yeomen families can show an unbroken succession for some 300 years. Fenton in 1811 states that Musselwick (Marloes parish) is 'now inhabited by a respectable freeholder of the name of Runawae.' They also took part in the brewing trade, sending a considerable quantity of ale to Liverpool in the late 18th century. There is still a farm in this parish called Rynaway's Kiln, and on the coast is Runaway's Cove.

Refs: Dwnn, i, p. 72; BM Egerton MS 2586, fo. 404; NLW, Pembs. Plea Rolls; LT 1786; Fenton, *Tour Pembs.,* 1811; Phillips, *History of Haverfordwest,* p. 180.

HOWELSTON, *Talbenny*

A farmstead on high land, a mile east of Talbenny village. During the middle ages from c. 1250 to 1509, seven generations of the family of Howell owned Howelston. Their pedigree, in the hand of G. W. Griffith is in the Wagner Collection in the College of Arms. In the second half of the 15th century Thomas Morris of Castle Villa in Dewsland married Margaret Howell of Howelston, and in 1497 she granted her lands and tenements in Talbenny and Howelston to her son, Henry Morris and they remained in the Morris family till the end of the 16th century, when it passed to the Scourfields of Castle Villa. In 1573 Ann Scourfield married John Meyler of Trewallterwen in St. Edwins parish, and Howelston was settled on her. In 1786 it was owned by the Owens of Orielton. Thereafter little mention is made of Howelston which was let to farming tenants.

Refs: Episcopal Registers of St. Davids; College of Arms MS; Wagner MS 2, 90 (G. W. Griffiths); NLW, Pembs. Plea Rolls, 1609-1614; Francis Jones, 'Castle Villa – Cas Wilia', *The Treasury of Historic Pembrokeshire.*

IVY TOWER, *St. Florence*

A residence a mile north of St. Florence village. The original name seems to have been Tor, a corruption of the word 'Torr' meaning a high rock or hill, and about a mile southwards is the farm of Tarr. It was rendered in deeds of 1603-25 as Ivie Torr and Ivetor. As to the element 'Ivy', the Cambrian Register 1706 states it may have been named after Paul Ivy an Elizabethan engineer sent to survey the defences of Milford Haven and Tenby, but 'the latter was not seen by Mr. Ivy nearer than two miles distance at a place, and some pretend to say, called from him Ivy Tower . . . where it was believed the voluptuous surveyor found a magnet of more powerful attraction than either Milford or Tenby.' It occurs in the deeds of the Williams family in the years 1727-1778. The farm Ivy Tower is first mentioned in 1771, and is known as such in the following years.

The founders of this family were ecclesiastical people having no blood relationship in the county. Bishop Robert Ferrar was burnt at the stake at Carmarthen in 1555. By his wife Elizabeth, the martyr had three children, Samuel, Griffin, and Elizabeth.

Elizabeth found her husband in the church. He was a Herefordshire man called the Rev. Lewis Williams who became Rector of Narberth, which position he held until his death about 1617, then being a very old man. His will was proved at Carmarthen on 31 March 1617. I have not been able to find out who his forebears were, but presumably they were in easy circumstances to be able to educate their son for Holy Orders. It is remarkable how many Pembrokeshire families start with attorneys and parsons, often of very humble origins. The first always gathered money, the second was eminently respectable, while both normally were able to marry the younger daughters of the county families, although many of the attorneys harvested heiresses and only daughters.

The Rev. Lewis Williams and Elizabeth Ferrar, his wife, had eight children: Robert Williams (Richard Williams in my will transcript), the eldest son, bought lands in the parish of St. Florence, and appears to have settled on the land. He maintained the clerical tradition of the family by marrying Elizabeth Whitchurch, niece of Archdeacon Robert Rudd of St. Florence. She was buried in September 1654, while her husband's will, dated 17 August 1654, was proved in PCC 7 July 1656. (Berkeley 268.) They had the following children:

1. William Williams; 2. Elizabeth Williams married John Howell of Llangludwen, son of Reynold Howell by Mary Barzey his wife, descendant of the Penybenglog stock. They had issue. Vide Howell of Trenewydd. She died April 1655, aged 44; 3. Jane Williams, married ... Ferrar. She died May 1691, aged 77; 4. Susan Williams married John Howells of Eastlake, Amroth. She died in August 1692, aged 70, and his will was proved 13 September 1692.

William Williams the eldest son, married in 1657 Jane, daughter of Arthur Stafford of Laugharne, (his will was proved in 1667). She died in March 1659 at the early age of 20. William Williams lived to the age of 73 and died in March 1689. He was assessed at four hearths in 1670. They left an only son, Robert Williams. Robert was born in 1657 and was educated at Trinity College, Oxford and was afterwards of the Inner Temple. He was an Alderman of Tenby. He married Elizabeth Hammond of Whitley, Yorkshire who survived her husband. Robert Williams died about 1710 when his will was proved at Carmarthen. Elizabeth his widow died before 1728 leaving three children. William Williams the eldest son; Thomas Williams, who in 1728 at the request of his late mother, gave £5, the interest of which was to be laid out in sixpenny wheaten loaves and household bread and given on every Good Friday for ever to the 'poor housekeepers of Tenby not receiving weekly pay'. He died unmarried in 1744. Elizabeth Williams married Griffith Williams of Panthowell, Carms. and Tenby by whom she had issue.

William Williams the heir, born in 1693 succeeded to Ivy Tower, married in 1727 to Elizabeth, daughter of Morgan Davies of Coombe, Carmarthen. They had seven children. The heir yet another William, was born in 1736 and became a well-known public figure. He was High Sheriff for Pembrokeshire in 1766

and four times Mayor of Tenby. He was senior Alderman of that town at his death, having been formerly for many years its town clerk. He was well versed in antiquarian, biblical and ecclesiastical learning. His 'Primitive History' had the approbation of the celebrated chronologist, Dr. Hales, and his 'Christian Code' and 'New Translation of the New Testament' justly merited the tributes they received. He gave valuable Hebrew and oriental books to the church and was active in church affairs. He was a great letter writer, and some, giving an account of his own ancestors may be found in *Arch. Cam.* Series 3, Volumes 4 and 5. He wrote to *The Cambrian* in November 1813, a letter about fortifying Milford Haven. He took a poor view of poachers and pretenders to the gentry as the notice in *The Cambrian* reveals, (printed on page 297 in *The Treasury of Historic Pembrokeshire)*. He married Maria Jermyn of Skrinkle by whom he had an only child and heiress, Maria Williams. He died on 16 November 1813 at an advanced age, leaving his daughter Maria and 'my acknowledged son', Thomas Rixon Williams, evidently by his housekeeper, Mary Rixon. Maria Williams was married at Clifton in 1808 to Orlando Lloyd Harris of Dursley, Gloucestershire. Orlando was High Sheriff of Pembrokeshire in 1824 and took the name Williams by Royal Licence. They had an only child who died in infancy. Maria died in 1849 and her husband in the following year. Ivy Tower was sold and by 1854 owned by John Leach, esquire. It was sold again and by 1894 and was the home of Colonel H. H. Goodere. Later it was sold again, and today is a holiday park hotel.

A well-built Georgian house of two storeys, a range of five windows on the upper floor, with a pillared entrance, flanked by two large windows on the ground floor.

Refs: B. G. Charles, *NCPN,* pp. 21-2; Pembs. RO Williams Deeds, HDX/833, LT List 1786; Cambrian Register, vol. II, 1796, p. 180; Burke, *LG,* 1850; C. S. Allen, *South Wales,* 1871, illust.; M.I. St. Florence Church; Francis Jones, unpublished essay, 'Williams of Ivy Tower'.

JEFFRESTON HOUSE, *Jeffreston*

Originally home of the Nash family, a cadet of Nash of Nash. The Nash heiress, Maud, married David Smith (d. 1556), and their descendants continued at Jeffreston until the end of the 18th century. John Smith, High Sheriff in 1753 subscribed to a copy of the Rev. William Evans's translation of *Canwyll y Cymry* in 1771. He left an only daughter and heiress Anne, who in 1759 married Philipp Philipps of Lampter Velfrey House, and their son, Thomas Philipps afterwards lived at both his parents' houses, and had ten children. The *Pembrokeshire Archaeological Survey* calls the house of the Smiths, Great House, Jeffreston.

JOHNSTON (HALL), *Johnston*

A village some three miles south of Haverfordwest, on the road to Milford. The mansion on the southern fringe of the village is marked as 'Hall' on modern OS maps. In the 15th century it was the home of the family of Tancred, well-known in the medieval history of the county. John Tancred of Johnston (still there in 1499) died c. 1510, having had the following children – John died young and unmarried, Elizabeth, co-heiress, married pre-1507 Morris Butler who was living at Johnston in 1507, Alicia, co-heiress, married Jenkin ap Owen, and Anne who died unmarried pre-1519. The Tancred arms were *gules* a chevron between three escallops *argent.* The main seats of the Butlers (descended from the Butlers of Dunraven, Glamorganshire) in Pembrokeshire were Johnston, Coedcanlas, Scovaston, and Tregadwgan; their arms *azure* three covered cups *or.* Morris Butler, who held several important public offices during the first half of the 16th century, was followed by six generations, and although living in the early 17th century at Scovaston, continued to own Johnston until Hugh Butler, a Royalist and 'a grand malignant' sold the property to Sir Roger Horsey about 1639. In 1668 Elizabeth Horsey married Arthur Owen (descended from the Orielton family), and he came to live at Johnston.

At that time the manor of Johnston comprised the manor house, and about 200 acres. In 1670 Elizabeth Horsey was assessed at ten hearths for the manor house, which shows it to be have been very large at that time. By 1703 Johnston had been sold to Francis Edwardes (a younger son of the Little Trefgarn family, M.P. for Haverfordwest 1722-1725) and was followed there by his son William Edwardes, prominent in public life, and created Lord Kensington in 1776. He died at Johnston in 1801, aged 90, having represented Haverfordwest in nine parliaments between 1747 and 1801. Several tourists found it worthy of mention.

A tour written c. 1800, now kept in the archives of the Society of Genealogists, London, contains the following entry: 'Aug. 21. Johnston Hall the seat of Lord Kensington. His Lordship seems an uncommon sloven if the Traveller may judge from the appearance of his House and Garden. Upon enquiry of an old man at the Turnpike, found His Lordship to be a miser, and Her Ladyship a spendthrift'. Malkin in his *Tour,* 1804, notes: 'Johnston is an ancient seat belonging to Lord Kensington, which should not be passed by without a visit.' Fenton wrote with some asperity in 1811: 'Johnston, the seat for many years of the Late Lord Kensington, but since his death let to a tenant. There is nothing in the situation to recommend it as an eligible residence as it lies rather low, close to the great road, and in a coal county, therefore a deep clay soil . . . It is to be lamented that the present nobleman, his son, is obliged to seek a residence in a neighbouring county [Westmead, Carm.]' In the same year, Carlisle writes, 'The only object of note is an old Family Mansion of The Right Honourable Lord Kensington, called Johnston Hall, which is now partly occupied as a Farmhouse, and the remainder is in a rapid state of decay': Lewis's

Topographical Dictionary, (1834, 1840) comments: 'Johnston Hall, an ancient mansion of the family of Edwardes, and for a long time the residence of the late Lord Kensington, is now the property of the present lord, and is in the occupation of Thomas Bowen Esq.'

In 1835 Lord Kensington then living at Noyadd, Llanarth, Cards., sold the estate for £10,000 to the Rev. James Morgan, clerk, of Talgarth, Brec., and on 21 February 1873 the parson's Trustees sold the manor and estate to Richard Carrow. The Carrow family held it for several decades. In 1894 Richard Carrow and his son Charles, (owner of the Brickworks at Johnston), were living there. In 1921 the mansion, manor and estate were advertised for sale, the vendor being Howard Gwynne Keppel Palmer, described as 'Beneficial Owner'. The sale catalogue describes Johnston Hall as built around a courtyard, comprising, on the ground floor, a hall, three reception rooms, cloak room, lavatory, servants' hall, kitchen, pantry; on the first floor six family bedrooms: stabling, garages, kennels, tennis court, gardens, orchards; in all 16 acres. The catalogue has two photographs of the house. The Milford Haven family of Brand lived there afterwards, and finally sold it.

Nowadays, the Hall, a double-pile building with a wing to the rear, is set in pleasant grounds; nearby are the old coach-house and other ancient outbuildings, one of which may well have been a dwelling-house (part of the hall) in earlier days, and close to this building is the old walled garden alienated during the 19th century. The owner-occupier the agreeable Lt. Col. H. J. Evans, M.B.E., D.L., retired Gurkha officer, welcomed me when I called there in 1986.

Refs: Dwnn, i, pp. 76, 110, 132, 179-80; Pembs. RO, LT records; NLW, Goswood MS, pedigrees; Eaton Evans and Williams Deeds; Floyd MS 1361C; PRO, Chancery Proc. C5 89/15; Anc. Deeds, vol. V; Carms. RO, GGMS; Picton Castle Deeds.

JORDANSTON (HALL) – TREWRDAN,
Jordanston in Dewsland

An ancient mansion in the vernacular style, with a small grove on a westerly slope overlooking the Western Cleddau, mid-way between the farms of Llangloffan and Trecoed. The mansion is close to the parish church. Nearby is a field called Castell where probably an early fortification had stood.

In 1326 Jordanston is described as a knight's fee. In 1411 the living of Jordanston was held by the Bishop of St. Davids, Lord of the Hundred, by reason of the minority of the son and heir of Ieuan ap Roppert ap Meyer (ap Tancred) late lord of Jordanston, deceased.

In the late 14th century the Wogans of Boulston who were the lords of the manor, owned the living and held it throughout the 16th century, but by 1621 the manorial rights had passed to the Gwynn family who owned the mansion and estate. The Gwynns, who came from Llanidloes, Mont., were owners of Jordanston from 1561, until the early half of the 17th century, Matilda Gwynn the ultimate heiress married John Vaughan of Lisswent, Rad., who settled at Jordanston.

John Vaughan and Matilda had three sons and a daughter, Sarah who married a Mr. Morgans. Jenkin who succeeded to Jordanston, married Grace Wogan of Llanstinan. Jenkin found himself arrested for murder in 1659 when a servant Theophrastus Mellychop, died under suspicious circumstances, and despite a post mortem declaring that he died of natural causes, Jenkin was charged with his murder. It appeared that Jenkin and Mellychop had left

Jordanston to call on Mr. Owen of Priskilly and 'returned thither between five and six of the clock in the evening'. They stood in the porch for some time speaking to Mr. and Mrs. Vaughan and then left. A little later Mr. Vaughan 'while he was taking his pipe full of tobacco' in the house looked through the window and espied Mellychop 'lying on his back in a swound over against the window of the parlour' and went to his aid. The unfortunate man died early the following morning. Others told a different tale of dispute and quarrels and hence Jenkin found himself arrested but was later exonerated. He died without issue on 24 April 1675 aged 42. After Jenkin's death the estate passed to his next brother Morgan Vaughan who died unmarried on 30 November 1678. The third brother, Lewis died in the lifetime of his two elder brothers. Generally known as Lewis Gwyn Vaughan he entered the Church and in 1659 became minister of Rudbaxton. He was suspended from his duties after a complaint against him by one Nicholas Roch but later, after a petition by his parishioners, re-instated. He had married an unknown wife, Cosmeda by whom he had one son, Gwynne. He left an estate valued at £39 8s. (detailed). Gwynne succeeded to Jordanston when still a minor, and married Mary, daughter of Dr. William Owen. He died comparatively young, his will being proved in 1702, leaving eight children 'now living' and an estate valued at £599 8s. Lewis Vaughan the eldest son succeeded, and married Grace Johnes of Llanfairclydogau. He was an active magistrate, High Sheriff in 1717, sat in Quarter Sessions and took a particular interest in the state of local roads and bridges. He died in 1755 without issue and Jordanston devolved onto his younger brother, John Vaughan. He married a Carmarthenshire lady of fortune, Anne, heiress of John Williams of Gellydowill. He resided wholly at his wife's estate and after his brother's death sent his eldest son and heir, Gwynne to live at Jordanston and conveyed a large part of his estates to his son.

John Vaughan and Anne had ten children. Gwynne, John junior, Charles, Daniel, who entered the army and rose to be Lieutenant Colonel of the 39th Regiment of Foot. After retiring from the army he returned to live at Jordanston, and was a captain in the Fishguard Fencibles at the time of the landing of the French in 1797; George Vaughan, Anne, Elizabeth, Rachel who married George Harries of Tregwynt and died without issue, Mary, Frances who married Richard Edwardes of Navy Hall, Cards.

Gwynne Vaughan the eldest son had settled at Jordanston in 1755, and in 1769 his father conveyed the larger part of the family's Pembrokeshire estate to him. He became a Justice of the Peace, Governor of Fishguard Fort, High Sheriff of Pembrokeshire in 1799, and in 1800/1 was Scavenger for the town of Fishguard. He had been associated with Fishguard Fort from its beginning. In 1779 the town had been bombarded by a privateer and forced to pay a ransom, an experience that led to a movement to establish a fort there to prevent a repetition of the unpleasant experience, and as a protection against any hostile naval operations against the country. The Members of Parliament for the county supported the project and the Government accepted the necessity for such protection. It was decided to build the fort on a headland dominating the approaches to the landing stages at the estuary of the river Gwaun. This land formed part of the Jordanston estate. On 18 July 1781 Gwynne Vaughan granted a lease to Sir Hugh Owen of Orielton, Baronet, of ground called 'the Castle Point' adjoining the sea, in a close called Park y Morva on the north side of the harbour, creek, or haven called Fishguard, for the purpose of erecting thereon a fort battery or place of defence for the better protection of shipping in the harbour and in the road opposite the harbour, and of the inhabitants of the town from such attacks as they had experienced from the war then being waged. The fort was accordingly built and eight nine-pounder guns installed. Gwynne Vaughan was appointed governor.

During the brief but lively episode of the landing of a hostile French force near Fishguard in February 1797, the Vaughans were involved with local defensive measures. On the eve of the landing most of the local notables including Colonel Knox of Llanstinan, commander of the militia, Gwynne and Daniel Vaughan of

Jordanston, were enjoying themselves at a ball held at Tregwynt, home of the Harries family. During the evening, news came of the landing of French troops at a secluded cove on the coast of Pencaer a few miles away. The guests departed hurriedly, Knox to join his troops, Governor Vaughan to see to the Fort, leaving behind a determined Daniel Vaughan who loaded all the firearms he could find to await the arrival of the hated foe should they penetrate so far inland. In the event the French surrendered without an engagement, and amongst the Council of War assembled under the commander, Lord Cawdor, at the Royal Oak Inn at Fishguard where the articles of surrender were signed, were the Governor of the Fort and his brother Daniel. The two brothers were personal friends of Colonel Knox whose conduct was sharply criticised. When he was forced to resign, the officers of the Fishguard Fencibles, among them Daniel Vaughan, signed a letter in support of their former commander. When, as a result of recriminations, Knox challenged Lord Cawdor to a duel in May 1797, Daniel acted as his second. The fort had not been involved as the enemy had landed in a cove several miles away, and in any case does not seem to have been adequately equipped to meet such an occasion. Accordingly Governor Vaughan wrote to the Duke of Portland pointing out that the Fort's ammunition supply was wholly inadequate, and asking him to remedy the deficiency.

On 15 November 1774 Gwynne Vaughan was married at St. George's, Hanover Square, London, to Margaret daughter of Thomas Gill of St. Marylebone, London, by Margaret daughter and co-heiress of Gervas Norton of Kettlethorp, Yorkshire. By the prenuptial settlement made on 29 October, the Jordanston estate was settled on the young couple and the heirs of their body. Gwynne died on 18 January 1808, and was buried at Jordanston where a tablet perpetuates his memory. The arms on the memorial is quarterly, 1 & 4 *gules* a lion rampant reguardant *or*; 2 & 3, a chevron, and on a chief a lion passant, over all an escutcheon of pretence, quarterly i & iv, blank, ii. & iii, a maunche. His widow died on 15 April 1826, and was buried at Little Gaddesden, Berkshire.

Gwynne Vaughan and Margaret his wife had two children, (although Gwynne had two 'base born' children by one Mary Lewis); his legitimate children were; Gwynne Gill Vaughan, born 24 April 1776 and Margaret Vaughan, born 31 July 1775; she never married and died on 18 November 1836, and was buried at Jordanston. By her will, dated 7 November of that year, she bequeathed the interest of £500 to be distributed every Christmastide among the poor of her native parish.

Gwynne Gill Vaughan matriculated at Magdalene College, Oxford on 11 July 1795, at the age of 18, and graduated B.A. in 1799. He was a Justice of the Peace, and in 1813 served the office of High Sheriff of Pembrokeshire. Few notices of him have come to my notice, apart from the fact that he gave a lease for 99 years of a Baptist chapel in Letterston to Henry Davies of Panteurig, Minister of the Gospel.

He died on 28 March 1837 in his 60th year and was buried at Jordanston where a memorial to him was erected by 'his old friend and sole executor, Major-General Sir James Cockburn of Langton, Baronet'. He was unmarried and the last of the Vaughans to live at Jordanston. Although he had kinsfolk, descendants of his aunts, he chose to alienate the estate from his family, and bequeath it to his friend Sir James Cockburn, Bt.

The fortunate legatee had a distinguished career. Born in 1771 he became Page of Honour to King George III, and afterwards entered the army. He became Colonel of the Scots Greys, Governor of Bermuda in 1811, Major General and Inspector of Marines in 1819. He died in 1852. By his wife, the Hon. Marianna Devereux, daughter of the 13th Viscount Devereux, he had a daughter, Marianna Augusta who succeeded to the Jordanston estate, and married Colonel Sir James John Hamilton, Bt., of Tyrone, and Plâs Llanstephan, Carms., who died in 1876. Thereafter the mansion became the property of gentleman-farmers, who have maintained the mansion in excellent style. While laying a new floor in the dining room in 1899 two horse's skulls were found under the old boards. It was the custom to do this to produce an echo or 'better sound' in the room in olden days.

Jordanston now belongs to the Raymond family. The mansion was assessed at five hearths in 1670, and in 1709 the estate consisted of the manor, advowson of the parish church, the capital messuage, 17 farms and houses, the wharf at Fishguard, with its royalties, and a water corn mill there. The properties lay in Jordanston parish and nine other parishes in the district. A sale catalogue of 1817 describes the mansion as comprising five reception rooms, two large kitchens, pantries, cellars and domestic offices; eight bedrooms; outhouses; a walled garden (2 acres); two carriage drives.

Refs: Pembs. RO, Deeds HDX/661, LT, 1876, Sale Catalogue, 1917; Cardiff Public Library, Deeds; NLW, Cwrtmawr Deeds; Carms. RO, GGMS; Francis Jones, 'Jordanston in Dewsland', *Pembs. Historian,* 1974, 'Lay Manors of Dewsland', *Journal Hist. Soc. of the Church in Wales,* 1969, and essay 'Jordanston in Dewsland'; Francis Jones, *Historic Carmarthenshire Homes and their Families,* and *Historic Cardiganshire Homes and their Families.*

JORDANSTON, *Llanstadwell*

In the Hundred of Rhos (Roose). A mansion (now a farmhouse) about half a mile southwest of Rosemarket village. I visited it on 19 May 1976 accompanied by Lt. Colonel Evans of Johnston Hall. It is a tall three-storeyed house, with ranges of five windows, a fine fanlight over the entrance door; an interesting projection to the rear has a stepped chimney-stack, older than the main block. Originally the home of the Jordan family after whom it is named. A pedigree by George Owen of Henllys starts with Leonard Jordan who married in the second half of the 14th century 'a daughter of John of Doomple Dale' (Dumple Dale was for many years afterwards home of a branch of the Jordans). Leonard's son Thomas Jordan married a daughter of Jenkin Lloyd of Cemaes (Blaiddbwll, *vide supra*) and had a son John Jordan who married Elizabeth Sturmyn. During the Wars of the Roses, John was an active Yorkist, and in 1469 accompanied Sir Henry Wogan to Banbury where both were slain. His son John Jordan the younger was about eight or nine years old when his father fell. He married Anne Elliot of Earwere. He too was engaged in political warfare, and 'went with the Duke of Buckingham, his master, against the King, and was beheddyd in the castell of Harfordwest, and left his son William Jordan but 4 years old'. Like his immediate forebears William met a mournful end. George Owen notes, 'William Jordan went with Sir John Wogan as capten to Terwin and Turney [in France], and there was slaine, and left his sonne Richard Jordan but 14 yeres of age'. No tragedy attended young Richard's life and he went on to marry Elinor (or Elin) daughter of Henry Morgan of Mudlescwm (H. S. Carms. 1544) by, Margaret daughter of Henry Wogan of Wiston. Richard avoided the perils of war, confined his attention to domestic matters with some vigour, and when he died, between 1566 and 1580, he left ten sons and two daughters.

In 1581 David Jordan of Jordanston, gent. son and heir of Richard Jordan deceased, and his widowed mother Elin Jordan alias Morgan, were involved in a law-suit relating to an annuity of 40s. charged on Dumpledale in Burton parish. David married Anne Lloyd by whom he had issue. His brother Thomas Jordan died suddenly without issue and his wife Alice Thomas was 'burnt in Carmarthen for poysening her husband'. However, the family was not destined to remain much longer at Jordanston. By the middle of the 17th century they had gone, and in the Hearth Tax list for Llanstadwell in 1670 the surname Jordan is not to be found.

In 1734 it was the residence of Thomas Bowen whose forebears lived at Haverfordwest. The Bowens remained at Jordanston until the beginning of the 19th century. By 1834 it was owned by William Henry Wilson of Leics., and they were still in possession in 1904 when Jordanston was owned by William Le Hunt Wilson who was then living at Dulwich.

Refs: BM Egerton MS 2586, ff. 384-5; Pembs. RO, LT 1786; NLW, Morgan-Richardson Deeds, i, p. 64; Francis Jones, *Historic Carmarthenshire Homes and their Families.*

KEESTON/KEYSTON (TREGETHIN), *Camrose*
A hamlet near the St. Davids-Haverfordwest highway, between Pelcomb and Roch. Home of the medieval family of Roblin, but the site is not known for certain. A report made of a survey, about 1900 tells us there was in the village a small overgrown ruin, suggested to have been the home of the Keating family who gave name to the place, 'there are three detached buildings, the best preserved, and the largest, a very long narrow structure, 20ft wide and 150ft (or thereabouts) long; the greater part is lying prostrate. It is entered by a ruinous semicircular porch. The place is so ruinous and overgrown with brambles that we are unable to take measurements and give the description that is due. When, some 20 years later, the inspectors of RCAM visited it they stated that the few features mentioned above 'have practically vanished'.

George Owen of Henllys, c.1600, gives the following pedigree – William Roblyn de Cestingston married Eleanor, daughter of Sir Walter Malefant and Dame Alice de Roch; their son was David Roblyn who was father of Harry Roblyn. Dr. Charles, who cites the name Ketingeston in 1295, states the name may be derived from Kething, possibly from the Welsh Cethin. The Welsh continue to refer to the village as Tregethin.

Refs: B. G. Charles, *NCPN*, p. 56; *Pembs. Arch. Svy*, 1896-1907; *RCAM Pembs.*, 1925, p. 48.

KILBARTH, *Rudbaxton*
A farmstead about a quarter of a mile west of the parish church. There is a reference to the property in 1326 when Kilbarth, Frowlynchurch, Scolton and Haythog, were counted as a single fee, formerly held by Guy de Brian, but is now in the hands of the Lord Bishop, and for Kilbarth John Symond paid yearly one penny. Much later, in 1566, Hugh Harries of Haverfordwest owned a messuage and a ploughland in 'Gilbawrgh' in Rudbaxton parish. William Phillips lived at Kilbarth in 1650, whose daughter Anne married John Codd who lived at his wife's home in 1669. Six generations of the Phillips family succeeded to Kilbarth, and were there until the first half of the 19th century when its two sons, Edward Picton Phillips (b. 1822) and his brother John William Phillips, solicitor, settled in Haverfordwest. It was afterwards the property of several yeoman families.

Refs: Black Book of St. Davids, 1326; NLW Pembs. Plea Rolls; WWHR viii, p. 107: Pembs. RO, LT 1786.

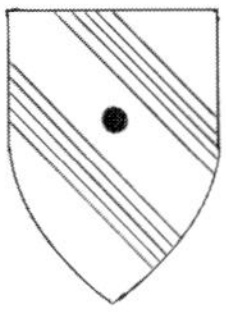

Canon

KILGETTY, *St. Issells*
Formerly a mansion on high ground just over a mile north of the hamlet of Stepaside. *RCAM* 1925, p. 375, calls this place 'an ecclesiastical residence of the canons of St. Davids.' Not so. In fact it was the residence of a very secular family, surnamed Canon, whose worldly attachment to commerce in Haverfordwest had enabled its members to purchase landed property and to set up as country gentlefolk. Originally a farm, it was acquired by the Barlow family towards the middle of the 16th century, and about 1620 was sold to Sir Thomas Canon of Haverfordwest.

This family, clearly of non-Welsh origin, came from the Carmarthenshire township of Laugharne where they had been engaged in trade and had acquired some freeholds. The first to move westwards was David Canon the elder, described as merchant of Haverfordwest in the first half of the 16th century. By his wife Gwenllian, daughter of Henry ap Gwilym of Laugharne, he had eight children, namely: Morris born about 1538; David of Haverfordwest, merchant, who in 1607 received from the Corporation a lease for life of the office of Weigher and Keeper of the Common Beam in the town with its fees and profits; Edward, lame and sick from youth and unable to work; William; Thomas; Anne; Katherine and Eleanor.

Morris Canon, the eldest son, became a man of substantial means. The advancement of a family may be gauged by acquisition of landed property, by the holding of senior public appointments, and particularly by its marriages which indicate acceptance by older and established governing stocks. Morris Canon's progress is milestoned by his description in contemporary official and legal documents: in 1566 of Laugharne, 'merchant'; in 1568 of Haverfordwest, 'merchant'; in 1577-82 of Haverfordwest, 'gentleman'; finally burgeoning into county respectability in 1584 as 'esquire'. He added to his property both in Laugharne and Haverfordwest. In 1564 and 1577 he bought lands, burgages, and orchards in the county town from Thomas Wogan of Austerslade; he acquired property at Fenton in Wiston, Thurston in Burton, Leweston in Camrose, and held a lease of Temperness, formerly part of the dissolved priory of Haverfordwest. In 1586 he bought the manor of East Pelkam in Camrose and the annual rents of three messuages and 320 acres, for £30 from John Howell of Haverfordwest, merchant; and shortly before his death he settled part of his estate which included the 'capital mansion and messuage' of Leweston, upon his second son Thomas with remainder (in default of issue) successively to his eldest son David, his third son John, his youngest son William and, in default of issue to these sons, to his (Morris's), brother David.

Morris Canon also graduated in the government of the town. He became a Common Councilman of Haverfordwest, High Constable in 1568, bailiff in 1570, town sheriff in 1576, and mayor in 1580. Marriage brought him into the ambit of the older gentry when in 1564 he espoused Elizabeth, daughter of John Voyle, landowner and merchant of Haverfordwest, by Margaret daughter of Sir James ab Owen of Pentre Ifan, among her kinsfolk being the Bowens of Llwyngwair and the Warrens of Trewern. The Voyles traced to the medieval landowner, Dafydd Foel of Trewern in Cemais, whose sobriquet in its pronunciation but not its orthography, was adopted as a permanent surname by his numerous descendants. Some people have claimed that the Voyles descended from a Fleming of that name. Not so; their ancestor was a bald-headed Welshman. Elizabeth brought her husband the modest dowry of £40, and under the marriage settlement Morris endowed her with an even more modest annuity of £5.

In his will made on 13 May 1587, Morris Canon expressed a wish to be buried in St. Mary's church, Haverfordwest, should he die in Pembrokeshire, but in Laugharne church should he die in Carmarthenshire. Among bequests was a sum of 40 shillings to the poor of Llanwnda to be paid by the hands of 'my aliesmen', Mr. Llewelin Lloyd of Llanstinan and Mr. Owen Jones of Trecwn. The will was proved in London on 10 July 1587. Elizabeth survived him, to marry one Rice Morgan; she died on 4 August 1597.

Morris and Elizabeth Canon had four sons, namely:

1. David Canon, bailiff of Haverfordwest in 1599, who settled at Fenton. He married Frances Hancock, and had four children, the eldest of whom we shall meet later at Kilgetty. Although George William Griffith of Penybenglog described David as *simplex,* 'a simple person', he was sufficiently able to make a will at Fenton on 28 October 1600 in which he mentions his wife Frances, his brothers Thomas, John, and William, his son and heir 'Morice' a minor, and his second son John. The will was proved at St. Davids on 18 November 1600. The widow later married, successively Hugh Merryman and Henry Jones, both of Wiston parish.

2. Thomas Canon, born c. 1567 – see later.

3. John Canon, studied at Clifford's Inn, entered the Middle Temple on 26 February 1596, became Town Clerk of Haverfordwest, and M.P. for that borough in 1601. He had mining interests, and on 4 September 1623 King James declared his pleasure that John Canon 'whose ancestors have long held land in Pembrokeshire where lead mining exists which yields lead and eight ounces of silver per bushel of ore', should undertake the working of the said mines, and ordered the sheriff of Somerset to send ten or twelve most skilful workmen from Mendip to assist him in the enterprise. He married Alice, widow of David Middleton of Middleton Hall, Carmarthenshire, and had issue.

4. William Canon, admitted to the Middle Temple on 14 March 1601; he was a tailor, Sheriff of Haverfordwest in 1620, and a feoffee of lands of the Free School in the years 1613-37. By his wife Jane, he had issue living in 1638.

Thomas Canon, the second son, became owner of Kilgetty. He was a remarkable man, but as he is not included in the *Dictionary of Welsh Biography,* perhaps I may be allowed to include some details concerning him. He matriculated at Jesus College, Oxford, on 5 February 1584/85, aged 17, and afterwards studied at Clifford's Inn and Lincoln's Inn. On his return to Haverfordwest he entered public life, became a Common Councilman, bailiff in 1589, town sheriff in 1597, and mayor for the years 1599, 1602, 1606, 1612, and 1632, was a feoffee of the lands of the Free School, and is among those named in the charter granted to the town by King James in 1609. In 1603 he was Deputy Constable of Haverfordwest Castle under Thomas Acton, and on 13 April of that year was appointed a Justice of the Peace and of the Quorum for Pembrokeshire, and was also a Deputy Lieutenant.

During his earlier days he acted as agent for Sir John Perrot, and in 1592 is described as one of the men who collected rents for that magnate. He also acted as lawyer for Sir John, and loaned several sums of money to him, which he found difficult to recover. Some trouble arose after Sir John's death in 1592, and Thomas Canon, John Griffith, and Anne Williams, widow, were charged in the Court of Exchequer with embezzling bonds, plate, and jewels belonging to the deceased knight, valued at £2,000; and it was further alleged that when Roger Williams (once Steward of the Household to Sir John) was mortally ill, his wife, the said Anne, prevented Roger's kindred from seeing him, and persuaded the sick man to convey all his personalty, valued at 1,000 marks, to the said accused and furthermore to convey to Thomas Canon lands called Rosedowne in fee simple.

Higher appointments were to come his way. In 1609 he was Surveyor General of Crown lands in the Principality, and in 1622, Prince Charles, Prince of Wales, appointed him Feodary for the Court of Wards in Pembrokeshire. In or about 1623 he received the accolade of knighthood, and in May-August 1625 and January-June 1626, sat as Member of Parliament for Haverfordwest; and he is probably the 'Sir Thomas Canon knight' who sat for Haslemere in 1628/29.

Sir Thomas acquired a reputation as an antiquary, and about 1620 produced historical evidences to support the claim of the princes of Deheubarth to the sovereignty of all Wales as senior representatives of the line of Rhodri Mawr, which stung Robert Vaughan of Hengwrt, some 40 years later, to take up the cudgels on behalf of the royal house of Gwynedd, in his well-known book *British Antiquities Revived.* This contention may have been of academic interest only, modern historians will thank Sir Thomas more for his efforts towards preserving monumental brasses in St. David's Cathedral.

Like his father he invested profits and liquid capital to acquire landed property and to develop its potentialities, with the result that he amassed a large personal and real estate. In 1590 he loaned £90 to his cousin Morgan Voyle, secured on Blaen Cilcoed with four messuages and a limestone quarry belonging thereto, and two messuages at Gellyhalog in Crunwere, and Ludchurch, which were conveyed to him in 1597; in 1594 he erected a weir 'on the river Dungleddy' near Kilbarth, between his own land on one bank and the land of John Hire of 'Kilbargh', on the opposite bank; in 1607 he acquired a lease of Deplesmore in Keyston, and in the following year Thomas Robyn sold to him a four-acre close in Laugharne; shortly before 1612 he bought from Evan Phillip Gwrwared, valuable properties called Llandilus, Croft Beynon, Hendre Glyngwytha alias Eldwall, Croft Bathoe, Carbiglye, Kilvaghe y Bonon, and lands between the 'lake or river' called Glyn y guyther and Glyncallet, all in Vaynor, Llawhaden. In 1610 he bought Little Eliadshill alias Aliardeshill from Sir John Wogan of Boulston, and in 1617/18 bought the manor of Begelly and lands in Williamston Elnor and Thomas Chapel from Sir William Wogan of Wiston. About this period he bought extensive lands in the south of the county from George Barlow of Slebech, which included Kilgetty. In 1620 he bought properties in the vill and fields of Templeton from Lewis Jones of Lampeter Velfrey, and on 23 November 1624 acquired an extremely valuable addition to his estate, when Sir James Fullerton of London and James Maxwell, one of the Grooms of the Bedchamber, granted to him the manor, reeveship and forest of Coedrath in Pembrokeshire, paying yearly to the King £11 3s. 2d. for the manor and reeveship, and £3 1s. 1d. for the forest.

In addition to buying property, he laid out money in mortgages. Early in the century he loaned £200 to Sir John Lewis of Abernantbychan, Cardiganshire, 'secured on the Carmarthenshire manor of Castle Lloyd and Marchynege', which was redeemed in 1610.

Sir Thomas owned a moiety of the manor of Maenclochog, which he charged in 1623 with a yearly payment of £10 to Jesus College, Oxford, 'for the maintenance of a catechism lecture in the College and for a sermon and communion in the chapel on every Thursday before the Act (i.e. Act Sunday) celebrated by the University'. He was less happy in 1634 when the Court of Star Chamber fined him £20 for the practice of private confession, and John Scourfield the High Sheriff seized his lands at Maenclochog under an Exchequer writ. In addition he held some leases, and in 1605 he and Sir William Lower of St. Wynnowene, Cornwall, received from the Crown a lease of the manor of Eastington in Rhoscrowther. According to Fenton, he entered into partnership on 12 March 1623/4 with his kinsman John Voyle to work silver mines at St. Elvis near Solva, probably connected with the Crown grant made to his brother John Canon in the previous year.

A few alienations were made, such as lands in Molleston near Narberth which he sold to John Philipps of Picton Castle in 1611; and two burgages he had acquired in the Cumberland towns of Keswick and Castlewig, sold in 1619 to Christopher Farlan of Keswick for £50; and in 1625 he alienated lands at Drewston in the Pembrokeshire parish of Nolton. Still, he had more than enough to spare, and an entry in the Haverfordwest Corporation Records, shows that Sir Thomas owned real estate producing an annual rental of £1,000, and a personal estate valued at £20,000. He was, thus, one of the richest men in South Wales. Many of the deeds and documents bear after his signature the seal of arms granted to him by the Garter King in 1614, namely *gules* on a bend *argent* double-cotised *or,* a pellet; with a cannon *sable,* mounted on a carriage *or* as a crest.

He lived at various places; in 1605/6 he is described as of 'Luelston' (Leweston), in 1624 as of London, and in 1626 as of Kilgetty, but he lived mainly in the town of Haverfordwest, for an entry in the Corporation Records made in 1650, states that he had lived in Haverfordwest for about 'sixty years and upwards', doubtless at 'the great house in town' listed with the Canon properties in 1645-51.

Sir Thomas never married. His will made on 20 October 1638 contained bequests to the poor of Haverfordwest, Burton, Camrose, Haroldston, Lambston, and Wiston; to St. Paul's Cathedral; to his brothers John and William and their children; to his uncle David Canon and Anne his wife; to his cousin John Beynon of Carmarthen, merchant; to his friends Hugh Owen of Orielton, Arthur Owen of New Moat, the Rev. Thomas Prichard, D.D., and Archdeacon Rudd of St. Davids; and bequeathed all his real estates to his nephew Morris Canon, son of testator's deceased elder brother. The will was ultimately proved on 23 February 1654/55 by Elizabeth, widow of the said Morris Canon the nephew.

Morris Canon the nephew inherited the property of his father David, as well as the great fortune of his uncle Sir Thomas. He studied first at the Middle Temple, and was admitted to Lincoln's Inn on 1 August 1614. During the early part of his life he lived in Haverfordwest, and later at Kilgetty. He may have kept rooms at Lincoln's Inn, for he was described as of that place on 30 August 1650 when, as executor of Thomas Boyland, he assigned a bond in £400 from the Earl of Manchester to John Robinson of London. According to the GGMS he married Elizabeth, daughter of John Wogan (of Wiston), and although the marriage is not mentioned by Mr. Green in his history of the family (WWHR, VI and VII) that is no reason for rejecting the union. They were married before 1643.

Little is known of Morris's career. At one time he seems to have been on uneasy terms with the Corporation of Haverfordwest who brought an action against him in 1647, alleging that he had possessed himself of all the real estate of his uncle Sir Thomas, and refused to pay a legacy of £120 that had been bequeathed to the town. Accordingly, in 1650 the Court of Great

Sessions issued a writ of sequestration against him, and the High Sheriff thereupon took into his hands closes of land called Cashfield and the farm called Temperance (Temperness).

In 1647 he leased a messuage called 'The House in the Greene in Lanteage Village', Crunwere parish, to John Poyer of Tenby, farmer, his wife Margaret Poyer alias David, and Henry David son of Maurice David of Chapel Hill, Narberth; in 1651 he gave a lease of lands at Penrath in St. Issells, to John Coale of St. Issells, his wife Margaret Coale alias Doole, 'kinswoman to Sir Thomas Cannon', and their son Philip Coale; and in 1654 he mortgaged lands at Ridgeway, Froghole, and Rowlesdon in Tenby, to Nicholas Lewes of Hean Castle, in the sum of £200.

Like others of his kinsfolk, Morris Canon was concerned with mining. When he came to live at Kilgetty he found coalmines on his doorstep as it were, and traces of some of them may still be seen on the slope just below the old mansion. They brought in an acceptable income to the family and continued to do so for the subsequent owners of the property. But it might have been well for Morris Canon had they never existed, for in January 1654/55, 'in the night-time when proceeding homewards' he fell headlong into one of the coal pits and was killed instantly. After the inquest his body was brought to Wiston for burial.

Morris Canon's will, dated 20 December 1639, was proved by his relict in PCC (26 Aylett) on the same day as she proved the will of her husband's uncle, Sir Thomas, as mentioned earlier. He left £100 between 'my half-sisters' Jane and Mary Merryman daughters of Hugh Merryman of Wiston, deceased, 'my father in law' *(recte,* step-father); £50 to his sisters Katherine wife of Thomas Gibbon and Janet wife of John Hoare; £400 to his brother John Canon; £100 to his friend Sir Henry Marten, Kt., of St. Botolphs without Aldersgate; he mentions his mother Frances 'now wife' of Henry Jones of Wiston, gentleman; he left the manors of Coedrath and Begelly to his wife Elizabeth for life, together with coal mines and lands, with remainder to heirs male and female of his body, and in default, to his brother John Canon, and in further default, to his godson Maurice Canon the younger, son of 'my great uncle' David Canon of Haverfordwest; he willed that 'my silver bason, ewer, and bowls to be heirlooms to my house in Haverfordwest'; and appointed his wife and Thomas Boyland (dwelling with Sir Henry Marten) to be executors.

Good provision had been made for the widowed Elizabeth, who was to enjoy the profits of 20 farms in the parishes of St. Issells, Amroth, and St. Mary, Tenby, for life, and afterwards they were to revert to the Canon family. Her widowhood proved brief, and before 1661 she had married Isaac Lloyd of Ynys-y-borde near Llandovery, a barrister-at-law, who came to live at his wife's Pembrokeshire home. Blome's *List of Nobility and Gentry* for 1673, contains the entry 'Isaac Lloyd of Kilgetty, Esq.'. Undeterred by mournful memories Elizabeth and Isaac opened several new coal mines in Begelly and Coedrath which provided handsome addition to her already well-laden coffers. Isaac died in the parish of St. Dunstan-in-the-West, London, in 1675, and administration of his goods was granted to the widow. Elizabeth survived him by about ten years, and administration of her goods was granted to her son on 7 May 1685.

Morris and Elizabeth Canon had an only child, John, born in 1643, and admitted at Lincoln's Inn on 19 June 1660. He lived for some time at Leweston, then at Kilgetty before marrying Ann, daughter of Owen Wood of Horsemore, Anglesey, esquire, deceased. The prenuptial settlement was made on 19 October 1663, her portion being £2,700. John Canon agreed to settle on Ann an estate of the yearly value of £400 secured on properties in Pembrokeshire, Carmarthenshire, and Haverfordwest, when she became 21 years of age.

The will of his great-uncle, Sir Thomas, continued to be a source of trouble, and in 1666 Morris Canon was obliged to institute an action in the Court of Chancery against Sir Hugh Owen and Arthur Owen, esquire, two of the executors.

John Canon died in 1690 and, as his wife had predeceased him, administration was granted on 16 June to his son-in-law Edward Philipps.

Elizabeth, only child of John Canon and sole heiress to the Kilgetty estate, married Edward, eldest son of Sir Erasmus Philipps, 3rd Bt., of Picton Castle, the marriage settlement being executed on 13 June 1685. After the wedding, Edward Philipps came to live at Kilgetty, and served the office of High Sheriff in 1691. His tenure at Kilgetty proved brief, for he died without issue at London on 15 April 1694 and was buried at St. Giles-in-the-Fields. The widow married again, on 9 July 1696, to Simon Harcourt of Lincoln's Inn and of Pendley, Albury, Hertfordshire, son of the Rev. Vere Harcourt, D.D. When she died, childless, on 17 August 1706, the Kilgetty estate became vested in her first husband's family.

Marriage with the Canon heiress had brought the valuable Kilgetty estate to the baronets of Picton Castle, chieftains of what was more of a clan than the usual county family. Kilgetty became a seat for successive sons and heirs who thus acquired experience of directing and managing property before shouldering the greater responsibility of the parent estate which in due course would be their primary concern.

As we have seen, Edward Philipps who married Elizabeth Canon was the eldest son of Sir Erasmus, 3rd Bt. Edward died in his father's lifetime in 1694; two years later the father died, and the baronetcy and the estates were inherited by Edward's younger brother, Sir John Philipps, 4th Bt.

The 'Good Sir John', so-called for his humanitarian attitudes and philanthropic works, had three sons: Erasmus, John and Bulkeley. Erasmus, who grew up to be an author of books on economic subjects, kept a diary which provides a few glimpses of life at Kilgetty. He tells us that Thomas Lewis, agent for the Kilgetty estate, died suddenly at Picton Castle in September 1724 having lived in the family for about 37 years, and later in that month, after John Williams had been appointed as successor, Erasmus Philipps, accompanied by his brother John and his cousin James Philipps of Pentypark, proceeded to Kilgetty to examine the property and settle the deceased agent's affairs. About this time negotiations were afoot for the marriage of brother John, when it was arranged that he should live at Kilgetty, and accordingly certain improvements were carried out to render the residence more agreeable to its new occupier. On 10 August 1725 Erasmus noted, 'Went with brother John to Kilgetty about planning some new outhouses to be built there, and altering and adding to the Mansion-House'. John's marriage to Elizabeth, daughter of Henry Shepherd of London, took place at Whitehall Chapel on 27 September, and they remained at London until the work at Kilgetty was completed. By the middle of the following year the house was ready to receive the newly-weds, and Erasmus entered in his journal, 'On 13 June 1726 Brother John with my sister-in-law and her mother set out from London for Kilgetty where they arrived on the 26th instant, came from Bristol by sea'. A rental compiled in 1735 shows that the Kilgetty estate produced £347 16s. 1d. annually.

John Philipps and his wife settled happily at Kilgetty and it was there that their three sons were born, of whom only Richard survived. John, known to his family and friends as 'Kilgetty', entered Parliament, was a prominent member of the high-Tory Society of Sea Sergeants, and was suspected of harbouring Jacobite sympathies. There is no doubt that there were grounds for thinking so, and copies of Jacobite poems and ditties among his papers have been preserved in the Picton Castle archives. However, discretion proved stronger than conviction and he held government appointments under two Hanoverian kings.

When the 'Good Sir John' died on 5 January 1736/37, his eldest son, Erasmus, the diarist, succeeded as 5th Baronet. He never married, and in October 1743 was drowned in the river Avon, and was succeeded by his next brother, 'Kilgetty', known to us as Sir John Philipps, 6th Bt.

Sir John died on 23 June 1764, and his only son Richard succeeded as 7th Bt. He became an eminent public figure, and was created Baron Milford of Ireland by Patent dated 22 July 1776. By his wife Mary, daughter of James Philipps of Pentypark, he had no issue, and when he died on 28 November 1823, the estates were left to a kinsman, Richard Bulkeley Philipps Grant, who took the name and arms of Philipps. The new owner was created a Baronet in 1828,

Baron Milford of Picton Castle in 1847, and ten years later died without issue. The estates passed to his half-brother, the Rev. James Alexander Gwyther, who took the surname Philipps and came to live at Picton Castle.

During the 18th century the Philippses greatly developed the mineral resources of the estate, and worked coal mines at Kilgetty, Saundersfoot, Ridgeway and Moreton (St. Issells parish), Kilanow and Little Merrixton (Amroth parish) and Kingsmoor (Begelly parish). Coal and culm was drawn in carts to the beach at Saundersfoot, and there loaded on to coastal vessels at low tide and carried to various ports. Sir John ('Kilgetty') had another use for his miners; he arranged for a number of them to be given votes – 'The Black Hundred' as they became known – to influence Parliamentary elections, and brought them in a menacing body to attend at the hustings where, in addition to casting their own votes, they could exert pressure on hostile or reluctant electors.

In the first half of the 19th century Kilgetty House ceased to be used as a residence, and was let to a succession of tenants. With the death without issue of Sir John Erasmus Gwynne Alexander Philipps in 1948, his sister, Lady Dunsany, became owner of the estate, of which Kilgetty continues to form a part.

A sketch of the mansion and its surrounding fields was made by John Butcher in 1743. It was then a tall house of six storeys, flanked by two long outbuildings, enclosing a large courtyard, from which a gate led to ornamental gardens, at the end of which was a fine belvedere, the ruins of which remain. From the mid-18th century it ceased to be used as a residence, became a ruin, which was removed, so that no traces now remain. Several other features such as the outbuildings, the gardens, and the belvedere, are still to be seen.

Refs: Francis Jones, 'Kilgetty, A Pembrokeshire Mansion', *Arch. Cam.,* 1976, pp. 127, 139, illust.; Francis Jones, *Historic Cardiganshire Homes and their Families; Pembs. Arch. Svy,* 1896-1907; Picton Castle Deeds; Curtis, *Laugharne,* 1880, p. 355; NLW, Slebech Deeds, Eaton Evans and Williams Deeds; F. P. Gwynne, *Sketches of Tenby,* etc., 1852, p. 139; Pembs. RO, Deeds D/Adams; Fenton, *Tour Pembs.,* 1811.

KILVELGY, *St. Issells*

Now a farm just east of Kilgetty. It is marked on Rees's 14th century Map as Kilvegy (Kilsketty). In the late 16th century it formed part of the Barlow of Slebech estate, and in 1613 John Barlow owned 'the manor of St. Issells alias Kilvelgy' containing a number of messuages, 500 acres of land, a corn mill, and a fulling mill. The next resident at Kivelgy was Jenkin Thomas, son of Evan Thomas descended from Brychan Brycheiniog. In 1670 he paid five hearth taxes, which shows it to have been a commodious residence at that time. He married Mary Barlow of Haverfordwest by whom he had an only child, Anne Thomas, who married Lewis Bowen of Haverfordwest. In 1658 John Bell the elder of Arnolds Hill is described as formerly of Killvelgie, gentleman; in 1679 one Samuel Thomas gentleman was living at Cilvelgy. The property remained in Barlow ownership and finally passed to Sir William Hamilton (who had married the Slebech heiress), who is described as owner in 1786, with John Hodges as tenant, and in 1834 William Hodges was tenant. In 1786 there was also Little Kivelgy owned by Lord Milford with David Welch as tenant.

Refs: NLW, Pembs. Plea Rolls, Nos. 184, 226; WWHR iii, 133; Taylor's *Cussion,* p. 97; Pembs. R.O, LT 1786; *Western Mail,* 1 May 1986, illust. of Kilvelgy farm.

KINGSTON, *St. Michael's, Pembroke*

Now a farm, 1¼ miles to the southeast of Pembroke town. In the second half of the 17th century it was held by the Meares family. In the 18th century it was owned by John Campbell Hooke (one of the Stackpole Court family) who is given as the owner in 1786, with Mr. Furlong as tenant.

Refs: Pembs. RO, LT 1786; Meares family ped.

LACERRY, *St. Twynells**

Initially owned by the Whites of Henllan; Thomas White was of Leserry, Esq. in 1673. In a deed dated 1 July 1659 Jane White of Lacerry, parish of St. Twynells, spinster, Anne Gwillim of same parish, widow and Margaret White of same, spinster, agreed with Henry White of Henllan, Rhoscrowther, Esq. the bargain and sale of Upper Loveston. They were still resident at Lacerry in 1670. By 1894 Benjamin George Roberts was of Lacerry, husbandman.

Refs: HT 1670; VL 1894; Pembs. Plea Rolls No. 78; Blome's *List* 1673.

LAMPETER VELFREY, *Lampeter Velfrey*

Lampeter House, formerly called 'Peniucha'r Dre' and 'Upper End House' due to its position in the village. In the 17th and 18th centuries it was home to the Philipps family (said to be a cadet of Picton Castle). In 1670 Anne Philipps was assessed at six hearths. Towards the end of the 18th century, sons of the family moved to Begelly, Jeffreston, and one son emigrated to South Africa. Another son, the Rev. Edward Philipps (1736-93) Rector of Lampeter Velfrey, was the father of a daughter who married Nathaniel Phillips of Slebech, and their daughter, Mary Dorothea, married the Baron de Rutzen who afterwards settled at Slebech. Another daughter, Louisa Catherine, married the Earl of Lichfield. Still an attractive residence, Lampeter House consists of an old part and a newer addition. The older part is in the rear, which had chimneys at either end and gables and a chimney *(simne fawr)* on the lateral wall with a massive chimney stack and the Philipps arms on one marble mantlepiece. The house was enlarged by Mr. Tudor Thomas in 1888.

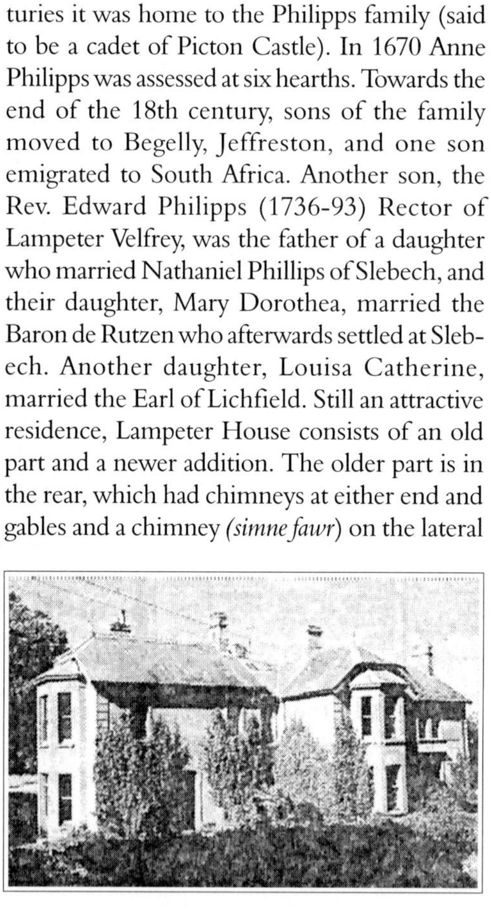

Refs: NLW, Slebech Deeds, Pembs. Plea Rolls; Pembs. RO, LT Lists.

LAMPHEY, *Lamphey*

There were three residences on the north-eastern fringe of Lamphey village, worthy of note, namely:

1. LAMPHEY PALACE

During medieval centuries this was a residence of the Bishop of St. Davids. Extensive ruins remain; among its noteworthy features are an early 13th century central hall, with an added camera block in the west, which, with its chapel and remodelling belong to the time of Bishop Vaughan (1509-13), and on the east an impressive first-floor hall, and remains of the chapel; a gatehouse and enclosing wall belong to the time of Bishop Gower (1328-47). A detailed inventory of the goods of Bishop Rawling, died 1536, lists the following rooms of the late Bishop 'at his manor place of Lantefey', with their contents, providing an idea of the extent of the building at the Dissolution, as follows – The Bishop's own chamber 'where he was accustomed to take his rest, and where he died'. The Chamberlain's chamber, Wardrobe, Checkered chamber, Great chamber, Gardine chamber, Gloucester chamber, next chamber to the Gloucester chamber, Parker's chamber, Steward's chamber, the next chamber, the Porter's chamber, Cook's chamber, Painter's chamber, Barbour's chamber, Brewer (chamber), Under Cook's chamber, Chapel chamber, the second chamber within the Chapel chamber, Chapel, Hall, Parlour, Wine Cellar, Buttery, Pantry, Kitchen, Larder House, Fish Larder House, Bakehouse, Brewhouse, Malthouse, Oxhouse and the Park.

Refs: Arch. Camb., 1888, pp. 363-7 which contains the above list and contents, ibid 1938, pp. 1-14, ibid 1977 p. 174; *RCAM Pembs.*, 1925, No. 362 illust.; Radford, *Lamphey Place* (official guidebook) illust.; *Carmarthenshire Studies,* 1974, pp. 47-8; Fenton, *Tour Pembs.,* 1811, edn. 1903, pp. 236-7, illust.; *Western Telegraph,* 21 April 1983, illust.

2. LAMPHEY COURT

A residence just north of the Palace. Several families lived at Lamphey, but whether in part of the old Episcopal palace, or in another house nearby is not known. It was the house of Devereux, Scarfe and Cuny families successively. George Devereux and Richard Cuny were High Sheriffs in 1580 and 1615.

The area belonged to the Devereux family, but on the attainder of the Earl of Essex late in the reign of Queen Elizabeth, the lands were purchased by Sir Hugh Owen of Orielton and remained in possession of his descendants until about 1821.

Due in great measure to election and political expenses Sir John Owen, Bart of Orielton found himself in deep financial waters, and among those he turned to for assistance was Charles Mathias from whom he borrowed £45,545 secured on the manor and lands of Monkton. Although this provided temporary relief to the anxious baronet it failed to arrest his progress towards the brink, and by 1820 the debts were so pressing that he found himself obliged to sell the manor of Lamphey as well as properties he owned in Llanstinan and Penally to Charles Mathias for £35,000. A sum of £25,545 was to be retained by Charles Mathias in order to reduce Owen's mortgage secured on the manor of Monkton. By 1821 Lamphey was owned in fee simple by Charles Mathias who decided to build a new mansion in the style popular at that period. There had been an older residence there known as Lamphey Court which had fallen into a sad state of decay by the time he acquired it. In 1826 the crumbling fabric was dismantled and an engraving of the ruins made by Gastineau appeared in Jones's *Wales Illustrated* in 1830. The new Lamphey Court was a large handsome mansion with a fine portico of four Ionic columns.

The squire of Lamphey Court took some part in public life, was a Justice of the peace, and in 1817 High Sheriff of the county. On 28 April 1812 he had married Mary, eldest daughter of John Bethell of Hassage, Somerset. Charles Mathias died on 23 July 1851; his wife in 1853 leaving ten sons and two daughters, all recorded in Burkes *Landed Gentry* 1952 where their marriages, issue and descendants are set forth

at large. Lewis Mathias succeeded to Lamphey and Llang-warren. Educated at Brazenose College, Oxford, he settled down to the duties of a Pembrokeshire landowner, becoming a J.P. and D.L. and High Sheriff in 1856. In 1879 his estate consisted of 4,562 acres with a yearly rental of £4,113. He married Emily, daughter of John Bennett Lawes of Herts, on 9 October 1845 and had seven children. He died in 1882 his wife having predeceased him. Charles Mathias, born 1849, educated at Harrow and Emmanuel College, Cambridge, returned to his Lamphey estates, was a J.P. and a Captain and Honorary Major of the Pembroke Yeomanry Cavalry in the years 1871-90. He married in 1875 Cecilia Stoke of St. Botolphs and had four children by her before dying in 1918. Their heir Charles Ronald Mathias, born 1877, was educated at Cheltenham College and spent some years in South Africa as a police official. He was also High Sheriff in 1937 and eventually Chairman of Pembrokeshire County Council. A kindly, highly popular man he was particularly interested in antiquaries. In 1913 he married Shelah Farewell, of Natal, South Africa and had two sons, Lewis and Anthony, who was a Pilot Officer in the RAF and killed in action over Germany in 1940. Charles Mathias was succeeded in 1949 by his surviving son, Lewis, who was High Sheriff in 1965.

Lewis Mathias was the last of the family at the mansion which he sold in 1978, and now lives in a house in the grounds. The mansion is now an hotel.

Refs: Lewis, *TDW,* 1835, 1840; *South West Wales, Guide,* Kyrian Rees, 1976, illust.; Jones, *Wales Illustrated,* 1830, engraving from a drawing by H. Gastineau of the Palace ruins, with part of the new Lamphey Court a short distance away. For illustrations see *Western Telegraph* 4 December 1980, 20 January 1983 and 4 July 1984; Francis Jones article 'Llangwarren'.

3. LAMPHEY PARK

A residence just north of Lamphey Court. In 1786 James Thomas was owner-occupier of Lamphey Park, and was still there in 1817 when he was described as gentleman. In 1834 Charles Poyer Callen was the tenant, paying a yearly rent of £50, and Lewis in 1840 states that Lamphey Park, 'the property of Mrs. Thomas occupies a pleasant situation.' It is now derelict.

Refs: Lewis, *TDW,* 1840; Pembs. VL 1834; NLW, Maesgwynne Deeds, No. 59.

LANCYCH, *Clydey*

On the banks of Afon Cych, to the east of Ffynnone. A residence built in the first half of the 19th century on the site of an earlier house. The first known owner was Morgan Llwyd who owned a large estate in the district, and is described as of Lancych in the years 1739-62, the occupier being Benjamin Davies, tanner. On Morgan Llwyd's death, Lancych passed to Sarah Lloyd his widow. In 1770 she married a second husband, David Griffiths of Vaynor, who moved to his wife's home. He was High Sheriff of Pembrokeshire in 1779, and died in 1782/3. Sarah remained there and her will was proved in 1802. Lancych passed to her relation Marianne Jones, who married in 1807 the Rev. Thomas Thomas, Rector of Jordanston in Dewsland, who came to Lancych where he died in 1813. The widowed Marianne continued there till her death in 1831. They had no children and Lancych estate was partitioned.

The next owner was Dr. Walter David Jones, M.D., an antiquary of repute, who died at Lancych in 1869. He left all the estate to his wife Ann for life, then to John Francis Jones 'who shall take and use the name and arms of Lloyd of Ffoshelig and Dole Llanerch, after the name of Jones.' J. F. Jones Lloyd was followed by his son H. A. Jones Lloyd, solicitor, who died in 1932. He was followed by Mr. Owen Jones Lloyd whose son now lives at Lancych. The irregularity of the plan and survival of some corbelling on the outside walls indicate the antiquity of the earlier residence, but in the 19th century it was reconstructed in the *cottage ornee* style, and the interior radically rearranged.

Refs: NLW, Lancych Deeds, Owen/Colby Records, Tithe Maps Clydey 1841; Pembs RO, LT 1786; B. Williams, *Hanes Casnewydd-Emlyn,* 1860, p. 58.

LANDSHIPPING, *Martletwy*

Landshipping is an area on the banks of the Eastern Cleddau where it meets the Western Cleddau. Landshipping Ferry (a) consists of a small quay with a few houses around it. About half a mile southwards is (b) Landshipping Quay, on an inlet, where ships carried on a lively trade in olden days, and about half a mile eastwards is the small hamlet near which stood an impressive mansion (c) until its demolition in the early half of the 19th century, marked as 'Landshipping Old House' on Colby's Map in 1831.

LANDSHIPPING FERRY

Some 50 yards above the shore, a new mansion was built about 1800 by the Owen family, to replace the older, ruined inland mansion. It is marked on Mudge's Map of 1819. In the parish tithe map of 1840, the ground plan of the house is given, then owned by Sir John Owen.

In 1857 it was advertised for sale, and thus described. 'Beautifully situate on the Banks of the River Cleddy and opposite Picton Castle containing sundry 'Bedrooms, Hall Parlour, Dining and Drawing Rooms, Library, Nursery, Servants' Offices, Range of Stabling, Coach House, Saddle Room with Granary over, Yard, Extensive Walled Garden, Orchard, works etc'; nearly five acres in all, in hand of the annual value of £30.

When I visited Ferry in 1974, I found the ruined mansion, its walls well preserved, and all the features still well defined. The house consisted of three storeys, and in the front were two bow windows which rose to roof height, the main entrance was between them. In the rear part was an extension, and to the rear was a wing still inhabited and in excellent condition. It was then owned by Mr. Leavesley of Worcestershire. Now in a parlous state the mansion has been recently purchased for renovation.

LANDSHIPPING HOUSE

Caput of the manor of Landshipping was held in the 16th century by the families of Nash and Wyrriot. From the latter it passed to the family of Owen of Orielton early in the 17th century and remained in their hands till its demolition a few years before 1840. The Owens lived there from time to time. It was then a structure of three storeys and in 1670 was assessed as containing 20 hearths, one of the largest Pembrokeshire residences.

A letter from Sir Hugh Owen to Sir John Philipps of Picton Castle, mentions the 'new modelling and a water folly at Landshipping' in 1696/7. Erasmus Philipps in his journal mentions on 3rd September 1729, 'I went to Landshipping, Mr. William Owen and his lady from home.' In the Land Tax List of 1786 the house is shown as being held by representatives of 'the late Sir Hugh Owen, Bart'. Thereafter Mr. Owen lived at Orielton, and Landshipping House soon required extensive repair, and an estimate of the work required there, made by Griffith Watkins, 'house builder', on 26th October 1789, mentions (*inter alia*) the following rooms in the mansion – nursery, Blue room, Plad (sic.) room, Lady Owen's room, Dressing room and closet, Plad rooms in the Gallery 'Charset', Yellow room, Gallery corridor, Red and Plad rooms 'on one floor', Sir Hugh's closet, Best Parlour, Hall, Drawing room, Common Parlour, Butler's Pantry, Housekeeper's room, Stewards hall, Servants' hall; a wing on the east side of the house consisting of kitchen, larder, dairy, brewhouse and bedchambers over, being 100 feet long and 20 feet broad; scullery; an old building east of the house, called The Curnal Stable, 22 feet long and 18 feet broad; lime house, coach house, malt house, carpenter's workshop, common stables, middle stables, pigs' yard and cot, pump and cover to the well, garden.

By 1789 the uninhabited mansions of Orielton and Landshipping were deteriorating rapidly, and the Owen 'Great House' at Tenby, and the Owen house at Haverfordwest, were similarly neglected by the Trustees of the Owen family. Some £2,009 16s. 0d. had been spent on repairs at Landshipping, but in January 1790 Lady Owen arranged for the principal rooms to be closed, the furniture to be covered with dust sheets, and dismissed the housekeeper, cook and other domestics, as well as the gardeners and farm hands, retaining only a female caretaker at the mansion. This was the swansong of the old residence, and Fenton noted in 1811 – 'Landshipping, where embosomed 'sacred to social life and social love,' formerly stood a very respectable mansion now unroofed and in ruins, a favourite residence of the late Sir William Owen, where the venerable baronet lived much.' A few remnants of the old mansion are still to be seen near Clare House farm (now belonging to Mr. Eynon). A good deal of the walling of the old mansion's garden still remain, and traces of fish-ponds on the south side below the landscaped and terraced grounds.

LANDSHIPPING QUAY

This house stood above the old quay. In the 18th century it was the home of William Thomas (will dated 1713) and Mary, his wife. They had three sons and a daughter, namely William Thomas (d. 1734), Hugh Thomas D. D. Master of Pembroke College, Cambridge (d.1780) and Walter Thomas, mining entrepeneur, who settled at Chester. The daughter Sarah Thomas, married in 1723, Henry Leach, mercer, of St. Mary's Pembroke, from whom descended the Leaches of Corston.

Refs: (for the three houses), Taylor's *Cussion*; Fenton, *Tour Pembs.*, 1811; Pembs RO, Deeds SMB/HL/C, LT 1786; NLW, Picton Castle Deeds and Papers, Owen/Colby Deeds, Tithe Map Martletwy Parish 1840; Census Return 1851.

LANGTON, *Manorowen*

Originally a modest late medieval farmhouse with a large walled garden, Scleddau Uchaf, became the property early in the 19th century of Sir James Cockburn, Governor of Bermuda. He added a wing on the north east side of the older building and renamed it Langton after the house in Lothian belonging to the family of his friend Sir John Hamilton with whom he had served during the Peninsular wars. He was the father of John James Hamilton who was to become Sir James Cockburn's son-in-law in 1834.

In 1837 on the death of Gwynn Vaughan of Jordanston (q.v.), Sir James Cockburn, who was his executor, inherited his estates and on the death of Richard Parry Bowen at Manorowen in 1837 bought further land in Scleddau.

When Sir James died in 1852 the entire estate passed to his daughter Marianna Augusta and her husband, Sir John James Hamilton. Their joint interest in the welfare of children and in promoting a Christian education led them to assist in the foundation of schools in Fishguard, Manorowen and Mathry, and to finance much needed repairs to the churches of Jordanston and Mathry. In 1855 they moved to Plâs Llanstephan which they rented from the Meares family and they used it as a Summer residence until her death in 1892. Sir James died in 1876.

After Marianna's death Langton passed to her Godson, James Hamilton Langdon Yorke. He was also the grandson of her first Cousin Georgiana Yorke (née Hawkins). On the strength of his son's inheritance, his father, James Charles Yorke, himself a descendant of the Earl of Hardwicke and great grandson of the Bishop of St Davids and Ely, brought his family to Pembrokeshire. He rented Trecwn from the Barham family while he set about adding to his son's house at Langton. He refused architect's advice and on the first attempt the masonry collapsed. In order to strengthen the structure, the surviving outside wall, including the window embrasures, were incorporated into the center of the building. The new building consisted of a large northeast facing wing of high ample rooms, including the apparently mandatory billiard room. Its other feature was a broad, highly polished staircase of New Zealand pine, whose treads sloped unaccountably downwards. The only south facing rooms in the building were the ones in the original farmhouse which became a series of kitchens, servant's rooms and larders. It had no architectural beauty but was a comfortable house for a family with 10 children and staff.

J. C. Yorke became High Sheriff in 1896 and was Chairman of Governors at Fishguard Grammar School until his death in 1932. Since the estate belonged to his son, the legal action which ensued after he began to dispose of some the property went to the House of Lords and became a classic in legal history. Sadly, this son, James Hamilton Langdon Yorke M.C. who served in the Pembrokeshire Yeomanry was killed in action in Syria in 1917. The property passed to his son James John Simon Yorke D.S.O., RN. Apart from a period during the 1939-45 war when the army requisisitioned it, the family lived at Langton until his death in 1963. He was then Deputy Lieutenant of Pembrokeshire. The house became a Baptist seminary and later a Nursing Home.

Ref: Mrs. A. Eastham.

Mr. G. Williams, coachman, with Mr. J. C. Yorke (right), outside the stables at Langton House

Barlow

LAWRENNY, *Lawrenny*

The mansion stood on high ground near the confluence of the rivers Cleddau and Cresswell, above the northern bank of the latter. A short distance away is the parish church, the South Transept of which is called 'The Lawrenny chapel'.

In 1587/8, Wogan of Wiston was lord of the manor of Lawrenny, while the freeholds of the district were in possession of the powerful family of Barlow of Slebech, a cadet of which was seated at Cresswell. The first to own Lawrenny appears to have been William Barlow of Cresswell, High Sheriff in 1612, who died in 1636 and was buried at Lawrenny. His son Lewis Barlow of Cresswell and Lawrenny, was High Sheriff in 1641 and 1668. Lewis's son John Barlow was High Sheriff in 1686, and a John Barlow was High Sheriff in 1705. The last named John Barlow was MP for Haverfordwest, and by his wife Anne daughter of Sir Hugh Owen, 2nd Bt., of Orielton, had issue. Lewis Barlow was assessed at nine hearths in 1670 which denotes that Lawrenny was then one of the largest mansions in the county.

The last male generation of the Barlows, Hugh Barlow, died without issue in 1763, and his wife, Elizabeth, daughter of Sir Arthur Owen of Orielton lived at Lawrenny till her death in 1788, and was buried with her husband in the parish church. Her sister-in-law, Anne Barlow had married Wyrriot Owen of Great Nash, and it was their son Hugh Owen who succeeded to Lawrenny, and took the surname Barlow.

Anne's youngest sister, Dorothy Barlow married John Lort of Pricaston and their daughter Elizabeth Lort married in 1767 George Phillips, M.P., of Haverfordwest, and their descendants ultimately succeeded to Lawrenny, namely the Lort-Phillips family who continue to own it to this day. Tourists of the late 18th and early 19th centuries have much to say about Lawrenny. In 1798 Shrine wrote, 'This place (Lawrenny), much improved by the taste of its present owner, Mr. Barlow, may justly be called the finest in Pembrokeshire, both from its internal decoration and its commanding position at the extremity of a high ridge clothed with thick woods'; Barber, in 1803, says much the same; and Fenton, notes, 'Lawrenny, the charming seat of Hugh Barlow Esq. M.P. for Pembroke, where he lives for at least seven months of the year . . . He boasts a park well stocked with venison, extensive and well managed hot-houses, and has the command of fish.' The house, though of that unpicturesque species of building peculiar to this country about a century ago, a tall cube, and in its external as to form not much entitled to admiration, yet is within disposed of with much taste and convenience, and is well connected with its offices; and from the breakfasting-room you walk into a neat conservatory well furnished with rare plants.'

On 3 June 1809 a notice read, 'To be let, Lawrenny-Hall (late residence of Hugh Barlow, Esq. deceased)', with, on the ground floor, a spacious dining parlour, drawing room, breakfast parlour communicating by a glass door with a conservatory, a library, commodious kitchen, steward's room, housekeeper's room, servants' hall, cellars, and other offices; on the first floor, four bedchambers with dressing rooms; on the second floor, seven bedchambers with three dressing rooms, and a store-room; in the attic storey, ten bedchambers; also coach-houses, stables, walled gardens, hot houses, pleasure grounds, paddock, park, and demesne lands, in all about 388 acres. In 1840, S. Lewis writes, 'Lawrenny Hall, the ancient seat of the late Hugh Barlow Esq. . . . and now a ruin. This fine estate is entailed on the family of Lort-Phillips of Haverfordwest'. The historian, Burke, states in 1858 that the original house 'Has lately been pulled down, and another is in the course of being created by Mr. Phillips in the castellated style'. This was George Lort-Phillips, M.P., whose family had inherited the property. This large towered and turreted mansion, typical of the mid-19th century,

known as Lawrenny Castle, remained until 1950 when it was demolished. The family continued to live there and to contribute to public life – J. F. Lort-Phillips was High Sheriff in 1880, Lt. Col. Patrick Lort-Phillips in 1954, and David Lort-Phillips in 1983. Mr. David Lort-Phillips, the present owner of the estate, lives at nearby Knowles Farm, a commodious farmstead.

Refs: Pembs. RO, Plan of Lawrenny Demesne by John Butcher, 1762, LT 1786, and D/Law/2, plan and design for Lawrenny Castle, 1851-58: C. S. Allen, *Photographs in South Wales,* 1871; T. Lloyd, *Lost Houses,* 1986, illust; *Western Telegraph,* 7, 14 March 1984, and 7 July 1985, illust.; *Contemporary Biographies of S. Wales & Mon.,* 1907, illust. Other refs. are included in the text above.

LECHA, *Llanhowell*

Near Afon Solfach, just north of Caerforiog, and some two miles from the seaside village of Solfach. Lecha is an interesting old farmstead, home of gentlemen farmers for many generations, and among its features is a pine-panelled room. In 1562 it formed part of the estate of Parry of Trecadwgan, and in the following century was the home of John Jones (whose father was a younger son of Jones of Brawdy) who lived there from 1625 to 1670. By the end of the 17th century ownership had passed to the Barlows of Slebech. In 1741 George Barlow leased the property to Thomas Barzey of Arnolds Hill, for the lives of his three children, George Barzey, Anne, and Sarah. George Barzey, who kept a pack of hounds at Lecha, died without issue in 1810 aged 71, and was followed by his sister Anne Thomas, the last surviving 'life', in 1820.

Ownership passed to (Sir) William Hamilton, in right of his wife, heiress of Slebech, and afterwards to the Hon. Robert Fulke Greville of Castle Hall near Milford, who, on 12 August 1857 sold Lecha to Stephen Thomas for £3,700. Stephen died in 1889, aged 74, and was followed by his son, the highly respected Dr. Thomas Nash Thomas (known locally as *O Lecha*), and finally to Mr. Elfet Martin of Lochmeyler (a great-grandson of Dr. Thomas's sister) who was the last local owner, but died, alas in 1986, having sold Lecha a few years previously.

RCAM Pembs. tells of ruins nearby: 'on the land of Lecha are the remains of a cromlech; the capstone measuring 15ft x 11ft and about 4ft in thickness. There is also a mound near, and it is said that there were two there formerly. About 200 yards south of the cromlech is the site of Caerforiog, encompassed by a moat 10ft wide now filled with water and mud. The outside measurements of the work are 25 yards by 24 yards. The interior, covered with dense undergrowth. The water of the moat rises about 9ft clear of ground level and runs into Afon Solfach, a few yards to the north of the enclosure, and forms the body between Llanhowell and Whitchurch parishes. On the opposite bank of the river is Llyn yr Alarch now much silted, but formerly a feature of the ruined mansion of Caerforiog. A dovecote is said to have stood on a mound within the moat but no trace remains'.

Refs: NLW, Slebech Deeds, Pembs. Plea Rolls and Fines GS, Williams and Williams, H'west, Deeds, Eaton Evans and Williams Deeds; Anc. Mon. Pembs.

LEWESTON, *Camrose*

In the east of the parish, between Wolfsdale and Great Treffgarne Mountain, Leweston consists of a group of farmsteads in close proximity. The name derives from Llewelyn and tun, and is marked on Rees's 14th century map as Leweleston, a lord's demesne, and is included as Lewelyston in the I.P.M. of the owner, Aymer de Valence, Earl of Pembroke in 1324 who was killed in a tournament at Compiegne.

There were four farms here, and in the Land Tax List of 1786, Upper Leweston was owned by the occupier Thomas Bowen Barry

Esq. and the other three called Lower Leweston were owned by the lord, Thomas Bowen, who lived in one of them. The Tancred family were living at Leweston in 1441, and were there in 1591 when Lewys Dwnn called to record their ancestry. In 1623 one of the farms was owned by the Prince of Wales who had let it to Sir Thomas Canon, an antiquary from Haverfordwest, and his homestead is described in that year as consisting of three principal rooms on the ground floor, '13 couples, and thatched'.

Later in the century it became a residence of the Bowen family from Haverfordwest, and by 1797 one of the farmsteads was owned by Joseph Fortune from the same town.

The early Fortunes were Quakers, and were in Pembrokeshire in the mid-17th century and were buried in the enclosure at Mount near East Hook. Some were tradesmen in Haverfordwest and amassed a good deal of money which they invested in landed property. In 1797 Joseph Fortune of Haverfordwest, tanner, became a J.P., D.L. and Mayor of Haverfordwest, and died at his house in Market Street in 1803. His son, William lived at Leweston where he died in 1826.

It was the seat of his descendants until the death in 1925 of Miss Marianne Fortune at the age of 88, her home described in that year as 'a quaint old 17th century house'. One of the Leweston farms became part of the estate of Jones of Brawdy, and was still owned by Frederick William Jones in 1904.

Refs: Essay by J. R. Poyer Penn in WWHR xi, 1926, pp. 1-36; ibid. Francis Green 'The Fortunes of Leweston', pp. 63-76; Pembs. RO, Deeds 1669-1728, LT Lists; NLW, Picton Castle Deeds, Morgan-Richardson Deeds; *NLWJ,* 1980, xxi, No. 4.

LINNEY, *Castlemartin*

Near the coast at the southwestern end of the Castlemartin promontary, just south of Linney Burrows, and overlooking the inlet called Black's Cove. Marked as a knight's fee on Rees' 14th century map; as Linney house on George Owen's Map, 1603; as residence of 'Row Esq.' on the maps of Bowen (1760) and Kitchin (1763). Fenton wrote in 1811, 'Nearer the sea is Linney, an old mansion, formerly the property and residence of the Rows, a family of middling fortune.' It became property of the Lorts, and in 1631 the owner was George Lort of Linney, gent. In 1670 John Leach was assessed at five hearth taxes for Linney, and his will was proved in 1675. The next was Richard Row, gent. who married Elizabeth Meares. He was High Sheriff of the county in 1729, and died before 1735. His wife died in 1750. They had two children, Francis Row, living at Linney in 1741, who died without issue, and Alice who married in 1721 James Bowen of Llwyngwair, and had issue.

The property was afterwards leased to George Phelps, gent. who was there in 1787 (the owner being John Campbell Esq.), and was followed by his only son John Phelps who had inherited 10 leaseholds and was living at Linney in 1804. Thomas Jones, gent, lived there in 1834. George Roch, farmer, was at Linney in 1851, and James Roch in 1904.

Refs: NLW, Morgan-Richardson Deeds, Eaton Evans and Williams Deeds; Fenton, *Tour Pembs.* 1811; RGC Pembs. 1925.

LITTLE MILFORD, *Freystrop*

To the northeast of Freystrop Cross, near the western banks of the Cleddau, and three miles south of Haverfordwest. This property formed part of the estate of the Perrotts of Haroldston from early times. In 1682 Susanna Perrott of Haroldston, widow, granted a lease of a messuage and garden in Freystrop to John Beavans of Little Milford, Yeoman. This is the first reference found to Little Milford.

In 1722 there are references to John Steward of Little Milford, gent. and his son, Charles. By 1756 it was the home of Caesar Mathias who was Mayor of Pembroke in 1767, and High Sheriff of the county in 1774. He died in 1795, leaving by his wife Alice, daughter of Henry Leach of Pembroke, whom he had married in 1754, a son Henry Mathias, who became a lawyer. Henry afterwards moved to nearby Fernhill, was Mayor of Haverfordwest in 1806, and in 1816 was High Sheriff of the county. During his shrievalty he presented an address from the county to the Prince Regent on the marriage of his daughter, Princess Charlotte, and was knighted. Sir Henry was the last protonotary of the Carmarthen circuit. His wife Katherine was daughter of Philip Jones of

Llanina by Katherine Warren of Trewern, Nevern, but they had no issue. Sir Henry died in 1832, aged 75, and Katherine in 1848, aged 83. His first-cousin was the Revd Caesar Morgan of Ely, whose wife, Mrs. Mary Morgan wrote her *Tour to Milford Haven* in 1791. In 1907 Little Milford, then comprising 319 acres, was the home of Joseph S. Roberts.

Refs: Hampton Deeds (Pakington); NLW, Corston Deeds; *Contemporary Biographies of S. Wales and Mon.*, 1907, p. 102, illust.

LLANDEILO, *Llandeilo*

Called Llandeilo Llwydiarth in early days, but earlier in the middle ages Llandeilo, and from about 1750 the farmstead near the old parish church ruin was known as Llandeilo Fach. There were two farms in 1786, both called Llandeilo, and in the Voters' Lists for 1894 and 1904 they were designated Llandeilo Uchaf (standing first north of the Llangolman – Maenclochog road) and Llandeilo Isaf (near the church ruin), the oldest farmstead in the parish. It stands to the east of Maenclochog, a little south of the ruined church in the farm of Blaenllwydiarth, one of the names applied to the parish in early times.

The parish comprises some 1,171 acres, and slopes northward to include the highest point in the Preseli range, namely Moel Carn Cerwyn. A famous well continues to bubble near the old church; Carlisle, in 1811, calls it 'a fine spring which the credulous still believe will cure coughs when the water is drunk out of the skull of St. Teilo, which is carefully kept clean and shining on the shelf of a farm home just by the well', and Thornhill Timmins writes in 1895, 'This curious relic was formerly held in high esteem as a cure for all manner of sickness, water being drawn from the saint's well, and drunk out of the skull.

The virtue of the draught was supposed to consist of its being administered by the eldest son of the house of Melchior, then, as now, the hereditary custodian of St.Teilo's skull.'

The livings of Llandeilo, Llangolman, and Maenclochog, were granted by David de Rupe, son and heir of Gilbert de Rupe, to the Abbey of St. Dogmaels. The grant had been made without Royal Licence, but on 30 October 1320, the Abbot received a royal pardon for this omission. Llandeilo later became a lay manor, but in 1898 no emoluments were derived from it, and the manorial courts discontinued. The parish was united to Maenclochog by Order in Council 11 July 1877. Some ruins of the old church are still to be seen near the farmstead. The earliest known family there was that of Cadigan who remained till early in the 17th century. Its successor was the Griffith family. Griffith ap Thomas (died c. 1649/50) had some remarkably enterprising sons who left the old home – John Griffith of London, in 1642 became Treasurer and Solicitor to Thomas Howard, Earl of Arundel who became Earl Marshal in 1646; William Griffith, Groom of His Majesty's Chamber in 1642; Thomas Griffith ancient of a Company in Ireland in that year, while another brother Maurice Griffith, *agricola*, stayed at home, and was executor of his father's estate in 1652. The son of William Griffith, called John, became one of the Guard of Charles I.

The next family there was that of Melchior, one of whom had married a daughter of Cadigan of Llandeilo in Elizabethan times. The Melchiors, a Welsh family, came from Newport, the first of this unusual name being Melchior ap Ieuan ap Howel ap Gwallter, who died on 3 April 1591 and was buried in Newport church on Easter Day. His sons adopted their father's Christian name as their permanent surname. The Melchiors continued to farm Llandeilo until well on in this century. Although they were custodians of St. Teilo's skull, they nevertheless sold the holy relic in 1927, for £50 it's said. In 1950 the Chetham family lived there.

Refs: NLW, Bronwydd Deeds, Poyston Deeds, Pembs. Plea Rolls; Pembs. RO, LT 1786, VL; Carms. RO, GGMSS, BM, Egerton MS 2586, C of A MSS, Protheroe v, xii; *Arch. Cam.* 1889 v, vi, 1893; Bacon, *Liber Regis;* R. Comm. on Land in Wales; Lloyd Williams, *Craydro Sir Benfro*; Carlisle, *TDW,* 1811; Timmins, *Nooks Pembs.,* 1895.

LLANDIGIGE FACH, *St. Davids*
Llandigige (fawr) and -fach, two farmsteads near each other, lying between Berea on the north and Carnhedryn on the south, marked on Colby's Map 1831. In 1326, Daykin and his co-tenants held at Llandegige Vechan three borates of land and paid yearly 3s., and 'suit at the Lord's mill'. Llandigige Fach was owned by John Warlow of Newgate in 1612, a minor gentry family. His son Thomas Warlow of Newgate married Jane daughter of William Jones of Brawdy, and their son John Warlow settled at Llandigige Fach and was living there in 1634. Six generations of Warlows lived there until the early part of the 18th century when Llandigige Fach was alienated. The property was then divided into two farms. In 1786 one of the farms was owned by the Widow Nash, with John Warlow (died 1816) as tenant. His brother Henry Warlow died unmarried in 1767; and the other farm was owned by John Parry, gent. with Henry Phillip as tenant. Later it became a unified farm again and therefore was home of farming tenants.

The last Warlow, the widow Mrs. Mary Warlow (née Martin) died in 1824 leaving Llandigige Fach to her friend James Propert of St. Davids. Henry Evans was occupier in 1894.

Refs: Black Book of St. Davids, 1326, p. 104; Warlows Pedigree (*penes me*).

LLANDIGIGE (FAWR), *St. Davids*
Location as in preceding entry. The addition *fawr* was discontinued, and the property was usually described as Llandigige. Few references have been found to this place. In 1326 Philip Vaughan, David ap Meilier and their co-tenants held a carucate of land at Llandigige free of rent, from the Bishop of St. Davids. In 1559 John Walter is described as of Llandigige. In 1612 Lewis Lloyd of Llandigige Fawr, gent. granted lands in the parishes of St. Davids and Llanhowel, to Thomas Lloyd of Kilkiffeth, Esq. John Harries of Llandigige, Esq. was a J.P. and a grand Juror in 1756 and 1767; and in 1786 it was the residence of George Harries, Esq. with Sir William Williams as tenant. Williams was born in 1755, and in 1782 married Mary Miller and in 1809-24 was described as Esq. and J.P. He died in 1835, and was followed there by his son John Williams who married Jane Makeig of Park y Pratt near Cardigan. He died in 1866, and his wife in 1872. None of their 21 children remained at Llandigige. Daniel Walters was living at Llandigige Fawr in 1894

Refs: Black Book of St. Davids, 1326; NLW, Owen of Orielton Deeds, Pembs. Plea Rolls, 1612; Francis Jones, *Historic Cardiganshire Homes and their Families.*

LLANDDINOG, *Llandeloy*
Now a farmhouse standing between Hendre and Caerwen, and to the south of Afon Solfach, marked on Rees' 14th century map as Landewank (*sic*) and on Colby's 1831 Map as Llandonoch. An interesting commodious old farmhouse, the interior was modernised during the late 1970's, but the exterior is largely unchanged. It was from medieval times a lay manor held of the Bishop of St. Davids as chief Lord of this fee. In 1347 it was held by a local landowner, Philip Cadigan, senior. The manor of Llanddinog was acquired by the Barlows of Slebech, and when it was held by John Barlow in 1613, the manor comprised the following properties – the capital massuage of Llanddinog, a corn mill (Felin Wen), and 21 acres in Hendre Issa, 18 acres in Tyre-aberthe and a messuage in Magwr Walter, both in Whitchurch parish; two tenements in Lochfaen and a tenement in Prewcawen, all in Brawdy parish, and two tenements in Croftufty (Whitchurch parish) and Mechelych (St. Davids parish); and the services of certain properties held in Llanddinog manor by knight's service in the parishes of Llandeloy, Whitchurch, St. Davids, Brawdy, Llanrhian, Mathry, St. Lawrence and Llanhowel. Thus, its manorial jurisprudence was extensive. The manor was occasionally united with that of

Trecadwgan. In 1629 Griffith Hawkwell of St. Kennox was Seneschall of the manors of Trecadwgan and Llanddinog.

The lords of the manor of Llanddinog continued to be the Barlows of Slebech, and in 1705 the manor and farm of Llanddinog formed part of their estate. In 1715 the farm and the mill was owned by James Harries of Haverfordwest, (son of John Harries of Porthiddy), who died in 1719, leaving the properties to his younger brother Dr. George Harries. His eldest daughter Jane Harries inherited and left the properties to her nephew George Harries Griffiths, who died without issue, and the properties passed to the kinsman Dr. George Phillips, M.D. of Haverfordwest in fee simple. Dr. Phillips is described in 1786 as owner of Llanddinog and its mill, with Thomas David (Davies) as tenant. The Davies' remained there for generations, and after them a series of farmers lived there. The manorial rights had long lapsed.

In 1842 George Lort-Phillips sold Llanddinog and the mill, with it to Thomas John of Caerwen for £3,225, who later experienced difficulties, and in 1855 granted the property to his creditors. Some local traditions state that – the first issues of the *Pembrokshire Guardian*, then called the *Dewsland and Kemes Gazette*, were printed at Llanddinog before the editor, John Williams, opened offices at Solva. A French emigré Count lived for a time at Llanddinog, and a letter from the Vicar of Llanddinog inviting him to dinner is extant. The remains of a building, said to have been a church, were over a field still called 'Weirglodd y Fynwent,' opposite the farmhouse; and a stone with an incised cross and an inscription, is said to have been a jamb in the gate.

Refs: WWHR iii, pp. 134-6; *RCAM Pembs.,* 1925; Francis Jones, 'Lay Manors of the Bishopric', *Journal Hist. Soc. of the Church in Wales,* 1969; NLW, Eaton Evans and Williams Deeds, Williams and Williams (H'west) Deeds, Court Rolls of the Manor of Llanddinog among Frances Green Deeds, Poyston Deeds, Tithe Map; Pembs. RO, LT 1786; *Black Book of St.Davids,* 1326.

LLANDRE, *Llanycefn*

Not to be confused with nearby Llandre, Egremont, Carmarthenshire. A residence to the west of the village of Llanycefn, near the road leading to Maenclochog. Home of the Twyning family from the late 17th century. Daniel Twyning married Anne Philipps of Southfield, and his son Griffith Twyning of Llandre married Elizabeth Griffith co-heiress of Bjax Griffith of the ancient house of Penybenglog. Five generations continued to live at Llandre, until William Henry Twyning sold his Llanycefn properties. His sons left Llandre – John Poyer Twyning, William Henry Twyning; James Hamilton Twyning who settled at Evesham as an ironmonger, and Charles Stephen Twyning of Haverfordwest, a master mariner, drowned in 1847. In 1786, Thomas Owen, gent, was the owner-occupier, and thereafter it was occupied by several persons.

Refs: Pembs. RO, LT 1786, VL; NLW, Llidiardau Deeds.

LLANEY, *Llanreithan*

A large farmstead to the southeast of Croesgoch and alongside the road to Llanreithan church. The name has been rendered in different ways, but today the local pronunciation is Llan-ey. Home of yeoman families. In 1326 the name is rendered as Llandener, where David Vachan, John ap Henry and their co-owners lived, holding one carucate of land. In 1459 the seal of David ap David Lloid ap Gwilym de Llandenoe, to a deed of that date, showed a stag. In 1672 John Thomas of Llandenay, gent. served as a juror in Great Sessions; in 1688 William Propert of Llandeney, gent. lived there; in 1786 Llandeney was owned by Samuel Harris Esq. and occupied by John Vaughan. On Colby's Map 1831 it is marked Llandenoi, and in 1838 Llandenoy Farm was owned by Mary Harries, with Captain Hugh Harries, occupier. By 1894 William Williams held the land and tenement of Llanhoy, and in 1950 Margaret and Clifford Thomas lived at Llannoy, who were very kind to me when I called there.

Refs: Black Book St. Davids, 1326; NLW, Eaton Evans and Williams Deeds, Tithe Schedule of Llanreithan parish 1838.

LLANGLOFFAN, *Granston*
Two farmsteads stood here from early days. It is not clear whether part, or whole, of Llangloffan once formed part of a lay manor. In 1587/8 'Stanguaveth alias Llangloffan' was owned by John Wogan, who in that year 'discontinued [the courts] the west part of the town and not the rest'. In 1585 William Griffith was plaintiff in an action with David Rees and his wife Margaret, concerning a messuage and 131 acres in Llangloffan -vawr and -vach. William Jones, and Thomas Lloyd, Esq. were concerned with three messuages, one toft and 192 acres in Llangloffan -vawr and -vechan. Jenkin Llwyn was plaintiff, and Thomas Lloyd and his wife Charity, defendants, respecting the manors of Jordanston and Stangenavied, and messuages and lands in Llangloffan. Part of the property was later owned by William Tucker of Sealyham, who, in 1666, granted a messuage and lands in Llangloffan to John Owen gent. of Henllan Owen near Eglwyswrw, for £100. The Land Tax of 1786 records Llangloffan Uchaf as being owned by Gwyn Vaughan, Esq. with John Harries tenant, and Langloffan Ishaf owned by William Jones Esq. with David Roberts tenant. The terms uchaf and ishaf are still used to distinguish the two farms there.

The place is now well known for its Baptist chapel. During the latter half of the 19th century William Didwith farmed Llangloffan Isha. His name was known in medieval times, and in 1326 Henry Dedewith was a juror of the neighbouring manor of Castlemorris. William Didwith died leaving three daughters only, and the old surname became extinct.

Refs: NLW, Papers of GS, Fines; *Black Book of St. Davids,* 1326; Francis Jones, 'Lay Manors', *Journal Hist. Soc. of Church in Wales,* 1970; *South West Wales, Guide,* Vywyan Rees, 1986, illust. Llangloffan farm.

Griffith

LLANGOLMAN, *Llangolman*
The parish is on high land of the Preseli Hills bounded on the north by Mynachlogddu, on the south by Rhydwilym. The farmstead of Llangolman is a short distance south of the parish church. In 1960 the dwelling was described as having a manorial aspect, *'ty-byw maenoraidd yr olwg'.* The Lewis and Griffith families were among the oldest in the parish. In 1638 Evan John Griffith, gent. served as a juror in Great Sessions.

In 1721 Stephen Lewis was High Sheriff of the county; he married Miss Griffith of Glanrhyd, Cilynaenllwyd, but died without issue. A book-plate of the Rev. Maurice Griffith (1721-98) seventh son of Evan Griffith of Llangolman, shows the following arms: *gules* a lion rampant regardant *argent,* with crest, on a ducal crown a griffin segreant *argent.* In 1786-88 Stephen Griffith of Llangolman is described as a J.P. He was owner-occupier of Llangolman farm in 1786, also owning Dyffryn Ffullbrook, Rosser's Hand, and Troedyrhiw.

In 1805 an inquest was held in the home of Stephen Griffith, before a coroner and jury, respecting the death of Mr. John Griffith, when it was recorded that deceased was found drowned in a pond called Llyn ucha in Llangolman parish. Later the farmstead had a series of occupiers – in 1894-1904 Daniel John, in the 1930s James John who bred black cattle, and was an accomplished leader of the local choir which won a prize in the Fishguard National Eisteddfod in 1936. After World War II a Pole, Capt. Michalski farmed there with his son Ioan Glyndwr Michalski.

Refs: NLW, Pembs. GS; Carms. RO, GGMS, Gwynfardd; Llwyd Williams, *Crwydro Sir Benfro,* 1960.

Broughton

LLANGWARREN, *Jordanston*

A mansion within a spinney on a slope above a stream, one mile to the southeast of the parish church. The property was once divided into two messuages, Llangwarren -Fawr and -Fychan, owned in 1543 by Griffith ap Hugh Broughton who bore the arms: *sable* a chevron between three owls *argent*. The property was sold to the Lloyds of Llanstinan. Llewelyn Lloyd of Llanstinan died in 1588, and Llangwarren passed to his daughter and co-heiress Jane Lloyd. She married, firstly, John Scourfield of Castle Villa, and secondly, Thomas Mathias of Glastir, Nevern. He was eldest son and heir of Mathias Thomas (d. 1588) descended from the ancient family of Young who were at Glastir in the middle ages. Thomas Mathias (born c. 1570) bore the arms of his Young ancestors, namely: *argent* a stag trippant *gules* between three fleurs-de-lys *or*.

After his marriage he settled at Llangwarren. Jane died leaving two daughters, and then Thomas married, secondly, Ursula, daughter of the famous antiquary George Owen of Henllys, Lord of Cemaes, by Elizabeth Philipps of Picton Castle. Thomas Mathias died in 1617 and was buried in the chancel of Jordanston church where he is commemorated by a stone bearing his paternal arms impaling those of Owen and Philipps. His funeral expenses came to £530. By Ursula, he had an only son and heir, John Mathias, who was followed at Llangwarren by 11 generations of his descendants.

The family took a leading part in public life, serving as Justices of the Peace, Deputy Lieutenants, militia officers, they also produced an Eschaetor for Pembrokeshire, a Steward of the Lordship of Dewsland, and eight High Sheriffs of the County. During the Civil War John Mathias was a Roundhead.

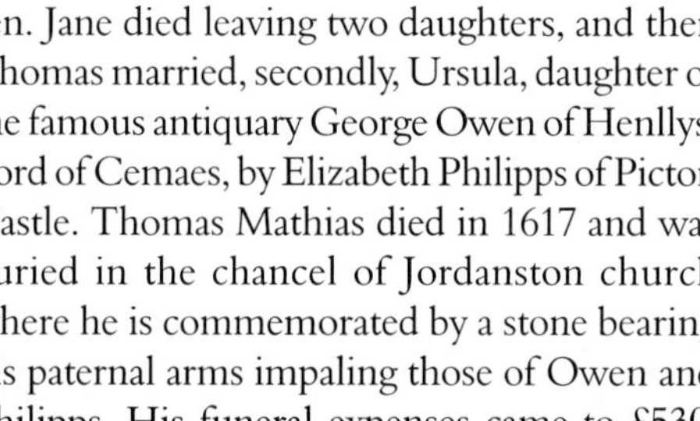

In due course his politics caught up with him when after the restoration he found the Bishop of St. Davids whom he had imprisoned during 'those unhappy times' was less inclined to look upon him kindly. The lands which he had held of the Bishop for over 50 years were surveyed and the Bishop had the rents adjusted. The case went before Great Sessions and eventually the Bishop won his case but getting the fine paid proved nigh on impossible. John Mathias died intestate and his will was proved in 1683. He left six children by his wife, and his only son, Lewis succeeded to Llangwarren. He married Mary Phillips of Trelewelyn after 1681.

Towards the end of the century Lewis Mathias was an active Jacobite; during the 18th century the family supported the Methodists and Howell Harris held services in the hall of Llangwarren. Several of the family helped the Moravians and one, David Mathias, became a worthy minister of that denomination. Several entered the armed services, and towards the end of the century, Colonel Henry Mathias, C.B. led the famous charge of the Gordon Highlanders on the heights of Dargai. For some years the mansion was in the hands of strangers, when in 1811 Lewis Mathias granted a lease for lives of Llangwarren to S. M. Phelps, who made improvements to the mansion which in due course reverted to the Mathiases.

Little is known of Thomas Mathias the eldest son of John and Margaret who seemingly succeeded to Llangwarren during his father's lifetime. Mystery too surrounds his departure from the old home and the circumstances that determined him to relinquish the estate. Yet the Llangwarren deeds trace in detail the steps taken in the matter. 'On 14 November 1747 Thomas Mathias of Llangwarren, eldest son and heir apparent of John Mathias esquire, agreed with his next brother John Mathias also of the same address, that for £700 he would quit claim all right and title to the capital messuage and lands of Llwyngwarren and all his other properties in Pembrokeshire, (certain houses and tenements in Letterston parish excepted), and to make over household goods, furniture, cattle, corn, implements of husbandry, and other effects in Llwyngwarren, (his own plate, moneys, securities, jewels, watches, rings and other like effects excepted); and it was further agreed that before the absolute sale of the premises the said brother John should pay £1,500 and interest thereon plus £25, due to Gwynne Vaughan, esquire, already secured by a mortgage; and further agreed that brother John should provide for and maintain Thomas and his sister Elinor Mathias for their lives, and that Thomas should have use of the Bed Chamber called The White Room, and the room within the White Room, also use of a closet under the stairs and a little cupboard, all in Llwyngwarren House, that Thomas should keep two horses for which brother John should provide grass, hay and ten bushels of corn yearly; and should Thomas choose to quit Llwyngwarren, then John was to pay him an annuity of £27 [per annum] for life'.

Shortly after the foregoing agreement had been executed, John paid the debts, and by deed dated 13 September 1751 Thomas formally relinquished the estate. Thomas may have remained at Llangwarren for a few more years for in 1753 he relinquished three further properties in Letterston to his brother. After this Thomas lived in Haverfordwest, probably at the family house in St. Martins, for it was there that he died unmarried and intestate in March 1832 and was buried at St. Nicholas. He was not wholly bereft of landed possessions, for among his property to be divided among his heirs-at-law were Trewallterwen, Tresaeson, Park Mountain, Ffynnon Gron, Rhosgranog and a house and two fields in Fishguard parish and a pew in the church of Haroldston and the tithes. John Mathias his brother died without issue in 1822, aged 82.

In 1810/11 Charles Mathias held Lamphey Court and by 1823 he owned it and commenced to build a new mansion there, which continued with his descendants until a few years ago, when it was sold. After the family returned to Llangwarren, Charles Mathias in the 1880s made extensive alterations and improvements to the ancient home. The last of the male line at Llangwarren was Charles A. S. Mathias, J.P. on whose death the estate passed to his only child and heir, Miss Leslie Mathias who married Mr. John Lloyd-Philipps a younger son of Dale Castle. He predeceased his wife, and when she died in 1985, Llangwarren passed to her two daughters, who in 1987 advertised for sale the mansion, which the family had owned for nigh on four centuries. Among the Mathias muniments is a drawing of the original mansion made in 1813 by John Tambyn of Haverfordwest, before any extensions and changes were effected. For a traditional tale of hidden treasure found at Llangwarren, see Francis Jones *Treasury of Historic Pembrokeshire,* pp. 210-211.

Refs: Dwnn, i, pp. 162, 243; WWHR, ii, p. 41, *Pembs. Arch. Svy*; Laws, *Little England,* p. 359; Charles *George Owen of Henllys,* pp. 31, 53; Pembs. RO Llangwarran Deeds; Cardiff Public Library Deeds; Carms. RO, GGMS; Dale Castle Pedigrees; Manorowen Pedigree MS; College of Arms, Wagner MS No. 3; NLW, Pembs. Papers of GS, Coleman Deeds, Tithe Maps 1843; Francis Jones essay 'Llangwarren'.

LLANION, *St. Mary Pembroke*

The former residence stood to the north of Pembroke and to the northeast of Pembroke Dock, near Biers Pool farm, and the inlet on the nearby coast called Lanion Pill. An early medieval Welsh manuscript records that at 'Llonyon ym Penvro' beehives and swarms of bees were kept, giving rise to the proverb *'o heid Llonyon'.* Another manuscript compiled in 1600-19, mentions the family of Bennet, the last of whom was Hugh, 'There were diverse knightes, as is said, of the Benetts, and their mansion howse was now a decaied howse at Munston, and they were lords of Mirian, Bernards pools in Landian alias Laniell (Lanion) iuxta Pembrook, and in diverse other places in Pembrokeshire'.

The last of the Benetts had three daughters and heiresses: 'the one married James ap Eynon of Kenerth, of whom Mores ap Owen is descended and inherited about 50 pound rent by that descent; the other married Bowen of Roblinston who hath the manor of Llanien; and Lutterell is heire to another daughter, and all three have lands in Merriam'.

For some years Llanion formed part of the estate of the Meares family. George Meares gent. was at Llanion in 1665 and five years later was assessed at four hearths. Edward Byam, an

Antiguan merchant, finally settled at Llanion where he died in 1768 and was buried in the parish church. His son and heir William moved to Sunny Hill near Manorbier.

The Holcombe family occupied Llanion for a few years in the period 1751-63. It then passed to the well known family of Meyrick who lived there occasionally. In 1786 J. F. Meyrick, Esq. is described as owner-occupier of Llanion, and the land let to Thomas Kinaston. However, by the first decade of the next century it had fallen into decay. Fenton informs us in 1811. 'Lanion, a seat of John Meyrick Esq. till of late years almost constantly inhabited by a succession of different tenants, temporary residents in the county, but now unroofed and suffered to fall into decay, as Bush, his principal family residence lies so near in a situation much more commanding than the other, though in some respects inferior in point of beauty'. Rees, writing in 1815 describes it as 'now in ruins'.

In 1905 the authoress Mrs. Stuart Peters wrote, 'to the east of Bierspool may be seen the ruined walls of Llanion House, the original country seat of the Meyrick family. Lord Nelson was sometimes a guest at this old house, and it is said that once or twice he was accompanied there by Lady Hamilton.'

On June 5 1846 an uncoffined skeleton was dug up in Llanion Park (now a cricket field).

Refs: Myfyrian Archaeology, 398.b, 56; NLW MS 1602D, fo. 171; Fenton, *Tour Pembs,* 1811; Rees, *Beauties of South Wales,* 1815; Stuart Peters, *History of Pembroke Dock,* 1905.

LLANMARLAIS, *Lampeter Velfrey*
Marked on Colby's Map 1831, on the eastern bank of Afon Marlais. A memorial in St. Clears parish church to the memory of Mr. John Evans of Llanmarlais in Pembrokeshire states that he married Mrs. Elizabeth Philipps of the House of Llwyn y Crwn, by whom he had surviving issue, three sons and two daughters who had been left motherless at a very helpless age: he died on 1 May 1734, aged 71: the memorial was set up at the sole expense of his son-in-law, Mr. Roger Jones of Laugharne. In the Land Tax List of 1786, Gwynne Vaughan Esq (of Jordanston in Dewsland) was the owner, and John Hall, tenant.

LLANNERCH (Y BLEIDDIE/BLEIDDIAU), *Newport*
Formerly a mansion, now a farmstead, standing in the upper valley of the Gwaun, overlooking a romantic glade at the foot of the northern slope of Carn Ingli. In George Owen's MS c. 1600, is a list of houses in 'Leppe, lowe, and close placis', among which is 'Llannercybleidde house'. The name meant 'Glade of the Wolves' but later it became Llannerch only.

The old mansion stood close to the side of the present farmhouse, and together with the outhouses, is said to incorporate some of the mansion. Few traces of the older building remain, but over the doorway of an outhouse is a massive stone with a chamfered lintel. Mr. Vaughan, the owner-occupier, told me that there was a tradition that a church had also stood there, probably the private chapel of the former owners, and that there had been a flight of stairs leading downwards to a room or crypt.

The original gentry family there was that of Bowen descended from Llewellyn y Coed (living 1369) ap Owen (living 1342) 7th in descent from the princeling Gwynfardd Dyfed. The grandson of Llewellyn y Coed, Owen, settled at Llannerch y bleiddie, and was followed there by seven successive generations of his descendants, the last of the family, Owen Bowen (living 1614) had been a ward of George Owen of Henllys. Owen was said to have wasted his inheritance (*omnia devastavit*) and had to depart from his home. After his day, Llannerch was occupied by a series of yeomen farmers. The arms borne by the Bowens were: *azure* a lion rampant *or,* and in chief three roses *argent,* based on the arms of Gwynfardd.

Refs: L. Owen, vol. i, pp. 34, 60-1, 105, 155, 162-3, 170; Chetham MS Pedigrees: Pembs. RO, LT 1786; Carms. RO, GGMSS, Gwynfardd; NLW, Bronwydd Deeds, Poyston Deeds, Trenewydd Deeds, Foley of Ridgeway Deeds, AE MS 12356E; *Trans. Carms. Antiq. Soc.* 1924-5, vol. xviii, p. 65.

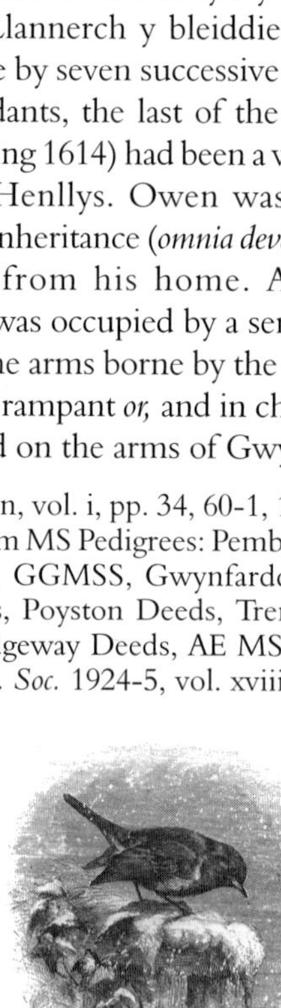

LLANREITHAN, *Llanreithan*

Within a sheltering grove in a truly rural spot close to the upper waters of Afon Solfach, between the farms of Clawddcam and Trenichol, stands the parish church and farmstead of Llanreithan. The church stands close to the site of the old mansion which stood near the stream, and had been the home of gentry families from the time of the first Tudor monarch down until 1780, after which it became ruinous, and about 1800 was dismantled and its stone used for enlarging the farmhouse and outbuildings. The walled garden is the only remnant of squirearchal dignity, the site of the mansion being a verdant stretch of pasture.

The farmhouse is an ancient and commodious structure containing some 26 rooms. In the early 19th century Nonconformist services and Sunday schools were held there, and the old wooden 'pulpit' is still kept there (1986). The earliest landowning family there was a branch of the Bowens of nearby Lochmeyler, descended from Bleddyn ap Cymfyn, Prince of Powys till his death in 1075. David Bowen of Lochmeyler (living 1506) was father of William Bowen, a second son, who settled at Llanreithan. William was followed by his son David who died without issue, and Llanreithan passed to his sister Crisli who had married Morris David Morgan of Clydey. Crisli's son, Morris ap Morris, was followed by his son Griffith Morris who was living at Llanreithan in 1599. He married Margaret daughter of James Bowen of Llwyngwair, and his son James Griffith was High Constable of Dewsland in 1650 and 1652. He died in 1658, leaving an only child and heiress, Anne Griffith, who, before 1641, had married John Laugharne who was the first of that family to settle at Llanreithan. They were an ancient stock, and bore arms: *gules* three lions' heads erased *or*, which they later quartered with the boar and hollybush of Henllys, as a result of John's son, Arthur Laugharne's marriage, with Elizabeth daughter and co-heiress of David Owen of Henllys, in 1678. The Laugharnes' motto was: *ostentare jugulum pro capite alteries*, in memory of their ancestor who had marched to Bosworth with Henry Tudor in 1485.

The family were at Llanreithan for five generations, the most exciting of them being

John Laugharne, High Sheriff in 1731. He strongly objected to the marriages of his sisters Anne (to John Lilly, a dancing master), Margaret (to David Benbow, an attorney from Aberystwyth), and Dorothy (to John Ashwall, of Lincoln, described by his brother-in-law as 'a tramp'). John wasted much money in legal proceedings against his sisters and their husbands, while they counter-attacked with numerous lawsuits, with the result that John Laugharne found himself heavily in debt, and kept a retinue of armed retainers to protect Llanreithan against attempts to serve further writs on their master. He was then declared an outlaw, and he was captured by a ruse by the High Sheriff and an armed posse and imprisoned in Haverfordwest Castle. He soon obtained his freedom, and is said to have discovered a 'crock of gold' hidden at Llanreithan, which he soon dissipated by supporting the Jacobites of whom he strongly approved. He was the last Pembrokeshire squire to have maintained a jester, known locally as *'ffwl Llanreithan',* whose sprightly antics endeared him to his master but proved a sore trial to guests and visitors. The squire had a fierce bout of fisticuffs with the vicar whose views he disliked. In 1751 he was obliged to sell the moiety of the Lordship of Cemaes to his opulent cousin Thomas Lloyd of Bronwydd. Then, suddenly, in 1752 he left for London where he married his concubine, a Mary Parry, and in the following year returned to Llanreithan, with a little baby daughter called Sophia. He did not survive long, and in December 1755 died leaving all his estate to his wife for life, and then to Sophia in fee simple.

Sophia Laugharne was the last of the family to own Llanreithan. She married John Popkin of

Trehyon, Carmarthenshire, and died a young woman in 1779 leaving four children none of whom came to live in Pembrokeshire.

In 1790 her widowed husband sold Llanreithan and much of what was left of the estate, thus severing the long connection of the Laugharnes with Llanreithan.

The mansion had been bought in 1751 by the Holcombe family, and some time after 1799 they sold it, and by 1840 it was bought by Thomas Harries of Trewilym and Mrs. Elizabeth John, wife of David John. Their only child, Mary Anne married in 1821 a Cardigan solicitor, Thomas George, who later divorced her for adultery. She lived at Llanreithan until her death in 1880 aged 80. She often strolled from Llanreithan to my grandmother's farm, New Inn, accompanied by 10 dogs all of whose names began with 'T' – Timothy, Titus, Tomore. She had had a special pet dog called Squire Bach that had unfortunately been drowned in the Leet, and she often lamented his loss to my grandmother. After her death one half of Llanreithan was owned by Thomas Harries and the other half by Phillips of Bolahaul, Carmarthen. Phillips eventually sold it to John Harries, son of Thomas, and it passed from him to his son, Mansel Harries, and from him to his son, John Mervyn Harries, a friend of mine who still owned it in 1981.

The farmhouse stands empty and decaying, the chapel unkept, but there are hopes that it will be restored as it has recently been offered for sale.

Refs: Francis Jones, 'Llanreithan', *Pembs. Historian,* 1970; Francis Jones, *Historic Carmarthenshire Homes and their Families;* Carms. RO, Trant Deeds, Castell Gorfod Deeds, Plâs Llanstephan Deeds; NLW, Eaton Evans and Williams Deeds, Poyston Deeds, Bronwydd Deeds, Maesgwyne Deeds, St. Davids Diosese Consistory Court Records, Tithe Map 1838-9; College of Arms, Protheroe MS iv, fo. 117.

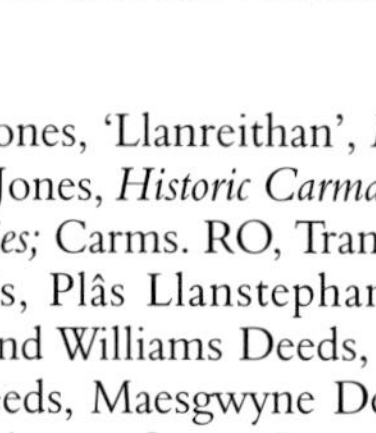

Laugharne

LLANSTINAN, *Llanstinan*

A mansion nearly two miles west of Trecwn, in the vale of Nantybugail, and three miles south of Fishguard. At the height of its prosperity the Llanstinan estate included properties in ten Pembrokeshire parishes, the manors of Llanstinan, Llanfairnant-y-gof, and Talbenny, the presentation to Llanstinan curacy, and the Lease of Tithes, and also properties in Cardiganshire and Breconshire. The earliest known family at Llanstinan were the Lloyds.

At the beginning of the 16th century William Lloyd was owner, succeeded by his son Morgan Lloyd (living 1548) who married the daughter of Thomas Madog, by whom he had a son, Llewelin Lloyd, who died in 1588. Llewelin's daughter and co-heiress, Jenet, received Llanstinan as her share, and married Rees Wogan, younger son of Sir John Wogan of Boulston. Rees was the first of the Wogans to settle at Llanstinan, where he was succeeded by five generations of descendants. One of the most successful of them was Sir William Wogan, younger son of Thomas Wogan of Llanstinan by his wife Elizabeth (Owen).

He was a barrister of Gray's Inn, appointed King's Sergeant in 1689, and knighted in the same year, and was Chief Justice of the Carmarthen Circuit of Great Sessions from 1689 to 1701. He died in 1708 without issue. An inventory of his possessions made in 1710, enumerates the rooms in Llanstinan, as follows – four garret rooms, Hopkins' room, room over the Oak-room, closet, room over the Little Parlour, withdrawing room, Great Parlour, Hall, Little Parlour, Study (with library), kitchen, dairy, cellar, outer-cellar, cellar under the stairs, servants' Hall, and (probably detached) storehouse and brew-house. It seems that Sir William had rebuilt the mansion, and John Lewis tells us 'I remember when my neighbour Sir William Wogan of Llanstinan was pondering where he should erect a new mansion instead of the old, grown ruinous, and was on the point of shifting the old site which was low, near water, and sheltering, to the summit of a hill that would give him a view of the sea, I was the means of prevailing with him to place it where it now stands, a few feet only elevated from the ancient habitation, for which persuasion, the current of fashion rather setting against me, I was much reflected on'. The last of the Wogans of Llanstinan, William, died without issue in 1710, leaving Llanstinan and its large estate to his nephew, John Symmons of Martel. The Symmons were an old local family, and by the marriage of John Symmons to Agnes daughter and co-heiress of William Prys of Martel, he settled at that mansion, which remained the home of his descendants for several generations. One of them, Thomas Symmons of Martel, married in 1669 Margaret Wogan sister of the Judge Sir William Wogan, and their son John Symmons in 1710 inherited Llanstinan from his cousin William Wogan. John married Martha Harries of Tregwynt, and was High Sheriff in 1713.

The last of the family were two brothers, John Symmons the heir, and the Rev. Charles Symmons, D.D., Rector of Narberth, who died in 1826. John the heir, inherited Llanstinan in 1766. About 1773 he married Anne Barlow of Slebech, and afterwards settled at his wife's home. He fell into debt, and in 1783 sold the mansion and estate of Martel to William Knox, and shortly afterwards, Llanstinan, to the same person. William Knox died in 1810, and Llanstinan and other properties were sold to Sir John Owen of Orielton.

Fenton wrote in 1811, 'Llanstinan a mansion which I remember embosomed in majestic woods now, alas! denuded, deserted, and rapidly hurrying to decay – a mansion that ever ranked in this county amongst the first class with regard to its pretensions in every respect'. Lewis stated in 1840 that 'The ancient mansion of the family of Symmons, which had been suffered to remain in a neglected state for some time, has been modernised or rebuilt'. It had been repaired by the owner Sir John Owen, Bt., and in 1856 he sold the Llanstinan estate (3,200 acres), and died in 1861. In 1891 it was advertised for sale, with 405 acres, the mansion being described as consisting of Ground Floor – Lounge hall, Library, Study, Dining and Drawing rooms, butler's pantry, WC.; First Floor – 5 bedrooms, 2 dressing rooms, linen room, bathroom, lavatory; Second Floor – 7 bedrooms; Basement Floor – servants hall, waiting room, kitchen, larder, scullery, dairy, 2 cellars, boot room, coal house, W.C.; Outbuildings – walled kitchen garden. The sale catalogue contains ground plans of the mansion and outbuildings.

The mansion was accidentally burnt down in 1940, and today is a gloomy ruin.

Refs: WWHR, vii, pp. 7-11; ibid. xiv, pp. 221-7; Fenton, *Tour Pembs.,* 1811, p. 188; Francis Jones, *Journal Hist. Soc. of Church in Wales,* 1969; Cambrian Register II, 1796, iii; College of Arms, Protheroe MS, iv to 92; Chetham MS No 97; Carms. RO, SC No. 914 & 485.

Davies

LLANTEG/LLANTEAGUE, *Crunwear*

In the small hamlet of Llanteg are two substantial houses, one the seat of the Davies family, the other, of the Hensleighs. Few early references have been found relating to the properties. In the years 1611-17, a farmer called Morris lived in one of the houses. Firstly, let us consider the Davies family, a branch of Davies of Newton, Laugharne parish, descended from the Cardiganshire magnate, Rhys Chwith, said to have been Esquire of the Body to King Edward I. Thomas Davies, the first to settle at Llanteg, was assessed at three hearths in 1670. Henry Davies was living at the 'White House in Lanteage in Crunwear' in 1671, and Chancey Davies the elder, was 'of Whitehouse in Llanteague in Crunwear' in 1708. By the mid-18th century they had left Llanteg. They bore as arms: *argent* three bulls' heads caboshed *sable,* horned *or.* In 1786 Lord Milford was the owner of three properties at 'Llanteague', and the Revd. Edward Philipps, of one.

We now turn to the Hensleighs who were at Llanteague in the same period as the Davies's. They came from Somerset to Pembrokeshire, and in 1670 John Hensleigh of Llanteg was assessed at two hearths. The last of this line, John Hensleigh, attorney-at-law, died on 28 January 1769, aged 64, at the Red Lion Inn, Carmarthen, and was buried at Llanddewi Velfrey. By his wife Catherine (daughter of the Rev. Thomas Philipps, vicar of Laugharne) John Hensleigh had an only child and heiress,

Elizabeth, who married John Bartlett Allen of Cresselly and had issue.

Refs: Picton Castle Deeds; Hearth Tax 1670; LT 1786; Francis Jones, *Historic Carmarthenshire Homes and their Families.*

LLANUNWAS, *Whitchurch*

A large double-pile mansion on high ground to the west of Solva Ucha, and overlooking St. Brides Bay. The earliest known family at Llanunwas was that of Crunn, a name found in western Dewsland from 1326 onwards. In 1597 Thomas William Crunn, yeoman, granted (in consideration of the marriage of his son John to Elizabeth daughter of John Bowen Cadigan of Henry's Moat) to Thomas Symmons of Martel, gent. and William James Harry of St. Davids parish, yeoman, three messuages and lands in the village and fields in Llanunwas -Ucha and -Isha, and Lethgell, and in Whitchurch parish, to be held to grantor for life, and then to the said John and Elizabeth. The said John Crunn had succeeded by 1613 when he held Llanunwas as of the manor of Llanddinog, the lord being John Barlow of Slebech.

The property afterwards passed to Elizabeth Crunn, widow. Her daughter and heiress, Anne Crunn, whose marriage to Francis Laugharne of Llanreithan 'Latelie had been solemnized' when their post-nuptial settlement was executed on 1 March 1670, the lands settled 'uppon the Bloved of the said Francis and Anne' were the two messuages of 'Llanywas -Ucha' and -Issa, and Hendre -Ycha and Yssa, in Llandeloy parish. John Wogan of Eweston, Brawdy parish, and Harry Thomas of St. Davids parish, gentry, were trustees. In 1716 the estate consisted of the two messuages of Llanunwas, the mill called Felin Porth-y-rhaw, in Whitchurch, Carnhedryn-Fawr alias -ucha, in St. Davids, and Hendre -Ucha and Isha, in Llandeloy parish.

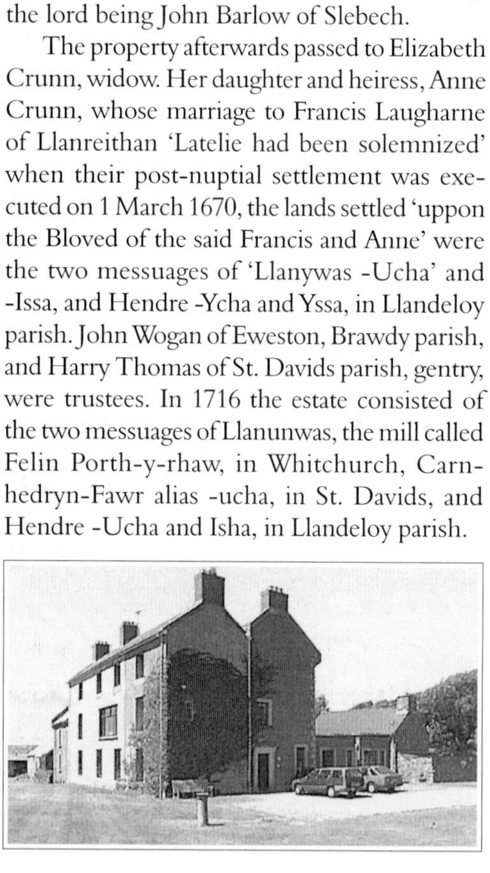

Francis Laugharne was followed by his son the Rev. Arthur Laugharne, rector of Dinas and Prebendary of Caerfai. He married Jane Lloyd of Cards. He died in 1753, Jane in 1757. The Rev. Arthur left one son and five daughters, the son, the Rev. William Laugharne was rector of Dinas, Manordeifi and Llanllawer, and died unmarried in February 1784/5, and was buried at Whitchurch. The inventory attached to his will, names the following rooms at Llanunwas – hall, parlour, closet, study, buffet, room over the parlour. Yellow room, middle room, green room, upper room, kitchen, loft over the kitchen, while the outbuildings included carthouse, poultry house, calves house, little stable, stoneloft, barn, malthouse, little loft, brewhouse, and the garden little house.

Llanunwas was sold shortly afterwards, and the owner-occupier in 1786 was Gilbert James, a younger son of John James of Lochmeyler and Dorothy Harries of Priskilly. An attorney-at-law he had also lived at Holloway near Narberth, and finally at Llanunwas. His wife's identity is unknown. He had two sons, John James who married one Mary Thomas, by whom he had an only child, Jane, and William Ford James, who died without issue, about 1785. John James died in his father's lifetime, and Llanunwas passed to his daughter Jane James, who in 1799 married Joseph Harries of Priskilly, who then settled at Llanunwas. He was High Sheriff in 1821. She died in 1821, her husband in 1824. Their eldest son, Gilbert James Harries, succeeded to Llanunwas, and died in 1856, leaving the estate to his eldest son Cecil Anson Harries who died without issue in 1908, and Llanunwas passed to his nephew Gilbert David Harries who was High Sheriff in 1892, and died in 1916. None of his children lived at Llanunwas.

Refs: Fenton, *Tour Pembs.*, p. 76; WWHR, iii, p. 135; *Black Book of St. Davids,* 1326; NLW, Bronwydd Deeds; College of Arms, Wagner MS 2; Cardiff Public Library Deeds (now in Glam. RO); Brawdy Deeds (Jones).

LLANWNWR, *Llanwnda*
A farmstead in the northwest extremity of Pencaer, just over a quarter of a mile south of Strumble Head lighthouse, and above the cove of Carregonen. There are traces of a medieval chapel and burial ground near the farmyard.

A report by *Ancient Monuments* 1925 tells us that 'a considerable number of flag-lined graves have been found, and after rains the outlines of burials can be traced. In 1883 when the Arch. Cam. Assn. visited the place, one of the graves was opened, and was not more than a foot in depth: some of the others were said to have contained ashes as well as bones. At the front of the farmhouse is a cross incised stone that was moved from the granary steps some few years ago'.

In 1326 Llanwnwr was described as a knight's fee (Welsh). In 1517 William Tucker of Sealyham granted a lease of a messuage and 40 acres in Llanwnwr to Rhys ap Lewis William, who, in 1533 alleged that he had received a grant, not a lease, from Tucker. In 1587 Thomas Tucker of Sealyham was des-cribed as 'lord of the manor of Llanwnwr in Pencaer'. Later, it changed hands, and the I.P.M. of William Scourfield of New Moat, stated that in 1622 he owned the manor of Llanwnwr. By 1659 Elizabeth Griffith, widow and her son John Griffith, were living at Llanwnwr, when John Vaughan of Jordanston granted properties in the parishes of Jordanston and St. Nicholas to them. The Griffith family continued at Llanwnwr to 1789 when Thomas Griffith, Esq, gave a lease of Llanwnwr (minerals excepted, and certain rooms reserved to lessor) to William Batine of Barretts Hill, Steynton, gent. for the lives of William's wife Dorothy, and their children Thomas and Mary Batine. Thomas Batine the son remained there till his death in 1885. The family of Mortimer (from Tre-howel) came to live there, and were followed in the 1890s by J. C. James of Caerwen. In the present century Mr. John Richards settled there, and the present owner-occupier (1986) is his son Mr. Morgan Richards of Llanwnwr.

Refs: Black Book of St. Davids, 1326; Taylors *Cussion,* p. 97b; *RCAM Pembs.,* 1925, p. 191; PRO, Early Chancery Proceedings; NLW, Llwyndyrws (Cards.) Deeds, Pembs. GF, Poyston Deeds; Pembs. RO, DCT Deeds.

LLAWHADEN, *Llawhaden*
Formerly a 17th century mansion, now a farmstead near the castle in the village of Llawhaden, contained a 17th century staircase and a panelled room and some stone vaulting. Near the house stands a dovecot. Across the road is a large walled garden of former times. Fenton wrote in 1811, 'enter the village and pass the mansion of William Skyrme, Esq, of a most respectable family in this county, whose ancestor, an eminent attorney in the Court of the Marches, settled here about two centuries ago, and laid the foundation of two or three families of that name now centering in this gentleman'.

Rees in 1815 noted 'In the village [Llawhaden] is a handsome mansion, the residence of William Skyrme Esq.' Lewis, in 1840, adds a little more – 'in the village is also a good family house belonging to a descendant of the Skyrmes whose ancestor accompanied Oliver Cromwell into the principality during the parliamentary war, and obtained a settlement at this place.' The Skyrmes came from Shropshire, and in the Pembrokeshire Great Sessions of 1640, William Skyrme of Ludlow, was an attorney in a case. John Skyrme of Llawhaden was High Sheriff in 1716. The Skyrmes left Llawhaden at the end of the 18th century, and thereafter was let to yeomen who used the house for farming purposes. The house has recently been destroyed by a fire in which the owner sadly perished.

Refs: Fenton, *Tour Pembs.,* 1811, p. 172; Rees, *Beauties of S. Wales,* 1815, p.807; Lewis, *TDW,* 1840, Pembs. RO, LT 1786; Buck's Engraving 1740, of Llawhaden Castle, includes a sketch of the mansion (illust).

LLETHER/LLETHR, *Brawdy*

About half a mile south of Brawdy church, stands Llether, a large double-pile mansion of three storeys, separated from Brawdy by a small *cwm* through which runs a tributary of Afon Newgale. To the south of the mansion is Newgale farm formerly a manor. In early times Llether was divided into two separate manors – Llether Superior, a manor, also called Llether Ucha (Upper), and Llether Gronw; this is the property described in this entry.

The lord of the manor of Llether Inferior in 1568-81 being John Barlow of Slebech; after this, the manor was united to Llether Ucha, the owners being the Jones family of Brawdy. Later the property included Llether Manor House (mansion), Llether Farm (home farm), and Llether Issa (farm), all in close proximity. The manorial juresdiction and rights lapsed during the 19th century.

The earliest known reference to Llether Ucha is in 1328 when John ap Philip granted to Adam the clerk (Parson) half of a building and garden, and one-third of a bovate, in Llethergrono, a stang in Roshingern (*sic*) to be held until John ap Philip paid certain monies to Adam.

In 1594 part of Llether Ucha was owned by William Jones of Brawdy, and part by the Warlows of Newgale. The lands of William Jones passed to his younger brother Gilbert Jones, and then to Gilbert's son and heir, William Jones. This William married Katherine Hergest of St. Davids, and the property passed in due course to their son and heir Richard Jones who sold it to his cousin William Jones of Brawdy in 1635.

John Warlow of Lower Llether married Catherine Voyle, daughter of John Voyle of St. Elvis by his wife Lettice Mortimer, and had two daughters, co-heiresses. The elder daughter, Lettice Warlow had Lower Llether as her share, and in 1652 married James Jones of Upper Llether second son of William Jones of Brawdy, and thence forth their descendants owned both properties. They were succeeded in 1699 by their son William Jones. The last of their descendants, and eventual heiress, Mary Jones, married George Roch of Butter Hill, and Llether remained in Roch hands. The last to live at Llether was Colonel Thomas James Roch who left Llether for Tenby after World War I.

The Llether estate was advertised for sale in 1919, the main properties being described as Llether Manor House: consisting of, on the ground floor – entrance hall, dining room, kitchen, scullery, pantry, larder, boot room, and on the first floor, a drawing room, four bedrooms, and dressing room, and on the second floor, three bedrooms, bathroom, and W.C.; the grounds included a large lawn tennis court, a walled garden with access to the first floor of the house by an archway.

Upper Llether Farm: (137 acres), the house containing a parlour, sitting room, kitchen, dairy, four bedrooms, with outbuildings, let to William Owen at a yearly rent of £130.

Lower Llether Farm: (175 acres), the house containing a parlour, sitting room, kitchen, meal room, dairy, five bedrooms, and outbuildings, let to Henry Williams at a yearly rent of £107.

When I visited Llether in the 1960s, the mansion was owned by the Morris family. When I examined Lower Llether I found a fine painting on the wall over a fireplace, of a mansion (late 17th or early 18th centuries). About 1970/71 it was sold to a Mr. Ling, who during his occupation 'modernised' the house, and by 1975 he was engaged in the sale of the property.

Refs: Francis Jones, 'Lay Manors of Dewsland', *Journal of the Hist. Soc. of the Church in Wales,* 1969, 1970; Fenton, *Tour Pembs.,* 1811; *Pembs. Arch. Svy,* 1896-1907; *RCAM Pembs.,* 1925; NLW Tithe Map 1842, Maesgwynne Deeds; Pembs. RO LT 1786, Deeds DB 13, 30; PRO, AD. E210, D5520; *Come to Pembs* (guide), c. 1936, illust.; History of Jones of Llether (unpublished), *penes me.*

LLETHER WOGAN, *North Pembs.*
Unidentified
Possibly in the district of Moat. N.B. there is a Llether farm in Mynachlogddu, and called Llether Ucha in the Tithe Map 1840; today they are called Llether Ucha and Issa. The only reference that I have found to Llether Wogan occurs in a Scourfield pedigree assembled by George William Griffith of Penybenglog. The pedigree reads as follows: Harry Scourfield married Etheldred Butler of Trecadwgan in Dewsland, and had a son and heir, John Scourfield of *Llether Wogan* (d. 1593) who married Katherine Wogan of Wiston, and had a son and heir John Scourfield, and a younger daughter Mary who married Owen ap Evan ap Jenkin, both living in 1591, and had four sons and a daughter, viz. Thomas ap Owen of Mynyddmelin (Llanychllwydog parish) bailiff of Cemaes in 1629, David, James, John, and Catherine. I place the above on record, hoping it will help some future antiquary to identify the elusive Llether Wogan.

Refs: College of Arms, Protheroe MS Nos. v, xii (G. W. Griffith); *Dwnn,* i, pp. 110, 176; Chetham Pedigree MS, appendix in Laws, *Little England;* GGMS; WWHR, ix, p. 145.

LLWYNBEDW, *Capel Colman*
An attractive well maintained 18th century residence, on a slope just southwest of Capel Colman church, and to the east of Boncath. A short distance northwards is Cilwendeg. The earliest known owners of Llwynbedw were the families of Morris and Morgan. On the marriage of Morris Morris of Ffynnone, gent. to Elizabeth daughter of Jenkin Jones of Rhosygilwen, among the lands settled was Tir Llwyn Bedw (post-nuptial settlement 1692). Jacob Jones (born 1743) youngest son of John Jones of Cilwendeg, settled at Llwynbedw, and died there in 1787. He was followed at Llwynbedw by his son, Rev. John Jones (1782-1844) rector of Llanfyrnach and Penrith, from whom descended the Joneses of Penylan and Llanmilo. Arms of Jones: *argent* on a chevron *azure* and two bear's heads between two bull's heads erased in chief, and a lion passant in base.

Llwynbedw was afterwards occupied by several owners, but their stay was short. Possibly their stay was influenced by the disturbing apparition that haunted the house. It was during the 1890s that Mr. S. Gwilly Davies stayed there as guest of John Daniel Jones, auctioneer, and agent to the Bronwydd estate. The ghost, said to be that of a lady who had been drowned at Glan-pwll-du just below the plâs. In the evening, the sound of a rapidly-driven coach could be heard from the house, then it stopped at the entrance, followed by a ringing of the house bells, and residents could hear the swishing of the ghost's skirts as she darted from room to room. One bedroom was never used as those who had slept there claimed that 'something' disturbed their repose. As a result the occupiers found great difficulty in recruiting house-servants from the district where tales of the 'Lady of Llwynbedw', were well known. Mr. Peter Gwynne Hughes lived there for many years, his sleeping hours seemingly undisturbed.

Refs: Buckley, *Sheriffs,* 1909; S. Gwilly Davies, *Wedi Croesu'r Pedwar Ugain, Atgafion,* 1967, pp. 18-19, 23-27; Monuments in Capel Colmon parish church; Pembs. RO, LT 1786; NLW, Tithe Map 1849.

LLWYNGOR(R)AS, *Nevern*
Now a farmstead on a hillside north of the river Nevern, and between Nevern church and the hamlet of Felindre; marked on Colby's Map as Llwyn-y-goras. At one time the property was divided into several farms – in 1632 we find the capital messuage of Llwyn y Gorres Issa, in 1740 Llwyn y Gorras Ucha, and in the Land Tax of 1786, we find three farms there, namely Llwyngorras [the plas] owned by Roger Davies Esq, occupied by William Davies, Llwyn y Gorras Fawr owned by Thomas Lloyd Esq of Bronwydd, occupied by John James, and Llwyn y Gorras fach owned by Thomas Lloyd Esq of Cwmgloyn, occupied by Enoch Rees. It was finally united into one property.

The earliest known owners of the property were the Bowen family, of whom George Owen of Henllys wrote about 1608 – 'Lloyn y gorres the mansion house of Morgan Bowen gentle-man (b. 1547), standeth for healthe and pleasure fayre upon the topp of a banck over lookinge a fayre and plessant valley, beinge the more pleasant for that it is his owne. This house was built about 30 yeres past [1578, which is carved on a stone in the wall of the house] by his elder brother Thomas George Bowen, a man who for his good hospitallitie, gentle behaviour amonge his equelles, his good advise to his distressed neyghboures, and other his good partes, was much lamented at his death who havinge yssue but one daughter, sould the same to this her uncle [Morgan Bowen] being third sonne to his father George Bowen, a man in his tyme of noe small rule and estimation who was the naturalle [illegitimate] sonne of John Bowen sonne and heyre to Sir James Bowen knight, and beareth the Armes of Pentre Ieuan with the due difference.' The bard Huw Llewellyn (c. 1552-94) wrote an elegy to the above Thomas ap George ap Owen of Llwyngorras.

In 1595 George Owen Esq of Henllys, confirmed to Morgan Bowen of Llwynygorres, gent, his right in 'a capital messuage called Llwynygorres', a messuage called Plâs Penywayn, and closes called Park yr Ithyn, Tir y vorwyn gloff, and Park Dol yspadrick Issa, all in Nevern parish, messuages called Tythyn Penyrallt, Tythyn yr Escair, and Vron Vawr in Dinas parish, and one-third of a messuage in Mynachlogddu. Morgan Bowen's will was proved in 1612, and not long afterwards his son Owen Bowen and Elizabeth Bowen sold Llwyngorras, to the Webb family. By her will, proved in 1632, Margaret Webb of Alleston (near Pembroke) bequeathed 'to my son Alexander Webb, the capital messuage of Llwyn y Gorres Issa, late in tenure of Melchior Bowen, and now of mine, in as large a manner as the same was granted to me by Elizabeth Bowen and Owen Bowen.' By the end of the 17th century, the property had been bought by a family named Davies. In 1705 Thomas Davies of Llwyngorras was a Land Tax Commissioner, and in 1715 was a Justice of the Peace. He died in 1730.

In 1762 the owner was Roger Davies, J.P., and he still held it in 1786. In 1789 the Llwyngorras estate was sold by the brothers Thomas and Mathew Davies to William Davies (no relation). William, described in several subsequent deeds as of Llwyngorras, Esq. died in 1826 aged 86. His widow, Martha, was described as the owner-occupier in 1840. His descendants, Grace Martha Davies and Jane Davies, were the owner-occupiers in 1894. Among other descendants were Susannah Gwenllian Davies who married Mr. R. T. P. Williams, the well known solicitor of Haverfordwest, and Captain W. Davies Evans inventor of a move in chess called 'Evans's gambit'. Since 1900 Llwyngorras has had a series of farming owner-occupiers.

Refs: George Owen, *2nd Book,* ed. B. G. Charles, *NLWJ,* p. 19; WWHR ii, p. 36; NLW, Pembs. GS, GF, Tithe Map 1840, Bronwydd Collection, manorial Court Rolls; Pembs. RO, LT 1786, QS Order Book 1740, Saunders-Davies Deeds; Carms. RO, GGMS, Gwynfardd; Francis Jones, unpublished article 'Llwyngorras'.

Bowen

LLWYNGWAIR, *Nevern*

A mansion on the north of the river Nevern, and a mile to the east of Newport. The Bowens are one of the oldest of Pembrokeshire gentry. The family settled at Coed in Nevern parish, and continued there until Ifan ab Owen built a residence at nearby Pentre Ifan which bears his name. He was living there in 1409. His great-grandson Sir James ap Owen, a strong adherent of Henry Tudor in 1485, bought Llwyngwair from the Cole family shortly after 1503, which thereafter became the main seat of the family. Llwyngwair had belonged to the Coles before 1326, one of whom discovered the value of marle as a fertiliser used afterwards for centuries on north Pembrokeshire farms, a productive activity continued by the Bowens such as James Bowen of Llwyngwair (High Sheriff, 1803) who encouraged the use of sea-weed and powdered bone as fertilizers on farms and supported local agricultural societies. Matthew Bowen, a younger son of Sir James, was the first of the family to settle in Llwyngwair, to be followed there by thirteen generations of his descendants. The Bowens of Llwyngwair took an active part in public life, providing seven High Sheriffs, a Lord Lieutenant, and numerous Parliamentary commissioners, magistrates, and deputy-lieutenants. In earlier times several bards were guests at Llwyngwair like Ieuan Brechfin, Dafydd Emlyn, and others wrote poems to members of the family in the 16th and 17th centuries.

During the 18th century the Bowens were sympathetic to the Methodists, and many of their leaders were guests at the home and held services there. George Bowen (1722-1810), for his support of this cause became known as 'The Nonconformist Churchman'. Among the visitors were John Wesley, Howel Harris, Daniel Rowland, and Williams Pantycelyn who is said to have composed his famous hymn,

'Dros y Bryniautywyll niwlog,
Yn dawel f'enaid, edrych draw',

while travelling over the Preseli hills to the comforts of Llwyngwair.

It was a commodious house of the traditional type. The antiquarian neighbour, George Owen of Henllys, commented in 1607, 'Llwyngwair the mansion house of James Bowen gentleman . . . the house and demaynes more than halff compassed with the ryver of Neverne yelding as well comoditie fishing as other pleasures. The seat pleasant for wood and water'. In 1670 it had six hearths which placed it among the largest houses in the parish. The tourist Malkin was less impressed when he wrote in 1804, 'Llwn Gwair, seat of George Bowen Esq has the advantage of shelter from some good timber by the side of the Nevern in a country where timber is scarce. In other respects it has nothing to distinguish it from the general style of gentlemen's houses on a small scale', while Fenton in 1811, described it as 'the beautiful seat of George Bowen Esq'. The mansion had been augmented from time to time, and in its heyday had 34 bedrooms. It has survived in excellent state, a long traditional building of two storeys and an attic storey, with ranges each of nine windows, and four dormer windows, with a large entrance porch of three storeys reaching to roof height, with wings extending to the rear.

It had been sold by 1957, and today is a hotel and holiday centre which has altered its outward appearance but very little. Alas, the Bowens have departed, leaving their memorials and coats of arms in Nevern church – *azure* a lion rampant *or* within an orle of eight golden roses, with the crest of a golden lion holding the well known Bowen knot in its forepaws – to remind us of the bygone centuries when the benevolent Bowens of Llwyngwair were toasted on the hearths of Cemais.

Refs: Dwnn, i, pp. 166-7, WWHR, ii, p. 87; George Owen, *2nd Book*; Baronia de Kemes; PRO, AD, iii BM Egerton MS 2586; College of Arms, Protheroe MSS III, IV, V; GGMS, Gwynfardd; Dale Castle Pedigrees; Cardiff Library Deeds; NLW, Picton Castle Deeds, Llwyngwair Deeds, Bronwydd Colln., Owen of Orielton Deeds, Foley of Ridgeway Deeds; Pembs. Papers of GS, H'west Corporation Deeds, Tithe Map Nevern 1844; Francis Jones, 'Bowen of Pentre Evan and Llwyngwair', *Pembs. Historian,* 1979, pp. 25-57, and refs there; B. G. Charles, *George Owen of Henllys,* 1973, passim; E. T. Lewis, *North of the Hills,* 1973, illust.; *Western Telegraph,* 15 July 1987, illust.

LLWYNIHIRION, *Nevern*

A farmstead just east of Carnedd Meibion Owen, and about 3¼ miles southeast of Newport. Home of some of the younger sons of Llwyngwair, John Bowen, second son of George Bowen of Llwyngwair, lived at Llwynihirion, and on 4 August 1648 married Elin daughter of George William Griffith of Penybenglog. Their son, George Owen, succeeded to Llwynihirion.

LLWYNYGORRAS, *Mathry**

Llwyngorras held by Rowland Laugharne, Esq. of the Bishop of St. Davids comprised 87 acres in 1722 tenanted by Essex Harries. The Harries family were there from the early 18th century when Essex Harries married an unknown Margaret who followed her husband to the grave, her will being proved in 1774. Essex had died in 1770 aged about 49. Their eldest son, another Essex succeeded them. He had been born 1 September 1752, and married Anne, sister of Peter Williams of Longhouse. Their eldest son and heir succeeded his father in 1833 and married Anne, daughter of David Walters of Wood, Roch. Thomas died young in 1852

aged 35 and his wife died at Castle Hill, Fishguard in 1896 aged 69. They left two known sons, Walter William Harries of Llwyngorras who died 17 July 1896, aged 48, shortly after his mother, and was buried at Treffynnon. Walter William and his wife Jane had had a son, Walter Cyril Harries who died aged 12 weeks in 1881. The younger brother succeeded to Llwyngorras, he married a (?Martha)Williams of Mabws Fach by whom he had three sons, Roger, Thomas, Hubert and a daughter Bridget.

On 17 July 1770 an inquest was held before William Jones of Llether, coroner, and a jury at Llwynygorras on the body of Essex Harries aged about 49. About 7 p.m. on Monday 25 June a couple of neighbours called at Llwynygorras on Essex Harries and stayed a little time. Essex complained he was not well and would not drink with them. On their departure he went out of doors with them having ordered his wife, Margaret to heat him a little beer against his return. The servant maid having some business to go out about two minutes after her master had gone, saw that he had fallen on his face into a small rivulet that was within about 14 yards from the door, 'upon which she hallow'd out to her mistress who immediately ran and found her husband quite dead supposed to be suffocated in a fit, he being subject to them for some years before'.

Llwyn-y-gorras was empty, and in the main, derelict by the 1980s when Mark and Anne Shuttleworth bought the house and buildings and restored them. The outbuildings are now dwellings.

Refs: Pembs. GS 1770; Terrier 1817 Carms. RO; Tithe Schedule Mathry 1842; *Svy. of Bishopric of St. Davids,* 1815.

LLYSTYN, *Nevern*

A farmstead south of the river Nevern, about midway between Llwyngwair and Trewern. In 1607 George Owen wrote 'Llistyn sygnifieth in Englishe a full Coort or pallace, a house now alltogether raynated and usid as a dayrie, in tymes past being of great acompt for this was the mansion howse and portion of Rees Llewelyn ap Owen one of the five sonnes of Llewelyn ap Owen aforenamed, and Rees Llewelyn ap Owen had this place called Llistin . . . he has also five sonnes . . . Gwilym ap Rees his eldest sonne had this house [Llystin] who was first and cheiffe awncester of the family of the Gwillims of this place, and had yssue Rees Gwillim [who] was father to Ellyw his sole heire wieffe to Harry Bowen of Lochmyler . . . the house and demeyns come to Owen ap Owen of Pentre Iewan esquior father to Thomas Bowen after whose death it fell to the parte of Jane Bowen [died 1624] youngest daughter and coheire to the saide Thomas Bowen and wieff to William Warren [of Trewern] who now in her right enioyeth the same as a grange or dayrie adjoining to his demeysnes of Trewern. I remember in my tyme a fayer grove of trees about the house which now is roted and the land tilled: out of this house of Lliston yo sprunge forthe dyverse houses of gentlemen'.

William Rees ap Gwilym ap Rees of Llystyn son of Llewelyn of Coed, lived in 1526 at Llystyn Ycha. From the 17th century Llystyn was let to a series of farming tenants.

Refs: George Owen, *2nd Book*, 1607, p. 275; *Dwnn*, i, pp. 60, 162-3, 170; Fenton, *Tour Pembs.* 1811; College of Arms, Protheroe MS V; WWHR, ii, p. 55.

LOCHMEYLER/LOCHMEILIR,
Llandeloy

About a mile west of Llandeloy village, and bordered by the farms of Trenichol, Rhosgrannog, Trevanner, and Treiva. Once the residence of landowning families, it is now an ancient commodious farmstead with a ground storey and upper storeys, with attractive dormer windows in the roof, which once formed part of the old residence. It is said to have been named after one Meilir, claiming descent from Bleddyn ap Cynfyn, Prince of Powys. Fenton wrote, '. . . Llech Meylir, built by a chieftain of the name Meylir of the house of Blethyn ap Cynfyn, who, joining some of the auxiliary armies from Powys, settled in this county and laid the foundation of a family of some consequence of the name of Bowen, whose sole heiress, Catherine, married John Scourfield, Esq, of New Moat, the property of whose descendant, Henry Scourfeld Esq. it now is.'

Meylir's descendants, nine generations of whom lived at Lochmeyler, took the permanent name of Bowen, were there from the 13th century and also owned Robleston Hall in Camrose parish. The last male of the family, Richard Bowen, died in 1564, leaving a daughter and heiress Catherine Bowen who was 24 weeks old when her father died. Margaret, mother of Catherine, then married Jenkin Reed of Carmarthen by whom she had five sons, and according to a contemporary manuscript 'he had also eightie base children . . .' Catherine brought Lochmeyler to her husband, John Scourfield of New Moat, High Sheriff in 1600. She died in 1607, and thereafter Lochmeyler was owned by her descendants, the Scourfields, until 1875 when it was sold by Sir Owen Scourfield to the then tenant Mrs. Harries, who, in 1915 sold it to her son-in-law Mr. Perry Martin, who was succeeded by his son Mr. Elfet Martin, M.B.E., J.P. who died in 1986. His widow remained at Lochmeyler. The owners of Lochmeyler enjoyed the privilege of being buried within the church of Llandeloy. In the 19th century the family of Harries, devout Congregationalists, held a lease of the old house, where they used to meet, and in 1838 the historian Dr. Thomas Nicholas preached several sermons there.

The Scourfields continued to live at their original residence, and leased Lochmeyler to responsible tenants. In the 18th century the family of James held it for three generations. On the death of Dr. Richard James in 1771, the property passed to his sister Bridget, surviving lessee. She had married in 1767 the Revd John Mathias, JP, vicar of St. Lawrence, and Lochmeyler passed to him, which he held till his death in 1805. His son, Richard moved to Castle Cenlas, and while there, his daughter, Letitia Mathias, eloped with the Rev. James Jones, vicar of Mathry. Meanwhile, Lochmeyler, had been leased to William Harries, a son of nearby Trenichol. Afterwards it became the property of the Martins as mentioned above.

Refs: Owen, *Heraldic Visitations,* i, p. 116; WWHR, XI, Francis Green 'Bowen of Lochmeyler'; ibid. IX, Francis Green, 'Scourfield of New Moat'; Francis Jones 'Castle Villa', *Treasury of Historic Pembrokeshire;* PRO Star Chamber Proceedings; College of Arms, Wagner MS 2; Pembs. RO, LT; NLW, Peniarth MS 156, Haverfordwest Deeds, Lucas Deeds, Parish Tithe Map, Llandeloy 1845.

LOCHTURFFIN, *Mathry*

A large square Georgian building, with a pillared porch entrance leading to a hall, drawing and dining rooms, and inner hall, sitting room, and kitchen; on the upper floor, seven bedrooms: from the kitchen there is access to an attached building which was the original farmhouse, containing a hall, dining room, kitchen, an inner hall, and a sitting room, and on the upper floor four bedrooms. Lochturffin stands in grounds with protecting trees, between Castle Cenlas and Treffynnon. From early times, Lochturffin comprised two farms, both farmsteads being on the site of the present building, one of them being attached to the main part. Among the properties forming part of the Lochmeyler

estate when the owner, Richard ap Owen, died in 1563/4, was a tenement and 20 acres in Loughtyrphyn. There were two farms there, one owned by the Scourfields of New Moat, the other by the Owens of Orielton.

In modern days they were combined to make one property. From 1610 to 1727 one of the farms was leased to a local yeoman family named Owen. When widow Owen died in 1727 her son, Henry Owen, 'gave up his bargain, upon which it was rented to Mr. Richard James of Lochmeyler at a rent of four pounds a year'. Richard James died in 1756 and was followed by his son Dr. Richard James who died without issue in 1777 leaving the lease of Lochturffin to his brother-in-law, the Revd John Mathias (died 1805). The other farm was leased by Henry Scourfield to Henry Warlow who died there in 1764, and was followed by his son Arthur Warlow.

Their descendants lived at Ewenny Priory, Glam. and took the name Turberville. At the Priory are the portraits of Warlows of 'Mathree' Pembs. (d. 1836) nephew of Gen. Sir Thomas Picton: and John Warlow of 'Landwyfain' (Lochturffin) 1770-1814 who married Catherine Picton of Poyston: and son of the latter, Thomas Warlow (d. 1836). See also 'The Picton Soldiers' in *The Treasury of Historic Pembrokeshire,* pp. 154-161.

In 1780 Henry John of Caerwen bought Lochturffin from Hugh Owen of Orielton, and settled there, and thereafter the property remained with his descendants, one of whom, Mary John, married the Baptist Minister, the Rev. T. E. Thomas of Trehale, whose son Henry John Thomas lived at Lochturffin where he died in 1893, and is now home of his grand-daughter Mrs. Mary Price (née Thomas), who in 1987 advertised the mansion, grounds, and 21 acres for sale.

Refs: NLW, Lochturffin Deeds, Scourfield Deeds, Lucas Deeds, Trenewydd (Pancaer) Deeds, Pembs. Plea Rolls; Pembs RO, LT 1786; G. H. Warlow, *History of the Warlow Family,* 1926.

LOCHVANE (LOCHFAEN), *Brawdy*

A farmstead lying in a small vale near the coast, between Pointz Castle and St. Elvis. In early times it had been an episcopal manor belonging to the See of St. Davids. By 1326 it had been amalgamated with the manor of Brawdy, and in 1652 it is recorded that 'the manors of Broodye, Pointz Castle, and Langvoyne' belonged to the Bishop of St. Davids, and much later, in 1861, 'manors of Brawdy, Pointz Castle, and Lloughvane' appears in the episcopal records. By 1613 there were two farmsteads (messuages) at Lochvane. In 1786 one of these farms was owned by John Jones of Brawdy, Esq, with George Howell as tenant, and the other

owned by Miss Anne Jones of Llether, with widow Berry as tenant, and 1845 one farm (25 acres) was owned by Benjamin James, the other (95 acres) by George Roch of Llether, with Thomas Beynon as tenant. A descendant of the George Howell of 1786, lives at Newport, Mon., and possesses several photographs of the old farmhouses and outbuildings (modernised). His ancestor, Thomas Howell, Master Mariner, born 1811, died of yellow fever and is buried at Matonzas, Cuba.

Refs: *Black Book of St. Davids,* 1326: WWHR iii, pp. 134-5; Francis Jones 'Episcopal Manors of Dewsland', *Journal Hist. Soc. of Church in Wales,* 1967, No. 22, p. 9 *et seq.*; NLW, Slebech Deeds, Pembs. Plea Rolls, Tithe Map of Brawdy 1845; Pembs. RO, LT 1786.

LONGHOOK, *Castlebythe*

Called Lanwg locally. A farmstead to the southwest of Castlebythe, and separated from the farm of Martel by Afon Anghof. In the 16th century the home of minor gentry families, and afterwards of well-to-do yeomen. The property formed part of the estate of Perrott of Haroldston. In 1625 Sir James Perrott of Haroldston granted (by way of exchange) lands in Upper and Lower Longhook to Margaret Symyns, widow, and John Symyns, gent. both of Martel. These properties are marked on Colby's map of 1831 as Longhook -fawr and -fach.

In 1677 Sir Herbert Perrott granted a lease for 21 years to Thomas Harding of Castlebythe, yeoman, and in 1691 Hesther Perrott of Haroldston, spinster, granted a further lease of Longhook and other lands, for 31 years. Longhook was later sold to William Knox of Llanstinian, Esq. and in 1786 he owned both Great and Little Longhook, the former being tenanted by William Myles, the latter by John Thomas. In 1831 Great Longhook was owned by Hugh Owen Owen, Esq. then of Llanstinan, who leased it to George Miles, farmer, for lives.

Refs: BM Egerton MS 2586; College of Arms, Wagner 71152; Pembs. RO, Deeds; Muniments of Lord Hampton, descendant of the Perrotts.

LONGHOUSE, *Mathry*

A large farm on a headland on the Dewsland coast, between Abercastle and Trevine. The lands of Longhouse lie on the border in Mathry and Llanrhian parishes, the farmhouse being in the former. It formed part of the possessions of successive bishops of St. Davids, and was a grange of importance. Longhouse was situated in the manor of Trevine which was also owned by the bishops. A survey of the episcopal estates in 1660 states: 'Trevine is a mesne Lordship and therein is a tenement and lands called Longhouse with the lands called Henllys, being a large ancient house, and the lands appear very good, all worth the sum of £35 per annum, and out of lease in August last 1660. The old tenant is Henry Garnons, the ancient reserved rent is £4 13s. 4d. which the said Garnons paid and is confirmed in possession.' The charitable attitude of the bishop is shown by a transaction in 1776 when the tithe, corn and grain of Trevine and Longhouse were conveyed to trustees to be used to help poor widows of Mathry parish.

Manorial court roles from 1824 onwards show that a mayor was annually elected for Trevine. Manorial courts were still held in 1896. Longhouse continued to be let on leases. It consisted of 357 acres in 1817, two fields near the house being Park Maenllwyd and Park Fagwr Hên. The leaseholder from 1695 was the Thomas family, who continued at Longhouse till the death of John William Thomas without issue in 1854. His niece, Ellen Anne Marychurch married H. P. Griffiths, who stayed at Longhouse for a short time before moving to Llanstinan. David Perkins of Pwllcawrog settled there. He was followed by his son Norman, High Sheriff in 1955, and by his grandson Peter who became High Sheriff in 1966.

Refs: Pembs. RO, LT 1786; *Black Book of St. Davids,* 1326; NLW, Records of the Church in Wales, Bishop's Surveys of 1660 and 1815, Title Maps 1842, Trenwydd (Pencaer) Deeds; Francis Jones, 'The Episcopal Manor of Trevine', *Journal of the Hist. Soc. of the Church in Wales,* 1967, No. 22, pp. 31-35.

LONGRIDGE, *Bletherston*

A large double-pile house, with a wing extending to the rear, on a slope near the confluence of Afon Syfynwy and the Eastern Cleddau. Now a well maintained farmstead. The name is topographical, 'long ridge', on which the mansion is situated. From medieval times onward Longridge formed part of the temporalities of successive Bishops of St. Davids who leased the property to various gentry and yeomen. In 1292 the Bishop's stud (*equaria*) was kept there. A survey of the episcopal temporalities made about 1660, states: 'Longridge Farm in the Baronry of Llawhaden is a Fair Tenement and dwelling with about 700 acres of land there, in possession of Griffith Twyning, gent. undertenant to ye Michels of Harescombe near Gloucester for 3 lives in being and Lawhadden mills for the same lives'. After Griffith Twyning came Joseph Twyning who was there in 1688 when he was granted a lease for 3 lives of 'The Grange of the Lordship of Llawhadden called Llangrige'. He was followed by John Twyning, living there in 1692. The Skyrmes were next at Longridge.

In 1728 John Warren of Trewern married Dorothy Scourfield of Moat; she had previously married William Skyrme of Longridge, and when John Warren died in 1743, she then returned to Longridge. Their son, William Warren married his cousin Jane Skyrme. He died in 1757 and his extensive estates were shared among his four daughters, co-heiresses. Catherine Warren who had married Philip Jones of Llanina (Cards.) in 1758, held the lease of Longridge for some years. It afterwards passed to her sister Jane who, in 1773, married Sir Basil Keith, Governor of Jamaica, and in 1786, described in the Hearth Tax List as owner with Benjamin Evans, tenant.

The Terrier of the estate of the Bishop of St. Davids compiled in 1817 shows that he still owned Longridge and adjacent 35 fields comprising 466 acres. The topographer Lewis writing in 1834 and 1840 states that in Bletherston parish is 'an estate called Longridge which belongs to the Bishop of St. Davids'. After this leases were granted to successive farmers.

Refs: Black Book of St. Davids, 1326; NLW, Records of the Church in Wales, Olven and Colby Deeds, Poyston Deeds, F. Green Deeds, Pembs. Plea Rolls; Owen, *Pembs.,* vol. 1; BM Egerton MS 2586; Pembs. RO, Deeds (RTP); Francis Jones, 'Warrens of Trewern', *Pembs. Historian,* 1974; Francis Jones, *Historic Cardiganshire Homes and their Families.*

LOVESTON, *St. Twynells*
Now a double-pile farmstead about half a mile south of St. Twynells church; to the west is Merrion, to the east is Sampson Cross. For some two centuries home of gentry families. In 1545 Thomas Watkin lived there. By his wife Joan Adams of Paterchurch, he had two daughters, co-heiresses, Elizabeth, married Thomas Adams who was of Loveston, *iure uxoris*, and died before 1562, leaving a son John Adams who lived at Loveston till his death in 1605, leaving a son Thomas who presented a paten to the parish church in 1611, and died in 1626; the other co-heiress, Margaret, married in 1545 Griffith White of Henllan, who died in 1590 leaving a son, Thomas White of Loveston in 1604.

The Whites continued at Loveston, and in 1680 Mary White, widow, paid five hearth taxes, which shows that the house was of a commodious structure. The Leach family then came there. Henry Leach (1700-87) was followed by his son Abraham Leach of Loveston, who bought Corston which became the family's chief residence. Loveston afterwards was let to farming tenants.

Refs: BM Egerton MS 2586; Pembs. RO, LT 1786; J. T. Evans, *Church Plate of Pembrokeshire,* 1905.

LYDSTEP PALACE, *Manorbier**
This building has been completely swept away. It stood in the hamlet of Lydstep and had long been in ruins so says RCAM in 1925. It was known as Ludsop in deeds and documents down to 18th century and its borders were, on one side where Lydstep Post Office car park stands. There are sketches and a description of the exterior in Laws *Little England* on pages 186-189. Peter Smith writing in *Carmarthenshire Studies,* (a volume of essays presented to Francis Jones in 1974), tells us 'Apart from the great hall of the Palace at St. David's it is the only building in Dyfed we have discovered which was without an enclosed fireplace to the hall, which must therefore have been heated by an open hearth. The house is built within a long rectangle with the exception of a small projection at one end housing a latrine. There are three vaulted basement rooms, one large room having the vault running axially, one small room roofed by a cross vault, and one small vaulted room under the latrine. Much of the first floor has been lost, but appears to have consisted of a hall and small parlour. The hall was reached by an outside stair. The stair itself has gone but the entry to the hall can easily be identified'. A Robert Ludsopp owned lands in Jeffreston and had a son Jenkin Ludsopp who left two daughters and co-heiresses, Alice and Elen who married David Nash of Nash and had a son, Thomas Nash who married Eva, daughter of Pierce Scourfield. No dates are given. The owner of Lydstep in the 19th century was the Philipps family. For plans of the house see P. Smith, *Houses of the Welsh Countryside,* 1975, p. 27.

MABWS FAWR, *Mathry*

A farmstead in a copse on a slope, a mile to the south of Mathry village, and above the upper waters of Cleddau Wen which borders its northern side. Several adjoined farms bear the names Mabus Fawr, Mabws Fach, Bont Dwr Fabws, and Penlan Fabws. To the east of Mabws Fawr is a hill fort, Castell Llynin Mabws, in a field still called Parc yr hen gastell, and near the house is Parc Ffynnon Dewi whose well was dedicated to the national saint of Wales.

In 1326 'Mabovis' was a fee of which the Bishop of St. Davids was lord; at that time the freeholders were Simon ap Philip, Ieuan ap David, and Rosa Russell who held two carucates and 7½ bovates there, and the Bishop held in his own hand half a bovate and half an acre there. They were to accompany the Bishop and his host in time of war, and to follow the relics of the Blessed David as far as the rocky outcrop of Carn Twrne. In 1560 the brothers William David and John, sons of Ieuan ap Owen of Mabws Fawr lived there, descended from Twdwr, Prince of Deheubarth. John left an only child and heir, namely Isabel who married David ap Thomas, gent. David settled at Mabws, and the property in due course passed to his granddaughter Margaret, who married Owen ap Melchior of Newport who settled at his wife's home. They had five sons and four daughters, the eldest of the sons, Charles Owen of Mabws Fawr, was Bailiff of Dewsland in 1631. Lewys Dwnn recorded the family pedigree in 1613, under the heading 'Y Plâs y Mabws'.

The property changed hands after 1634, and about the middle of the century it became part of the estate of the Tucker and Edwardes families of Sealyham, and Mabws Fawr was leased to yeomen families of Dewsland. The best known of these was that of Evans, who obtained a lease of Mabws Fawr in the first half of the 18th century.

John Evans (1715-75) variously described as 'gentleman' and 'yeoman' was a Land Tax Commissioner in 1768, and was succeeded at Mabws Fawr by his son, John who married Martha Mathias of Pencnwc, a descendant of the powerful squirearchal families of Wogan and Ford of Stone Hall, by whom he had a son, John who succeeded to Mabws Fawr.

This John Evans was an enthusiastic Baptist who held services at Mabws Fawr. By his wife Anne Howell of Treddiog he had highly gifted children including John Brown Evans (b. 1831) who emigrated to South Africa where he became an extremely successful farmer and laid the foundations of Angora goat farming in Africa, and to keep his herds under control invented a special wire known as 'Evans Patent Fencing' now called 'barbed wire'. When he died in 1888, *The Times* described him as 'the largest farmer in the world', his lands extending to 260,000 acres.

His younger brother, Morgan Jones Evans, (1835-99) succeeded to Mabws Fawr, was a progressive farmer, and produced an improved breed of Welsh Black Cattle, known as 'the Mabws breed'. He founded and edited the journal called *The Country Gentleman*, and was a noted contributor to *The Field*, and a well known poet. He was succeeded at Mabws by his sister, Rebecca Sophia Evans, better known as 'Rebecca Mabws' and was one of the first women to become public lecturers in Great Britain. She married the Rev. Thomas Williams, and died in 1874. Her only son, H. A. Williams, chemist, Justice of the Peace, County Councillor, died, without issue, at Haverfordwest in 1937 aged 67. In the early 1960s Mabws Fawr was sold to a stranger, who demolished the old house, and erected a new farmhouse. The outbuildings have all now been converted to dwellings.

Refs: Dwnn, i, 112; *Black Book of St. Davids; RCAM Pembs.*, 1925; Pembs. RO, LT 1986; NLW, Morgan-Richardson Deeds, Tithe Map Mathry, 1842; Francis Jones, 'Mabws Fawr' in *Trans. Cymwr.* 1970, 112-129, and refs there.

MANORBIER CASTLE, *Manorbier*

Normally this building, which is mainly a ruin, would not be within the scope of this work but as parts of it have been restored to make it once again a family home then it qualifies on these grounds for inclusion.

Fenton described Manorbier as 'the most perfect residence of an old Norman baron with

all its appendages; church, mill, dovehouse, ponds, park and grove, still to be traced'.

It looks today much as depicted by Samuel and Nathaniel Buck in 1740. Nothing much has been added to the building since about 1300 except making part of it habitable again.

Manorbier's greatest claim to fame is as the birthplace of Giraldus de Barri (c. 1146 -c. 1220), otherwise known as Giraldus Cambrensis or, more popularly, Gerald of Wales. Gerald was a grandson of Odo de Barri, a Norman who is said to have founded Manorbier. His father, William de Barri, married Angharad, daughter of another Norman, Gerald de Windsor and granddaughter of Rhys ap Tewdwr (d. 1093), Prince of South Wales.

Gerald wrote, *(inter alia) The Journey through Wales* and *The Description of Wales*. Both these, written in Latin, are very readable in the late Professor Lewis Thorpe's translation. Gerald waxes lyrical when describing his birthplace with lavish praise.

The de Barri family (whose arms were: *argent* three bars gemels *gules*) and their descendants occupied Manorbier for about 200 years, their connection ending in 1399 when the castle and lands were confiscated by Henry IV. Thereafter the Castle changed hands several times but by the late 1530s it was already in ruins with no one living there. Cromwell's soldiery siezed Manorbier in the Civil War but it was not besieged or slighted. The Castle does not have a keep and is built around a large courtyard with a surviving round tower and gatehouse.

Lady Dunsany, widow of John, Baron de Rutzen of Slebech, married secondly Lord Dunsany, lived here for a number of years.

MANOROWEN, *Manorowen*

A mansion within attractive woodland, one mile southwest of Goodwick and two miles from Fishguard, overlooking the road from Goodwick towards St. Davids, and a distant view of Fishguard Bay and the coastline to Pen Dinas. Although the name as spelled at present suggests that of an ancient manor such was emphatically not the case. Originally it was a maenor, an early Welsh tenurial unit, and not to be confused with the later Norman Manor.

In 1326 it was a knight's fee called 'Maynornowan'. Local Welsh folk call it 'Farnawan', more faithful to its origin than the modern 'official' form. The spelling Maenornawan occurs in numerous early documents down to the mid-18th century. The latter part is derived from the name of a man called Nawan ap Gnawan, spelled Grawan on the Elizabethan chalice of the parish church.

The Goodwick-St. Davids road passes the present mansion and the church. The original residence stood near the east end of the church, and was flanked on the other side by a large walled garden, which, with a gazebo, has lasted to the present day.

In 1326 it was 'Maynornawan, a knight's fee (English)', but no further references have been found to the property, until the 16th century. The first family of note at Manorowen was that of Williams who were there early in the reign of Elizabeth I. Ievan ap William son of William Walter, was one of the coroners of Pembrokeshire from 1575 and is usually described as 'gentleman' in contemporary records. He engaged in numerous property transactions in the parish of St. Davids and nearer home seems to have farmed on a scale sufficiently large to enable him to sell produce in distant markets. We read in the *Welsh Port Books* that on 29 April 1586 the *Sunday de Washford* sailed from Phiskard (Fishguard) to Aberme (Barmouth) and elsewhere carrying 40 quarters of wheat and 40 quarters of rye from Ievan Williams of Manernawne. He died about 1600. By Joan his wife, he had an only son, William and a natural daughter Margaret verch Ievan who married a freeholder, Phillip John of Llambed y moch near Mathry. William Williams succeeded to Manorowen and married Elizabeth, daughter of William Warren of Trewern before 1610. William was one of the parishioners responsible for the upkeep of the Train Band, the Home Guard of those times, and in 1609 was ordered to pay 1s. 10d. because of defective armour. Poor William came to an unhappy end; on 20 July 1622 the coroner held an inquest at Manorowen on the body of William Williams, gentleman and found that he 'at the instigation of the devil' had killed himself with a knife on 19 June, and accordingly returned a verdict of felo de se. It appears that he left no heir. His widow remarried less than a year later to James Phillips who came to live at Manorowen and died before 1638 when a new man was living at Manorowen. This was another William Williams whose relationship, if any, to the preceding William Williams is unknown. This William is said to have been an ardent Royalist and eventually fled overseas with Prince Charles leaving his wife and small son, Lewis at Manorowen and is believed to have died on the Continent before 1654.

Manorowen passed briefly into the hands of George Owen of Scleddau, a descendant of the Williams family, and he sold the estate on 6 December 1665 to the family of Lewis descended from the medieval chieftains of north Pembrokeshire. The new owner was kin to Bowen of Llwyngwair and Pentre Evan, and other leading landowners. The Lewis's had lived at Henllan Owen in Eglwyswrw, the first of the family to settle there being Lewis ap Richard, great-grandson of Jenkin ap Howel of Nevern who fell at the battle of Banbury in 1469. His son, George Lewis, the first to adopt that permanent surname, sold Henllan Owen to his cousin-german George Bowen of Llwyngwair. It was his descendant, John Lewis the younger who bought Manorowen and came to live there. He married Diana, daughter of John Lloyd of Cilglynen before 1643. He became a J.P., and was Mayor of Fishguard on ten occasions between 1641 and 1675, builder of the second mansion at Manorowen, and developer of the fishing industry at Fishguard and Goodwick. The older residence was totally abandoned and not a single stone remains to indicate the site.

John Lewis was an antiquary of some merit, and was particularly interested in archaeological remains to which he guided scholarly friends who called at Manorowen from time to time. He took Sir Richard Bassett, a Glamorgan magnate of a similar bent to see the cairns and megaliths of Nevern parish. A history of the life and style of John Lewis in the new mansion was later written by his great-grandson, Richard Fenton the antiquary, who wrote of him, that he was, 'the friend of Bishop Gibson and Edward Lhwyd; but his principal claim on notice is as a magistrate and a country gentleman, in which view of him he makes a distinguished figure . . . he discharged the office of Justice of the Peace during the whole of James the Second's reign with inflexible integrity and firmness; and having been bred to the law knew so to temper its rigour . . . As a country gentleman his style of living and hospitality were of a character then but little known to men of his moderate fortune, and now, I am sorry to say, almost faded out of society.

As he farmed his demesne, and produced his own grain, he could vouch for his malt, and piqued himself on having the native and staple liquor of the country in a perfection that made it proverbial, and for which that house long continued to maintain a reputation; nor was the more ancient and heroic beverage of Wales, mead and bragawd, making no inconsiderable accession to his cellar, overlooked, which as well as his made wines of every sort, was of the first quality; and his pickles, preserves, syrups, and cordial waters had an equal title to excellence . . . having very extensive orchards well cropped, he made his own cyder and perry . . . the successful culture of his hop vintage . . . his gardens supplied him with common fruits, some of which existed to within these few years, with abundance of filberts, walnuts and mulberries found in his dessert. Fish he never lacked, being entitled to the tithe of all taken at Fishguard as lay impropriator of the parish. Besides a plentiful poultry court and farmyard, a well stocked dovecot, ponds for wild fowl, and glades, of which I remember three in use for taking woodcock in winter, and a sheep walk famed for its sweet mutton at a place called Cronllwyn . . . furnished his table with the substantials most in demand . . . and enabled him to indulge his hospitable disposition in a most enviable degree, by entertaining his superiors in rank and fortune at an expense scarcely perceptible; so his house became the frequent rendezvous of the first families of the country during the festive months of winter.

He had six daughters whose education . . . equally fitted them for the drawing-room and the mysteries of the family receipt-book, and whose useful accomplishments procured them respectable matches; to each of whom he assigned a province in the management of his household: by which means . . . it was conducted with a precision and a consequence that gave it the air of a much greater establishment, and freed him from the petty drudgery of "chronicling small beer", leaving him time for more important avocations. Even after the marriage of his daughters, the only one who lived near, my grandmother, who, when single, had the care of the brewery department, was regularly sent for to settle the October operations; the produce of which could not be admitted into the cellar till sanctioned by her approbation.'

The precise dates of the deaths of John and Diana Lewis are not known but they were both gone before the year 1733, leaving six daughters, Martha who married Thomas Parry of Pembroke; Jane married the Rev. James Williams; Ursula married David James of Cilhedryn; Anne died unmarried; Diana married Richard Fenton of Fishguard, grandfather of the antiquary, and a daughter who died young.

Martha and her husband Thomas Parry succeeded to Manorowen which continued as a family seat until early in the 19th century when the Bowen-Parrys built a completely new residence just in front of Lewis's residence, which was used thereafter for domestic purposes, and continues to be so used to the present day. The last of the family at Manorowen was Richard Parry-Bowen who died heavily in debt in 1837 leaving four children; and his heirs and his creditors sold the estate. The only son, Richard Parry-Bowen is believed to have emigrated to New Zealand and died without issue.

The capital messuage, demesne, and lands, the home farm, and eight other properties in the vicinity, were sold to Dr. Moses Griffith for £14,000 in 1841 and later on he improved and extended the mansion on its western end. This is the excellently maintained mansion (the third at Manorowen) that greets our eyes today. Dr. Griffith, a member of the family of Griffith of Rickeston and Pointz Castle, served for 31 years as an army surgeon, and for several years in India. He never married and died in 1883, aged 94, leaving the Manorowen estate to a son of his bailiff, the Rev. Thomas Johns, vicar of Manorowen, till his death in 1905. The new owner was followed by his son Mr. V. G. J. Johns, solicitor, who died in 1946, leaving Manorowen to his eldest son Captain Graham Johns, T.D., D.L. The family remains at Manorowen today.

Refs: Black Book of St. Davids, 1326; BM Egerton MS 2586, p. 295; Fenton, *Tour Pembs.*, 1811; Lewis, *TDW,* 1833 and 1840; *Welsh Port Book,* p. 132; See *Historic Houses of Pembrokeshire and their Families*, 1996, and Francis Jones article 'Manorowen'.

MARLOES COURT, *Marloes*

The home of farming families; the very earliest of whom were the Marloes of Marloes. The first family of whom we know any details are the Malefants. Sir Walter married Dame Alice de Roch and their daughter Dame Alson Malefant married Sir William Morlasse of Rowse. They in turn had a daughter Margaret who married Hick Howel and they had a son, Richard and a daughter Margaret who married William Barrett of Pendine.

The Bevan(s) family lived there in the latter half of the 18th century. David Bevan of Marloes Court, a farmer viv. 1753 married twice. By his first wife, who is unknown, he had a son, David who was Master of HM Sloop

Petterell. He had a younger brother Cornelius and a sister Esther. The house was owned by Hon. William Edwardes, afterwards 3rd Lord Kensington. His tenant was James Dean Wathen in 1834. After the Wathens came the James family who were there between 1885 and the 1920s.

MARTEL, *Puncheston*

The present farm of Martel is about half a mile east of Little Newcastle and one and a quarter miles southwest of Puncheston. The site of the former mansion is on the northern bank of the stream called Afon Anghof, between Martel Bridge and Allt yr Hwc. A railroad from Letterston passes alongside the site.

The earliest known family here was that of Martel after whom the property was named. John Martel of Martel, living there in the late 15th century. His daughter and heiress, Agnes, married William ap David, member of the family of Llystyn near Newport, who was living at his wife's home in 1557. The estate eventually passed to his three daughters and heirs, one of whom, Agnes had Martel. She married John Symmons, described as 'Husbandman, of Martel' in 1566. The name is also spelt Symins and Symyns.

Their son, Thomas married Margaret, daughter of Griffith Gwillim of Pembroke, prenuptial settlement dated 1580, and he died 6 August 1612 aged 63, leaving a son John who married in 1604, Margaret, daughter of David Lloyd of Cilciffeth; he died 10 May 1664 aged 72. Their son, Thomas married four times; firstly to Anne daughter of John Owen of Trecwn, and widow of George Warren of Trewern, by whom she had had three children. Thomas and Anne had a son, John who died in 1669, and a second son who died aged 16. Thomas married secondly, in 1668/9 Elizabeth Owens of Wenallt; and thirdly Margaret, the daughter of Thomas Wogan of Llanstinan by whom he had an heir, John born 13 April 1670. He was High Sheriff in 1715 and married Martha, daughter of George Harries of Tregwynt; his will was proved in 1730. John and Martha had two sons, Thomas, born 1694 who went to Pennsylvania and died in 1741 and John Symmons (1701-64), a member of the Society of Sea Serjeants, owner of the estates of Martel and Llanstinan (where he went to live), and about 1773 married Maria Philipps of Sandyhaven. He was followed by his son and heir, John Symmons, who was the last of the line as a major landowner. He married Anne Barlow of Slebech and went there to live and rebuilt that residence.

In 1783/84 he sold the estates of Martel, Llanstinan and Slebech, to William Knox (see DNB). The original residence, Martel, had been abandoned, and had become ruinous. By a lease dated 1782, John Symmons leased to Edward Davies of Castlebythe, a turner, part of the messuage called Martel, except a small plot of ground and the old garden on the bank of the brook (Anghof), at a spot between old Martell (mansion), and Martel Mill, and in 1799 William Knox of Llanstinian granted a lease to John Llewellin of Letterston, farmer. In 1811 or shortly after, the trustees of the late William Knox, sold that worthy's estate to Sir John Owen of Orielton. The land of Martel was thereafter owned by successive farmers. The coat of arms of Symmons of Martel are engraved on the chalice (hall-dated 1725) of Puncheston church, namely party per fesse *argent* and *sable* three trefoils two and one counter-changed.

Refs: Evans *Church plate of Pembs.,* 1905, pp. 81-2; *Dwnn,* i, 192; Chetham Pedigrees; WWHR, ii, p. 44, XIY pp. 207; Fenton, *Tour Pembs.,* 1811; Carlisle, *TDW*; Lewis, *TDW,* 1840; BM, Egerton 2586; College of Arms Protheroe MS IX, pp. 89, 99; Pembs. RO, Deeds HDX/686, No. 2; NLW, Bronwydd Deeds, Cwrtmawr Deeds; Noyadd Trefawr Deeds, Pembs. Plea Rolls, Eaton Evans and Williams Deeds; Poyston Deeds, F. Green Deeds.

MARTLETWY HOUSE, *Martletwy*

Stands to the north of the village, northeast of the parish church, and near to the Vicarage. Home of the Philipps family, derived from Picton Castle, in the 17th Century. On 1 September 1631 John Philipps of Molleston, Thomas Philipps of Martletwy gentlemen, with four others, assigned hogs and swine and 'wild honey' within the forest of Narberth, to John Barlow of Slebech, Esq. On 8 April 1666, the said John Barlow mortgaged 'a capital messuage called Martletwy House' to George Meares of

Nangle, gent. and on 12 January 1669/70, the said Meares and Barlow, realised 'the capital messuage and lands called Martletwy House' to Thomas Carpenter of Lincoln's Inn, Esquire, to be held in trust for William Barlow of Mynwear, Esq. In 1670 John Barlow of Slebech paid hearth taxes for seven hearths in Martletwy. In 1682 William Barlow, gent., is described as of Martletwy. By 1786 it was owned by William Knox, with Joseph Davies as tenant.

Refs: NLW, Slebech Deeds; Pembs RO, LT 1786.

MERIANOG, *Meline*

On a northern slope of the Preseli hills, below Carnalw, and two miles east of Brynberian. Also spelled as Bryianog in earlier documents. There were several farms in the vicinity called Merianog-fawr, -ganol, -fach, and in the 19th century the name -west had been added. The name occurs as Breuanog-fawr, (1412), Bryanog (1600), Bryanog fach and issa (1560-1620), and two farms called Vrianog (1786). The earliest notice I have seen occurs in a deed of 10 May 1412 when Philip ap Howel ap Jenkyn granted the messuage and land of Brenanog-vawr, and four acres at Henllys Morgan with the wood there, to Owen ap Gwilym Ddu (ancestor of the Owens of Henllys, died c. 1447). Thereafter several yeoman families lived there. In 1583 Thomas ap Rees (descended from Howel Gawr, and Gwynfardd Dyfed), described as of Merianock-ycha and yssa was made a ward of George Owen of Henllys, who, nine years later, sold the wardship to William Warren of Trewern. In 1638 Thomas ap Rees and his sons James ap William Thomas (descended from Gwynfardd Dyfed) are described as of Merianog-Issa, and later the said son James Thomas, living at Merianog-fach with his son William Thomas and daughter Chrisley and Margaret. Later the father sold Bryanog. The prenuptial settlement of Griffith Morris gent. of Cwmcerwyn and Catherine, daughter of William Lewis of Rhosymaen, formerly of Vronianog-fawr, was made in 1721, and in 1760 the post-nuptial settlement was made between Thomas Morris of Whitchurch and his wife Martha, one of the daughters and co-heirs of Thomas Lewis gent. late of Vrianog-fawr, deceased.

The Land Tax of 1786 records Thomas Williams of Treleddyn, St. Davids as owner of two messuages at Vrianog, and one messuage there owned by John Rees. By 1837 the owners were William Williams of Merianog-fawr, Phoebe Bland of Merianog-fach, and Western-Merianog, and Thomas Rees of Merianog-ganol. The Voters' List of 1950 shows four messuages, viz. Merianog-fawr, -fach -ganol, and -West.

Refs: Carms. RO, GGMS I; Pembs. RO, LT 1786; NLW, Bronwydd Deeds, Tithe Map Meline 1837; College of Arms, Protheroe MS IV and XII.

MERRION COURT, *Warren*

Half a mile southeast of the parish church. A Manor belonging to Henry Wogan, (died in 1499). With the death of John Wogan in 1559 it passed to co-heiresses who sold the property to Thomas Bowen of Roblinston who was lord of the manor in 1587. Some time after 1623 it was sold to the Lorts of Stackpole Court, from whom it descended by marriage to the Campbells, (Lords Cawdor). Fenton wrote in 1811 – 'Merian Court, the head of a manor now belonging to Lord Cawdor, and therefore of a still more baronial appearance, as part of the ruin presents a species of masonry of a very superior quality that indicates something more highly finished that what is generally met with'.

Refs: y Cymmr. 1903, pp. 95-105; Fenton, *Tour Pembs.,* 1811; Taylor's *Cussion,* fo. 98; BM, Egerton MS 2586.

Callen

MERRIXTON, *Amroth*

One and a quarter miles west of the parish church. The original name was Meyrickston. In 1760 it was the home of Evan Williams, Esq. J.P., and in 1773 of John Martin Esq. J.P. In 1786 William Callen Esq. was the owner-occupier, and his wife Anne (née Poyer), and there was another residence nearby also called Merrixton and owned by H. Skyrme, Esq. with Thomas Cosens, tenant. The tithe map of 1844 gives Sir Richard Bulkeley Philipps as owner, and William Brock Swann as occupier, while a nearby property, East

Merrixston was owned by Charles Poyer Callen with David Edwardes tenant. In 1848 William Brock Swann Esq. is described as of Merrixton House.

Refs: NLW, Slebech Deeds; Morgan-Richardson Deeds; Pembs. RO LT 1786.

MILTON HOUSE, *Carew*

A residence, half a mile northwest of Carew Cheriton church, marked on Colby's Map as 'Milton House' within grounds on the edge of Milton village. Comparatively modern, it was owned by the Rev. William Holcombe in 1786, with William Phelps as tenant. By the early 1830s William Bowen was living at Milton House, being the first of that family there who was to continue there for nearly a century and a half. Lewis wrote in 1834: 'Within the parish are several gentlemen's seats of which the principal are Milton House formerly part of the extensive estate of Upton Castle, and now the property and residence of William Bowen Esq. an elegant modern mansion pleasurably situated within grounds . . . '

William Bowen's sister had married James Summers of Haverfordwest, Clerk of the Peace, and it was to his nephew, James Summers, he left Milton House. James Summers then added Bowen to his name; James Bowen Summers settled there and was High Sheriff in 1874. He was followed by his son, Sutton Bowen Summers, who sold Milton House after the 2nd World War. In 1950 it was the house of Colonel St. L. G. Hawkes.

Refs: Pembs. RO, LT 1786; Lewis, *TDW,* 1834 edn.; VL 1904 and 1950.

MILTON, *Burton*

Formerly a residence, 1¼ miles northwest of the parish church; it is now a farm. The earliest known family there was that of Wogan. Richard Wogan of Milton married Maud Philipps of Picton Castle. He died without issue, and his widow then married Morgan Jones who was of Milton, (*iure uxoris*) when he was High Sheriff in 1547. Morgan predeceased Maud and was followed at Milton by his son William Jones, gent. William died in 1577, and his will mentions his brother Thomas Jones of Harmeston, his son Henry Jones, a minor, and his mother Mrs. Maud Philipps Wogan, gentlewoman, who proved the will. Little else is known of Milton, and it was let to farmers. The owner in 1786 was David Hughes Esq. (of Harmeston), and Richard Fields as tenant.

Refs: Picton Castle Deeds; Pembs RO 1786; *Dwnn,* i, p. 229.

MINWEAR/MINWERE, *Minwear*

This consists now of the ruins of a former monastic property and a farmhouse north of the parish church. Minwear manor and the lands of Cadwgan in Minwear, and the church were granted by Robert, son of Lodomar, to St. John of Slebech about 1150 (and confirmed 1241-45), with freeshare in all Minwear Manor and the wood in the manor.

The Ancient monuments survey of 1925 wrongly and erroneously, attributed the ruins of the mansion as a Tithe barn. I visited Minweare in April 1974. The farm was still part of the Slebech estate. The ruins of the former mansion are a considerable distance from Minwere farm which is by the church. The ruins are extensive, part of the dwelling house remains, built over an under-croft. There are remains of large outhouses, the largest one being a huge building of two storeys, 35 yards x 9 yards with slit ventilations. Two large walled gardens; a well with masonry around, and an overflow pool (gofer). The ruins are in a woodland on the bend of the Cleddau, opposite Slebech House. It is locally called 'Sisters House'.

In 1538 Roger Barlow was living at Slebech but in 1546 he bought with other properties, the manor and rectory of Minwere. In his will dated 1553 he left the dairy house at Minwere with the stock and cattle to his wife Julgan. In 1583 George Barlow of Minwere was admitted to the Inner Temple and afterwards inherited the Slebech estate (q.v.) from his father. Fenton wrote: 'Exactly opposite to the house of Slebech there are considerable remains of a respectable mansion, once inhabited by a brother of the Barlow who resided at Slebech. They are said to have lived in such harmony with each other that their bills of fare were mutually announced by trumpet, and the place of dinner fixed by the predominated excellence of the publication'.

In 1613 records show that John Barlow owned *(inter alia)* 'The manor of Mynwere containing one capital messuage called Sistern House: 290 acres of land; 300 acres of woodland; 10 acres of salt marsh; one corn mill; two messuages in Mynwere and 50 acres; a parcel called Mynwereshill and 100 acres; five cottages and much else'. Sistern House was probably a corruption of Sisters' House as there was once a nunnery there, the ruins being in Minwear parish.

The history of Minwere and Slebech are closely linked. The Barlows of Slebech were created baronets (see Burke's *Extinct and Dormant Baronetcies*).

In 1786 Mrs. Ann Barlow was the owner of Minwere but William Knox owned Minwere House.

Minwere latterly belonged to the Lewis family and to Baron de Rutzen of Slebech Hall.

Refs: Slebech Deeds Nos. 556, 742, 693, 743, 555, 693, 3901-2, 3527, 12462; PRO Pat. Roll No. 798; Taylor's *Cussion.*

Scourfield

MOAT/MOTE THE/ NEW MOAT, *New Moat*

A residence in grounds close to the southern side of New Moat, now a complete ruin. The earliest, and main residence of the Scourfield family from the late 14th century to our time, a period of over 550 years. At the end of the 14th century John Scourfield lived there and in a deed of 1438 the parties are described as John Skorffyll the elder of Nova Mota, his wife Isabel and their son John Skorffyll, junior, and before the end of that century the name was spelled as Scourfield which influenced the family to adopt a canting coat of arms: *gules* three greyhounds *argent* ('couring the field'), with a crest of a silver greyhound holding the word 'Ffydlon' in his mouth. In 1591, the then head of the family signed his name to his pedigree as 'John Schourthefyld'.

That their residence was commodious is indicated by the fact that it contained eight hearths in 1670. The Scourfields owned the New Moat estate for at least 14 generations. About 1780 William Henry Scourfield went to live at Robeston Hall near Milford, leaving, (but still owning), New Moat which became ruinous. On his death in 1805 he was succeeded by his son also named William Henry Scourfield the last member in the male descent of his family. In 1843 he died without issue, leaving the New Moat estate to a descendant of his sister, Elizabeth Anne Scourfield. She had married Col. Own Phillips of Williamston (Burton parish) in 1804, and had a son John Henry Phillips who received New Moat. This John Henry took the surname Scourfield in 1862, and was created Baronet on 18th February 1876 which he enjoyed for a very short time for he died in June of that year. He was succeeded by his son, Sir Owen Henry Phillips Scourfield, 2nd and last Baronet, who died without issue in 1921, leaving the New Moat estate to his cousin Henry George Saunders-Davies, of the Pentre family, who took the name Scourfield by R.L. in 1922. He was followed by his son, Col. David Gwyn Davies-Scourfield, M.C.

The New Moat estate was advertised for sale in 1925, but not sold. At this time the estate consisted of 49 properties. The mansion had become ruinous, and in 1926 was demolished. A few references to the old mansion occur during the 19th century.

In 1811 Fenton wrote: '. . . Moat, a straggling village, below which I see with regret the shell of one of the most ancient houses in the mountain district, now unroofed, where still within these forty years the family of Scourfield from the time of Edward the First had continued to reside in the midst of a very large contiguous property and a wealthy respectable tenantry. The house of its sort and its age ranked among the very first, and its situation was truly a noble one on an eminence looking down on Haverfordwest about nine miles off . . . near a handsome church, the advowson of which was in the family, and in a parish entirely, or with a very small exception, their own property ... Mr. Scourfield now resides at Robeston, about six miles below Haverfordwest, where he had no other property but his demesne with a mansion house on one side most unpleasantly circumscribed; and, for this, was abandoned the feudal importance of the upland situation'.

The next writer, S. Lewis, writes in 1840 – 'Moat: the ancient mansion of the Scourfields who resided here from the reign of Edward I till within the last 60 years when they removed to Robeston Hall near Milford, has been taken down, and is now erecting a spacious and elegant mansion on the same site to which the family will remove when it is competed; the house which is surrounded with thriving plantations and with groves of ancient timber, is delightfully situated at the foot of the southern declivity of the Precelly range of mountains, and commands a fine view over the whole of the lower part of the county.'

Refs: Fenton, *Tour Pembs.,* 1811; Lewis, *TDW,* 1840; *Cambrian Journal,* 1862, p. 241; *Dwnn,* i, pp. 110, 175-6; WWHR II, p. 64; ibid. IX, p. 145; Carms. RO; SC 636, 1925; PRO, Anc Deeds; T. Lloyd, *Lost Houses of Wales,* 1986, Photo.

MOLLESTON, *Narberth*

Now a farmstead, called Great Molleston, about two miles southwest of Narberth town. Formerly a gentry residence. Towards the end of the 16th century it was the seat of Owen Philipps, a younger son of Morgan Philipps of the Picton Castle family. He died before 1621, and was survived by his widow, Priscilla Philipps (née Chester), and their son, John Philipps who succeeded to Molleston, married Jane Elliott and they were still living there in 1644. They had a son and heir, Owen Philipps. On 1 December 1635, John Philipps, gent. of Molleston, his mother Priscella Philipps, widow of East Moor, Manorbier, and their son and heir Owen Philipps, agreed to convey the farm of Molleston and pennage of hogs and swine and wild honey in the forest of Narberth, to John Barlow, Esq. of Slebech. Owen Philipps is the last known member of the family at Molleston.

On 14 June 1704 Evan Lewis of Laugharne, yeoman, and Thomas Davies of Molleston, assigned to John Barlow, Esq. of Slebech, for a term of years, a messuage called Molleston, and lands 'near Great Molleston mansion House', and a piece of land called Trebaron in Narberth parish. In 1765 Thomas George and his wife Margaret, (formerly widow of Robinson Lloyd of Vaynor), were living at Molleston. In 1786, William Knox of Slebech, is described as owner of Molleston, with William George, tenant there. In 1834 William Hand is described as owner of Great Molleston.

Refs: Pembs. RO, LT 1786, VL; NLW, Pembs. Plea Rolls, Bronwydd Deeds, Slebech Deeds.

MONKTON OLD HALL, *Monkton*

About one hundred yards southeast of Monkton Priory. In 1811 we are informed by Fenton, 'the prior's mansion, a little to the west of the Cemetery, now converted into a farmhouse, is of a singular form, uniting the architecture of various fashions and ages. It is ascended by a flight of steps, at the foot of which on each side are the remains of very curious pillars. The basement is all vaulted; and the outbuildings, together with the walls that enclosed the whole, give us an idea of the prior's great estate.

The monastic precinct, or rather prior's liberties, occupying a very large tract, formed a paddock well walled round, commanding a fine view of the estuary, castle, and town of Pembroke, [and it] must have been a sumptuous and delightful residence. A dove-house of large dimensions, an inseparable appendage to houses of the first note in this country, still exists entire, just without this paddock. The Priory Farm now rents at £400 per annum;' and Carlisle says, 'There is a building, joining the churchyard on the East, called Monkton Hall;

but it is doubtful whether it belonged to the Priory: it has the marks of considerable antiquity, and has long been in the possession of the Owens of Orielton, which is in the parish of St. Nicholas.' Timmins describes Monkton Old Hall in detail in 1895, and suggests it may have been the 'hospitium or Prior's dwelling'.

Refs: Dwnn, i, p. 137; Fenton, *Tour Pembs.,* 1811, p. 206; Carlisle, *TDW,* 1811; *Pembs. Arch. Svy,* 1896-1907; Timmins, *Nooks Pembs.* 1895, pp. 61-63, illust.; Laws, *Little England,* 1888, pp. 119, 143, illust.; *Arch. Cam.,* 1880, pp. 248-252; ibid. 1881, pp. 86-7; ibid. 1977, p. 172; 'Carmarthenshire Studies', 1974, essay by Peter Smith, pp. 49, 85, figs; Peter Smith, *Houses of the Welsh Countryside,* 1975, pp. 22-30, plans and figures pp. 28-9, photos, plates 4 and 5; *RCAM Pembs.,* 1925, pp. 236-7.

MOOR, *Castlemartin*

Now a farmstead southeast of the church and marked on Colby's Map, The LT Pembs. 1786, gives Moor and Moor Hays farms, owned by John Campbell, Esq. with Thomas Edwardes, tenant. Fenton writes in 1811, 'Turn to the left (from Castlemartin church), to see Moor, one of the chief mansions of this district about two hundred years ago, of a very irregular form, with many ruinous and extensive outbuildings, once entered by a gateway now stopped up, leading to a porter's lodge. With very few exceptions, this may serve as a model of the style of building their houses among the greatest of that era in this country, which invariably appears to have been surrounded by a high court wall having a large arched gateway, and essentially differing from the form of the principal houses of the date, in the upper part of the country; where, notwithstanding the Norman encroachment, presumptuously called a conquest, as the strongest proof of their never having been subdued, the natives retained their language and the British fashions in everything continued evidently predominant.'

Nearly a century later, Timmins wrote in 1895, '. . . Moor Farm, where once stood a goodly mansion, of which scarce a stone has been spared.' In the 18th century it was the home of John Prout, (will proved 1780), whose daughter, Elizabeth married John Leach of Brownslade and had issue.

Refs: Fenton, *Tour Pembs.,* 1811, p. 223; Timmins, *Nooks Pembs.,* 1895, p. 91; LT 1786, Pembs.; Colby Map.

MOOR, *Walwyn's Castle*

Between the villages of Walwyn's Castle and Tiers Cross, on Colby's Map. Home of the family of Summers, descended from William Summers of Moor whose will was proved in 1713. Richard Bowlas of Llanstadwell, and others sold two farms and a ploughshare called Honeyhook Lambrough, in 1718, to John Summers of Moor in Walwyn's Castle parish, yeoman. In 1786-97 the owner of Moor was Mr. Thomas Bowlas. The Summers and Bowlas families intermarried and continued to own the property. In 1834 William Bowlas Summers lived at Moor until his death in 1836 and was the last of the family at Moor. His younger brother settled at Rosemoor in the same parish, which became the main seat of the Bowlas-Summers family.

Refs: NLW, Poyston Deeds; Pembs. RO, LT 1796.

MOOR, *Rosemarket*

In his will, dated 1696, Thomas Tasker of Moore, Rosemarket parish, gent. mentions 'my capital messuage called Moore' which had been settled in 1688 on the said William on his marriage to Katherine Roch. William died before 1699, and the widowed Katherine then married Philip Rice (who owned lands in the parishes of St. Dogmaels and Moylgrove), who then settled at Moor, *iure uxoris.* In 1712 Mary Tasker, spinster, granted to Sage Tasker, both of Moor, a lease for 21 years of a moiety of Moor in Rosemarket and a moiety of Clareston in Freystrop, at a rent of £15 p.a.

Refs: NLW, Eaton Evans and Williams Deeds, No. 43884; Tithe Map.

MORFIL, *Morfil*

Now a farmstead on the lower slopes of Mynydd Morfil, above Pontfaen in the Gwaun valley. The former mansion stood about 200 yards lower on the slope, due south of the parish church. Towards the end of the 18th century it became a ruin, and only a few mounds and stones remain to indicate the site. Across the vale is Mynydd Casfuwch, and through the vale runs Afon Anghof. From early times this area has been a land of hill farms, and the environment is still wholly unspoilt. Fenton wrote in 1811: 'Morville, memorable for the gallant stand the Welsh mountaineers made against the Norman usurper, as the portion of a younger son of Cilceithed, whose great-grandson, in compliment to a lowland lady of Castlemartin, whom he married, left his native highland, and there continued to settle, which . . . became at last, united to the vast estate of Orielton'.

During the Middle Ages, Morfil was a seat of noblemen descended from Gwynfardd Dyfed.

The first of the family to use the name Lloyd (Llwyd), was Ieuan Llwyd, son of David Ddu of Cilciffeth. The name was borne by twelve generations of his descendants who lived at Cilciffeth, Morfil, Pengegin, Cilglynen, and finally at Grove near Pembroke. The last in direct descent was Elizabeth Lloyd, daughter and heiress of Thomas Lloyd of Grove, who married in 1725 William Owen of Landshipping, who later became Sir William Owen, 4th Baronet of Orielton. In 1786 Morfil is recorded as the property of Lady Owen, with William Greenish as its tenant. It was a commodious house, and is described as of five hearths in 1670. The family produced several High Sheriffs: Thomas Lloyd of Cilciffith (son of Owen Lloyd of Morfil), in 1596 and 1613, and to mark the last occasion founded and endowed the Haverfordwest Grammar School which lasted to our own times; Thomas Lloyd of Grove in 1700, and his son Thomas Lloyd in 1709. The Lloyd arms were *azure* a lion rampant *gules* within an orle of roses *or.* After the gentry ceased to live at Morfil, it was let to farming tenants, William Lewis, yeoman, in 1750, and in 1834-40 William Williams was tenant of Morfil (then 528 acres).

Refs: Francis Jones, 'Lloyd of Cilciffeth', *Pembs. Historian,* 1873, pp. 30-62; Fenton, *Tour Pembs.,* 1811, p. 312; *Dwnn,* i, pp. 167-8; Pembs. RO, LT 1786; NLW, Slebech Deeds, Orielton Deeds.

MORGANS,

Now in Williamston East, but formerly in Begelly

Earlier deeds describe Morgans as being in the parish of Begelly. From 1291 Williamston East was a chapelry of the rectory of Begelly, and in the 19th century formed into a parish.

Morgans, formerly home of yeomen and minor gentry, is now a farm. In the 17th century, a pedigree shows Thomas Adams of Morgans and his wife Joan, daughter of Stephen Barlow of Arnolds Hill. In 1653, Thomas Adams of Morgans was a freeholder of the manor of Redberth, on the northwest of Williamston East (Colby Map 1831). In 1670 Thomas Adams of Begelly parish was assessed at three hearths. In 1676/7 Thomas Adams the elder of Morgans in Begelly, gent. Katherine his wife, and Thomas Adams their son and heir were living there. In 1762 John Williams of Morgans, Esq. J.P., was a Grand Juror, and in 1769 a Land Tax Commissioner for the county, and was still living there in 1786. John Adams of Loveston St. Twynells (a cadet of Paterchurch), was living in 1591, and had two sons – Thomas Adams of Loveston, (will proved 1627), and John Adams of Morgans in Begelly.

Refs: RCAM Pembs., 1925; WWHR, I, p. 241, IV, p. 245; Lewis, *TDW,* 1840; Picton Castle Deeds; Pembs. RO LT 1786; NLW, Pembs. GF 1762, 1772; Tucker MS (peds.).

MORGENAU, *Cilgerran*

This place is named after a brook called The Morgeney but it was formerly known as Rhosygilwen. In 1904 John Colby of Ffynonne sold Rhosygilwen, Penalltfedw, Cilast Fields and Cnwegyrn, in all about 200 acres, for £8,000 to Charles Evans Davies Morgan-Richardson, J.P., a solicitor. When he occupied the property he re-named it Morgenau.

Morgan-Richardson was the author of the novel *Henry Vaughan, a Story of Pembrokeshire.* He died on 28 September 1913 aged 56. His son and heir Charles Lethbridge Ernest Morgan-Richardson (b. 1888), succeeded to the property and lived there until his death in 1961, apart from 1914-18 when it was let to tenants. After his death the house and contents were sold.

Refs: South Wales, Historical Biographical Pictorial, c. 1908, photo; *Contemporary Biographies of S. Wales and Mon.,* 1907, photo of house p. 154.

MOUNTON, *Mounton**

The surname Callen or Callan is probably English and its appearance in south Pembrokeshire suggests that the first of the family came with, or in the wake of the Norman and English occupiers of that district. However as the name first occurs in the late Middle Ages, it is probable that the Callens came as traders or farmers. The area of their settlement was in the parishes of St. Florence, Mounton and latterly Narberth.

In 1424 a rental of lands in the lordship of St. Florence was compiled at Pembroke and among the entries is the name of David Vawre who held a messuage and 22 acres which had been lately held by Richard Callan at a yearly rent of 20s. 8d. Over a century passes by before we again meet with the name.

In 1532/3 a rental of Newhouse alias Newton, shows that Owen Callen, a free tenant of that manor paid a yearly assize rent of 8s. and rendered one and a half days for the duties of reaping and harrowing. In the Petty Jury lists for the Great Sessions held for Pembrokeshire in 1586 and 1613, we find the names of John Callen and William Callen respectively, both of the parish of Mounton, south of Narberth.

In 1670 Thomas Callen was assessed at two hearths and he was probably the man mentioned in the prenuptial settlement made between John Callen, heir of Thomas Callen and Mary his wife of Mounton and Jane, the second daughter of John Beynon of Llether Gloyne in the parish of 'Llampeter Welfrey', yeoman. Later in the same year the family sold the capital messuage of Mounton for £80.

On 24 June 1741 William Callen of Mounton, gent. granted a lease to the Rev. Nathaniel Rowlands of Llangeitho, the Rev. Peter Williams of Carmarthen, Evan Lewis of Pentlepoir and others, of a chapel commonly called and known as 'Mounton Chappel', mineral rights excepted for the lives of Marychurch Callen son of the lessor, Anne wife of William Callen, another son of the lessor, and John Callen, son of the last named William Callen and grandson of lessor. The rent was £2 yearly, and the lessees were to pay all taxes, rates and repairs and maintain the chapel. The name Marychurch Callen suggests that there had been intermarriage with the ancient family of Marychurch of Norchard, Llawhaden and Haverfordwest where they were glovers and mercers. William Callen, born about 1723, married before 1746, a wealthy wife namely Anne daughter of John Poyer of Grove. She became the ultimate heiress of the Poyers. They settled, after 1765, at Merrixton, in Amroth parish. William died at Merrixton on 10 January 1793. In his will, after settling his realty, he left one guinea each to his family to buy mourning rings. His widow died aged 79 in 1808 leaving all her real estates to her eldest son for life, and afterwards to her second son and his issue male and female.

The eldest son, John, born about 1746 died unmarried and intestate in 1822. There is a monument to his memory in Mounton church. The younger son, Charles, born about 1764 lived at Loveston before he inherited the Grove estate on his elder brother's death in 1822. He married Eliza Ormond of Amroth in 1792 and died in 1824 leaving six children; John who died unmarried at Merrixston aged 31 in 1824; Charles entered the army and was a captain in the 71st Highlanders. He lived at Underdown and married Anne Mansel but had no issue. The third son, Daniel Poyer Callen succeeded to Grove and Molleston. He married firstly in 1830 Caroline Bell Webb-Bowen of Camrose and had three children. He married secondly at Wiston, his servant maid, Elizabeth Lloyd, an event not greeted with acclamation by his kinsfolk. He died intestate on 28 December 1849 aged 42. His younger brother Richard died unmarried in 1832; the daughters of Charles and Eliza Callen were Eliza who married John Lewis of Henllan and Anne who died aged 20 at Bath in 1823.

The three children of Daniel Callen and Caroline were; John, educated at Rugby, and entered the 71st Highlanders. He lived at Grove and was a J.P. for Pembrokeshire. He died unmarried; Anne Eliza who inherited Camrose from her maternal uncle, married in 1853, Lewis William Penn, R.A. later a colonel and a C.B. The third child was Katherine who married her first cousin, John Lennox Griffith

Poyer Lewis of Henllan, barrister-at-Law. They had no issue.

Refs: Francis Jones unpublished article 'The Callens of Mounton'.

MULLOCK, *St. Ishmaels*

A farmstead to the west of Butter Hill mansion. The earliest known reference to it is in 1234-42 when the name is spelled Milnhochdich, and in 1295 as Mulhok. In the late 16th century it was the home of George Jenkins, (2nd son of Philip Jenkin of Roch parish), living in 1551-99. In 1610, Sir Walker Rice of Carms, mortgaged a messuage called Lytle Mullock (in tenure of Henry Browne) in £14 10s. to George Jenkins of Great Mullock, gent. George signed his pedigree for Dwnn in 1613, and was followed at Mullock by his son Philip Jenkins gent. who was there in 1623.

In 1660, Adam Hawkin held the lease of Great and Little Mullock at £33 p.a., and John Davies, miller, held the lease of Mullock Mill at £17 p.a. In the 18th century it formed part of the Stackpole Court estate, and in 1767, the Hon. Pryse Campbell granted to Gilbert Davies of St. Ishmaels parish, yeoman, a lease for three lives, of Great and Little Mullock, Sivershill, and Mullock water grist mill, all in St. Ishmaels Parish.

In 1786 Mullock was owned by John Campbell, Esq. with Mr. Harry Davies, tenant, with the same owner (then Lord Cawdor), in 1797, with Cornelius Davies, tenant. In 1802 the property was advertised for sale by Lord Cawdor, described as Mullock Farm, (254 acres) 'with a convenient dwelling-House, well fitted up suitable for a gentleman farmer, into offices, farmyard, and proper outbuildings', in possession of Henry Davies, aged 39, on lease for his life, at a yearly rent of £60. It was bought by William Bonsfield, Tooley Street, London for £4,050.

On 6 September 1813 John Dedwith of Jordanston parish, Dewsland, farmer, 2. John Dedwith Gibbs, 3. Henry Davies of Mullock, and 4. John Philipps Laugharne of Orlandon, assigned a term of years of Southfield and Thornhill, in St. Ishmaels, and on the same date the said properties were conveyed and surrendered to the said Henry Davies and his trustee the Rev. James Summers, cleric, of Haverfordwest.

The first of the Davies (Davis) family at Mullock, was Henry Davis, who was followed by his son, Henry, born c. 1760. The second Henry Davis of Mullock was High Sheriff in 1819, and died on 16 May 1825, and was buried at St. Ishmaels. His eldest son was Thomas Henry Davis, who was followed by his brother Gilbert William Warren Davis, High Sheriff in 1839, J.P., who built a new mansion at Trewarren, and about 1842 went to live there. He died in 1886.

Fenton records a local tradition regarding Mullock Bridge 'under the arch of which the gallant Sir Rhys ap Thomas, in order to fulfil an old prophecy importing that Henry (VII) must go to the crown over this illustrious Welshman's back, condescended to crouch (for it is very low), that his future sovereign might have the full benefit of the prediction'. A sketch of the bridge was made by Timmins in 1895.

Refs: Fenton, *Tour Pembs.*, 181, p. 96; Timmins, *Nooks Pembs.*, 1895, p. 120; B. G. Charles, *NCPN*, 1938, p. 76; Pembs. RO Deed 1, Nos 22-3, 38; LT 1786; NLW, Calendar of Dynevor Documents, 1610.

MUSSELWICK,
also called **MUSLICK,** *Marloes*

A farmstead to the north of Marloes village, and overlooking Musselwick Bay. Marked on the maps of George Owen (1603) as Muselwick (Marloes); Kitchin (1763) as Moselywick, (Marloes), and on Colby's (1831) as Muslewick, (St. Ishmaels), on the coast looking towards Dale.

Although there are several references to the property in medieval times, there is insufficient information to enable a pedigree of the owners to be made. More such evidence occurs from the 17th century onwards. The first known family there was that of Moore. John Moore was there around 1650, and was followed by his son Francis Moore who was living there in 1670. In 1714 he was a Parliamentary voter, and died about 1744 when his will was proved. Francis's son, John Moore, gent. married in 1744, Anne Bowen of Glanduad, Nevern. He was the last in the male line of his family, and was survived by three co-heiress daughters. The eldest, Alice Moore married Phillip Powell, gent., who then settled at Musselwick, where he died some time after 1793, and the widowed Alice died at Kidwelly, Carms. in September 1828 in her 82nd year. The second sister Anne Moore was unmarried, and went to live in Haverfordwest; the third sister, Elizabeth Moore, married before 1771, the Revd. William Rees, clerk, of Newgale in Brawdy, where he died without issue in 1781, and Elizabeth in 1793. Musselwick, which was mortgaged, became part of the estate of the Philipps Laugharne family of Orlandon, later of St. Brides mansion, and Musselwick was leased to a series of gentlemen farmers – Morse (1802), Bowen (1834) and Scale from 1842 when the owner was Charles Allen William Philipps, with John Scale as tenant. At that time 'Muslick' comprised 236 acres and three of the fields bore the names Beacon Park, Brawdy Park and Church Park.

In 1920 the St. Brides estate was advertised for sale and Musselwick is described as a farm of 225 acres held by George Scale on a 21 years lease granted in 1914; the farmhouse was built of stone, and slated, with five bedrooms, three sitting rooms, kitchen, scullery, dairy, a garden and farm outbuildings. The Scale family continued at Musselwick, and in 1950 the following were living there, Colin Scale, Hugh, Kenneth, William and Mary J. Scale.

Refs: NLW, Poyston Deeds, J28; Pembs. Plea Rolls No. 2884; Pembs. RO, LT 1786-1802, Deeds HDX 194, Nos. 1-3; VL 1950.

MYNYDDMELYN, *Llanychllwydog*

Home of the Bateman family, a cadet of the Batemans of Honeyborough.

Philip Bateman of Honeyborough married Jane, daughter of Sir John Wogan; their son, also John married Jane, daughter of John ap David of Llystyn. Their son, owned lands in Trenewydd in 1586/7 and married Ann daughter of John ap David of Fishguard. They had an extensive family of ten. Thomas the heir, viv. 1591, will proved 1610, married Anne daughter and heiress of Rhys ap Ieuan and they had two sons, John and Lewys both viv 1591 when John Bateman signed his pedigree for Dwnn, paying him 3s. Their arms were *argent* three escallops *sable*. The family were also at Trellwyn and Trenewydd in Llanllawer.

There was a grant on 1 September 1582 from 'George Owen of Henllys gent. to John Bateman of the parish of Llanychllwydog and Owen ap Ieuan Jenkin of the parish of Llanychllwydog, gentlemen, for 20 marks of the wardship of Annes verch Rees and Elizabeth verch Rees, daughters of Rees ap Ieuan Jenkin late of the parish of Llanychllwydog, gent. deceased, together with the mansion or capital tenet wherein said Rees lived called Klyn venog in parish of Llanychllwydog, and lands belonging, a water corn mill on the said tenet, a tenet at Trellan, a tenet at Penmonyth mawr, a tenet near Holmws in Newport parish, all of which David Rees ap Ieuan ap Jenkin held of George Owens's barony of Kemes by knight's service. The said John Bateman and Owen ap Ieuan Jenkin were natural uncles of the said infants, and tutors appointed by the will of the said Rees ap Ieuan Jenkins over them'. Owen ap Ieuan Jenkins married Agnes to Thomas Bateman, son and heir of John Bateman who 'now enjoys all the lands in right of said Agnes'. Agnes's sister, Elizabeth, died a spinster and her share of the lands passed to Agnes. Thomas Bateman had two sons, David, who married a sister of Thomas Williams of Haverfordwest; her mother was Elen Tucker; and Eynon Bateman who married Ursula, a daughter of Jenkin Lewis of Castell Moel. Eynon Bateman was assessed for three hearths in 1670.

In 1786 Thomas Nicholas was listed as owner-occupier. Later the families of George and Evans were associated with the property.

Refs: Dwnn, i, p. 173; GGMS Gwynfardd; Protheroe XII (GWG) fo. 55; LT 1786; Bronwydd Deeds No. 1298; Pembs. GF; Landowners Return 1873; GGMS *Adv. Pem.* I, p. 28.

NANTYBUGAIL, *Llanfairnantygof*
Formerly a substantial farmstead, about half a mile west of Trecwn hamlet. Belonged to the estate of Trecwn, and was leased to yeomen and minor gentry families. In the second half of the 16th century it was owned by the Jones (or Johns) squires of Trecwn, and later the estate passed to the Vaughans (through a distaff descent), and from them to the Foster Barhams who held the estate till 1933 when Captain C. H. S. Barham and his only son and heir were tragically killed in a road accident near Coventry. Trecwn was afterwards bought by the Admiralty. Nantybugail is included in the Trecwn rentals in the 19th century, but does not appear in the estate sale catalogue in 1939. Among the earliest folk at Nantybugail was the yeoman family of Cynfrig who were there in 1595. In 1663 Thomas Owen Esq. of Trecwn granted a lease for 99 years of Nantybugail and Cnwc y Berllan to John Lewis the elder, of Nantybugail.

The Lewis family came from Henllan Owen near Eglwyswrw, and were descended from the ancient owners of Pentre Evan. John Lewis the elder was the first to settle at Nantybugail, and after his death in 1664, was followed by his son and heir, John Lewis the younger, gent. a solicitor, who played an active part in local life, and was coroner for the county for several years. In 1666 a lease of the farms of Nantybugail and 'Trevorvoll' was granted to John Lewis and his wife Diana (née Lloyd of Morfil), who had bought the Manorowen estate near Fishguard, and about 1670-80 left Nantybugail and settled at Manorowen. He became a J.P. and was Mayor of Fishguard on ten occasions. He died leaving six daughters, one of whom became grandmother of the well known historian Richard Fenton of Glyn y Mêl. In 1739 the leaseholder was Robert Thomas, yeoman, in 1786 James David, in 1859 William Symmons. After this, very few references are found to Nantybugail.

Refs: NLW, Bronwydd Deeds, Coleman Deeds, Poyston Deeds, Vairdre Book, *Extent of Cemais,* Pembs. Papers of GS, NLW MS 1390D; Pembs. RO, LT 1786, VL.

NANTYLLADRON, *Clydey*
The name Nantylladron has not been found in post 17th century records. In more modern times appears the farm of Nant-y-lledfron, one and a half miles north of Clydey church, and half a mile west of Dugred-isaf. It is likely that Nant-y-lledfron represents the earlier name. The will of Griffith ap Evan ap Howell, of Clydey parish dated 22 July 1555, mentions 'my son and executor Morris Griffith, and my daughters Elizabeth verch Griffith, and Margaret verch Griffith, and the tenement where I now dwell called Place Nantylladron'. A pedigree in the GGMS of Morris ap Griffith ap Ieuan ap Ieuan ap Howel ap Einon of Rhosychen, Carms, descended from Cadifor Fawr, was followed by his son James who was father of David and Abel James of Werngoy in Clydey; this David was followed by his son Morris of Nantylladron in Clydey. James Morris of Nantylladron married Elizabeth daughter of David Parry of Noyadd Trefawr. Morris James of Nantylladron had five sons, one of whom, Thomas Morris was, assessed at four hearths in 1670. The Land Tax for 1786 shows Nantylladron owned by Thomas Colby Esq. and John Jones M.D., with John Mathias as tenant. Nant Lledfron is included on Colby's Map in 1831, and is spelled thus in Voters' Lists for 1894 and 1904.

Refs: Carms. RO, GGMSS (Cadifor Fawr and Gwyddro); *Dwnn,* i, p. 217; Pembs. RO, LT 1786; Francis Jones, *Historic Carmarthenshire Homes and their Families, & Historic Homes of Cardiganshire and their Families.*

NARBERTH – PLÂS, *Narberth*
The former residence stood on rising ground just above the parish church, within a bow shot of the medieval castle at the southern entrance to the town. It was occupied, (perhaps built during Elizabethan days), by John Vaughan a member of the Vaughan family of Pembrey (Carms.), descended from the Breconshire chieftain, Moreiddig Warwyn. John Vaughan died in 1580/1 leaving six daughters, coheiresses. His daughter Jane received the mansion as part of her share, and married John Elliot of Earweare (Amroth) who settled at his wife's home which remained in possession of

their descendants until the latter half of the 18th century when the estate passed to the Meares family. In legal documents the property is variously called Narberth Place, Narberth Place House, Narberth House and also as Place and Plâs.

In its heyday it had been commodious, and in the Hearth Tax List of 1670, it contained six hearths. The division of the demesne into holdings had been made in the first half of the 18th century. In the prenuptial settlement, dated 1743, of the last owner, Alexander Elliot and his wife-to-be, Jane Barlow of Lawrenny, the names are rendered as 'Narberth Place House'. Alexander died in 1755, without issue, and the widowed Jane moved to Haverfordwest.

The next owners, the Meares, did not come there to live, and let the mansion and land to local tenants. In 1786 William Meares was the owner and the tenants were Gregory Gale, John Roberts, John Evan and Thomas Thomas.

The present Plâs, as it is now called, is a two-storeyed, L-shaped farmhouse, with a projection from the front, at the northern end, while the rear wall, clearly part of the old mansion, contains the remains of a large decorated window in freestone, together with some Elizabethan corbelling. A ground plan of the Plâs made in 1871, includes an extension to the rear of the house, but this has been removed subsequently. In that plan, the property, described as 'the Plâs Demesne (49 acres)' was advertised for sale, and the tenant then was Mrs. Francis Lewis, at a yearly rent of £105. The estate then comprised the 'excellent dwelling house and offices, Lower Hays, Orchard Park, Hop Yard, Moor, Western Hills and a cottage by the toll gate tenanted by Jason Williams at £4 4s. per annum'.

An antiquary recorded his impressions of the house in 1889-91, as follows. 'An ordinary dwelling house now occupies its site, but a portion of one old wall seems to have been incorporated in the existing house. A small bit of massive masonry and portions of a mullioned window in freestone at the back of the house on the garden side remain to attest the fact that the Plâs was once a mansion of considerable strength and beauty . . . The last of the Miss Elliots did a very good thing for Narberth by making over to the town for ever, a large piece of common, on the edge of which the Board schools are built, on the side of the Haverfordwest road. I think it is commonly called Town Moor'.

The Pembrokeshire Archaeological Society (1896-1907) marked the site of the original mansion in a field to the north of Plâs farm, adding 'Here stood the house of the Elliots: there are only the faintest traces of the house to be seen'. However when I examined the alleged 'site' in 1974 I was unable to discover any trace of a previous building, and neither had the occupier of the land ever heard of any tradition relating to it.

Ref: Dwnn, i, pp. 122, 204; Picton Castle Deeds; NLW, Slebech Deeds; *Carms. Notes* 1889-91, p. 21; *Pembs. Arch. Svy,* 1896-1907; Pembs. RO, LT 1786, Deeds, Sale Cat. 1871; Francis Jones, *Historic Carmarthenshire Homes and their Families.*

NASH, Great, *Llangwm*

Marked on the Colby's Map of 1831 are Great Nash near a crossroads about one mile west of Llangwm village, and about a mile west of Great Nash is Little Nash, and about half a mile south of Great Nash is Nash Mill on the banks of a stream. According to Dr. Charles who quotes numerous examples of the name between the years 1324 and 1566, the name is derived from 'cotton ash'. The mansion house, Great Nash eventually became an uninhabited ruin. RCAM Pembs. 1925, p.136 states that a few fragments, including a vaulted cellar of the original mansion, can be traced immediately behind the present building now a large farmhouse probably built in the 17th century; in the farmyard is a 16th century dovecote about 20 feet high.

Great Nash was the residence of four wealthy landowning families. The first was that of Nash, the surname being probably derived from the property. The Nash family lived there in the 15th and the early 16th century. Arnold Nash was followed by his son Richard, and he by another Richard who was the father of the daughter and heiress Jane Nash. She married Alban Philipps third son of Morgan Philipps of Picton Castle. Alban settled at his wife's home, and their son and heir, named Alban after his father, was living at Great Nash in 1648, and he married Dorothy Laugharne. The next owners of the property was the family of Corbett descended from a Merionethshire squire.

Thomas Corbett, one of ten children of Robert and Bridget Corbett of Ynys y maengwyn Mer., and his wife Dorothy, daughter of William Laugharne, were living at Great Nash in 1670, the house being then assessed at six hearths, so that it was then a commodious dwelling. He was followed by his son, Erasmus Corbett who, in 1681, married Anne Mathias of Llangwarran, and had three daughters and co-heiresses, the eldest of whom, Dorothy Corbett succeeded to Great Nash. She married Charles Owen, son of Sir Hugh Owen of Orielton, and both were living at Great Nash in 1704, and were followed there by their son and heir Wyrriott Owen who married his cousin Ann Barlow of Lawrenny Hall whose surname he adopted in lieu of Owen. The said Wyrriott Owen (died 1773) had four sons and one daughter. The eldest son, Charles Owen died without issue in 1757, and was succeeded by his next brother Hugh Owen who owned Great Nash in 1786, and died without issue in 1809.

An interesting lease between Sir Richard Walter, knight of Shenfield, Essex and Charles Owen of Great Nash dated 2 May 1704 details the 'lease of free liberty of driftway 18 feet wide for all carts, wagons, with cattle to drive, lead and carry all and all manner of coale, culm, lime, and other goods: from the Pitt Parke to Mooreshead and thence to Black Tarr Rock, and the liberty to use a limekiln at the east end on a field called South Knap, and the liberty to load and unload ships at Black Tarr Rock, for 21 years, in exchange for a lease of parcels and lands in Llangwm'. The prenuptial settlement of Wyrriott Owen and Anne Barlow details the settlement of the following properties to the use of the marriage: 'Pencarnan, Clegr, Hendre, Trelerior, Clegermoya, Trevaithan, Treluid, Upper and Lower Treginnis, Tresissil, Trehale, Clynfoone, Longhturfield, Olmarch, Rosewig Williamston [Trewilym] in parishes St. Edrins, Mathry, Llanhowel and St. Lawrence: Northnap and The Hall, other messuages and land and a moiety of the water corn mill called Langum Mill in Guilford in Burton: a quarter part of messuage and land called Williamston and Barnlake and other messuages and land in Burton, a messuage and garden in Key Street, parish of St. Margaret Haverfordwest: a messuage and curtillege in Sheep Street in parish St. Thomas, Haverfordwest'. The whole totalled 30 messuages, 3 dovecots and 2,430 acres in the above parishes.

In 1811 Ann Barlow of Lawrenny Hall granted a lease of Great Nash to Thomas George for the lives of his three daughters, Elizabeth, Anne and Cecilia. It was at this stage in the house's history that Richard Fenton commented: 'Less than a mile from the village is the mansion house of Nash, now unroofed and in ruins and perfectly denuded, its woods having been recently cut down. The house, of the most fashionable form of mansions in this county of its date, a sort of cube, was large and habitable within these few years, as it was meant to have been fitted up for his residence by my friend Mr. Wyrriott Owen, the late worthy possessor . . . what this place was at first called I cannot learn but it took the name of Nash from a family of that name, Advenæ, who came into possession of it about two centuries since. It after came to the Corbets, then to the Owens, and now belongs to Hugh Barlow, Esq. the legal representative of the late proprietor.'

Refs: Dwnn, i, 202; WWHR, ii, pp. 36, 62; Fenton, *Tour Pembs.,* 1811, pp. 134-5; GGMS Adv. Carm. fo. 226; Chetham MS, No. 102; Pembs. RO, Deeds; B. G. Charles, *NCPN,* 1938.

NASH, LOWER, *Nash*

Origin of name as in above entry. A small parish situated between Upton and Pembroke town. The main properties were Lower Nash alongside the parish church, and Upper Nash in the east part of the parish: in 1363 the former was called Nether Ash, the latter Over Nash. In 1526 they appear as 'Lower and Upper Asshe'; and in 1607 as Over and Nether Nash, then owned by Henry Bowen of Upton Castle. From the later part of the 16th century the names appear consistently as Nash. The most important property was Lower Nash, today a large farmhouse retaining architectural features of the Tudor period. In 1670 it was assessed at three hearths, the occupier being William Davies, Esq. J.P., a member of the ancient family of Davies of Cwm, (Carms.) who traced to Rhys Chwith, Esquire of the Body to King Edward I. His son, Thomas Davies was a Grand Juror in 1731, and High Sheriff of Pembrokeshire in 1737. He died on 27 April 1741 in his 71st year; his wife was Jane, daughter of David Gwynn of Pentre, Llangathen, Carms. A memorial tablet to Thomas Davies in Nash Church, is engraved with the family arms: *argent* a chevron between three bulls heads caboshed *sable.*

The Davies' were probably leaseholders, for Lower Nash continued to form part of the Upton Castle estate. In the latter half of the 18th century, Upton was divided between four daughters and co-heiresses, and parts of the estate were sold. In 1786 Henry Leach owned Lower Nash, with John Roch as tenant, while Upper Nash was owned by the Rev. William Holcombe. The will of Mary Roch of 'Lower Nash Farm' was dated 17 October 1800 and she mentions 'my brother John Roch of Lower Nash'. In 1840, Lower Nash (then 178 acres), was owned by Abraham Leach, Esq. with Richard Llewelin as tenant.

In 1974 the house was renovated by the new owner, Mr. Eddie Gibby, O.B.E, J.P., D.L., who lived there till his death in 1984. An interesting piece of vernacular architecture is a stone staircase, rising from alongside a fireplace, leading to the upper storey. The building is in excellent state and the home of Mrs. Sheila Gibby in 1986.

Refs: Pembs. RO, Deeds, LT 1786; NLW, Tithe Map 1840; B. G. Charles, *NCPN,* 1938; Peter Smith, *Houses of the Welsh Countryside,* 1975, p. 473, and map, No. 33; Francis Jones, 'Cwm (Coomb)', *in Carm. Historian,* 1970; Francis Jones, *Historic Carmerthenshire Houses and their Families.*

NEESTON, *Herbrandston*

Home of the families of Davies and Bowen (Cadet of Upton Castle). Sadly this historic house was demolished by the Esso Oil Company who owned the land upon which it stood.

The Rev. William Davies. LL.B., parson of Narberth, was father of Griffith Davies of Neeston who died in 1606, his property being described as 'the Great House in the South part of Neeston'. Griffith's granddaughter and heiress, Joan, married in 1635 Henry Bowen; Neeston passed to the Bowens and by descent to the Jordans.

Barrett Bowen Jordan, of Neeston, son of James Jordan and Jane Bowen of Haverfordwest, had five daughters and co-heiresses by his wife Martha, daughter of John Adams of Whitland, whom he married in 1773. Martha, the third daughter, married in 1803 the Rev. William Wilson, of Knowle Hall, Warwickshire. Wilson's mother was a daughter of the Rev. William Harris of Bryn Hyfryd. The Wilsons, thereafter, quartered Bowen of Neeston in their arms: *gules* a lion rampant within an orle of cross crosslets fitchee *or.* The Wilson family is recorded in Burke's *Landed Gentry* for 1875.

Barrett Bowen Jordan became heavily in debt, and fled the country. In 1784 he is described as 'late of Neeston' and 'resident of Ghent in Flanders'. Yet two years later he is still recorded as owning Neeston and was assessed for Land Tax. He died aged 53 in 1802 and is buried at St. Thomas, Haverfordwest. By 1805 the owner was recorded as Thomas Philipps Esq. eldest son and heir of the Rev. Edward Philipps of Lampeter.

Refs: WWHR, ii, p. 42; Pembs. Plea Rolls No. 175; Pembs. RO DB/13 No 118; NLW 1362B; ibid. 12357 (Alwyn); GGMS (Urien Rheged fo. 18); Burke, *LG,* 1850 SN; ibid. 1850, Vol. 2, p. 1608.

NETHERWOOD, *St. Issells*
A square house of two storeys with a verandah at one side. It figures in *Photographs in South Wales*, 1871.

Once the home of the Stokes family it belonged to a Mrs. Vickerman in 1852 and later became the home of General Sir George Richards Greaves, G.C.B., K.C.M.G. (b. 1831). The General served at Peshawar during the Indian Mutiny, was Chief of Staff in the Ashantee Expedition and was Chief of Staff in Cyprus 1878/79.

Netherwood later became a school.

Nevern Cross

NEVERN, *Nevern*
Site unidentified, but it is known that the mansion stood near the parish church at the edge of the village. The Nevern estate was owned by a family descended from Gwynfardd Dyfed. In 1442 Howel ap Jenkin the elder and his wife were living at Nevern. He was followed by his son Jenkin ap Howel who took an active part in the Civil War on the Yorkist side, and was slain at Banbury in 1469.

The estate passed to his son, Howel ap Jenkin the younger, who was living there in the years 1470-91.

George Owen of Henllys was at the townred of Nevern in 1603/4, and wrote 'Here was the mansion house of Howell ap Jenkin ap Roppert, the younger, the greatest man of lyving in his tyme in all the countrie, and now his heires growen to that povertie that they are scarse knowen who they are, if any be lyvinge. The said Howel ap Jenkin the younger built a fayre house, but died before the same was fynished . . . He had yssue a sonne named William who consumed the whole inheritaunce, and it is said that Howell ap Jenkin the father, being a learned man, died at the birth of his son William, cast at his nativities, whereby he pesentlied toued his wieffe that she had borne a sonne that should consume and spende all that he and his auncestors had gathered; and thereupon, as it is reported, the said Howell ap Jenkin determyninge to prevent fate, made somme estate of his landes, such as he thought his sonne might not sell the same, and did especiallie repose trust in one Morgan Taylor, a meane and base fellowe mantayned by his almes, and was parishe clerke and wholilie fedd and releeved by the said Howell ap Jenkin, and therefore so much tyed to the said Howell ap Jenkin, that he thought noane might be better trusted than he. After the death of the said Howell ap Jenkin, his sonne William fullfilled his foreseen fotrune and left not one foote of landes unsould, and the said Morgan Taylor do joine in sale of the landes, and this maketh many to muse at this daie to see these ffeoffmentes made by them both, yet well knowen to be Howell ap Jenkin's landes, this being the onelie cause, so that to prevent the determyned will of God no worldlie pollicie can prevaile, and who so trusted base mynded people shalbe served of them in their kynde . . . ' *(2nd book,* c.1603-4, pp. 273-276).

It seems that the ruins of the old mansion were still to be seen in 1811 when Fenton mentions among trees near Nevern village are 'the ruins of a venerable old mansion . . . belonging to and begun to be built by Howel ap Jenkin ap Roppert, of the princely stock of Gwynvardd Dyfed, and a man then of the greatest property and command in the country, but who died before it was finished . . . his one son William, who by a most profligatt course of life, dissipated his vast inheritance'. The profligate William married Elen Fychan daughter of Thomas Howel ap Owen Fychan of Argoed in Nevern parish by whom he had three children – Owen, (blind), and Lewis both died unmarried, and Jane who married firstly, Owen nephew of the vicar of Nevern, and secondly, William James. By the first Jane had a daughter Llewen who married twice, and by the second, Owen William, who sold relics of the Nevern estate, Cwmeog and Trefaes to William Owen of Henllys, (father of George Owen). And so the line of the Nevern family was extinct by 1600.

Several bards addressed odes to members of the family. Hywel Surdwal mentions going to the church of Nevern and the mansion nearby: Rhys Nanmor mentions the mansion as being near the river; and Lewis Glyn Cothi who says he looks forward to his meal at Nevern. But one of the family, Howel ap Jenkin ap Robert, seemingly gave short shrift to the bards as shown by his *englyn*:

Gan Howel gythrel gidag ethrod – gwrdh
Fe gae gerddor gernod,
Gan ei dad, gleisiad ai glod
caid nobol o ai adnabod.

The Squires of Nevern bore the arms of Gwynfardd: *azure* a lion rampant within orle of roses *or.*

Refs: NLW, Bronwydd Deeds, Llanstephan MS 38B; BM, Egerton MS 2586; P.RO, AD D, No. 827; Chetham MS, ped. No. 11; Carms. RO, GGMS Gwynfardd.

NEVERN CASTLE (Castell Nanhyfer), *Nevern*

In 1181 Giraldus commented: 'the ancient and chief castle which the princes of Wales possessed in this part of the country was *Ceastrum de Lanhever,* where still remain the ruins of a very strong hold surrounded on three sides by a very deep moat, evidently cut out at a vast expenditure of labour, which even to this day contains water'. About 1603/4 George Owen of Henllys wrote, 'Nevarne Castle, now utterlie defased, yet doth the seat thereof shewe of what strength yt was in tymes past, being seated on a hieghe hill unacessable on the one parte, and strengthened with a meightie dytck hewen out of the mayne rocke of the other partes, this was the cheiffe house of the lordes of Kemes in the tyme of the lord Rees . . . and this is that same Castle called Castle Llanhyver . . . which castle of Llanhyver, being see thence utterlie decased and rased, so known but of a few'.

Refs: George Owen, *2nd Book,* p. 276; *Arch. Cam.* 1859, p. 334; *Anc. Mon. Pembs.,* 1925, p. 260; Laws, *Little England,* 1888, p. 97.

NEW HOUSE, *(formerly called* **Red Castle**), *Newton North*

Mudge's Map 1819 and Colby's Map 1831 locate New House on the southern edge of Canaston Wood, and marked as Redcastell on Dineley's Map 1684, and as Redcastle on Speed's Map 1611. Richard Fenton, having left the village of Minwear says 'Hence I pass over a new road carried through very beautiful woods to the ruins of a once very consequential mansion called New House . . . It is a large pile of excellent masonry, seems to have been moated, and one of the earliest habitations of the uncastellated form. In some writings, I have seen it briefly noted that New House was formerly called Red Castle . . . '; he suggests that it may have been the residence of the Canaston family, and afterwards became part of the Barlow of Slebech estate, (*Tour Pembs.* 1811, pp. 164-168).

There are several references to the manor of Newhouse in the 16th and 17th century deeds of the Barlows. In 1657, John Barlow Esq. leased to his fifth son, Lewis Barlow, 'a messuage called New House formerly called Redd Castle, in Newton parish' for 99 years.

During 1896-1907 the following description of New House ruins was made: 'The basement is 15 yards by 10 yards: there is a fire-place to the east of the stairs on the south-west side; a window on the west, three windows on the north, a door and loophole to the south: the hall had two chimneys on the east, two windows on the south; stairway on the south-west, and three more windows; a part of the building at the east end is cut off by a dividing wall which seems to be of later work: on the east of the basement is a door in a ruined wall, two windows; the wall at the east is gone. A moat encompasses the building.' A more professional description was made by the Commissioners of Ancient Monuments in June 1920; 'Castell Coch. About 250 yards north-west of the modern farmstead called Newhouse is a perfect example of the country gentry's residence of the 13th-15th centuries . . . The moat at Castell Coch, which is an almost exact square of 270 feet, is aligned to the cardinal points . . . within the square area was built a residence, now a complete ruin, which was succeeded by the Newhouse already mentioned. This was followed, probably in the days of Elizabeth, by a small mansion, which, with many later alterations and additions, can still be traced on a plan executed in 1912, on the occasion of the clearance of the site by the county Ancient Monuments Society. The building then consisted of a large hall (43½ feet by 25 feet internally), and kitchen. The former was of two storeys above the ground floor, the latter of only one. In the north-eastern corner of the hall was a flight of circular stairs. The main entrance was in the centre of the north front, but the smaller room had a separate entrance from the west. The great fireplace was in the partition wall between the hall and the kitchen. The withdrawing rooms were on the first floor above the hall . . . As the necessity for complete isolation gradually ceased, the mode of entrance and exit was improved, and a roadway made across the moat. To the south-east, just beyond the moat are traces of the fish stew.'

Plan of moat and house, (*RCAM Pembs.*, 1925, pp. 278-9).

Refs: NLW, Slebech Deeds; Francis Green 'The Barlows of Slebech', WWHR, III; and refs. given in the text above.

NEWGALE, *Brawdy*

Now an ancient farmstead, (formerly a manor house), just below the crest of a high slope, with a fine view over the vale below Newgale Sands and St. Brides Bay.

Recorded in 1326 as a 'a knight's fee (English)', and thus marked on Rees's 14th century map. It became a lay manor, its lands in Brawdy parish. The first known family, to hold the property was that of Sutton, from about 1430 to 1560. John Sutton, the last of the family in the male line died leaving his estates to his daughter and heiress Thamoyng who married Rees ap Morgan of Haverfordwest, gent. and on 10 May 1560 they sold estates in Brawdy parish and elsewhere to John Voyle of Haverfordwest, whose IPM taken on 6 May 1681, includes 'Domine Newgale', whose lands were held by William Ieuan and William Jones of Brawdy, tenants.

Later in that year John Voyle of Haverfordwest was described as lord of the manor, and was followed by his son Morgan Voyle who was described in 1588 as Lord of the Manor of Newgale, and of three other manors in Dewsland. Morgan lived mainly in Haverfordwest, was Mayor in 1585, and Sheriff of the town in 1582. His son and heir, John Voyle, mined for silver in St. Elvis in 1624. Some time later the Voyles sold their interest in Newgale manor, which was held by the Owens of Orielton for a short while.

The Warlow family were farming tenants at Newgale as early as 1568, and became lords of its manor in the early 17th century and moved to live at nearby Llether. John Warlow's granddaughter, and heiress, Lettice Warlow, married, about 1652, James Jones, a younger son of Brawdy. Their descendants remained at Llether, and held the manor of Newgale *(inter alia)*, until the first half of the 20th century, the last manorial lord being Mrs. Nest Massy, daughter of Colonel Roch of Llether.

In a sale catalogue of the Llether and Brawdy estates in 1919, Newgale is described as part of the Llether estates containing about 207 acres in the occupation of T. Jenkins, (Jenkins Mawr), at £133 per annum. The farmhouse contained: 'a sitting room, parlour, kitchen, dairy, three bedrooms, a five stall stable, barn, cow house, feeding shed, calves sheds, corn loft, two pig cotts, and two workman's cottages. There are available beds of brick and china clay on this farm'.

Refs: NLW, Papers of GS, Pembs. 1670; Poyston Deeds; Pembs. Arch. Svy 1896-1907; *Dwnn,* i, p. 177; Francis Jones, 'Records of a 16th Century Pembs. Estate', *BBCS,* XIII, May 1949, pp. 93-104.

NEWPORT CASTLE, *Newport*

Standing on the slope of Castle Hill overlooking the town of Newport and Cardigan Bay. Seat of the Martins and their descendants the Owens and Lloyds. This ancient stronghold lies in the old hundred of Kemes invaded and conquered by the Norman Martin de Tours not long after the Norman Conquest of England. Martin first built a castle at Nevern of which only fragments remain, but it was his grandson, Sir William de Martin, who constructed a fairly substantial stone fortress nearer to the sea at Newport. Kemes became a Norman March – defended border territory against the native Welsh. Subsequent owners became known as Lords (or Ladies), of the March of Kemes of Cemaes.

In 1215 Llewellyn the Great captured Newport castle but three years later it was restored to the de Martins and their descendants who lived there quietly until 1357 when another Prince Llewellyn, last of his name, again attacked the place. Thereafter the family was left in peace. William Martin, son of Nicholas, served in the Scottish Wars and was summoned by writ to Parliament in 1295 as Baron Martin. His son, also William succeeded him as second Baron, but on his death in 1324 the barony fell into abeyance. The title of Lord Marcher of Kemes passed to Lord Martin's nephew, the 2nd Lord Audley.

Sometime in the 14th century the family moved out of Newport Castle, leaving it in the care of a Constable. The castle had the traditional keep on a motte with a moat and drawbridge. The Great Banqueting Hall still has traces of a 13th century fireplace.

The Lords Audley remained in possession of the now ruined castle until James, 7th Lord Audley, was beheaded in the reign of Henry VI. His estates reverted to the Crown but were restored to Lord Audley's son who sold it to the Owens of Henllys who were descendants of the Martins, thus as it were, 'keeping it in the family'.

Although for a time the fabric of Newport Castle was kept in order, by the early 15th century it had begun to decay. George Owen (1552-1613) the historian of the County, and author of *Description of Pembrokeshire* and *Cataloge and Genelogie of the Lordes of Kemes* was a Lord Marcher of Kemes and owned the Castle. His father, William Owen (d. 1574), compiler of *Le Bregement de Statutis* (1521), had recovered the Barony of Kemes after a nineteen-year legal battle. Unfortunately for him, George Owen was, for a time, imprisoned in his own dungeon.

From the Owens, Newport passed by descent to the family of Lloyd. Sir Thomas Lloyd was created a baronet in 1863. His son, the second and last baronet, Sir Marteine Owen Mowbray Lloyd, Bt., delineated his descent in *Burke's Peerage and Baronetage* from Martin de Tours and stated that he, by right of tenure, was the 24th Lord of the Barony of Kemes and that 'the Barony of Kemes is the only Lordship Marcher now in existence in the Kingdom, and the lords thereof still exercise a portion of their rights, and annually appoint, under their hands and seals, the Mayors of Newport'.

Sir Marteine's only son and heir fell in the Great War and the baronetcy became extinct. The first baronet had inherited a ruin, but in 1859 he repaired and made habitable part of the Castle, using stone from a demolished gatehouse. For the first time in centuries Newport Castle became a family home again. Sir Marteine's youngest daughter, Joan married Philip Saxon Gregson-Ellis of Bryddyffrin, Denbighshire. The latter's daughter, Mrs. John Gregson-Ellis who died in 1975, was Lady Marcher and has been succeeded by her daughter, Mrs. Hyacinthe Hawkesworth.

The castle has a ghost known as 'The Lavender Lady' with a fondness for children; she carries with her the scent of lavender from a posy she holds. The castle is currently tenanted by Mr. and Mrs. H. B. Holt, who have restored and repaired the building.

Its remains include the Hunter's Hall, the Great Tower, a crypt, the 'goale for felons' and the main gateway.

NEWTON, *Llanstadwell*

Formerly a gentry residence, about three-quarters of a mile east of Newton-ness, (now called Newton Noyes), and half a mile south of Waterston village: today Newton is enveloped by an oil refinery. In 1811 Fenton states: 'Newton was once the residence of the princely family of Craddock, lineally descended from Howel Dda, lords of this place, whose descendant Sir Richard married Emma, daughter and co-heiress of Sir Thomas Perrot of Eastington, and dropping Craddock, took the name of Newton, and was Chief Justice of the Common Pleas. This led him to settle in England, and dispose of his property in Wales. He died 14 December 1444 (according to DWB, at an advanced age, between 11 November 1448 and 10 June 1449) and lies buried in a chapel on the south side of Bristol Cathedral. This place (Newton), boasting of the most delightful views on the harbour, now the comfortable residence of Lewis Child, Esq. retains nothing of any pristine dignity in point of habitation . . . I learn from Mr. Child that in the churchyard of Llanstadwell church there was a sculptured tombstone, bearing an effigy almost overgrown with the turf, which was removed to make place for the internment of his uncle Mr. Bowlas, the late proprietor of Newton, he having directed his body to be laid there, as if from tradition he had understood that this was formerly the burial place of the ancient lords of the place; for in a pedigree of that family there is mention made of one buried at Newton, meant I presume for Lanstadwell'. The judge married, firstly, Emma daughter of Sir Thomas Perrot of Haroldston St. Issells, Pembs., and secondly, Emmota, daughter of John Harvey of London, and had issue by both. Emmota survived him, and died in 1475; in the church of Yatton, Somerset, is an altar tomb with the effigy of a judge, wearing the collar of SS, and his lady by his side (DNB). Sir Richard owned lands in Somerset and Gloucestershire.

Among his descendants was John Newton of Gonerby, Lincolnshire, from whom descended the illustrious Sir Isaac Newton. Sir John Wynn recorded, 'William alias Wilcocke Crados married an inheretrix in Pembrokeshire where his posteritie remained ever since. Havinge by the house called Newton named themselves Newton Cradocke both in Pembrookshire and Somersettshire.' The next family at Newton was that of Bowlas, a minor gentry family, who were there from 1554 (possibly earlier), until 1795 when it passed to their kinsfolk the Child family by will of Samuel Bowlas in 1794, to Lewis Child, Esq. who was living at Newton in 1795.

The last of the family at Newton was Elizabeth Bowlas Child who, by will dated 16 October 1861, proved 13 June 1862, left all her realty and personalty to her sister Jane Child, and the said Jane Child (sister of William James of Fishguard, Esq.) whose will dated 27 May 1865 (with three codicils), was proved on 4 May 1871, the executors being the Revd. Henry Lewis of Stowmarket, Suffolk, and John Child of Roch. Particulars of Sale of the Newton Estate appeared in 1871. A sale catalogue offered the Newton Estate in Llanstadwell parish for sale on 21 August 1900; the estate was on the shores of Milford Haven, with a frontage of nearly two miles: the family mansion of Newton House, with lawn, garden, conservatory, wash house, stables, farm building, cottages and lime kilns (416 acres, on shores of the said Haven), with four other pieces of land, all in occupation of Roch Davies, Esq.

Refs: Pembs. RO, Newton Deeds and documents 1554-1871, LT 1786; NLW, Poyston Deeds, Pembs. Plea Rolls 1686; *Dwnn,* i, pp. 44-5, 274-5; Fenton, *Tour Pembs.,* 1811, p. 152; Lewis, *TDW,* 1840; Sir John Wynn, *History of the Gwydir Family,* 1927 edn., pp. 32-3.

NEWTON, *Rudbaxton*

A residence about 1¼ miles south of Scolton mansion, and about half a mile north of The Rath. Near The Rath are Newton Hall and Little Rath farms marked on Colby's Map 1831. The mesne manors of Newton and Rudbaxton were held in 1587 by the lords Stanley and Havard as of the manor of Fletherhill. In 1631/2 Owen Edwardes of Little Treffgarn bought Newton manor from Thomas Stanley of Knockin. At the time of his death, pre-October 1649, Owen owned four messuages and 495 acres in Newton, as part of the large Little Treffgarn estate, and in 1786 William Mortimer Edwardes owned Newton Hall and Newton Lodge near The Rath, and Rowland Edwardes was owner-occupier of Newton.

Today (1987), the owner-occupier of Newton is Mr. Peter Higgon, son of the late Col. Higgon of Scolton.

Refs: Picton Castle Deeds; WWHR, VIII, p. 194; Owens, *Pembs.,* ii, pp. 400, 519; Pembs. RO, LT 1786; VL 1894, 1950; Taylor's *Cussion,* 1587-88, p. 96a.

NOLTON, *Nolton*

A coastal parish overlooking St. Brides Bay, between Newgale on the north and Broadhaven on the south. The village and parish church are located about three quarters of a mile inland. Fenton has written of two ancient houses:

1. 'The glebe house is situated exactly opposite the church separated by a road only; and with no pretensions above the character of a cottage, yet furnishes most unexpected and comfortable accommodations. It has marks of great antiquity, being vaulted; and was formerly approached by a gateway opening into a quadrangle, walls five feet thick, and cement as

hard as a rock . . . It is remarkable that a family of the name of Grant from Scotland, in the time of the unfortunate Mary, settled in this mansion, and that his descendant now occupies part of the property: the only large enclosure in the parish was called Grant's Park before the whole parish was enclosed, 1750 . . . '

2. 'On the north side of the churchyard was the old manor-house, the mansion of the lord of the vill . . . of which, perhaps, not a vestige would have remained but for a water-closet entered from the first floor, as at the parsonage, a peculiarity in the old mansions of the country. The property of Nolton, of which this old mansion was the head, before the great rebellion, was in the family of Crowe, but being forfeited, it was bought by the City of London, under condition of paying the usual quit rent to the Crown, still paid; of the city a Mr. Cozens of Robeston West bought it; from this purchaser it devolved on Thomas Kymer, Esq. who sold it to Mr. Barlow of Lawrenny; and Hugh Barlow, Esq. member for the town of Pembroke, is now the possessor'.

Refs: Fenton, *Tour Pembs.,* 1811, pp. 87-8; *RCAM Pembs.,* 1925, s.n. Nolton.

NORCHARD, *Manorbier*

Just south of The Ridgeway, and north of Lydstep. Formerly a commodious residence of an ancient landowning family, built over a continuous vault. It is now a farmhouse. The earliest residence of which we have any record was that of Looney, also spelled as Lynny and Lang. Thomas Looney left no sons and Norchard passed to his daughter and heiress Isabel who married Lawrence Marychurch who settled at his wife's home. Between 1400 and 1600, eleven generations of his descendants lived at Norchard. The origin of the family is unknown, and the name was often rendered as St. Marychurch by Dwnn. Five of the name served as Mayors of Tenby in the period 1501-26. When Dwnn recorded the pedigree and arms a fawn couchant, on 10 November 1591, John Marychurch signed, and gave five shillings to the herald for his travail.

The family remained at Norchard until the latter half of the 19th century. In 1670 William Marychurch was assessed at seven hearths for Norchard, and Maud Marychurch and Francis Marychurch were each assessed at one hearth apiece. The male line seems to have failed shortly afterwards, and Mary Marychurch married on 1673, John Williams of Gumfreston, and Pant Howel (Carms.), who then settled at Norchard which passed to Mary's descendants. Mrs. Mary Meyrick had two daughters who married two brothers – Mary to John Meyrick (d. 1732), and Alice who married Francis Meyrick (d. 1741). In 1786 Norchard was owned by John Meyrick Esq. (of Bush), with Nicholas Roch as tenant. Thereafter Norchard was farmed by a series of tenants.

Refs: Dwnn, i, p. 124; WWHR ii, 37; Chetham Pedigree in Laws, *Little England*; Picton Castle Deeds; Pembs. RO, LT 1786; Peter Smith, *Houses of the Welsh Countryside,* p. 23; BM, Egerton MS 2586; *Come to Pembs. Guide* (c. 1936), p. 28, illust.; Francis Jones, *Historic Carmarthenshire Homes and their Families.*

NOTE: A family of Marychurch lived in Haverfordwest from the 17th century, where they were successful tradesmen, mercers and glovers. William Marychurch, a Royalist, was elected Mayor of the town in 1653, but was fined and ousted from the post at a suit in Haberdasher's Hall, London. In 1694 William Marychurch was Sheriff of Haverfordwest, and Mayor in 1694; in 1829 Joseph Marychurch was town sheriff, and in 1865, Mayor of the town. The family also owned property at Llawhaden.

NORTH DOWN, *Lamphey*

In 1840 this was described as a genteel residence owned by Colonel Kemm and occupied by the Rev. B. Byers.

Henry Rowe of Lamphey and Pricaston who died in 1705 had a son, Lewis, whose administration was granted 10 July 1714, and who lived at Northdown. By his wife 'Sebell', he had four sons, John, Henry who was born at Lamphey in 1699, was M.A. of St. John, Cambridge, and vicar of St. Petrox and Burton. He married Alice Meares of Corston. The third son was Thomas who lived at St. Petrox and died 1767, and the youngest son, Richard married on 6 June 1736 at Rhoscrowther, Magdalene Howells and they lived at Kilpaison. John Rowe married twice, firstly to an unknown wife by whom he had a son Richard, who was Mayor of Pembroke in 1766, 1775, 1781 and

1786. By his second wife, Elizabeth Leach, John had four children of whom little is known. The daughter Mary Rowe (1720-1810) married Richard Hood of Bangeston and had issue.

His second son (b. 1699) was the Rev. Henry Rowe, Vicar of St. Petrox. John's son Richard, inherited North Down.

Refs: Pembs. Plea Rolls No. 160; Lewis, *TDW,* 1840; VL 1904.

ORIELTON, *Hundleton*

Formerly in St. Nicholas, Monkton parish. A mansion on high ground one mile south of Hundleton village, and three-quarters of a mile north of St. Twynnells. Pembroke town is 2½ miles to the northeast. Fenton wrote in 1811, '. . . Orielton, a mansion that has maintained high rank for centuries . . . probable that it was originally inhabited by some powerful follower of Arnugh de Montgomery, of the name of Oriel, a name now almost worn out, and only found among the vulgar . . . in the reign of Henry the second, it was possessed by a man of note, of the name of Wyrriott, whose descendants continued to occupy it till the reign of Queen Elizabeth, when, by the marriage of Sir Hugh Owen, Knt, with the sole heiress of that great estate, Elizabeth Wyrriott, it changed the name of its owner. Sir Hugh was a younger son of the ancient house of Bodeon, Anglesea', Orielton continued to be their chief residence, where they intermarried with the first families and shared the highest honours of the county. While a fair amount of evidence exists concerning the owners, little has been found about the early edifice. George Wyrriott was in residence in 1188 when Gerald of Wales called and mentions the ghostly visitants at the house. An 'unclean spirit' was said to haunt the house, conversed with men, and in reply to their taunts, upbraided them by recounting their secret doings which they wished to keep from the knowledge of others.

In 1300 Sir David Wyrriott of Orielton attended the court of Joan de Valence, Countess of Pembroke, and was living in 1323, and may have been Sheriff of Carmarthen in 1314 and 1317. In 1384 Richard Wyrriott of Orielton was instructed to deliver Manorbier castle to the King's hands; and his great-grandson Thomas Wyrriott was Sheriff of Pembroke in 1459. Thomas Wyrriott had been an officer in the bodyguard of Humphrey, Duke of Gloucester, and on the arrest and murder of the Duke in 1447, Thomas was imprisoned in London, but later released. The next owner, Henry Wyrriott married Margaret natural daughter of Sir Rhys ap Thomas K.G. of Dynevor. He led troops during Henry VIII's war in France, and became High Sheriff of Pembrokeshire in 1549 and 1559.

When the herald, Fellowes, called at Orielton in 1530 he recorded the arms of 'Harry Weryote of Oryalton' as: *argent* a lion passant *sable*, with several quarterings, and the Crest: a hairy man holding a branch on his shoulder.

The last of the family at Orielton, in the male succession, George Wyrriott, was a J.P. and High Sheriff in 1577; by his wife, Jane Philipps of Picton Castle, he had a daughter and heiress, Elizabeth Wyrriott, who married in 1591, Hugh Owen, a younger son of the Owens of Bodeon, Anglesey, who settled at Orielton. At the time of her marriage the Orielton estate comprised four manors, 80 farms, four water corn mills, a fulling mill, and 5,200 acres in south and mid-Pembrokeshire, to which Hugh Owen added many more properties. Hugh was a J.P., High Sheriff in 1583, was later knighted, died on 8 February 1613/14; and buried in Monkton churchyard.

Hugh and Elizabeth had eight children; John the heir predeceased his father; William inherited the Bodeon estate; Morris died in 1588; Sibyl married Sir William Wogan of Wiston and had twelve children; Jane married, evidently much to her discomfiture, David Lloyd of Forest Brechfa and Pengwernoleu, Carms. Her father kept delaying handing over her marriage portion of £300, which so enraged the disappointed husband that he revenged himself on the hapless Jane, throwing her down the stairs at Forest, 'bust' her head with a cudgel, wounded her with a rapier, knocked out four of her teeth, trampled her underfoot, and wrenched the hair from her head 'in whole locks', so the victim alleged before the courts in 1595/6. Her family took counter measures and in 1597/8 David Lloyd sued his father-in-law, Hugh Owen, Thomas Vaughan of Llether Cadfan and his wife and other for forcibly breaking into Forest and abducting the luckless Jane. How the affair ended is not detailed but David Lloyd died and Jane remarried William Griffith of Penrhyn.

The sixth child Anne married John Lewis of Presaddfed, Anglesey; Janet married John Laugharne of St. Brides. Their son was Major General Rowland Laugharne, the Parliamentary commander in the Civil War. The eighth child, Frances, married Morris Wogan of Boulston.

Hugh Owen, (son of John, who predeceased his father); was a minor when he succeeded to Orielton on the death of his grandfather in 1613/4. He took a prominent part in local affairs, was High Sheriff in 1634 and was created a Baronet in 1641. The struggle between King and Parliament was to lead to much inconvenience and peril for the new baronet and although there can be little doubt that his sympathies lay with the monarch who had bestowed the accolade on him, he seems to have been animated by a powerful urge to survive, come what may, so that we find him now for the king, now for Parliament, seemingly switching loyalties to contrive to be on the winning side. His discretion proved stronger than his conviction, so that he survived the misfortunes that attended those more deeply committed to the causes they espoused.

On the outbreak of the war he took the side of Parliament, and it was on the orders of Sir Hugh Owen and John Wogan, members for Pembroke borough and the county respectively, that Haverfordwest was garrisoned during the autumn of 1642. In the following year he signed two of the six resolutions of loyalty addressed to the King from Pembrokeshire landowners, but shortly afterwards veered back to the Parliamentary cause. Following Royalist successes in west Wales, including the capture of Haverfordwest, Sir Hugh was lodged in that castle and according to Simon Thelwall's letter to Cromwell suffered the 'most uncivil and ungentle usage' despite protestations by Lord Carbery the supreme Royalist commander in west Wales. Thelwall's letter proceeds to describe some of Sir Hugh's tribulations on this occasion 'He was unbreasted and in his pantables preparing for bed at Haverford, when Sir Henry Vaughan of Derwydd, a Royalist commander and another man with a mountier drawn over his face takes him by the shoulders and calling him "Dissembling Traitor", some musketiers having presented their muskets at him, compelled him downstairs, and then on horseback, not permitting him time to put on his boots, nor his virtuous lady (a character justified in her pious resolution to share her fortune and declines with her husband) suffered to have a pillion to ride upon behind him . . . They stayed but little on their way and were early next day at Carmarthen', where he was kept under restraint. While there be suggested conditions for cessation of hostilities, but nothing came of them, and he was still a prisoner in February 1643/4 when the House of Commons resolved that the Lord General take steps to exchange prisoners for Sir High Owen and Sir John Price.

We know nothing of his activities in the years immediately following his release but it is clear that he transferred his sympathies to the Royal cause. Information laid against him on 19 April 1648 alleged that 'he sat with the junta at Oxford, left home when the county was under obedience of Parliament and went to Anglesea, then in obedience to the King'. Further information on 18 July of the following year stated that 'he gave the late King £800, sued out his pardon under the Great Seal of Oxford, and then lived in North Wales till most of the garrisons were reduced to obedience. That he countenanced Poyer and had him continued Governor of Pembroke till his revolting, and after he was proclaimed traitor by Parliament, sent him provisions during the siege. That contrary to the order for malignants to leave London, he was in town all the last insurrection and did not help the Parliament army in the siege of Pembroke. That he was excepted from the Act for a general fine for South Wales because he was sequestered for acting with Laugharne and Poyer, and from the Anglesea articles because he did not surrender in February 1646, corresponded with Gerard. That his house is a refuge for notorious delinquents, and that he now harbours Laugharne's wife in his house in Dean's Yard Westminster and she is constantly railing against Parliament though she received much favour from the Lieutenant General when in the county'. The Information ended with the request that 'his estate in Anglesea worth £1,000 a year should be sequestered, and that the State may not be moved by his deceitful allegations trying to excuse himself'.

This condemnatory document had its effect, and in 1649 when Parliament fined delinquents and pardoned others, Sir Hugh was excluded from pardon, and on 6 May. 1651 his estate was sequestered. However, he made his peace with Parliament and was allowed to hold important public appointments under the Commonwealth. From 1650 to 3 July 1653 he was Custos Rotulorum for Anglesey, High Sheriff of Pembrokeshire in 1654, Mayor of Haverfordwest in 1657 where he had been a common councilman for many years. The compiler of the 'True Character' says – 'Sir Hugh Owen, as much as is understood of him, a royalist, so habituated to reservedness that it is thought he cannot now extricate himself if he would from it, a lover of the country and justice; but noted by some to be too sparing or too modest to bear the burthen of the affairs of his country'.

Whatever his true political attachment may have been he was in possession of his estates at the Restoration, and lived unmolested until his death in the latter half of 1670 at the age of 66. By his will, dated 9 September 1670 and proved in PCC on 9 June following, he appointed his wife Katherine and son Hugh to be joint executors.

Sir Hugh married, firstly, Frances daughter of Sir John Philipps, Bart, of Picton Castle, who died in 1629; and secondly, Katherine widow of John Lewis of Prescoed, daughter of Ivan Lloyd of Yale, Denbighshire. By Frances, Sir Hugh had four children, two sons who died without issue and two daughters. By his second wife, Katherine he had two sons, Hugh and Arthur, and a daughter Mary. Katherine was living at Landshipping in 1671 when her son, Sir Hugh granted six farms to her. The second Baronet, Sir Hugh lived mainly at Land-

shipping, participated in the coastal trade owning a three-eighth share of new vessel called *The Factor*. He was High Sheriff in 1664 and several times served as M.P. He married his second cousin, Anne, only daughter and heiress of Henry Owen of Maesoglen, and she was also heiress of her uncle Colonel Hugh Owen of Bodeon thereby reuniting the estates.

The Owen arms were: *gules* a chevron between three lions rampant *or.* Orielton was a large commodious mansion, assessed for 17 hearths for taxation in 1670. A tourist in 1802 wrote of Orielton – 'The house is neither ancient nor modern, being fronted with brick, and the frames of the windows and the corner stones of freestone; somewhat in the stile (*sic*) of Llanvorda (Denbs.) before it was burnt. The house has plantations up to its very front . . . ' The Owens of Orielton were a family of considerable distinction producing several Justices of the Peace, Lords Lieutenant, High Sheriffs, and an ADC to Queen Victoria, Members of Parliament, and were rewarded with baronetcies and governmental appointments. The first baronetcy, granted in 1641, was borne by successive descendants until 1851 when Sir William Owen, 8th Bart, died without issue. However, Corbetta Owen, sister of the 7th Bart, had married John Lord, of Pembroke in 1774, and their eldest son, John Lord, inherited the Orielton estate in 1809, when he adopted the name and arms of Owen and was created a baronet (of the 2nd creation) on 12 January 1813. About 1809 he took down the old edifice, and erected a new mansion. Unfortunately he became heavily in debt, and in 1857 Orielton and what was left of the landed estate was sold to M. A. Saurin of Cilwendeg, sometime a Gentleman Usher of the Privy Chancellor. However his baronetcy survives in the person of Sir Hugh Owen, 5th Bart.

Orielton had remained in possession of descendants of the Wyrriotts for some 750 years, and it was the first time that it had ever been sold. Among the descendants living today is Captain Mark Phillips, first husband of Princess Anne, the Princess Royal.

At the time of the sale in 1857, Orielton had been deserted by Sir John Owen and becoming ruinous, the new owner made several improvements, and restored it as a residence. Mark Anthony Saurin of Orielton was High Sheriff in 1867, and his son Morgan James Saurin held the same office in 1883. One of the later owners of Orielton was A. G. Gaddum, High Sheriff in 1943. The property was later sold, and is today a Field Centre.

Refs: Dwnn, i, pp. 247-8, ii, 95; WWHR, ii, p. 95; Peter Smith, *Houses of the Welsh Countryside,* 1975; Francis Jones, 'Owen of Orielton, *Pembs. Hist.* 1974; Timmins, *Nooks Pembs.,* 1895, p. 74, illust.; *Black's Guide,* 1851, p. 304; Fenton, *Tour Pembs.,* 1811, p. 216; Phillips, *Memoirs of the Owen Family*; C. S. Allen, *Photographs in South Wales,* 1871; *The Welshman* Newspaper, 26 Aug. 1842; *South Wales Daily News,* 7 Jan. 1911; NLWJ, 1968, illust.; NLW Maps, Prints and Drawings, Orielton c. 1810; *Pembs. Arch. Svy* 1896-1907; NLW, Pembs. Plea Rolls 1544; MS 1730, Tour (AD 1802); BM, Egerton MS, 2586.

ORLANDON, *St. Brides*

About a mile to the southeast of St. Brides inlet. It was also called Humprey. In 1603 there is reference to 'the lands of Hugh Butler, Esq. at Humproughe'; and in 1668 John Hopkins, gent. instituted a law-suit against Walter Roch, Yeoman of Humpra in the parish of St. Brides. It afterwards became a property and residence of the Laugharnes descended from William Laugharne who had married the daughter and heiress of the family of John de St. Brides, and in 1832 'the capital messuage and demesne called Orlandon alias Humprey', belonged to the Laugharne family.

During his Pembrokeshire tour, Fenton reached 'Orlandon or as it was formerly called, Humprey, the seat of my old friends, J.P. Laugharne, Esq. whose hospitality I was engaged to share for a few days, and from whose

inexhaustible source of ancient lore I was permitted to draw largely . . . After experiencing the most hospitable reception from my friend, and a night of such refreshment as the antiquarian traveller can but seldom command . . . I sat out . . .' Some 70 years later, in 1882, a local historian wrote, '. . . where stood till of late an old mansion worthy of note, Orlandon, once the seat of the Laugharnes' . . . The Orlandon property, which was once the most extensive in the county, has all been sold. It was at one time the boast of the family that they could ride from sunrise to sunset without going outside it . . .'. Thornhill Timmins, who called there about 1895, had this to say, '. . . Orlandon, where the skeleton of a large old mansion rises grimly above a group of wayside cottages. In its palmy days Orlandon was the home of the Laugharnes, a family of some celebrity in their time, but now extinct in this locality.' The Laugharnes had been established in Haverfordwest in medieval times, and later became landowners with seats at Pontfaen, Llanunwas, Llanreithan, St. Brides Hill, and Orlandon.

In the late Middle Ages, William Laugharne married the daughter and sole heiress of John de St. Brides, and settled at St. Brides Hill and Orlandon, both in that parish. They bore arms: *gules* three lions heads erased *or.* In 1762 Rowland Philipps Laugharne of Orlandon, was High Sheriff; John Philipps Laugharne of Orlandon was High Sheriff in 1788 and 1797. On 15 April 1835, Sir William Laugharne Philipps of Haverfordwest, Bart., released in trust for sale 'Orlandon otherwise Humprey' in St. Brides parish, and lands elsewhere in Pembrokeshire. The Tithe Schedule for the parish, in 1839, records William Charles Allen Philipps as owner-occupier of Orlandon, and a ground-plan of the commodious mansion is also given. The family abandoned it, and a sale catalogue of 1920 of the St. Brides Estate includes, 'Orlandon, the mansion, now in ruins, the early home of the Laugharnes'.

Refs: Dwnn i, 73, p. 184; Fenton, *Tour Pembs.,* 1811, pp. 96-7; Timmins, Nooks Pembs., 1895, p. 119, sketch of the ruins; Phillips, *Haverfordwest and its Story,* 1882, pp. 29-30; Pembs. RO, Deeds HDX 194, No. 17; NLW, Papers of GS, Pembs. Plea Rolls 1668; Poyston Deeds.

PANTYDERI, *Llanfairnantgwyn*
A mansion, three-quarters of a mile to the east of the parish church. Commodious, built in the traditional Welsh style, it is of three storeys with ranges of five windows, and still has the original oak beams, and a fine oak staircase; it overlooks a well-tended lawn and a trout pool. The earliest mansion is said to have occupied a site at a place called Hendy, a short distance away. Nicholas noted that the present building contains parts of considerable age, that several additions were made, the last about 1840 being the most extensive.

For over seven successive centuries Pantyderi was a residence of gentry families. The first descended from Gwynfardd Dyfed, and by the distaff from the Cantingtons of Eglwyswrw. Madoc ap Hywel was living at Pantyderi in 1289, and from him descended Canvey John, son of John ap Gruffyrd or 'Gnts', whose descendants finally adopted the permanent patronymic of Jones. Thomas Jones, solicitor and coroner, was at Pantyderi in 1694, and married to Grace Lewes of Llysnewydd, and had *(inter alia)* a son and heir, John Jones, also a coroner for the county. John died without issue, and by his will (2 Feb. 1721) and codicil (6 Dec. 1728) left Pantyderi to his unmarried sister, Anne for her life and then to testator's nephew, Thomas Bowen, second son of Joyce Jones by her husband, Thomas Bowen of Gwern Ffulbrook in Llanfairnantgwyn parish. Their descendants, the Bowens succeeded to the Pantyderi estate.

In 1786, Thomas Bowen was owner-occupier of the mansion. From the Bowens, the property passed to the well known Colby family of north Pembrokeshire. In 1837 Thomas Frederick Colby was the owner-occupier of Pantyderi, the mansion and lawns, and demesne of 147 acres, two of the fields being known as Park Castell Coch, and Park Ffynnon Goch. The last of the Colbys at Pantyderi was a notable character, Thomas, usually known as 'Twm Colby', some of whose idiosyncrasies have been recorded by H. M. Vaughan in *South Wales Squires*, pp. 89-90. The eccentric squire died on 4 April 1912, aged 82.

The owner-occupier in 2001 was Mr. M. Jones and his family. The house is in excellent condition, and well maintained and used as a holiday centre.

Refs: Dale Castle MS; Manorowen MS; Nicholas, *County Families,* 1875 edn.; Lewis, *TDW,* 1840; H. M. Vaughan, *S. Wales Squires,* 1926; Carms. RO GGMS (Gwynfardd); Pembs. RO; LT 1786; VL; Deeds D.RTP; Saunders-Davies Colln.; College of Arms Colln.; Protheroe MS IV fo. 155; NLW, Morgan-Richardson Deeds, Cwrtmawr Deeds, Alwyn Evans Ped.

PANTEG (PANTEAGUE),
Llanddewi Velfrey
A residence in a dingle east of Plâs Crwn, south-east of Llanddewi Velfrey, and about a mile from the A40 road from Whitland to Haverfordwest. A photograph taken in 1987, shows Panteg, a large commodious double-pile Georgian house of two storeys and an attic storey; ranges of five windows, set within lawns and attractive grounds; now called Panteg Farm (309 acres).

The first known owners were the Stepneys of Prendergast near Haverfordwest. In 1619 Sir John Stepney sold Panteg to Henry Hensleigh whose family had come to Pembrokeshire from Paxton, Somerset. Five generations of the Hensleighs remained at Panteg, until 1763, when Elizabeth only daughter and heir of John Hensleigh, married John Bartlett Allen of Cresselly, and their descendants took the surname of Hensleigh Allen. The Hensleighs had been quickly successful, and by the 18th century had become Esquires. They took little part in local life apart from supporting worthy causes. Thus, John Hensleigh subscribed for four copies of the Rev. William Evan's translation of *Canwyll y Cymry* in 1771.

Henry Hensleigh had married Dorothy Kymer and their only son and heir, John, viv. 1670, succeeded to Panteg. He married a kinswoman, Barbara Kymer of Cwmsaeson by whom he had a son, Robert who died in 1685, and a daughter Barbara. Robert married Jenet, daughter and heiress of Thomas Evans of Glanmorlais by whom he had a son, Henry and three daughters. Henry married Margaret daughter of John Lewis of 'Lan' and they had two sons, John (1705-69) an attorney, and Thomas who took Holy Orders and died in 1762; and three daughters, Barbara, Anne and Mary. It was John's daughter Elizabeth, by Catherine, daughter of the Rev. Thomas Philipps of Laugharne who married John Bartlett Allen.

In the following century, Panteg was let to tenants. The house was bought in 1987 by Mr. Plowden formerly of Vron (qv).

Refs: Pembs. RO, LT 1786; NLW, MS 6462 (George Owen); College of Arms, Protheroe MS IV, ff. 84, 86.

PANTIRION, *St. Dogmaels*

A residence to the northwest of St. Dogmaels village, between Granant and Clawddcam; marked on Colby's Map 1831. Little has been discovered about it in early times. In the second half of the 18th century Pantirion was the home of Richard Jones, described as land surveyor and owner-occupier in 1786; Later it became home of the Jenkins family, a branch of the Cilbronnau family. In 1875, Richard Jenkins, J.P. of Pantirion, (son of Griffith Jenkins), lived there, took an active part in local life and was 13 times Mayor of Cardigan. By the end of that century Pantirion had passed from the Jenkins and in 1904 was the home of one Griffith Lewis.

Refs: Nicholas, *County Families,* 1875 edn, p. 903; NLW, Bronwydd Deeds No. 2093; Francis Jones, *Historic Cardiganshire Homes and their Families.*

James

PANTSAESON,
also **PANTSAISON,**
Monington

The residence is marked on Colby's Map of 1831 among woodland on a long southerly slope, three-quarters of a mile north of Monington parish church, one and a half miles north of Glandwr farm, and one and a half miles northeast of Moylgrove village. About ten years ago Plâs Pantsaeson was described by Mr. Hugh Lloyd Howell (of the Glaspant family) as follows: 'The approach to Pantsaison is well wooded with trees on both sides of the drive, which through neglect is now rough and uneven. This Georgian mansion has a pillared portico, with scroll-work on the wall above. A stone staircase with metal banisters goes down to a tiled entrance hall; several spacious reception rooms open on to the hall, with a smaller room that has a moulded ceiling of floral design; most of the bedrooms are large and sunny with ample head-room; while the servants' quarters at the back of the house are extensive with stairs leading to the upper floors. Traces exist near the present residence of an older house, probably Jacobean'.

The industrious Thomas Nicholas restored the history of the family and residence in 1875, as follows: 'This family (James), has been resident at and in possession of Pantsaison beyond any record to the contrary. There is a tradition in the family that there were thirteen William James's in succession before the last two Johns: Col. John James (d. 1819), and John T. W. James (b. 1812), but it does not seem to have had very extensive possessions or to have arrogated to itself a place among the chief families of the county . . . At the west end of Pantsaison there is a scarped earthwork . . . The present house of Pantsaison is of the Italian villa style, and was built in the year 1836. Two or three (probably more) successive houses have been standing on or near the same spot.'

The 6 inch OS Map of 1904 marks 'The site of manor house', to the northwest of the present residence, and near a cluster of outbuildings. *The Pembrokeshire Archaeological Survey* (1896-1907) reported, 'a farmyard and building of no archaeological import occupies the site of old Pantsaison house. The property has been in the James family for many generations. Their predecessors were the Peverils, who lived in a house between Pantsaison and the sea, the very site of which is in dispute'; the foregoing is noted in *RCAM Pembs*., 1925, p. 235, but adds no further information.

The Peverils were a well known family in the district in medieval times, but no connection with Pantsaison has been found. My own researches reveal no early connection with the James family. They show that Thomas Lloyd of Pantsaison was living there on 13th July 1614; and in 1615 Thomas William Lloyd, yeoman was living there; later in the century William Rowland of Pant y Sayson, who was assessed at two hearths in the Hearth Tax List of 1670. The eldest daughter of Thomas Rowland, Mary, married William Garnons, member of a well known landowning family in North Pembrokeshire. In 1721/22 a Mary Rowland married William James, and their prenuptial settlement, dated 28 February 1721/22, includes the following properties settled on the couple: 'Trevarrld-Ucha and -Issa, and other lands in the parishes of Monington, Llantood, and Bayvill.' Although the bridegroom is described as of Pantsaison, it was not included among the properties settled. From this marriage onwards, six generations of their descendants continued at Pantsaison. One of the family, Col. John James, in 1799 fought a duel on the field called Fortune's Frolic, killed his opponent, and had to flee to the Continent. He returned to Pantsaison, and died in 1819.

The last owner, William Frederick Lloyd James (b. 1872) sold Pantsaeson to Mr. and Mrs. Robertson Williams, and left the district to live in Herefordshire. His sister, Mary Ellen James (b. 1874) married Mr. J. M. Philipps of Treffith, J.P., C.C. She died at Tenby in 1924; she was author of *The Fishguard Invasion*. The arms of James of Pantsaeson as given by Nicholas are as follows: *Sable* a dolphin naiant, embowed *or,* between three cross crosslets *or,* quartering those of Bateman, Vaughan and Taubman; Crest: a demi bull rampant *sable,* horned and hoofed *or*; motto, *Ffyddlon et y gorffen,* (faithful to the end).

Refs: Nicholas, *County Families,* 1875 edn. p. 902; BLG, 1850; *RCAM Pembs.,* 1925, p. 235; *Pembs. Arch. Svy* (1867-1907); *Alumni Oxoniensis;* Pembs. RO LT 1786; VL 1894, 1904, Deeds 1808, 1813; Landowners Return 1873; NLW, Tyllwyd Deeds; Mrs. Ethel Jones Deeds, Morgan-Richardson Deeds, Alwyn Evans MS 12357 E, pp. 14 -16, Papers of GS.

PARC CYNHAETHW(Y), *Manordeifi*

Now a farmstead about half a mile southwest of Cilfowyr. Little is known of its early history. In the 15th and early 16th centuries it was owned and occupied by freeholding families, from whom the property passed by marriage to one of the leading gentry families of southwest Wales.

On 15 October 1543, Llewelin ap William Thomas of Cilrhedyn (Carms.), released a tenement and land at 'Perthkynaythoo' in Cilgerran Hundred, to Philip ap Ieuan ap Meredydd of Kilvowyr. It became the property of David of Park Kynhathwy son of Griffith ab Ieuan. He was followed by his son, Thomas ap David who married a daughter of Griffith of Whitechurch parish, by whom he had two daughters, co-heiresses; the elder co-heiress, Janet, married Thomas Philipps son of William Philipps, son of Sir Thomas Philipps of Picton Castle, descended from Cadifor Fawr of Blaen Cych. After the marriage Thomas Philipps moved to Parc Cynhaethwy, and was living there in 1587-91, and later. He was followed by his son Eynon Philipps whose name appears in the Manordeifi Muster Roll in 1613. The will of a neighbour, John Beynon, son of Eynon ap Griffith of Cilfowyr, dated 3 April 1615, left two messuages called Tythynod Park Kynhoethwy within the territories of Kilvowir (formerly in tenure of Thomas Philipps, gent. deceased), to testator's nephew, William White. Very few references have been found to Parc Cynhaethwy in later times.

Refs: Dwnn, i, p. 105; WWHR, ii, 85; Pembs. RO; LT 1786; VL 1834; Carms. RO, GGMS (Adven. Perw) fo. 231; NLW, GS, Pembs. Plea Rolls, Nos. 52, 59; Eaton Evans and Williams Deeds, No. 34; Francis Jones, *Historic Carmarthenshire Homes and their Families.*

PARK COURT, *Llanrhian*

Today a farmstead within the village of Trefin. From medieval times Trefin has been an Episcopal manor directly under the governance of the Bishop of St. Davids, who is said to have had a residence here which, according to local tradition, stood on the site of the present Park Court, a name said to derive its name from the manorial Court held there from time to time; the courts were held in different houses in Trefin, – in 1720 it was held 'in the house of John Thomas, in 1722, in the house of David Thomas, in 1824-28 in the house of Sarah Francis, and in 1895 at the Ship Inn, Trefin'.

In 1686 John Thomas, of Trefin, gent. sued John ap Rice of Rickeston, Brawdy, Esq. for £20 damages, for entering with force of arms on a messuage of plaintiff called *le Court* and on an acre called *le Orchard* (now Old Orchard, a farm adjacent to Park Court), and departed with cattle, took away trees and traves, (i.e. beams), and six couples. Total value of the manor in 1306 was £16.

From the records of the court we learn that the animal fair was held in the village on the feast of St. Martin, and lasted for three days, a mayor was appointed annually. The court was still held in 1898 under the Bishop's authority, to whom tolls and dues were paid. The Bishop held the adjacent farms of Longhouse and Henllys where he kept cattle and horses, and grew harvests of corn and other grain. Park Court was leased to the family of Garnon for many years. Latterly owned by the Davies Family.

Refs: Black Book of St. Davids, 1326, pp. 57, 71, 105; Fenton, *Tour Pembs.,* 1811, pp. 19, 55; NLW, Archives of Courts of GS; Francis Jones, *Journal of Hist. Soc. of Church in Wales,* 1967, pp. 31-5.

PARK GLAS, *Crinow*

'The parish, with the exception of a very small portion, belongs to Roger Eaton, Esq. whose elegant mansion of Park Glas is situated within its limits', (Lewis, *TDW,* 1840). Eaton left daughters and co-heiresses. His wife, Mrs. Dorothea Eaton presented a chalice to Crinow church in 1844. The house had been built by an earlier Roger Eaton, of Clynpathal in 1743.

Memorials in Crinow church give clues to the subsequent descent and ownership of the estate. Charles Delabere Prichett Jones of Park Glas was the only son of the Rev. David Jones, Rector of the Parish. He died in 1867. Algernon Romilly Jenner of Park Glas died in 1872 and Charles Eaton Vaughan Shield, only son of H. R. and A. M. Shield of Park Glas died at sea in 1900 aged 25.

There is a photograph of it by C. S. Allen of Tenby in *Photographs in South Wales,* 1871.

PARSELE/PARSELLE, *St. Edwins*

A farmstead on high ground about a mile east of the parish church. Home for many generations of yeoman families. On 29 December 1559, Jenkyn Morgan ap John of Penderyn (Brec.), yeoman, stole cattle from John Llewellyn David ap Gwilym at Pursellay, Pembs. He was apprehended, and in June 1560, with others, was tried, pleaded guilty, and placed in

Haverfordwest goal, from whence he managed to escape.

In 1596 John Wogan, gent. sued Thomas David Morgan and his wife Margaret, re: three messuages, two tofts and 34 acres in Perselick and St. Edwins, and in 1598 the said John Wogan sued Thomas Bowen, gent. and his wife Janet, concerning three messuages, two tofts and 34 acres and a rent charge of 1s. 10d. in Treddiog, Perselly, and St. Edwins.

In 1601 John Wogan sued Richard Howel and Thomas David Morris of St. Edwins parish, yeoman, for trespass and depasturing on Wogan's lands at Persellick in St. Edwins to the value of 40s. In 1613 John Wogan, gent. gave 6s. 8d. to agree with Thomas David Morris and his wife Margaret, re: a messuage and 33 acres in Persellick.

Nothing further is heard of the property, until 18 November 1765 when Julien John of Parselle, widow, signed her will, leaving a chest to Lettice, daughter of John Harry of Little Newcastle parish, and the residue of her goods 'to my nephew by law, George Evan and my niece Jane Harry, they to be executors of my will'; which was proved on 25th December 1765. At this time the Morse family lived at Parsele, descended from the Morses of Trein-deg. Three generations lived at Parsele, one of whom, Henry Morse, gent. was described as a Parliamentary voter, of St. Edwins parish, in 1760, and as owner-occupier of Parselle in 1786. The Evans family came from Scleddau, and were interested in antiquities. Edward Evans of Parselle died in 1914, leaving a son George Morgan Evans, (died unmarried in 1960), and Margaret Evans (d. 1939), aged 56, having married Edwin Morse, son of Thomas Morse of Pantybryn.

Edwin Morse who held Parselle *iure uxoris,* sold the property and retired to Letterston where he died in 1960, whose son Edward Llewelyn Morse married Lily Scale of Tre-wallterwen, and whose daughter, Elizabeth, married Owen Reynish of Churchlands. Edward Evans of Parsele kept an interesting diary full of information about farming at Parsele and the surrounding district; he was the first to draw attention to an inscribed stone in the farmyard of Llangwarran in 1896.

Refs: PRO, Cal. Pat. Rolls 1560-63, p. 522; NLW, Papers of GS, 1596-1613; Pembs. RO LT 1786, Survey by Henry John, Head Surveyor 1787.

Roch

PASKESTON, *Cosheston*

A residence about a mile northwest of Milton village, built in the Georgian style, with a modern extension to one gable end. The first known folk at Paskeston were yeomen, probably tenants, namely David Scurlock, yeoman (1559), George Ellys, gent. (1617), and William Jermin, gent. (1626) son of Rees Jermin, yeoman, after which came John Rossant, (1659) son and heir of James Rossant of Cosheston, yeoman. The Rossants belonged to the minor gentry and lived at Paskeston during the period 1659-1780, and acquired a small estate, the last of whom we find at Paskeston, being John Lewes Rossant, gent. and Mary his wife and John Rossant and John Lewes Rossant, gent. all of whom were living there in 1780.

It is likely that there was a farm as well as the mansion, as early as 1724; Nicholas Roch of Paskeston, was High Sheriff in 1729, and in his will, proved in 1759, he mentions his sons, Nicholas, Mark, and George, and 'my kinsman' Thomas Roch of Butterhill. He was succeeded by his son Nicholas Roch of Cosheston, who succeeded his uncle (who was still there in 1815), Nicholas Roch of Paskeston died there in 1866, and was followed by his son, also named Nicholas Roch who is included in the Landowners' Return of 1873 as owning 944 acres.

The next gentry family there was that of Allen (kinsman of the Cresselly stock), who were mentioned at Paskeston in 1894. Newton Seymour Allen, D.S.O., of Paskeston was High Sheriff in 1919 and died in 1934.

Refs: Pembs. RO, LT 1786; Deeds LLC/1, and D/LLC; NLW, Picton Castle Deeds; Rogers of Pembs. G.J., Plea Rolls; *RCAM Pembs.,* 1925; D. Miles, *Sheriffs of County of Pembs.*

PATERCHURCH, *St. Mary, Pembroke*
The former residence on the west of the town, overlooking the estuary, and in the 19th century became included within the area of the Pembroke dockyard. The earliest families there were known by the name of the property.

This was the main residence of the Adams family. The earliest known resident there was David de Paterchurch whose daughter and heiress, Elen, married in 1422/3 John Adams, son of Nicholas Adams of Buckspool (q.v.) in Bosherston parish. John settled at his wife's home, and became Lieutenant to Henry Wogan, Steward to the Earl of Pembroke and in 1448, was followed by his son, William Adams who married Alice, daughter of Sir William Herbert of Troy, Mon., Steward of Pembroke, natural son of William, Earl of Pembroke. William's grandson, John Adams, served as M.P. for Pembroke Borough in 1541-44, and was still living in 1553; his wife was Catherine, daughter of

Thomas ap David Goch ap Meredith ap Madoc, Baron of Stapleton Castle, near Presteigne, Rad. The bard, Lewis Glyn Cothi, addressed a poem to David Goch whose ancestry he traced to Rhodri Mawr, a prince of Wales.

Breiniawl wyt o'r barwnwaed
barwm ystelptwn nos deed.

David Goch was a noted Lancastrian who raided all Yorkists within range until eventually slain at Pennal field near Pennal, Mer.

The last of the family there was Rhys Adams whose will was proved in 1698. The house was not used as a residence after that date, having passed to his son, also Rhys, who sold it to Richard Gwynne of Gevenifa, Carms., who made his will on 9 September 1702, and states . . . 'I have lately purchased of Rice Adams, gent. a capital messuage or mansion house called Paterchurch, heretofore mortgaged unto John Owen late of Berllan, Esquire, deceased, upon which mortgage there is still £1,350: Paterchurch is to go to my grandson, Thomas Gwynne'. The demesne of the old mansion contained the private cemetery of the Adams family, the last to be buried there, 'in their own burial ground', being Roger Adams, son of William Adams, on 11 January, 1731/32. Many bones and skulls were disinterred later, especially when the foundations of the Royal Dockyard were made in the years 1820-44, and again in 1889. The Gwynne family alienated the property before 1731, when it was owned by the Owens of Orielton who held it until part of their estate was sold by Sir William Owen to the Government by Act of Parliament of 1757, and thereafter remained Crown Property.

The Adams line seems to have wilted towards the end of the 17th century as Rhys's two brothers, William and Nicholas, were apprentices in London in 1698 and nothing further was heard of them. However some members of the family still had connections with Paterchurch in 1731, after which they exchanged land there with the Meyrick family, it is said as a result of gambling, and on the Meyrick land they built Holyland (q.v.) early in the 18th century, and it became the chief residence of the family.

The old mansion was decaying fast and was offered to the Hon. Charles Fulke Greville, who in a letter on 1 September 1802 wrote to Lady Cawdor that he was '. . . surprised at the dilapidation, the house has neither roof, doors, or windows; the wind and thieves have been so diligent since my last visit that I do not know how my villa will become elegant', and the idea of purchase was abandoned. In Mrs. Stuart Peters' *History of Pembroke Dock* (1905), it tells us that: 'In 1854 the crumbling walls of the old ruined mansion of Paterchurch were pulled down with the exception of the tower. The old place had served many purposes: it had been a residence and later had been used as a store and also as a modeller's shop.' The gateway to Pembroke Dockyard was part of the old mansion. Much of Pembroke Docks now cover the site of the house and park.

In 1900 Allen noted, 'The gate tower of the old house (by some mistaken for the belfry of a church), was enclosed within the royal dockyard at the south-west corner'. It can still be seen there.

Refs: Dwnn, i, pp. 92, 130, 172; WWHR, ii, 76; *Pembs. Arch Svy,* 1896-1907; Sketch by Norris in Cardiff Public Library; Parish reg. St. Mary, Pemb.; Mr. & Mrs. S. C. Hall, *Tenby,* p. 9; Mrs. E. Stuart Peters, *Hist. Pemb. Dock,* 1905, pp. 1-4, 12, plan & photo; *RCAM Pembs.,* 1925; Allen, *Sheriffs of Pembs.,* 1900, p. 18; Pembs. RO, VL; Deeds HDX 589, Nos. 9-10, 12, plan & sketches; Mrs. Barbara Gordon, (née Adams of Holyland) has a good water-colour of old Paterchurch c.1800 which she kindly showed to me when I called on her in April 1974. For photo and account of the Tower see *Western Telegraph,* 6 Jan. 1983.

PEMBROKE CASTLE, *Pembroke*

It is not strictly within the scope of this work to include the great ruined fortresses of the County but I feel that an exception must be made in this case. Not only is Pembroke Castle the largest Norman stronghold in Pembrokeshire, it is also of great historic importance as the birthplace of Henry Tudor, later Earl of Richmond and eventually King Henry VII, first of the Tudor monarchs.

Gerald of Wales writes authoritatively about the Castle as his grandfather, Gerald of Windsor, was appointed castellan by Arnulph, son of Roger de Montgomery who founded the Castle in 1093.

King Stephen created the first earldom of Pembroke, a title which passed to some of the most powerful magnates of the period including William Marshal and Aymer de Valence.

Jasper Tudor became Earl of Pembroke in 1454. He was second son of Owan Tewdwr and Queen Catherine of France and therefore half-brother of Henry VI. Jasper made parts of the Castle into more comfortable living quarters. His older brother, Edmund Earl of Richmond, married Lady Margaret Beaufort, a descendant of Edward III and it was here that Edmund's widow gave birth to Henry Tewdwr who was to change the dynastic history of England and Wales. You can see the actual room. For a fuller account there are many sources but Robert Innes-Smith's *Pembroke Castle* (Pilgrim Press, Derby), the Castle's guidebook, gives a succinct summary of its history and architecture.

Henry Tudor

Oliver Cromwell did his best to demolish the Castle but it was too big a task. A great deal of damage was done and the local people used the ruins as a quarry for stone.

Pembroke Castle remained a romantic ruin until 1880 when J. R. Cobb of Brecon carried out a scheme of restoration. Nothing further was done until 1928 when Major-General Sir Ivor Philipps, K.C.B., D.S.O., bought the ruins and began further extensive restorations. After the death of the Major-General his daughter, Mrs. Basil Ramsden, inherited the building and in 1959 handed over its administration to trustees who open the Castle regularly to the public. At the time of writing the trustees are represented by Major Ivor Ramsden, M.B.E., the Major-General's grandson. (*Vide* Cosheston Hall.)

PENALLT CADWGAN, *Cilgerran*

Lewis Wogan of Wiston married, as his second wife, Anne, daughter of James Lloyd of Cilrhiwe. She died in 1703, then living at Penallt Cadwgan. By Anne, Lewis Wogan had four children – Lloyd Wogan, baptised 1786, died young; Anne married Thomas Lloyd of Bronwydd, Bridget married Lewis Powell of Greenhill and Katherine married John Warren of Trewern. In 1894 one Ivor Evans held the land and was tenant of Penallt Cadwgan.

Refs: WWHR, vi p. 217; VL 1894.

PENALLTCYCH, *Clydey*

Sometimes also called Penrallt Cych, and so marked on modern maps. Now a farmstead on high land to the west of Pont Cych and the hamlet of Cwm Cych. The first known family there was David ap David 'alias Dwbl Dys' of Penallt Kych, who married Mary, daughter of Lewis Philips Howel of Blaenythan, Cards., but nothing further is known of them.

Towards the middle of the 17th century David Llewelyn, gent. a minor squire, owned the property, and in 1684 he bought the nearby mansion of Clynfyw and went there to live. He died about 1716, having made his will on 30 April of that year. His eldest son, Thomas Davies, succeeded to Penallt Cych, and his second son Llewelin (Leoline) Davies succeeded to Clynfyw. Thomas married Elizabeth Bowen daughter of Canon James Bowen M.A., member of the Bowens of Pontgynon, and was followed at Penallt Cych by his son, James Davies. James, married Anne, daughter of Thomas Howell of Bryn y Ceirch and Llether Moel, Cynwyl Elfed, and had two daughters and co-heiresses.

On her death in 1731, she was followed at Penallt Cych by her daughter, Anne Davies, who married Henry Williams of Trelech, son of Andrew and Janet Williams. Henry then settled at his wife's home and died there before April 1764. On 9 April 1764, the widowed Anne left Penalltcych to Evan Humphrey of Cynwyl Elfed farm at a rent of £20 yearly, 6 fat hens, two fat geese, to carry three horse loads of coal yearly to Penalltcych, the lessor to have liberty to graze a horse there. They had three children, Henry Williams, (d. 1773), Thomas Williams (d. 1778), and Margaret (heir of the brothers), who married Thomas Howell of Cynwyl Elfed who came to live at Penalltcych, and died in 1816. Margaret died in 1815, aged 72, and Penallt passed to their heir Thomas Howell who built a mansion at 'Glaspant otherwise Tythinpabyog' where he went to live, and the family remained there until some two decades ago when it was sold by the head of the family, Mr. H. W. Ll. Howell, J.P.

After the departure of the Howell family, Penalltcych was leased to the Rev. John Morse, B.A., Fellow of Hertford College, Oxon., who kept a school there where pupils paid 18 guineas per annum and one guinea entrance fee. During some alterations to the house a number of horse heads were found beneath one of the floors, believed to have been placed there as protection against an 'echo' in the room.

Refs: Carms. RO, GGMS, i, fo. 12, J. Francis Deeds, No. 567; Carms. Ant. Soc. Deeds; Pembs. RO LT 1786. NLW, Griffith Owen Deeds, Nos. 6229, 7789, Tithe Map, Pembs.; WWHR, ii, pp. 40-1; Manorowen MS p. 149; Curtis, *Laugharne,* p. 124; *The Cambrian,* 1 Feb. 1806; Francis Jones, 'Diary of a Doctor's Wife' *Carms. Hist.,* 1981; MS Hanes Cisdal Capel Iwan. gan. Parch; D. G. Roberts 1970 in Carms. RO, Maps, Mudge 1819, Colby 1831; Francis Jones, *Historic Carmarthenshire Homes and their Families & Historic Cardiganshire Homes and their Families.*

PENALLTY LLYN/PENRALLTYLLYN, *Manordeifi*

Spelt as Penralltyllyn on modern maps. A farmstead on a slope just south of Cilfowyr, and flanked by the farms of Parc Cyneithw and Cilast Issaf. Home of the family of Lloyd, descended from Lloyd of Dolau Llannerch, Clydey, tracing to Cadifor Fawr of Blaen Cych. Six generations lived at Penalltyllyn from Elizabethan days to 1685. They were minor gentry and the estate was a modest one. The family deteriorated and shortly after 1685 sold the property.

Griffith Lloyd married a daughter of Thomas Lloyd of Trewern, by whom he had three sons, none of whom were able to forward the fortunes of the family; namely Jonathan Lloyd, a weaver, living at Penrith in 1685, Jenkin and John of whom nothing is known after their departure from Penalltyllyn. The downward trek had started as early as 1622 when John Lloyd and his wife Jane, mortgaged a quarter of Penalltyllyn, where they dwelt, also called Plâs Pen Allt y Llyn, and a messuage call Tirt y Skybor hên, and a quarter of a close called Park Dawkins, all in the territory of Cilfowyr. After the eventual sale of the property the farm was let to farmers.

Refs: Dwnn, ii, p. 45; Dale Castle Deeds MS fo. 127; Manorowen MS p. 154; Pembs. RO, LT 1786, VL 1834, 1894, 1904; Carms. RO GGMS; NLW, Morgan-Richardson Deeds and MS 12356, p. 154.

PENALLY ABBEY, *Penally*

This fine mansion built in the Gothic style in the 1790s adjacent to the church and with fine views over Carmarthen Bay has abbatial remains in the grounds including a ruined 13th century chapel dedicated to St. Deneilol and a Flemish chimney. Its early history is obscure but from 1916 to 1924 it belonged to the Jameson whiskey family. It has been restored and sensitively converted into a country house hotel by Mr. & Mrs. Steven Warren.

PENALLY COURT, *Penally*

The earliest known owner of this property was Lord Milford in 1786, with Thomas Rowe as tenant. Thomas Rowe died in 1791 aged 64, and by his wife Anne, daughter of the Rev. Philip Elliott of Annikel, he had a son, Rev. Thomas Rowe who succeeded to Penally Court, and died in 1810. Thomas's son, George Rowe, became a doctor at Haverfordwest. In 1834 William Wakes was living at the Court and in 1852, R. Waters, Esq. lived there and was Mayor of Tenby. The next owner was John M. Griffith, a yeoman, progressive farmer, breeder, show judge, and member of the Welsh Land Commission. His daughter, Mary May Griffiths, when aged 25, was appointed by Queen Victoria, Superintendent of the Royal Dairy at Balmoral, in 1896. Now tenanted by Mr. Evans, and known as Penally Court Farm, the ruins of the old court can still be seen.

PENARTHUR, *St. Davids*

A farmstead to the northwest from St. Davids, near the road leading to Porthmawr. In earlier days there were three farms here, Penarthur (also known as Maen Arthur), Penarthur-Ucha and -Issa; owned by yeomen and minor gentry. In 1608 Thomas Price, Esq. agreed with David John Howell, Theodore Howell and Thomas John Howell, in respect of two messuages, two tofts and 176 acres in Maenarthyr Ycha alias Penarthur, Treleddyd Fawr, St. Davids, and Carnedryn Issa.

Thomas John Howell succeeded to Penarthur-Ucha, and later owned Penarthur-Ucha and -Issa, Trelethed Fawr, Tir y Gof, Trewellwall, Carnedren-Issa, Llanvwgar, Caerfarchell, and Clegyr Owen. By his wife, Jane Mathias (a widow in 1637) he had three sons and two daughters. Towards the end of the century, Thomas Howell lived at Penarthur Issa and on his death in 1695 was succeeded by his eldest son, John Howell, who settled at Penarthur Ucha, where he died in 1703, leaving two daughters, co-heiresses, Elizabeth who married Evan Davies of St. Davids, Esq. and Esther who married a Mr. Colby. The said Evan Davies, Esq. was described as of Penarthur in 1739 when he was a Grand Juror. Some of the family seems to have slipped down in the social scale, such as James Howell of St. Davids, blacksmith (*faber lignarius*), described in 1710 as administrator of the goods and chattels of John Howell of Penarthur, husbandman, who had died intestate. In 1725 Esther Howell the elder, widow, lived at Penarthur-Usha. By about the mid-century the Howell family had left the area. In 1786 William Davies, gent. owned Penarthur, with the Rev. Canon Holcomb as tenant. Thomas Colby, Esq. was owner of Penarthur-Ucha, the tenant being John Lewis. A little after this, William Davies left Penarthur and established himself at Barry Island which formed part of his estate.

On 3 November 1798, William Davies of Barry Island, Esq. granted a lease of messuages called Penarthur-Ucha, -Issa, and Penarthur, two cottages at Trelethid Fawr, a field called Six Acres, and the Bishop's lands in Penarthur called Tyr Lleech, Arthur's Stone, and Penygroes, to William Nash. Thomas Nash died in 1825, leaving his widow Dorothy and their three daughters. In 1848, the widow sold her share of Penarthur to her relatives, Henry and Margaret Harries and their children.

In 1862 Penarthur and its adjacent lands, were offered for sale (title to commence with the will of William Davids of Barry Island, dated 19 October 1800). The property was described as Penarthur, 126 acres, (Ebenezer Williams, tenant held by lease dated 27 September 1850), and a leasehold interest in three pieces of ground called Tyrneach, Penygroes and Arthur's Stone (Maen Arthur) containing five acres.

At one time, the Hergest family of St. Davids, held one of the three messuages called Penarthur, but references are rare. Towards the mid-17th century, Thomas Hergest, vicar-choral of St. Davids, is described as of Penarthur; and later, one Margaret Hergest of Penarthur (living 1696), married Gilbert Tegan of St. Davids parish, by whom she had Thomas Tegan, yeoman, John, and Margaret Tegan, all living in 1703.

Refs: Pembs. RO, LT 1786, Sale Cat. 1862; NLW Papers of GS (Pembs), William and Williams (H'west) Deeds, Spence Colby Deeds.

PENBEDW, *Llanfihangel Penbedw*

Penbedw farmstead marked immediately south of the church on Colby's Map 1831. Home of the antiquary George Owen Harry in late Elizabethan times, rector of Eglwyswrw and Llanfihangel Penbedw. He was a well known historian and genealogist, author of *The Genealogy of King James I* (1604), and *The Well Springs of True Nobility*. A manuscript in the hand of David Edwards, kept in the College of Arms, contains a pedigree of Hopkin of Gower which states 'this pedigree was drawn by George Owen (Harry) of Pen Bedowe ye 18th day of November anno domini 1603'. By his will, proved in 1655, Thomas David Morgan, gent. of Manordeifi parish, bequeathed to his grandson John Llwyd. 'My capital messuage called Penbedwin Llanfihangel, Penbedw parish, and lands within the free chapel of Llangolman Penbedw called Plâs Cilvachwrnele and Tir y Ffynon Fawr, now in my occupation, to my son-in-law Thomas Lloyd and Elizabeth his wife, my daughter.' Grandson, Griffith Lloyd is also named. The Lloyds remained there till the end of the century. The Land Tax List of 1786 gives James Bowen Esq. as owner, with Rev. Lewis Walters as tenant. The following are commemorated on a tombstone in Eglwyswrw churchyard – Evan Protheroe of Penbedw in Llanfihangel Penbedw parish, died 4 January 1831, aged 88; and the Rev. David Protheroe, vicar of Eglwyswrw, died 28th September 1855, aged 86. During the years 1894-1904, William Thomas lived at Penbedw.

Refs: College of Arms MS, Box 36/X; WWHR, ii, pp. 242-4; DWB, p. 343, s.n. Geo. Owen Harry; B. G. Charles, *George Owen of Henllys,* 1973.

PENBERRY/PENBERI & PENBURY,
St. Davids

Marked on Colby's Map of 1831 as Pen-berry. A farmstead on the east side of Carn Beri, a carn on the coast near Penclegyr. The earliest known resident was Arnold Jones, gent. younger son of William Jones of Brawdy by his wife Mary Warren. He was there prior to 1584, and married Anne Wogan of Stone Hall. He was High Constable of Dewsland in 1605, and was still living in 1615. He was followed by his son Henry Jones of Penberi. In 1599, Thomas James of Penbury, yeoman, sued one David Harry for trespassing and depasturing at Porthiddy Fawr in Llanrhian parish.

Thomas James (Harries) of Penbury made his will on 7 March 1616, which was proved in the following year, he left four sons and one daughter, all surnamed James, one of whom Lewis James, gent. owned Penbiryvawr, Penbiry Golman, Rosegolwyn, Tregweyth, Tir Prior, Herglodd Ycha, Whitchurch, and Trevadog, in 1631. It was owned by John Harries in 1776, when John Warlow surveyed Penberry and in

1811 an amended table of acreages of fields was made by John Tamlyn, surveyor. The Land Tax list of 1786 records John Harries, Esq. as owner of Penberry, with Phillip Beynon as tenant; the widow Margaret Beynon and her two sons, John and William, were still there in 1807-11. In the first decade of the 20th century, William Propert Williams lived at Penberry (1904).

Refs: Pembs. RO; Deeds HDX 1588, No. 1, LT 1786; NLW Papers of GS, Plea Rolls and Fines.

PENBLEWYN, *Llanddewi Velfrey*
Now an abandoned ancient farmhouse at Penblewyn crossroads; a modern farmhouse has been built nearby. For several generations the old house was the residence of the Jones family who also owned Caermaenau and other local properties. In 1656 it was the home of John Jones, gent. who married a daughter of John Philipps of Woodstock locally called *Shon butsh goch*. By 1786 it was owned by John Dunn, gent. with Edward James and David Jones, tenants.

Ref: Photo of Penblewyn, *Western Mail,* 18 Feb., 1987; Francis Jones Archives.

PENCELLI (CAPEL), PENCELLY, *Eglwyswrw*
There was a chapel called, in 1612, 'the chapel of Penkethllie Vaughan', attached to the benefice of Eglwyswrw. In a deed dated 6 June 1407, it is described as 'the chapel of Pencelli', *ad magnam viam de vadu leprorsuro ad villam de Pencelli*. (College of Arms, Wagner MS No. 12). It stood between Pencelli and Trewilym Uchaf, but became a ruin, and is described in 1914 as 'heavily covered with undergrowth.'

Refs: RCAM Pembs., 1925, p. 94; College of Arms, Wagner MS No. 12.

PENCELLI FAWR, PENCELLY, *Eglwyswrw*
A farmstead to the northwest of the village and near to Pencelli forest. The name is rendered in earlier legal documents as Pencelli Fawr. Although several references occur to the property, insufficient evidence has survived to enable a coherent genealogy of the folk who dwelt there. Between the years 1579 and 1597, George Owen of Henllys bought Pencelli fawr which lay within Owen's manor of Eglwyswrw. In 1786 Cefn Pencelli and Pencelli fawr were owned by 'Mrs. Hay and Mrs. Price', with Llewelyn Williams as tenant; through marriage to an heiress of Henllys the property passed to Lloyd of Bronwydd, Cards., and in 1834 Thomas Lloyd of Bronwydd was described as owner. In 1894, Pencelli was held by William Morgan, and in 1950 by Guildford M. Morgan, when it was spelt as Pengelly.

Refs: B. G. Charles, *George Owen of Henllys,* 1973, pp. 33-4, 37, 39, 46, 56, 69, 71; George Owen, *2nd Book, NLWJ*, 1948, p. 2791; NLW, Bronwydd Mun. Kemes Court Rolls; College of Arms, Protheroe MS iv, fo. 89 and Wagner MS No. 12; Francis Jones, *Historic Cardiganshire Homes and their Families.*

PENCELLI FOREST,
PENCELLY FOREST, *Eglwyswrw*
Just north of the village, in the manor of Eglwyswrw. In George Owen's time it enclosed 500 acres, within which were 13 'glades or cockshuts' where woodcock nested. By 1786 it had passed to the Lloyds of Bronwydd.

Refs: Fenton, *Tour Pembs.,* 1811, p. 293; B. G. Charles, *George Owen of Henllys,* 1973, and refs. there.

PENCELLI FYCHAN *or* **FACH,**
PENCELLY, *Eglwyswrw*
Near Pencelli Fawr, into which it was later absorbed: the name is now lost. George Bowen was father of Robert Bowen who lived at Pencelli Fychan in late Elizabethan times, where he was succeeded by his son John ap Robert Bowen, who married Mary daughter of William Griffith of Penybenglôg. John died early in 1615 owned two messuages called Pencelly Fychan, two other messuages called Cippill Gwynt, and a messuage called Tŷ Mawr, and 500 acres. He

died c. 1615 and left two daughters co-heiresses, called Jane Robert alias Bowen, and Joanna Robert alias Bowen, aged respectively six and three years, who became wards of George Owen of Henllys, lord of the manor of Eglwyswrw.

During the 16th century the Young's who came from Tregaman, held Pencelli Fychan; John Young married Margaret Bowen, and their son Philip settled at Pencelli Fychan, where he was followed by his son, John Young, whose daughter and co-heiress married Owen ap Owen of Glanduad. Very few references occur to the property after this, and as it no longer exists, it is likely that its lands were absorbed into neighbouring farms.

Refs: WWHR, ii, 92 s.n. Pencelli fach; NLW, Kemes Court Rolls, 4 May 1615; Dale Castle Ped. Book, fo. 163; BM, Egerton MS, No. 2586; Bronwydd Deeds MS 699.

PENCNWC, *Mathry**

The farmstead of Pencnwc occupied the site of the old 'castell'. Held of the Bishop of St. Davids and leased to the Mathias family. Edward Mathias of Castle Morris, married Lettice, second daughter of Richard Ford, Esq. of Exeter by Mary Wogan his wife of Stone Hall. They are buried in Mathry churchyard. Their granddaughter Martha born 1752 and died 1815 married John Evans of Mabws. The prenuptial settlement of Jacob Jones of Carmarthen, the brother of Morgan Jones of Cilwendeg, and Anne Mathias, the second daughter of John Mathias of Penykwok, gent. gives her portion as £200. Lands in Llwynbedw were settled on the marriage. In 1784 John Mathias was of Penyknwok, gent. and his wife, Maria, daughter of Anne Davies of Trellys, St. Nicholas.

By the early 19th century Abraham Leach was the lessee at Pencnwc, a survey and valuation of his estate in 1842 shows Pencnwc then comprising 296 acres, 3 rods and 30 perch. William Evans was tenant.

Refs: Carms. RO; Mathry Tithe Schedule 1842; Pembs. RO D/LLC/674; Saunders-Davies Papers at Pembs.. RO.

PENCRAIG, *Llangolman**

There is a Pencraig shown on Colby's Map of 1831 about three quarters of a mile southeast of the parish church. It was the home of the Protheroe family who came there from Dolwilym in the late 17th century. The first there was Philip, a younger son of Evan ap Prydderch (will dated 20 January 1651), and Jenet Eaton. Philip married c. 1709 Catherine, daughter of Thomas Lewis of Pencraig by whom he had three sons, John, James who was vicar of Eglwyswrw, married Elizabeth Edwards and died in 1764/5; and Simeon (1719-85) who married Mary Phillips. The eldest son, John married Anne James in 1769 and they had seven children. John died in 1800 and his wife in 1819. Their heir, another John, (1769-1800) married Maria Griffith, and they had three sons and four daughters. The eldest son, James, (b. 1790), died unmarried in 1817 and Lewis Protheroe succeeded to Pencraig which he mortgaged in 1831 and sold in 1842 to Essex Nicholas of Garndwyren, Letterston parish.

Refs: Mrs. J. Daniels; Pembs. RO D/LJ James of Narberth solicitor Deeds.

PENLAN, *Lampeter Velfrey**

The home of Lewis John in 1670 when he paid tax on nine hearths showing it to have been a commodious residence. His will was dated 24 January 1695/6 and there is a M.I. in Lampeter Velfrey church to his memory and to his wife 'Joan' by whom he had five sons and two daughters; William, George, Reignald, Griffith, Roger, Mary and Anne. William the eldest son, was a citizen of Bristol. He was knighted in 1703, High Sheriff in 1708, Mayor of Bristol and a soap maker. He married Bridget, daughter of Edward Baugh, a Bristol linen draper in 1679; her portion was £500. They had two sons, John and Joseph and four daughters. The following lands were settled on the marriage, 'Penn Llan with closes (named), three cottages, a water grist mill in Diffrine Gwaithmoe near the rivulet called Gwaithinge, in the parish of Lampeter Velfrey; a messuage in Kiffig, Carms.; and two other messuages in Lampeter Velfrey'. They married before 8 December 1679. By 1786 Penlan was owned by Rev. Dr. Lewis and tenanted by Richard Jones.

PENLAN CYCH, *Manordeifi*★

In 1720 Penlan Kych was part of the Noyadd Trefawr estate and in 1771 a lease for 21 years was granted by Mrs. Frances Gwynne of Noyadd Trefawr, now of Bath, widow, to David Davies of Penlangych, farmer at a rent of £35 p.a. Frances Gwynne was the daughter of David Parry of Plâs Newydd, St. Dogmaels and widow of Marmaduke Gwynne. In 1796 she mortgaged Penlan Cych to Eleanor Mathias of Fishguard, spinster in £400, and later the same year she agreed to sell the property to the tenant David Davies.

Refs: Noyadd Trefawr Deeds, 1771, 601-2, 2710, 985; Francis Jones, *Historic Cardiganshire Homes and their Families.*

PENNAR, *Pembroke St. Mary*★

Home of the Meares and Ferrior (also spelt Ferrier) families. The Ferriors who were here in the late 17th, 18th and 19th centuries were widely settled in south Pembrokeshire, below Milford Haven. Annabella la Ferrior held lands in the manor of Lamphey in 1326; in 1402 John Ferrior was one of the bowmen guarding Narberth Castle; they are found in Pwllcrochan, Castlemartin, Carew, Manorbier, Tenby, and Pembroke as well as Pennar from c. 1650 to the end of the 19th century. 'Pennar manor house, is now a farmhouse. Near the old manor house of Pennar is a rath composed of three high works or ramparts, parallel to each other in straight lines,' so says Silas Davies in *Wales* published in 1897.

In 1345 William de Rupe of West Pennar granted yearly rents from burgages in Pembroke held by Walter Cole and John Peverill to his son, Henry. There were two houses, East Pennar and West Pennar. Arthur Meares of Pennar and Margaret his wife moved to Golden and they died pre-1765 when George Meares was at Pennar. In 1745 George Meares of West Pennar, Esq. and he was High Sheriff in 1739. In 1765 he endowed a school for 12 poor children with £12 per annum charged on Pennar which was then an estate of 300 acres. By 1786 Hugh Meares was owner and the tenant was the widow Williams assessed at 18s. 10d. in Land Tax.

The Ferrior family produced some distinguished soldiers. Two sons of Jenkin Ferrior of Pennar, Colonel Samuel Ferrior born 1773, entered the 1st Life Guards and was killed at Waterloo whilst leading a charge. Colonel Charles Ferrior, born 1782, fought in the 43rd Regiment, H.M.I.S. and died in 1863. Their father, Jenkin was a Land Tax Commissioner for Pembrokeshire in 1769.

Refs: LT 1786; VL 1834; Charities Report 1819-37; PRO. AD. D1755 & D2142.

PENPEDWAST, *Meline*

A farmstead to the northeast of the parish church, on high ground above the valley of the rivers Cynon and Nanhyfer. The house, now an empty ruin, was built on a rocky outcrop and faced eastwards. George Owen of Henllys purchased a house and some lands at Penpedwast in 1578, and added to it by further purchases there in 1584 and 1595. What had been a remote hamlet of two or three households became a single holding which Owen leased in 1584 to the Rev. Miles Thomas, rector of Meline, who built 'about 20 years past a mansion house wherein he now dwells'.

Originally, the property was owned by local freeholders; on 20 October 1465 Lewis ap Gwilym ap Res (sic), Res ap Gwilym ap Res, and David ap Gwilym ap Res, granted to John ap Howel ap Jenkyn, a moiety of a messuage and lands on Pant Bedewas in the fee of Meline, which lately belonged to Oweyn: on 21 September 1577 Melchior ap Ievan ap Howell of Newport, yeoman, granted to Owen Johnes of Trekoner, gent, a messuage at Pant bedwast then in tenure of Owen Lewis, and on 10 March

1577/78, Owen Johnes released to George Owen [of Henllys] a messuage at Pantbedwast and a close and two acres at Allt y claffe in Meline parish. On 5 May 1584 George Owen granted a lease for 21 years of three messuages and lands at Pantbedwast to the Rev. Miles Thomas. Thus the conglomeration of dwellings and lands became a single holding.

By 1612 the parson had departed, and in that year George Owen settled Penpedwast and Henllys-issa on his sons George, William, and Evan. Penpedwast continued in the descendants of George Owen (d. 1613) until the death, without issue, of William Owen of Henllys, c. 1681, when the estate passed to his two sisters, co-heiresses – Elizabeth who married Arthur Laugharne of Llanreithan (d. 1699) and Anne who married Thomas Lloyd of the Bronwydd family who settled at Penpedwast. The eldest Lloyd granddaughter and heiress Anne (b. c. 1738) daughter of William Lloyd of Penpedwast, married, c. 1737, her kinsman Thomas Lloyd of Bronwydd, who, in 1750 purchased the moiety of the Barony of Cemaes from his wife's cousin, John Laugharne of Llanreithan. Thereafter it continued as property of the Lloyd family. Thomas lived mainly at Bronwydd, and Penpedwast was leased to tenants. In 1834 William Jones, gent. held it under a lease for lives. In 1883, plans and specifications were produced for 'the new buildings at Penpedwast farm'. By 1894 it had been sold to Morris James, described as owner-occupier of Penpedwast.

When I called at Penpedwast in April 1986, it was owned by Mr. Phillips who farmed the land, but lived at Tremain near Cardigan. The house was empty and would become ruinous in due course; the hallway was still panelled, as was the *neuadd* – relics of bygone gentry times. There were four bedrooms. The nearby outbuildings were still in use. The old orchard was on the slope close to the house.

Refs: NLW, Bronwydd Deeds and Documents, George Owen, *2nd Book,* Llwyngwair Deeds, Hampton Deeds, Tithe Map Meline, 1838, B. G. Charles, *George Owen of Henllys,* 1973; Francis Jones, *Historic Cardiganshire Homes and their Families.*

PENRALLTRHEINY, *Cilgerran*

Today the name used is Allt-y-Rheiny. A commodious residence built in the traditional Welsh style, a short distance to the southeast of Cilgerran. About 12-15 yards away is a two storeyed building, once a dwelling house, probably 16th century, and now used for lumber, at the top end of it a modern garage has been added. The present mansion is of two storeys and a spacious attic storey, all in excellent state. When I called there in May 1983 it was the home of a retired banker, Mr. P. L. M. Davies, O.B.E. and his wife, kindly hosts, who later sold the place and in 1985 moved to Fishguard.

The first family of any note at Penralltrheiny was that of Garnons, an English border family, they settled in Cilgerran parish 1559-69, and in Elizabethan days John Garnons, Attorney of the Great Sessions, became M.P. for Haverfordwest in 1571, and of the county of Pembroke in 1574. He was Clerk of the Peace for the county in 1575. He married Elen daughter and co-heiress of John Davids of Trefin and Penralltrheiny by his wife Alice Revell daughter of Thomas Revell. By Elen (d. 1618/19) he had nine children.

The Garnons left Penralltrheiny towards the end of the 17th century; in the first half of the 18th century it passed to a Miss Garnons, heiress of her two brothers who had died without issue; she married William Phillips of Fagwr Eynon, Monington, gent. who moved prior to October 1766 to his wife's home, and was described as owner-occupier in 1784. Their eldest son, William Phillip married Francis Maria Gower of Glandovan by whom he had two sons and two daughters. On William's death in 1803, he left the estate to his *second* son, John, to the exclusion of the eldest son William who was allowed an annuity of only £25. The reason for this somewhat unusual procedure, is, that William, shortly after birth, had been put out to be nursed with a woman who had a baby son of her own, and it was believed that she had substituted her own child for that of Penralltrheiny.

John Phillips, a major in the Royal Pembs. Militia, died unmarried in 1848, leaving the property to his sister's son, William E. Williams,

commander of a steam vessel on the Ganges for many years, who, on inheriting, resigned the post and returned to live at Penralltrheiny; he married and had issue.

The family of Howells of Ffynnonfelen, (Carms.) owned Penralltrheiny for a short while in the mid-18th century (about 1753-64). During the 18th and 19th centuries, the mansion was enlarged and improved. When it was advertised for sale in July 1917, the particulars and plan described it as 'a Gentleman's residence', with 84 acres attached. It was approached by a wooded drive, at the entrance of which stood the Marine Lodge. The mansion contained on the ground floor, entrance hall, drawing, dining and breakfast rooms, and domestic offices; on the first floor, the East Wing contained a sitting room, two double bedrooms, bathroom, housemaid's closet, cupboards and in the West Wing, a double bedroom and two smaller bedrooms. On the second floor were four bedrooms and two attics. There was adequate stabling including a dairy 'fitted with slate shelves'. The pleasure garden and grounds included tennis lawn, herbaceous borders and shrubs, and a walled kitchen garden with fruit trees. Also for sale, was a modern farm house 'erected about 20 years ago' (c. 1897), with, on the ground floor, a small sitting room, large kitchen, scullery, pantry, and on the first floor, three bedrooms; and outhouses.

Refs: Francis Jones Archives.

PENRHIW/PEN-CW, *Llanwnda*

A farmstead on high ground called Pen-cw, overlooking Fishguard Bay. The modern village called Harbour Village was built on Pen-cw at the beginning of the 20th century.

The earliest known owner of Penrhiw was Jonathan Thomas living then in 1699. Jonathan and Anne his wife gave a lease of 'Goodig' in 1702 to William Rogers. Jonathan Thomas moved to Haverfordwest, then to Natt's Hook, Walton West parish, where he made his will in 1722. He was succeeded by his son and heir John Thomas who married Margaret Brazell of St. Ishmaels parish, and by their post-nuptial settlement, dated 5 February 1716/17, the two messuages called Penrhiw, and Goodwick, were settled to uses of the marriage. John left two daughters and co-heiresses.

The first daughter, Anna Thomas, married William Rogers of Goodwick, and on 16 January 1744/5, they mortgaged their moiety of Penrhiw to Miss Margaret Thomas of Cilciffeth; the mortgage was assigned on 29 May 1759 to Lewis Dedwith of St. Nicholas, husbandman, who, on 3 January 1760, assigned the mortgage to William Lewis, gent. of Penyrallt, Nevern, and on 16 November 1767 William Rogers and Anne (owners) sold Penrhiw (comprising a moiety of two messuages, one orchard, four gardens, 130 acres) to Sparks Martin Esq. of Withybush. In 1786 Sparks Martin is described as owner, with Thomas Thomas as tenant.

The second daughter, Elizabeth Thomas, married in 1742 William Moore of Haverfordwest; their son Edward Moore, on 2 February 1803, sold the moiety of Penrhiw to David Harries who, in the following year, purchased the other moiety, so that the whole of Penrhiw became his property where he came to live. His daughter Dinah Harries married G. B. Meager of Oystermouth, near Swansea, and their great-grandson Captain John Meager of Carmarthen, is living. Finally, the moiety of Penrhiw was sold on 15 December 1804 to David Harries of Dinas Island.

Today Penrhiw, still a flourishing farm, is owned by Mr. Arthur Perkins, now of Penysgwern, Llanwnda parish.

Refs: LT 1786; Wills; Trenewydd Deeds; pedigree penes me; *RCAM Pembs.,* 1925, p. 185.

Jones

PENTOUR (PENTOWER), *Fishguard*
A wholly modern residence of the late Sir Evan Davies Jones, Bart., J.P., High Sheriff in 1911, Lord Lieutenant of Pembrokeshire. It was sold after the Second World War by his son and heir, Sir Thomas Jones, Bart, and described as comprising, on the ground floor: a tiled entrance hall, dining room, lounge, morning room, sitting room, kitchen, and domestic offices; half-landing: drawing room; first floor: six bedrooms, bathroom. In the early 1960s it was used as a hotel; in the early 1970s it was sold to Mr. Wynford Vaughan Thomas, the television personality, who died in 1987. It stands on high ground with a view over Fishguard Bay, Dinas head, Pen Morfa, Cwm Gwaun, and part of the river Gwaun. In the distance northwards the Preseli Hills.

Saunders-Davies

PENTRE, *Manordeifi*
A residence in the south-eastern part of the parish, on high ground overlooking Cwm Cych. Its original name was Pentre Ifan, and is thus described in deeds and legal records of the 16th and 17th centuries. Not far away is Castellan called Castellan Ifan in the first half of the 17th century. Pentre has been the home of three gentry families from the late Elizabethan period down to the present century. The earliest of these was the family of Parry descended from Harry ap Philip of Blaen Cych and his wife Anne Clement.

The first of the Parrys at Pentre was John Thomas Parry (ap Harry) who was living there in 1610, and died about 1625. Thomas's grandson, David Parry of Pentre (living 1643), married Mary daughter of Jason Lewes by Temperance Saunders daughter and heiress of Nicholas Saunders, and had a son and heir Thomas Parry of Pentre who was assessed at three hearths in 1670, so that the house was then of modest size. By this time the Parrys had slipped down the slope a little. Thomas, by his wife Anne Voyle of Llanelly, had three sons – 1. Rowland Parry, a tanner, 2. David Parry, 'in service at Cilrhiwe' in 1698, and Roger Parry of whom nothing is known. By this time the property belonged to the Saunders family. David Saunders, third son of Tobias Saunders of Ceyn-y-Felin, Cilrhedyn, weaver (d. 1719), lived at Pentre where he died in 1750. David was succeeded by Erasmus Saunders who married in 1746 Jane Phillips of Moelifor, Cards. Erasmus died in 1759, aged 40, and left Pentre to his three daughters, co-heiresses – Bridget and Magdalen, both died unmarried, and Susanna, ultimate sole heiress, (1755-1823) married Dr. David Davies, M.D., Doctor of Physic, of Carmarthen, son of Rhys Davies of Llandovery. After the marriage Dr. Davies moved to live at Pentre, and took the surname Saunders-Davies. He died in 1829, aged 74. A letter dated 29 October 1805 from Dr. David Davies written to a friend says that his son has just gone to Harrow and that the boy will soon be as good a scholar as any of the English boys, 'although they sometimes call him "Welsh Rabbit"; the masters say he has been very well grounded by Mr. Ferrior, Harrow is in the highest state of discipline'.

Five successive generations of the family succeeded to Pentre. After the mid-20th century, they left Pentre, which was sold. For a time it became a private girls' school, known as 'Pentre Manor School'. Later, Pentre was purchased by Mr. Parkes-Gibbon, a tradesman of Carmarthen.

Little is known of the mansion until we come to the 19th century. Rees wrote in *Beauties of South Wales,* 1815, 'a new mansion is now erecting on the site of the old by Dr. Davies, the present occupier who married the only surviving heiress of this house . . . its gardens and walls are of the old style and greatly admired. The grounds are pretty, surrounded with woods and thriving plantations' (p. 870).

Alterations were made by C. R. Cockerill, in 1824/25. Tho. Lewis, author of the *Topographical Dictionary of Wales,* 1840, wrote that it was 'a handsome and substantial modern edifice erected on the site of the old mansion'.

In Francis Green's admirable account of 'The Saunders of Pentre' there is an illustration, made in 1853 of Pentre, but since that time further additions and changes have been made. *The Tivyside Photographic Souvenir,* 1871, by C. Allen, contains a photograph showing Pentre as a low two-storeyed house, with ranges of five windows and a pillared porch-entrance. It was enlarged, and stone-cased in 1879, and an attic storey added.

Refs: Lewis, *TDW,* 1840; F. Green, 'Saunders of Pentre', WWHR, ii, p. 161 ff. & illust. op. p. 181; Thomas Lloyd, *The Lost Houses of Wales,* 1986, with photograph on p. 73; Rees, *Beauties of S. Wales,* 1815.

PENTRE IFAN, *Nevern**

Other than Nevern no Pembrokeshire parish can boast of having been the home of a family that has survived in the male line within its bounds for a period of 800 years. The lineage of the Bowens of Pentre Ifan and Llwyngwair may be traced from the early 12th century down to the present day with no break of succession, and thus may be accorded the blue riband of the oldest landed family in the county. The power of survival of this north county stock which established itself in as many as 24 residences in and around the Nevern district, provides a subject that may well deserve the attention of students of heredity no less than of genealogists and historians.

In all genealogies the name of Gwynfardd Dyfed, said to have been a lord or prince in Dyfed, is given as the founding ancestor of the family. He is a shadowy figure, and if he existed at all, would have lived during the latter half of the 11th century. His alleged son, Cyhylyn, is more substantial, and as he is named in a legal record we may safely accept, not only that he lived in north Pembrokeshire, but that he was a man of importance. As his grandson was living in the years 1175-1203, we may accept that Cyhylyn lived in the first half of the 12th century.

Cyhylyn's two sons were certainly men of standing, and George William Griffith tells us – 'Theis two brethren, Gwrwaret and Lhewelyn lyved in the tyme of K. Hen. 3, and by their valor recovered the Comons of Perselley from Nicholas Martin Lo: of Kemes, settling the same in themselves and their heyres to the use of the Commoners of Kemes' *(Trans. Cymmr.* 1939, p. 128), and a confirmation of the deed relating to this transaction is included in the Baronia de Kemes, and later enrolled in the records of the Pembrokeshire Great Sessions for 1568. The confirmation, made after 1243, reads 'to the heirs of Gwrwared and Llewelyn sons of Kyhylyn' which indicate that the brothers were dead when the confirmation was made. He was followed by his son Gwilym whose name is also rendered in its English form, William, a somewhat turbulent character, for in about 1195 he led a mass-trooping foray into the prebend of Mathry which he plundered, seized the prepositus of the prebendary Giraldus Cambrensis, and held him to ransom. Although the Bishop of St. Davids refused to excommunicate the raiders, we are told that the Lord and the Blessed David within three or four days administered vengeance on them, more especially on William Abwuraret, described as the ringleader (Giraldus, *Works,* i, p. 320). What form the divine vengeance took is not recorded. He was followed by his son Gwrwared II.

According to the genealogies, Gwrwared II married Gwenllian a daughter of Ednyfed Fychan (d. 1246) seneschal of the princes of Gwynedd, and although there is no confirmation of this, the dates suggest that it was perfectly possible. He had a son, Gwilym, whose name is sometimes rendered in its English form.

This Gwilym had a distinguished career as 'a king's man', as numerous entries in contemporary records testify. In September 1233 William ap Gwrwared, Galfrid de Rupe, Jordan de Kersetun, and other Pembrokeshire magnates, united to check the unwelcome incursions of Maredudd ap Owain of Ceredigion (Shirley, *Letters of Henry III*, 426-7). He appears in 1244 as the royal bailiff who administered the lands of Maelgwn around Llanbadarnfawr for the King. In 1252, described as the King's seneschal over the lands of the young prince Maelgwn, he led a successful expedition against

the men of Elfael who claimed the pasturage of Maelienydd as of privilege. In 1258 Gwilym was appointed to enquire into the breaking of the truce between the King and the prince Llywelyn ap Griffith, and empowered to punish offenders (Cal.; Close Rolls, *Henry* III, 1446/7). Two years later, Prince Edward ordered the Justiciar and Treasurer of Ireland to pay £100 to William, son of Gwrwared then constable of Cardigan who had alleged that hitherto he had received only ten pounds of salt (Sweetman, Cal.; Documents, Ireland, ii, p. 108). In 1267 he was one of the men appointed to treat with the Welsh rebels in south Wales (Cal. Pat. Rolls, AD 1266-72, 114).

From all this we see that he was a trusted officer of the Crown, and being on the winning side, received adequate rewards. Perhaps the most noteworthy of his appointments was the constableship of Cardigan castle, a post rarely entrusted to a man of Welsh blood during that turbulent period. According to the GGMS he served in France where he 'gott arms wch he gave for his owne (viz) *gu*: a chevron inter 3 dellisses, and in chief *or* a lion rampant", and later built the house of Towyn near Cardigan.

Gwilym ap Gwrwared had several children, namely: 1. Einion Fawr; 2. Ievan who married Catherine, daughter of Stephen Perrot, from whom the family of Voyle descends; 3. Gwrwared; 4. Howel Gawr, father of Rhydderch (*viv.* 1325) who was father of Rhys of Penybenglog *(viv.* 1370); and 5. Gwilym dew, from whom the Bowens of Eglwyswen and Pantyderi descended.

The location of the family's caput during this early period, has not been determined. That it was in Cemais is certain, and probably in the wooded area known as Coed Cilruth of which Pentre Ifan was about the centre. Einion's house stood near to the present farmhouse of Pentre Ifan, and an inquisition made soon after the death of Einion's descendant, Thomas Bowen (d. 1586) includes among his possessions 'the manor or capital tenement of Pentreyvan and Kilyryth and 300 acres of land in Nevern parish'.

He married Tudo or Dido daughter and heiress of a Cardiganshire magnate Cadwgan Ddu lord of Aberporth, and had the following children – Owen; Gwilym who had two sons, Llewelyn buried at St. Dogmaels in 1346, and Gwilym Gam father of Dafydd ap Gwilym the poet (fl. 1340-70); Griffith living in 1302; Gwilym (William); and Robert.

Owen ab Einion Fawr, living in 1302, is described as 'o'r Coed', and apparently, earned the same epithet as his father, for we read in Lewys Dwnn (*Heraldic Visitations,* i, p. 23) Owain Vawr, son of Einion Vawr o'r Koed, slew 26 sergeants (or collectors) of Kemes, for which he received the blessing of the Hundred of Kemes, and afterwards slew the wild wolf near the Stone of the Wolf. In the same source the massacre of the *penceisiaid* is attributed to his father.

The name of Gwrwared, third son of Gwilym, occurs in Baronia de Kemes in 1273 as a witness to a grant of lands in Bayvil, and in 1278 as one of the free tenants who witnessed a Cemais charter. He is said to have married Gwenllian daughter of Sir William Cantington of Trewilym in Eglwyswrw, a settler family well-known in the annals of Cemais. Her brother is named in the Pembrokeshire Lay Subsidy of 1292 as 'Griffith Cantington alias Hir-Sais', i.e. 'otherwise the tall-Englishman'.

Gwrwared was followed by his son Robert who married Lleucu, daughter of Llywelyn ab Owen, and had a son Owen.

A transaction recorded in George Owen's *Description of Pembrokeshire* (vol. ii, 1897, pp. 469-472) contains valuable information, proving four generations of the family's pedigree and specifying the properties that made up the estate. It is a final concord made in the court of the Earl of Pembroke on 22 July 1342, between Owen ap Roppart ap Gourwareth, plaintiff, and David ap Gwilym ap Cronewas, deforciant, to enable the former to settle the family estate consisting of 73 messuages, 14 carucates, a mill, and half a mill, on his four sons and their heirs.

From this settlement it is clear that the caput of the estate was Cilrhyth, settled appropriately on the eldest son. This document contains the earliest known reference to Pentre Ifan, and as it was settled on the second son, Ifan, it is not unlikely that it was he who gave his name to the property. In the event Ifan died without issue and Pentre passed to the heirs of his brother Llewelyn.

Here we are concerned with Llewelyn, generally described in genealogies as Llewelyn o'r Coed, i.e. Coed Cilrhyth, which can only mean that he continued to live in the main homestead.

Llewelyn's name occurs several times in the *Baronia* (pp. 88-90), firstly under 1364, lastly under 1400. Together with his kinsmen Howel ap Waryn and Evan ap Waryn, he is described as one of the free tenants of the fee of Trewern, the land so held being divisible among heirs male 'according to the custom of these parts', i.e. gavelkind. By his wife Nest Fychan daughter of Howel Fychan ap Howel ap Gwilym (descended from Bleddyn ap Maenarch), Llewelyn had several children – Rhys who received Llystyn (*'a gavodd Llystin'*, *Dwnn*, *op. cit.*, i, p. 60), a property that eventually reverted to the Pentre Ifan branch of the family; Owen Fychan who settled at Argoed in Nevern; Philip who settled at Panteg in Llanddewi Felfre; Howel 'surnamed Howel Fawr for his valour; he slew Wadinmill, Justice of the County Palatine of Pembroke. Also he slew the said Justice his porter, and before that time killed 14 persons for whom he was not questioned because of the swaie that he and his followers, and his brother, being then Steward of Pembroke, did beare in those dayes', (Protheroe MS IV fo. 84); Evan, whose name is also rendered as Ifan and Ievan, whose fortunes we shall follow; and a number of daughters.

Sometime during the second half of the 14th century, Evan otherwise Ifan, son of Llewelyn ab Owen built a new homestead which became the chief seat of the family for several generations. Whether built directly on the site of the earlier house, once owned by his uncle Ifan, or near to it, is not known, but clearly it was not far away. He is named in the *Baronia* as foreman of a jury empanelled to enquire into the estate of John Touchet d'Audley, lord of Cemais (d. c. 1409), and his elder brother Rhys is mentioned in the same document. According to the GGMS he was living in 5 Henry VI (1426-27), and Llanstephan MS 101 adds that he was steward of Pembroke under Humphrey, Duke of Gloucester, who died in 1447.

Evan of Pentre Ifan married Margaret Arnold of Hubberston, and had a son Gwilym. Gwilym ab Evan who succeeded to the homestead and married Agnes daughter of James ap Howell of Trellwyn (Trefloyne) in Penally parish by Janet Stradling of Bristol. Practically nothing is known of his life, and the same is true of his son and heir Owen, who is said to have married Janet, daughter and heiress of John ap Harry ap Llewelyn of Gumfreston near Tenby, not far from Trellwyn.

The names of the children of Owen and Janet were: James ab Owen, eldest son; Mathias ab Owen who married Dyddgu daughter and co-heiress of David ab Owen ap Meredith of Trerickert in Nevern, and settled at his wife's home where he died in November 1540. He was followed by his son Owen Fychan who married Margaret daughter of Rhydderch Warren of Cardigan, and had a son Morgan; Thomas ab Owen who settled at Trellwyn (Trefloyne) before 1490, and established there the line of Bowen; Elizabeth married Henry Wogan of Wiston (d. 1499), and had issue; Catherine married John Devonald and had issue.

The elder son became an eminent man. In 1485 he supported the Earl of Richmond on his march to Bosworth. James ab Owen of 'Pentreth Ievan' became a pledge for the good behaviour of Jenkin ap Gwilym ap Griffith goch of Whitechurch in Cemais who had received a pardon in the court of Jasper, Earl of Pembroke, held before Edward Newton, Esquire of the Body to the King, and Steward of Pembroke, for all offences committed by him after 6 May 1488 (Cardiff Free Library Deeds, No. 1101). In 1506 he was serving as an officer of Sir Walter Herbert, then Lord of Cemais. He was knighted, and, as 'my trustie and welbeloyd frend and steward Syr James a Bowen, knight' was appointed on 6 May 1514 by John, Lord Audley to be auditor and attorney of the barony of Cemais, and with John 'Dabegwillim' and Richard Verney, to be one of Audley's deputies, to enquire into the tenures of the barony and to punish those who had transgressed against the franchises of the lord (*Baronia*, p. 108).

Pentre Ifan had always been a haven, and a fitting rendezvous for strolling poets and story-tellers, whose host boasted Dafydd ap Gwilym among his kinsfolk. Many poems were produced in praise of the hospitable host and his family. Sir James died between 1518 and 1532, as shown by a deed executed in the latter year which refers to properties at Gumfreston and near Tenby, bounded by lands 'of the heirs of Sir James ap Owen, knight'. He had been married twice. By his first wife Jane daughter of Jenkin Perrot of Caerforiog in Dewsland, member of the powerful family of Perrot of Haroldston, he had four sons and five daughters (*Dwnn,* i, pp. 61, 169), namely: John the eldest son, Owen, William, William Wen iangaf, Alson married Rhys ap Rhydderch of Towyn near Cardigan, Annes married William Vaughan of Trimsaran, Carmarthenshire; Elizabeth married (i) John Reed of Roches near Laugharne, and (ii) Reynold Morgan; Elen married (i) Rees ap Jenkin of Llanerch-y-Bleiddie, Nevern, and (ii) John Howel David Thomas of Wernan, Cardiganshire; Elizabeth junior married Henry Mores of Castle Villa, Brawdy.

Sir James married secondly, Mary daughter of John Herle of Brecon by Margaret daughter of Thomas ap Griffith of Dynevor, widow of Sir Richard Herbert of Coalbrook. Mary's inquisition post mortem was taken on 25 June 1547. By her, Sir James had four sons and nine daughters (*Dwnn, op. cit,* i, p. 169), namely: 1. and 2. William and Lewis Bowen, both died issueless; 3. Mathias Bowen who settled at Llwyngwair; 4. Nicholas Bowen, died issueless; 5. Elizabeth married William Philipps of Pendibarch (Pentypark); Jenet married David Thomas of Park y Pratt (he died 10 May 1601); Jenet the younger married Elisse ap Morris of Clenennau, Caernarfonshire, and had issue; Alice married Richard Edward Howel of Vaynor and Berriew, Montgomeryshire, and had issue; Catherine married (i) Griffith son of William Vaughan of Cilgerran and had a daughter, (ii) John ap Rees Fychan of Penbryn, Cardiganshire, and had a son Morgan John; Joan married John Vaughan of Pontfaen (settlement 1541) and had issue; Jane married (i) David Young of St. Dogmaels, and had a son Richard, (ii) Lewis David Lloyd of Cilie Aeron, Cardiganshire, and had a son Hugh; Margaret married John Voyle of Haverfordwest, merchant (his will proved in 1579) and had issue; Jane, junior, died young. In addition to this ample quiverful there was a natural daughter, Margaret who married firstly Philip Perkin of Dewsland and secondly Griffith ap Ievan ap Howel ab Eynon.

John Bowen, the eldest son by the first wife, never succeeded to Pentre Ifan as he died in his father's lifetime. According to Dwnn *(Heraldic Visitations,* i, p. 169) he married Jane one of the three daughters and co-heiresses of Sir Harry Wogan (of Prendergast, Haverfordwest), but the marriage is not mentioned by Francis Green (WWHR, VI, pp. 194-6). However it is known that Sir Harry died in 1518 (his wife Katherine Mathew of Radyr having predeceased him by six years), when his inquisition stated that he had a daughter and heiress named Jane, being then aged 11 years and upwards, and 'heiress of her mother'. This is the only Jane daughter of Sir Harry Wogan that I have found, and perhaps is the one who became John Bowen's wife. John Bowen had a son, Edward Bowen who died young, and two daughters, Elizabeth and Jane. He was also father of a natural son (by Nest daughter of David ab Eynon) named George Bowen who established a family at Llwyngoras in Nevern (Papers of Great Sessions, Wales 28, 163-1). As John died without legal male issue, the Pentre Ifan estate passed to his next full brother Owen Bowen.

However, the devolution of the property was later challenged in the Great Sessions by the great-grandsons of John Bowen's two daughters, namely John Williams of Gumfreston and Panthowel (d. 1638) and Thomas Vaughan of Cwmgwili. Owen Bowen second son of Sir James, succeeded to Pentre Ifan on his father's death. He married Maud daughter of Sir John Wogan of Wiston by Anne daughter of the Yorkist courtier Sir Thomas Vaughan, Chamberlain to the Prince of Wales from 1471 to 1483 when he was executed. Owen was the first of his family to become High Sheriff, an appointment he filled in 1545. He was alive in 1555, but died some four or five years later, for the Cemais Court Roll dated 24 February 1570 records that Owen ab Bowen of Pentre Ifan, esquire, had died, and at the time of death owned a messuage and 60 acres called Pentre Ievan, and that his son and heir, Thomas Bowen was of full age. The object of the entry was to establish formally the succession of the heir as a free tenant of the barony, and although only the main residence (the caput) is mentioned, his full estate, was extensive. He left two children, Thomas who succeeded to the property, and James who never married, but, given to sauntering, left three illegitimate daughters, Margaret, Elen, and Jane.

Thomas Bowen of Pentre Ifan, Justice of the Peace and of the Quorum, was High Sheriff in 1569. An active supporter of his kinsman Sir John Perrott of Haroldston, he became involved, about 1571, in an affray at Haverfordwest between the Perrot faction and that of Alban Stepney of Prendergast. Thomas Bowen married twice: firstly. Anne Philipps daughter of John Philipps of Picton Castle by Elizabeth daughter of Sir William Griffith of Penrhyn in Caernarfonshire, by whom he had two daughters; secondly, Margaret daughter and heiress of Rhydderch ap Rhys Fychan, who died without issue.

The Cemais Court Rolls tell us of Thomas's death, and give an indication of the extent of his estate. The entry states that Thomas Bowen of Pentreyvan died on the last day of February 1586.

The heirs of deceased were his two daughters Elizabeth and Jane. He also owned lands elsewhere in the county, outside the jurisdiction of Cemais, as George Owen informs us – ' . . . the Land of Dinas . . . (and) the Lland of Barrye in the parish of Llanrian, both of late years being the inheritance of Thomas Bowen of Pentre efan, Esquire, after whose decease these Llands were shared between his two daughters, each taking one . . . the Lland of Barry is in the demesne and parcell of the manour of Llanrian in Dewisland which manor and Lland fell to the parte of the yongest daughter of the saied Thomas Bowen, being sometimes the patrimonie of the Wogans of Wiston and sould by the last John Wogan to the said Thomas Bowen' *(O. Pembs.,* i, p. 115).

Thomas Bowen was survived by his wife Margaret who later married Thomas ap Harry by whom she had a son, Stephen Parry of St. Dogmaels. By his first wife Annes Philipps, Thomas Bowen left two daughters, co-heiresses: Elizabeth Bowen *'a gadd Pentre Ievan'* (Dwnn, *Heraldic Visitations,* i, p. 170); Jane Bowen *'a gas Llystyn'* (ibid.), married William Warren, J.P., of Trewern, and had issue. William died in 1611, Jane in 1624.

Elizabeth the elder co-heiress, married, firstly, Lewis Philipps (b. c. 1553) son of Eynon Philipps of Cardigan, a branch of the Picton Castle family. The wedding had taken place before 10 June 1586. Lewis Philipps was mayor of Newport in 1588-90, and died before 1599 leaving 11 children. The widow then took a second husband, Rees Lloyd of Llanfair-clydogau, Cardiganshire, by whom she had two sons. The second marriage had taken place before 1600, for Rees Lloyd is described in that year as 'of Pentre Ifan' (*iure uxoris*); he died in 1619, and his coat of arms is included in George Owen's armorial (NLW MS. 136878 fo. 71).

Elizabeth survived her second husband by many years. In 1636 Elizabeth Bowen alias Lloyd, widow, her son Thomas Philipps, gentleman, his wife Anne, and his son Henry Philipps, all of Pentre Evan, enfeoffed John Lloyd of Trefach, gentleman, in the capital messuage of 150 acres called The Island of Dynas in the fee of Dynas, probably as part of a family settlement. She died not long afterwards, and the Cemais Court Rolls for 11 October 1638 record that Elizabeth Bowen alias Lloyd, widow, had died seized of the capital messuage called Pentre Ievan and 200 acres, a tenement and 20 acres called Place y Coed (doubtless the old plâs of Coed Cilryth), and another tenement and 16 acres there called Knwck y Clydy, and two tenements and 30 acres at Penywern, all in the fee of Trewern; and that her heir was her son Thomas Philipps, then of full age. She had held these lands in dower, and they now passed to the heir on whom the rest of the estate had already devolved. Thenceforth the Philippses held Pentre Ifan. Thomas Philipps, their great-grandson was the last of the line at Pentre Ifan for which he was assessed at four hearths in 1670. According to a genealogy he 'sold away his estate' . He was mayor of Newport 1713-21 and was buried at Nevern on 2 April 1717 and his wife in 1733, being described as 'formerly of Pentre Evan'. What became of their children, William, Frances and Mary is not known.

Thereafter the house was let to farming tenants and formed part of the estate of the Warrens of Trewern in 1759, and passed to William Warren's eldest daughter and heiress, Catherine who married Philip Jones of Llanina, Cards. Mrs. Jones is shown as the owner in the Land Tax of 1786. Her will was proved in 1793 and the property passed to her only son, Edward Warren Jones of Llanina and Trewern.

In 1839 Benjamin Rees of Pentre Evan subscribed to the Works of Rev. Joseph Harris, (Gomer); he was the tenant of the joint owners Thomas Lloyd and Charles Longcroft farming 209 acres. The Rees family were prominent Baptists and one of the family, the Rev. David Rees, born at Pentre Ifan in 1758 settled at Froghole and became an eminent minister.

The survey made in 1925 of the old buildings at Pentre Ifan states that 'in the farmyard is a tiled building of two storeys, remains of stabling attached to the former building, the upper floor is approached by outside stone stairs and has numerous small openings for light.' There is an illustration of the barn in *Arch., Cam.* 1867, iii, p. 374.

Refs: Dwnn, *Heraldic Visitations of Wales,* i, pp. 23, 59-61, 166-170; *WWHR,* VI, pp. 38, 62, 81-2; Dale Castle MS 22, 36, 41-3; NLW, Peniarth MS, 140, 63, 293-4; Llanstephan MS, 101, 21-2; NLW MS, 1602 D.189b; BM, Egerton MS. 2586; George Owen MS in *Arch. Cam.,* ser 2, vol. 38; Barony of Cemais records and George Owen's MSS, preserved in the Bronwydd Collection in NLW; *Baronia de Kemes*; George William Griffith's MSS in the College of Arms Protheroe Collection, III, IV, and V; Challenge pedigrees among the Papers of GS and in the GGMS, and on medieval records. The more modern period, from about 1500, is based mainly on Probate records and the collection of Llwyngwair Deeds and Documents, and similar collections in The National Library. Other sources are cited in the text. For the middle period the statements by Dwnn are authoritative, the information having been mainly obtained by him at first hand from members of the Bowen family in 1591, from George Owen and George William Griffith, two antiquaries whose works were largely based on original documents, many of them no longer available for present day historians; Francis Jones, *Historic Cardiganshire Homes and their Families.*

PENTRE ITHEL, PANT ITHEL,
Mynachlogddu

Marked as Pentrithel, to the west of Mynachlogddu parish church, and northwest from Dyffryn Filbro farm. Now a farmstead. Both name the ancestor of the first family at Pentre Ithel, as Griffith John Llewellin of Blaenygroes, succeeded by his son Thomas Gitto, and he, in turn, by Lewis Thomas Gitto who lived at Pentre Ithel until he was 'kill'd by a gret mischaunce with a gunne'. His wife was Catherine, daughter of Lewis Philipps of Pentre Ifan (Mayor of Newport 1588-90); She married secondly Thomas Jones who was living with his wife at Pentre Ithel in 1622. A younger son of Pentre Ithel, Stephen Jones, moved to Rhosygilwen. The Jones family remained at Pentre Ithel until the latter part of the 17th century.

The property was owned in 1786 by 'the heirs of Morris Bowen, Esq. of Upton Castle; in 1840 Morris Morris and Griffith Morris owned it, being then 148 acres, the tenant being Benjamin Thomas; in 1894 one Evan Thomas lived there; in 1904 Stephen Davies of Dyffryn Fylbro owned 1/6th part of Pentre Ithel, and soon afterwards it passed to the Owens of Cwmglôyne. The Cwmglôyne estate, owned by Morris Williams Lloyd Owen, then of Haverfordwest, advertised the estate for public auction, including Pentre Ithel (144 acres). During the 18th century Baptists held religious meetings at the house.

Refs: Pembs. RO, Deeds BD, 13, 98; LT 1786; VL, 1894, 1904; Carms. RO, GGMS (Gwynfardd); NLW, Tithe Map 1840, Mudge Map 1819, Colby Map 1831; College of Arms, Protheroe MS, iv.

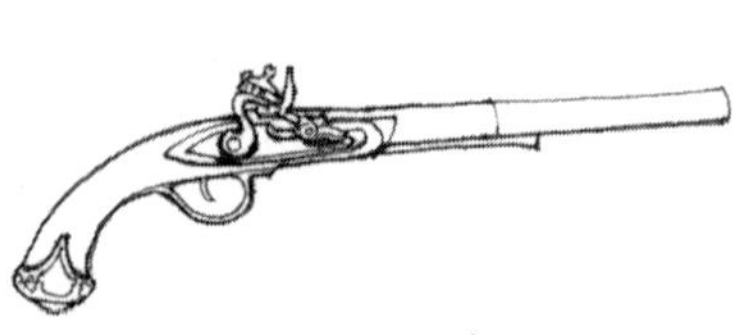

PENTYPARK/ PENTYPARC, *Walton East*
A mansion on a spur about five miles northwest of Haverfordwest, and just over one mile southwest of the parish church of Walton East. For nearly 500 years from 1500 to the present day, Pentypark was the seat of landowning families. The first known family, that of Rogers, there in the late 15th century, and John Rogers and his three children, John, Jenkin and Alice, were living at 'Bentclergh' in 1501-3. Jenkin was followed by his son, Jenkin Rogers junior, who may have been the father of Thomas ap Jenkin Rogers. This Thomas and Isabella his wife, were described as of 'Bentyberche' in 1554, being the last of the line of Rogers. Shortly afterwards James Philipps, son of William Philipps, second son of Sir Thomas Philipps (d. c. 1519) of Picton Castle, was seated at Pentypark. He was called variously James Williams and James Williams Philipps, according to the Welsh custom of nomenclature. He married Jane, daughter of Edmund Griffith of Cichele, a north Wales landowner. James died before 1572 when Jane Williams of Bentiborth, widow, alias Jane Philipps then of Woodstock and her son, John Williams Philipps, were administrators of the goods of James Williams of Bentyborth, gent. who died intestate.

The said son John succeeded to Pentypark, became a J.P., and was High Sheriff in 1622. He married Grace, daughter and heiress of Richard Vaughan of Carsygedol, by whom he had four sons and two daughters; the eldest son James Philipps succeeded to Pentypark, and their male descendants continued there until the death of James Philipps J.P. (High Sheriff 1787), who left an only daughter, Mary Philipps, who married Sir Richard Philipps of Picton Castle, created Lord Milford. She died, in 1815, her husband in 1823, without issue.

John Philipps, son of James and Elinor, (Butler), who succeeded to Pentypark, and paid two hearth taxes in 1670, was a wild and dissolute young man. He kept a band of adventurous retainers who roved the countryside freeing any impounded stock and serving their master's interests. He also kept a pack of fox-hounds at Pentypark. His troubles were recorded in a suit in the Court of Exchequer in the Easter term of 1668. He took a mistress Bridget Vaughan whom he pretended to have married until she became pregnant with his child. He then threw her out and disowned her. She was taken in by John Bowen of Wolfdale who was promised recompense if he reared the child, named Vaughan Philipps. After ten years, having received no funds from the protesting father, John Bowen went to court and was awarded £6 per year for the ten years he had raised the child. Unfortunately John Philipps declined to pay and John Bowen took the law into his own hands and raided the Pentypark estate by night taking away 12 cows, four heifers, seven young cattle, 12 calves, 17 horses and mares, four colts and 360 sheep which he drove to the village of Camrose to be valued and sold. The values set upon the stock were too great, they remained unsold, and even worse being 'wild and untamed', escaped and returned home. Some of the beasts were claimed by others who then sued John Bowen; and his fellow raiders also wanted a cut of the value of the unsold stock as they had been promised. The situation deteriorated with writs flying in all directions. John Philipps had taken another mistress, Mary Howell, by whom he had five or six children and whom he eventually married. The outcome of the dispute is not recorded, but John Philipps died in 1695, naming Mary Howell as his wife and leaving his estate to his eldest son, John Philipps then a minor. There was no mention of the illegitimate son, Vaughan Philipps. According to the Golden Grove Deeds he lived at York, married in England and had a son also called Vaughan

Philipps who is said to have married a Herefordshire heiress.

It was during this period that Fenton wrote about Pentypark, (1811): 'Pentypark, a mansion embosomed in woods, since the death of the late possessor (James Philipps, d. 1794) now seldom inhabited but by servants placed there to air it, belonged to a branch of the ancient family of Kilsant ... finally inherited by Lady Milford (d.1815) and her sister Mrs. Jane Philipps'. The property passed to the Lloyd family of Ffosybleiddiaid, Cards., one of whom, John Lloyd, had married Mary only sister of James Philipps of Pentypark (father of Lady Milford). It was inherited by Colonel James Philipps Lloyd who came to live at Pentypark where he died in 1837. The property afterwards passed again to the Lloyds, the last in the male line being Richard Llewellin Lloyd (High Sheriff Pembs. 1912, d. 1938), who left three daughters, one of whom, Grace, married Mr. Trevelyan Jones of Pentypark.

The earlier mansion was destroyed by fire in the 18th century, and the present residence was built in 1710: during the early 1870s it was restored and enlarged by Capt. F. L. Lloyd-Philipps (High Sheriff in 1877). When I called there last in 1981, the house was in excellent state, but what amused me was to find that one of the attics housed a large colony of bats. The walled garden, originally comprising three acres, had been reduced in size.

Refs: WWHR, ii, p. 67; Fenton, *Tour Pembs.*, 1811, p. 178; Lewis, *TDW,* 1840; Lloyd, Family Pedigrees and Records 1913, p. xxvii; *S. Wales, Hist. Bio. Pictorical,* c.1908, illust. of Pentypark; D. Miles, *Sheriffs of Pembs., 1541-1974*; J. Steegman, *Portraits,* vol. II, Cardiff, 1962, illust. of some 30 portraits in Pentypark; NLW, Slebech Deeds, Papers of GS, Pembs. Pleas Rolls; Noyadd Trefawr Deeds; Francis Jones, unpublished essay & *Historic Cardiganshire Homes and their Families.*

PENYBENGLOG, *Meline*

The mansion of Penybenglog stood on a bluff above Afon Nanhyfer, between the ancient fortifications of Castell Penybenglog and Castell Clwyd. It continued as a gentry seat from the Middle Ages until the end of the 18th century. Fenton, in 1811, wrote '. . . another mansion, Penybenglog, ranked with the first in its day; which, though it has long ceased to be inhabited by any of the descendants of its ancient possessors and has often changed masters, yet by having had the good fortune to find a succession of respectable tenants, it has been kept in a state of decent repair, and till within these few years one of its windows exhibited the pride of ancestry in painted glass . . .' Fortunately, a poem describing the heraldic window on 23 April 1642, has survived, while the long window, lighting the main staircase in the house, has also survived, but without the coats of arms. The house mentioned by George Owen of Henllys about 1611 – 'in Nevarne standeth Penybenglog the mansion house of William Griffith' (d. 24 March 1608). William was followed by his son George, who greatly improved the property and of whom it was written by a contemporary, 'George William Griffith, after the death of his father, lived at Penybenglog: repayred the Ruines of the decayed buyldinges, erected and bestowed charge upon ffences, hedges, and moundes upon the demesne thereof, and for enlargeinge the same demesne purchased certeyne tenements and lands in Meliney and Nevarne, amountinge to the value of £300 and upwards.'

The earliest owners of Penybenglog descended from the 11th century chieftains Gwynfardd Dyfed and Cyhylyn ap Gwynfardd. Howel Gawr held the property in 1342, and his grandson Rhys (living 1370) owned Penybenglog, Glanduad Ucha, Cwmgloyn and Cruglass Issa; he was followed by his son Llewelyn (living 1451-81), whose son and heir, David ap Llewilyn, left an only daughter and heiress, Dyddgu (d. 1538), married Rees of Dyffryn Tâf, son of David ap Howel ap Jenkin Lloyd of Blaiddbwll who, in her right, succeeded to Penybenglog. The said Jenkin Lloyd descended from Cyhylyn ap Gwynfardd and bore arms: *azure* a lion rampant *or* within an orle of roses *or,* but as 'he was a zealous partisan of the House of York, changed the colour of the roses to *argent*'. Rhys of Penybenglog died in 1520, and his wife Dyddgu in 1538; their grandson Griffith inherited Penybenglog where he died on 28 November 1569, and was followed there by five generations of his descendants who all bore the permanent surname of Griffith. Of these the best known was George William Griffith, J.P. (b. 1584) noted scholar, historian, antiquary and genealogist, who married Maud Bowen of Llwyngwair in 1605. He died in 1654/55, and many of his manuscripts have survived among the Bronwydd Archives (now in NLW), in the British Museum, and in the College of Arms.

His great-grandson, Robert Griffith, was the last male of the family at Penybenglog where he died without issue in 1737, when the estate passed to his three sisters, co-heiresses, each enjoying a share, namely Anne who married Thomas Merchant, gent. of Manorbier-Newton; she died on 26 November 1761, aged 74; Elizabeth who married Griffith Twyning of Llandre, Llanycefn, gent. had issue; and Lettice who married John Williams of Cardigan. Over the succeeding years the co-heiresses sold their shares of the estate to various buyers, mostly from West Wales. The mansion of Penybenglog, and its demesne continued intact. The mansion was commodious and in 1670 contained six hearths, and in 1744 Thomas and Anne Marchant conveyed one-third of the estate with other properties in Meline and Nevern, to Thomas Parry of Aberystwyth; by 1756 Penybenglog was owned by George Summers of Haverfordwest, who, in that year sold it to his only daughter, Mrs. Elizabeth Parry, widow.

During the years 1759-71 the tenant of Penybenglog was the rector of Meline, the Rev. Watkin Lewes (father of Sir Watkin, Lord Mayor of London, M.P.). In 1773 the Revd. John Lewes of Whippingham, Isle of Wight, Doctor of Law, sold Penybenglog, probably for a term of years, to the Rev. James Bowen, rector of Meline. The freehold continued in the Parry family until the death of George Parry of Scovaston, near Milford, solicitor, who by will made in August, 1816, bequeathed 'my messuage called Penybenglog' in Meline, and a house and garden in

Haverfordwest, to his housekeeper (and paramour), Miss Elizabeth Elson, widow. She did not keep it long, and by 1828 Penybenglog had been bought by John Hughes, Esq. of Alltlwyd (Cards.), who still owned it in 1837 with a Thomas Hughes as tenant. In the early part of the 19th century the old house seems to have become ruinous. Over the kitchen door is a stone inscribed 'Rebuilt 1828 J. Hughes Esq. (owner), William Lewis tenant'. Whether this meant it was totally or partly rebuilt is not clear, probably the latter, for the house with its ancient cellars and other features, clearly survives still on the original site. A local farming family of Hughes owned it at this time.

Penybenglog was bought by Mr. Stuart Wilson (its owner-occupier when I visited in 1986), who improved and repaired the three-storeyed house, retaining the long window that once contained ancestral coats-of-arms, tastefully extending and improving surrounding lawns, flower beds, grassy ground and walks, retaining the ancient style of historic Penybenglog.

The last 'official' notices of the house were made by *The Pembrokeshire Archaeological Survey* (1896-1907), as follows: 'Penybenglog mansion. An old pedigree house. The existing house is of the 18th century. It has good panelled ceilings, a charming old china closet, dados etc. A hideous new wing was added some time ago and the old entrance (relic of an earlier house) destroyed. Overhead was a beam, fortunately preserved, on it the date 1623, and in a vase-shaped figure the initials G.G. Outside is a nicely carved pew-back brought from Meline Church when this edifice was restored, on it is the following legend: *SED: MATHILD: UX: GEO: PER (resti GRI) PENYBENGLOG: G.E. 1626,* 'At the rebuilding of the church (1865) this pew-back was removed to Penybenglog'. (Visited 1920, *RCAM*, 1925, p. 226).

Refs: George Owen, *2nd Book,* p. 227, B. G. Charles, Ed., *NLWJ,* 1948; *Dwnn,* i, pp. 151, 184; WWHR, ii, p. 54; Fenton, *Tour Pembs.,* 1811, pp. 309-310; Francis Jones, 'Griffith of Penybenglog, *Trans. Cymmr.,* 1939, pp. 125-153; NLW, Llanstephan MS 138E, fo. 35; Alltlwyd Deeds; E. T. Lewis, *North of the Hills,* 1973, contains a photo of Penybenglog; Francis Jones, *Treasury of Historic Pembrokeshire,* pp. 59-67 & *Historic Cardiganshire Homes and their Families.*

PENYRALLT, *Nevern*

In the Cilgwyn quarter of the parish. Early in the 17th century it was the home of Thomas Vaughan, son of Lewis Vaughan of Fagwr Goch in Morfil, branch of the medieval family of Vaughan of Bredwardine, Herefordshire, whose arms were: *Sable* a chevron *argent* between three boys' heads affrontee proper each with a snake *vert* entwined round his neck. The arms are described in one of Lewis Glyn Cothi's poems before 1450. The chevron is sometimes omitted. Thomas Vaughan of Penyrallt married Margaret daughter of Thomas Mathias of Glastir. Their son Robert Vaughan married a daughter of George Perwyn of Dinas and their daughter, Eleanor to Griffith Andrew. Robert Vaughan had five sons, James, Owen, Francis, Thomas and Morris. Francis (1685-89), succeeded to Penyrallt, and married Eleanor, daughter of John Vaughan of Farthingshook by whom he had two sons and a daughter. By 1786 Penyrallt had become the property of the Le Hunte family.

Refs: Carms. RO, GGMS, I, fo. 3; College of Arms MSS; Protheroe MS IV ff. 148-9.

PENYRALLT, *St. Dogmaels*

A farmstead marked on Colby's Map as Pen'rallt, on the northern outskirts of St. Dogmaels village. Once the home of minor gentry families. In the 15th century it was owned by John Philip Thomas David, who was succeeded by his two daughters, co-heiresses, one of whom married Rees Young son of Howel Young of Cemaes, and the other married Morris ap Owen ap Howel ap Jenkin Lloyd of Cenarth. Later, the owner was one William Young, who, by his wife Elizabeth Morgan, had two sons, one of whom, Rees Young, 'sold Penyrallt to Thomas Young of Tregamon' (*Golden Grove* ms). Afterwards it passed to the Davies family, and in 1670 Nicholas Davies was assessed at five hearths, which indicates that Penyrallt was then a commodious residence.

In 1739 John Ladd, only son of Dr. James Ladd, M.D., is described as 'late of London but now of Penyrallt', unmarried, he had three sisters – Martha Ladd died young, Jane Ladd married after January 1724, Rice Lloyd of Chancery Lane, and Elizabeth Ladd who married about May 1727, James Lloyd of Cilrhiwe. In 1786 the owner was Sir Watkin Lewes who let Penyrallt to a tenant farmer.

PENYSGWARN(E), *Llanwnda*

Now a large farmstead alongside the highway from Goodwick to Harmony (Pencaer) and sits within a well-grown protecting copse, and formerly a minor gentry residence . . . In 1326 Pensgwarn is described as a Knight's fee (Welsh). In 1636 Pensgwarn (then comprising two farms), formed part of the estate of Philips of Trelewelyn, and continued as such until 1814 when shortly afterwards it was sold to the Mortimer family. In 1748 the tenant was Peter Meyler, husbandman, whose eldest son James Meyler of Pensgwarn married Ann daughter of Morris Davids of Llanwnda parish in 1748.

In 1786 the tenant was William George. After 1814, it was sold to John Morgan Mortimer gent. described as owner in 1834. However he was somewhat improvident, and on 16 November 1849 he was obliged to grant Pensgwarn and four other farms in Llanwnda parish, two farms in Fishguard parish, as well as properties in Nantcwnlle and Llanddewi Brefi parishes (Cards.) to trustees to provide funds for payment of grantors debts. The Mortimers left Pensgwarn, and in 1894 Edward Perkins held the messuage and lands, and today it is owned by his descendant Miss Nesta Perkins J.P. The farmhouse is commodious and well kept, as are the attractive well-preserved outbuildings.

Refs: Black Book of St. Davids, 1326; NLW, Trenewydd Deeds; LT 1786; Francis Jones, 'Trellewelyn' (unpublished essay) & *Historic Cardiganshire Homes and their Families.*

PHILBEACH,
also rendered as **FILBETCH,** *Marloes*

In the Dale peninsula, between Marloes village and Crabhole, about a mile from the seacoast. From about 1200 to about 1800, Philbeach was the residence of gentry families, but was later adapted to farming purposes. In the 13th century it belonged to the de Vale family overlords of the Dale district. The earliest spelling is Filbech and Fulbuche, which later is rendered as Filbeach, Fulbech and finally Philbeach. Dr. Charles suggests that the meaning of the name was 'hay field', which well describes the residence which stands on high ground overlooking a small valley. Robert de Vale, Lord of Dale, had a daughter Sara, who married William (de) Ffilbech, and had a son Sir William Ffilbech, knight. The knight was followed by an only son, Henry Ffilbech, who had an only child, Joanna, the last of the line to live at Philbeach. She married David Barrett of Dudwall, Camrose parish, who settled at his wife's home. They were followed at Philbeach by their son Peter Barrett who was living there in the reign of King Henry VI.

Peter had two daughters, co-heiresses; Margaret Barrett the elder daughter inherited Philbeach and married William Voyle, and Agnes Barrett the younger daughter inherited Dudwall and married Philip Tancred, whose descendants were still at Dudwall in 1591. William Voyle settled at his wife's home and was the first of the Voyle family at Philbeach who remained there till the latter end of the 17th century. The last of the main line there was William Voyle, living in 1647 and his wife Barbara daughter of Sir William Chancey, knight. They had no children and the estate passed to William's brother, Matthew Voyle who married Grace, described as widow in 1706; they had two daughters only, and Philbeach was sold to the Wogan family of Boulston.

In 1773 it was owned by John Wogan, with Alice Davids, aged 80, as tenant and comprised 197 acres. The last Wogan owner was Elizabeth Wogan described as owner-occupier in 1786. By 1790 it had passed to a Mr. Cotton; in 1802 Major Robert James Acland was owner, with Evan Parry as tenant; in 1840 Robert James Acland was owner, with William Cale as tenant.

Thereafter the property was occupied by farmers. The owners were Mr. and Mrs. James to whom I am grateful for their kind welcome when I called in 1977. The old mansion is now empty, and its interior partly ruined, and the owners live in a house built on the hillside a short distance away.

In 1811, Fenton noted '. . . near Dale . . . Pass by Crabhole an ancient mansion where once lived Phillip de Crabhole . . . and farther on by another venerable house, William de Filbatch by marrying Sarah daughter of Robert de Vale of Dale, became possessed of a vast addition to his own property . . . In this old house till very lately remained the old baronial hall, with a long oak table placed across the floor at the upper end, raised as in college halls, on a dais or steep'. *The Pembs. Archaeological Survey* (1896-1907) states, 'A round chimney and some portions of the old house are still standing', and continue to the present day. When I visited Philbeach on 6 September 1977, I found the old house empty, and in one part the ceiling over 'the best room', the bedrooms and the main staircase had been removed; the cellar below had been covered and cemented over. It was a large house extended on to a higher level in later times. The large old chimney at the end of the older part still survives, as does the walled garden nearby.

Refs: Francis Green, *Wogan of Boulston*, 1902, illust.; Sale Cat. June 1733; *Anc. Mon. Pembs.,* 1925, p. 218, photo showing the round chimney; Peter Smith, *Houses of the Welsh Countryside,* 1975, maps 8, 9, 28; *Dwnn,* i, pp. 71-2; WWHR, ii, p. 58; Dale Castle Pedigrees No. 137; Carms. RO, GGMS (Adv. Pembs.); Pembs. RO, Deeds; BM, Egerton MS 2586, 398-399; PRO, Anc. Deeds; NLW, Papers of GS, Plea Rolls, GF, Tithe Map (Marloes) 1842, Cwmgwili Deeds; Cardiff Library, Deeds.

Philipps

PICTON CASTLE, *Slebech*
Seat of the families of Wogan and Philipps. This is undoubtedly one of the premier country houses in Pembrokeshire, if not in the whole of Wales. It was a fortified house in the reign of William II and from that time to the present has been occupied by families in direct succession from the Norman owners.

That it has always been tenanted by descendants of the original owners lends a further distinction to Picton. No king or Baron entered its hall other than as guests, and the heraldic ensigns that fluttered above its towers – the golden martlets of Wogan, the silver wolf of Dwnn, and the sable lion of Philipps – proclaim that despite its location in 'English' Pembrokeshire it has always been the seat of families of Welsh ancestry.

The earliest known owner of Picton was a member of the distinguished family of Wogan, derived from the Breconshire chieftain, Gwgan ap Bleddyn, whose name in modified form became the settled patronymic of his Pembrokeshire descendants. The main residence of the Wogans was at Wiston where ivied fragments of their castle are still to be seen, whose memory is preserved to this day in the Welsh form of its name, Cas(tell) Gwish. It was probably the 'castle in Wales' belonging to Sir David Wogan mentioned in the Irish Patent Rolls for 1409. The family acquired extensive possessions in Slebech parish and elsewhere in Dungleddy through intermarriage with the heiresses of the knightly houses of Wizo the Fleming and the Norman de Staunton. A Wogan is described as 'lord of Pykton' in 1302, and it seems clear that he held it some years previously. Wogan after Wogan, knights, justiciars, and royal officers, succeeded to Picton until the second decade of the 15th century when the heiress, Katherine, brought it to her husband, Owen Dwnn, a Carmarthenshire landowner who traced his lineage to the princes of pre-Norman Dyfed.

Their son Henry Dwnn ventured on the turbulent waters of baronial politics and during the internecine struggles that disgraced the name of the later Plantagenets gave his support to the cause of the White Rose. He fell in a skirmish on Monday in the Vigil of St. James the Apostle, 1469, being the eve of the affair at Banbury where the Yorkists suffered a severe reverse. The inquisition taken after Henry's death, preserved among the muniments of the Duke of Rutland, states that the heir was William Dwnn aged 5 years. The lad, however, died in infancy, and his extensive properties in Pembrokeshire and Carmarthenshire passed to his sisters, Joan and Janet.

The elder co-heiress, Joan, 'golden daughter of Harri Dwnn' as Lewis Glyn Cothi calls her, inherited, among other properties, Picton. Sometime before 1486 she married Sir Thomas ap Philip of Cilsant in Carmarthenshire, descendant of Cadifor Fawr of Blaen Cych, a powerful noble whose obit is recorded in the *Chronicle of the Princes* under the year 1189 (1191). From this union came the wide spreading family of Philipps. Picton castle has always remained the principal seat of Sir Thomas's descendants to the present day.

The Wogans took a prominent part in the subjugation of Ireland and Sir John Wogan was Justiciar of that country from 1295. Six successive generations of the family lived at Picton.

Thomas's descendants took the name of Philipps. The fortunate Thomas ap Philip was a descendant of Cadifor Fawr, lord of the Seven Royal Courts of Dyfed, whose death is recorded in the *Brut* under the year 1089. His son Bledri ap Cadifor acted as interpreter between his countrymen and the Normans. Bledri's grandson, Aaron of Cilsant, took part in the Crusades, and it was he who added the crown and chain to the lion in the family coat-of-arms. His numerous descendants spread in a vast network over south Wales, and the *Golden Grove Book* devotes nearly 100 folios to them. Over 280 households were established in Wales and an indeterminate number to the east of Offa's Dyke. Sir Thomas was a man of consequence, Esquire of the Body to King Henry VII, Coroner and Eschaetor of Pembroke, Bailiff-in-eyre of the Lordship of Haverford, Receiver of Llanstephan and Oysterlowe. He commanded a force in the French war of 1513. His son John who adopted the permanent surname of Philipps, succeeded to several of his father's offices, was High Sheriff in 1542, and held appointments in the Royal Household, starting as Server, and becoming Steward of the King's Bedchamber.

They descend from the princely stock of Cadifor ap Collwyn who was Lord of Pembrokeshire and died in 1089. The Philips/ Philipps family produced numerous cadet lines and many distinguished public servants including two Lords Lieutenant, 25 High Sheriffs, several Members of Parliament, innumerable J.P.s, military and naval officers, barristers and other important posts and several were granted knighthoods, baronetcies and peerages.

During the Civil War Sir Richard Philipps garrisoned Picton for the King and the castle sustained a long siege. It collapsed as the result of a Parliamentary trick. Sir Richard's baby son, Erasmus, was being nursed by a maid-servant. As the maid watched the besieging forces through the window she was spotted by a trooper who approached the window, which was on the lower floor, carrying a flag of truce and brandishing a letter. In good faith the girl opened the window, still holding the child, to receive the letter. Suddenly the trooper lunged forward and snatched Sir Richard's heir and rode off. A genuine message was then sent threatening that if the castle was not immediately surrendered the child would be killed. Sir Richard had no alternative but to give in. The Parliamentary general's conscience was so stricken that he refused to give the order for the castle to be demolished, which is why it still stands today. Sir Richard's father, John, was created a baronet in 1621. The 7th Baronet, another Sir Richard, was raised to the peerage as Lord Milford in 1766. As he died without issue the barony became extinct and the baronetcy passed to a cousin. The Rev. Sir James Erasmus Philipps, 12th Baronet of Picton, had six sons. The eldest succeeded as 13th Baronet and was elevated to the peerage as Viscount St. Davids. The second son, Sir Ivor was a distinguished soldier and Governor of Pembroke Castle which he bought and restored. His only daughter, Marjorie, married Lt. Col. Vincent Basil Ramsden and their son, Major

Ivor Ramsden is of Cosheston Hall (q.v.). The third son, Owen, was created Lord Kylsant, a title which became extinct at his death. The sixth son, Sir Laurence, was created a baronet and had the barony of Milford re-created for him. His son, the 2nd Baron was well-known for his eccentricites and sat in the House of Lords as a Communist.

The earliest surviving picture of the Castle was sketched in 1684 when the Duke of Beaufort called there. It shows a building within a walled enclosure. The entrance to the front of the Castle was between the two main flanking towers. The 18th century Lord Milford made several changes and built a dining room and drawing room at the east end. He swept away the old portcullised entrance, the moat and the drawbridge and replaced them with a classical portico with Grecian columns. However, in 1840 the portico was replaced by a 'Norman' doorway which remains today and is more in keeping. Fenton was allowed to see over the Castle and, in the manner of the time, was refreshed with fruit and wine. Another who feasted on peaches and nectarines and took some away was Sir T. Cullum who commented on a strange horned owl which not only hatched its own eggs but also sat on chicken's eggs, hatched them, ate them and was 'rather savage to strangers'.

Refs: The Treasury of Historic Pembrokeshire, pp. 53-9, and various published and unpublished articles by Francis Jones.

Philipps

PIERSTON/PEARSON, *St. Brides*

A farmstead on the headland south of St. Brides Bay, to the east of St. Brides, and near to Hoaton farm. The villages of Marloes and Dale are situated to the southwest of Pierston farm. In medieval times Pierston was a manor forming part of the possessions of the de Brian family. In 1270 an agreement was made whereby one-third of the manors of Pererston (Pierston) and Popleton were granted to Andrew Wake and his wife Johanna, for their lives, with ultimate reversion to the heirs of Guy de Brian. Few references occur to Pierston thereafter.

In the years 1717-26 Pierston was the home of Thomas Bowen, gent., and his son and daughter, Henry and Frances. By 1756 it was owned by George Lloyd Meares, High Sheriff in that year, and in 1769 Hugh Meares of Pierston was a Commissioner of Land Tax for the county.

In the years 1786-97 George Meares Esq. was the owner, with James Roch, gent. as tenant, and later it was bought by Lord Kensington of St. Brides mansion. The topographer, Carlisle noted in 1811, 'the manor belongs to Lord Kensington in right of his purchase of Pierston, although Mr. Laugharne contends to have a mesne lordship in the single tenement of Little Marloes only, where he claims a jurisdiction exclusive of the Lord paramount'; and in the same year, Fenton noted in his *Tour* that he 'passed Pearston, once the residence of a family of considerable respectability in the county, Meares, but by purchase now the property of Lord Kensington'. Thereafter the house and attached lands were leased to farmers.

In the sale catalogue of the St. Brides estate (Lord Kensington) in 1920, Pearson Farm (282 acres) is described as 'The spacious, stone built, rough cast and slated house', sheltered by plantations, and containing five bedrooms, two sitting rooms, kitchen, back kitchen, dairy, and offices, and 'charming old walled and well timbered gardens', together with farm outbuildings, held on 21 year's lease by W. P. Richards.

Refs: Carlisle, *TDW,* 1811; Fenton, *Tour Pembs.,* 1811; Pembs. RO; LT 1786; NLW Maesgwynne Deeds No. 96; Dr. Rees, 14th century maps; H. Owens, *Old Pembroke Families,* 1902, p. 83.

PISTYLL MEIGAN, *Llanfairnantgwyn*

A large three-storeyed house, with eight bedrooms in the heartland of Cemaes, near the road from Eglwyswrw to Boncath, are three farms whose names commemorate a local saint – Pistyll Meigan, Dyffryn Meigan and Penanmeugan – about half a mile eastwards of the parish church. The most important of them is Pistyll Meigan, marked on Rees' 14th century map as the chapel of 'Llan Meugan'. As will be shown later, Pistyll Meigan was divided into two farms.

The chapel and holy well continued to function down to the close of the 16th century, but the bell was tolling on 14 July 1592 when the following letter was dispatched: 'These are to will and requier you being gentlemen to us knowne to be well affected and forwarde in her Majestie's service and good of the countrie, forthwith with all convenient spede to repaire to the place called St. Meugans where somtyme offringes and superstitious pilgrymages have been used, and there to cause to be pulled downe and utterlie defaced all religues and monuments of that chappell, not leaving one stone therof upon an other, and from tyme to tyme to cause to be apprehended all such persone and persones of what sexe, kinde, or sorte whatsoever that shall presume hereafter continue to the tenor and purporte of the said honourable commission, to repaire either by night or daie to the said chappell or well in superstitious maner, and them to bring or sende before us or envie of us'. Signed by 'your very loving ffrends George Owen (of Henllys), Alban Stepneth (Prendergast), John ap Rees, Haverfordwest'.

When the Commissioners of Ancient Monuments called there in 1914, they reported 'a strong spring still flows in the foldyard of Pistyll Meugan Farm, but no trace of the chapel remains above ground'. In 1618 it was reported that 'at Saint Meigan yng-Hennys fair are said to have been held on Ascension Day, the Thursday after Trinity Sunday, and the Monday after St. Martin's Day'. Tolls from St. Meigan's fair were paid to the Lord of Cemaes; in 1600 George Owen received £3 15s. 7d. and another relic of Elizabethan times was noted by George Owen of Henllys who tells us that two games

of Cnapan were annually played at St. Meugans on Ascension Day and Corpus Christi Day, between the men of Cemaes against the men of Emlyn (hundred) and the men of Cardiganshire.

Few references have been found to the property in more modern times. In the 18th century it was part of the estate of the Bowens of Llwyngwair. In 1726 James Bowen, Esq. granted a lease for 21 years of 'Pistill Moygen otherwise called Llanvoigan', to John Evan, mercer, and in 1758 George Bowen Esq. owned the property. Not long after it was sold. In 1786 there were two farms called Pistillmoyan, one owned by John Jones, gent. with Daniel Evans, tenant, the other by Thomas Lloyd, Esq. with David Bowen tenant; and Llanvoygan by Walter Rice, Esq. with David Morris tenant.

In 1837 Pistill Megan was owned by Mrs. Anne Evans, with Morris Williams tenant; two of the field names 'Castell Coch' may commemorate an early Celtic fortification and 'Park Pensylvanea' which suggests 18th century Quaker associations.

In 1894 Thomas and John Vaughan held Pistyll Meigan, jointly. When Pistyll Meigan was put up for sale in 1981/82, the sale catalogue showed a commodious three-storeyed 19th century house with a projection to the front rising to roof height, with an entrance porchway leading to a hall, drawing, dining, and breakfast rooms, study, two kitchens and offices; on the first floor, five bedrooms, and on the second floor three bedrooms; to the rear were outbuildings, stables, cattle sheds etc.

The house is surrounded by two acres of grounds, and included an orchard and it was sheltered by a small grove of mature trees. It can be seen from the roadway. When I gazed at it I thought of earlier days when Pistyll Meigan's hallmarks were the chapel, holy well, pilgrimages, gaiety, and pugilistic endeavours.

Refs: George Owen, Vairdre Book MS, NLW; *Llyfr Phygain,* 1618; Owen, *Pembrokeshire,* I, p. 271, note 7; B. G. Charles, *George Owen of Henllys,* 1973, and *2nd Book* of George Owen's 'Description of Pembs.', *NLWJ,* vol. V, No. 4, winter, 1948; Dillwyn Miles, *A Pembs. Anthology,* 1983, p. 220; Fenton, *Tour Pembs.,* 1811, p. 282; Pembs. RO, LT 1786; *Western Mail,* 4 June 1981, 15 April 1982, illust.; Francis Jones, *The Holy Wells of Wales,* 1954, p. 209; NLW Llwyngwair Deeds.

PLÂS CRWN, *Llanddewi Velfrey*

A mansion in wooded countryside southeast of the village of Llanddewi Velfrey. Sometimes called Poys-cwm. The first known owner, Philip Lewis Thomas, was living there in 1613-47. His son and heir John succeeded and left an only daughter, the heiress Elizabeth, who married Reynold Lewis (descended from Gwynfardd Dyfed) of Clynpottal, High Sheriff in 1678, who settled at his wife's home, where he was still living in 1693. His two sons died without issue, and Plâs Crwn passed to his daughter Elizabeth who married James Woolley and had five daughters. The property continued in the family until about 1733 when they made arrangements for selling the estate. The next owner was Thomas George, gent. who was at Plâs Crwn in 1759 and made improvements to the old mansion.

His son and heir, Evan George, succeeded and died in 1859, leaving Plâs Crwn to his son, Owen William George who married Catherine Margaret Beynon of Trewern; Evan had two daughters, Frances Margaret who married Dr. Thomas Rees-Thomas of Lampeter House, and Catherine Mary George who remained unmarried. Frances had issue, and Plâs Crwn passed to her son Frank James Gordon Thomas who married Katherine Geraldine, eldest daughter of Col. Lewis W. Penn, C.B., of Camrose, by whom he had a son, Frank Griffith Thomas, who spent part of his childhood at Plâs Crwn, which he left about 1910, when Plâs Crwn was advertised for sale. F. G. Thomas had a daughter Pamela Thomas who married a Mr. Brownrigg, and they were living at Little

Marcle, Oxfordshire, in 1981 when I had the pleasure of meeting them.

The sale catalogue, dated 1910 describes Plâs Crwn as having a tiled floor conservatory with a doorway in the centre, and at each end passes by means of French windows into a dining and drawing rooms, hall and smoke room; pantry, kitchen, scullery, servants' hall, housemaids' pantry, dairy, with passage to the back door; there were two cellars. On the half-landing was a bathroom and convenience; on the first floor were five bedrooms, and on the second floor two bedrooms, nursery, and china pantry. There was a walled garden, outbuildings, stables etc. In front of the house a 'ha ha' separated the house from the field beyond. When I called there in 1976, Plâs Crwn was empty, falling into a ruin.

Refs: Carms. RO, GGMS, LT 1786; Sale Cat. 1910; Pembs. RO, Deeds; College of Arms MS, Protheroe MS; Landowners' Return 1873; information ex inf. Mrs. Brownrigg, and Rev. M. G. R. Morris, vicar of the parish; NLW Llwyngwair Deeds.

PLÂS IWERILL (Y WERILL), *Llanfihangel Penbedw*

In the wooded glen of Iwerill. The site of the Plâs is now unknown. There were several other farms in the near vicinity; Tythyn Dyfryn ywerill and Tythyn Gwaun Ywerill (1640), all in Gwestfa Iwerill (1640-42), and Dyffrin Rhiwerill. In 1634 Philip Gruffydd ap Edward, gent. of Eglwyswen parish released the messuage and lands called Plâs y Werill to Rutherch ap Richard of Llanfihangel Penbedw.

In 1642 James Davids of Eglwyswrw parish (grandson of Rutherch ap Richard) and his mother Ellen Davids, owned Plâs Blaen Iwerill, and other properties in the parish and chapelry of Llanfihangel Penbedw, and in Gwentfa Iwerill in the said parish. In 1659 James David of Llanfihangel Penbedw, gent. owned Plâs y Werill. In 1662 the said James David and Temperance his wife, mortgaged Plâs Ywerill in £50 to Thomas Jones of Brithdir, gent. to be held in as large a manner as Rutherch ap Richard (grandfather of John Davids) purchased the same from Phillip Griffith ap Edwards; and on 3 October 1663 James Davids, gent. and Ellen Davids, widow, both of Llanfihangel Penbedw, in consideration of £70 released Plâs Iwerill to Thomas Jones of Brithdir, gent. In 1665 James Davids then of Eglwyswrw parish, held a mortgage in £28 on Plâs Blaen Iwerill and two other properties in Gwestva Iwerill.

The property passed from Jones of Brithdir to Jones of Cilwendeg, but the name Plâs Iwerill was no longer used. In 1786 Dyffryn Rhiwerill was owned and occupied by Anne Morris. In the parish Tithes Schedule of 1837 Dyffryn Rhiwerill was owned and occupied by Morgan Jones, (of Cilwendeg). No traditions of the Plâs have been found, and its very site is unknown.

Refs: NLW, Bronwydd Deeds; Tithe Schedule 1837; Pembs. RO, LT 1786.

PLÂS Y BERLLAN, *Manordeifi*★

Situated about half a mile east of Cilfowyr and shown on Colby's Map 1831. This was the home of John Williams of Blaenheiny. He was born 1737 and died 20 December 1781 leaving a son, Thomas (1768-1835), who married Sarah . . . (1772-1851). Their son, Rev. John Williams was born 1800 and was curate of Clydey. He married an unknown Anne who was born 1891. They had two sons, John, baptised 26 September 1855 and Walter and Jane, both the last named died on the same day, 20 April 1857, followed one week later by their mother. Their father John died on 2 July 1866.

PLÂSYMEIBION, *Llangolman*

A farmstead on a slope just north of Ponthowel bridge built over the upper waters of the Eastern Cleddau. The house sometimes called Ponthowel. The property came to prominence for the first time during the 18th century when it became the home of the yeoman family of Gwynne. The Plâs is a commodious building of two storeys with a range of four windows; at the side extends a lower two-storeyed building which seems much older, and may well have been part of the original structure. It is used as the kitchen and other domestic purposes, and is entered through a large traditional porch; a tablet in the outside wall is inscribed 'G.G. A.D. 1756'. (i.e. Griffith Gwynne), and on another tablet are the words 'Rebuilt by T. James AD 1871'

I visited it in 1973 and made a sketch of the house. In 1786 Thomas Gwynne is recorded as owner-occupier. On 21 June 1797, Richard Jones made a survey of Plâs Meibion demesne and adjoining farms, (Pont Howell Mill, Cnwe y Deryn, Plâs Hwdog, Tir Coch, and Wern), being the estate of Thomas Gwynne Esq.

The estate was put up for sale at Narberth on 3 August 1797. However, Plâs Meibion was not sold then, and in 1801 it was owned and occupied by Thomas Gwynne. However the Gwynne family moved to Cilciffeth, and Court Llanychaer. Plâs Meibion was occupied by several yeoman families in the 19th century; in 1834 James Gibby was living at 'Place Meibion'; in 1873 Daniel James was owner-occupier; in 1894 David Griffith and William Philips were occupiers; and in 1904 Benjamin Davies was of Plâs y Meibion.

Refs: Pembs. RO, LT 1786; NLW, Mrs. Thomas (Pencaer) Deeds; Landowners' Return 1873; Griffith Gwynne, *Place y Meibion,* subscribed for a copy of Rev. Wm. Evan's English Translation of *Cannwyll y Cymry*, 1771.

POINTZ CASTLE (CAS BWNSH),

Brawdy

A farmstead on high land near the road from Haverfordwest to St. Davids. The farmland slopes to the coast washed by the waters of St. Brides Bay. On the western side lies the parish of St. Elvis (Llansilo) and just beyond is the picturesque village of Solva.

Pointz Castle is named after an early owner, Pointz, whose name suggests Norman or Flemish origin. Near the entrance to the farm is a mound called Pointz Castle, which probably marks the remains of an earthwork fortification; the field abutting it on the west side is known as Parc y Castell. It guarded the entry to the dwelling house which stands a hundred yards or so beyond.

It was a large commodious long house built in the vernacular style, and around its front was a wall enclosing a courtyard. It was a capitular manor belonging to the Bishop of St. Davids, who kept livestock there, the demesne land and the house being let to yeomen.

A record dated 1292/3 shows that the Bishop possessed 280 cattle and sheep and grain at Pointz Castle, valued at £46 17s. 2d., a considerable sum in those days. By 1326 it was

united with the neighbouring manor of Tynewydd, and the combined manors were united to that of Brawdy whose caput stood alongside the parish church a short distance away. In 1326 the manors of 'Castrum Poncins and Nova Vida' are given as one manor; the demesne consisted of four carucates, each of 89 acres; there was a water grain mill; among the tenants were David Bowen, David Parys, David and Adam the millers, Cadifor ap David, Daykyn ap Howel, John Fawr; the Lord (Bishop) owned 24 cattle, 7 horses, and 500 sheep; the tenants had to wash the sheep; they were also to follow the relics of the Blessed David so far as Garn Twrne, and pay duties and attend courts, etc. Most of the lands specified were part of the manor of Pointz Castle. In 1545/46 Walter Wythyn, husbandman, held Pointz Castle, and in 1582 it was let to John ap Rhys of Rickeston, and in 1584-88 William Martin lived at Pointz Castle. Afterwards it was held by various members of the Rickeston family of Rhys, and they were succeeded by the family of Griffith, an old highly respected yeoman stock who lived at Hendre in Llandeloy parish.

Evan Griffith of Hendre had a lease of Rickeston in 1745 and came there to live. His son, Samuel Griffith, was the first member of the family to live at Pointz Castle, and was succeeded there by his son, Essex Griffith. In 1861 a new lease was granted to Essex for the lives of two of his sons, Samuel Griffiths then aged 26 and James aged 25. Essex built more modern outbuildings at Pointz Castle in 1867, roofed with Carnarvon slate which had come from a wrecked ship called *The Two Brothers*. The slate is said to have been a gift to Essex for his hospitality to the wrecked crew. Essex died in 1875 and was succeeded by his son Samuel who died in 1918. The last of the family there was his son, George Griffiths who retired in 1946.

Finally, on 29 July 1940 Pointz Castle was transferred from the Bishopric to the University of Wales who are now the owners. The tenants in 1986 were Mr. and Mrs. Leslie Raymond. The ancient family of Griffith was, at the time of writing represented by three ladies, the daughters of Mr. and Mrs. George Griffiths of Pointz Castle namely: Mrs. Mabel Thomas, Mrs. Iris Morgan, and Miss Dorothy Griffith.

It is a pity to have to end on a sad note. During a violent storm the roof of the historic manor house of Pointz Castle was badly damaged and the University decided that the best thing to do was to demolish the house that for many centuries had been a landmark of Dewsland, and to build, some distance away, a new house with no trace of the vernacular in its appearance.

Refs: The Black Book of St. Davids, 1326; NLW, Tithe Map, LT, and Church in Wales Records; Information from Griffiths of Pointz Castle family papers; Francis Jones, 'The Lordships and Manors of Dewsland'.

PONTFAEN, *Pontfaen*

An attractive commodious mansion standing near the parish church on a steep slope above the upper waters of the river Gwaun which flows for some seven miles to reach the sea at Fishguard. Behind the mansion, the land rises to the northeast, to the hill tops of Mynydd Morfil and Mynydd Cilciffeth, and before it, across the river the land rises to Mynydd Melyn in Llanychllwydog and Mynydd Dinas in the parish of that name. The original mansion stood there in early medieval days, and, with a few architectural changes, has retained its status to the present day. The house is protected by a copse of well grown trees.

In 1811 Fenton observed: 'Pontvaen which was inhabited by a family of considerable influence in this country within these sixty years, of the name of Laugharne, the heiress of whom married Rowland Philipps Esq. of Orlandon, whose son John Philipps Laugharne Esq. my old friend and school-fellow, is the present proprietor'. Some 30 years afterwards S. Lewis wrote, 'Pontvaen House, formerly residence of the Laugharnes, and now, by purchase, together with the estate, including the whole of the parish, the property of Henry Rees, Esq. is a handsome mansion, pleasantly situated and surrounded with thriving plantations'. In 1863 the Pontfaen estate in Pontfaen, Morfil, Llanychllwydog, and Llanychaer parishes, was advertised for sale, comprising 1,155 acres with an annual rental of £530 p.a. and 'we are informed the demesne having been in the proprietor's (Henry Rees) own hands for some years, has been farmed, drained, and improved at a very considerable outlay, under the best system of husbandry, and is now in splendid condition. The mansion and offices having been built of late years and in thorough repair . . . '

Pontfaen had been the house of three successive families for many centuries. The first known proprietors descended from the Dyfed princeling, Gwynfardd Dyfed, whose arms were: *azure* a lion rampant *or* between an orle of eight roses of the second, was borne by his descendants.

In the years 1350-1400 the owner was Rhys ap Robert ap Owen, said to have been the first of his line to settle at Pontfaen, and was followed by his son Gwilym Vychan who was there in the 1440s. His son Llewelyn, succeeded him and the estate passed to his only child, the heiress, Llenca. She married shortly before 1491, John Vaughan of Abergavenny descended from the Breconshire chieftain, Moreiddig Warwyn whose coat of arms is: *gules* three boys' heads each with a snake proper entwined around each neck. John settled at his wife's house, and was the first of the Vaughans there. In those days Pontfaen was a substantial building, and in 1670 contained five hearths. Six generations of Vaughans continued at Pontfaen which eventually passed to the ultimate heiress, Lettice Vaughan who married in 1625

Francis Laugharne, younger brother of Major General Rowland Laugharne, who took a prominent part in the Civil War in west Wales. Ann Vaughan, grand-daughter and heir of the said John and Llenca, married her kinsman, John Laugharne of St. Brides. Six generations of Laugharnes lived at Pontfaen until the marriage of the ultimate heiress, Anne Laugharne in 1750, to Rowland Philipps of Orlandon a cadet of the Picton Castle family, who there upon adopted the surname Philipps Laugharne. Later descendants inherited the baronetcy of the Picton Castle family, the last of them being Sir Godwin Philipps who died aged 17 in 1857.

Most of the properties of the Laugharnes lay in St. Brides and Haverfordwest, and the later generations took little interest in their Pontfaen inheritance and in 1823 the Pontfaen estate was sold to Henry Rees of Roch parish. Thus after over five and a half centuries, Pontfaen passed to a stranger. Some time after 1845, Henry Rees sold Pontfaen to the Gowers of Castle Malgwyn in North Pembrokeshire. In 1863 it was sold to Richard Arden, a wealthy London lawyer. It eventually came to the Buckinghamshire family called Camm. In 1941 C. B. Camm sold Pontfaen and part of the estate to Major John Francis, D.L., of Carmarthen, father of Captain John Francis, O.B.E., D.L., whose daughter is the owner at the time of writing.

Refs: Pembs. RO, LT 1786; *Dwnn,* ii, pp. 172-3, 244; NLW, Poyston Deeds; Francis Jones, 'Pontfaen', *NLWJ,* 1977; Fenton, *Tour Pembs.,* 1811; Lewis, *TDW,* 1835, 1840.

PONTGYNON, *Meline*

The farmhouse of Pontgynon stands at the northern end of the parish, on the lower slopes of the Preselis, above the waters of Afon Nanhyfer, between Eglwyswrw and Crosswell. On Rees's 14th century map it is marked as Trefgynon, a Knight's fee (Welsh). When my wife drove me there on 2 January, 1977, a beautiful sunny day, we found a picturesque old two storeyed structure with a range of three windows, very vernacular in appearance. The floors of the rooms slope with the terrain, and walking through them we approach the eastern banks of Afon Nanhyfer; ceilings are low, there are massive well-preserved old oak-beams. Mr. John Williams, the present owner-occupier, is a descendant, through his mother, of the Rees family who had claimed a lease of Pontgynon in 1786 and later acquired the freehold.

Originally the residence of gentry, we are told by the antiquary Geo. Owen, in 1603/4: 'At Pontgynon upon Nevarne banke dwelleth William Bowen, second sonne of Mathias Bowen of Lloyn gwayer . . . the house he dwelleth in was builded by himself about 28 years past (c. 1575), the lands thereof was partlie geaven him by his father, but much amplified by his own purchases'.

The Bowens remained there till the end of the 17th century, and a document of the period describes the Pontgynon estate as follows: the capital messuage and mansion called Plâs Pontgynon; a messuage west of Pontgynon Bridge; a messuage known variously as Eskybor Fawr alias Eskybor Pontgynon; a field called Park y Tynkr; a messuage called Tythyn Pantyrhiw fechan alias Tyther yr Allt grach; a water corn mill called Pontgywn Mill alias Felin Newydd alias Felin Killallyn; these were mortgages and for a time were owned by Griffith of Penybenglog which thereafter became the home of farmers who held it on leases for lives.

John Warren of Trewern was the owner in 1736. Early in 1786 it was owned by Rees Stokes, and later in that year John Rees Stokes and his wife Frances (née Warren of Trewern), Catherine Warren his sister-in-law granted a lease of Pontgynon to the then tenant, Thomas Rees, for the lives of lessors, and of John Rees (aged 7), son of Henry Rees of Penffordd, and another John Rees (aged 6) son of Evan Rees of Rhosmaen fach. In the early 19th century, the property was owned by the Lloyds and Williamses of Cwmglôyn, while the Rees' remained as tenants. The Rees family continued at Pontgynon as occupiers, James Rees in 1834 and in 1894 by William Rees, and was bought by them shortly afterwards. By 1950 it was owned by David R. Williams, a kinsman.

Refs: Pembs. RO, LT 1786; Carms. RO GGMS (Gwynfardd); NLW, Bronwydd Deeds, Tithe Map Meline 1837; WWHR, ii, 37; George Owen, *2nd Book*, 1603, p. 276, PRO, Chancery Suits 5, 451/85.

PONTYGAFEL, *Llanfyrnach*

The valley of the Tâf, through which that river runs, forms the boundary between the shires of Pembroke and Carmarthen. The vale was well known for its gentry and yeoman families some of whom have survived to the present time.

The residence of Pontygafel stands near the hamlet of Glandwr, whose nonconformist chapel contains a memorial tablet adorned with the coat of arms of John Devonald of Graig who lived there in 1757 – an unusual exhibit in a nonconformist chapel. Nearby also is Derlwyn owned by later owners of Pontygafel and used by them as a residence for the widows of the family. During medieval times Pontygafel was a residence of descendants of Jenkin Lloyd of Blaiddbwll who derived from the Chieftain Gwynfardd Dyfed.

Nine successive generations of the lineage of Jenkin ap Llewelyn held Pontygafel from early medieval times down to the latter part of the 17th century. Morris ap Howel of Graig married Morfydd daughter of Rhys ap David ap Hywel Jenkin Lloyd of Blaiddbwll, and their daughter Janet married John ap Eynon of Pontygafel, whose descendants continued there for four generations, the last members of the line adopting the surname Evans in the late 17th century.

The property passed to William James whose son John James lived at Aberclwyn from 1702 to 1767, and with Pontygafel continued in the James family until the 1970s when it was sold by the then owner, Mr. E. O. James. From circa 1700, seven successive generations of Jameses continued there, highly respected, the last generations were eminent solicitors, barristers, senior civil servants, and local government officers.

Refs: GGMS; Protheroe MS, xix, ff. 48, 53; MSS of H. E. James, B.A.; Deeds in Pembs. RO, HDX; Colby Map 1831.

POPEHILL, *Johnston*

A tall commodious residence in a rural area, near the roadway leading from Haverfordwest to the town of Milford. To the north of the residence is Dredgeman Hill, and to the south, the village of Johnston. From time to time several gentry families have lived at Popehill, but none remained there for long. In 1431 William Aftecote, described as son and heir of Margaret Cadell 'late of Apehill in Wallia', quit claimed all his lands in Treenhill, (now Dreenhill), in the lordship of Haverfordwest, once owned by Phillip Lloyde, rector of Herbrandston, Co. Pembs. In the following century the property passed to the family of Lewis.

In 1566 Hugh Lewis lived at Popehill, having married Maud, widow of Thomas Butler, gent. (son of Arnold Butler of Johnston), she was the daughter of John Harries of Haverfordwest. Hugh held the property in 1597, after which it passed to Thomas Canon, gent. who was still there in 1604. Afterwards it passed through several hands. In 1725/6 Popehill was owned by William Bowen, gent. later of Mullinger, a cadet of the Bowen family of Upton Castle. In 1762 it was held by Mary, described as widow of Thomas Williams gent. of St. Davids parish, and since 1733 of Popehill and of Haverfordwest, where she was then living with her eldest son, Thomas Williams.

By 1773 the owner-occupier was Thomas Wright, still there in 1807. It changed hands again, when bought by William Edwardes of Johnston Hall (created Baron Kensington in the peerage of Ireland on 20 July 1776), descended from the chieftain Tudor Trevor of North Wales. He died in 1801 and was succeeded by his son and heir, the second Baron, who left Popehill, and settled in the neighbouring county of Carmarthenshire where he died in 1861. Thereafter Popehill became the home of local yeomen; one of them was deacon of Bethesda Baptist Chapel who permitted religious services to be held at Popehill before Horeb Chapel was built in 1817.

Refs: Picton Castle Deeds; Carms. RO, Trant Deeds, Lucas Deeds; Pembs. RO, Papers of GS, Plea Rolls; LT 1786, 1797; NLW, Francis Green Deeds No. 3; Roberts, *Baptist Hist. Sketches in Co., Pembs.,* 1907, p. 34.

PORTH CLAIS, *St. Davids*

The cove and the farm are situated on the coast south of the cathedral city. In 1326 Porth Clais was a lay manor of the See of St. Davids. In 1587 and 1599 John Garnons was lord of the manor. The Garnons family held lands at Trefin and also Cilgerran. John was a successful attorney-at-law, and was Clerk of the Peace for Pembrokeshire in 1575; M.P. for Haverfordwest in 1571. He held the manor of Porth Clais, and in 1603 a Final Concord was made of the manor and lands between John Phillip and John Owen, plaintiffs, and John Garnons and Ellen his wife. Ellen (also called Ellin), was a daughter and co-heiress of John David of Trefin. John died in the first decade of the 17th century, and was followed by Ellen in 1618. Very few references have been found to Porth Clais in later records. In 1786 Porth Clais was owned by the Rev. M. Williams, the tenant being Henry Arnold.

Refs: Black Book of St. Davids, 1326; Taylor's *Cussion*; PRO Records Wales, 3, 0214; see Francis Jones, 'Lordships and Manors of Dewsland', *Journal Hist. Soc. of Church in Wales,* 1970, p. 9.

PORTCLEW, *Lamphey*

An imposing house in the southern end of the parish on high ground overlooking the cove of Freshwater East and the waters of the Bristol Channel beyond. Lewis in 1840 speaks of 'Portclew, a modern mansion, the residence of Thomas Parry Esq. is beautifully situated on an eminence commanding a fine view of the sea.' In 1326 Thomas Wettar of Portclew was described as a landowner in the fee of Lamphey, part of the temporalities of the See of St. David's. In 1560 Edmund Poyer and John Philips are described as 'of Portclew'. By 1595 it was held by Lewis Bishop whose descendants remained there until the death of another Lewis Bishop after 1771.

The Bishop family had come to Pembrokeshire in about 1600 and bore arms: *argent* on a bend cotised *gules* three plates (or besants). The well known family of west Wales landowners, the Parrys, succeeded the Bishops when John Parry married Margaret, daughter and heiress of Lewis Bishop and came to live at his wife's home. John became High Sheriff in 1772. Their

son William Parry married Ann Kemm, second daughter of Henry Kemm of Northdown, their marriage settlement having been made on October 22 1801. Their daughter, Mary Ann Parry married at Lamphey on 26 January 1830 the Rev. Francis George Leach, son of Abraham and Catherine Leach of Corston. Francis died in 1876 aged 80 and his wife died in 1894 aged 86. By the mid-19th century the Parrys had left Portclew and Portclew House became the home of Col. William Morrison whose descendants were still there in 1904. The district around Portclew had a number of properties which bore the name. In 1786 John Parry was owner-occupier; Sir Hugh Owen owned East Portclew; Sarah Bastin owned Little Portclew and Abraham Leach owned another farm of the same name. In 1894 there were four properties in the area: Portclew; Portclew Burrows; Upper Portclew and Little Portclew. By 1950 most of these properties remained including Portclew House, occupied by the Uphill family.

Owen

PORTHIDDY (PORTHEIDDY) FAWR *and* **FACH**, *Llanrhian*

A large farmstead on the boundary separating the parishes of Llanrhian and St. Davids, with lands in both parishes. The capital messuage was Porthiddy Fawr, with Porthiddy Fach, the small adjacent farm forming part of the larger property The lands are on the coast near the cove called Abereiddy, bordered on the northern side by Ynys y Barry, and on the southern by Cwmwdig.

Several references to the property occur in medieval deeds and documents. In 1383 Philip ap Philip Meugan granted lands at Porthiddy fawr, Llanmyon Frân, and 'Trefftheyaw', all in the lordship of Pebidiog to Margaret daughter of William ap Philpyn. In 1450, Walter ap Jenkin Lloyd owned lands in Porthiddy fawr and two years later he released to John ap Ieun Gwyn ap Rhys four stangs at Porthiddy Fawr, called Tyrhende, Penvrce, Martle and Fford Fychan, and several other properties within the lordship of Pebidiog; and in the same year he released to John ap Oweyn of Porthiddy Fawr, 'lands in Porthiddy Fawr where the hall of John ap Oweyn is'.

In 1459 David ap David Lloyd of Llanderoe (now Llaney near Croesgoch), released 16 virgates in Porthiddy Fawr to John ap Oweyn. In 1523 Dafydd ap Ievan ap Meredydd granted to his daughter Margaret 'a messuage and lands in Porthiddy Fawr and Fach'.

The property seems to have changed hands fairly regularly during these early days, but in the 16th century it passed to a local yeoman, and remained in successive generations of his descendants for nearly two centuries. This was the family of Harry, later known as Harries.

The first known ancestor was David Harry James the elder of Porthiddy Fawr who was there during the period 1588-1630, and is variously described as yeoman and husbandman. Of his wife all that is known of her is her Christian name, Margaret. They had two sons, David Harry (James) the younger who was at Porthiddy Fawr from 1637 till about 1679 when he died. He had a brother, George Harry; described in contemporary deeds as 'gentleman', he married a member of a well known gentry family; Grace daughter of Thomas Jones of Brawdy, and sister of John Jones. Their prenuptial settlement was made on 30 March 1629. Their two sons, David and John adopted the surname Harries, and their daughter Elizabeth married David Perkins of Trevaccoon (d. 1694). John succeeded to the property and is described in 1663 as 'gentleman'. He was assessed for four hearths in Porthiddy Fawr in 1670. His will, dated in 1685, was proved in the year following. John Harries married Jane daughter of a wealthy landowner, Thomas Phillip of Trelewelyn near Manorowen, their marriage settlement being dated 25 July 1658. He died in 1686, and Jane died about 1716/17.

They had three sons and five daughters. The eldest son, David Harries, received only £10 under his father's will, while Porthiddy and Treglemais, with other properties were left to his widow absolutely. David moved to London where he married a lady much in debt for which he was arrested. After this he went to Holland and became a favourite of the Prince of Orange, who became King William III of Great Britain in 1694. David continued to enjoy Royal favour, and in 1701 is described as a Page of the Bedchamber in Ordinary. He lived in London but little is known about him or his wife. He had two sons, the younger being John Harries, a Colonel in the Army, but neither had any association with Porthiddy or the county. James Harries, the second son went to live in London where he fought a duel. As a result, he returned to his native county, and married Elizabeth Harries, widow of Haverfordwest. He lived at Haverfordwest for the remainder of his life, and died in 1719. He had no issue.

The third son, George Harries, entered the medical profession and practised as a physician in London. On the death of his brother James, he inherited the paternal estate of Porthiddy, and then settled in Haverfordwest. Very little is known of him or his wife; their two children were Jane and Caroline Harries; the elder daughter lived in Carmarthen, and died unmarried some time after 1763; the second married Thomas Griffiths of Coed, Llandyfaelog, Carms., and had a son and a daughter. The five daughters of John Harries and his wife Jane (Phillips) were Elinor, Mary, Ursula, Anne and Elizabeth, all of whom married

Pembrokeshire landowners and clergymen. Elinor, the eldest daughter, married firstly, Thomas Higgon, and secondly, Owen Phillips of Haverfordwest (d. 1740), by whom she had three sons, from one of whom, George Phillips, a clergyman, descend the well-known county family of Lort-Phillips.

The Porthiddy estate passed eventually to Lort-Phillips; in 1786 George Phillips, Esq. was the owner, and in 1801 John Lort-Phillips is described as owner of Porthiddy Fawr and Fach, and it continued in possession of that family until finally sold.

There is a tradition recounted by Francis Green, in a letter written in 1894 to J. W. Phillips, that when a Mr. Harding married an unknown daughter of a Harries of Porthiddy he is said to have 'ploughed up a rich treasure' on Porthiddy land; a field on Porthiddy is still called Park Harding.

Refs: Pembs. RO, LT 1786 et seq.; NLW, Morgan-Richardson Deeds; Eaton Evan and Williams Deeds; Papers of GS, Plea Rolls; WWHR, VIII, pp. 141-146; Essay by Francis Green who erroneously ascribes the origin of the Porthiddy Fawr family to the Harries of Cruglas; Francis Jones, *Historic Carmarthenshire Homes and their Families.*

POSTY, *Bletherston**

Home of the family of Thomas, now a farm. Known as Poysty Bach and Poistye in the 17th century. John Rickert of Posty married a daughter of Piers Scourfield of Moat and their daughter Janet married Rhys ap Jenkins who settled at Posty and had a son, David ap Rhys living in 1591. In 1658 Arthur Lewis of Bwlchyclawdd had married an heiress of Posty and in 1648 Lewis Rees was of Posty Mawr, gent. In 1674 Rice Lewis of Posty Mawr Anne his wife and their son, John Lewis of same place, gent. mortgaged Posty Mawr and closes in parish of Bletherston to Laurence Colby, gent. of Bletherston. In 1678 they sold Posty Bach to Laurence Colby and in the following year released the said lands. Thomas Vaughan became the tenant of Posty in 1683, and in 1742 John Colby settled Posty (inter alia) on his pre-nuptial settlement when he married Grace Davies. Vaughan Thomas was a Land Tax Commissioner for Pembrokeshire in 1769, and High Sheriff in 1782. The Colby family still owned Posty in 1811.

Refs: Spence Colby Deeds; *Dwnn,* i,.176; NLW Trenewydd Deeds Nos. 107, 108, 2; Pembs. Plea Rolls Nos. 182, 231.

Stevenson-Owen

POYSTON HALL, *Rudbaxton**

The earliest references are 'ville de Poytynges-ton' in 1476 and 'Poythenston' or 'Poytington' in 1480. The name is probably a corruption of 'Poytyns farm', certainly a Henry Poytyn was living in the Haverfordwest area in 1340. By 1592 the place was referred to as 'Poiston' or 'Poyston', later it became known as 'the hall house of Poyston' (1671) or just 'the Hall' (1679).

It is difficult to determine the form of the house that existed here before the 18th century, probably whatever it was became incorporated within the structure of the rear service rooms of the house. Still visible are several blocked up windows and a doorway, with possible evidence of vaulting. The latter visible on the kitchen chimney stack suggests antiquity. The site is also suggestive of age, being low down, not far from water. A will in the early 18th century refers to an 'oak room'.

The three-storey front of the house with its Georgian symmetry is obviously 18th century. It faces south at a right angle to the axis of the old house. Thomas Picton, the owner of Poyston in the middle years of that century, sold two farms, Scollock (192 acres) and Triffleton (69 acres) for over £600 in the 1750s, so perhaps this financed his building. Certainly he had a large family so the size was useful. Superficially the house now looks much as it did in his time because although it was later totally upgraded

General Picton

and improved in the 19th century, the refurbishment respected the Georgian feel of the house. The Georgian interior was probably fairly plain with modest room sizes. The stairs to the top floor and some internal doors survive from this period. Externally there is still some slate hanging (a typical Pembrokeshire vernacular feature) dating from then, together with zig-zag brick cornicing under the eaves at the rear of the house. There are two small vaulted cellars under the front hall. Up until the Victorian changes there was a stone porch with some classical decoration, banded rustication in the stucco up to the first floor string course and a bust of General Picton mounted over the middle window over the porch.

In the mid-1800s the house, along with Withybush House, was acquired by William Owen, a highly successful architect, builder and joiner who had decided to completely retire from trade and become a gentleman. He was one of the founders of the *Western Telegraph* weekly newspaper. His son, Henry Owen, eventually settled at Poyston and it was during his time that the last phase of development took place. He added the dining room with the galleried library above making an impressive room two storeys high and embellished with heraldic crests, a gilded overmantel displaying the Owen crest and a collection moulded fireplace with Dutch tiles. He thoroughly overhauled the rest of the house adding panelling, a stained glass window by Dix on the stairs, an ornate plaster fireplace and overmantel celebrating the battles of General Picton in the front hall, etc. He added many 'high tech' features of his age including a bathroom, an acetylene gas generating plant, the hydraulic ram system which pumped water up to the greenhouse, and an electric wind direction indicator linked to the dragon weather vane on the library roof. He also added an attractive lodge (now called The Rose Gate) and gates and piers at the end of the front drive. This drive was known as The Avenue and whilst it was improved by Henry Owen, its route is identical to that shown on the 1830s tithe assessment map. An interesting feature almost now disappeared was a stone and iron bridge that crossed the public road and linked Poyston, via a path to Withybush House, the other Owen property. Dr. Henry Owen of Withybush, later of Poyston, was D.C.L. and Ll.D. of Oxford. He was a great antiquary, Governor of Haverfordwest Grammar School and Trustee of Sir John Perrot's charity. He was author of *Old Pembrokeshire Families* and editor of *Owen's Pembrokeshire.* He died in April 1919 aged 75. He was one of four brothers, Judge Stevenson Owen, George Leader Owen and the Revd. James Owen of Cheltenham College. His sister became Mrs. Pugh Evans of Carmarthen.

There is a story in the public record office dating from Victorian times told by a gamekeeper that the ghost of General Picton dressed in a cloak and carrying a sword appears on the front drive on the anniversary of his death at Waterloo. Also associated with the legend of General Picton is the blackened skull of a horse that still exists under the floor of the drawing room. This is supposedly his horse from the battle of Waterloo. Tradition has it also that the rest of the horse is buried under the big lawn.

The grounds amount to 15 acres. Laid out in the 18th century the whole is surrounded by a belt of trees. Below a partially walled kitchen garden, lawns slope down to a small lake that in Victorian times boasted a boat house. There are several ornamental trees still surviving, the best being a Tulip tree growing close to the dining room.

Refs: D. Ellis; Francis Jones Archives.

Stepney

PRENDERGAST,

Prendergast

The ancient residences, known as Prendergast House and Place, stood on low ground on the western bank of the river Cleddau which divides Prendergast parish from the Borough of Haverfordwest. The property derived its name from the medieval owners, the last of whom to reside there, Maurice de Prendergast, accompanied Strongbow to Ireland where his descendants remained for successive generations and had no further connection with Pembrokeshire.

Prendergast Manor and its accompanying estate passed to the family of Joce (or Joyce), then to the Wogans, and in early Tudor times to the family of Cadarn or Catharne. Henry Catharne of Prendergast became Constable of the Pebidiog Hundred (now Dewsland), and Clerk of the Courts of Haverfordwest and Roose. He was lord of the manor of Prendergast and held manorial rights, including a gaol beneath his tower at Prendergast; and all other privileges: all having been held by Sir John Joce and his son, Thomas Joce, Esq. who were his predecessors at Prendergast. He held the manor of Bulhook: one quarter of the manor of Dale, and rights of wreck there, half the fishing of the Cleddau by the side of the river where his land was.

His will, dated 17 April 1525, was proved in the following year. He was succeeded by his son Thomas Catharne, High Sheriff of Pembrokeshire in 1565, and M.P. for the county for a long period before he died on 24 February 1567/8. By his wife Jane, daughter of Sir John Wogan, he had four daughters, co-heiresses, and Prendergast House passed to his daughter Margaret (b. 1546), who married in 1565 Alban Stepney, the first of an English family from London and East Anglia to settle in west Wales.

On 31 December 1561 the Bishop of St. Davids appointed Alban to be Receiver-General of the diocese for life. By his marriage he acquired Prendergast House and other portions of the estate which Margaret his wife had enjoyed as daughter and co-heiress of Thomas Catharne. She died before 1573, and by that year Alban had married his second wife, Mary, daughter of William Philipps of Picton Castle. Alban was also High Sheriff of the county in that year, an appointment he held again in 1590 and 1605. Active in public affairs, he was M.P. for Haverfordwest in 1584 and 1586, for Cardigan county in 1589, for Carmarthen County in 1597, and for Pembroke County in 1603. He added to his estate in 1579 by purchasing lands near Prendergast, and in Haverfordwest, and in the parish of Roch. Alban Stepney died in 1611, was survived by his wife, Mary (Philipps), by whom he had four sons and two daughters. His will, recited in detail by Mr. Francis Green, shows that he owned an extensive estate in Pembrokeshire and Carmarthenshire. His eldest son and heir, John Stepney, born in 1600, received a Knighthood in 1621, and on 10 November of the same year, advanced to a baronetcy. The baronetcy was borne by his descendants, and terminated with the death of Sir Thomas Stepney, 9th Bart, on 12 September 1825, without issue. Sir Thomas had been Groom of the Bedchamber to Frederick, Duke of York, for thirty years.

The family property then passed to descendants on the female side who had married into the Gulston family who lived at Derwydd, Carms. They took the name of Stepney-Gulston, and later Cowell-Stepney. On 22 September, 1871, John Cowell-Stepney was created a baronet, and left two sons. James Charles Murray Cowell-Stepney, Page of Honour to King William IV, was a Lieutenant-Colonel in the Coldstream Guards, and was killed at the Battle of Inkerman in 1854, aged thirty. His brother, Emile Algernon Arthur Keppel Cowell-Stepney, succeeded to the estate, and on the death of his father Sir John Cowell-Stepney on 15 May 1877, Emile succeeded to the baronetcy. He was somewhat eccentric, dropped his title, and emigrated to the United States where he died in 1909.

No remains of Prendergast House have survived, and few references to it in earlier sources have been found. In 1530, we learn that Henry Catharne, Esq. Lord of the Manor of Prendergast, kept a gaol under the tower of his house. There is a long gap to the next reference. This is in June 1662 when John Ray speaks of 'a fair house of Sir John Stepney'. In 1670, Prendergast then the house of Sir John Stepney, is described as containing nine hearths. During the 18th century the Stepneys spent most of their time in Carmarthenshire, and ceased to reside at Prendergast which became ruinous, finally derelict. A tourist who saw it in October 1767 speaks of it as 'now in ruins'. A few parts of it continued to exist in 1811 when Richard Fenton notes '. . . I descend to the margin of the rich meadows whose banks the Cleddau washes, to see the small remains of the mansion called Prendergast Place . . . where nothing is left but the shell of a spacious barn, and one fragment of a portion of the old house, with a few small apertures by way of window cased with freestone, and part of a lofty garden or orchard walk . . . (after the departure of the Stepneys) the old mansion of Prendergast was suffered to fall into decay, and the property annexed to it sold'.

Samuel Lewis, the topographer, found little there of interest in 1840, when he noted as follows '. . . of whose mansion some remains may still be traced . . . (on the family moving to Carmarthenshire) 'the ancient seat, being deserted soon fell into decay.'

The only relic of the early days to have survived is 'The Lady of the Ghyll', a ghost in the form of a vaporous cloud, said to walk along a footpath in Prendergast; the small tract of land that harbours her is called 'The Ghyll'.

Refs: Dwnn, i, pp. 89, 135, 180. GGMS, Pembs. Pedigrees; Fenton, *Tour Pembs.,* 1811, p. 120; Lewis, *TDW,* 1840; NLW, LT 1786, Poyston Deeds No. 157, Burke, *Landed Gentry,* 1969 (Stepney-Gulston); Francis Jones, *Historic Carmarthenshire Homes and their Families.*

PRISKILLY, *Mathry*

John, son of Robert Goch of Preskyli held land in the manor of Castle Cenlas in 1342. In 1661 the Bishop of St. David's granted a lease to John Owen, of Priskilly, of lands including the wood or forest of Priskilly. The parcel consisted of about 400 acres and Owen '. . . hath built a pretty litle tyled house thereon'. Later the area seems to have been divided into three sections: Priskilly Forest, Priskilly Fach and Priskilly Fawr. In the 18th century ownership was divided between the Bishop of St. David's, the

Scourfields, the Vaughans, the Lloyds, the Morses and the Howells. In 1815, 297 acres of Priskilly Forest was held by Moses Mathias and 520 acres of Priskilly demesne by J. H. Harries Esq. 'The ancient mansion of the family of Harries of Priskilly Forest is now the property of John Hill Harries Esq.' (Lewis, *TDW,* 1840). 'The house is of no regular order of architecture, and when the present occupier came into possession of it, had grown much dilapidated by age. He immediately set about repairing and improving it, and it now presents the appearance of a comfortable country residence such as befits the habits and requirements of a private gentleman of fortune. It stands embosomed in wood and skirted by the Western Cleddau. The grounds are extensive and, like the gardens, kept in the best possible order.' (Burke, *Heraldic Visitations*, ii, p. 231, 1853). The Harries family were in possession in the 1880s (*Vide* Walford, *County Families*).

Fireplace detail, Priskilly

RAMSEY ISLAND
(YNYS DEWI *and* YNYS TYFANOG)

Lying off the St. David's Peninsula, across Ramsey Sound. Home of the Whitton family. Thomas Whitton (d. 1673/4) married Lettice, daughter of James Wogan of Stone Hall and his wife, Ursula, née Laugharne. Thomas had a son, also named Thomas, (d. 1684, will proved 1684/5) who married Anne, (d. 1699). They had four children, Thomas, the heir, who died in 1734, Christopher who was of Ramsey Island when he married in 1698/9, Katherine Voyle of St. Elvis, widow of James Warlow of Llether. The daughters were Elizabeth and Anne of whom nothing is known.

In 1543/4 Nicholas Jenkins, Philip Lewes, Thomas Blethryn, Geoffrey Walter, John Vechan, Thomas Gwilym Owen, Thomas Walter, John Voyard, all of the City of St. David's, mariners, were summoned to answer William Browne of St. Davids, for 'taking his goods at Ramsey, on 23 May, 1543, viz. 50 puffins eggs, 60 puffins, and 500 gulls at Ramsey, to the value of £10'.

The Rev. James Summers who held a lease of Ramsey Island (1822) under-leased it for £65 per annum to John Mathias and David Morgan, trustees and executors of the late John Summers Esq. In 1832 there is record of a lease from the Bishop of St. Davids to William Bowlas Summers of Walwyn's Castle, (son of James Summers, deceased), of Ramsey Island, and in 1833 he instituted an action that the lease to John Mathias and David Morgan be set aside. In 1848 J. B. Summers leased the Island to the family of George Phillips , farmers of Rosepool for the life of Elvi, wife of George Phillips at £226 10s. 6d. rent p.a., but George Phillips surrendered the lease in 1851. On 20 June 1891 William Williams of Grove Hotel, St. Davids, innkeeper, granted a lease to Luther Bowen Rees of Clegyr, farmer of Ramsey alias Ynys Trevanog, and the small islands called the Bishop and his Six Clerks; being the prenuptial settlement of said L. B. Rees and Elizabeth Mary, daughter of William Williams. On 1 February 1901 there was a notice in the *County Guardian* - 'Ramsey Island to let, together with the outlying islands of North Bishop, South Bishop, Cantwr, and Walltog. Ramsey is well stocked with rabbits and feathered game of every description. The area of Ramsey is about 600 acres, arable and grazing, and is well watered and fenced. For further particulars apply to Mrs. Martha Williams, Grove House Hotel, St. Davids, or to Mr. John Reynolds, Treglemais, Croesgoch'.

The Black Book of St. Davids (1326) states 'They say that the Lord (Bishop) has in the Island of Ramsey two carucates of Land containing 100 acres and each acre worth to let 2d. per year, and there can be kept there 10 horses, 100 head of great cattle and 300 sheep and the pasture for each head of great cattle is 2d. and for every 10 sheep 2d., and they say that the Lord (Bishop) is able to take thence 100 loads of rushes and heath; each load is worth 3d. and the Lord is able to take there, without injury to the stock, 500 rabbits for cooking and they are in actual value worth 33s. 4d. Total 75 shillings'.

Fenton's *Tour Pembs.* records: 'The old house where I have formerly made one of many a pleasant party is in ruins, and a new farmhouse is built near'. *The Cambrian Travellers Guide'* (1813), says that the place is the home of the peregrine falcon, that puffins were few and that the local cheese was 'excellent'.

The Queen and her family picniced on the island on 9 August 1977, when the royal yacht, *Britannia* put in on her way to Northern Ireland.

Refs: Fenton, *Tour Pembs.,* Vol. 2, p. 69; Pembs. Plea Rolls No. 238; 35 Hy 8; W & W (H'west) Deeds 12052 & 12072; *County Guardian* 1901; Terrier in Carms. RO; *The Cambrian Travellers' Guide,* 2nd edn., 1813; *Blacks Picturesque Guide,* 1853, p. 292; *Country Quest,* Oct. 1967; H. Moll *Deser of Wales;* 17 HO, p. 262; *Black Book of St. Davids*, 1326, pp. 15-17; Cardiff Public Library Pembs. Deeds, Pembs. RO HDX Deeds, & HDX/80.

Mathias

RHOS Y BAYVIL, *Bayvil*

Shown in Colby's Map of 1831. Home of the Peverill and Mathias families. These Peverills are descended from the great but now extinct Norman house. George Owen in his *Second Book* says '. . . now the dwellinge place of Thomas Mathias ap Owen. The house is now more simple in vyor than the partie is auncient by descent as heyre male to the auncient famylie of the Peveralls whose auncestor was of those of Devon who was one of the knights that came with Martyn Toures to the Conquest of Kemes and had to him geaven this, Tregamman and diverse other landes, but tyme had greatlie dessinguished the lyving and estimasion of this famylie. His father Mathias was sonne to William sonne to Gwillim sonne to Owen Peverell third sonne to John Peverell'.

John Peverill in 1427/8 divided his large estate between his three sons. The youngest, Owen Peverill received Rhos y Bayvil, (amongst other lands). From him descended paternally Mathias ab Owen of Rhos y bayvil whose children adopted the permanent surname Mathias. The arms are: quarterly *gules* and vair, a lion rampant *argent*. George Owen finds a later version of the Peverill arms as: *Sable* four besants in chief, on an escutcheon of pretence gyronny *argent* and *gules*. Owen's son Gwilym married Alson, daughter of Owen Ievan Lloid of Treyordan. Their son, William, had a son and a daughter. The heir, Owen William married Margaret, daughter of Jenkin Llewelyn of St. Dogmaels, and their heir was Mathias ab Owen who married Gwenllian, daughter of Thomas Mathias Bowen. They had three sons, Thomas, the heir, Owen and John. By 1786 William Rowland gent. was owner occupier assessed at 8s. 11d. Land Tax.

Refs: Wagner MS 2. GO; George Owen, *2nd Book*, p. 269.

RHOSDWARCH, *Meline*

South of Rhosmaen, shown on Colby's Map of 1831. Formerly the home of the Watkins family descended from Ieuan ap Llewellyn, (to Howel Gawr). In 1602 William Watkin, son and heir of Watkin ap Ieuan, late deceased, was of 'Rose Towardr'. William married Elizabeth, daughter of George Thomas, and they had two sons, George, 'begotten before marriage' and who married the daughter of William Gwyn of Pwll y Cregin and had a son William Watkin of Cardigan. The second son was Ieuan. A daughter of Ieuan William Watkin of 'Kest Weyrch' and Elen his wife, the daughter of William Bowen of Pontgynon married the son of John Howell of Cilymainllwyd. By 1718 John Howell, (will dated 19 April 1718) was of Rhostwarch. He married Elizabeth and had one son, John (viv. 1752), and three daughters, Mary, Anne and Grace. John Howell married Martha, daughter of William Lewis of Bwlch y Clawdd, prenuptial settlement dated 2 October 1720. She had a portion of £100. They had four sons and two daughters. The eldest son was the Rev. John Howell who was of Rhostwarch in 1752 and of Bridgwater where he died in 1804, having had one son, John, who died without issue, and four daughters. The second son of John and Martha was Roger Howell (d. 1762) who had a son, George living in Spanish Town, Jamaica in 1809. In the 1786 Land Tax the Rev. John Howell is shown as owner and the tenant as John Griffiths. In the Voters List of 1834 David Phillips is shown at Rhostwarch and is still there in 1894.

Refs: Mudge Map 1819; *Anc. Mon. Pembs.* p. 226; GGMS (Gwynfardd); ibid. I, Tydwal, fo. 5; Bronwydd Deeds No. 1294; LT 1786.

Hergest

RHOSLANOG FAWR *and* **VACH,** *Mathry*

Home of the Hergest and Wogan families. John Hergest was assessed at one hearth in 1670. Lewis Wogan of Boulston, (d. 1702), names Thomas Wogan of 'Treslanog' as a remainder-man to his estate. The arms of Hergest: *argent* a dragon passant, wings raised *sable* langued *or*. The arms of Wogan: *or* on a chief *sable* three martlets of the first. Crest: A cockatrice.

In 1326 Rhoslanog Fawr was a knight's fee. In 1560 William ap John ap Ievan John ap Ievan ap David, William ap Ievan ap David, all yeomen, Isabella verch Ievan ap David, housewife, Jenett verch Philip John ap Rees, housewife were all of Rhoselannoke Vawr. By 1593 Hugh Wilkins yeoman released Roslanog Vawr and Vechan to Rees ap Rees of Mathry, and in 1614 Rice ap Ievan was sued by William Perkin, gent. for trespass and depasturing. The will of Thomas Phillips of Trelewelyn, (will dated 24 November 1681), included two messuages in the occupation of John Hergest who had been there since 1641; Thomas Hergest held Rhoslanog Vawr in 1697. By 1747 Sparks and Martha Martin of Withybush leased Rhoslanog Vawr in the townred and fields of Rhoslanog to Edward Lawrence of Mathry, and in 1792 James Lawrence held the lease from Gwyn Vaughan of Jordanston, Esq. being the only surviving life, for the lives of said James, Phoebe Skeel of Trewilliam and Edward Lawrence, nephew of James Lawrence, the rent being £40 p.a. 6 fat hens or pullets at Shrovetide, keep a dog, two cartloads of coat or culm to Jordanston, suit of mill at Garn Mill and paying accustomed toll for same. However by 1792 Gwyn Vaughan had leased Rhoslanog Vawr Issa and Garn for lives of lessee, to John Roch, Lettice his wife and Thomas Roch their son. James Roch assigned the lease in 1837 to Joseph Roberts of Carnachenllwyd who had married Rachel, daughter of James Roch.

In 1839 Treslanog Vawr, was owned by Sir James Cockburn, Bt. with James Roch as tenant. The Voters List 1834 shows James Roch at Roselanog, lease of lives on Roslanog Lower Farm. In 1801 Thomas Williams of Rhoslanog Vach, yeoman bought the estate for £654. He bequeathed the moiety to his natural daughter Mary (1829). She married David Bateman who then came to Rhoslanog Vach. David Bateman, (d. 1869) and Mary who died in 1870, left their two sons, Thomas and John the farm of Rhoslanog Vach. Thomas had a son, William, who was a mariner living at Rhoslanog in 1887, when his father lived at Trellwyn, Mathry.

Refs: Black Book of St. Davids, 1326; LT 1786; Maesgwynne Deeds; Pembs. Plea Rolls. 1543 Nos. 3, 18, 21, 84; W & W (H'west) Nos. 8466 & 8467, 8468; 8470; 8474; 1874; Fines in Pembs. GS; VL 1824; Cwrtmawr Deeds Nos. 1416, 1104; Mathry Tithe Schedule 1842; BM Egerton 2586 fo. 343.

RHOSYGILWEN, *Cilgerran*

Home of the Lloyd, Jones, Colby and Morgan-Richardson families. Jenkin Lloyd, grandson of Howel ap Jenkin Lloyd of Blaiddbwll and second son of Owen Lloyd and Elin his wife was first known owner of Rhosygilwen. He married firstly Lleucu, daughter of David Glyn Gwalter, who traced back to Cadifor Fawr, and secondly Margaret, daughter of Jenkin ap Owen John of Clynhenllan. Their son Thomas inherited and his son, Jenkin Thomas Lloyd, 'of ye Place' married Angharad and had three daughters, co-heiresses. Margaret who married Stephen Jones, son of John Griffith of Clydey who came to Rhosygilwen, Crysli who married Thomas Griffith John of Panterlys, Llandygwydd, and Anne who married Alton Hughes, son of Hugh Griffith Morgan. Margaret and Stephen Jones had three sons and one daughter, Anne whose prenuptial settlement was dated 3 November 1654. She

married David Morris Griffith ap Eynon. Thomas, the heir, married twice but had died without issue by 1676. The second son, Captain Jenkin Jones was of Rhosygilwen, and married Rebecca Weld of Buckinghamshire. In 1670 Jenkin Jones, grandson of Howel ap Jenkin Lloyd, was assessed at three hearths. His will was proved 25 June 1689. He left one son and heir, Theophilus Jones, viv. 1698, a minor in 1689. He married twice, firstly to Elizabeth, daughter of William and Dorothy Warren of Trewern by whom he had a daughter, Anne, who married John Colby of Bletherston who came to Rhosygilwen, and a son of whom nothing is known who died without issue. Theophilus married secondly, Elizabeth, daughter of Thomas Jones of Pantyderi, coroner, by whom he had a daughter Ada who died without issue.

In 1740 there is a report of an inquest at Kilgerran before Thomas Lewes, coroner, and a jury, (Edward Garnons a member), 'on body of Theophilus Colby who ever since he was four years old was subject to convulsion fits; on 1 September 1740 he came alone to a bank of a rivulet called Cwm Croess, had fits and immediately died'. On 22 July 1756 is recorded a lease for a year of Rhosygilwen and other properties between Thomas Colby and another Thomas Colby, both of Rhosygilwen and Hugh Owen of Landshipping and George Bowen of Llwyngwair.

Lewis in *TDW* tells us that 'Rhos y Gilwen the elegant modern mansion of John Humphreys Esq. who obtained this estate by marriage with Catherine, daughter of the late Thomas Colby Esq. of Ffynnone and erected the present house'. J. R. Phillips says, 'The old house which at the present day would hardly merit to be called a respectable farmhouse, stood a little below the present edifice which was erected about 35 years ago by Mr. Humphreys, a brother-in-law of the present Mrs. Colby. This house is a neat specimen of what is generally termed domestic Gothic, and its interior arrangements are commodious and well arranged'.

In 1904 Morgan-Richardson bought Rhosygilwen from the Colbys for £8,000. The house was renamed Morganau while in the ownership of Morgan-Richardson. He died in 1913 and C. L. E. Morgan-Richardson who followed died in 1961. In 1983 when Major Jones visited it, the owner-occupier was Mrs. Jane Creswell Evans, who lived there alone with a tenant in part of the house. The Colby arms were shown in a painted glass window overlooking the stairs. It was offered for sale in July 1984, but was destroyed by fire in 1985. The house has since been rebuilt and is now run as a retreat. There is a photograph of the exterior in *Contemporary Biog. S. Wales and Mons.,* Morgan-Richardson 1907, p. 154, and the portraits are recorded in *Steegman*.

Refs: WWHR, i, p. 53; GGMS I, (Gwynfardd), p. 20; Bronwydd Deeds 1503, Nos. L733, 1746; Morgan-Richardson Deeds, ii, p. 425; Pembs. GF 1740; J. R. Phillips, *Hist. of Cilgerran,* 1867, pp. 125-6, 166-7; Kitchin Map 1763; Lewis, *TDW,* 1840, 1834; Steegman, *South Wales*, Vol. II, 1962; D. L. Baker-Jones, *Ceredigion,* 1977, pp. 147-180; Owen & Colby Deeds, p. 380; Carms. RO, J. Francis Colln. Nos. 577, 221-2; VL 1894; LT 1786; Thomas Lloyd, *Lost Houses of Wales,* 1986, p. 71.

RHOSMAEN, *Meline*

Rowland Philipps of Velindre and Blanche his wife, daughter of William Sait, had four sons, the fourth son, also Rowland, married Mary, daughter of Eramus Philipps of Rhosmaen. She was the co-heiress of her brother George Philipps. Rowland and Mary had two sons and one daughter. Rowland the heir died without issue, Eramus Philipps was of Haverfordwest, (and gave this pedigree to E. Protheroe in 1826), and their daughter Mary, heiress of her brothers married Thomas Field of Milton, in the parish of Burton. They had a sole heiress, also Mary who married James Davies of Millfield, Moat. He was originally of Cork Street, Westminster and a tailor. In 1594 John Lloyd was of Rhosymaen. He married Jenet, daughter of Thomas Mathias of Glastir, (died 1617), by Jane, daughter of Llewelyn Lloyd. Thomas Lloyd their son died in 1613, his brother David was his heir. On 20 July 1621 David Lloyd of Rhosymaen, gent. Margaret his wife, and James Lloyd their son and heir conveyed Rhosmaen Ucha and Issa and other properties to James Bowen of Llwyngwair by way of mortgage. It was never redeemed and Rhosmaen and the other lands became part of the Llwyngwair estate.

In the will of Lewis Rees, Gent. of Newport, Pembrokeshire: 'To my nephew John Owen of Rhosymaen, Nevern, a house in Newport now in occupation of Evan Owen, officer. Residue to my said nephew, William Owen of Newport, and make him executor', 24 November 1786.

'Rhosymaen . . . the mansion house of Thomas Bowen, an infant now in ward, the sonne of Owen James, son to James Lewis, natural son to Lewis David, son to David ap Griffith ap Evan ap Madoke ap Howell ap Owen ap Gwillim Dew ap Gwillim ap Gwrared of Kemes and so paternally descended of the ancestors of Pentre Ivan gave the coats (of arms) of that house with the due difference. The mother of the said Thomas was the natural daughter of Thomas Lloyd, Esq. his grandmother paternal was daughter to George Owen, Gent. The inheritance of this house was in our father's age accounted next the best sort of livings though now lately many new purchases have left him behind, and yet is the same not diminished'. The Land Tax records 1786 show Thomas Williams, Esq. of Trelethin as owner of Rhosymane, Thomas Lewis tenant assessed at £1.0.3. and the Tithe Map of Meline 26 October 1837 shows Rhosmaen as 60 acres, Phoebe Bland owner, Stephen Lewis tenant.

Refs: LT 1786; George Owen, *2nd Book,* p. 278; Protheroe MS IV, ff. 148-9; ibid. V; Wagner MS, 2, GO; Bronwydd Deeds No. 774.

RHOSMOELED, *St. Dogmaels*

Lewis Griffiths, (no dates given), died seized of Rosymoyled, and his three daughters and co-heiresses held the lands jointly in co-parcenary. Two of the daughters married: Elen firstly to William Thomas Woolcock and secondly to William Powell. Thomas Powell, son of the second marriage, inherited his mother's moiety and sold it to William Thomas Griffith. Jane the younger daughter, married Morris ap Howell Ddu whose son Thomas Morris sold his moiety to his cousin Jenkin William, son of Elen and William Woolcock. Jenkin William had a son and heir, Thomas who died young and a daughter, Grace who married John Browne, scribe to George Owen c. 1600.

The 1786 Land Tax shows that William Rowland, gent. was the owner occupier and in the Voters List 1894, Owen James.

Refs: Francis Jones Archives; BM, Egerton 2586 fo. 318; LT 1786; VL 1894.

RHYDYDRISSI, *Whitchurch-in-Cemaes*

Home to descendants of Madoc Gwilym viv. 1289. Madoc had two sons, David Fychan and Ievan viv. 1366 from whom descends Thomas Jones, coroner, of Pantyderi. David Fychan had a son, Philip David Fychan who married a daughter of David Gwilym Rees and had an heir Ievan ap Philip who married Mably, daughter of David Llewellin Gwilym of Whitchurch in Cemaes. They had a son, Edward who had three sons, Griffith Edward, Philip and James. Griffith Edward was of Rhydydrissi and he married Catherine, daughter of Philip Thomas. They had two sons, Philip the heir who died without issue, and John who married a daughter of George Owen Harry of Dinas. Their daughter Gwenllian married David Morgan. No dates are given.

Refs: GGMS II, Adv. Pembs. fo. 231-2; WWHR II, 85.

RHYDLANGOEG, *Amroth*
Vide **Colby Lodge** *supra*

RHYD YR HARDING, *Mathry*
Shown on Colby's Map of 1831 and situated just over half a mile west of Priskilly Mansion. Rhyd yr Harding was the home of the Thomas and Jenkins families subleased from the Priskilly Forest estate but in the ownership of the Bishops of St. Davids. David Thomas paid tax on one hearth in 1670, his son, also David, was buried at Mathry on 17 December 1760. He had a son, David (1753-72), who had three sons and one daughter, Anne (buried Mathry 23 March 1753). The heir, David was born 1772 and buried at Mathry 14 September 1830, the second son, John viv. 1830 and Thomas the youngest son, also buried at Mathry 23 March 1753. David Thomas had four sons, David, James, Ebenezer and William, and four daughters, Phoebe, Anne, Hannah and Mary. David the heir, baptised at Mathry 1791, married Martha, a herbalist of Barnsley and had one son, William, and three daughters, Maria, Mary and Hannah who married William Jones of Penymynydd, Mathry the great-grandfather of Francis Jones. William Thomas shown as being of Bengal, married in 1850, Mary Jane Davies of St. Dogmaels, and had a son, David who died in Fishguard in 1954 aged 94, and four daughters.

The Jenkins family became tenants of Rhyd yr Harding in the early 1800s, bought the freehold of the property in the Church Commissioner's estate sales of 1886, but again reverted to tenancy with the sale of the freehold to Arthur Griffiths of Letterston in 1900. In 1945 however Arthur and Gladys Jenkins last of the family to live at Rhyd yr Harding, repurchased the freehold and they then remained in the property until its sale in 1962. Since 1971 David Green has owned the house, modernised its interior and extended it into adjoining historic outbuildings.

Refs: Francis Jones Archives; Mathry Parish Tithe Schedule 1842; VL 1894; D. Green.

RHYDGARNWEN, *Llantood*
The earliest known owner was William Gruffydd ap Jenkin of Llantood, gent. who released three acres lying between 'Ryde garne wenne and Croese filly vraen' in Llantood on 7 May 1573. In the will of Rowland Jenkins, husbandman of Bayvil dated 19 June 1657, he leaves land called Rhyd y Garne in Llantood to his sons, James and Owen. In the 17th and 18th centuries this was the home of the Morgan family. John Morgan married Elizabeth, daughter of John Lloyd of Hendre (d. 1638) and had a son, George who married Joan, daughter of Jenkin Jones of Cardigan. Their son and heir John, married Mary, daughter of William Rowland of Cilgarthen. They had two sons, George and David and two daughters Jane and Joan all viveus 1733. David Morgan married a daughter of George Lloyd of Cwmgloyne and had issue viv. 1755.

In 1786, William James, gent. was owner and David Richard was tenant. In 1873, William Griffiths George was owner of 138 acres. His descendant, John Picton Meredith George, solicitor of Cardigan died in 1934. He had married Sarah, daughter of Benjamin Evans of Cidigell. She died in 1939.

In 1975 it was the home of Dr. and Mrs. Brownlie who sold it in 1980 to Mr. and Mrs. Hugh Jones who used it as a guest house. They advertised it for sale in 1988. The present house was built in the early 19th century near the older farmhouse of which no trace now remains.

Refs: PCC, Wrotton bg 5; Manorowen MS (peds); VL 1834; Eaton Evans and Williams Deeds, 58; Landowners' Return 1873.

Le Moigne

RICKESTON, *Brawdy*

We know nothing of the first settler Rickart except that he gave his name to the place, but it is likely that he was of Norman ancestry and arrived in the early 12th century. During this time it became home to a family surnamed Le Moigne, sometimes written Le Mayne and Le Maen. The coat-of-arms borne by the Le Moignes: *or* six martlets *gules*, three, two and one, suggests an affinity with the baronial house of De Valence, Earls of Pembroke. They may have been kinsmen, or on the other hand retainers, for the latter often adopted arms based on those borne by their superior lords. According to Dwnn 'Gwenllian le Maen sol eyr of Ffylip le Mwyn o Dre Rickart' married Robert Martin. The Martins continued at Rickeston for nearly two centuries during which time they acquired further properties by intermarriage with substantial landed families like Marlos, Ramsey, Dyer of Fishguard and Warlow of Bernards Well in Henry's Moat. In 1326 it was a Knights fee, English, and in the *Black Book of St. Davids* it is recorded that 'Wenllion Martyn holds the manor of Ricardiston, pays 12d., and service, follow[ing] the relics to Garnturney'. The last head of the main line was Arnold Martin who married Isabel verch Owen of Lochmeyler in Llandeloy parish. Their only child Alice, called Alson in the Welsh fashion, became heiress of Rickeston.

The extent of the manor is unknown. Its caput was Rickeston, and it is clear from references in various documents that some of its constituent members lay in several surrounding parishes. In 1347 *Kaervaga* is described as being in the tenement of Riccardistoun. In 1593, part of Castle Villa (Brawdy parish) and Rhoscynefin (Llanreithan parish) formed part of the manor of Rickeston, Tremanhir and Fogwr Walter formed part of the 'Lordshipp of Rickardston in Dewisland' in 1665 and Caerwen. But it was far more extensive than this. A document dated 20 January 1538/9, describes it as 'the chief manor called Riccardistowne with appurtenances, and 7 messuages, 800 acres of land, 100 acres of meadow, 200 acres of pasture, 60 acres of wood, and 40 shillings rent' which shows it to have been of considerable extent.

About 1490, Alice married David ap Rhys, a natural son of the illustrious Sir Rhys ap Thomas, K.G. of Dynevor, by a daughter of Gwilym ap Harry ap Gwilym Fychan, a landowner of Court Henry in Llangathen, Carmarthenshire. On his father's side Sir Rhys came from distinguished lineage tracing to the British prince Urien Rheged, and through his mother descended from the same stock as the Tudor dynasty. Henry VII owed much of his fortune at Bosworth to the partisanship of Sir Rhys whom he loaded with honours and appointments, while his son, Henry VIII continued to extend friendship and favour to 'good father Rhys' as he termed him. Owing to his enthusiasm for unconventional dalliance, Sir Rhys became father of a considerable number of natural children, most of whom found no difficulty in marrying aristocratic wives and founding families of their own. Among these was David ap Rhys.

The Rickeston line adopted the name Rhys as their permanent patronymic, and in records the name appears as Rhys, Rees, Price, sometimes with and sometimes without the 'ap'. The family always used the form ap Rice which it had adopted before the end of Elizabeth's reign and, in order to avoid confusion, I have retained that nomenclature throughout except when quoting directly from documents. They also bore the arms of the Carmarthenshire knight, *argent* a chevron *sable* between three ravens proper, with a cheerful disregard of the heraldic rule of differentiation.

ap Rice

These arms, based upon the legend of the raven army of Owen ap Urien Rheged, were well known throughout Wales, and the old genealogists referred to the families who bore them as *Gwaed y Fran* (Blood of the Raven).

David ap Rhys settled at his wife's home, and does not appear to have taken an active part in public affairs. He had seven children, the youngest being born about 1500. He died, probably not long after this, and his widow remarried Thomas Bateman of Honeyborough near Llanstadwell. Bateman was married four times, Alice being his third wife. She died before 1541.

David ap Rhys and Alice (Martin) had seven children: 1. Thomas; 2. William; 3. Lewis, died without issue; 4. Lewis the younger, died without issue; 5. Harry, died without issue; 6. Janet, married William Warren of Trewern near Newport, and died on 12 January 1569/70, leaving issue; 7. Alson, married John ap . . . by whom she had a son Rhys ap John.

The eldest son, Thomas ap Rice, had considerable trouble in taking seizin of the property. During the years 1533-38 he brought actions against the Bishop of St. Davids, seeking redress for the relief of the manor of Rickeston, and land in Tancredston, which he held by knight service of the Bishop, alleging that by local custom the existence of a life tenant in reversion barred such relief. In 1546 he sued Thomas Richard Symond and Thomas Symond for three messuages and 145 acres in Ambleston, and Llewellyn David Gwilym for a messuage and 167 acres in Castlebythe, all of which had been owned by Richard Warlow of Bernardswell, plaintiff's great-grandfather by the mother's side.

He had to meet a more serious threat in 1540, when his kinsman William Martin of St. Davids sought to recover the capital manor of Rickeston, seven messuages, 1,200 acres of land, and an annual rent of 40 shillings in Rickeston. Claimant was the son of Owen Martin, younger brother of Arnold, and so cousin-german to Alice Martin the heiress. He produced a pedigree tracing him back to Robert Martin who had married Gwenllian le Moigne, alleging that the estate had been entailed in the issue male, so that it should have descended to him as senior male representative of the family. The action dragged on until 1548, and on 3 February of that year, the court decreed that the lands should be given to William Martin who was to enjoy them until Thomas ap Rice could produce a better title; ordered Thomas to pay the costs of the lawsuit provided William allowed him to harvest the grain he had sown on the said lands, and give him permission to remain at Rickeston for a further year during which he was to remove all his goods and chattels. This was a severe blow to Thomas. Whether he eventually produced a better title or whether the parties came to an arrangement is not known, but one thing is crystal clear – he never gave up Rickeston or the land in dispute.

More tribulations were in store. He was next assailed by his younger brother, William ap Rice, who sued him in the Great Sessions in September 1554, for his share of the Rickeston estate, then comprising 35 messuages, 2 grain mills, 1 fulling mill, and 790 acres of land in Brawdy, Whitchurch, St. Elvis, Llandeloy, St. Edrins, Fishguard, 'Llanllawell', Henrys Moat, and Castlebythe, which he said had been held by Alice Martin, mother of the parties, 'by Welsh tenure', and accordingly should descend in equal shares to the sons. He was careful to state that Alice had died before the feast of the Nativity of John the Baptist 33 Henry VIII, (24 June 1541), after which the practice of gavelkind in Wales was barred by statute. Thomas denied the claim, and maintained that the lands descended by primogeniture.

Here again, the result is not known, but as we shall see Thomas managed to retain the patrimony. He and his wife Agnes, daughter of John ap David ap Gwilym of Trecwn by Jenet Devonald, were both alive in 1565. Their only child died in infancy. After her husband's death between 1565 and 1570, his widow married Owen Phillips of Llanfihangel Penbedw in north Pembrokeshire.

Before he died, the harassed Thomas came to an arrangement with his younger brother William who is sometimes described, for instance in 1553, as 'William ap Rs formerly of Richardiston gentleman, alias William ap Rs of Haverfordwest merchant'. In 1563 he sold the estates to William. This transaction had to pass through the Great Sessions, and records of the court contain a description of the extensive property owned by the family. In that year Richard Bateman and Morris Walter a corvisor of Haverfordwest were plaintiffs, William ap Rice deforceant, and Thomas ap Rice and Agnes his wife tenants in possession, when a Recovery was suffered of the manors of Rickeston and Tancredston, 29 messuages, 2 grain mills, 1 fulling mill, and 7,380 acres of land in Rickeston, Tancredston, Brawdy, Caerpylsey, Greshylde, Tremaenhir, Ffynnon-ddewi, Trefgynwyll,

Wynehouse, Llanvunus, Penpant, Llanrithan, Caerfarchell, Cronllwyn, Bondwenhooke, Rhydygele, Llether David, Llether Gronw, Trehale, Percellycke vaure, Percellycke vache, Corpixe land, Pencoyd melin, Bernardswell, Henrysmoat, Castle-bythe, and Westfield. Thomas and Agnes conveyed these lands to William ap Rice for an annuity of £6 and all heriots, fines, and other casualties incidental to the properties. An exemplification of the Recovery was made on 9 July 1565.

As a result of these transactions, William ap Rice, the second brother, enjoyed the estates. Described as 'de Brydeth, gentleman', he served on a jury in the Great Sessions in 1550/51, and in 1566/68 was escheator for the county. He married before 1548, Elizabeth daughter and co-heiress of Thomas Bateman of Honeyborough, by Catherine Reed his first wife. This was the Thomas Bateman who had married the widowed Alice of Rickeston so that he was stepfather as well as father-in-law to the bridegroom. William ap Rice died about 1570, leaving the following children: 1. John, died without issue; 2. William, died without issue; 3. John, see later; 4. Margaret; 5. Ellen, married, firstly, David Dew ap Gwilym Dew, secondly, Thomas Nash of Sandyhaven, and had issue by both husbands.

John ap Rice, third but eldest surviving son, succeeded to Rickeston. The Martin cousins seemed inclined to re-open the question of succession, and Owen Martin of St. Davids took steps towards that end in October 1570, but nothing came of it. He married Katherine Perrot, born in 1530, daughter and sole heiress of John Perrot of Scotsborough, a large mansion in Gumfreston parish, near Tenby, and owner of a valuable estate in south Pembrokeshire. This union allied John ap Rice to some of the best-known houses in west Wales.

John ap Rice was one of the two resident Justices of the Peace in Dewsland in 1575, and George Owen described him as Justice of Oyer and Terminer and Justice of the Peace for Marine Causes in the counties of Pembroke, Carmarthen and Cardigan in 1598. As a magistrate he took part in suppressing Popish practices to which many Pembrokeshire people still adhered, and in 1592, together with George Owen and Alban Stepney, caused St. Meugan's chapel on the border of Cemaes and Emlyn, to be denuded of 'superstitious relics and monuments', and prepared to prosecute all people still attempting to use the place for religious purposes. He was very friendly with the lord of Cemaes, and was trustee to the marriage settlement of his son Alban Owen of Henllys and Lettice Mercer, signed on 24 September 1596. He served as High Sheriff for the county in 1582 and 1593.

John ap Rice died in 1598, his will dated on 13 June of that year being proved in PCC on 8 December following. He desired to be buried in Brawdy church, towards the repair of which he bequeathed 6s. 8d.; he gave 35s. 4d. to each of the churches of Hayscastle and Whitchurch; 20 shillings towards the maintenance of a house of correction or workhouse in Dewsland; 20 shillings to the Corporation of Haverfordwest towards purchasing the fee farm of the rectory of St. Mary's there; and 10 shillings to the Corporation of Tenby. The transeptal chapel on the south side of the chancel in Brawdy church is still known as the 'ap Rice chapel' where he was doubtless buried. His widow survived him by nearly sixteen years and was buried with her Perrot ancestors in Gumfreston church, where an inscribed slab records that 'Katherin Parat wife of John Apris esquier' died on 17 September 1614. They had the following children: 1. Thomas, 2. William (died about September 1607) married a daughter of Sir John Perrot, by whom he had a son, William; 3. Janet, who was dead in 1597; 4. Elizabeth, married William Barlow of Creswell (High Sheriff in 1612, died on 7 March 1636-37) and had issue; 5. Mary, married Lewis Powell of Lamphey, barrister-at-law of the Middle Temple, M.P. for Pembroke in 1620 and 1625, and for Haverfordwest in 1624.

Thomas ap Rice, the eldest son, of Rickeston and Scotsborough was High Sheriff of the county in 1610, and a Justice of the Peace. In 1598 he married Margaret, daughter of William Mercer of Lancashire. She died in childbirth on 1 May 1610, in her 30th year, 'after she had lived twelve years in wedlock with me and borne ten children, of whom seven survive' – so said her husband who caused these facts to be inscribed on their monument in St. Mary's Church, Tenby. He married secondly Alice, daughter of Lewis Thomas ap John of Cwmgwili near Carmarthen, but they had no issue.

Thomas ap Rice added to his inherited property. On 8 December 1601 Thomas Philipps assigned to him a Crown lease of the pannage of hogs, swine, and wild honey within the forest of Narberth and also the rents and farms of the tenure of Molston, parish and Lordship of Narberth, each the possession of Rees Griffith, Esq. attainted of high treason, which pennage and lands held of the Queen by a lease for lives of Owen Phillips, Alban Phillips and the said Thomas Phillips of 'Picton'. Thomas ap Rice was the eldest son of John ap Rice and his wife Katherine Perrot. The date of his birth is not given but he was High Sheriff of the county in 1610 and a J.P. Thomas ap Rice owned considerable estates; when he suffered a Recovery of his estates in the Great Sessions in 1627 he owned 40 messuages, 10 cottages, 3 grain mills, 20 gardens, 10 orchards and 6,120 acres of land with further properties in St. Davids and Castlebythe. He leased Ramsey Island (q.v) which the Bishop had leased to him in 1619 for the lives of himself and his children, Lettice, John and William at a yearly rent of £3. Thomas was troubled by various 'assaults and outrages' over the years and was often in court. During the Civil War he played the role of a 'Shoni bob ochor'. In 1642 he was for Parliament, but by the end of the following year he had declared his intention to exert his utmost to reduce Pembroke town and castle to His Majesty's obedience, and in September of that year was numbered among those who subscribed £2,000 for the King. Thomas ap Rice 'being of great years' made his will on 27 March 1650 and died shortly afterwards. They had eight children of whom the eldest son, Perrot ap Rice, died during his father's lifetime, and so never succeeded to the estates.

Few references to him have been found. In 1619 he acquired from Rice Rudd and Thomas Brinley, both of London, eight acres of pasture and eight acres of land in Llandeloy and Llanhowell parishes, formerly in occupation of the vicar, and also an annual rent of 5s. 4d. According to the deed 'these lands were formerly for the priests to pray in the pulpit of Llandeloy and Llanhowell'. He too had his troubles. In July 1636 he sued Thomas David who had unjustly deseized him of a messuage and 180 acres in Knightston and Tenby for the preceding 20 years. Perrot was often sued for debt in the Great Sessions, and the last reference I have found to him was in March 1640 when Gilbert Jones, one of the Brawdy family, sued him for the return of £640. He probably died shortly after.

Perrot ap Rice married Margaret, daughter of Sir Edward Littleton, sister of Sir William Littleton, Lord Keeper. She was still living in 1662. They had 13 children, of whom James ap Rice, the eldest son of Perrot, succeeded his grandfather to the Rickeston and Scotsborough estates. He was High Sheriff of the county in 1655, and a Justice of the Peace. He was dilatory in business matters. In 1654 Roger Pillcorne, vintner, sued him for £36, and Rees Jones, gentleman, sued him on a bond made in 1649 which James ap Rice tried to repudiate alleging he had been forced to sign the bond 'under threat to his life'. In 1657 Timothy Littleton, Richard Jones, Rees Jones, and Roger Lort sued him for £541. His tenure was of short duration. On 1 June 1658 he made his will, which was proved in PCC on 26 July 1660. He desired to be buried in St. John's church, Gloucester, and bequeathed to 'my dearest heart my wife Anne', all the estate he had inherited or purchased from his paternal uncles John and Bartholomew, and authorised her to sell part of the property to pay his debts. Accordingly, on 15 November 1660, Anne ap Rice sold the manor of Skyfog in St. Davids parish, and two messuages and a tucking mill in the townred of Skyfog, and two messuages in Hendre Griffith, to William Davies of Carew, gentleman for £15,028. Anne was cousin-german to her husband, being the eldest daughter of Sir Rice Rudd of Aberglasney. She had married James ap Rice in 1654, and their prenuptial settlement was dated 14 July of that year. She married secondly, James Lewes of Abernantbychan, Cardiganshire (his will dated 1669) and thirdly, Colonel James Philipps of Tregibby, Cardiganshire. She died towards the end of 1673, and her will dated 14 November 1673 was proved on 5 May of the following year. As James ap Rice had no children, the estates passed to his next brother, John.

John ap Rice married Elizabeth daughter of Thomas Newsham of Abersannan, Carmarthenshire, who came of a prosperous burgess family trading in the county town. John was constantly in trouble, and over a long period we find him appearing either as defendant or plaintiff, mainly the former, in the Courts of Great Sessions. He also found rent-paying distasteful. On 22 September 1659, James Lewes of Abernantbychan and Anne his wife demised a messuage called Park House and 'the White Close of Kingstown' in the Out-liberties of Tenby, to John ap Rice for 40 years at a yearly rent. Having taken possession, the lessee refused to pay any rent, with the result that he received a summons to appear in the Great Sessions for 1667/68 to answer for the default.

His troubles came to an end in 1670, for he died on 2 June of that year, at the age of 37 and was buried in St. Mary's church, Tenby. His name is carved on the Scotsborough monument which his widow repaired. By his will, dated 21 May 1670, and proved on 12 July following, he left the mansion house of Scotsborough, Cornish Down, and two messuages in St. Mary's called Cams Mills, to his wife for her life, with remainder to his son and heir James and his male issue in tail, and in default to the heirs male of the ap Rice family.

John and Elizabeth ap Rice had five children, James ap Rice the heir, born about 1657/58, was involved in difficulties throughout his life, constantly in debt, constantly concerned in litigation, and set his family on the road that led to its final ruin. In 1675 when still a minor, a bill was exhibited in the Court of Chancery by his tutor and guardian, John Beachfield of Elderfield, Worcestershire, which stated that the minor's uncle, James ap Rice, was indebted in considerable sums to several persons at the time of his death. Having no issue the said James agreed that part of the estate be sold to pay debts, the residue of the property to be settled on his nephew, James. The minor's mother was in the house when the said James died, and with Arthur Bateman and Mary his wife, Thomas Newsham, and others, took possession of the deeds of all the estates, denied the deceased ever made a will, and combined to keep the property in their possession. The minor's aunt, Anne ap Rice (née Rudd) was also said to be party to the conspiracy. The minor's mother told the story rather differently; the estates were held in trust to secure the widow's dower and the portions of the younger children; and she complained that the plaintiff wished to deprive his younger brother and sisters of their substance.

To enable him to meet his more pressing occasions he created several mortgages, which proved to be the millstones which finally submerged the family. Financial straits did not prevent him carrying out the normal public duties of a country gentleman. He was a Justice of the Peace, and a pretty active one, his signature often appearing on warrants. In 1682 he committed one Margaret Thomas to gaol for stealing 7½ strikes of barley and malt, and, what was far more dangerous, 'for cursing her Neighbours and suspected to be a notorious witch'.

James ap Rice was Bailiff of Tenby in 1678, and Mayor in 1681/2. In July 1688 he became High Sheriff, and on this occasion bought from Joseph Edmondson, tailor, of St. Clement Danes, very smart uniforms for himself, his son, and the javelin-men who were to attend him on his public appearances. The tailor who did not know anything about him, received a bond guaranteeing he would receive payment 'in due course'.

Alas, James neither paid the tailor nor redeemed his mortgaged estates. He died suddenly in 1692, and on 13 September administration of his goods and chattels was granted to his widow, Eleanor ap Rice. He is described in the document, as of Rickeston, esquire, having ceased to reside at Scotsborough in 1689 when, with the consent of the mortgagee, he leased the house, for three lives, to Thomas Smith, gentleman.

James had made a good marriage, his wife, being Eleanor Powell daughter of Captain William Powell of The Hill, Ludchurch, by Mary daughter of Richard Vaughan of Cwrt Derllys, near Carmarthen, related to the Earls of Carbery; they had five children. The eldest son, James ap Rice who lived at Tenby, having let Rickeston to a tenant, failed to retrieve the estates from the morass of mortgage into which his father had thrown them. In 1692, Streynsham Master, the London mortgagee brought an action in Chancery against young James, his grandmother Elizabeth ap Rice, John Philipps of Carmarthen, Griffith Dawes, Griffith Hawkwell, and Margaret Meares, in order to secure the interest due. The evidence of Griffith Hawkwell revealed an example of duplicity practised by the late James ap Rice. He stated that James had mortgaged Tancredston, Butler's Lands in Rhydygele, Caerwen, and Gryssillt to him on 28 May 1684, and made a further mortgage to him on the same lands on 4 June 1689 – but James had told him nothing about the other mortgages he already had on those properties. The sins of the father were now being visited on the son.

In 1706 James ap Rice found that he owed Sir Streynsham Master, Knight, the sum of £2,200 made up of the capital and interest on a mortgage created in 1687. Sir Streynsham appears to have behaved very well, and said he was prepared to accept £1,600 and to forgive the remainder of the debt. However James could not find that sum. With the word 'Ichabod' ringing in his ears he turned to John Rickson, a wealthy merchant of Pembroke, and asked for help. Rickson agreed to satisfy Master, and also Griffith Dawes of Bangeston, provided James conveyed the estates to him absolutely. To this the harassed man had to agree. Rickson then paid the £1,600 to Master. On 6 May 1706 James ap Rice, described as of Tenby, gentleman, conveyed the manor of Scotsborough, Cornish Down, Cames Mill, Rickeston (in tenure of Richard Bateman), tenements in Brawdy, Whitchurch and Llandeloy (in tenure of William Cole and Thomas Williams) to John Rickson, who paid the mortgage money owing to Dawes. On 14 June of the same year he conveyed his estates in Brawdy, Llanhowell, Whitchurch, Hayscastle and St. Mary's Tenby, to Sir Arthur Owen of Orielton, Baronet, and George Moore of Eastington, esquire, to hold in trust for John Rickson, and agreed to make a further deed to ratify that gentleman in possession.

The curtain finally fell on 8 October 1706, when a deed of ratification was signed between James ap Rice of Tenby, and Cecilia his wife of the first part; John Rickson of Pembroke, merchant, Sir Arthur Owen, Baronet, and George Meares of Eastington of the second part; John Barlow of Lawrenny and Charles Owen of Nash, esquires of the third part. By this, the following estates were conveyed to Rickson, in fee – Knightston, Tanners Cross, White Close, Heywood, Salters Close, Moysland, and other properties in St. Mary Tenby; Tancredston, the manor, lordship, and mansion house of Rickeston (then in occupation of Henry Richards), Prengwyn (in occupation of Thomas Williams and William Cole), the manor and capital messuages of Rhydygele of the East and West side, and the manor of Grinton alias Peningegrose (both in occupation of Richard Bateman), Caerpylcher in Brawdy and Whitchurch (in occupation of Henry Richards and Henry John), the manor of Trewilym and Gwryd in St. Davids, the capital messuage called Caerwen, all the Grissell and a piece of arable land between the Grissell adjoining to the Old Lane and abutting on the end of Caerpylcher hedge containing about 3 acres and adjoining to Caerwen, all in Whitchurch parish, and a corn grist mill in the parishes of Brawdy and Hayscastle.

Thus the lands that had been held by his ancestors for over four and a half centuries passed to a stranger. The unhappy landless man and his wife left Pembrokeshire soon afterwards. The last reference I have found to him is on 22 August 1707 when James ap Rice described as late of Tenby, but then of the parish of St. Margaret's, Westminster, and Cecilia his wife, and George Meares of Eastington, made a further release to John Rickson of certain properties specified in the previous deed.

The identity of his wife Cecilia, remains unknown. They had at least one child, a son known as George Price. The will of Elizabeth ap Rice of Tenby (1712) contains a bequest of £20 to 'George Price son of my grandson James Price'. After this, silence.

The fate of Rickeston, cradle of the race, is gloomy. In 1706, John Rickson of Pembroke became owner of the property, but never came to live there. The occupiers after the departure of the ap Rice's were a respectable people of near-gentry, called Bateman, followed by Henry

Richards, a yeoman, and then by Evan Griffith of Hendre, near Cross Jack, who came there about 1740. Joseph Rickson having occasion to raise money, mortgaged Rickeston to Esther Williams of Haverfordwest for £500 on 10 October 1740. On 30 May 1745, Anne Rickson of Pembroke, widow of the said Joseph, on behalf of her son William Rickson, an Ensign in Major-General Onslow's Regiment then serving in Germany, granted a lease of Rickeston to Evan Griffith for the lives of lessee, his wife Anne, and the life of a kinsman, Thomas Griffith (born 1736) son of William Griffith of Hendre, at a yearly rent of £30.

On 11 May 1754, William Rickson, Anne Rickson, widow, Joseph Rickson, and Esther Williams, in consideration of £501 (being the principal sum of the mortgage referred to earlier) and also of £499, making a total of £1,000, sold Rickeston outright to Lettice Barlow of Rosepool, widow. The new owner was the daughter of William Jones of Llether, a Justice of the Peace, and High Sheriff in 1744. She had married in 1719/20, Thomas Edwardes of Summerhill, a cadet of Edwardes of Treffgarne, and after his death married William Barlow of Rosepool about 1723. She was again a widow before 1754, having had no issue by either husband.

By her will dated 2 December 1765 and proved 4 December 1769, Lettice bequeathed 'Richardston and the manors purchased from William Rickson Esquire' to her nephew James Jones, a sporting attorney better known to his contemporaries as 'Shemmy' Jones. 'Shemmy' died without issue in 1781, leaving the properties to his brother William Jones of Llether, J.P., one of the coroners for Pembrokeshire. The coroner died in 1804, and his ultimate heiress, his younger daughter Mary, became lady of the manors. She married George Roch of Butterhill. On 31 July 1785, William Jones sold Rickeston for £1,200 to the tenant Samuel Griffith who was also farming Pointz Castle. Since that time the property has been the freehold of the Griffith family, who bestowed on it the name Rickeston Hall.

Like the family, the mansion has disappeared and not a stone remains to mark the site. A plan of the property made in 1775 for James Jones, by Thomas Lewis and surveyed by Charles Hassall, shows the house to have been a large L-shaped building set amidst lawns, surrounded by trees, with a few outbuildings near by.

A new farmhouse with extensive outbuildings was built by Samuel Griffith who died in 1824, and I have been told that a good deal of the stones and other materials from the old mansion were used for that purpose. Certainly, a stone shield bearing a chevron between three ravens, the coat of arms of ap Rice, was placed in the wall of an out-house, and although visible at the beginning of this century, the emblems are now indistinguishable. The mansion stood at a distance of 166 yards to the SSW of the present farm buildings, and its site has been largely incorporated into the Brawdy airfield.

A few vague memories of the ap Rice's survive. The side chapel in Brawdy church is called the ap Rice Chapel, and the architecture suggests that it was built in the late sixteenth or early seventeenth century, probably by the family. When an archaeological survey was made by some Pembrokeshire antiquaries in 1896, they had a chat with John Gibbon of Solva, formerly of Tremaenhir. The old farmer, then aged 83, said he had heard that during the lifetime of the last 'Price' of Rickeston, his steward murdered a shepherd in a field at a place called Rhos Mwnk; Mr. Price, though he knew of the steward's guilt, nevertheless defended him, and Mr. Price 'never afterwards had any luck'. What truth lies in this tradition cannot be determined, but it is in harmony with what we know of the later ap Rice's and of the social climate of Dewsland during their reign.

Inventories tell us how Rickeston was furnished in the years 1650 and 1673, and help to convey an idea of the internal arrangements. The ground floor consisted of the hall, parlour, dining-room, kitchen, upper kitchen, buttery, larder, little larder, and the dairy – which may have been detached from the house itself. We do not know the size of these rooms, but their contents suggest that they were pretty roomy. Rickeston was the largest house in Brawdy parish in 1670 when it was assessed at 5 hearths in the Hearth Tax list.

Reference to the 'dyneing room' at this early date is interesting, for it was not until well on in the following century that dining rooms as we know them came into use in the country houses of west Wales. Before then, meals were usually taken in the hall or the parlour. It will be noted that the hall and parlour contained beds. Beds in downstairs rooms of the country houses occur frequently as late as the 18th century. The cupboard-bed in the hall of Rickeston in 1673, was a closed-in structure, probably with sliding doors to exclude draughts. The bedchambers proper were on the first floor at Rickeston, and consisted of the Great Chamber, the Master's Chamber, the gentlewomen's chamber, the chamber over the buttery and the chamber over the hall door. In the 1673 Inventory the Yellow and White Chambers are included. Several 'lofts' are mentioned, some in the house, others over outhouses such as 'the Chamber over the Stable' and 'the plowmen's Chamber'. The cockloft, a little room or garret open to the rafters, is still known as 'coglofft' in the district.

The contents of the rooms suggest they were comfortable, and, to an extent luxurious. There were carpets and rugs, Kidderminster hangings, arras, silk-fringed curtains, and coloured valances, cushions, couches, covered chairs, feather-beds, linen which included tablecloths and napkins. A pair of virginals stood in the parlour. There was 'one trunck with bookes' and a little desk.

Refs: Anc. Mon. Pembs. p. 29; Slebech Deeds No. 236; Fenton, *Tour Pembs.*, 1811, p. 23; Griffith Owen Deeds (iii); *Dwnn,* i, 74; WWHR ii, 63, 75; JHSCW 1970; LT 1786; Dineley, *Progress,* p. 256; *Royal Com.,* 1898 p. 473; *Arch. Cam.,* 1897, V, xiv, pp. 133, 329, illust.; ibid. 1898, V, xv, p. 93; *Black Book of St. Davids,* 1326, pp. 110, 111; Brawdy Tithe Schedules 1842; NLW 13681 B. Griffith Owen's Armorial; PRO, Wales 3, No. 3214, Fines; PRO No. 3289; NLW, Maesgwynne Deeds, No. 33; PRO, Pembs. Plea Rolls, No. 63; PRO, Chancery Proc. C.10, 103, 18; PRO, Early Chancery Proc. Cr. 857, No. 18; Cardiff Free Library, *Handlist,* p. 12; Francis Jones, 'Rickeston and Scotsborough', *Pembs. Hist. Soc.* 1966, *Historic Carmarthenshire Homes and their Families, Historic Cardiganshire Homes and their Families, Treasury of Historic Pembrokeshire.*

RICKESTON HALL, *Robeston West*
Home of the Roch and Harries families. The Roch family provided two High Sheriffs for the county, Nicholas Roch in 1675 and a namesake in 1733. On 3 October 1611 a grant was made from 'Thomas Lloyd of Kilkethed Esq. to Robert Bowen of Llanchaelt, gent. and Thomas ap Owen James of Meline, gent. of the following properties – four tenements called Great and Little Richardston in Robeston Park in Rowse, in tenure of John Fortune, Nicholas Rotch and Patrick Sinett; and Richarston Myllne, on trust for said Thomas Lloyd for life with remainders'. In 1683 Thomas Roch of Rickerston was murdered by Vaughan Phillips, gent. probably in a duel; in 1689 the owner was George Roch; in 1738 is recorded a prenuptial settlement between 'George Roch of Riccaston, gent, and Martha Allen daughter of William Allen of Gelleswick', and Rickeston was the home of the Allen family from the early 19th century; Charles Allen of Rickeston Hall is recorded on the 1904 Voters List.

Refs: LT 1786, 1797; Pembs. Plea Rolls No 99; NLW, Eaton Evans and Williams Deeds No. 1270; Pembs. GS, VL 1894; Deed in Cardiff Library now in Glam. RO; TM Brawdy ph. 1845; Pembs. RO D/LP/-.

Foley

RIDGEWAY, *Llawhaden*

Home of the Foley family. On 30 August 1711, Richard Fawly the elder of Ridgeway, gent. Sir George Barlow of Slebech, Bt. and William Phillips of Haythog, esq. and Richard Fawley the younger of Ridgeway, gent. agreed the release of lands in Pembrokeshire, including the capital messuage called Ridgeway alias Lletherston, to trustees to the use of Richard Fawley the younger to enable him to make 'a competent settlement on any woman he may happen to marry and may bring a Fortune into the family'. The earliest recorded member of the family was John Foley, granted lands by Bishop Hoton of St. Davids and John Foley was Constable of Llawhaden Castle 1383. He was succeeded by his son and heir, William; his son, Thomas and in turn by his son John viv. 1512. In 1615 Richard Foley was a member of the Train Band of the Hundred of Dungleddy. Enthusiastic royalists, five Foleys were killed at the battle of Colby Moor. In 1661 William Foley paid a Benevolence of 20 shillings, and nine years later Richard Foley paid tax on 3 hearths. In 1691 John Foley was declared an outlaw for contempt of Court. The Foleys owned extensive property in Pembrokeshire and in 1719 John Foley was elected an Alderman of Newport, Pembs. Thomas Foley entered the Navy and accompanied Anson on his voyage round the world in 1744. His nephew achieved far greater fame. This was Sir Thomas Foley, born at Ridgeway in 1757. He entered the Navy, took part in numerous sea battles and received sufficient prize money to enable him to buy the Abermarlais estate in Carmarthenshire. He became one of Nelson's captains and fought at Toulon and Cape St. Vincent. His ship *Goliath* led the British fleet at the Battle of the Nile in 1798, and was prominent at the Battle of Copenhagen 1801. He was promoted to the rank of Admiral and knighted in 1815. He married a younger daughter of the Duke of Leinster. He died in 1833 and was buried in a coffin made from the timbers of one of his ships. The last descendant of the Foleys at Ridgeway was Sir Richard Foley-Philipps, Baronet, who died in 1965.

The original house stood at some distance from the present mansion which was built in the 18th century by John Foley, and was a plain house on high ground. The modern Ridgeway house was completed in 1741, the ancient mansion having stood in the now stable yard. Fenton describes it as '. . . the elegant residence of my estimable friend, J. H. Foley, esq., crowning it amidst groves chiefly of his own planting'. John Herbert Foley was High Sheriff in 1795. Ridgeway was advertised to let in 1809 with a full description of the accommodation including eight bedrooms, library, large Drawing Room, Servants Hall, coach house, stables, walled garden, pleasure grounds and plantations – in all about 350 acres. In 1871 it was the seat of R. P. Davies, and a photograph appeared in C. S. Allen's *Photographs of South Wales.*

Major Jones visited the house in 1981 and wrote of it: 'The front of the house is surrounded by a ha-ha. In the rear is a dog graveyard, one of the stones bearing the date 1887. The west wing of the house seems much older than the rest, and has a large old chimney stack of stone which is clearly very old. There are some drip labels in the wall alongside the chimney. The mansion is empty but in excellent state, and divided into flats, and is internally much changed. It is now a Home for Aged people.' The house is said to be haunted by the ghosts of the Foley cavaliers who had fallen at Colby moor, and there are tales of phantom horsemen galloping along the old drive.

Refs: CRO Glasbrook Deeds. No. 9; Schedule p. 5; Carms. RO; Nicholas *County Families,* ii, p. 950, 1875; Fenton, *Tour Pembs.,* 1811; C. S. Allen, *Photographs of South Wales,* 1871; Burke, *Visitation of Seats,* iv, 1858, p. 40; Francis Jones, *Treasury of Historic Pembrokeshire,* pp. 178-180; Glasbrook Deeds. Nos. 9, 10, 29, 16; Rees, *Beauties of South Wales,* 1815, p. 806; *The Cambrian,* 22 July 1809; Pembs. GS C9F; Pembs. Plea Rolls Nos. 52, 54, 163, 246; Landowners' Return 1873.

RINASTON, *Ambleston*

Due west from Ambleston village, near the road to Little Newcastle. In 1308 the house was called Villa Reyneri, and occupied by John Reyner, tenant. Called Tre Reina or Tre Rina in 1566, and called today by Welsh, Tre-einer. In 1230 there is mention of *Capella de villa* Reineri, and the remains of the church can be seen in an enclosure 120ft x 100ft now within the yard of the farmhouse, and a burial took place within the church in 1789 a few years before it was abandoned. There is an old tombstone in the farmyard inscribed 'David Morse of Reneaston, died 30 July 1785 : Martha his wife died 11 January 1789'.

In 1384, Henry, son of John Cole of Reineriston is owner, and the family were still there in the early 16th century. In 1503 Jane Cole of Rhinaston married Harry Howel of Llysyfran, and their daughter Jane married John Scourfield of Moat. By the 17th century Wogans and Powells were associated with the property, and after them the Morse family. Phoebe, daughter of David and Martha Morse married John Evans of Trevayog, St. Nicholas, farmer, prenuptial settlement dated 21 December 1776, and they had three sons the youngest of whom, John Evans is described as 'of Rinaston'. By 1786 in the Land Tax lists, William Phillips Esq. is shown as owner, with John Evans as tenant. The house is now a farm.

Refs: NLW, F. Green Deeds; LT 1786; A. Cam. Ser. 11, iii, p. 261; *Anc. Mon. Pembs.*, vii, p. 3; Pembs. Plea Rolls No. 136; PRO, Ancient Deeds, D 5116, D8038; Taylor's *Cuisson*, 96a, 1587-88.

RHINDASTON, *Hayscastle*
see **TREINDEG**

Fowler

ROBESTON HALL,
Robeston West

Fenton in his 1811 *Tour Pembs.* writes '. . . Robertson Hall is about five miles from Milford, in a pleasant English like looking country and we understood in a good neighbourhood. The garden is extensive, but this year except in the Peach and grape Houses, quite destitute of fruit. It seems well sheltered and has high Quick hedges to break the force of the wind, but it seems the blights from the sea are so injurious to the trees, that a crop except under glass cannot be depended upon'.

In Carmarthen Museum is the frieze of a mantelpiece from Robeston Hall of late 18th century work. It bears the carved arms of Fowler: quarterly *azure* and *or*, in the first quarter a hawk's lure and string *or*. Crest: an ostrich head *or* between two wings *argent*, the beak holding a horse-shoe *azure*. Hugh Fowler, who presented the parish church with bells in 1719, inherited the estate from his mother in 1703, Martha, wife of John Fowler of Haverfordwest, merchant will proved 1707, née Couzens whose father, Thomas Couzens (alias Cozens) (d. 1677), of Robeston Hall, was assessed for six hearths in 1670.

Hugh Fowler, of Gray's Inn died without issue and the property went to his nephew Thomas Keymer, (b. 16 July 1722), who sold Robeston to William Scourfield in 1782 and went to live at Kidwelly where he died February 1784. The latter was High Sheriff in 1812, the year in which he advertised Robeston Hall for sale. The particulars of sale give a fairly detailed description of the estate which comprised 338 acres including 12 acres of plantation, hot-houses, peach houses and a conservatory. 'The mansion house is a substantial stone building containing spacious breakfast, dining and drawing rooms, servants' apartments, extensive offices, stabling, coach houses . . .'. Land Tax records show Henry Scourfield owner occupier in 1797. In the 1834 Voters List William Henry Scourfield is owner. For four years from October 1792 the house was leased to Charles Fulke Greville, at £20 per annum.

The house was destroyed by fire on 24th August 1921 - a barn and an ice-house survive.

Refs: Thomas Lloyd, *Lost Houses of Wales*, 1986, p. 73, illust.; Slebech Deeds 867; Pembs. RO D/LP/

T; Taylor's *Cuission,* 1587-8; Blome List, 1673; LT Lists; Lewis, *TDW,* 1840; *Cambrian Journal,* 4 April 1812 & *Cambrian Journal,* 1862; Griffith Owen Colln.; Arch. Cam., 1924-5, p.45; Pembs. RO Deeds DX/181, NLW 5446C; Fenton, *Tour Pembs.,* 1811.

ROBESTON WATHEN HOUSE,
Robeston Wathen

On an eminence close to the church and village. The mansion of Robeston Wathen was erected about 1815. In 1840 this was the seat of the Rev. J. W. James, and in 1867, the home of Ven. George Clark, Archdeacon and Prebendary of St. Davids. It had many owners including the families of Barlow, Rice, Colby, Philipps and Lord Kensington but was generally occupied by

tenants. Sale particulars give details in 1866 and 1929. It was described as a 'very commodious and substantially built mansion with very extensive stabling, coach house and other outbuildings, a large walled garden and lawn, shrubberies, woods and plantations, with 39 acres of meadow and pasture land. Also several cottages and gardens. There were seven principal bedrooms on the first floor and some grand reception rooms and a conservatory. From 1977 it has been a country house hotel.

Refs: Nicholas, *County Families,* 1875 edn., p. 897; VL 1904; Sale Cat., 1866; Lewis, *TDW*; Francis Jones Archives.

ROBLINSTON, *Camrose*

The ruins stood about half a mile north west of Camrose Church. Original home of the Roblin family. William Robelyn having held half a Knight's fee in 1251/2. In 1324 Alexander Roblyn held (inter alia) 'certain parts of a fee at Robelingston' also held in 1325 by his son and heir then a minor. In 1366 William Roblyn held half a fee in the vill of Robelyn, Joan his daughter married James ab Owain of Lochmeyler. Her mother was Eleanor, daughter of Sir Walter Malefant of Upton Castle. The elder branch of descendants of James ab Owen remained at Roblinston until they removed to Wolfsdale.

In the reign of Henry IV Jane Roblin, daughter and heiress of Alexander Roblin married John ab Owen whose son Morris Bowen was ancestor of the Bowens of Roblinston. Morgan Bowen murdered John ap Rice but was pardoned and died in 1609. His son, John Bowen settled at Wolfsdale. Fenton in his *Tour Pembs.* (1811), writes '. . . a large ruinous shell of a house called Roblinston of a plan and dimensions much exceeding what was generally the character and size of the mansions of this county at the time when we may venture to date its erection about two centuries ago, inducing us to form a very respectable opinion of the builders spirit and taste. It was, when in a different form, once the residence of the family of Roblyn . . . that became extinct in Joan, the daughter and sole heiress of William Roblyn, who married John Bowen of Llech Meyler, about the time of Henry the Fourth, of which house the Bowens of Wolvesdale and Camrose were off-sets. I have called it a shell, as it appears never to have been finished, or at least never inhabited as I could learn, no memorial of it in that state having been preserved anywhere'. The arms of Roblyn are: *Gules* a 'shoular' *argent.*

In 1926 it was recorded that nothing remained of the house and that the site was occupied by a modern house.

Refs: Fenton, *Tour Pembs.,* p. 86; *Dwnn,* i, pp. 116, 121; WWHR ii, pp. 48, 172; XI, 1926 II; XI, pp. 16-17; XI, 37 ff; *Dwnn,* i, p. 116; Opem Fam. 24; Opem ii, p. 382; Pembs. Plea Rolls VII Edw. III; Poyston Deeds No. 140b; LT 1786.

St. Davids

ROCH, *Roch*

Former home of the Walter and Stokes families. This was probably the house near the castle now used as a farm house and formerly part of the castle demesne. The castle itself, a mere tower, was restored, and an extension added for domestic purposes by Lord St. Davids in the early 1900's, and Major Jones and his family leased the tower for a period after World War II.

The earliest record shows Henry Barett who was probably of Cuffern, as being of 'la Roche', he owned lands in Folcaston which he had of the gift of Adam Barett, and he authorised John Morse of Hylton to deliver seisin of same to John Reynboth of Folcaston.

By 1550 the Jenkin family was at Roch, Phillip Jenkin, Husbandman who was accused of murdering Joan Codd of Roch parish, a servant of Roger Webb. He was one of the five sons and three daughters of George Jenkins and Katrin daughter to David Tew ap Gwilym Tew o syr Vercheiniog. They signed for Dwnn in 1597 and Dwnn visited again in 1613. George was the second son of Philip Jenkin, grandson of Gwallter o Grychan y Kastell, and Anne, daughter of Huw ap William o Dal y Kowth ap Sion ap Tomas ap Gruffydd ap Nikolas. Philip the eldest son married Marged daughter of John Knevet by Elizabeth, daughter of Huw Gardarn of Bryngest. Philip and Marged had two sons, Morgan and Hari.

Philip and Anne had two younger sons, Tomas and John and a daughter Anne, who married Lewys Ieuan. All were alive when George Jenkins signed for Dwnn in 1597.

In about 1601 William Walter bought from the de Longueville family the manor of Roch and the advowson of the church plus a quarter share in Dale Castle and the manor of Eweston and an eighth share in the manors of Hodgeston and Barton. The Walter family were shoemakers and tradesmen in Haverfordwest and the said William was, in 1611, described as 'yeoman'. William Walter, (d. 1650), married Elizabeth Protheroe niece of 1st Earl of Carbury, and his daughter, Lucy (b. 1630), was the mistress of Charles II. William Walter and his wife were

estranged for the latter part of their marriage and constantly short of money. Elizabeth spent much of her time at her family home, Derwydd where she could live a more gentil life.

Richard Walter was High Sheriff in 1657. On 6 September 1665, Richard Walter of Ravensdale, Carms, and Bridget his wife, mortgaged the capital messuage called the Demesne of Roch, and another messuage in Roch, (containing three and a half ploughlands) to Anthony Stokes of Roch, gent. for £433 6s. 8d; and on 15th May 1725 Sir Richard Walter leased the capital messuage called the 'the Demesne of Roch to Constant Stokes for 21 years at £52 p.a. In 1732 Joseph Walter, Richard's son and heir, is given as being 'of Rosemarket'.

In 1735 Joseph Walter of St. Thomas, Haverfordwest gave a lease of possession to

Lucy Walter

William Owen of Landshipping and Lewis Barlow of Lawrenny, of the Manor of Roch, the capital messuage called Roch Castle and Trevrane, and other lands in Co. Pembroke. This Joseph's sister, Bridget Walter, married Anthony Stokes of Haverfordwest, and left (inter alia), a daughter Thomazina Stokes who married John Jones of Brawdy. Deeds show that by April 1754 Joseph's widow, Elvi, (née Barlow), had married secondly, Alexander Elliott of Earwere and Narberth. Alexander Elliott and Elvi his wife released to Benjamin Stokes of Haverfordwest the capital messuage and Demesne of Roch with the castle or site called Roch castle for £1,300 and one third of coal and culm during lives of said Alexander and Elvi in survivorship. By 1786 the Land Tax records show two messuages called Roch and three messuages called Roch Gate owned by Hugh Savage, Esq. tenant Henry Mathias, Esq. and Henry Rees, and seven messuages also called Roch owned by William George Phillips and Miss Anne Lort. Lewis in *TDW* tells us 'The castle with its demesnes became the property of John Harries, Esq. from whom it passed by will to the late John Rhys Stokes, Esq. of Cyfern'.

The castle is currently used for holiday letting and is owned by Mr. & Mrs. William Berry.

Refs: Dwnn, *Heraldic Visitations*, i, pp. 135, 192, 202, 228; Papers of GS, GF; Pembs. Plea Rolls, Nos. 8, 12, 77, 119, 128, 136; AD iii, 452; Tithe Map Roch 1837; S. A. Allen, *Photos*, No. 363 1871; Griffith Owen List (iii); WWHR V, p. 271 ff; Morgan-Richardson Deeds, i, pp. 139, 141, 145; LT 1786; Lewis, *TDW*, 1840.

ROSEMARKET, *Rosemarket*

Rosemarket Manor and church, granted by William, son of Haion; Robert, son of Godebert and Richard, son of Tancred, c. 1140-1160 to the Hospitallers of Slebech.

Home of the Walter family, although they ceased living there before 1670. Sir Richard Walter was High Sheriff in 1727. On 12 August 1735 Joseph Walter gave a lease of possession to William Owen of Landshipping, of (inter alia) the capital messuages called Walter's Hall and the Hall of Rosemarket. Fenton in his *Tour Pembs.* 1811, '. . . here Sir Richard Walter had a mansion whose remains speak it to have been highly respectable about a century ago, and possessing all the appendages of a great man's house in those days'. Again 'The ruins of this mansion are now the property of Mrs. Owen Barlow who is the principal proprietor of land in the parish.'

Francis Jones visited the ruins on 19th May 1976. He described them as extensive with a massive chimney stack. 'Mr. Sidney Pawlett of Cross Farm remembered it well and had played in the ruins when a child. About twenty years ago the ruins were swept away and the present farmhouse erected partly on the site of the old mansion. It stands on a rise at the edge of the village and in an adjoining field the old dovecote still stands.' He goes on to say: 'Cross Farm, adjoining the parish church, is an interesting survival. It has an undercroft, (once used as a dairy) and above it was the main chamber, now the parlour. This is very ancient. The owner-occupier, (1976) is Sidney Pawlett, an agreeable person.'

Refs: CRO Trant (Yelverton) Vol. 1, No. 1275; Pembs. RO Deeds D/LLW, Nos. 178, 292, 309; *Anc. Mon. Pembs.*, 1925, p. 314; WWHR XIV; Carlisle, 1810; Fenton, *Tour Pembs.*, p.110; Lewis, *TDW*, 1840; Morgan-Richardson Deeds I, 139, 142; Rees St. John, 1947 p. 106;

ROSEMOOR, *Walwyn's Castle*

This stands near the road about half a mile south of Walwyn's Castle church. In 1786 Thomas Bowlas was owner and later it was the home of James Bowlas Summers, (d. 1878), with 1540 acres worth £2,355 per annum. He was the son of John Summers of Moor (qv). Alice May, daughter of J. B. Summers was married in Cawnpore, India, to Capt. R. W. H. Ronaldson, only son of J. T. Ronaldson of Hawick Grange, Northumberland on 14 December 1895.

Refs: LT 1786; Landowners' Return 1873; Francis Jones Archives.

ROSEPOOL, *Walwyn's Castle*

This originally belonged to a family called Row, but later became the home of the Bateman and Barlow families. In 1541 William Bateman, (of the Honeyborough family), is described in the Picton Castle archives as of 'Rowispole'. In the 17th century this was the seat of a younger branch of the Barlows of Slebech. Thomas Barlow was assessed at five hearths in 1670. On 3 April 1685 William Barlow of Walwyn's Castle borrowed £100 from Lettice Barlow and in the following year a further £100, granting her lands in Walton West as security. She died before redemption was made and her interest descended to John Barlow son and heir of John Barlow, and nephew of Lettice Barlow. On 23 November 1693 William Barlow granted by way of mortgage in £60, the messuage called Rosepoole being then two ploughlands and in the tenure of William Tasker, gent. William Barlow died before repaying and his estate came to his son, also William. William married Lettice, widow of Thomas Edwardes of Somerhill, and daughter of William Jones of Llether, she was a lady with a 'considerable fortune'. William Barlow died before 3 August 1737 without issue, when his widow agreed with Lewis Barlow, son and heir of John Barlow who inherited the mortgages on Rosepool, to let Lettice have Rosepool and the mortgaged lands for life on payment of £15.17s 6d per annum. On the death of Lewis Barlow, his brother and heir, Hugh Barlow of Lawrenny continued the arrangement until Lettice's death in 1769 when it reverted to the Barlows of Lawrenny. By 1779 Barbara Surman, widow of Thomas Surman of the same place, gent. was of Rosepool and the Land Tax records of 1786 show Mr. J. Cozens, owner, Mr. Roch, tenant. By 1834 William Cozens of Sandyhaven owned Rosepool and the house was offered for sale in 1837.

The house had a fine walled garden. On Colby's Map 1831 a colliery is marked just east of Rosepool house and demesne.

Refs: Pembs. Plea Rolls Nos. 53, 83; LT 1797; VL 1834, 1894, 1904; Sale Cat. Pembs. RO DB/13 No. 101; *Anc. Mon. Pembs.* 1925, p. 407; Eaton Evans and Williams Deeds; Picton Castle Deeds; Mudge Map 1819.

RUDBAXTON, GREAT, *Rudbaxton*

Close to the parish church, just east of the house is a 'motte'; c. 1150-1200 Rudbaxton was the fee of Alexander Rudebac. The Welsh called, (and still do), the place, Rydbac.

It was probably Great Rudbaxton which the Haywards acquired by marriage with the Goddard heiress, and later went to Fletherhill. Fenton describes Great Rudbaxton as 'one of the largest tenements in the county and in the best conditioned'.

Sir William Lewis was the owner of Rudbaxton in 1786 Land Tax lists, with Mr. Charles Gibbon, tenant, as was James Llewellin in 1834 at a rent of £50 p.a. James Williams occupied Rudbaxton farm in 1904. David Llewellin, the former rally driver, now is owner occupier.

Refs: LT 1786; VL 1834, 1904; Francis Jones Archives; Fenton, *Tour Pembs.*, 1811.

RUSHACRE, *Narberth*

The local Welsh folk call this 'Rhydsiacer'. Griffiths Howells, gent. owned extensive lands here, (no dates given). His mother had been born there and was probably the daughter of William Jones of Carfellgarw, Llanglydwen Parish. There is a photograph of Rushacre in *Hanes Carmel Penfro* on page 32.

Refs: Francis Jones Archives; *Hanes Carmel Penfro* p. 32, R. D. Hughes 1935.

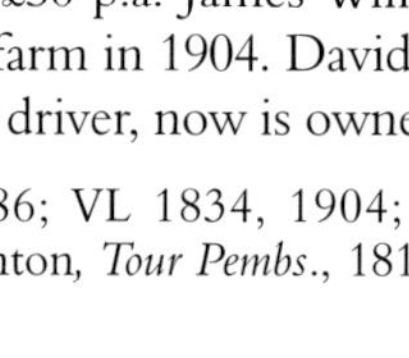

ST. BOTOLPHS, *Steynton*

The earliest reference to this residence is that of William Howell of St. Baddoggs, yeoman in 1617. The Howells were followed by the Elliot(t)s. The Rev. Phillip Elliot obtained St. Botolphs by marriage with Mary his first cousin, daughter of John Howell of St. Botolphs and his wife, Lettice. She was heiress of her father. Her grandfather William Howell was taxed on 2 hearths in 1670. The Rev. Phillip Elliot took his M.A. at University College Oxford and became Rector of Treffgarn 1739-1767 and also of Rudbaxton 1743-1767. Phillip and Mary had a large family, The eldest surviving daughter Anne married Thomas Rowe of Penally, The second daughter Lettice married Rev. John Voyle, Rector of Lawrenny and several of their grandsons joined the Indian Army. The youngest daughter, Mary married the Rev. Moses Grant, Rector of Nolton and Vicar of Roch. They were the grandparents of Richard Bulkeley Grant afterwards Philipps who became Lord Milford of the 2nd creation, inheriting Picton Castle.

The only son of Philip Elliot to have issue was Dr. George Elliot of Laugharne. Two of his sons, John and Phillip, married daughters of Dr. Lettsom, a fashionable 18th century medical man. Their elder brother George was sent to India and had three children by his Indian mistress, whom he sent to London to be educated. His son joined the navy and was killed in the West Indies at the age of 24. One of his daughters married a Voyle cousin and had a large family by him, two of whom became Major Generals in the Bengal Army. Some of her descendants were living in Tenby in 1915.

The younger daughter of Phillip and Mary, married John Leach of Pembroke and her son, another John Leach was of Ivy Tower and High Sheriff of the County in 1855. John Elliot and his wife Mary Lettsom had 12 children. John Elliot was proprietor of Elliot's Brewery in London. His eldest son, also John was a founder member of the Athenaeum Club in 1824. A younger son, Henry spent most of his life in the service of the Hon. East India Company

becoming Sir Henry Elliot K.C.B. In 1847 he was gazetted Foreign Secretary to the Government of India. His health failed and he died at Cape Town aged 45 on his way home.

The will of William Howell of Hubberston Park dated 8 August 1654 and proved 14 November 1656 tells us that he wished 'to be buried in the Park chapel, . . . my sons William and David Howell, my daughters Rebecca and Jennet (to be kept at school till she can read the bible), . . . To my son William Howell all my lands at Boothockes in the parish of Hubberton, and to be executor'. The Land Tax records that George Elliott was owner occupier in 1786 and 1797 being assessed at £0.12s.8d.

Fenton tells us of ' . . . a newly erected mansion built on the site of the old chapel of St. Budock by Mr. le Hunte, a gentleman of Ireland who, since the troubles in that country, has resided in Pembrokeshire where he possesses a valuable property inherited from an ancestor in the time of Charles I, who married an heiress in this county though none of it lies in the neighbourhood of his residence'. General le Hunte acquired the mansion through the marriage of a forefather to a co-heiress of Lloyd of Cilciffeth.

le Hunte

Lewis (*TDW*) says that 'In the western part of Steynton parish is St. Botolph's 'the seat of A. L. Stokes, Esq. by one of whose relatives it was purchased in 1826 from the representatives of General le Hunte. The present mansion was built in 1800, about a hundred yards to the west of the ancient edifice, and partly on the site of a monastery . . . and part of the walls of the ancient monastery, which are still remaining, have been incorporated with the outbuildings of the modern mansion'.

Anthony Innys Stokes, was High Sheriff in 1827, and Major A. V. W. Stokes, (d. 1947) was a distinguished sportsman of the old school and once rode in the Grand National. He was born at St. Botolphs and lived there all his life. After his death the property was bought in the following year by his cousin, Mrs. Lee Roberts. The house was, in 1976 a hotel.

A word must be said about the name St. Botolphs. There was, on the property, an old chapel dedicated to St. Budoc, rendered in the vernacular as 'St. Buttock'. When the private house was built this name did not seem appropriate so it was re-named St. Botolphs.

Refs: PCC Berkeley 385; *English Speaking Students of Medicine at the University of Leyden,* R. W. Innes Smith; Pembs. Plea Rolls No. 109; Laws & Edwards, *St. Mary Tenby,* p. 241; *Contemporary Biographies,* 1907, p. 107, photo; Laws, *Little England,* p. 56; *Anc. Mon. Pembs.,* 1925, p. 391; Lewis, *TDW,* 1840; VL 1904; Fenton, *Tour Pembs.*; *Western Telegraph,* Aug. 1984; P. D. Edwards Palmour; ibid. 19 August 1948.

ST. BRIDES, *St. Brides*

Called le Hill in 1298, and home of the St Brides, then by marriage to Russell, then by marriage to Laugharne, the name is often rendered as Lacharn, being the Welsh form of Laugharne in Carmarthenshire whence doubtless the family came. Fenton in his *Tour Pembs.* wrote '. . . rode to visit the old mansion of St. Bride's formerly the residence of John de St. Bride's whose daughter and sole heiress . . . enriched the family of the Laugharnes who came into Pembrokeshire from Cornwall. There is a tradition that he was shipwrecked on the coast and that the lady who afterwards honoured him with her hand, discovered him almost lifeless on the shore, and had him removed to her father's mansion not far off, where he experienced the most hospitable treatment and being a handsome man soon captivated the lady . . . the habitable house, exclusive of offices, seemed at one time to have formed the sides of a quadrangle enclosed by a high embattled wall, with a walk all round at top, having an arched gateway in front, and another leading to a walled garden of considerable extent. In front of the house was a paddock, including a bowling green and fishponds, and bearing marks of having been laid out in walks between venerable oak trees of large girth, though of stunted growth in point of height, and bending under the pressure of age and the western, almost irresistible, breeze, for it faces that aspect of the ocean that here almost washes the walls of this enclosure'.

The pedigree given in *Dwnn* and signed by John Laugharne in 1597, begins with the 14th century Thomas Lacharn who married Siwain, daughter and co-heiress of Krabol (Crabhole). The Laugharnes were for several centuries burgesses and merchants in Haverfordwest. Francis Laugharne was High Sheriff in 1568 and 1578; Rowland in 1586, Walter Laugharne in 1594 and John in 1631. Branches of the family settled at Llanreithan, Llanunwas, Walwyn's Castle and Pontfaen. Rowland Laugharne of St. Brides was assessed at 11 hearths in 1670 suggesting that St. Brides was, even then a very large house. The last of the family, John, died without issue, and the estate passed to his sisters and co-heiresses. Albania inherited the mansion as part of her share, and married William Philipps of Sandyhaven and Haythog, (High Sheriff in 1736), and he became owner in right

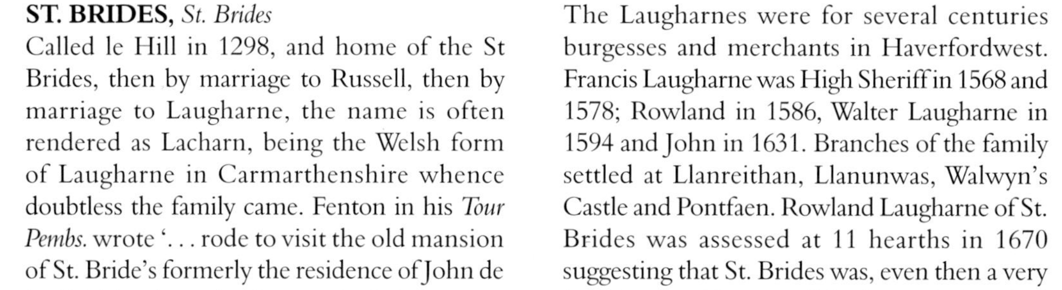
Here lye the bodys of Morris Wo
HERE LIE THE BODYS OF MORRIS WOGAN AND FRANCES
OWEN OF ORIELTON HIS WIFE WHICH MORRIS WAS SON OF SR IOHN WOGAN THE
YOVNGER AS ALSO ABRAHAM WOGAN ESQ AND IANE MANSELL OF MARGAM HIS WIFE
AND ALSO LEWIS WOGAN ESQ AND KATHERINE PHILLIPS OF CARDIGAN PRIORY HIS WIFE
AND ALSO FOVRTEEN OF THEIR CHILDREN ONE DAVGHTER WAS BVRIED AT
SAINT BRIDES THE SAID LEWIS WOGAN DIED MARCH THE 25TH 1702
LEAVING BEHIND HIM ANNE HIS ONLY CHILD AND SOLE HEIRESS MARRIED
THE 26TH OF DECEMBER 1698 TO IOHN LAVGHARN OF SAINT BRIDES
IN THIS COVNTY ESQ WHO CAVSED THIS MONIMENT TO BE ERECTED

Boulston Church Inscription

of his wife. He died in 1739. Fenton tells us that 'On the shore on the ascent to the west of the church stands Hill, the seat of Charles Philipps, Esq. the owner of St. Bride's, commanding a most charming view over St. Bride's Bay and the opposite coast, and though in so bleak an exposure, backed and skirted with a thriving belt of plantation, open only to a beautiful lawn of great extent gradually sinking to the creek . . . The peninsular point of land forming one side of the fretum between it and Skomer, belonging to Hill, is converted into a deer park . . . When the great estate of St. Bride's passing to co-heiresses became divided, the part that included St. Bride's fell to the share of a descendent of the princely house of Cilsant . . . who finding the site of St. Bride's low, and the house and the offices too large and ruinous for an income, abandoned the ancient mansion and gave rise to Hill, an elegant modern structure that will always derive consequencies from its relationship and vicinity to the venerable remains of St. Bride's'. William's son, Charles Philipps married Anne, daughter of Thomas Skyrme of Vaynor. Charles Philipps died in 1750 leaving three sons and two daughters. William who was High Sheriff of the county in 1790; Charles who died in 1791; Thomas who died 1742 and Anne and Elizabeth. All but Anne died without issue. She became the heiress and married Joseph Allen who assumed the name of Allen-Philipps and was High Sheriff. Anne died in 1796. Joseph and Anne had among other issue, a son Charles who inherited St. Brides Hill and was High Sheriff in 1809. His son William was also High Sheriff in 1844 and, having no issue devised St. Brides Hill to his nephew, The Rev. Gilbert Charles Frederick Harries, a member of the Harries family of Llanunwas, near Solva.

The 4th Baron Kensington purchased the castle in 1880, and the 6th Baron Kensington sold the estate in 1920. It then consisted of 'A Baronial residence, Skomer Island, Midland and Grassholm and Gateholm Islands, twelve farms, 22 small holdings, 40 cottages, manorial and foreshore rights, in all 3,662 acres; the rents were recorded at £2,901 15s. 7d.' It was for a while known as Kensington Hospital.

R. M. Lockley, says that: 'St. Brides was formerly the site of a local herring fishery; a chapel stood on its shore but

When St. Bride's chapel a salt house was made,
St Bride's lost the herring trade;

more than that, the sea swept in and devoured the chapel and much of its graveyard, so that even today the odd gravestone is seen peering out of the eroded shore, near the ancient lime kiln.' It is now holiday apartments.

Refs: SC436 Carms RO; Lewis, *TDW,* 1840; A O iii, 1256; Pembs. RO I, 62; LT 1786, 1797; B. G. Charles, *NCPN,* p. 74; Steegman, *S. Wales,* Vol. II, 1962; Rees, *Beauties S. Wales,* 1815, p. 816; *Pembs. Arch. Svy;* Griffith Owen Gentry List c. 1600; BM, Egerton 2586; R. M. Lockley, *Pembrokeshire,* 1957 p. 121; *Dwnn,* i, 73; Fenton, *Tour Pembs.,* pp. 96-8; Colby Map 1831; H'west Corp. Deeds.

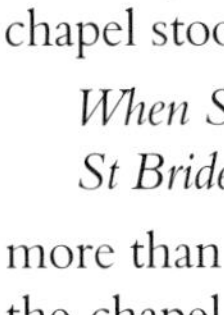

Bradshaw

ST. DOGMAELS, *St. Dogmaels* In the 16th century this was the property of the Bradshaws, a Lancashire family who settled first at Presteigne, Radnorshire. In 1536/7 John Bradshaw described as 'of Ludlow' was granted a Crown lease of St. Dogmaels Abbey and Caldey. On 10 November 1543 he received a grant in fee of both properties for the sum of £512. 2. 10d. His son John sold Caldey to Walter Philips of Tenby. John's two sons, Edward and John, were both captains in the army and were captured at Pill in 1643. Their sisters married into the families of Owen ap Henllys, Gwynne of Taliaris and Lloyd of Llanstephan. The arms of Bradshaw are: *argent* two bendlets *sable*, a martlet in chief. However, the seal to a bond from William Bradshaw to Thomas Canon of Haverfordwest in 1607 shows a shield charged between what seem to be three martlets. High Sheriffs from this house were John Bradshaw

1571. Edmund Winstanley 1591 and Julius Deedes 1703.

By 1670 St. Dogmaels Abbey had become the property of Thomas Parry who was assessed at six hearths in that year. The actual monastery was suppressed in 1535 and the church adapted for parochial use. Most of the Abbey buildings fell into ruins and the secular mansion house was probably where the vicarage now stands.

Refs: Fenton, *Tour Pembs.,* p. 282; Griffith Owen List (iii) MP Cardigan Borough 1604; Blome List 1670; Dale Castle Ped. 132; Pritchard, *St. Dogmaels*, p. 185; St. Dogmaels Abbey HMSO pamphlet 1962, pp. 10 & 21; Pembs. RO HDX/661 No. 1; Picton Castle Archives; Francis Jones, *Historic Carmarthenshire Homes and their Families.*

ST. ELVIS, *St. Elvis*

For several generations this was the home of the Voel family, descended from Dafydd Foel or Voel ('The Bald') of Trewern, Nevern. John Voyle gent. was owner in 1605 and still there in 1621 but by 1652 William Voyle was the owner. He married Margaret, daughter of Peter Barrett. In 1670 Margaret Voyle, a widow, was assessed for three hearths. Their son, Owen succeeded and was followed by John Voyle who married Margaret, daughter of Sir James ab Owen. Their son and heir, Morgan married Elizabeth, daughter of Francis Laugharne and their daughter Elizabeth married Morris Cannon. Morgan and Elizabeth had a son, John who succeeded and five daughters. John married firstly a daughter of Sir John Wogan by whom he had a son, William and a daughter Elizabeth; and secondly Lettice Mortimer, a widow of a Dr. Voyle by whom he had two sons, Bartholomew and Thomas, and two daughters Jane and another, name unknown. William Voyle, the son and heir of the first marriage succeeded. He married a cousin, Margaret, daughter of Dr. William Voyle and had three daughters and co-heiresses, Lettice, Elenor and Anne. St. Elvis became the property of the Williams family of Trelethyn. In 1788 Thomas Williams leased to David Morris of St. Elvis, yeoman, the farm of St. Elvis, (except the Store house near Quadan), with power to build a 'wear' in some part of St. Elvis river, to be reserved for lessor, and lessor also to have engress and egress, and to cut down and 'stoak furze' if necessary) for life of lessee, Jane his wife, and Ann their daughter at the rent of £70 p.a. and six fat hens at Christmas.

Refs: W & W No. 23318; LT 1786; Slebech Deeds No. 173; Pembs. GS & GF; Pembs. Plea Rolls No. 86; ibid. 116; ibid. 169; W & W No. 23318; Cwrtmawr Deeds No. 1104; Pembs. RO D/RTP/SKY. No. 162; Tithe Schedule 8 Nov. 1837; VL 1894; Francis Jones Archives.

ST. KENNOX (ST. KENOX), *Llawhaden*

'A farmhouse set amidst ancient trees on the west bank of the Eastern Cleddau'. Former home of the Hawkwells and the Owens, cadets of Henllys. It is now a farmhouse standing on the site of what was once known as The Chancellor's House where once lived the Rev. Rhys Pritchard when Chancellor of St. Davids (1620). The house had been annexed to that dignity. The Vicar used to preach from 'the rocky eminence near the house to an audience which no church could contain'. In 1551 William Hawkwell, yeoman, was summoned to answer for a debt of £34. The Hawkwells were still in possession in 1702. In 1786 Sir William Hamilton was owner. Lord Nelson took the opportunity to visit Milford Haven whilst being entertained here by Lady Hamilton. Sir William Hamilton was a true patriot, even being prepared to lay down his wife for England. In 1843 the Rev. William Houghston was owner. The property was sometimes called 'St. Enochs'.

Refs: Anc. Mon. Pembs., pp. 137 & 143; *Eminent Welshmen,* p. 425; NLW Eaton Evans and Williams Deeds, Nos. 1240 & 1246; Pembs. Plea Rolls Nos. 9, 99, 238, 270; Foley of Ridgeway Deeds, VL 1834, 1904.

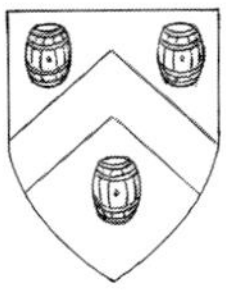

Button

SANDYHAVEN, *St. Ishmaels*
Home of the Rhys, Button and Philipps families. William Rhys was High Sheriff in 1557. On 28 October 1641 Miles Button, of Cotterell, Glamorgan was owner in fee and granted a lease to Thomas Stepney (brother of Sir John Stepney, 2nd Baronet for life at £30 p.a. The arms of Button are: *argent* a chevron between three tuns *gules*. Thomas Stepney was still living at Sandyhaven in 1649 and his will was proved on 5 July 1669. His son, John, eventually succeeded to his uncle's baronetcy, now long extinct. Sir John Stepney married a daughter of Sir Anthony Van Dyke, the portrait painter. In 1786 John Campbell, afterwards lst Lord Cawdor, was owner with William Cozens as tenant. In 1802 Lord Cawdor sold the property, then a substantial farmhouse, with the Cozens family still as tenants, at a yearly rent of £130, for the sum of £4,556. In the sale catalogue it was described as 'Sandy Haven Farm . . . with a roomy farm house and offices, garden, large farm yard and convenient buildings for the Husbandry Business'.

They were still tenants in 1839 when Thomas Lloyd owned the estate, then 348 acres. From the 1850s to the 1870s the Philipps family, (a cadet of Picton Castle), were owners. They had left by 1890 when the Perkins family were at Sandyhaven they bought the property and were still there in 1917. Major Jones visited Sandyhaven in 1974 and again in 1976. He was disappointed to see that the outer walls had been cemented. Mr. Beer, a farmer, was in residence at that time.

Refs: St. Ishmaels Tithe Schedule 1839; LT 1786, 1797; Blome List 1673; B. G. Charles, *NCPN*; ibid. GO; Cawdor (L) 26/995; Slebech Deeds No. 162; VL 1904; Pembs. Plea Rolls No. 18; WWHR viii, p. 107; Bronwydd Deeds No. 1851; Pembs. Pub. Records 1, 42, 43; ibid. No. 125; *O Pembs.,* ii, pp. 157, 549, 563, 572, iii, 185.

SCLEDDAU, *Manorowen*
Home of the Owen family, a cadet of Trewern, probably the farmhouse near the crossroads. Colby's Map of 1831 shows Scleddy Ucha and Issa. In 1731 George Owen Esq. was in possession of Scleddy Ucha, but the property was let to a number of tenants. In the Land Tax Lists of 1786 Dr. Edwards is shown as owner, Thomas B. Parry, Esq. as tenant. The Voters List of 1834 shows Timothy David of Sklethy, lease of lives of part of Sklethy Issa; Daniel Francis of Sklethy Ganol, lease of lives of house and lands of Sklethy Ganol; David Griffith of Sklethy, lease for lives of Sklethy Ucha Farm.

Refs: GGMS (Gwynfardd); LT 1786; TM 1837 Manorowen; VL 1834; Francis Jones Archives.

SCOLLOCK, *Ambleston*
The Joyces were in possession during the Middle Ages followed by the Instance family and the Gwy(l)lims . John Joce de Scolhog was witness to a deed in 1383/4. He married Isobel Newton of Bullhook. His heir, also John, married Alicia Bola and had a son and heir, also John, who married Alice, daughter of Philip Howel of Llysyfran by Alice Eliot. Their son Henry Joyce had a sole heiress, Alice. Richard Gwylim is shown as being an 'Alderman of Pembroke'. His daughter Mary married Thomas Barlow. Richard's father was John Gwillim of Scollock and his mother Katherine, daughter of Lewis Powell of Pembroke by his third wife Katherine, daughter and heiress of John Hall. The Instance family descended from William Instance who married Jenet Philip of Stone Hall; their son Thomas was of Scollock, he married Elizabeth Jenkin of Yerbeston. Thomas was one of 16 children. Alson Instance, heiress of Thomas married four times, firstly to John Vougler of Colby who died 1592, by whom she had a son Richard; secondly to Thomas Merryman of Wiston; thirdly to John Roblyn of Scollock by whom she had three sons; and lastly to Thomas Philpyn of Scollock by whom she had one son. In 1786 Thomas Picton is listed as owner. In 1834 Thomas Llewellyn had a lease of Scollock farm. On Colby's Map of 1831 New Scollock, Old Scollock, Scollock Cross and Scollock Bill arc all shown.

Refs: BM Egerton 2586 H 363, 367, 367a, 368; GGMS Adv. Pembs., 1, 16; LT 1786; VL 1834; Protheroe MS v, fo. 181; GGMS (Gwynfardd).

SCOLTON MANOR, *Spittal*
Now well known as the Scolton Manor Museum and Country Park. The museum is devoted to Pembrokeshire and serves as a local history research centre. 'Scaneton' was a knights fee. The Francis family was of Scolton; David Francis will dated 18 April 1749, proved 27 May 1754 had three sons, John, Joseph and David and five daughters. His heir John was succeeded by David Francis who was in his 60th year in 1793 when he was of Scollock Bill.

The Higgon family have lived hereabouts since at least the 16th century. On February 6th 1609/10 William Higgon of Scolton gave evidence in a case against one George Wadin. Higgon and his neighbours said that they had long suspected Wadin was 'a sheepe stealer and did lead a lewde life'. The case showed him to be, indeed, a very bad lot. Thomas Higgon was assessed for four hearths in 1670 but it is not certain whether he lived at Scolton. The first recorded member of that family to live there was James Higgon (d. 1732). The old house was destroyed by fire in the mid-18th century and the Higgons went to live in Haverfordwest. They did not rebuild the house until 1840 at a cost of £3,000. John Higgon was High Sheriff in 1793; John Donald George Higgon in 1889 and Lt.-Col. J. H. V. Higgon in 1951. The Colonel sold the estate in 1972 to Pembrokeshire County Council who converted it into a museum. The pedigree is outlined in *Burke's L.G.* 1972 and the Scolton portraits are listed in Steegman. Lewis in *TDW* states that

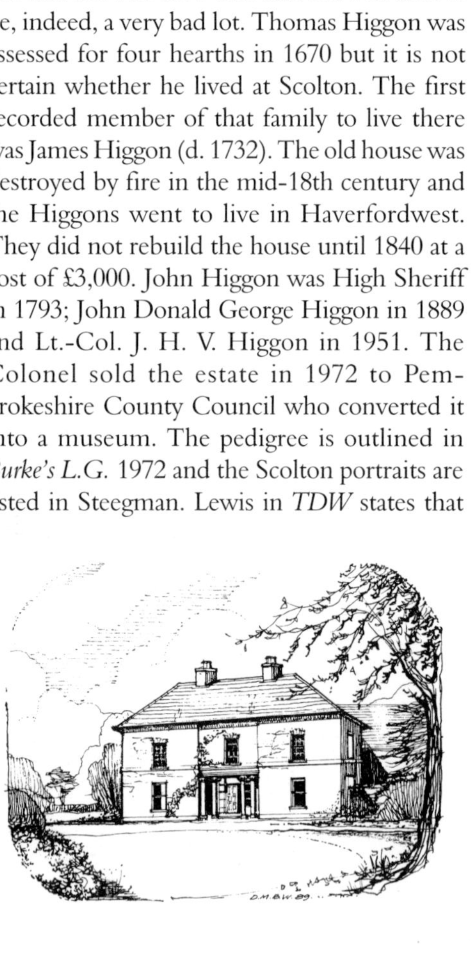

'near the road from Haverfordwest to Cardigan is a place called 'Scolton Gallows' where tradition states the heir of the family was hung for slaying the heir of Haythog on that spot in a duel'.

Refs: Pembs. GF 9 Jas. 1; Nicholas, *County Families,* 1875, p. 902; Pembs. RO HDX/648 Nos. 1-59; ibid. D/HLG No. 295, ibid. D/Hig. No. 2, *see also* D/Hig. No. 1 Svy of Scolton in 1769; *Pembs. Arch. Svy;* Pembs. Plea Rolls 36, 80 101, 124, 252; Morgan-Richardson Deeds 78-9; Steegman, *S. Wales,* Vol. II, 1962; Lewis, *TDW,* ii, 376.

SCOTCHWELL, *Prendergast*
Originally a farm, marked on Colby's Map of 1831 and rebuilt in the 19th century by the Stokes. Home of the Surman and Stokes families. The Surman family were tenants and later owners of Scotchwell.

In 1736 James Barlow leased the messuage and tanyard called Scotchwell comprising 17 acres and adjacent lands to Lettice Surman of Scotchwell, gentlewoman and Simon Surman aged about 3 years, son of Thomas Surman of Prendergast for lives of lessees. In 1762 Sir William Owen of Orielton, Bt., and Thomas Keymer of Robeston Hall Esq. conveyed Scotchwell to Hugh Barlow for the use of Thomas Surman, farmer. Thomas Surman of Scotchwell is described as 'gentleman' in 1754 and Simon Surman served as a Grand Juror in 1783, in 1788 he was Surveyor of Highways in Prendergast Parish. In 1786 he was assessed as owner-occupier for Land Tax at 4s.

On 15 January 1794 Paul Surman conveyed Scotchwell to Thomas Stokes. Henry Stokes of Scotchwell, who died in 1823, married Anne, daughter of Dr. George Phillips, M.D. His second son, John Lort Stokes, born 1812, achieved fame as an Admiral who served on H.M.S. *Beagle* with Charles Darwin and was badly injured by an aboriginal who speared him. Admiral Stokes not only helped Darwin chart various areas of Australia but was later to command his own ship and sail to New Zealand. The name 'Cptn Stokes' is carved on the trunk of an old tree in the grounds. Fanny Anne Stokes, daughter of the Admiral married in 1865, Louis Sampson, barrister. He was High Sheriff of the county in 1893 and a J.P. Their

son was Sir Edward Marley Sampson, a barrister, born 1869 and died 19 March 1925 at Scotchwell.

It is ironic that Simon Surman was Surveyor of Highways in 1788. Exactly two centuries later there was a battle against building an eastern by-pass for Haverfordwest. The then owner, Mr. Steven Llewellyn, who inherited Scotchwell from his father, battled to stop the by-pass claiming it would damage the house.

Refs: NLW, Eaton Evans and Williams Deeds; VL 1904; Maesgwynne Deeds No. 15; Pembs. GS; LR 1873; *Western Mail,* 28 Nov. 1984.

SCOTSBOROUGH, *Tenby*

Once the home of the Perrot and ap Rhys families. John Perrot was High Sheriff in 1551; Thomas ap Rhys in 1610; James ap Rhys in 1655 and another James ap Rhys in 1688.

It was described as 'Scotsborough – whence its imported name we cannot say – is merely the picturesque ruin of an ancient house, which belonged to the honourable and far-descended family of Ap Rhys whose monuments are in Tenby church. The ruin consists of crumbling walls, many of them held together by twisting fronds of ivy – the ivy being remarkably fine. As an example of the strong dwelling of a period when, although defences of domestic buildings had become less a necessity than they had been, it was still a policy and a duty to be always prepared for attacks; the old house of Scotsborough will be examined with interest'.

John ap Rice, third but eldest surviving son of William ap Rice and Elizabeth, daughter of Thomas Bateman, married Katherine Perrot, born in 1530, daughter and sole heiress of John Perrot of Scotsborough, a large mansion in Gumfreston parish, near Tenby, owner of a valuable estate in south Pembrokeshire. The Perrots had held Scotsborough since the latter half of the 14th century. In 1405 Thomas Perrot of that place negotiated a truce with Owen Glyndwr, and eight years later served as Mayor of Tenby; his descendants intermarried with the families of Verney, Wogan of Wiston, Wyrriot of Orielton, and Lloyd of Tenby. This union allied John ap Rice to some of the best known houses in west Wales.

Thomas ap Rice of Rickeston and Scotsborough, son of John, was High Sheriff of the county in 1610, and a Justice of the Peace. In 1598 he married Margaret, daughter of William Mercer of Lancashire. She died in childbirth on 1 May 1610, in her thirtieth year. James ap Rice, eldest son of Perrot, succeeded his grandfather to the Rickeston and Scotsborough estates. He was High Sheriff of the county in 1655, and a Justice of the Peace. On 1 June 1658 he made his will, which was proved in PCC on 26 July 1660. He desired to be buried in St. John's church, Gloucester, and bequeathed to 'my dearest heart my wife Anne', all the estate he had inherited or purchased from his paternal uncles John and Bartholomew, and authorised her to sell part of the property to pay his debts. As James ap Rice had no children, the estates passed to his next brother, John.

John was constantly in trouble, and over a long period we find him appearing either as defendant or plaintiff, mainly the former, in the Courts of Great Sessions.

John ap Rice married Elizabeth, daughter of Thomas Newsham of Abersannan, Carmarthenshire, a prosperous burgess family trading in the county town. He was constantly short of money and in the courts. His troubles came to an end in 1670, for he died on 2 June of that year aged 37 and was buried in St. Mary's church, Tenby. His name is carved on the Scotsborough monument which his widow repaired. By his will, dated 21 May 1670, and proved on 12 July following, he left the mansion house of Scotsborough, Cornish Down, and two messuages in St. Mary's called Cams Mills, to his wife for her life, with remainder to his son and heir James and his male issue in tail, and in default to the heirs male of the ap Rice family. James ap Rice, born about 1657/58, was involved in difficulties throughout his life, constantly in debt, constantly concerned in litigation, and set his family on the road to ruin.

James ap Rice leased Scotsborough in 1689 to Thomas Smith, gentleman, Jane his wife, and Jane their daughter, for their lives. On 12 July 1693, Thomas Smith sublet the house to Henry Hilling, yeoman, and on 15 February 1698/99, Hilling disposed of his interest to Walter Middleton of Tenby, esquire. It was during this time that Edward Lhuyd the Antiquary, stayed at Scotsborough while undertaking archaeological searches in Wales. One of his letters, dated at Scotsborough on 23 February 1697/98, states he had travelled in Glamorgan, Carmarthenshire, and Pembrokeshire, 'but ye country people in Several places took us for Jacobite spies'.

From 1706 Scotsborough remained in the hands of the Ricksons until 1764 when William Rickson conveyed it to his brother-in-law, the Rev. Hugh Thomas, D.D., then Master of Christ College, Cambridge. Dr. Thomas left the property to his son, William, whose widow, having married on 19 March 1800, Matthew Campbell (cousin of the first Lord Cawdor), settled it under specific trusts, on Richard Parry, son of Richard Parry by his wife Mary, daughter of the said Dr. Thomas.

On 3 September 1810, Richard Parry sold Scotsborough to John Owen of Orielton (created a Baronet in 1813), who sold it on 13 February 1817 to Jacob Richards of Tenby. Later, Charles William Rees Stokes and his wife Harriette Jane, daughter of the Rev. John Phelps, vicar of Carew, and granddaughter of Jacob Richards, bought the property from the representatives of William Henry Richards, a grandson of the said Jacob.

Scotsborough originally stood on the verge of an inlet called The Ritec. The area has been reclaimed from the sea, but is today a swamp, through which the river Ritec continues to run. After the departure of the ap Rice's, Scotsborough was never inhabited by gentry and gradually decayed so that it was largely ruinous by the early part of the 19th century. The west front was converted into cottages to house a number of working people but in or about 1824 an epidemic of smallpox broke out in these tenements, and the occupiers fled in panic, never to return. The building soon became a total ruin. Scotsborough had been a large strongly fortified house, and the loopholes in some of the walls are probably of pre-14th century origin. All that remains to recall the splendour of Scotsborough and its occupiers is the fine monument in St. Mary's, Tenby, which fortunately escaped the ill-fortune that attended the family and its residence.

In 1906 the huge growth of ivy was removed to reveal the original building and there are illustrations of what the ruins looked like at that time. Between 1930 and 1934 when Major Jones lived in Tenby he visited the ruins many times and they were then much as they were in the 1906 illustrations.

Refs: Francis Jones 'Rickeston and Scotsborough', *Treasury of Historic Pembrokeshire* and *Pembs. Hist. Soc.,* 1966.

SCOVASTON, *Steynton*

Marked with three dwellings on Colby's Map of 1831; Upper, Middle and Lower Scovaston.

Home of several families including the Butlers and Mordaunts. Thomas Butler was High Sheriff in 1644. In 1658/9 Hugh Butler of Scovaston sold large parts of his estate to William Mordaunt and Anne his wife. In 1670 William Mordaunt was assessed at seven hearths at Scovaston. Scovaston was formerly a considerable mansion. Fenton tells us '. . . the venerable buildings, that, in the remembrance of many living, occupied the site, have been transmuted into farmhouses'. It belonged to the Mordaunt family who owned 21 ploughlands. The last Mordaunt to own Scovaston is said to have had 21 children. This family was probably a branch of the Mordaunts who were formerly Earls of Peterborough. In 1685 William Mordaunt brought an action against Rice Gibbon for saying to Mordaunt's servant 'Your master is but a poor pitiful knave and has nothing but what he picks out of other men's pockets'. In 1700 Rice Gibbon of Scovaston, gent, 'died in the fields of Scovaston of the convulsions and fitts while working there on 4 May last'. In 1826 Scovaston was offered to let with 'about 180 acres, with lime kiln, fish pond, walled garden and house with 6 bedrooms and dressing rooms'. By 1863 the house had been rebuilt and was occupied by William Rees who was High Sheriff in that year.

Just before Christmas in 1985 tragedy struck Scovaston. The then owners, Richard Thomas and his sister Miss Helen Thomas were brutally murdered and the house set alight. It was completely gutted. The estate and ruins were put up for sale in May 1986 and have since been restored.

Refs: Western Mail, 28 Dec. 1985; *Western Telegraph,* 1 Jan. 1986; NLW Quaritch Deeds (1922) No. 368; Pembs. Plea Rolls, Nos. 103, 237, 245, 247 271, 278; Blome List 1673; NLW Morgan-Richardson Deeds No. 262; ibid. I, 86; Fenton, *Tour Pembs.,* p. 197; LT 1786; *Carmarthen Journal,* 28 July 1826; VL 1904; PRO AD (unpub.) 10802. PRO, Anc. Deeds.

SEALYHAM, *St. Dogwells*

Situated in woodland in a small valley through which runs the Afon Angof which fills a small lake.

Home of the Tucker family and world famous as the place where Sealyham terriers were first bred. Originally a small house containing only two hearths. The present large building is of 18th century construction and in the first half of 20th century was used as a tuberculosis hospital and later as a home for the elderly before closing in 1964.

The earliest member of the family to come to prominence was John Tocker, reeve of Trefgarne in 1405-07. The first of the family to be associated with Sealyham was Owen Tocker of Selyham, gent. in 1544/5 who owned lands in Haverfordwest where the Tockers were merchants. John Tocker, otherwise Tucker, was described as 'gentleman' in 1560. An 18th century Tucker – Admiral Thomas Tucker, R.N. achieved renown by killing the notorious pirate 'Blackbeard' in the West Indies. He went on to capture Spanish ships with rich cargoes and died in 1766. An heiress married an Edwardes, descendant of Owen Edwardes, grandfather of the 1st Lord Kensington, and they took the name of Tucker-Edwardes (Vide *Burke's Peerage*). In 1840 the house was described as 'an elegant modernised mansion'. The ghost

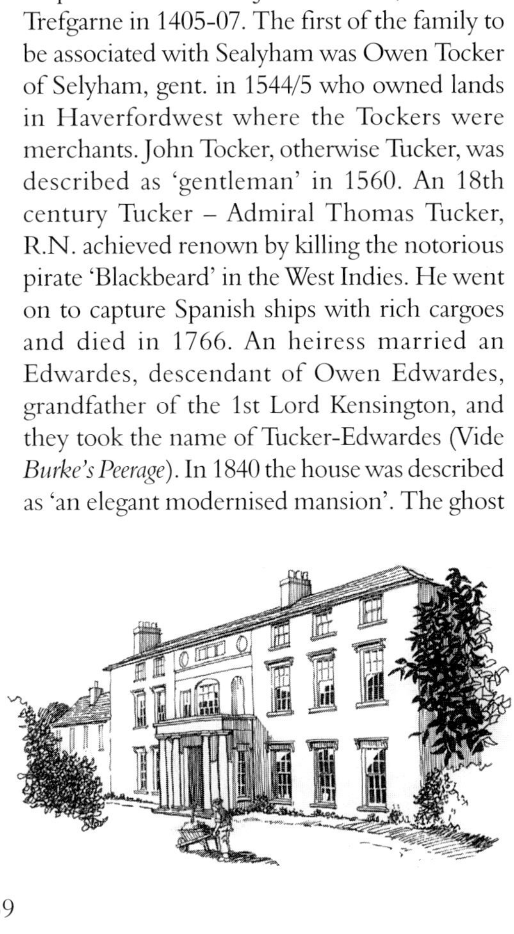

of a woman in white used to haunt the drive, the tradition being that a daughter of the house, Grace Tucker, had fallen in love with the coachman. Her angry father is said to have built a small cottage off the drive with barred windows in which he consigned his daughter 'to cool her off'. This little building, Major Jones reports, became a ruin but had for a time been used by Captain John Owen Tucker-Edwardes as kennels. He was the first man to breed Sealyham terriers. The late Mrs. C. O. Higgon once told Major Jones that she and a friend had actually seen the ghost gliding across the drive on a winter's evening in 1897. Rowland Edwardes was High Sheriff of the county in 1747 and a Sea Sergeant, John Tucker was High Sheriff in 1763, and William Edwardes Tucker in 1829.

The Tucker-Edwardes family sold Sealyham to the King Edward VII National Memorial Assn. in 1920. It changed hands in 1970 and again in 1988 when New Zealanders Sam and Valerie Richards bought it and now run it as an Activity Centre.

Refs: Lewis, *TDW,* 1840; *Dwnn,* i, p. 192; WWHR ii, p. 40; ibid. viii, pp. 177-208; *Contemporary Biographies of South Wales and Monmouthshire,* 1907, p. 93; Pembs. Plea Rolls No. 19; NLW, Eaton Evans and Williams Deeds; Picton Castle Deeds No. 83.

SIMPSON/SIMPSTON, *Roch*

In the Autumn of 1604, Morgan Bowen, described as 'of Symston, gent.' was granted a pardon for killing John Rees of Roblinston, yeoman, in a duel at Haverfordwest. In 1724 Thomas Jones of Cremina, Llanddewi Velfrey purchased absolutely the Simpston estate in Roch parish for a large sum from Ralph Price and others. The Land Tax returns for 1786 give Francis Meyrick Esq. as owner. Now known as Simpson.

Refs: Morgan-Richardson Deeds Nos. 55, 57, 66; Pembs. GS; Pembs. Plea Rolls No. 109.

SION HOUSE, *St. Mary's, Tenby*

Here we have a lost Nash house. The architect designed it for William Routh in about the year 1792. In 1810 it was put up for sale. 'Lately the residence of Mrs. C. Routh, deceased, with crock house, stable, garden and shrubbery. The mansion consists of a spacious entrance hall, eating room, breakfast parlour, library and china closet on the first floor; a handsome drawing room, (commanding beautiful prospects of the Mall, the Pier, Sir William Paxton's baths, Carmarthen Bay and the adjacent picturesque country), a music room, two bedchambers and a dressing room on the second floor; two bed chambers and three servants rooms on the second floor; two bed chambers and three servants rooms on the attic storey; a large kitchen, servants hall and two cellars on ground floor; convenient attached and detached offices, built within the last 18 years under the direction of a very eminent architect and no expense spared . . .' Originally a high, three-storeyed classical house it was enlarged and its symmetry spoiled later in the 19th century. It even had a change of name as Wooferton Grange and was for a time a girls' school. On March 24 1938 the house was totally gutted by fire. The site is now a block of flats. A photograph of the ruin can be seen in Thomas Lloyd's *Lost Houses of Wales.*

Refs: The Cambrian, 14 July 1810; Poyston Deeds No. 405; Thomas Lloyd, *Lost Houses of Wales,* 1986, p. 72.

SLADE *see* **ANASTASLADE**

de Rutzen

SLEBECH, *Slebech*

Home of the families of Barlow, Symmons, Knox, Phillips and de Rutzen. Mrs. Morgan writes in her *Tour of Milford Haven,* 1791: 'It is an exceedingly handsome house and has accommodations for a vast many people. I think they told us there were 25 bedrooms with each a dressing-room adjoining; and likewise two parlours, a study, a drawing room, a dining room and a billiard room, besides offices and accommodations of every other kind'. A more precise description appears in May 1792 when the estate, of over 7,000 acres, was put up for sale by public auction by 'Mr. Christie at his Great Room, Pall Mall'. The sale particulars are very detailed both of the house, its interiors and the curtilage. The mansion had three regular fronts with flights of stone steps to the principal floor. The north and south fronts each extending to 88 feet with uniform semi-circular bows.

On 4 June 1546 Roger Barlow and his brother Thomas bought the Commandery of Slebech and certain monastic properties in Pembrokeshire from the Crown for £705 6s. 3d. A note in the pedigree compiled by Joseph Lord in 1739 reads 'This Roger Barlow being an adventurer by sea, on his putting in to Milford Haven, purchased a very good estate at Slebech of King Henry VIII, and was the first of the Barlows in the county of Pembroke'. The estate remained in the Barlow family, and eventually came to Anne, daughter and heiress of George Barlow. In 1758 she married William Trevannion of Caerhays, Cornwall, who died without issue, and in 1773 she married John Symmons of Llanstinan and by him too, had no issue. John Barlow of Slebech was High Sheriff in 1562 and 1575; George Barlow in 1618; Sir John Barlow in 1681; George Barlow in 1752. Several later owners also held this post including Baron de Rutzen.

On 4 May 1784 John Symmons sold the Slebech estate to William Knox of Soho Square London, for a total of £90,834 5s. 0d.

In 1795 Knox sold the mansion to Nathaniel Phillips of Gloucester Place. Nathaniel Phillips aged 66 and a widower for 30 years married Mary Dorothea daughter of Rev. Edward Philipps of Lampeter Velfrey, a cadet line of the Philipps of Picton Castle, then about 19 years of age. In the same year he was High Sheriff for the county. Nathaniel and Mary had four children, Mary Dorothea born 1797, Nathaniel born 1798 who was educated at Eton and graduated at Christ Church, Oxford in 1817 became High Sheriff of Pembrokeshire in 1820 and died unmarried in 1824 at the Hotel of the Arms, Amsterdam from concussion and bruises occasioned by a severe fall; Louisa Catherine, born in 1801, married in 1819 Thomas William, Viscount Anson, created Earl of Lichfield in 1831 and had issue, and Edward Augustus born in 1802, died unmarried in 1830. Nathaniel Phillips the father died on 30 December 1813 aged 83.

Mary Dorothea Phillips, the eventual co-heiress of the estate, with her sister Louisa, married in 1822, Charles Frederick Baron de Rutzen born 3 March 1795 at Niederbartan in Courland. They had seven children and by 1830 had become sole owners of Slebech. The estate then known as Slebech Hall comprised of 3,700 acres and produced a rental of £5,300 per annum. In 1834 he arranged for the Duke of Brunswick to send him two wild boar. The boar were let loose in the Canaston woods. This was unpopular with the tenants but de Rutzen persuaded them to allow him to cull them by hunting them. They took 'an unconscionable time a-dying' and the Baron enjoyed several years of sport. The Baroness died in 1860 and the Baron in 1874. Their eldest son, Baron Frederick Leopold Sapieha Manteuffel born at Brighton on 10 June 1825 succeeded to Slebech, was a J.P. and served as High Sheriff in 1871. He died unmarried on 20 May 1890 and was

succeeded by his brother Rudolph. Rudolph born 6 September 1828 was a BA of the University of Cambridge and a barrister of the Inner Temple. He was High Sheriff in 1895 and a J.P. He to died unmarried in 1915 and was succeeded by his nephew Alan, son of Albert Richard Francis Maxmilien de Rutzen, born 1830 and a barrister who had a distinguished career and was knighted in 1901. He married Horatia Augusta Stepney Gulston of Derwydd, Carmarthenshire, and Alan was the eldest of five children. Alan de Rutzen was born 1876 and succeeded his uncle Baron Rudolph in 1915 while serving overseas as a Lieutenant in The Pembroke Yeomanry. He was killed at the battle of Kattia in 1916. He had married in 1908, Eleanor Etna Audley Thursby-Pelham of Abermarlais Park, Carms. and they had one son, John Frederick Foley de Rutzen, born on 27 January 1909. He was educated at Eton College and in the University of Cambridge. On 23 May 1918 he received a Royal Licence for himself and his heirs male of his body on succession, to use the title Baron de Rutzen within His Majesty's dominions. John, Baron de Rutzen fell in action near Battaglia on 11 October 1944. He was a talented man, widely read and a poet with a strong attachment to his lands and tenants and the discharge of his public duties. He served in the Welsh Guards during WW2 and saw active service in North Africa and Italy. He had married Sheila Victoria Katrin, daughter of Sir Henry Philipps, Baronet of Picton Castle and by her had an only child, Victoria Anne Elizabeth Gwynne de Rutzen. His widow married Lieut.-Col. the Hon. Randal Plunket, later the 19th Lord Dunsany and his daughter married Sir Francis Dashwood, Bt., of West Wycombe. Lady Dunsany inherited Slebech and eventually sold it to the Hon. William Philipps, C.B.E., who made some interior alterations. Mr. Philipps, who died in 1974, was the fourth son of the first Lord Milford. He was High Sheriff in 1968. Extensive further information is given in *The Treasury of Historic Pembrokeshire.*

Refs: Mrs. Morgan, *Tour of Milford Haven,* 1791, pp. 296-7; Francis Jones, 'Slebech & Some Further Slebech Notes' & *Treasury of Historic Pembrokeshire,* pp. 162-176 & *Historic Carmarthenshire Homes and their Families.*

SODSTON HOUSE, *Narberth*

Called Sottisdoune in 1282. Marked on Colby's Map of 1831 and the Mudge Map of 1819. Sodston House enjoys a quiet rural setting a few miles north of Narberth. In 1705 the messuage and land called Sottston was part of the Barlow of Slebech estate. On 7 November 1768 Ann Trevannion of Slebech, widow, mortgaged Sodson and other messuages to Bridget Foley of Ridgeway, widow.

It was the home of the James family; in 1786 William James, gent. is described as owner-occupier. This is a T-shaped house. A sale notice in *The Cambrian* on 9 June 1808 describes the house as a substantial modern mansion house with three spacious parlours, eight bed-chambers, garrets and closets. There were, of course, the usual outhouses and gardens and about 100 acres in all. Over the next century the house changed hands frequently being mortgaged and remortgaged. Its occupiers were at different times a branch of the James's of Pantsaeson, 1798- 1811; John Phelps who died 1830; William Frederick Northey, the Ward family, and Elizabeth Jane Roch of Cheltenham.

George Devonald was of Sodston when he died on 7 August 1836. He left all personalty and realty to his wife for ever and £30 per annum for establishing a school in the parish of Narberth. His widow, Martha mortgaged for £1,400 the messuage called Sodson House to Miss Ann Harvey of Haverfordwest. Martha Devonald died 26 March 1848. The Mortgage was unredeemed and came to Thomas Noot, trustee who paid the money to said Ann Harvey who reconveyed Sodston to Thomas Noot acting as Trustee of the will of Mrs. Devonald. The mortgage was transferred by Thomas Noot in 1851 to Mr. James of Woodson; in 1856 to Mr. Northey; in 1858 from Mr. Northey to Robert Ward and back again to Northey, in 1862 from Northey to Ward again; in 1886 and 1888 transferred yet again. In 1905 Webb-Bowen conveyed Sodston to Colonel Bernard Robert Ward, R.E. Latterly it was owned by W. Benyon Evans of Narberth who sold it to David Davis who conveyed it to Anthony Ward of Lower Broadmoor. Mr. Williams, owner-occupier, lent the deeds to Francis Jones in 1976. In 1985 the estate was up for sale again as a whole or in lots. It is now owned by Mr. & Mrs. MacNaghten and their family.

Refs: Slebech Deeds No. 727; VL 1834, 1904; Nicholas, *County Families*, 1875 edn., p. 840; Pembs. RO ii, 96, 1609; ibid. 127, 146; Sodston Deeds courtesy of Mr. Williams of Sodston.

SOUTHFIELD, *Llysyfran*

For long a Wogan possession, Southfield was in the ownership of one Henry Jones in 1562. He was the son of Richard Jones, merchant of Haverfordwest who died before 1552 and Janet, daughter of William Wogan. Richard Jones's brother was Standard Bearer to Henry VII. Henry Jones's younger brother was Richard Jones of Brawdy. Henry seems to have been twice married, firstly to Elizabeth, daughter of John Scourfield of Mote, and secondly to Dorothy, daughter of Thomas Vaughan. He produced one son and heir, Thomas Jones who in 1617 was Under Sheriff to William Scourfield. He was also Steward to Sir William Wogan of Wiston who owned two fifths of the Barony of Dungleddy and as such was entitled to hold a Court leet at Wiston. He and Sir William Wogan were the defendants in an action for £100 damages in 1622 brought by Sir John Philipps of Picton on the grounds that Thomas Jones had prevented Sir John's Steward from holding a Court. Thomas Jones died in about 1633 leaving two daughters Anne and Elizabeth as co-heiresses. Anne Jones married Thomas Philipps of Velindre, son of William Philipps of Castlebythe and grandson of Morgan Philipps of Picton Castle. They had two sons, James Philipps 'of Southfield' and William Philipps later described as 'of Kilbarth' in Rudbaxton. William Philipps's son married Phoebe Picton of Poyston, her brother being the grandfather of Sir Thomas Picton. The other co-heiress of Thomas Jones, Elizabeth, married firstly, Philip

Lloyd and secondly John David Llewellyn 'of Kilywendog'. After James Philipps came five generations of Philipps ending with John Philipps (1820-94). Successful in business, including the establishment of a tanyard near Southfield Villa, he left land totalling approximately 1,000 acres. He was a prominent Methodist, building at least four chapels as well as two schools. On his death, Southfield passed through his sister Letitia Melchior's line to her grandson William Melchior James, the son of her daughter and a David James living at Enfield, Portfield Gate. The Melchiors from Llandeilo (Pembs.) were descended from William Melchior, Bailiff of Newport in 1605. From 1658 they were the holders of an ancient skull believed to be that of St Teilo, and healing powers were reputedly given to those who used the skull to drink water from the well close to Llandeilo farmhouse. William Melchior James's son David Melchior James (1898-1978) inherited Southfield in 1963 but died childless leaving Southfield to Norman James (1933-94). It is now owned by David Ellis of Poyston, the great grandson of William Melchior James. David Ellis married Jane Woollen in 1987 and they have two children Sophie and Thomas. Major Jones visited Southfield in 1974 and described the existence of two houses, an older, smaller one and a larger one higher up the slope built in about 1840. He was told by Mr James that the original mansion lay below the present buildings and he writes 'I found no traces of it above ground, but around the alleged site a large number of daffodils and other flowers grew in profusion'. In 2001 Southfield House is being restored.

Refs: Coleman Deeds, No. 353; *Dwnn*, i, 78, 178; Pembs. Plea Rolls No. 112; VL 1834, 1904; GGMS I AD; Mr. D. Ellis.

Campbell

STACKPOLE COURT,
St. Petrox

This, without doubt, was one of the grandest houses in Pembrokeshire, if not all Wales. The earliest known owner was a Crusader, Sir Elidur or Leonard de Stackpole (his effigy is in the local church). His family did not remain long at Stackpole and the estate passed through an heiress to the Vernon family of Haddon Hall in Derbyshire. The Vernons preferred the comforts of Haddon to the then fortified house which was built by the Normans to keep out the Welsh. The family's steward, George Lort, originally from Staffordshire, was left in charge. Lort in the mid-16th century bought Stackpole from his employers and took up residence. He once wrote to a fellow steward that the best crop to plant in Pembrokeshire was agents because they clung to the land and thrived.

On 17 November 1591 Lewys Dwnn called at Stackpole and recorded George Lort's short pedigree. George Lort married Margery Eddow or Eddoe and had four sons, Roger, Thomas, George and Sampson. Roger the heir had succeeded his father by November 1601 and was High Sherriff in 1607. He married Abra, daughter of Hugh Burrows of Findon and had three sons and four daughters. Henry Lort the heir, said to be about 23 years of age in 1614 succeeded his father in 1613. He was High Sheriff in 1619. He added greatly to his estates and was a rich man. He married Judith, daughter of Henry White of Henllan and had seven children, five sons and two daughters. Roger Lort, born 1608 was the heir. He supported the Royalists in the Civil War and garrisoned Stackpole for the King until forced to surrender. He was among the few Pembrokeshire men to be accorded a place in the *Dictionary of National Biography*. In addition to making valuable additions to the family estate, he took an active part in public life and although a Royalist at heart, his dexterity during the troubled years of the Civil Wars and the Commonwealth ensured the survival of his family and estates and brought him offices under Cromwell and a baronetcy from Charles II. Roger matriculated at Wadham College, Oxford on 3 November 1626 at the age of 18 years. He graduated B.A. in 1627 and in that year became a student in the Middle Temple. He was a Latin scholar of considerable merit, a poet, and in 1646 published his *Epigrammatum Liber Primus*. He was High Sheriff in 1652 and a J.P. Roger Lort, the first baronet, (bestowed upon him by Charles II), was, when he died in 1663 one of the richest men in South Wales. He owned extensive estates in Pembrokeshire and Carmarthenshire, owned 1,000 cows, steers and heifers, 10,000 sheep, 50 horses, corn worth £3,000 and goods valued at over £7,000.

Sir Elidur de Stackpole

John Lort, 2nd baronet was the son of Roger and his first wife Hester Annesley. He was born around 1638, was admitted to Lincoln's Inn and was knighted on 17 January 1662 some six months before his father received a baronetcy. Sir John married Susanna Holles, a bride with a fortune of £4,000, daughter of the second Earl of Clare. Sir John died in 1673 leaving his estate to his only son, Gilbert and his heirs, and in default to his only daughter Elizabeth and her issue. Sir Gilbert Lort was born in Clare House, London on Easter Day 1671. He never married and died in his 28th year and was buried in Westminster Abbey. On the death of Sir Gilbert Lort, Bt., in 1698 without issue, Stackpole

Cawdor

passed to his sister and heiress, Elizabeth who was married to a Scot – Sir Alexander Campbell, yr. of Cawdor. Her husband was descended from the 3rd son of the 2nd Earl of Argyll who had married the heiress of the old Thanes of Cawdor of Cawdor Castle. Through her marriage the Campbells thus attained substantial estates in Wales which remained with their descendants until recent times. She died in 1714. John Campbell, son of Sir Alexander and Dame Elizabeth represented Pembrokeshire in Parliament from 1727-47, was Commissioner of the Admiralty from 1736-42. He replaced the old house at Stackpole with a new Georgian one. John Wright, bailiff wrote to Pryse Campbell, son of John Campbell in 1735, 'Since the pulling down of the old house the rats that used to run behind the wainscot are gone abroad'. Pryse Campbell predeceased his father who died in 1777. Another John, later the first Lord Cawdor, (created 1796), succeeded. He was a keen agriculturist and enjoyed shooting and sailing. He took part in the defeat of the French troops at the landings at Fishguard in 1797. Nelson visited the Cawdors in 1802 as did Fenton who wrote 'the house is distributed into a number of very noble apartments, and the library is large and well furnished . . . The offices are all well arranged, and the stables forming a detached large quadrangular building, are in a style of princely pretension. Of Stackpool, without straining compliment, it may safely be said that there are few places which display more magnificence without, or more sumptious hospitality and elegant comforts within.'

The Campbells rebuilt Stackpole and further enlargements were made in 1821 by George IV's architect Sir John Wyattville and his assistant Henry Ashton. John Frederick Campbell, who celebrated his coming of age in 1811, succeeded his father in 1821. He was a Fellow of the Royal Society and created Earl Cawdor and Viscount Emlyn in 1827. He was succeeded by his son, another John Frederick who was in turn succeeded by the 3rd Earl, Frederick Archibald Campbell. The 4th Earl

contested Pembrokeshire in the Conservative interest but without success. The 5th Earl Cawdor spent most of his time on his Scottish estates and after World War II his son decided that the 150-roomed house would have to go, largely because of the heavy taxation in force at the time. The sale of contents in 1962 was one of the most important ever to be held in southwest Wales. The great house itself was demolished in the same year – a needless and wanton act. The estate was sold in 1976. The National Trust now owns the park.

Refs: Francis Jones, 'Stackpole Court and the Lorts', *Treasury of Historic Pembrokeshire,* pp. 256-294; Thos. Roscoe, *Wanderings & Excursions in S. Wales,* 1836, pp. 156-9; *The Cambrian Tourist,* 1821 edn., pp. 109-111; Timmins, *Nooks Pembs.,* 1895, pp. 66-8; Laws, *Little England,* p. 141; *Dwnn,* i, p. 125; WWHR ii, 60; Lewis, *TDW,* ii, 376; Llwyd, III, p. 5; *Western Telegraph,* 5 October 1983; Fenton, *Tour Pembs.,* pp. 229-230.

STONE HALL, *St. Lawrence*

Hidden within a little glade, girdled with lawn, leaf and blossom, the mansion stands on a slope immediately above the Cleddau-wen. Overlooked by no height or habitation, this friendly hermitage is connected to the highway by a tree-lined drive, and according to the older folk, a *ladi wen* haunts the entrance gateway at dusk, often to the discomfort of those privileged to meet her, by moving slowly and deliberately towards the 'victim' into whose eyes she peers intently, looking, so 'tis said, for a person whose eyes are of differing colours, one blue, the other brown, and to the happy possessor will be revealed the whereabouts of a vast treasure *(trysorau di-ben-draw).*

Stone Hall provides an example of a traditional residence of the older Welsh gentry,

and fortunately has escaped the fate that overtook so many country houses in Pembrokeshire, mainly during the 19th century when they were transformed from modest, but adequate, accommodation into grand edifices which by today have become too burdensome to maintain or to fulfil functions peculiar to the conditions of the times that produced them.

While few features of its medieval predecessor survive, it is possible that an internal stone staircase, a wing and part of the walls – in places over four and a half feet thick – may have formed part of the original fabric. Substantially built, of stone as the name implies, it was never palatial, and the assessment in the taxation list of 1670 at four hearths (like the residences of Brawdy, Llangwarren, Llanstinan and Priskilly) shows it to have been typical of the more modest manor houses built for accommodating the household of a country gentleman mainly occupied with estate and farming concerns and local administration. Its fine walled garden has survived.

The site has been occupied continuously, at least from about 1400, and from that time to our own, the history of the residents is fully documented. This two-storeyed house consists of a central block facing eastwards, with wings extending to the rear of the premises, enclosing what once had been a courtyard. The central block contains the hall and main reception rooms; on the exterior wall of the south gable-end is a sundial engraved with the letters W.F.E., the date of 1704, and the legend *Tacit Surr (exit).* The initials are those of William Ford and his wife Elizabeth; the date probably commemorates the year when the sundial was placed there rather than any rebuilding, although the possibility of the latter must not be wholly discounted. Throughout, the rooms are commodious, low-ceilinged, with massive oak beams. The northern wing is the oldest section, mainly used for domestic offices, seemingly Elizabethan in character, adapted from an even earlier period. On two occasions at least, the southern wing has been extended as indicated by distinct variations in the roof height of the extensions.

Within the house, just off the hall and near the entry into the northern wing, a spiral stone stairway built into the wall leads to an upper storey, an undoubted feature from a remote age. The main staircase is wide, with easy, shallow treads; the lower rooms, hall, sides of the stairway, and some upper rooms and passages, contain modern panelling which replaced older woodwork, parts of which have been incorporated into the newer panels and some of the window shutters. Several oaken floorboards in the upper storey are very wide, clearly of considerable antiquity as also are some of the rafters in the attics. Chaff was used as insulation in the ceilings.

Changes had been made by successive owners, Wogan, Ford, Peel, and there is ample evidence of internal rearrangements effected in the mid-19th century. In 1858, when occupied by the Peel family, it was described as 'a place of great antiquity . . . The house is a good large, commodious family residence built and altered with no other view than internal comfort. The present proprietor, following the example of his predecessors, has made considerable additions, with the same disregard of outward appearance and architectural beauty. So ancient are some portions of the house that it is impossible to ascertain the date of its first erection, and so solid that the walls are four feet thick'.

According to *Peniarth MS 156* and *Golden Grove MS,* the earliest known family at Stone Hall traced its lineage to the north Pembrokeshire prince Gwynfardd Dyfed, and the first of his descendants to settle there seems to have been Philip ap Gwylim at the beginning of the 15th century. Philip married Jane, daughter of Philip Elliot of Earewere (Amroth) by Jane daughter of Sir Thomas Perrot of Eastington in Rhoscrowther. He died at Stone Hall on Thursday before the day of St.

Lawrence the Martyr, Henry VII (1486) leaving five children. Gwilym ap Philip inherited from his father in 1487. By his wife Margery Tancred he had an only daughter and heiress Anne who married Sir John Wogan of Wiston who was a Gentleman Usher of the King's Chamber also Bailey Itinerant of the Lordship of Haverford-west and in 1525 was appointed Bailiff of the Manor of Roosc in consideration of his services in England and abroad. He was High Sheriff of the county in 1543; 1550 and 1554, and of Cardiganshire in 1541 and 1555. He died in 1557 and was succeeded by his second son Morris Wogan. The Wogans remained at Stone Hall for a further four generations, the last to live there being William Wogan whose only son died young and his two daughters Dorothy and Mary became co-heiresses. Dorothy married William Ford, of Crewkerne, Somerset without consent of her mother who regarded Ford as unsuitable as a consort for a Pembrokeshire heiress of high degree. Mary, however, approved of her sister's choice, and to emphasis this married his brother Richard Ford. The estate was partitioned and the Hall formed part of Dorothy's portion. The Fords remained at Stone until the last of the male line, William, died in 1793 aged 76 leaving the estate to a relation by marriage, one of the Protheroes of Dolwilym. The Rev. William Ford Protheroe died heavily in debt in 1823, his only daughter having married George Roch of Butter Hill.

Stone Hall eventually became the home of Thomas Bowen who, in 1824, had a lease from Sir John Pakington (Vide *Burke's Peerage* – Hampton B), of coal pits and storehouses at Little Milford Quay. Later it belonged to John Entwistle Peel but in 1873 he sold it to the Rev. Edward Peacock, son of the Rev. Edward Peacock by his wife Anne, daughter of William Lort Mansel, Bishop of Bristol. There have been several owners since then, among them the Rev. Murray A. Mathews M.A, F.L.S, member of the British Ornithologists Union, who had resigned his living of Bishops Lydiard in West Somerset owing to long ill-health, and was author of *The Birds of Pembrokeshire and its Islands* (1904). The Seton family sold out to Dr. McGeoch in about 1951. Dr. McGeoch sold what remained of the estate to Richard Lloyd, an antiques dealer who was living there in 1981. He eventually sold it to Dr. and Mrs. Alan Watson who converted the house into an hotel and restaurant in 1985.

Refs: Francis Jones 'Stone Hall', *Pembs. Hist. Soc.*; Pembs. RO DB/13/108; ibid. D/RTP/SKY Nos. 116, 279, 287; ibid. HDX/197 No. 143; ibid. HDX/695 No. 6; ibid. DB/13/108; NLW Trenewydd Deeds No. 648; Burke, *Visitations,* IV, 2419, 1858; Nicholas, *County Families,* 1875; WWHR VII; ibid. ii, 35; *Dwnn,* i, pp. 106-7; LT 1786; VL 1834; Protheroe MS IV, ff. 148-9; BM Egerton, 2586. ff. 367-9; NLW Slebech Deeds No. 271.

Phelps

STUDDA, *Steynton*★

In 1392 the Prior of Pill held 15 bovates at Studah by knight's service held of the manor of Pill. It was long the home of the Phelps family. John Phelps of Studda, Esq. married an unknown Penelope by whom he had a son, George. John Phelps died 7 October 1765 aged 60 years and his wife in 1782 aged 82. Their son, George married Martha who died aged 67 on 6 October 1802, her husband having predeceased her on 14 November 1798 leaving their son, John and his wife Elizabeth. John died 7 March 1814 aged 49 and his wife 4 May 1813 aged 36. They had one surviving child, four children having died as infants, John Freeman Phelps was of Sodston, Narberth, when he died aged 22 on 11 May 1830. On a memorial inscription in Steynton church above the Phelps monument is a shield of arms: dexter a fess 3 garbs, sinister impaling a lion rampant *or* crowned; Crest, a garb *or.* The Phelps had sold Studda by 1786 when a Mrs. Meylett was shown in the Land Tax records as owner-occupier, she was the widow of William Meylett, a parliamentary voter in 1760. A descendant, Henry Arthur Meylett Evans of Haverfordwest owned the freehold house and lands of Studda in 1904.

The Voters List of 1834 shows a William Simleat of Studda, occupier of lands at Studda at a rent of £50 p.a.

Refs: VL 1769, 1834, 1904; Bowen Map South Wales c. 1760; LT 1786; Deed in Cardiff Library now in Glam. RO.

SUMMERHILL, *Roch*

Nearly one mile south of Cuffern – Colby's Map 1831.

Fenton wrote in *Tour* '. . . I pass by Summerhill once the residence of a respectable branch of the family of Edwards, descended from Tudor Trevor'. There are some walls of this old house incorporated in the comparatively modern farm. In the 14th century 'Somerhill' was owned by the Knights Hospitallers. In the latter half of the 16th century this was the property of a family called Hurd(e). By 1613 John Barlow of Slebech owned the Manor of Summerhill and the services of two carucates there. By 1642 we find Thomas Edwards, gent. described as 'of Somerhill'. He died intestate. At the end of the 18th century the Rev. Owen Edwards was owner but by the beginning of the next century the seat had become a farmstead. In 1838 the tenant was Thomas Owen. It was occupied by the Owen family, throughout the 1800s. In the 1894 and 1904 V.L. the tenant was William J. Owen who held a lease for lives, he died in April 1957, his wife was Annie Owen, née Rees.

Refs: Pembs. Plea Rolls Nos. 18, 24, 38, 61, 117, 139, 157, 165, 168; Fenton, *Tour Pembs.*, p. 87; *Pembs. Arch Svy;* Pembs. GF 1610; WWHR iii, p. 133; Pembs. Papers of GS; Pembs. RO. HDX/197 No. 3; ibid. HDX/750 Nos. 1-59.

SUMMERTON, *Little Newcastle*

On the 6 inch OS map, Summerton House otherwise known as East Summerton is marked, and close on the west side is Summerton Farm, about a mile north east of the village of Little Newcastle. There is an early earth castle on the land of this farm.

James ap Rees of Sommerton was sued for 10/- in 1594/5. The property is mentioned in the will of Laurence Hyer, farmer, of Sommerton in 1606. In 1786 Sparks Martin is listed as owner with Martha Mathias as his tenant. In 1894, one Daniel Luke was owner. It was offered for sale in 1913 and at that time the house was described as '. . . originally a mansion and is still very commodious and with little expense could be renovated'.

Refs: SC 451 Carms. RO; *Anc. Mon. Pembs.,* 1925, p. 147; KCR 37 Eliz.; Pembs. Papers of GS; Pr. W. fo. 89; Protheroe V, 158; VL 1894; LT 1786.

SUNNY HILL, *Manorbier* ★

Home of the Byam family lineally descended from Caradoc Frei'chfras. The son of William Byam of Antigua, Edward Byam born 1712, married mid-1734 his cousin, Lydia, daughter of Edward Byam, Governor of the Leeward Islands. He died in 1768 at Llanion, Pembroke St. Mary's parish where he was buried, leaving a son, William Byam sometime of Sunny Hill, who married Martha, daughter of Edward Rogers of Llanwnda. He predeceased his wife dying in 1779 leaving Sunny Hill to his widow, where she was accessed for 4s. 4d. in land tax in 1786. They had two sons and a daughter. Edward Byam born in 1767 was of Antigua, and married Christian Ryan of Dublin. They had a son, William viv. 1850 who served in 15th Hussars in France and later at Waterloo where he was wounded. He married 8 February 1815 Martha, daughter of Thomas Rogers of Antigua. William and Martha's second son, Samuel was D.D., vicar of Catterick, Yorkshire, and Chaplin in Ordinary to the King and died in 1816.

By the early 19th century the Leach family were of Sunny Hill afterwards of Milford. Henry Leach qualified as a magistrate for the county in 1801, and sold Sunny Hill in 1806. He married Mary Brand Jones, a co-heiress of Brawdy and had five children all born at Sunny Hill. The house was sold to Edward Stokes, will dated 29 August 1822, who by his wife, Cecilia had three children, Adrian, Sarah and Celia.

Refs: Pembs. Qtr. Sessions Order Book; Burke, *LG* 1850; VL 1834, 1904; LT 1786.

SUTTON LODGE, *Haverfordwest*

William Summers, of Sutton, gent. was assessed at £1 6s. 3d. in Land Tax in 1786. John Arthur Allen (b. 1802), son of John Allen of Gelliswick, settled at Sutton Lodge and married Mary, daughter of Stephen Thomas of Lower Haythog. In the mid-19th century it was the residence of John Penry Jones, J.P., D.L., (d. 1872) descended matrilineally from the Penry family of Cwrt y Ceidrim, Llanedy, Carmarthanshire. In the 1980s it was a hotel.

Refs: Francis Jones, *Historic Carmarthenshire Homes and their Families*; Burke, *LG,* 1898, ii, p. 1174; LT 1786; VL 1904; Protheroe, Beynon Deeds No. 200.

TALBENNY HALL, *Talbenny*
South of Talbenny village. The Howell family lived here in the 14th century and were still there in the early 16th century. The Howells were descended from Lodovicus Talbenny, Dominus de Talbenny and Brodmore. Lodovicus had two sons who split their inheritance. The elder was William and the younger, Howell whose great-grandson, Henry Howell was of Howelston in 1416 and married Alice daughter

of 'Dominus Taneard de Hospital'. Their son, Walter (viv. Henry VII), married Agnes daughter of William Filbech and they had four sons, Gilbert, Henry, William and John. According to the Land Tax records of 1786 Hugh Owen Barlow Esq. was owner but in 1797 one Adam Wathen described as 'gent.' was owner-occupier. In 1805 James Wathen of Middle Hasguard and Adam Wathen were of Talbenny Hall but by 1834 William Cole, of Philbeach was owner of the freehold.

Refs: Wagner MS 2 (GO); LT 1797, 1786; VL 1834, 1894.

TALYBONT, *Llawhaden*
Home of the Hawkwell family, the first of whom came to Pembrokeshire as an official of Bishop Barlow who first settled him at St. Kennox. From there they moved across the Cleddau to Talybont. In 1551 William Hawkwell of Llawhaden, yeoman, was summoned by John Snyy of Bristol, gent. administrator of Martin Pollard, gent. for £34. John and Katherine Hawkwell were assessed at two and three hearths respectively in 1670. Griffith Hawkwell was High Sheriff in 1663 and 1690. Fenton wrote: 'The mansion of Talybont, almost facing the church on the opposite bank of the river, and now belonging to John Meares Esq. was first built and inhabited by a family of Hawkwell . . . None of that respectable family to whom it now belongs (Meares) have resided there for these forty or fifty years; and like many of the deserted houses in this county too good to be pulled down, it has experienced in that time a fluctuating succession of occasional tenants.' The Meares family of Eastington, acquired Talybont by marriage, but preferred living at Eastington and the deserted house deteriorated accordingly.

In 1770 William Hawkwell Meares carried out considerable repair work to the building. This was because a Dr. Berkenhout from London had, the year before, approached the family with a view to renting the place. The rent was to be £10 p.a. and the lease to run for six years but the Doctor stipulated that the considerable repair work required was to be carried out by the owners. The ground floor rooms had suffered badly as a result of flooding when the river burst its banks. Fifteen loads of slate were delivered for re-roofing, at a cost of £2 7s. 0d., and 20 deal boards costing £2 10s. 0d. The following were tiled – outer kitchen and malt houses, kiln house (one side new), one side of the parlour new, pig cott all new, part of the mansion on the leads and part of the half roof, the south side of the mansion on the leads and part of the half roof, the south side of the mansion and the half roof: the following were painted: outside of the parlour, staircase, front of the mansion, stable, dairy, coach house, and one side of the kiln house; and 17 feet of glass costing 17 shillings was used.

In the Land Tax List of 1786, Upper and Lower Talybont both owned by John Meares Esq. and both tenanted by Isaac Ormond, assessed at £1 4s. 7d. and 17s. 4½d. respectively. In the Voter's List of 1894 Daniel Davies of Talybont, dwelling house, and Henry Thomas James of Talybont, dwelling house are recorded.

Refs: Fenton, *Tour Pembs.,* p. 175; VL 1834, 1894, 1904; Poyston Deeds No. 72; Pembs. Plea Rolls No. 9 1551; ibid. No. 178; Picton Castle Deeds; LT 1786; BM Egerton MS 2586, 1591.

TANCREDSTON, *Brawdy*

This place is named after one Tancred, a name found in 12th-13th century Pembrokeshire records. In 1326 a fee at Tankardiston was held in chief of the Bishop by William Martin of Rickeston, while his wife the lady Wenthliana Martin held also a knight's fee at Tankardyston. They had been held by the family of Le Moigne of Rickeston, whose heiress was the lady Gwenllian. The Martins held Tancredston until about 1480, when the heiress, Alson Martin brought it to her husband David, illegitimate son of Sir Rhys ap Thomas.

In 1565 Thomas Ap Rice and Agnes his wife were vouchees in connection with a recovery of estates which included the manor of Tankerdeston, and in 1569 a recovery was suffered between Richard Bateman and Maurice Walter, demandants, and William Ap Rees gentleman, tenant, in respect of the manors of Rickardston and Tanckardeston and other lands in Pembrokeshire. On 9 August 1585 a Final Concord was made between John ap Rice plaintiff and Henry Martin gent. deforceant, in respect of 'the manors of Rickardston and Tanckardston' and other lands. In 1587/88 the manor of Tancardston was held by John ap Rees.

The lords of the manor had some trouble with the family of Castle Villa, seat of the influential family of Morris and later of the equally influential Scourfields. In June 1550 Thomas ap Rhys of Rickeston sued John Scurfyld and Katherine his wife for £40 damages. He deposed that Henry Morris had held one messuage and 46 acres of land in Tankeston, held of the manor of Tankeston by homage and fealty and payments of 40s. and 2s.: and also a messuage and 42 acres of land and 4 acres of wood in Castlevillia, held of the same manor by homage and fealty and payments of 40s.; and a messuage and 139 acres in Roskaneven, held of the said manor, and payments of 4s. and 2s. Henry Morris died leaving as his heiress, his grand-daughter, Agnes Richard (daughter and heir of Richard Morris son and heir of the said Henry, who had died in his father's lifetime), a minor, whose wardship belonged to Thomas ap Rhys as lord of the manor of Tankeston. However John Scurfyld and Katherine took the guardianship and the profits into their own hands, to the lord's loss of £40. The result of the case is not known, but some arrangement must have been made for the Scourfields were able to marry their son William to the little heiress.

Old buildings at Tancredston

Forty years later a similar situation arose which obliged the lord of the manor once again to take legal action to support his rights. According to the evidence in the suit which was pleaded before the Great Sessions at the end of 1592, John Scourfield, son of William Scourfield of Castle Villa by Anne (Agnes) Morris, his wife, married Jane, daughter of Llewellin Lloyd of Llanstinan, by whom he had a daughter and heiress, Anne, born about 1580. From his mother John Scourfield had inherited a messuage and two carucates of land in Castle Villa, held of John ap Rhys of Rickeston as of his manor of Tancredston. John Scourfield died at Castle Villa in May 1588, leaving the said Anne, then aged 8 years, as his heiress. John ap Rhys as lord of the manor claimed the infant's marriage. However her kinsfolk did not agree with this and when the little girl disappeared, John ap Rhys brought a charge against William Scourfield (aged 50 years) and John Jenkin of New Moat yeoman (aged 30 years) for abducting her from the house of her guardian William Walter Glyn and Gwenhwyfar Lewis his wife, at Manorowen, and further cited Thomas Mathias (who had married the widowed mother of the infant), John Scourfield of Moat, and John Meyler of Trewallterwen in St. Edrins parish for aiding and abetting the offence. Unfortunately the result of the case is not given, but the Scourfields seem to have emerged victorious, for the little girl was later married to her kinsman Thomas Scourfield who turned out an irresponsible rake.

In 1706 the manor of Tancredston, (with other properties), was sold by James ap Rice of Rickeston to John Rickson of Pembroke; in 1754 William Rickson sold it to Mrs. Lettice Barlow of Rosepool, widow, who by her will dated 2 December 1763 left it to her nephew James Jones of Haverfordwest, son of William Jones of Llether. James Jones died intestate in 1781 and the manor became vested in his brother William Jones of Llether. In 1784 William Jones of Llether Esq. deputed Thomas James to his gamekeeper for the manors of Rickeston, Tankiston, and Rhydygele, and on 27 January 1802 deputed John Richards, yeoman, to be his gamekeeper for the preceding three manors as well as for his manor of Llether. His daughter and ultimate heiress, Mary, married George Roch of Butter Hill, and the Roch family became lords of the manor of Tancredston and the three other manors named above. The last court for these manors was held about 1860, the revenues being described as 'small'.

The origin of the Hicks family who farmed Tancredston is obscure. There is no doubt that they were English by extraction. There is a tradition that the Pembrokeshire family descends from the Rev. John Hicks, a clergyman who was ejected from the living of Saltash in Cornwall soon after the Restoration as he objected to taking the oath. I have found nothing to connect him with Pembrokeshire.

The first established family of this name is to be found at Tancredston. The earliest reference is in 1661 when Owen Hicks of Brawdy parish paid 2/6d. towards a Benevolence. His Christian name suggests that he had Welsh ancestry and it is possible that his mother was a Pembrokeshire woman. He had a brother called Erasmus Hicks. The will of Owen Hicks dated 14 August 1685 was proved at Carmarthen on 13 November following. He mentions his wife, Elizabeth whose maiden name appears to have been Griffiths. They had one son, Erasmus, and three daughters: Dorothy, Elizabeth and Lettice. Erasmus Hicks of Tancredston married Anne, sister of Thomas Rees of Kerbyd. His will dated 2 April 1718 was proved at Carmarthen on 16 April following. He left the following children: James Hicks, the eldest son who was farming Tancredston in 1726; David Hicks and three daughters, one married David Howell; Anne and Lettice. David Hicks farmed Tancredston in 1726/7. His lease expired at Michaelmas 1730 when the farm was granted to Llewellin Harry. David Hicks had the following children; Abel, Thomas, who farmed part of Tancredston, and Erasmus. Abel married Elizabeth, daughter of the Vicar of Brawdy, the Rev. Lewis Evans of Tremanhire in Whitchurch parish. Abel embarked on trading ventures and owned a coastal vessel which did considerable trade. He also owned collieries in the county and became a man of some substance. In 1752 he became the owner of Tremanhire, and in the right of this freehold voted for Owen of Orielton in the parliamentary elections of 1765 and 1768. He died in 1788, aged 74 and his wife in 1802 aged 86. His will dated 2 October 1788, in which he is described as of Haverfordwest, mariner, was proved at Carmarthen on 28 March 1789. They had three children, Henry, Thomas and Dorothy.

There is a tradition that the Evans family had been at Tancredston for some four centuries but I have not been able to trace them back beyond the 18th century. It is also said that the Evans's formerly of Olmarch and Carforiog are of the same stock. It is from the Estate Books of the Scourfields who owned Tancredston that we find the earliest references to tenants named Evans. Llewellyn Harry died in 1731 and his widow gave the land up and it was then rented to Griffith Evan and his partner, Richard William at the yearly rent of £54. At Michaelmas 1733 they divided the farm between them, henceforth farming separately. The next tenant was George Evan who held it under a lease of £54 a year and was living there in 1771. The other farms at Tancredston during 1771-74 being held by Thomas Hicks and Henry Skeel. George Evan was assessed at £1 4s. 8d. in Land Tax in 1787. Administration of George Evan's estate was granted at Carmarthen to his son, John, now Evans, on 12 May 1795. John had three children, Thomas, Susanna, who married George Harries of Trenichol, and Sarah who married Richard Gwyther of Brawdy. Thomas was born in 1799 and married Sophia, daughter of William Edwards of Penfeidir. Thomas also farmed Treddiog and may have lived there for some time. They had five children, George, John, Margaret, Sarah, and Mary Anne. George the youngest but one child was born in 1847 and farmed Tancredston. He married Mary Anne, ninth child of Henry Jenkins of Kingheriot. George Evans was a very popular man and a member of Trefgarn Owen chapel and a very good musician. He was master of the chapel choir. He died on 2 January 1918 and his wife on 5 December 1922. They had six children, Minnie, a twin brother to Minnie who died an infant; Lillian and Kitty her twin sister, Gwennie and Susanna who died in July 1974.

The Scourfields were still in possession of Tancredston in 1842.

Refs: Francis Jones, 'Evans of Tancredston' and 'Hicks of Tancredston'; Francis Jones Archives; Scourfield Estate Books; Pembs. Plea Rolls Nos. 102, 234; Pembs. papers of GS; Lucas Deeds; PRO, Wales 3, No. 3214, Fines; PRO, Pembs. Plea Rolls, June 1550; *Black Book of St. Davids*, 1326, pp. 95, 103; Taylor's *Cussion,* fo. 97a; B. G. Charles, *NCPN*, p. 28; NLW, Maesgwynne Deeds, No. 33; PRO, Wales 4.776/5, Pembs. GF, and Pembs. Plea Rolls No. 63; Pembs. QS Records, Game Licences.

TARR, *Penally*

A substantial house, standing in a prominent south facing position overlooking the castle, beach and headland, just southeast of the hamlet of St. Florence. Home of the Dunn family, (branch of Dunn of Crickwarren). In 1786 Tarr and West Tarr were owned by Lord Milford with John Dunn occupier, and West Tarr with Henry Evans as occupier. John Dunn of Tarr (1810-89) owned Crickwarren, Maidenwells, and lands in St. Mary and St. Michael's, Pembroke; in Llanddewi Velfrey, Narberth, St. Florence and Penally; he was succeeded by children of his next brother Thomas Dunn.

In the Voter's List of 1834, John Gwyther is of Tarr, lease of lives of Tarr and West Tarr farm, an old tower-house. In 1894, Thomas David Bowen is of Tarr Farm, tenant.

In 1986 Tarr Farm was offered for sale as a substantial 19th century country house, with three reception rooms and 6 bedrooms and two bathrooms, also offered were two cottages and 6 acres of land, then being used as holiday accommodation.

Refs: LT 1786; VL 1834, 1894; *W. Telegraph,* 1 October 1986.

TEMPLE DRUID
see **BWLCH Y CLAWDD,** *Maenclochog*

THE MOTE,
see **MOTE/MOAT,** *New Moat*

THORNE, *St. Twynells*

This is one of the houses in danger mentioned in Thomas Lloyd's *The Lost Houses of Wales.* It is, he says, '. . . a small but very sturdy late medieval hall with stone screen passage, pointed doorways and massive chimneys'. He goes on to say that it was (1986) 'empty and in disrepair'. In the late 18th century John Moody was listed as owner, and in 1894 John Vaughan.

Refs: Thomas Lloyd, *The Lost Houses of Wales,* 1986 p. 68; LT 1786; VL 1894.

THORNTON HOUSE, *Steynton*

A three-storeyed house about two miles north of Milford. First mentioned in 1618 with John Scone of Thornton, yeoman; in 1623 David Baten, yeoman is of Thornton. Francis Andrew, gent. will dated 28 March 1788 and proved 1793, whose father was a farmer of Priory, Steynton (d. 1770), lived at Thornton in the 18th century. Francis Andrew was a Grand Juror in 1783. His family was succeeded by the Crymes family in the person of Captain John Crymes, R.N., who lived at Thornton at the beginning of the 19th century. He was son of the Rev. Amos Crymes of Buckland Monachorum, Devon. The house was for sale in 1818, described as a 'desirable and modern built residence'. The vendor was the Captain's son, the Rev. Amos John Crymes (d. 1856). His agent was his brother-in-law, Morgan Rice James, a solicitor who had married Mary Anne, the eldest daughter of Captain John Crymes. Of Mr. Crymes's children, his son John became a naval officer and one of his daughters married in 1849, Lt. Col. Anthony Bowen Owen Stokes of St. Botolphs. Mr. Crymes lived at Haverfordwest and let Thornton first to a family called

O'Grady from Ireland and then to the Rev. Thomas Richards, M.A., who ran a boys' school there. After Emmelin Crymes married Colonel Stokes, the couple moved into Thornton, but they left when the Colonel became Chief Constable of Pembrokeshire. Emmelin died aged 22 at Thornton. Elizabeth Crymes died unmarried and Louisa married James Summers, solicitor and County Treasurer. The Land Tax records 1786 show Sir William Hamilton as owner of part of the estate, tenant J. Roch.

Thornton was again let and eventually sold to William Rees who built Thornton Baptist Chapel in 1867. Richard Poyer Lewis Penn of Camrose lived there in the 1880s, and Captain Charles Lewis William Allen Penn was born there in 1887. Other residents were Joseph Thomas of Haverfordwest and Broad Haven, another Baptist stalwart who passed it on to his daughter, Mrs. Colborne wife of a Congregationalist Minister. Mr. E. Picton Bamkin was owner until his death in 1927 and his sisters, Mrs. Cole and Mrs. Daysh inherited, and eventually sold in 1948. These two ladies used to show visitors a table in their sitting room 'upon which Lord Nelson placed his hat'. The purchaser in 1948 was the Milford Dock Manager, J. C. Ward whose widow sold it to Dr. Williams of Haverfordwest who was living there in 1976.

Refs: Pembs. Plea Rolls Nos. 111, 120; LT 1786; VL 1894.

TORBANT, *Llanrhian*

A farm house now very much altered, it serves as a ten bedroom guest house. In 1624 Torbant first comes to notice; On 15 June of that year John Morgan of Cilgwyn, labourer, stole from Torbant in Llanrhian, five white lambs the property of Elizabeth Owen of 'Llanryan', widow; and in 1631 David Lewis of Llanrhian, labourer, servant, of William Laugharne of Jordanston, gent. was in charge of sowing his mother's corn. He took a peck of wheat to Haverfordwest and sold it for 22d. He also confessed that he took from his master's house at Torbant, a 'plow chippe' belonging to his master, and sold it for 4d. Sadly, there is no record of the punishment for these light-fingered employees.

In the early 17th century George Owen and Elizabeth, née Gwillim, were the owners but there is a lease dated 25th July 1678 from Timothy Halton, D.D., Archdeacon of Brecknock to William Skyrme, gent. for the lives of the said lessee and of his daughters Mary and Elizabeth Skyrme. In the Land Tax returns of 1786 Francis Skyrme Esq. is listed as owner with Thomas James his tenant. In 1842 the Rev. Richard Davies, Archdeacon of Brecon was the owner. In the 20th century it belonged to Captain Cecil Charles and remains in the hands of his descendants.

Refs: Pembs. RO D/RTP/PIC; NLW Quaritch Deeds (1922) No. 339; Pembs. GF; Llanrhian Tithe Schedules, 1842; VL 1834, 1894.

TREBRITHIN, *Manorowen*

Now a farm house this was, in Tudor times, the home of the family of William Walker Glyn whose descendants moved to Plâs Manorowen near the parish church and took the permanent surname of Williams. In old deeds this place is sometimes referred to as Tre Aberithin. On 25 May 1602 David Hugh of Kilyglynen, gent. and William Williams of Manernawan, gent. were held in bond for possession of a decayed messuage and land in townred and fields of Tre David, Park y Baython, and Trebreythyn, in Manernawan. Lawley Phillips is shown as 'of Trebrithin' by his will dated 4 February, 1688, proved 28 May 1689; in the Tax list of 1786, Mrs. Joan Mathias owner, John Morris, tenant; and in the Voter's List of 1834, William Francis of Trebrithin, has a lease for lives of Trebrithin Farm.

Refs: Cwrtmawr Deeds No. 1121; Fines in Pembs. GS; VL 1834, 1894.

TRECADWGAN, *Whitchurch*

Trecadwgan is a farm on the high ground to the northeast of the village of Solva. During the Middle Ages it was the home of families of local importance, and from Tudor times to the first half of the 18th century of the gentle family of Parry. After that it was inhabited by various farming families, and in this century was acquired by Pembrokeshire County Council who converted the property into various holdings.

This manor had a royal origin. David, Bishop of St. Davids I (1147-77) 'gave his uncle Caducan the fee which is called the fee of Cuducan'. This Cadwgan was the son of Rhys ap Tewdwr (slain 1193), Prince of Deheubarth, and so brother of the Princess Nest, grandmother of Giraldus. There is no doubt that it received its name from Prince Cadwgan; in later times people surnamed Cadwgan lived there, and it is possible that they were descendants of the original owner.

In 1326 Phillip Cadigan held from the Bishop in capite 6½ carucates of land at Cadyganiston in Pebidiog. Philip ap Cadogan who had lands in Lochvane, was a man of considerable importance.

How long this family continued to hold Trecadwgan is not known, but in the 15th century the family of Butler, a cadet of the Glamorgan family had acquired it. On 16 September 1560, John Butler granted to John Barlow of Slebech the manor of Trecadwogan and 6 messuages, 1 water corn mill, 300 acres of land, 16 acres of meadow, 100 acres of pasture, 200 acres of furze and heath, and a rent of 4d., in Whitchurch and Trecadwogan, for £240, the clear annual value of the properties being £12. In 1566, and again in 1570, when John Barlow had to answer a writ of *Quo Warranto* regarding 'the barony of the manor of Trefodogan in Dewisland', he stated that it had been formerly held by John Butler of Coedcanlas Esq. who had inherited it from his ancestors, and had been sold by him to the said John. The two separate manors of Trecadowgan and of Llanddwnog were held by '*Barb*' in 1587/88.

The IPM of John Barlow of Slebech, taken October 1613, shows that he held the manor of Trecadowgan, containing one capital messuage, 210 acres of land, one corn mill called Salvagh Mill, one fulling mill, 5 tenements in Kingheriott, Rosegolwen, Penley, Treneweth, and Carvoriock alias Keshill.

The manor or lordship of Tregaddwogan, the lands of Tregaddwogan and others had been mortgaged by John Barlow and his trustees for £2,360 to Simon Lord Harcourt, who on 29 October 1715 assigned the same to James and Thomas Harries of Haverfordwest.

In 1716 James Harries, second son of John Harries of Porthyddy by Jane Phillips his wife, brought from Sir George Barlow Bart and John Barlow, Esq. the manors of Tregaddwoggan and Llandonock, and 20 messuages, 30 gardens, 2 grain mills, 1 fulling mill, 759 acres, courts baron and view of frankpledge in the parishes of Whitchurch, Brawdy, St. Davids, Llandeloy, Mathry, Llanwnda, Amroth, Llanychaer, Dinas and Newport. By his will, proved 1719, James Harries left Trecadwgan and other lands in Whitchurch parish to his younger brother Dr. George Harries. Dr. Harries had two children, Jane, and Caroline who married Thomas Griffiths of Iscoed, Carmarthen. Jane died at Haverfordwest and her will dated 27 May 1763, recites a deed of 19 June 1736 whereby her father had settled the manor and other lands on her sister, and she devised the reversion to Dr. George Phillips of Haverfordwest.

On 12 June 1752, Jane Harries of Haverfordwest, spinster, Thomas Griffiths and Caroline his wife of Carmarthen, granted a lease to Thomas Raymond, of Trecoedwogan and the whole Green thereto belonging, lands called Park y Bigail, Park y Cerrig, and Ffynnon Ddegwel, in all 150 acres in Whitchurch parish, for the lives of lessee's sons William (20), Michael (10) and Thomas (8) at £30 a year, 10 strikes of good black oats and market measure every Christmas, 10s. in lieu of a heriot, and suit at court at the Leet courts of the Bishop or of the manor of Trecadwgan

As Thomas and Caroline Griffiths died without surviving issue, the manor descended to their devisee, Dr. George Phillips M.D. ancestor of the Lort-Phillips family. In 1785 and 1786 he appointed Thomas Evans of Kerbyd, yeoman, to be gamekeeper for the manors of Trecadwgan and Llandonok.

Refs: Pembs. QS; Game Licences; Gir, Vita Davids, II, R.S, III p. 432; Jones of Brawdy MS, XXIII, p. 28 penes me; PRO, Pembs. PRO Rolls No. 298; Wales 3, 3411, Fines; NLW, Eaton Evans & Williams Colln., No. 4357; Jones of Brawdy Documents, I, 60; WWHR, III, pp. 133-4; NLW, Slebech Colln. No. 248; NLW, Poyston Deeds, No. 4; Taylors *Cussion*, fo. 97a; Barlow PRO, Plea Rolls, Nos. 28, 32; Deeds in C.F.L. *Handlist*; PRO, Ancient Deeds, iii, D 470; ibid., p. 12; Francis Jones, *Historic Carmarthenshire Homes and their Families.*

TRECLYN, *Eglwyswrw*
Situated just to the east of the village. In 1678 Thomas Griffith of Treclyn, great-grandson of William Griffith of Penybenglog was involved in a long Chancery case. He married Elenor, daughter of John Thomas of Treclyn and Margaret his wife, a daughter of Philip Bowen of Llanycefn. Mrs. Hay and Mrs. Price were joint owners in 1786 with tenants, John Rees and James Bowen. In the Voter's List of 1834 John Rees owned the freehold of Treclyn Isha. In 1894 William Rees was the freeholder and David Rees in 1904.

Refs: Chancery Proc. 5, 491/106 PRO March 1678; BM Egerton MS 2586; VL 1904; LT 1786; GGMS I (Gwynfardd); Pembs. Plea Rolls No. 119.

TRECWN, *Llanfairnantygof*
Known as 'Homestead of the hounds', at the foot of a steep slope on the northern banks of the Nantybugail brook. Richard Fenton writes in his *Historical Tour* (1811) 'Trecoon, a mansion . . . in point of situation yields to very few spots in the county, as possessing every ingredient of fine scenery, being situated on the edge of a steep hill, having a higher at its back, sheltering it from the north above the narrow vale which the little river Cyllell rises in and runs through, having the boundaries on each side nobly wooded, till where the vale terminates in a bold, craggy rock, that projects from a tract of healthy upland, affording ample room and subject for amusement to the sportsman . . . under this roof I pass the night, enjoy company and conversation rarely to be met within so retired a situation, and experience the same kind and hospitable reception (from the Barhams), as I have been accustomed to meet within that house from my childhood in the time of its former possessors (the Vaughans).'

In 1595 there is a confirmatory document concerning Owen Johns' right in 'a capital messuage called Trekoone'.

The earliest known family at Trecwn was that of Owen. They were followed by kinsfolk, the Vaughans of Farthingshook and when that family failed in the male line, the succession devolved on descendants through the female line, the Foster Barhams. Each of these families descended from its predecessor at Trecwn, so

that the property had remained in possession of the same kin for nearly four centuries until sold in 1939 for the first time in its recorded history. The Owens traced their lineage to the medieval chieftain Gwynfardd Dyfed whose overlordship extended over most of Pembrokeshire. From him descended many of the gentry of Cemais who bore in one form or another, Gwynfardd's heraldic coquizances of *azure* a lion rampant *or* within an orle of golden roses, and *gules* three true-love knots *argent*. It was his descendant John ab Owen who purchased Trecwn and settled there. His wife, Margaret was the daughter and co-heiress of William Clement of St. Davids by Elizabeth, daughter and co-heiress of William Dyer of Fishguard. In 1562 John ab Owen brought an action in the Court of Star Chamber concerning the abduction of a young lass aged between 12 and 16 years, which is particularly useful as it confirms the identity of his immediate forebears. John was described as 'John ap Owyne David ap Gwillim of Trecoon'. John and Margaret had nine children all of whom bore their father's Christian name, (rendered as John, Johns and Jones), Owen John the heir, William John living in 1591, Gruffydd Johns who married Jane daughter and co-heiress of John William of Bonville's Court, and had four children all surnamed Griffith. The fourth son, John Jones was murdered during a brawl at Newport on 16 June 1578 by Griffith Philipps of Pentypark, who was hanged for the deed. Thomas Johns living in 1591; Elizabeth who married Harry David Thomas of Llanstinan; Margaret married Thomas John Vaughan of Plâs Pontfaen, (will proved 1598), whose descendants ultimately were to inherit Trecwn. Anne (Agnes) who married John Adams of

Loveston; Jane who married Robert Recorde of Tenby who signed for Lewys Dwnn in 1597. He was nephew of the famous Dr. Robert Recorde, M.D., the eminent mathematician, author of several books, and inventor of the (=), and who was physician to Queen Mary before his death in 1558. Owen, the eldest son whose surname is variously rendered as John, Johns and Jones succeeded to the estate. He took an active part in public life and was coroner for the county, Steward or seneschal of Cemais and in 1605 it was stated he had held that appointment for about 30 years. He married a sister of George Owen, Lord of the Barony of Cemais. By 1603 he was a J.P. He added to the estate considerably and although he suffered occasional financial embarrassments was respected by his contemporaries. He married twice, firstly to Jonet, daughter and heiress of Owen Philipps of Longridge by whom he had an only child Margaret, who married John Davids, a rich burgess of Carmarthen. Jonet died young and he then married Katherine Owen. Owen Jones died on 13 March 1622/3. At the time of his death he owned 15 messuages in Fishguard alone plus numerous others including Trecwn. His heir was John Owen, then aged 48 years one month and six days at the time of his father's death. He was the eldest of the 7 children of Owen and Katherine.

John Owen born about 1575 married Lettice, daughter of Sir John Philipps of Picton Castle by Anne daughter of Sir John Perrott of Haroldston. Little is known of his career, and he died sometime after 1641. They had five children, George Owen the heir to Trecwn who matriculated at St. John's College, Oxford on 13 November 1629 aged 16 years. He married Elizabeth, daughter of Henry Lort of Stackpole Court by whom he had an only child George 'who died in minorite'. George Owen senior had no other children and on his death the estate passed to his brother Thomas. Thomas married in 1648, Anne, widow of William Wogan of Stone Hall and daughter of John Owen of Orielton. Thomas made his will on 11 March 1665/6 and died not long afterwards. Thomas and Anne had two daughters only, Lettice and Dorothy. Lettice died without issue before 1665 and accordingly Dorothy inherited Trecwn. She married her cousin, John Owen of the Orielton family, son of Arthur Owen of New Moat and Mary Philipps, widow of John Scourfield. John Owen came into Trecwn *iure uxoris,* and was assessed at seven hearths in 1670. He was MP for the county in 1678/9, and High Sheriff in 1684. His wife predeceased him. His will was dated 1695/6. They had an only daughter and sole heiress, Mary. She married firstly Hugh Wogan, son of Thomas Wogan of Llanstinan, and secondly a Mr. Lucy of whom nothing is known. The will of the childless widow, Mrs. Mary Lucy of Trecwn was dated 11 March 1695/6 about two months after her father had dated his will. The Trecwn estate passed to the next heirs of the Owen family, namely the Vaughans of Farthingshook.

Although the family of Owen had become extinct in the male line, its connection with Trecwn was by no means ended, for the successors were indeed doubly descended from the Owens through distaff lines. The Vaughans derived agnatic descent from Moreiddig Warwyn, a Breconshire noble who had lived in the 12th century. One of Moreiddig's descendants bearing the surname Vaughan married the heiress of Pontfaen in the Gwaun valley. Their descendants on more than one occasion intermarried with members of the Owen family. John Vaughan who inherited the estate in 1696 was the great-great grandson of Thomas John Vaughan and Margaret, daughter of John ab Owen of Trecwn. In 1701 when about 20, John Vaughan became a student of Gray's Inn. He came of age shortly and as Mrs. Lucy in her will made no reference to the Trecwn estate it was clearly entailed and would revert to the nearest of kin, the 'right heirs' of the Owen family, and consequently the estate was divided among three members of that family, namely John Vaughan, his sister Mary and a third Vaughan whom I have been unable to identify. John Vaughan came to live at Trecwn and married at Nevern church on 8 May 1706 Joan, daughter of Erasmus Corbet of Great Nash, Llangwm. In 1710 he was High Sheriff of Pembrokeshire, and in the parliamentary election for the county in 1714 voted for his kinsman Barlow. They had 12 children only one of whom married. He died on 13 February

1734/5 and by his will left a life interest in Trecwn to his widow who released her life interest in May 1739 to her eldest surviving son and heir, Erasmus. Erasmus matriculated at Christ Church College Oxford on 18 November 1731 aged 16 years. In 1737 he and his mother subscribed towards buying an organ for St. Mary's Church, Cardigan, and two years later he was sworn a burgess of that town. In 1752 he was a member of the high Tory Society of Sea Sergeants. Friendly with the Barlows of Slebech and with the Hon. William Hamilton who had married the heiress of that family, Erasmus kept an eye on the administration of the Slebech estate during the absence of the owners. In a letter to Hamilton, (then British Envoy at Naples), Ann Barlow wrote, 'Mr. Vaughan is the only honest steady man I know in the county'. Erasmus never married and when he died on 29 August 1775 at the age of 63, the estate passed to his next brother John. Many years ago Herbert M. Vaughan showed me Erasmus's armorial bookplate depicting the family arms, with a boy's head as crest, and the motto *Post funera virtus.*

John Vaughan born about 1713, entered the Royal Navy, and although his career was not distinguished by any personal exploit or participation in any spectacular naval operation, he rose to the highest ranks the service had then to offer, retiring as Admiral of the Blue in 1787. Dates of his appointments are given in *The National Maritime Museum's List of Commissioned Sea Officers 1660-1815.* John Charnock's *Biographia Navalis,* printed in 1797 provides some further details 'John Vaughan was on the 11 August 1746 appointed Captain of the *Solebay* frigate. He is one of those officers who have lived to reach, with the greatest credit to themselves, the highest rank in the service without ever being fortunate enough to experience a single opportunity of acquiring that celebrity every gallant man is ambitious to obtain. So little mention is made of him while he continued on the list of private captains, that we have not been able to collect any account whatever even of his appointments except that he at one time commanded the *Subtile*, a frigate of 26 guns taken from the enemy by the *Portland* at the end of the year 1746; and at another period the *Juno* of 32 guns. Undistinguished as these are, so high was the opinion entertained of him, and from private information we have received it appears most justly, so that he was promoted according to his seniority on the list, through the several ranks and degrees of a flag-officer till he at length reached that of Admiral of the Blue'. Charnock adds that 'in 1771 on the prospect of a rupture with Spain' he was appointed regulating-officer for the port of Milford and the district of South Wales. He was J.P. for the county and sympathetic towards Wesleyan Methodism, and John Wesley frequently visited Trecwn. There is a stone memorial underneath an oak tree on the estate commemorating a sermon preached there in 1777. He considered it to be one of the loveliest places in Great Britain.

Admiral Vaughan, according to John Wesley in his Journal (18 Aug. 1784) who tells of life at the old mansion 'where the Admiral governs his family as he did his ship – with utmost punctuality, the bell rings and all attend without delay whether at meals or at morning or evening prayers'. Latterly the Admiral suffered severely from gout which hastened the end of his days. Still, he lived to a good age, and a memorial in the parish church commemorates the 'Admiral of the Blue whose earthly tabernacle was dissolved on 2nd November, 1789 aged 76 years'.

As he was last male heir of the line of Vaughan, the succession devolved on his sisters. Dorothea was the only member of this generation to marry, and it was her son who succeeded to Trecwn in due course. They derived descent from a Northumberland border clan whose name was variously rendered as Forester, Forster and Foster. From this line came Col. John Foster, a wealthy planter settled in Jamaica where he owned large properties which he administered with the help of his brother Thomas. The Colonel married Elizabeth Smith of Barbados, and two years after her husband's death in 1731, at the age of 50, she married Dr. Henry Barham, a physician, and also a Jamaican planter, son of Dr. Henry Barham F.R.S. descended from the Barhams of Barham Court, Kent. Elizabeth and Col. Foster had several children , the fifth son Joseph, born in

Jamaica, inherited extensive estates from his father, uncle Thomas, and his stepfather, Dr. Henry Barham who required him to take his surname, which he did by Act of Parliament in 1750 being thereafter known as Joseph Foster Barham. His estates in Jamaica then amounted to 6,496 acres. On 1 July 1754 Joseph Foster Barham married firstly Dorothea Vaughan, younger daughter of John Vaughan of Trecwn, and in her descendants, ultimate heiress to that estate. Joseph and Dorothea had seven children; Joseph Foster Barham, the eldest son born 1 January 1759, received part of his education at Gray's Inn to which he was admitted in 1777. He took an active part in public life and had an interesting, somewhat grasshopperish political career. A humane man he advocated the abolition of the slave trade in his book *Considerations on the Abolition of Negro Slavery* (London 1823), though failed to lead the way on his own plantations. His public conduct received the approbation of the great reformer Wilberforce who described him as 'really a generous fellow'. He married in 1792, Lady Caroline Tufton, daughter of the 8th Earl of Thanet. On the death in 1803 of Miss Martha Vaughan, last heiress of Trecwn, he inherited the estate. Trecwn became the main family home from that date. Joseph was active in local politics, a member of the 'Blue' party in Pembrokeshire, active in his West Indies estates. Both he and his wife died in 1832 leaving five children.

John Foster Barham succeeded to Trecwn, he was also active in his West Indies estates and in local politics. He died without issue in 1838 and the estate passed to his next surviving brother, Charles who also died without issue. Trecwn passed to his nephew, Francis William Robins, son of his sister Caroline. Francis Robins, born 1841 at St. John's Wood, entered the army serving in the 60th Rifles retiring with the rank of Captain. On inheriting Trecwn he took the surname Barham. He had married in 1868 Mary Agnes Cook of Montreal. He died on 8 December 1926 and the estate passed to his only son, Cyril Hugh Sackville Robins (Barham), born at Croydon in November 1873. Cyril Barham entered the army, retiring like his father with the rank of Captain. He took an active part in public affairs. He was a fearless and enthusiastic advocate of views that appealed to him with the result that he occasionally figured in the Law Courts and local disagreements. He established the hamlet of Tufton to commemorate his connection with the Earls of Thanet of which family he was ultimately the sole representative. The Barham male line was tragically ended in 1933 when Captain and Mrs. Barham, and their son were killed while travelling from Trecwn towards Oxford where two of their children were at University. Near Coventry they stopped to visit a hostelry, and when crossing the road a motor-car ran into them with the result that Captain Barham, his wife and son were killed. As a result of this tragic event the house was sold by the surviving daughters to the Admiralty.

There is a record of a curse laid on Owen ap David the original member of the family to settle at Trecwn. It is said that he ruthlessly destroyed many local habitations in order to render his lands more suitable to the arts of the chase. An ancient hag, with the reputation of a witch, thereupon cursed him, saying that, though the lands would remain in his descendants, the name of the family would constantly change owing to the lack of male heirs. This has been strikingly exemplified by the subsequent history of the family.

Trecwn was a very fine-looking seat, but relatively modern. The tithe map drawn in 1838 shows the mansion and outbuildings much the same as they were until the third decade of the 20th century. According to the *Pembrokeshire Archaeological Survey Map* made about 1900, the site of the original mansion was about 150 yards to the southwest of the present one, but the *Ancient Monuments Commissioners Report for Pembrokeshire* (1915) calls Trecwn 'a modern mansion on the site of the one visited by Fenton'. The earlier house must have been of substantial proportions, for in the hearth tax of 1670 it is listed as possessing seven hearths. That has completely gone. A photograph of the later house taken in 1871, shows a large double-pile structure of three storeys with attics above, a range of seven windows on each storey, with the main entrance at one gable end adorned by a pillared porch. By 1889 a long wing projecting westwards had been added to the mansion, while the grounds on the north side are marked as 'aviary'. Magnificent tapestries hung in the Drawing Room and the house's destruction by the Admiralty was a tragedy. The house is illustrated in *Photographs in South Wales,* 1871 by C. S. Allen and also in Thomas Lloyd's *The Lost Houses of Wales*.

The estate then known as R.N.A.D. Trecwn was resold in the 1990s; its future is uncertain.

Refs: Abridged from Francis Jones's unpublished essay on Trecwn; Fenton, *Tour Pembs.,* p. 189.

TREDAFYDD, *Llanychllwydog*

This property is mentioned in a document dated 13 April 1464. Phillip ap Ievan granted to Ievan ap Gwilym ap Eynon 'all his messuage in Teffdavid in fee of Menyth Melyn'. The latter's descendants are mentioned in a charter of 19 November 1519 – 'Gwilym ap Ievan ap Gwillim ap Eynon of Trefllan in Kemeys, yeoman, and his son James ap Gwilym ap Ievan ab Gwilim ab Eynon, Grant of three messuages viz. – one called Trefddavid Yssa, the other lying at the upper head of Trefddavid, and the third called Plâs y Dyffryn, and also six acres which he lately had of the gift of Ievan ab Rees ab Lln ap Phillip between Gwern Pennyll on the west and the way called Forthsayson on the east, and also the wood which he had between Pant y Moch on the west and the water of Cwm Llewelyn on the east, in parish of Llannchloydock in the fee of Menethmelyn.'

Tredafydd was later owned by inheritance by Ursula, wife of John Owen of St. Kennox, and on April 3 1684 they sold it to John Higgon. The Higgon family were still in possession in 1822, having had various tenants occupying the property. In the Voter's List of 1834 William Higgon is shown 'of Tredavid, freehold house and land'; he was a J.P. in 1820. However by 1828 William David Esq. J.P. was owner. In the Voter's List of 1894, John Gwynne is of Tredavid Uchaf, land and tenement there, and John Phillips of Tredavid Isaf.

In the Spring of 1632, Jenkin Gwynn of Jordanston Esq. gave 60s. to agree with David Hughes of Cilgelynen, gent. and Thomas Lloyd, gent. and Charity his wife, in respect of the manor of Tredavid alias Manernawen, and other lands in Co. Pembroke. 'On 26 March 1632 a Final Concord was made between the aforesaid parties in respect of the manor of Tredavid alias Manernawen, 17 messuages, 3 tofts, 1 mill, 1 dove cot, 20 gardens, 20 orchards, 500 acres of land, and 1,555 acres in Tredavid alias Manernawen, Rhoslunwen Cassegan, Trevelgar, Tremarchoge, Llanunda, St. Nicholas Sciber, Letterston, Trevedlem, Carneycha, Carnissa, Martherie, Priskylly vawr and vaughe, Isklethey, Trebrithyn, Patrick fford alias Trerhose, St. Lawrence, Fishguard and Kilsavey; the fine being £400.'

On 12 April 1669 Jenkin Vaughan gent. plaintiff, and John Mathias Esq. and Joan his wife of Llangwarran, deforceants, 'made a fine in respect of the manor of Tredavid alias Manernawen and its appurtenances, 20 messuages, 1 water grain mill, 1 dove cot, 20 gardens, 20 orchards and 2,030 acres in Fishguard alias Fishingard, Manernawen, Llanunda, Jordanston, St. Nicholas, Granston, St. Lawrence, Mathry, and Letterston'.

In the period 1688-1707, the manor or lordship of 'Tredavid alias Mannernawen' was still in existence.

Refs: Bronwydd Deeds No. 1173; Pembs. PRO; Pembs. Plea Rolls, No. 138; PRO, Wales 3, 3342, Fines; ibid., 3297, Fines; Roll of Wards WO & GO.

TREDDIOG, *St. Edrins*

This is probably the manor of Trefnogh in Pebidiog, held by Griffith de Cantington and his co-parcener William, from the Bishop, in 1332. In 1587/8 'Scourfield of Castle Villa' was lord of the manor of Treddiog. It is called 'the manor of Saynt Eddryns' in a deed dated 1583/4.

On 30 March 1584 a Fine was made between Llewelyn Lloyd of Llanstinan and John Phillips, gentlemen, plaintiffs, and William Scourfield and Anne his wife, John Scourfield senior and Katherine his wife, in respect of 'the manor of Saynt Eddryns', and other lands in Co. Pem.

In September 1614, John Wogan gent. gave 10s. to agree with Thomas Scourfield, gent. and Anne his wife, in respect of the manor of Treddiogg alias Tretheogge, and 2 messuages, 3 gardens, 106 acres of land, one-quarter of one messuage, and 30 acres in Williamston, Patricksfoord alias Trerhos, Tretheog alias Treddiog St. Lawrence and St. Edrins.

The IPM of William Scourfield of New Moat (ob. 22 March 1621/2) held 10 August 1622 shows that he owned a messuage and 12 acres in Tretheog held of William Wogan gent. by knight service as of his manor of Tretheogg, being of the clear annual value of 6s. 8d.

In 1833 Daniel Davies of Foxhill and Lettice his wife gave a lease of Tredduog (136 acres) to George Harris of Tredduog for the lessee's life. On 20th October, 1847 Lettice Davies late of Foxhill, widow, now of The Burrows in Walton West, mortgaged to William John of Prendergast, gent. Tredduog in £500. On 7th October 1844, John Phillip of Mathry, farmer, mortgaged to Phoebe John of Trehale, widow, the messuage in parish of St. Edrins called Clyn ffwon, being part of the messuage of Tredduog purchased by John Howell gent. from William Ford Protheroe, clerk. A sale catalogue of 1863 includes 'the manor or reputed manor of St. Edrins otherwise Treddyog'.

In 1984 the property was sold with 211 acres, outhouses and farm buildings. The vendors were Col. and Mrs. Chaldecot. Mrs. Chaldecot had inherited the estate from her mother, Mrs. Thomas, heiress of the Trehale estate (q.v.).

Refs: NLW Poyston Deeds, No. 72; PRO, Pembs. Plea Rolls, No. 104; PRO, Wales 3, 3211, Pembs. Fines; NLW, Lucas Deeds; Taylor's *Cussion,* fo. 97a.

TREDEFAID, *Llantood*

Home of the Parry and Lewes families descended from Gossawl to Owen ab Evan who married Gwenllian daughter of Llewelyn ap Rhys Llewelyn. They had two daughters and co-heiresses, Cari who married Rhys Fychan of Towyn, Cardiganshire, and Elen who married James Griffith ap Howel. Their great-granddaughter, Margaret married Thomas Parry and their son, John Parry was of Tredefaid. He married Jane, daughter of Griffith David of Llanarth, Cards. His will was proved in Carmarthen in 1641. They had four daughters and co-heiresses, Anne, Jane, Lettice and Elizabeth. Lettice married Thomas Lewes, third son of John Lewes of Llysnewydd who came into Tredefaid in right of his wife, and the house devolved to their descendants.

In the late 18th century the Rev. William Lewes, Rector of Newport, was in occupation. His son, Sir Watkin Lewes, became Lord Mayor of London and in 1809 was living at Belvedere House in Southwark. In 1975 Major Jones and his wife visited Tredefaid. In that year the owners, Mr. and Mrs. John Woodhead, sold to a Mr. and Mrs. Gould, of Kent. There is a date of 1698 on the house.

Refs: Morgan-Richardson Deeds, ii, 339; P. Smith, *Homes*, map 29; Pontfaen Deeds; VL 1834; Pembs. GF; Bronwydd Deeds No. 828; ibid. 3370; ibid. 1873; WWHR ii, pp. 92-3; Dale Castle MS, 163; Francis Jones, *Historic Cardiganshire Homes and their Families.*

Young

TREDRISSI, *Nevern*

Home of the Young family. Howel ap Jenkin Young who had inherited Tredrissi (no date given) had five natural sons, who, in spite of their illegitimacy, married well and established families. Howel, after the birth of his fifth son, married his paramour but she produced only one daughter, Elen who, being the only legitimate child, inherited Tredrissi on her father's death. Elen married David ap Evan David by whom she had a son, Rhydderch, who sold the property to his uncle Thomas Young, (the fifth natural son of Howel). His descendants continued there into the 17th century. 'This famylie of the Youngues were in tymes past noted to be men tall of person, fayer of complexion and gentle of behavioure but now declyne from the same'. The arms of Young of Nevern were: *azure* three bulls' heads caboshed *or*. Rhydderch signed for Dwnn on 23 September 1591. From the Youngs descended the Mathias family of Llangwarren, and James Mathias is recorded in 1840 as owner-occupier with 65 acres.

Refs: George Owen, *2nd Book*, p. 273; *Dwnn* i, p. 162; Wagner MS No. 6; Tucker MS; VL 1834, 1904; GGMS I AD, fo. 28; ibid. AD. Pembs. i, 12; TM Nevern ph. 1840; GO Roll of Wards.

TREFACH, *Llanfairnantgwyn*

Lying southeast of Pantyderi and the home of the Lloyd and Williams families. Thomas Williams of Bridell, gent. had two sons, William viv. 1723 will dated 20 August 1738 who married on 17 July 1723, Anne, daughter of William Morgan of Blaenbylan by his wife Margaret, daughter of David Morris of Ffynnone. They had three sons and four daughters all minors in 1738. William Williams, (1732-99), was Baptist Minister and J.P. for Pembrokeshire and Cards., and for Borough of Cardigan. He was 19 at the time of his first marriage to Jane, sister of James Bowen of Llwyngwair, who died within a year of her marriage; William Williams became Minister of Blaenywaen chapel. By 1768 Ebenezer Chapel was built on the Trefach estate. He helped to start a Baptist mission in North Wales in 1776, of which he was Treasurer and organiser. About 1774 he went to live in Cardigan and founded a Baptist chapel there in 1775/6, and another in Verwig in 1797. He published several religious tracts and pamphlets; died 13 August 1799 and is buried in Ebenezer chapel burial ground. He had married secondly, Eleanora, daughter of Rev. D. Morgan of Garragh, Co. Londonderry, and one of the heirs-at-law of Rev. Thomas Pardoe of Jesus College, Oxford; she died without issue in 1780 and he then married Dorothy, daughter of Thomas Lewis of Llwyngrawys, Cards. in October 1784 and they had four children, one son and three daughters; William Morgan Williams of Trefach, the heir, was High Sheriff of Cardiganshire in 1784, died without issue in 1820 and his estate passed to his nephew James William Bowen, Q.C., son of Mary Anne Williams who married Thomas Bowen of Pantyderi, Captain 10th Hussars. Jane and Elizabeth Williams both died without issue.

In the Tithe Schedule of 1837 Thomas Bowen Esq. and John Bowen Esq. M.D. were shown as joint owners with Thomas Harries as tenant of 161 acres, 2 rods and 33 perches. He was paying £50 p.a. rent. Benjamin Harries was farming Trefach with Thomas Phillips in 1894 and was still there in 1904.

Now a farmhouse, it is a large square building with protruding stepped chimneys at each gable end. A slate stone in the wall states: 'Trevach built by J. W. B. Esqr. 1872.' A date stone on an outhouse has '1853 J. W. B.' (James William Bowen, Esq. shown on the Tithe Schedule of 1837 as owner of Trefach, tenanted by Thomas Harries.) There is a photograph of it as it was in 1972 in E. T. Lewis's *Mynachlogddu: A Guide to its Antiquities* (1972). Major Jones visited the house in 1985, a Mr. Jones being the owner.

Refs: Morgan-Richardson Deeds, ii, 533, Nos. 2335 & 2697; VL 1894, 1904; E. T. Lewis, *Mynachlogddu: Guide to its Antiquities*; Bronwydd Deeds Nos. 1671-2; Clynfyw Deeds NLW; Tithe Schedules, Llanfairnantgwyn ph. 1837; DWB; Francis Jones, *Historic Cardiganshire Homes and their Families.*

TREFACH, *Nevern*

Home of the Lloyd family in the 17th and 18th centuries. John Lloyd was assessed for five hearths in 1670. In 1638 he had placed his daughter Elizabeth with Richard and Dorothy Jones to be educated but was sued by the latter in 1642 for refusing to pay the tuition fees. John Lloyd was the grandson of Jenkin Lloyd of Llanfair Clydogau, Cards. Jenkin had two sons, Rees and Walter, who married Joyce, daughter of Griffith Lloyd of Forest, Carms. Rees who was of Trefach married Elizabeth Philipps widow, the daughter of Thomas Bowen of Pentre Ifan. They had a son and heir John who married Elizabeth, daughter of Alban Owen of Henllys in 1632, and Dorothy who married Thomas Lloyd of Llanfair Clydogau, Cards. John and Elizabeth had three sons and one daughter, Rees who succeeded to Trefach, John, Elizabeth and another Rees. Rees the elder, married Margaret, widow of Thomas Williams of Haverfordwest, mercer in 1654. They had a son, John, viv. 1682, and a daughter. John was still at Trefach in 1712 and he had one son, Thomas, will proved 1 April 1738, and three daughters, Elinor who married John Foley of Ridgeway, prenuptial settlement dated 21 April 1712, Margaret viv. 1713, and Rebecca who married Rev. William Laugharne of Treprisk.

In the 18th century the Bowen family were in possession – Lewis Bowen of Trefach is mentioned in 1743. His daughter and heiress, Catherine, married firstly John Lewis of Egremont and secondly Thomas Lewis who was 'of Trefach' *iure uxoris*. David Lewis, son of the first marriage succeeded. He married Jane, daughter of John Nicholas and Jane his wife, prenuptial settlement dated 18 November 1743. In 1771 Stephen Lewis of Trefach; subscribed towards two copies of the Rev. William Evans's translation of *Canwyll y Cywry*. He was sworn a burgess of Cardigan in Easter 1756 and had died by 1794. His only child Anne married John Evans, son of Rev. James Evans of Mathry in 1794. By 1840 Thomas Davies is listed as owner-occupier of Trefach a holding of 309 acres.

Refs: Francis Jones Archives, Vol. 14, pp. 140, 330; Francis Jones, *Historic Cardiganshire Homes and their Families;* TM Nevern ph. 1840; NLW Foley of Ridgeway Deeds Nos. 83, 112, 34, 46, 114, 62, 60, 64, 67, 68, 86, 93, 99, 206-7; Pembs. Plea Rolls No. 153; ibid. No. 147; Pembs. Papers of GS; Morgan-Richardson Deeds ii, 499; Bronwydd Deeds No 678; NLW, Dale Castle MS Ped. 138; GGMS III Lucas Deeds; WWHR ii, 58-9; ibid. ix, 130; VL 1894.

TREFAES, *Moylgrove*

In 1602 James Perrott of Haroldston, Esq. sued Ievan ap Rees of Trefaes for trespass and in 1614, 1615 and yet again in 1635 the Rees's of Moylgrove were involved in litigation for trespass. John Phillip Thomas, who by his second wife Jenet, daughter of Hugh Harry of Haverfordwest, had two children, Margaret John, who married David Perkin of Menevia, they had a son, Thomas Perkins, whose only son, William was hanged for murder (*ben mores*). John Phillip Thomas's younger daughter also called Margaret, married Eynon David Thomas of Park y Trapp, and 'devorsat suos, and as thei saye was devorsed and then married one Hughe Phe ap Ievan Jenkin in the liff of her husband Eynon David, and had by him a son named David and then she died, the said Eynon David surviving her'.

After this unfortunate saga the house became the home of Jenkin Lloyd who was assessed for six hearths in 1670. The property passed to the James family, William James's will dated 12 December 1726 and proved in 1729, had three sons and four daughters. The line descended to his grandson, William James the owner in 1786. He married Jane, daughter of William ap Howell ap Jenkin of Nevern. They had a son, Owen William, who died without issue but sold Trefaes in his lifetime to William Owen Esq. of Henllys. The James family had moved to Treprisk by 1786. Another pedigree however, tells us that although the James's had left Trefaes, they still had an interest there in 1904.

Refs: Wagner MS 2; Moylgrove Manorial Rolls 29 Oct. 1602; Bronwydd LGP, iii; KCR 6 April 1605; BM Egerton 2586. fo. 311a; LT 1786; VL 1834; *Anc. Mon Pembs.,* 1925 p. 240; *Aberglasney* p. 131; Morgan-Richardson Deeds, ii, 456.

TREFAWR, *Llanfyrnach*

The land formerly belonged to Whitland Abbey in Carmarthenshire. This building, standing southeast of the parish church, is now a farm. The Gwilyms owned this property in the 16th century; David Gwilym, married twice, the name of his first wife being unknown, he had by her six children, and by his second, Lleucu verch Philip Weith of Trehendy, four more; one, Katherine, 'had a base daughter by Morgan Bowen, now sowing in Havfordwest 1592, a semster', and John his son, had 'a daughter yt goeth abeging'. His eldest son by his first marriage, Morris 'dyed an old man 20 year past'. [c. 1572] inherited Trefawr and the family remained at Trefawr for several further generations; they were followed by the Lloyds, (no dates given). In 1786 Thomas Jones was owner-occupier. William Jones, probably his son, was the freeholder in 1834.

Refs: BM Egerton MS 2586, ff. 315 & 307a 11 April 1592; VL 1894; Bronwydd Deeds 2099; GGMS I (Gwynfardd).

TREFAYOG, *St. Nicholas*

A substantial farmhouse, former residence of the gentry family of Griffith, kinsfolk of the Warrens of Trewern and Bowens of Llwyngwair, and for a time from about 1745, the home of John Mathias of Llangwarren, who married Margaret (born 1700), daughter and co-heiress of Richard Williams of Clegyr Mawr. They had 15 children; Anne, his tenth child, was of Trefayog where she died unmarried. She became a Moravian in 1768; the year of her death is unknown.

Evan Griffith is mentioned as owner in the 1610 Plea Rolls; he was still alive in 1652. He had one son, William, and a daughter Anne who married John Tucker of Sealyham, will dated 1654. William, married Ursula Warren of Trewern, and they had three children, William, George and Jane. William married Margaret, daughter of John Scourfield by Catherine, daughter of Richard Bowen of Lochmeyler.

By 1670 it had passed into the ownership of the Mathiases of Llangwarren, John Mathias having been assessed for two hearths in 1670. In 1756 and 1759 John Mathias of Trefayog was a Grand Juror, and in 1773 John Mathias Esq. was a J.P. By the end of the 18th century Trefayog was largely occupied by tenants, including the families of William David – Voter's List 1834; in the late 18th/early 19th century the family of Evans. In 1894 Voter's List James Perkins is of Trevayog, house and land. When Major Jones called the owner was Mr. Idris Davies.

Ref: Pembs. GF; VL 1834, 1894; LT 1786; Francis Jones Archives.

TREFELLYN, TREFELYN, *Mathry*

The earliest reference is in 1326 when David ap Ievan ap Gr' (sic) held four bovates at Trefellyn. In 1632 Jenkin Gwynn of Jordanston bought a number of properties, some 1,555 acres in all, which included Trefellyn, Garn Ucha and Issa in Mathry parish from David Hughes of Cilychynen, Thomas Lloyd and Charity, his wife of Cilciffeth. Thus these properties merged with the others as part of the Jordanston estate which passed from the Gwynns to their kinsfolk the Vaughans. Trefellyn Garn remained in their possession until well into the 19th century. Trefellyn was owned by Sparks Martin of Withybush who gave a lease of Rhoslanog Vawr, Ucha and Trefellyn to Edward Lawrence for lives; by 1786 the Vaughans were back in possession. Trefellyn was tenanted by the Evans family, William Evans being of Trefellyn and Garn (400 acres) in 1786. He was buried at Mathry 19 August 1796; administration of his goods was granted to his only child, John who moved shortly after 1811 from Trefellyn to Haverfordwest. He had married after 1784 his first cousin, Martha Evans of Mabws Fawr by whom he had five children, the eldest, Morgan was born at Trefellyn 28 November 1811. Another pedigree is given of the family of John David, tenant of Trevellin who died aged 62 in 1728. He had had three sons, Thomas, Rees and Henry and two daughters, Mary and Anne. Thomas died 21 May 1776, leaving a son, John David (died by 1851), leaving two daughters, Mary and Jane.

In 1842 Sir James Cockburn was the owner and subsequent owners were Protheroes and Thomases. Trefellyn was put up for sale in 1983 and described as 'an outstanding and substantial dairy and arable farm of 470 acres. An aerial view shows the modest six-bedroom Georgian house dwarfed by huge ranges of modern out-buildings.

Refs: Owen of Orielton Deeds; Pembs. Plea Rolls No. 14; *Black Book of St Davids,* 1326, pp. 99, 103; PRO Anc. Deeds E210, D1734; Fines in Pembs. GS; LT 1786; Cwrtmawr Deeds 716; Tithe Map Mathry 1842.

TREFEUGAN, *Llanhowel*

In the 16th century the armigerous family of Propert lived here, and the line descended from Harry William Propert, viv. 1546 who married Mary, daughter of Thomas Jones of Brawdy, to his grandson, Thomas Harry Propert viv. 1691 who paid tax on two hearths in 1670. He had two sons, David, will proved 1688 and Gilbert. David who succeeded to Trefeugan, had two sons, William, will proved 1691 who married Elizabeth Harries and had two children, John and Catherine. William and Elizabeth had one, son, David (1686-1760) who married Elizabeth Hughes of Pantperthog; and two daughters, Mary and Martha who were both minors in 1691. David and Elizabeth had 14 children; their eldest son and heir the Rev. William Propert, clerk, will proved 1780, married in 1730, Grace, daughter of Richard Harding of Trevaccoon. They had a son, Richard (will proved 1762), and a daughter Elizabeth who married John Harries of Cryglas. In 1838 the property was part of the marriage settlement of William Evans when he married Mrs. Jane Mathias.

Refs: Pembs. Plea Rolls Nos. 6, 11; VL 1760, 1834, 1894; LT 1786; *Dwnn,* i, p. 197; W & W (H'west) No. 25910; *Anc. Mon. Pembs.,* 1925 p. 177; Pembs. RO HDX/197/No. 131.

TREFFGARN (LITTLE), *St. Dogwells*
Also known as Trowgarn Fach – one of the supposed homes of Thomas ap Owain, scion of the royal house of Deheubarth. Fenton wrote: 'Little Trefgarn, a single mansion-house on the top of the hill, the east side of the vale, is held under lease from the Precentor of St. David's by John Edwards Esq. whose ancestor, when he fillest stall in the cathedral, having made it his residence, his descendants for near two centuries continued to inhabit it and in my remembrance, in a style of great hospitality, till the present possesor, leaving it for Sealyham (q.v.), the seat of his lady in the neighbourhood, it has dwindled into a farmhouse'.

On 16 September 1140, a community was formed which furnished Wales with its first Cistercian house. An offshoot of the abbey of Clairvaux, it found a temporary home in 1144 at Little Trefgarn where Bishop Bernard of St. Davids settled on it lands belonging to his *See—locum apud trefgarn in dauglethef.* About 1151 the community moved to Whitland.

In 1259, Bishop Richard Carew, with the consent of chapter, granted to Richard the Precentor and his successors, 'their land of Trevegar', in lieu of 15 marks which he used to receive yearly from the chapter, on account of his personal residence as Precentor, and ordered that he and his successors should demand nothing more, except their share or dividend out of the common estate belonging to the canons resident.

On 29 July 1268, Bishop Adam Hoton bestowed on the Precentor out of the church of Cilycwm (Carms.) after the death of the then rector, 20 marks yearly, for his personal residence, and decreed that as soon as the Precentor should receive this annual payment, the estate of Trefgarn and Landredeon should return again to their ancient state and be annexed to the Episcopal table.

From subsequent records, it is clear that the manor was restored to the Precentor.

In 1535/36 the Precentor, held (*inter alia*) – *et ratione ejusdem dignitatis tenet maneria de Landredeon & Trefgarn Owen Cononwer per nomen medietatis unius foed' inilitar' et valet per annum in omnibus exitibus ulta reprisis, cum 3s. et 4d. communibus annis de perquisitis curarium ibid. em £4 3 8.*

On 26 April 1579, Thomas Huet, Precentor of St. Davids, granted to Thomas Edwardes, a lease for 3 lives of the manor or lordship of Trefgarn in Dewsland hundred, at £6 13s. 4d. per annum. The lease included all the manorial rights (except rents, services, lettings and settings of land, fines, forfeitures, escheated goods and chattels, goods and chattels of felons and fugitives, deodands, heriots, and reliefs due on the lordship of Llandrydion, and also the use, sale and occupation of the woods in the lordship of Trefgarn, and the spiritual jurisdiction of the lordship of Trefgarn, and the spiritual jurisdiction of the lordships of Trefgarn and Llandrydion) together with the stewardship of those lordships and the forestership of their woods: the lessees were also given the right of necessary ploughbote, castlebote, hedgebote, and plants of 'quycksets' for their own use, and for their fires 6 truckle-loads yearly out of the said woods: the lessees were also to be free from all heriots, reliefs, and all customs and duties on the death of any of the lessees.

This lease was renewed in favour of members of the Edwardes family of Treffgarn until 12 February 1880 when they acquired the freehold, the manor then comprising of 1,026 acres and 28 perches.

In 1587/88 the Precentor was lord of the manor of Trewgam East. On 17 April 1735, the Rev. John Pember, chantor of St. Davids cathedral church, leased to John Edwardes the lordship of Treffgarne alias Trawgarne, the capital messuage of Little Treffgarne (in St. Dogwells parish), and the lordship of Llanridian (in St. Davids parish) for 3 lives, at a yearly rent of £6 6s. 8d. for Treffgarne and £4 6s. 8d. for Llandridian. Under a marriage settlement dated 30 May 1746 these lordships were granted to John Symmonds and John Harries to be held in trust for the marriage of Rowland Edwardes and Anne his wife.

According to a survey made by one Thomas Lewis in 1778, the manor of Little Trefgarn comprised a little over 1,023 acres.

In about 1777 his descendant, John Owen Edwardes, having married one of the coheiresses of John Tucker of Sealyham, moved there to live. It is one of the rare instances of a county family living on leased premises for over three centuries and owning considerable property elsewhere in the county. John Edwardes was High Sheriff in 1702, Rowland Edwardes in 1747. The property was advertised for sale in 1893 and Charles Rice Saunders, of Hazel Grove owned the house and land in 1904. In Law's *Little England* there is a description: 'Little Trefgarn . . . and a long narrow building still stands though in a very ruinous state, which may have served as a gentleman's residence in the 14th century, for though there are no architectural details such as windows or arches, the masonry appears to be of very great antiquity. This building is now used as a cattle shed.' In the G.W.R. publication *South Wales, the County of Castles*, a photograph shows Little Treffgarn as a substantial farmhouse with a courtyard in front and a wing attached to the rear portion.

Refs: Arch. Cam., 1961, pp. 102-128; BM Cotton MS, Dom i, 147a (2); NLW, Eaton Evans and Williams Colln. No. 3861; WWHR, VIII, p. 192, Chapter Acts; Taylors *Cussion*, fo. 97; *Menevia Sacra,* p. 125, Stat. Men, p. 164; Welsh Episc. Acts Vol. I, D 645, p. 401; Stat. Men, p. 35; Valor Eccles, IV, p. 379; *JHSCW,* 1968; Francis Jones, *Arch. Cam.,* 1961, pp. 102-128; Francis Jones article 'Trefgarn Owen'; Laws *Little England,* 1888, p. 192; Fenton, *Tour Pembs.,* p. 181.

TREFFGARNE, *Lampeter Velfrey**
Home to the Willy family. Simon Willy was High Sheriff in 1704 and married Penelope Lewis, and was succeeded by their son, Henry who in turn was followed by Richard Willy, who married in 1762, a kinswoman, Priscilla Willy. Richard died in 1807 and his wife in 1811, leaving a son, John, who died in 1839 and three daughters and co-heiresses; Anne who married William Jones; Priscilla who married James Lewes of Cwmhyar, Cards. and had issue; and Elizabeth who married firstly, Henry Twyning, (d. 1819), son of Joseph Twyning and secondly Thomas Reece Thomas, surgeon in 1823. Elizabeth died in 1847.

James and Priscilla Lewes had two sons, John (d. 1860), who married Mary Bowen and James (d. 1844) who married Martha Jane Davies by whom he had a son, James Willy Lewes and a daughter Priscilla Willy Lewes, who married in 1856 Lloyd Price of Castle Piggin, Carms.

Refs: Pembs. RO James of Narberth Solr. Papers; Morgan-Richardson Deeds ii 496; LT 1786; Carms. Deeds in Pembs. RO; VL 1894.

TREFFGARNE HALL, *Treffgarne*
Home of the Evans family in the 19th century, and until 1914. The house has been the home of several prominent personalities, the present building having been constructed for Dr. David Evans in 1824. The existence has been suggested of a much earlier house 'The old road to Fishguard passed over the hill, through the village of Trevgarn, where a tradition prevails that it was once the seat of Cambrian royalty; which receives some countenance from the circumstance that in 1798, on pulling down some buildings, used as a barn and out offices, the massive walls were found to be built upon circular arches almost buried in the earth, and these were supported on some rude stone columns: on digging up the floor of the subterraneous pile, a quantity of coins and silver and gold trinkets were discovered and secreted by the persons employed'.

A subinfeudated portion of the feudal lordship of Haverfordwest, the manor was described as Traueger among the *feoda forinseca* of Haverford in the IPM of Alymer de Valence taken in 17 Edward II (1323/4). The earliest known lord of the manor, Sir Robert de Vale viv. 1268-92, was the descendant of a Norman family established in Pembrokeshire as early as 1130. The de Vales held extensive properties in the lordships of Haverfordwest, Walwyn's Castle, Cemais and filled important local appointments. Sir Robert's lands fell among his four daughters, co-heiresses, one of whom, Elen who had married Llywelyn ap Owen, received Treffgarne as her inheritance. This Llywelyn was the lord of Iscoed Uchirwern in Cardiganshire, son of Owen ap Meredydd ap

Owen ap Gruffydd ap the Lord Rhys, prince of Deheubarth, and so, ironically, Llywelyn became *iure uxoris,* the lord of a tract of land of which his ancestors had once been deprived by those of his wife. Llywelyn died in 1309 leaving two sons, Owen and Thomas. Owen, the elder son died without issue before August 1358, his lands passed to his nieces Elen and Margaret, children of his younger brother Thomas of Iscoed who had predeceased him. The elder daughter Elen, married Gruffydd Fychan, by whom she had the redoubtable Owen Glyndwr. The younger daughter Margaret, married firstly William de la Pole, lord of Mawddwy, a descendant of the Powysian royal family, and secondly Tudur ap Gronw of Penmynydd, ancestor of the Tudor dynasty. Since the manor of Treffgarne formed the share of the younger daughter, Owen Glyndwr as son of the elder daughter could not be lord of that manor as often asserted.

William de la Pole became *iure uxoris,* lord of Treffgarne, which descended to his son John de la Pole who died in 1403, leaving the lordship to his only son, Fulk. When this Fulk died without issue about 1414, the inheritance devolved on his only sister, Elizabeth, wife of Hugh Burgh. Their son, Sir John Burgh died in 1471 leaving four daughters, co-heiresses, the third of whom, Elizabeth, inherited Treffgarne which she brought to her husband William Newport of High Ercall in Shropshire, whose descendants continued as the lords of Treffgarne for the next two centuries. Between 1663 and 1673 the Newports alienated the manor and it changed hands frequently from that date: Thomas Cozens 1673, Martha Fowler, widow 1715, James Jones of Brecon 1720, Eleanor Jones of Haverfordwest, widow 1739, Thomas Kymer 1767 and it finally passed into the hands of the Evans family in the early 19th century.

The previous house had belonged to Rhys Evans, described as 'a substantial yeoman', and another family member, John Evans, established a number of Baptist chapels in the county. His will dated 18 March 1815 showed that he owned properties in Clydey, Penrith and Treffgarne. These were subsequently sold to Morgan Jones of Cilwendeg for £9,680. Rees Evans had a son and heir, John (d. 1816), who married Phoebe Morse of Rinaston. Their son David described as 'late of Rinaston but now of Treffgarne Hall 1820' was a J.P. and died in 1831. He had married Bridget, daughter of James Higgon of Spittal and built the new house in 1824. Nothing further is known of their eldest son, John Evans who was still at Treffgarne in 1894 described as 'lord of the manor and proprietor of the whole parish'.

Originally the estate was about 26 acres and the demesne around Treffgarne about 30 acres. In 1903 the estate was 1,200 acres with £800 p.a. rental value. In 1931 Mr. Victor Higgon, a relation of the Evans family, lived here and was High Sheriff in that year. This handsome symmetrical Georgian house has six principal bedrooms with a particularly attractive coach house.

Refs: Francis Jones, *Historic Cardiganshire Homes and their Families,* and article 'Trefgarn Owen'.

TREFIGIN, *Monington**

The earliest reference to this house was in a release dated 1 May 1345 between Madox ap Kerheragoch who released to 'Master Griffith de Caunteton, archdeacon of Carmarthen, a messuage and lands which said Griffith holds at Trefoegin in fee of Manington in Kemeys, one witness was William ap Gourwared Loyd'.

Here resided the Lloyd family the first at Trefigin being Alban Lloyd, third son of John Lloyd of Hendre who married Jane of Panty-rhys, Llandygwydd. Alban took as his wife, Elizabeth, daughter of Sir John Perrot and by her had a son, James Lloyd and grandson Ieuan Lloyd who married twice, having by a daughter of David Bowen, a son William Lloyd who was a parliamentary voter in 1760 and was assessed for land tax in 1786. Elizabeth Lloyd was assessed at two hearths in 1670 at Trefigin.

In 1854 a lease for 10 years of lands and farm of Trevigin and Castell comprising 270 acres in all at a rent of £180 p.a. was agreed between Thomas Askwith Jenkins of Trevigin, Esq. late Deputy Quarter Master General of the Madras Army and Thomas Nicholas of Trevigin and Castell of Haverfordwest, gent. Major Thomas Askwith Jenkins of Trevigin was born at Trevigin on 10 July 1809. In July 1851 he succeeded to Trevigin on the death of his uncle, Thomas

Morris of Trevigin and Bachendre in that year. Thomas Morris had been at Trevigin since 1803. He was the son of Thomas Morris (d. 1817), and Hannah his wife. There is a photograph in *Y Cymmrodorian* 1906 opposite page 98.

Refs: LT 1786; WWHR ii, p. 56; Bronwydd Deeds No. 811; Nicholas, *County Families,* 1875 edn., p. 903; NLW F. Green Deeds No. 442; Carms. RO, J. Francis Colln. No. 276; GGMS (Gwynfardd).

TREFIN, *Llanrhian*

Home of the Richard family. Henry Richard of Trefin (1732-1812) was Circulating Minister and C.M. preacher for 60 years. By his second wife he had a son, the Rev. Ebenezer Richard (1781-1837), who became private tutor in 1806 to one of the Bowen family. He was ordained in 1811 and retired from the ministry in 1830. His brother, the Rev. Thomas Richard (1783-1858) published two volumes of his sermons in 1866. Ebenezer's son, Henry Richard (1812-88), was M.P. for Merthyr Tydfil from 1868 to the year of his death. He died without issue and is buried at Abney Park, London. Recent distinguished residents were Mr. Edgar Phillips, member of the Gorsedd of Bards and Archdruid of Wales, and the Rev. Lloyd Evans – schoolmaster, poet and author – formerly Colonel Lloyd Evans, Deputy Chaplain General to the Forces and Honorary Chaplain to H.M. The Queen.

Refs: Francis Jones Archives.

TREFINERT, TREVINERT, *St. Davids**

It was a Lay Manor in 1587, Jones of Brawdy was Lord. The courts had been discontinued by that year. George, the younger son of Thomas Rees of Cerbyd, (will dated 1686), was of Trewinard, he was still there in 1676. The Rees family was still of Trefinert in 1834 when Henry Rees had a lease for lives of the house and land from the Mortimer family. In 1850 the Rev. Thomas Mortimer made a Statutory Declaration regarding the title to Trevinert. By 1852 Emily Mortimer, Spinster and Benjamin Mortimer, farmer were both of Trevinert.

Refs: Pembs. Plea Rolls No. 100; Taylor's *Cussion* 97a; GGMS II Adv. Carm., fo. 214; VL 1834; LT 1786; Pembs. RO Deeds D/JP/113; ibid. D/JP/116.

Bowen

TREFLOYNE, *Penally*

Home of seven generations of the Bowen family, descendants of Pentre Ifan. The ancient mansion of Trefloyne stood amidst trees on the northern slope of the high ridgeway which runs through the parish of Penally and extends westwards towards Pembroke. The comparatively modern residence is built a short distance above the old mansion, whose ruins, shown in early 19th century sketches, stood in what is now a small meadow. Every trace of the mansion has disappeared, but higher on the slope, near the present outbuildings, are remains of the base of the old dovecote, some 15 feet square, with three or four rows of nest holes. The site of Trefloyne is of great antiquity, for its earliest associations belong to the age of saints, when the disciples of St. Teilo and St. David were competing for ascendancy in Dyfed. The association between the Pentre Ifan family and southeast Pembrokeshire probably owes its origin to the marriage in the mid-15th century of Owen Fychan ap Owen to Jenet, daughter and heiress of Ievan Harry Llewelyn of Gumfreston. Their eldest son, Sir James ap Owen inherited the paternal estate of Pentre Ifan and their third son, Thomas ab Owen received Trefloyne being the first to settle there in the latter half of the 15th century and was still there in 1501.

During the Civil War Thomas Bowen was a Royalist and was one of the 24 Pembrokeshire gentlemen who signed a Protestation of loyalty to the King and of opposition to Parliament. In June 1644, a decree was nominated by an ordinance of Parliament for the defence and safety of Pembrokeshire, Carmarthenshire and Cardiganshire, among the signatories was

Thomas Bowen. However he did not carry out the orders and remained Royalist. Trefloyne was garrisoned in 1643 for the King and held by Lord Carbery and his 'damme boys' as Mr. Laws calls them. Early in 1644 at Trefloyne, Laugharne, the Parliamentary commander attacked and stormed the house which was held by 150 foot and horse. During Laugharne's approach march to the house Lord Carbery attempted a sally from Tenby, but was forced to retire. After collecting booty, Laugharne caused the walls to be slighted and withdrew to Pembroke. As a result Thomas Bowen was considerably embarrassed. In a letter written about 1645 he complained about 'the unhappy times' saying he had been plundered of his personal wealth, and in 1646 leading men in County Pembroke petitioned Parliament for consideration to be extended to Thomas Bowen of Trefloyne, 'a gentleman of a very fayre and eminent forturne in the country', whose house and estate had suffered greatly in the war. In 1648 Captain Henry Addys imprisoned several Royalists including Thomas Bowen and took ransom from them. Despite this he remained loyal to the King and took part in an action near St. Nicholas where they were defeated and Thomas Bowen was taken prisoner. He died in 1650 leaving his widow Abra and the four children by Mary (Daston) of his first marriage. Abra in her will dated 1676 'gave to this Town 250 pounds, ye interest thereof to continue for ever for ye maintenance of three poor, aged sober people born in ye said Town [of Tenby]'. The last of the main line, Thomas Bowen, heir of Thomas Bowen the Royalist and Mary his wife, married Anne, daughter of Sir Erasmus Philipps of Picton Castle. When he died without issue in 1677 the estate became the possession of his widow's family. The mansion contained eight hearths in 1670. The arms of the Bowens of Trefloyne consisted of two coats: *azure* a lion rampant within an orle of roses *or*, and *gules* a chevron between three true-love knots *argent*. John Bowen was High Sheriff in 1553 and 1560, Thomas Bowen in 1603 and Charles Bowen in 1628.

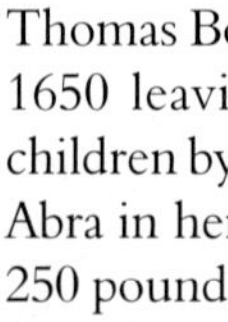

Bowen

The Philippses lived only occasionally at Trefloyne which they let to tenants. In 1714 Sir John Philipps gave a lease of Trefloyne, with the hall part of the dwelling house and the loft over it, the outer kitchen, the room called 'Mr. Philipps' Chamber' and the room over it . . . and the barn, stable, oxhouses, carthouse . . . orchards, gardens and the marsh adjoining to Margaret Marchant, widow, Penally. In 1754 Sir John Philipps leased the mansion to Rev. John Williams at a rent of £50 p.a.; Anne Williams of Penally, widow, by will dated 28th January 1765, left to 'George Williams, Clerk, son of my husband, John Williams, clerk, the freehold lease of Treloyn in Penally parish which I hold under lease from Sir John Philipps, Bt. and after his decease to his sister Anne, wife of George Scawe, mariner'; will proved at Carmarthen 24th May 1769.

Trefloyne was later alienated by the Philipps family and was in the 20th century, the property of Dr. William Thomas C.B., who added to the estate. Born 1890 Dr. William Thomas, a native of Llandissilio in Pembrokeshire had a distinguished career. Educated at the University College of Wales, Aberystwyth he graduated with first class honours in Chemistry and became a Doctor of Science and Fellow of the University. During the First World War he served in France in the Cheshire Regiment and was for some time a prisoner of war. He also studied at the Royal University of Holland and the University of Aberdeen and was a research exhibitioner at Emmanuel College, University of Cambridge. He became Chief Inspector of schools for Wales and was appointed Commander of the Bath in 1951. In 1965 he gifted Trefloyne to the University College of Wales.

A water colour made about 1800-10 shows part of the old house, then mainly in ruins. Materials from the old house were used to build the farmhouse and in 1800 a crude figure of a Virgin and Child was found in the rubble. Over the fireplace in the principal apartment was a carved escutcheon: a chevron between three escallops. All that now remains is a fragment of a gable containing a pointed window, and near the house is the base of a dovecote.

F. P. Gwynne, in *Sketches of Tenby*, 1852, says 'It is now a desolate ruin, entered by an archway; some parts of it have been repaired, and are now tenanted by two labouring families. A good view of this extensive ruin is obtained by ascending the hillside at the back of the courtyard. There is an old well halfway up this hill, hidden by a clump of trees and shrubs'.

Refs: Abridged from Francis Jones's unpublished essay 'Bowen of Trefloyne'; *Arch. Cam.,* 1877, p. 314; *Anc. Mon. Pembs.* p. 291; *Dwnn,* ii, pp. 20, 169; WWHR ii, 81; F. P. Gwynne, *Sketches of Tenby,* 1852, 127; LT 1786; Table of Pious Benefactors to this Corp. St. Mary Tenby 228; Picton Castle Deeds Nos. 4, 29; VL 1834, 1894; Dineley, *Progress,* p. 256; Blome List 1673.

TREFRAN, TREVRANE, *Roch*

In 1441 there was a grant by Thomas son of Walter Jurdan to Sir Richard Newton, Chief Justice of the Common Pleas and Robert Hoggetyn, clerk, of lands in Capriston, Bikton, Sutton and Trevrane in the Lordship of Haverfordwest. William Walter, yeoman, is listed as 'of Trevrane' in 1612. In that year a case was brought against his wife, Elizabeth Harries for abuses towards Jane Walter, alias Laugharne, wife of William Walter of Roch Castle.

Elizabeth is said to have come from Trefran near to the house of William Walter at Roch, where the common pound was situated, crying loudly 'Where are the thieves, the servants of Jane Walter who have stolen my cattle?' She then fell on her knees and prayed that the curse of God might fall on Jane Walter. Next she climbed into the pound shouting 'God's wounds I will kill all the cattle'. At this point William Walter, bailiff of the manor, stopped her but she still rounded on him shouting that he and all the others present were thieves and rogues. On another occasion this harridan again fell on her knees and cursed Jane Walter and used 'many execrations and wild and indecent speeches'.

The family of Walter were still there in 1733 when Dame Thomazine Walter, a widow, and Joseph Walter leased Upper Trefran (three ploughlands) to Stephen Thomas, husbandman. The Thomases, and in 1804, Stephen Thomas (junior) surrendered the lease to John Higgon, the then owner. The Tithe map of Roch parish 1837 shows James Higgon, Esq. owner of Trevrane, with John Thomas, tenant, of 48 acres; Crick-a-franc, James Higgon, Esq. owner, John Nicholas tenant, 23 acres, and Trevrane, James Higgon, Esq. owner, Richard Tew tenant of 181 acres.

A chapel subordinate to Roch parish is said to have stood at Trefran – *'Parochiale Wallicanum' in Y. Cymmr.* xxii, p. 26. The site is shown on the 6 inch OS map to be on Newgale Sands, about half a mile north of Trefran Colliery, and close to the culm pits which have practically obliterated the site. It is probably to be identified with a shallow oblong depression traceable in dry weather. This was St. Caradoc's Chapel mentioned by Giraldus. Fenton mentions 'the trifling ruins of Cradock's Chapel'.

Refs: Parochiale Wallicanum', *Y. Cymmr.,* xxii, p. 26; PC No. 103; Morgan-Richardson Deeds I, 142, AD 1735; VL 1834, 1894, 1904; Pembs. Plea Rolls Nos. 118, 251; PRO, Anc. Deeds 4938; NLW Cwrtmawr Deeds 1128; Fenton, *Tour Pembs.,* p. 81.

TREGAMAN,
also **TREGAMMAN,** *Nevern*

Tregaman derives its name from the river Caman which flows past it.

Home of the Peverill and Young families. Tregaman formed part of the estate of the family of Peverill. John Peverill, grandson of John Peverill viv. 1250, and son of David Peverill, divided the estate in 1427 between his three sons, Howell, Jenkin and Owen. The eldest, Howell, received Tregaman which was inherited by his only child Eva, (Agnes), who married Rees Morgan of Cardiganshire. By him Eva had two daughters and co-heiresses: Nest married to John Cole and Morfydd married to William Thomas Philpin. Their issue, after inheriting, sold Tregaman to Thomas Peter of Nevern, grandson of Rhys Glin Prys of 'Llysdin'. He married Gwenllian, daughter of Evan Lloyd ab William of Bayvil. He was of 'Tregamon' in 1587 and his IPM was taken in 1595. Thomas Peters' daughter, Sage, inherited. She was married to Thomas Philip Young who, says George Owen, '. . . likelie hath builded a new house upon the same'. Court records tell us that 'Thomas Young [was] killed at Eglwyswrw Faire upon Ascension day 13th May 1602 by John Bowen and Hugh Bowen the sonnes of James Bowen his uncle, brother to his mother, who were both executed for the same act at Haverfordwest XVIIIth of July anno prd'.

William Young who came into Tregaman *iure uxoris* was aged 59 in 1607 and the son of Philip Young by Anne his wife, daughter of Meuric ap Heilin. He was assessed for four hearths in 1670.

Thomas Young and Sage had two sons, Owen who was aged 30 in 1607 and of Tregaman; he married Margaret, daughter of Lewis Philipps of Pentre Ifan, and the younger son, William was of Haverfordwest. Owen and Margaret had a son William viv. 1685 who married Elizabeth, daughter of Arnold Tankard of Haverfordwest, mercer, and they had three children, the heir, Bartholomew whose will was proved in Carmarthen in 1678 by his widow Jane, daughter of David Scurlock of Cardigan, and a daughter and son of whom nothing is known. Bartholomew and Jane had four daughters and co-heiresses, all of whom were of Cardigan and unmarried in 1683. The Youngs remained in possession until the 1760s.

In 1764 we find John Morris of Haverfordwest, drover, listed as owner. He was then in financial straits and wrote to a cousin asking for help. He died in that year unmarried. Owen Owen was owner in 1840, with John Owen occupier; Sale particulars in 1908/9 tell us that Tregaman formed part of the Cwmgloyne estate; the tenant being Mr. Thomas Lloyd at rent of £148 p.a.

Refs: WWHR ii, 47; GGMS Adv. Pembs., i, 13; Pembs. RO DB 13, 98; Wagner MS 2, GO; Bronwydd Deeds Nos. 900, 901; Pembs. Plea Rolls No. 7, ibid. Nos. 177, 204; LT 1786; VL 1834, 1904; KCR Moylgrove Manor 37 EG2; George Owen, *2nd Book*, p. 272; Protheroe IV.

TREGENDEG, *Bletherston**

The Land Tax lists of 1786 show an Upper Tregendeg, Thomas John, gent. owner-occupier, Lower Tregendeg, Francis Skyrme Esq. owner, William Beynon tenant, assessed at 7s. 1½d. and £1 1s. 0d. respectively. The Griffith family was there from 1603 when Morris Griffith of Tregindege, gent. still extant in 1622, served as a juror on the IPM of William Scourfield of Moat; and Henry Griffith in 1640.

By 1709/10 when he married Sarah, daughter of Griffith Lewis of Carmarthen, Alderman, John Thomas was of Tregendeg, gent. His will was proved in 1730 and he left Tregendeg to his brother, Bodam Thomas of Llanboidy. The Thomas family were of Upper Tregendeg as shown on the Voter's List of 1834, with John Beynon and his wife Rosamund, née Beddoe at Lower Tregendeg. The Beddoes were related to the Thomas family, William Thomas of Bletherston, husbandman having married in 1655 Jane, daughter of George Beddoe of Lampeter Velfrey. He was originally a yeoman of Clogyvraen, Carmarthenshire. Owen Thomas of Llanuwchllwydog, gent. in his will dated 1675/6 names his nephew George Beddoe of Tregindeg in Bletherston.

Refs: Maesgwynne No. 161; VL 1834, 1904; Pembs. Plea Rolls; Spence Colby Deeds; Poyston Castle Deeds 72; LT 1786.

TREGINNIS ISSA *or* **LOWER,** *St. Davids**

In 1771 Upper and Lower Treginnis formed part of the estate of Wyrriott Owen of Great Nash with James Roberts, tenant. His rent was then £24 p.a., supplying Wyrriott Owen with 4 strikes of beams p.a. and 10s. in lieu of other duties. He then moved to Upper Treginnis and the owner of Lower Treginnis was Henry Harries, gent. His widow, Elizabeth Harries was in occupation by 1801 with her son, also Henry who was 65 in 1841. By 1861 Thomas Llewhellin, then aged 54 years owned Lower Treginnis and was described as 'Farmer and Commissioner'. He had been granted a lease of three lives of Ramsey by James Summers in 1860 and continued to farm Treginnis. By 1871 he had left Treginnis and had been replaced by the Bowen family, who did not stay long. By 1881 the farm was 200 acres and had passed to the 65 year old David Arnold and his wife. The Arnolds had left by 1893. In 1902 Martha Lewis, widow of Thomas Lewis had Lower Treginnis. In 1914 Lower Treginnis was owned by J. B. Evans of Cardiff and farmed by Francis Thomas, and after the war his two sons, James Henry Thomas and William Howard Thomas, farmed it.

Ref: Francis Jones Archives.

TREGINNIS UCHA, *St. Davids*★

Lies southwest of St. Davids near Porth Lisky and was the home of the Davids family. Once a lay manor held by William Philip Robin in 1587. Lower and Upper Treginnis formed part of the estate of Wyrriott Owen of Great Nash in 1771, the farm was then a holding of 230 acres. By 1780 the estate was owned by Hugh Owen, Wyrriott Owen's uncle. The Land Tax records show that in 1796 James Roberts was the owner. He was the son of the Rev. James Roberts, vicar choral of St. Davids who died 9 December 1763 aged 62. By his wife, Anne Harries whom he had married at St. Davids on 29 April 1729 he had three sons and five daughters. His eldest son, James born 1732, married 18 July 1766 Martha, daughter of John Harries. They had an only son, John of Treginnis Ucha, baptised 1767, viv. 1832, who owned a moiety of Treginnis, and also owned Trefinert and Trelethin fawr. He married 29 July 1797, Jane Phelps and they had a sole heiress, Emily baptised 1800, who married firstly, John Mortimer on 21 March 1816, by whom she had a son, John Mortimer of Treginnis. She married secondly, Henry Rees. In 1841 John Mortimer and his wife, Sarah both aged 30, were living at Treginnis with their infant son, the first of five children, and six servants. By 1902 Upper Treginnis was owned by William and Martell Roberts, the latter being still there in 1931.

Ref: Francis Jones Archives.

TREGLEMAIS, *Llanhowel*

As will be seen this was an Episcopal manor, but by the end of the 16th century it seems to have acquired the status of a lay manor.

The tun of one Clement, the property is often described in records as Villa Clementi, Clementson, Treglemes, and as Carn Fawr. Carn Treglemes is a prominent outcrop of rock in a field called Parc y gain fawr, nearly half a mile northwest of the parish church: near this rock are two other fields called Parc y gain and Parc y gain fach.

In the *Valor Eccles.* of 1535/6, under 'Archdeaconry of St Davids', the manor of Villa Clementis, (Treglemes), is described as worth 44s. 8d. per annum, held by Richard Wogan of Bolyston (Boulston) but for many years lapsed and paying nothing.

Villa Clemento is shown as Episcopal property in 1584, together with a rent of 23s. 8d. in Polletarock alias Poulletar which Richard Wogan formerly of Boulston held.

In 1587/8 the manor of Carn vawr alias Treglemes (Sir John Wogan of Boulston, lord), is listed as a lay manor.

On 11 September 1609, a Final Concord was made between Sir William Wogan, John Owen Esq. plaintiffs, and Sir John Wogan, Frances his wife, and Maurice Wogan their son and heir apparent, deforceants, in respect of the manor of Treclemmeys with view of frankpledge, and other lands in Pembrokeshire.

On 16 November 1610, William Walter of Trevrane, Roch parish, conveyed to Thomas ap Rees Esq and Revd Morgan Walter clerk, *inter alia,* a rent of 4s. from a messuage in Treglemes held in free socage as of the King's manor of East Greenwich, being of the annual value of 2s.

The IPM of William Scourfield of New Moat (d. 22 March 1621/22), shows that he held two messuages and half a carucate in Kerbett and Treglemes, held of Sir John Wogan by knight service as of his manor of Treglemes alias Carn Vawre, of the annual value of 10s. The IPM, taken 9 January 1637/8, of Sir John Wogan of Boulston shows that he owned the manor of Treglemes, and one carucate of land and one corn mill in Treglemes and Carnevaure, held by knight service and suit at the court of the

Bishop, worth £1 yearly. In August 1702 Richard Sparkes and Thomas Bowen agreed to render to Charles Phillipps and John Meyrick Esq. the manor of Treglemes and other manors and lands in Pembrokeshire. In 1785 Thomas Evans of Cerbyd, yeoman, was appointed gamekeeper by George Phillips M.D. for his manor of Carn Vawr and other manors in that vicinity, and in 1786 Samuel Harries Esq. was appointed gamekeeper of the same manor by the same lord. George Phillips was the ancestor of the Lort-Phillips family.

In 1737 David Reynolds, grandson of John Reynolds of Church Hill, tenant of Sir Edward Philipps of Picton, and son of John Reynolds, was living in the parish. He held a lease of Treglemais. David Reynolds was a man of pious nature and a supporter of Nonconformity in the locality. On 15 January 1739/40 the Quarter Sessions ordered that the dwelling house of Evan David called Treglemeys be recorded as a place of meeting for Protestant dissenters from the Church of England. What relationship Evan David had to the Reynolds, if any, is not known. It is possible that David Reynolds may have been the sub-tenant. In 1741 David Reynolds was High Constable of the Hundred of Dewsland. Little else is known of him and we do not know who he married. He was buried at Llanhowel on 1 April 1767. He had five children; four sons and one daughter, Mary, who married John Evans of Fagwr Goch Fach in Morfil and had eleven children. Francis Reynolds the eldest son of David succeeded to the lease of Treglemais and became High Constable of Dewsland in 1762. He was married twice, firstly to Martha Williams of Tancredston, by whom he had six children four of whom died in infancy, and secondly to Eleanor Warlow of Haverfordwest by whom he had no issue. John Reynolds the eldest son, born 21 December 1758 succeeded to Treglemais and married firstly Anne, daughter of the Rev. David Lewis, Baptist minister of Llangloffan but she died without issue in 1782. He married again shortly afterwards on 16 October 1783, Elizabeth, daughter of William Raymond of Trecadwgan. From an early age John Reynolds had shown a great interest in the Holy Bible and was an ardent Baptist. He became one of the leading religious ministers in West Wales. He was ordained in 1785 and built a new chapel at Felinganol and ministered there until his death in 1824. He was thought to be a French sympathiser and supporter of the landings at Fishguard in 1797 and Treglemais was searched by troops seeking proof of his involvement but nothing of a compromising nature was found.

By his second wife, Elizabeth, John Reynolds had three children, William, David and Phoebe. William Reynolds married on 27 June 1815 Mary, posthumous daughter of William Harries of Croftufty. After some years William moved to his mother's old home, Trecadwgan where he died in 1851. They had six children, two of whom were sons. The heir, the Rev. William Reynolds born 1820 lived at Trecadwgan and was a prominent Baptist. David, the second son of John and Elizabeth Reynolds remained at Hendre throughout his life and was well known as a successful farmer and breeder. He married Elizabeth, daughter of John Williams of Treyarched. They had two sons, John born 1837 and William. John succeeded to Treglemais and married Anne, daughter of George Scale of Capeston. She died in 1922 aged 76. They had seven children, four of whom died as infants. Philip, the eldest son, was the last to live at Treglemais. He married Rosamund Skeel Williams of Rudbaxton and they had three children, a son who died at birth and two daughters, Eileen born 1921 and Nesta baptised 1918. The property was sold after the Second World War.

Refs: Francis Jones unpublished essay, 'Reynolds of Treglemais'; *Black Book of St. Davids,* 1326; NLW, Eaton Evans and Williams, Nos. 92, 1294; Pembs.

QS Order Book; Landowners' Return 1873; NLW, Morgan-Richardson Deeds, No. 237; BM, *Harl* 6696, fo. 13a; Taylor's *Cussion,* fo. 97a; PRO, *Wales* 3, 3254, 3389, Fines; Pembs. QS, Game Licences; WWHR, iii, p. 274; NLW, Poyston Deeds, No 72; *Y Cyminrodor,* 1902, p. 128.

TREGROES, *Fishguard*

Between Fishguard and Manorowen on Colby's Map of 1831, about one-and-a-quarter miles southwest of Fishguard town.

The Courts Leet of the Royal Manor of Fishguard were held at Tregroes, probably for the Welshery. The manor was originally held by the Abbots of St. Dogmaels, but in 1536-40 came to the Crown and was divided into two: the Manor of English Fishguard and the Manor of Welsh Fishguard. In 1653 a Court Leet was held in the house of William Phillips 'neare ffishguard'. In 1814 the Steward of the Manor was Lord Kensington and a map of the Manor which was made in that year shows a group of three buildings at Tregroes, one of which is called 'Manor House'. Courts were still held there in 1859.

In 1568-1600 John Phillips was of Tregroes, and on 19 August 1616, James Phillips stated in a law suit, he then living in the parish of St. Edrins, a husbandman, '. . . has known manor of Fishguard for last 48 years. Born at Tregroes, when 20 years old he moved to St. Edrins . . . about 40 years ago'.

Ann Williams was shown as owner-occupier in 1786 Land Tax records paying 2s. 6d. The family of George and the Gwynnes were also sometime occupiers of Tregroes. They were all strong supporters of the Hermon Baptist Chapel – the first to be built in Fishguard in 1776 by the Rev. John Williams and Henry Morgan Esq. of Tregroes. Henry Morgan always gave a sovereign in the collection which he modestly covered with a penny.

Refs: Fishguard and Goodwick Silver Jubilee Tribute, 1977, pp. 4-7; Law Suit, PRO *History of St. Dogmaels Abbey*; NLW, Eaton Evans and Williams Deeds No. 1235; Protheroe MS IV fo. 89; LT 1786; NLW F. Green Deeds No. 9; VL 1894, 1904.

Gates

TREGWYNT, *Granston*

Tregwynt is one of the earliest inhabited sites in the area. A 14th century map designates it as a manor house. Situated in a delightful, if somewhat secluded spot, it is surrounded by tall trees which shelter it from the Atlantic storms that sweep over the little bay of Abermawr. The Harries family derives its descent from the famous Fleming, Wyzo, who during the reign of Henry I conquered the Hundred of Dungleddy. Wyzo built a stronghold known at Wyzo's tun or Wiston, and the castle was the centre of resistance to the Welsh and it was Wyzo who organised that resistance. His fortress was strong enough in 1146 to defy all attacks until Howell, son of Owen Gwynedd 'a person famously remarkable for martial endowments' came to their assistance with 'certain battering engines'. Wyzo left two sons, Walter who

appears to have died without issue and Phillip who left three children, Henry, an unknown son, and Margaret. Henry had two children, Robert who died without issue and a daughter who became the ultimate heiress of the patrimony of Wyzo the Fleming. Her name is not known but she married Sir Walter de Harford who was witness to Earl Walter Marshal's charter to Gilbert de Vale in 1241-45, and held the Barony of Wiston in 1247 and was present in the attack on Cardigan in 1244. He also accompanied Strongbow in his Irish conquests. There were only daughters from this marriage, and one of these, Hilary de Harford married Adam Stanton or Steynton, Lord of Steynton. From this marriage there were three co-heiresses, Margaret, Isabell and Nest who married Fermand or Fromand Brown. Nest and Fromand had two children, Thomas and a daughter who married Henry fitzHenry. Sir Thomas Brown married Ellen, daughter of Peter Russell of Brimaston. Sir Thomas lived in the parish of Granston, and there can be little doubt that his root tree was Tregwynt. It was his descendant eight generations later who was the first Harries of Tregwynt. This was Harry ap Thomas, son of Thomas William ap Phillip and Joan Bowen. Harry ap Thomas married about 1580, Anne, daughter of Lewis William of Panthowel and had four sons, and one daughter. Lewellyn Harry or Harries of Tregwynt, the heir was an energetic and enterprising man and added considerably to the fortunes of his house. He was a member of the Train Band of the county and we find references to him in the militia papers. In 1609 he had to pay eightpence for a rest for his musket, and in 1613 the muster rolls show that his armour was defective, and he 'wanteth a Rest and a Muskett.' He owned several properties in the Barony of Kemes and he had to do suit at Court as a free tenant. His wife was Elinor, daughter of Richard Philipps of Woodstock, a younger brother of William Philipps of Pentypark, which was a cadet branch of the Philipps family of Picton. They had 12 children. Thomas Harries, eldest son of Llewellyn and Elinor, predeceased his father. He married before 1635 Mary, daughter of George Bowen of Llwyngwair. She died before her husband. The will of Thomas Harries was administered by his father on 15 April 1659. Among other bequests he left £5 to be shared between his 'supposed children' and the residue of his estate to his lawful children, George and Elizabeth Harries. The Harries family continued to prosper and produce male heirs in direct line into the 18th century.

The only event to ruffle the calm was the landing of the French at Carreg Gwastad in 1797 in the time of George Harries and Eliza Gates his wife. The Gates family was an old stock, and their arms according to Edmondon's Heraldry (1780) were, per pale *azure* and *gules,* three lions rampant, guardent *or,* two and one. Eliza Harries was buried at Granston on 11 February, 1806.

The landing of the French at Carreg Gwastad, in the neighbouring parish of Llanwnda in February, 1797, caused some consternation at Tregwynt. The Tregwynt MSS. of Mr. Nelson George Harries, of Wolverhampton, contains an interesting reference to this event: 'In 1797 the even tenor of the lives of the Pembrokeshire folk was upset by the French Invasion of Fishguard. On the same night, Mrs. Harries of Tregwynt was giving a ball. Miss Mary Gwynne Harries, whom the writer met at Tenby on 29 March, 1902, and who was then about 80 years old, remembered having been at Tregwynt before 1830. She knew a Mrs. Bird who was a niece of an old servant of the family who was lady's maid to Mrs. George Harries and in the house on the night of the ball in 1797. This servant told Mrs. Bird that she was serving tea in an ante-room on the news of the French landing and that the hostess and guests at once took to their carriages and horses, leaving the lights all burning and the supper just laid on the table. The only one who remained was an old member of the family said to have been in the Army, who said that he would wait for the French, and did so, having loaded all the firearms in the place. Fortunately for him, the French troops went further up the coast and Tregwynt was saved from the destruction which overtook many other houses. Mrs. Harries with her two sons, George and Thomas Frederick, got into their coach with what valuables they could collect and drove to Narberth, where they heard that the French had surrendered, and they then returned to Tregwynt.'

There is no doubt that the 'old member of the family said to have been in the army' was Colonel Daniel Vaughan (brother of George Harries' first wife, and brother of Gwynne Vaughan of Jordanston and Governor of Fishguard Fort). Present also at the dance was Colonel Knox of Llanstinian who commanded the militia, and who left to collect his forces. From Knox's account of the affair, Colonel Daniel Vaughan stayed behind as 'his infirmities would not permit him to follow Colonel Knox'.

There were only two children of the marriage of George Harries and Eliza his wife, George and Thomas. George Harries was baptised at Dedham, Essex, on 9 October 1782. After succeeding to the estate his affairs became straitened with the result that Tregwynt was sold by auction at the Coffee Tavern, Cornhill, London in 1830. It was bought by Richard Llewellin Purcell-Llewellin, Esq. who was owner for a short time, and High Sheriff in 1840. The estate was sold in 1877, and bought back by descendants of James Harries and Elinor Griffithes his wife, of the Priskilly branch of the family. It then totalled 2,746 acres 2 rods 4 perches with a yearly rental of £1,735.

Mr. John Harries-Burrington, descended from the distaff side of the family, died in 1984 and left the estate to his relations the Gabbs. In 1986 it was put up for sale and much of the land was acquired by the National Trust. The house has since been restored by Mr. and Mrs. Sayer. Several hundred gold coins were found buried in the grounds in the 1990s, all predating the Civil War. Also found was a ring inscribed 'faith before false face'.

Refs: Francis Jones, 'Harries of Tregwynt', *Trans. Hon. Soc. Cymmr.,* 1946; Burke, *LG*.

TREHAIDD, *Nevern**

This was the home of the James family. James Lewis owned Trehaidd, Dolgau and Mountain Hall. He had two sons, David James, the eldest son, married Mary daughter of Henry Richard of Haverfordwest, the post-nuptial settlement dated 21 February 1697/8. He died without issue and Trehaidd passed to his younger brother, Lewis James viv. 1747, who married Elizabeth, marriage settlement dated 4 August 1725. They had a son, Lewis James of Trehaidd who married firstly, an unknown wife by whom he had three children all of whom died without issue. He married secondly, Mary, daughter of John Pryse of Blaendyffryn, Cardiganshire, by whom he had three sons and a daughter; John Pryse James who succeeded to Trehaidd, his will being proved in 1815; the other children being Rice, David and Maria who married Enoch Francis and was of Trehaidd in 1834. David James was of Trehaidd in 1904.

Refs: VL 1834, 1894; LT 1786; NLW, Eaton Evans and Williams Deeds No. 644; Pembs. Plea Rolls No. 273; Francis Jones, *Historic Cardiganshire Homes and their Families.*

Thomas

TREHALE, TREHAL,
St. Edrins

This property formed part of the estate of Scourfield of Castle Villa and Trewilym, and in 1611 a fine was suffered of two messuages and 99 acres in 'Trehayle' between James and Thomas Scourfield and the latter's wife. It remained a farm but at the end of the 17th century it was the home of Lewis Williams, tenant in 1695, owned by Mrs. Mary Lucy of Trecwn. Thomas Williams of Trehale, physician, was son of Lewis, son of James William, a son of William of Ffwrneithin, Cards. Descended from John Webley, of the Saer y Cwm family.

Dr. Williams and his wife were early members of Albany chapel, Haverfordwest; their daughter Mary was born at Trehale on 31 May 1710; they emigrated to Pennsylvania in 1725 and had died by 1737. It became the property of Hugh Owen by 1787 and of John Roberts by 1799. The eldest son, William Roberts became an Officer of Excise and served in various parts of Britain. While at Portsmouth he became involved in some difficulty, with the result that he was obliged to resign. He returned hurriedly to Trehale, and afterwards always went around armed with a pistol for fear of arrest. However he was not molested and when he died, was buried in St. Edrins church, his pistol with him. During the rebuilding of the church in 1846 his grave was disturbed and among his remains was the pistol.

Some time before 1797, Trehale had been bought by Henry John, the younger of Lochturffin who had bought it from Owen of Orielton. On his death in 1813 Henry left Trehale to his second son, Abel John who settled there. On Abel John's death in 1841 the property passed to his only child, Mary who had married in 1839 the Rev. T. E. Thomas, a Baptist minister eminent for his piety and charitable disposition. The present house was erected by him in about 1844 or 1845 on or near the older farmhouse. He was the second son of Henry Thomas born 6 November 1757 at Alltybeili, near Whitland, a Baptist minister for 73 years. He had married Mary, daughter of Evan Mathias of Penderi.

Theophilus Evan Thomas and Mary his wife had eight children, Henry John, Abel, Theophilus, Phoebe, Margaret, Mary, Anna and Elizabeth. Henry John born in 1841 was of Lochturffin and died there in 1893 having had eight children whose descendants are still prominent in Pembrokeshire affairs. Abel the second son, born in 1848 was a K.C., M.P. for East Carmarthenshire, B.A. of London University 1870, J.P. for Pembrokeshire and called to the Bar in 1873. A letter from T. Angus of the University of London to Theophilus Thomas on 17 January 1867 tells of a terrible accident when the ice broke 'on the water in our park' drowning more than 35 men. 'Among them was your son. He and four other students all fell in; but all reached the shore. Abel deserves special praise, if that is not too weak a word. One of his fellow students was in imminent peril, and it was largely owing to your son's care that he reached land. I understand also that after [he] had reached land, he went in and rescued another man. One student fell in, in the . . . middle, and saved himself by breaking the ice and swimming, 8 or 10 minutes being employed in that way. We put all to bed, giving them what was needful, and I am thankful to say all were quite well the next morning'. Abel married in 1875 Edith Pollock by whom he had three children.

The youngest son of Theophilus and Mary Thomas, another Theophilus Evan Thomas born 1853 inherited Trehale; he was a J.P. for the county and married Edith, daughter of George Blayney of Swansea. They had a son, Lionel who was killed at Ypres aged 19 years and a daughter, Marguerite who married Major John Francis. He died in 1960 and she died in 1944 leaving three children, John, Peter and Louise who married Col. Gilbert Chaldecot and lived at Trehale. The property included a chapel and yard and amounted in all to 270 acres. The arms of Thomas of Trehale are: *argent* on a chevron engrailed *azure* two griffons passant. On a chief *azure* three cinquefoils.

Refs: Francis Jones, *Historic Cardiganshire Homes and their Families,* p. 117; Francis Jones Archive essay notes; NLW, Lochturffin Schedule 1938; ibid. Lochturffin Deeds Nos. 3, 5, 6, 8, 17, 20, 28, 29, 30-31, 33, 34, 36, 37, 38, 39, 40, 43, 45, 46.

TREHENRY, *Llanfyrnach*

Shown on Colby's Map of 1831 as about three-quarters of a mile southwest of Llanfyrnach church. Home of the father and grandfather of the famous Jenkin Lloyd of Blaiddbwll in the same parish. The father, Ievan Fychan (or Lloyd) ap Ievan Llwyd, described as of 'Pentre Henry in Trayan Canol in the fee of Dyffryntaf' is mentioned in a deed of 14 Richard II, (1390/91).

Philip John ap Rees settled here in 1584. The prenuptial settlement of Lewis Philip John, son of Philip John ap Rees of Llanfyrnach *ar dafe*, gent. and Jane, daughter of John Phillipps of Llanvirnach, gent. dated 1584 tells us that, 'The said Lewis Philip John grants to Reignald (or Reynald), Lewis of Llanvirnach ar dafe, and Llewelin ap Morris of the same place, yeoman, my messuage called Tre Henry in Ll'virnach, a messuage called Frynondeg and lands, being an entail on the prospective bride and bridegroom and the heirs of their bodies'. A lawsuit arose between Richard Lewis plaintiff v. James Lloyd relating to the said lands in Llanvirnach; reciting the above settlement and entail, which lands on the death of the said Philip and Lewis and Reignald Lewis junior, (son and heir of the said Lewis and Jane), and Richard, brother and heir of said Reignald junior, descended to Richard Lewis. Lewis died in 20 Charles II (1644). Reignald Lewis died without issue.

According to the Land Tax records of 1786 Trehenry was owned by Lady Jane Keith, tenanted by James Lewis. The Lewis family were still at Trehenry in 1894 when another James Lewis was tenant.

Refs: Protheroe MS (GWG) XII, fo. 35; LT 1786; Bronwydd Deeds, Nos. 2085, 2087, 2088; VL 1894; Picton Castle Deeds.

TREHOWEL, *Llanwnda*

The families associated with this property include Lloyd, Williams, Harries and Mortimer. In 1603 William Thomas Lloyd had an interest in Trehowel. On 30 May 1638 Jenkin David of Trevasser Clethe Coch, yeoman, granted Rice William Lloyd and his son, both of Trehowel, all their title and claim to two messuages and other lands around. There was a Chancery suit between Lettice Rees, widow of William

Mortimer, gent. and Elizabeth his wife, and William Williams, an infant, plaintiffs against Ann Williams, widow and William Williams, an infant defendant in the years 1769-74. The case concerned a lease, part of a marriage settlement which was granted by David Harries of Trehowell, gent. and Mary his wife on 20 November 1732 to William Williams, yeoman for 21 years. David Harries had on his death left the enjoyment of the rents of the properties in the lease to his wife, Mary. At the time of her death in 1752 she was visiting her sister at Walterston, and her papers fell into the hands of William Williams and John Williams, the son, who were living at Trehowel. As she had died intestate they kept all the title deeds and altered the dates on the marriage settlement so that they could enjoy the property for a further 50 years. The claimants alleged that the word twenty in the lease was, about the time of the expiration of the lease, clandestinely and fraudulently altered by, or on behalf of the tenant to seventy and they won their case with costs in 1774. The lands in dispute were one third share of Trehowell, 'Castle Gladdis and Briskarn Vach', Llanwnda parish which plaintiffs claimed in remaindership. David Harries was the son of William and Alice his wife, and the eldest of their four children, the others being Elinor, who married William Williams, Mary who married John Propert and Lettice, who married George Rees. David Harries described as 'a good natured man', died without issue 1739.

Trehowell was inherited by John Williams, described as 'a drunken wicked fellow', son of Elinor and William Williams, and a fellow trustee with his uncle of the marriage settlement. William Williams, gent. was 'of Trehowel' in 1748 and William Mortimer, gent. as tenant in the Voter's List of 1834 and the Land Tax List of 1786. The *Cambrian Tourist*, says '. . . we passed a neat house called Caergwynt, (sic but recte Tregwynt), belonging to Mrs. Harris. The kind attentions of a farmer in the neighbourhood of this memorable spot claim our warmest acknowledgements. Having finished a most comfortable meal at Mr. Mortimer's house (which, during the confusion, was considered the headquarters of the French), he explained all the minutiae respecting this circumference, and very obligingly printed out the situation of their camp, and related many entertaining and interesting anecdotes. Deeply impressed with gratitude towards Mr. M. for his facilities, we soon arrived at Goodric sands'.

Refs: Cambrian Tourist, 1822 edn., p. 136; NLW, Eaton Evans and Williams Deeds No. 1254; Fines in Pembs. GS; VL 1834. W & W (H'west) No. 7221.

TREINDEG *alias* RYNDASTON, RHYNDASTON, *Hayscastle**

In 1326 Rindaston was a knight's fee occupied by John Reyner. By 1580 it formed part of the estate of Francis Laugharne of St. Brides. Morris Owen was of Rhindaston when he made his will on 11 August 1658; will proved 11 December 1660. Morris Owen had five children, Thomas, John, Peter, Lawrence, executor of his father's estate and taxed on one hearth in 1670, and Catherine. Morris mentions in his will the following grandchildren, Anne, Mary and Elizabeth Owen, Thomas and John Gofth.

By the 18th century the Nicholas family lived at Treindeg. Thomas Nicholas, second son of Henry Nicholas married Margaret Williams of Camrose on 30 June 1756; a witness to their marriage was his elder brother William. Thomas and Margaret had at least four children, Thomas the heir who married Elinor Morse of Hayscastle, (1786-1826), by whom he had three children, John, Essex and Thomas; the second son, John Nicholas was of Treindeg, the third son, William was of Priskilly fach, will proved 1839 and a daughter, Martha (1754-1827) married John Pointz (1758-1828) by whom she had a son, William of Barnards Hill. Thomas Nicholas made his will 9 October 1788, proved 30 May 1795. He voted for Philipps in the parliamentary elections in 1765 and 1768.

In 1786 there were five tenants at Rhindaston owned by Mrs. Julia Rooke, daughter of John Harries, Capt. 9th Foot (d. 1768) who had owned Rhindaston among other lands. She was the widow of Thomas Elbridge Rooke. The lands were occupied by John Punch and Thomas Nicholas, William Edward, William Evan and Evan William. Thomas and Julia Rooke had a daughter, Julia Ellbridge Anne Hort Rooke who married Henry Fleming

Pinkston Bartlett of Haverfordwest on 1 May 1806 at Haverfordwest.

Refs: PRO AD D4688, D8025; Poyston Deeds No. 210; LT 1786; Picton Castle Deeds 1362; Pembs. Plea Rolls Nos. 119, 235.

TRELEDDYN, *St. Davids*

A double-pile 17th century house with a smugglers' tunnel allegedly leading to Porthseli. For many years this was the property of the Williams family but other families such as Bleddyn, (1529) Tucker, and Bland were connected with it. On January 16th 1799 Thomas Williams of Treleddyn, owner of the sloop *Phoebe,* of the Port of Solva, proved '. . . that ten hundred or 33 bushels of salt taken on board for the curing of herrings were lost through stormy and tempestuous weather'.

One of the Williams family, a merchant farmer, is said to have been the first man to sight the French fleet in 1797 as it approached the coast of Pembrokeshire in its vain attempt at invasion.

In the late 18th century the famous actress, Mrs. Jordan, leased the house and was regularly visited by the Duke of Clarence, her lover, afterwards King William IV. It is said that one of the ceilings was emblazoned with the royal coat of arms, but this has disappeared, if it ever existed. A map of Trelethin (Treleddyn) was made in 1762 by Henry John. There is a photocopy in Pembrokeshire Record Office. The property was put up for sale in 1884. The house, then Upper Treleddyn was mentioned in the *Black Book of St. Davids*.

Refs: Pembs. Plea Rolls No. 106, 274; NLW, Eaton Evans and Williams Deeds No. 1340; Coleman Deeds Nos. 1491, 418; Cwrtmawr Deeds Nos. 1740, 1735; Maesgwynne Deeds No. 280; *Dwnn,* i, pp. 194, 1613; LT 1786; *Black Book of St. Davids,* 1326, p. 49; Pembs. RO HDX 1000; ibid. HDX/695 No. 3; VL 1834; W & W (H'west) No. 11773; Pembs. QS. Order Books.

Phillips

TRELLEWELYN, *Manorowen*

Said to be named after a Prince Llewelyn who stayed there while on a pilgrimage to St. Davids but more likely to have been named after a freeholder or perhaps a *breyr* who made his home there. There are several legends relating to the house and family in medieval days. Some of the lands that later became incorporated into the Trellewelyn estate, were at one time owned by several persons. Thus, on 20 January 1558/9, David ap Lewis and Thomas Llewelyn granted to David Morris Rees 'all messuages and lands in the vill and fields of Fynnon y gribe, Trefllewelyn Penmeythyn, Kaergowill and Pant Yago in the parishes of Llanwnda and Manernawan' for grantor's life, then to descend to his son, Maurice ap David and Maurice's children by Lleycue verch Thomas Morris. Whether these messuages were held in their entirety is not clear, but they had been acquired by the Trellewelyn family before the end of Elizabeth's reign, probably by purchase. The family of Phillips was certainly in possession of Trellewelyn at least 15 years before the above-cited settlement was made.

The pedigree of Phillips of Trellewelyn, recorded by the deputy-herald, Lewys Dwnn between the years 1588-1614 shows that the family descended from Rhys ap Tewdwr, prince of Deheubarth who fell in battle against the Normans in 1093. A branch of this royal house, shorn of pretensions, settled in the Newport district where its members lived in comparative obscurity as minor freeholders. Thence they moved to Trellewelyn, but whether that property was acquired by purchase or through marriage has not been determined. They bore the coat of arms of their princely ancestor, namely *gules* a lion rampant *or* within a border engrailed *or*.

The first of the family to settle at Trellewelyn was Ieuan ap Rhys ap Robert ap Gruffydd ap Henry of the parish of Newport. When he was there is not known but it was before 1543 for his name appears in the Lay Subsidy List for the parish of Manorowen in that year as 'Ieuan ap Price Ropert', assessed at £14 on which he paid a tax of nine shillings and fourpence. It was the highest valuation in the parish. Ieuan ap Rhys ap Robert married Lleucu, daughter of David ap Gwilym of Trecwn in Llanfairnantygof. His father-in-law described in 1488 as of Brimaston in Hayscastle parish, afterwards moved to Trecwn, and among that family's possessions were several farms in Manorowen parish so that the marriage may have led to Ieuan's settlement at Trellewelyn. They had an only son, Gruffydd who married Anne(s), daughter of Rhys ap Lewis 'o'r Gynkhordie', a place that has defied identification, but is probably meant for Cynheidre, now Cefnydre near Fishguard. Anne and Gruffydd had an only son Phillip who succeeded to Trellewelyn in due course. The marriages of Phillip ap Gruffydd allied him to leading families of the county. His first wife, Catherine, was the daughter of Owen Lloyd of Hendre in St. Dogmaels, by Jane, daughter and co-heiress of David ap William ap Perkin of Cwmgloyne, and by her he had five children. His second wife was Jonet, daughter of James Philipps of Pentypark in Walton East, a cadet of the influential house of Picton Castle; by her he had an only child, a daughter. Phillip died before 1598 for in the Spring Great Sessions of that year, Jonet was described as widow. Phillip ap Gruffydd's children adopted their father's Christian name as their permanent patronymic, afterwards borne by all their descendants. The eldest surviving son, Owen Phillips who subscribed his name to Dwnn's pedigree, succeeded to the estate. Described as 'gentleman' his name occurs as a juror in the courts of Great Session from 1611 to 1638, and is included in the muster rolls of the Train Band for Manorowen in 1613. In 1619 and again in 1632, he served as one of the High Constables of the Hundred of Dewsland.

Owen Phillips is thought to have married twice, firstly to Elizabeth, daughter of Thomas ap Owen of Roblinston, and secondly to a Margaret whose parentage has not been discovered. Owen pre-deceased her dying at Trellewelyn in 1638 leaving a considerable personalty, including £323 in cash which his son and heir Thomas, took in charge and 'unjustly detains' from his stepmother, Margaret who instituted an action to recover the money and sued Thomas for dower being namely one-third of 8 messuages, a mill, 18 gardens, 18 orchards and 1250 acres in the parishes of Manorowen, Llanwnda and Fishguard this being the extent of the Trellewelyn estate.

By his wife, Elizabeth, Owen had two children, Thomas and Jane, both born before 1612. Thomas succeeded and married Elen, daughter of Llewelin Harry of Tregwynt, the prenuptial settlement dated 6 November 1636. Thomas Phillips added greatly to the estate and ended his days as an 'esquire'. He was High Sheriff of Pembrokeshire in 1667. Thomas's reputation as a harvester of acres and guineas lingered for many generations and Fenton's *Tour Pembs.* contains this unflattering thumbnail sketch: 'once the residence of a family as noted for their talent for sordidly accumulating wealth as their neighbours were for a liberal circulation of it . . . Thomas Phillips [was] as noted for his avarice as his usury.' By extending the estate so considerably Thomas Phillips raised his family to the ranks of the higher gentry. He was assessed at five hearths in 1670, which suggests that Trellewelyn was of substantial size. He died in 1681 leaving his estate entailed to his eldest son, John Phillips and the 'heirs male of his body for ever, and in default of such issue, to the right heirs of the said John, for ever'. Thomas and Elen had seven children, John, the heir, George, James, Jane who married John Harries of Porthiddy fawr, and whose eldest son, David Harries went to Holland and became friendly with William of Orange in whose train he landed at Torbay in 1688. After the Prince's coronation as King William III, David was appointed Page of the Bedchamber.

The next daughter of Thomas and Elen was Ursula, then Mary, whose descendant Colonel Henry Harding Mathias led the charge of the Gordon Highlanders on the heights of Dargai in 1895; and finally Anne who married William Thomas of Clynfyw and had two sons, Thomas 'an innocent' and John Thomas.

John Phillips the eldest son succeeded; he took part in public life, served as High

Constable of Dewsland 1660/1 and was one of the Justices of the Peace ordered by the Court of Great Sessions in 1691 to issue warrants to search for soldiers' clothing, arms, ammunition and provisions belonging to Their Majesties or any of the officers or soldiers on the ship, *Durham Yard* wrecked near St. Davids, the articles in question having been appropriated by predatory country folk. John Phillips was, like his father, disinclined to part with money even when legally obliged and was sued in the courts for overdue bonds. He married Mary, daughter of the Rev. Evan Owen, an illegitimate son of the antiquary, George Owen of Henllys by Ancret Obilet of Carmarthen. Evan Owen was Chancellor of St. Davids from 1645 till his death in 1662. His brother was George Owen, York Herald at Arms.

John Phillips died in 1706/7 leaving two sons and four daughters; Thomas the eldest son succeeded briefly to the estate, dying without issue in 1709 leaving his estate mainly to his sister Elizabeth. His niece, daughter of his brother Charles challenged the right of her aunt, Elizabeth to the estate but her claim was defeated. Elizabeth married a gentleman described by Francis Jones as 'elusive'; nothing whatsoever is known of him except that he had died by 1729 as she is described in that year as 'Elizabeth Phillips of Trelewellin, widow'. She had three daughters, Martha, Diana and Mary. Elizabeth Phillips died in 1734 leaving all her reality to Martha Phillips, spinster 'who lives with me at Mr. Thomas Rees' house in Haverfordwest, and whom I do hereby own and solemnly declare to be my eldest daughter', and to her heirs forever, provided she did not marry any son of John Thomas of Ystrad, Carmarthenshire. Martha married Sparks Martin of Withybush (q.v.), (see also *Treasury of Historic Pembrokeshire* pp. 197-8), late in 1738 or early in the following year. They had an only child, John who died an infant. Martha predeceased her husband who inherited Trellewelyn. One transaction which is of interest is a lease he granted to William George of Tresinwen on 2 December 1783 of the farm of Rhosycaerau for the lives of lessee, Mary his wife, and their son, David George then aged about three years, at a yearly rent of £10, rendering two couple of fat hens, and providing two persons to make hay at Trellewelyn, and two persons to reap in the corn harvest there yearly. The lessee who signed in a good clear hand, was the great-grandfather of the statesman, Earl Lloyd George of Dwyfor.

Sparks Martin died 1 June 1787 and left the Trellewelyn estate to his youngest sister, Mrs. Elizabeth Phelps, widow, on condition that she took the name and arms of Martin only. The arms were: *Argent* a marten proper, collared *gules* between 2 bars *gules*: crest, a marten. Elizabeth's eldest son, John Phelps served as High Sheriff in 1794 and after his mother's death in 1809, took the name and arms of Martin.

By 1814 the capital messuage of Trellewelyn and other parts of the estate had been sold to the Bowen family of Manorowen. Alas that family were harassed by formidable debts and the estates were sold in 1841 to a member of the Pointz Castle family (q.v.), Dr. Moses Griffith, a retired army surgeon. He was a J.P. and deputy Lieutenant and died unmarried in 1883. He bequeathed the estate to the Rev. Thomas Johns, M.A. (Oxon), vicar of the parish, whose grandson, T. G. V. Johns, T.D., D.L., was the owner in 1978.

Major Jones's notes say 'The old tree-lined drive to the mansion is now cut by a railway line and disused. The present farmhouse is a substantial building but the former residence stood a little distance below in the woods, so I was informed by the owner, Captain T. V. G. Johns, of Manorowen, but no trace remains'. He later revises his opinion by considering that the present building is, in fact, on the site of the old and might even incorporate parts of the original. He also tells us that while visiting J. W. Phillips, solicitor of Portfield House, Haverfordwest, a descendant of the Phillips, he saw a portrait of Martha Martin in the dining room, she was described to him as 'the last of the Trellewelyn family'.

Refs: W & W (H'west) No. 23886; Mudge Map 1819; Tithe Map 1837; Francis Jones unpublished essay on Trellewelyn.

TRELLWYN, *Llanllawer*

Trellwyn Fawr and Fach, about one and a quarter miles east of Llanllawer on the southern slopes of Mynydd Dinas overlooking Cwm Gwaun, marked on Mudge's Map of 1819 and Colby's Map of 1831.

The earliest reference shown is in 1394/95: 'A grant by Howell ap Griffith ap Henry of Trellwyn, Dinas to David Mille, chaplain, of lands in Penrynzovy, Penmonethvawr, and Treflloyn – Dated at Penrynzovy, Tuesday next after the feast of St. Clement the Pope 18 Richard I.' It was the 17th century home of the Lloyd family, descended from the Lloyds of Cilciffeth and Morfil. Morris Lloyd of Trellwyn, living 1613, was foster father of his cousin Thomas Lloyd of Penygegin who later succeeded to Cilciffeth. At one time the Batemans, (descended from the Honeyborough stock), lived here. Life did not always go according to plan, the 'Disposition of Margaret Williams of parish of Dinas, widow, taken at Trewern 20 November 1837, and another, Ellen Young of Nevern, widow, said she was in a place when Mr. Robert Prichard, Bachelor of Divinity, Vicar of Nevern, on 30th October last, when Margaret Williams, widow and Owen Battman of Llanllawer, yeoman, were contracted for matrimony, and they then delivered themselves to give and pledge their troth, and as they were going to church to be married, Thomas Perkin drew the said Margaret away and would not suffer her to be married with Owen Battman'.

In the 1894 Voter's List, Martha Phillips is shown as of Trellwyn fawr and in the 1904 Voter's Lists, James Phillips and David Phillips of Trellwyn fawr are shown as joint owners of land and tenement; the Phillips family still farm there.

Refs: PRO Anc. Deeds, D4932; GGMS I (Gwynfardd); VL 1834, 1894, 1904; Pembs. GS.

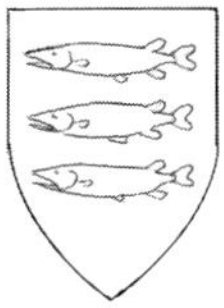

Picton

TRELLYFFA(I)NT, *Nevern*

Home of the Picton family. 'Trellyfain is the mansion howse of Owen Picton as yt hath ben to 3 or 4 of his auncestors before, and in auncient times the landes of Howell ap Jenkin of Nevarne . . . The coate of the Pictons is: *gules* three pikes nayant *argent.'*

Owen Picton was aged seven in 1595. On 16 October 1595 the Queen granted his marriage and wardship to Hugh Lewis, gent. he decided to marry the ward to Elizabeth, daughter of John Symons gent. but the ward declined and entered upon his property which consisted of a carucate in Nevern whereupon Hugh Lewis, in 1612 brought an action against him in Great Sessions to recover £200 damages. Owen Picton was the son of John ap Owen Picton who had married Jenet, daughter of James Philipps of Pentypark. Jenet outlived her husband and applied for administration of her husband's estate in 1587. Owen Picton married twice. Firstly to Mary, daughter of Thomas Young by whom he had one son, and secondly to Elizabeth, daughter of John Bowen by whom he had four sons and seven daughters. Owen Picton died in 1639 when his widow, Elizabeth then living in Newport, applied for administration of his estate.

Fenton writes: '. . . I proceed to Trellyffan . . . to see the figure of a toad, well sculptured in black marble, which is introduced into a chimneypiece and was formerly covered with glass to preserve it from any injury. It is said to have been brought from Italy, the work of a foreign artist. My enquiries as to the date of its introduction here were fruitless, and all I could learn was that it had filled its present station for some centuries . . . Whether the present occupiers of Trellyffant are descendants of the original family, one of whom was the unfortunate victim of Giraldus's account, I cannot pretend to say, but they have lived there for some generations. The respectable clergyman, our companion, The Rev. Mr. Owen, visiting his native county after 21 years, (who traces to the same stock), tells me they bear a toad for their crest . . . He says that if bodily peculiarities are hereditary, then the present proprietors may be descended from Syssyllt Esgair who became a meal for the toads . . . there can be few instances adduced of tallness being continued in a family so long as this, every one of the present as well as the former generation being upward of six feet and even a female of only nineteen years of age nearly as tall'. There was a carving in dark green veined marble about the size of a woman's hand, reputed to have been the work of an Italian artist. This had been brought back from Italy by Sir Richard Mason, Knight of the Green Cloth in the time of James II to his relatives at Trellyffant who bore a toad as their crest. It was exhibited at the Cardigan meeting of the Cambrian Archeological Association in 1859.

The Owens still owned Trellyffant in 1840 with a tenant, William Morris farming 370 acres. In the 1890s the owner was Morris Owen Lloyd Williams of Cwmgloyne who lived at Haverfordwest, but by 1909 it was advertised for sale then worth £28 p.a. in rent. His widow died in 1942 and Francis Jones was unable to trace the whereabouts of the toad.

Refs: George Owen, *2nd Book,* p. 273; Pembs. Plea Rolls 50, 96, 154; WWHR X, 44-5; Fenton, *Tour Pembs.,* p. 295; Timmins, *Nooks Pembs.*, 1895, pp. 155-6 sketch of toad.

TRENEWYDD, *Crunwear*

Home of the Howell family descended from Cadifor Fawr of Blaen Cych. Reginald Howell bought Trenewydd in 1686. Of his sons, John the eldest inherited the estate. He was made a bankrupt and a deed of 15 July 1756 tells us of the Ratification of Release of the real and personal estate of John Howell in return for £2,272; by 1772 John Howells was living in Haverfordwest on an annuity of £70 raised on his estates. He was descended from Howel ap William of Ffynnonwen whose will was proved 1595, and who left two sons, Reynald and William of Llandaf. William had a son John who married his first cousin Elenor. Their son, Reynald Howell purchased Trenewydd, and married the daughter of Arthur Stafford. His will was proved in 1686. His second son, Robert viv. 1702 married Mary, daughter of George Phillips of Waunberri and they had two sons and two daughters. John Howell, the bankrupt was the eldest, and he died without issue in 1795. George Howell the second son, of Haverfordwest, was a surgeon. The elder daughter, Anne, married the Rev. John Phillips, Rector of Talbenny and the other, Margaret, married a surgeon with the splendid name of Essex Devereaux Jones. By 1786 The Rev. John Phillips was the owner, but 60 years later Robert Morgan is described as of Trenewydd. He owned a 7/8ths share in the smack called *The Penelope* and three quarter share in the brig called *The Elizabeth* of Saundersfoot. His descendant, Frances Elizabeth Morgan was born in 1843, was the first woman in Wales to become a doctor and died in Brighton in 1927.

Refs: GGMS (Cadifor Fawr); Pembs. RO SMB/HC/C Nos. 95, 97; Maesgwynne Deeds 200;

TRENEWYDD, *Llanllawer*

In 1586 John Bateman owned this property. He was the second son of Philip Bateman of Honeyborough by his wife Jane, daughter of Sir John Wogan of Wiston. John married Jane, daughter of John ap David ap Gwilym ap Rees of Llystyn in the parish of Nevern. Their eldest son, John succeeded, and married Anne, daughter of John David Walter Jeffrey of Fishguard, viv. 1591. John and Anne had at least three sons, Thomas the eldest succeeded his father whose will was proved in 1609/10. The family steadily declined in the social scale and the last of his line, Price Bateman was a husbandman whose will was proved on 8 July 1745. He left an only daughter, Martha. In more prosperous days the Batemans made alliances with old local families such as the Mortimers of Coedmore, the Wilkins and the Bowens of Trefloyne. The estate was sold in June 1866 then comprising 189 acres with a rent value of £60 per annum and three couples of fat hens at Christmas yearly. David Davies was the surviving tenant with a lease of three lives, aged 71.

Refs: Pembs. GS (GF) 1653; Bronwydd 831; SC June 1866. Pembs. Plea Rolls No. 230.

TRENEWYDD FAWR, *Llanrhian*

A traditional stone farmhouse, the centre of a large dairy farm. Records go back to 1326 when the place was known as Froches or Vrothes. On 9 October 1414 John Stephen of Dewsland, yeoman conveyed two messuages and 32 acres in Vroches in the Hundred of Dewsland, which 'he was seized in fee', to Henry Wogan (d. 1499), of Boulston, Esq. 'The said Henry Wogan, in couson [sic] of a marriage to be had between him and Elizabeth Bowen, one of the sisters of Sir James Bowen of Pentre Evan, and by deed dated 3 June 1415, granted the said lands to use of Henry Wogan for life, remainder to Richard Wogan, (son and heir of said Henry Wogan), and his sons, remainder heirs of said Henry and Elizabeth'. On Henry's death the property descended to said Richard Wogan who afterwards died in 1541, and before his death Sir Richard Wogan of Boulston, son and heir of said Richard Wogan, entered on the lands and demised them to Meilir Lloyd of Dewsland, gent. his then servant, to be held at will, who was then appointed Sir John Wogan's reeve, bailiff or rent gatherer in the Hundred of Dewsland. The said Meilir rendered several accounts for Vroches at yearly rent of 14s. 4d., and duties and services. Meilir died so possessed, and his son and heir Rowland Lloyd continued in the office of rent gatherer to Sir John Wogan and paid him the small rent of 13s. 4d. and other duties for the said premises. Sir John Wogan died and was succeeded by his son and heir, Sir John Wogan of Boulston and he allowed Rowland Lloyd to continue the office and possession of the premises. Rowland Lloyd then died and his base son Robert Lloyd, together with Morris Howell, both of Llanreithan parish, 'by colour of having by casual and indirect means gotten into their hands the ancient entail made by Henry Wogan Esq. and other deeds, and on 17 August James I, (1619), entered on Vroches and expelled Sir John Wogan's tenants therefrom'.

Rowland Lloyd died in 1610 leaving four or five base children by two different mothers, Harry and Thomas, who succeeded to Trenewydd Fawr, and Mary, Sage and Robert by another mother. Rowland's wife, Anne, daughter of Lewis Powell of Pembroke apparently died without issue. The Lloyds continued at Trenewydd until the mid 19th century when the direct line tailed out with the daughters of William Samuel Lloyd (d. 1876), and Mary his wife, daughter of John Williams of Treyarched. They were of Tyllwyd and Longhouse, William's father Thomas (d. 1815), apparently being the last of the family to farm at Trenewydd. William and Mary died leaving two co-heiresses Mary Anne who married Henry Thomas of Lochturffin, and who had a son, Lloyd Thomas of Lochturffin and a daughter, Anna who married V. J. G. Johns of Manorowen; and Letitia who married the Rev. William Morris Lewis of Hendre. The Land Tax records of 1786 show that Barrett Bowen Jordan Esq. was the owner of Trenewydd with Samuel Lloyd tenant paying £2 4s. 8¼d. By 1842 John Hill Harris owned Trenewydd and it was occupied by James Morgan farming 337 acres.

In 1975 the owner-occupier was George Richards and his son Morgan. In 1982 Trenewydd Fawr was on the market with 365 acres. The farmhouse is described as 'traditional' and has two reception rooms and five bedrooms.

Refs: Chancery Proc. Jas I. H31, No. 18. 16 Nov. 1620; TM 1842; GGMS (Gwynfardd); *Dwnn,* i, p. 109; LT 1786; Pembs. GS; Pembs. Plea Rolls.

TRENEWYDD MANOR, *Llanwnda*

Built on a slope overlooking the unspoilt coastline of Pencaer in North Pembrokeshire, Trenewydd is one of the oldest homesteads in the district. On high ground above the house are the remains of a large prehistoric fort and the memorials of local chieftains of pre-Christian days. Below are the ramparts of Castell Cleddyf, (Castle of the Sword), and the holy well of Sant Degan, while on the cliff edge above St. George's Channel is an inscribed stone commemorating the last invasion of Britain by the French in 1797.

A short tree and shrub lined drive leads to the property from the district road and sweeps around a central lawn. There is a walled garden and, prior to the sale in 1985, an attractive stable block and farm buildings now partially converted into dwellings. The house dates from circa 1500 and has been extended and improved over the centuries, resulting in its present

graceful appearance. The house includes some different styles of architecture and intricate plaster work. A novel feature is the guard goose house in a back passage, a relict of medieval days and the old wooden salting table nearby. The house retains it simne fawr and has oak beamed rooms from successive periods.

Trenewydd was a large farm from Elizabethan days, home of successive yeoman families. During the 17th century it was occupied by the family of Hughes, followed in the early 18th century by that of John, and some fifty years later by the Reeds. Before 1830 it had passed to the ownership of the landowning family of James of Trefelgarn, St. Nicholas parish whose descendants continued there until recently. Georgiana Margaret, daughter of J. C. Yorke, who married firstly, Hugh Mortimer Thomas from Cwrt, Llanllawer, and secondly Herbert David Johns, M.C., a cousin of Graham Johns of Manorowen and the Perkins of Penysgwarne, lived there. On her death she left the house to her daughter by her first marriage, Katherine Anne Royston Brown who lived there until 1985 when the house, coach house and buildings were sold in separate lots.

Refs: Francis Jones Archives; VL 1834, 1894; LT 1786; Pembs. Plea Rolls; Mrs. A. Eastham.

TRENICHOL, *Llandeloy*

Early references to 'Trenicol' show that originally the property consisted of two holdings, Ucha (Upper) and Isha (Lower), a small part of which was owned by the Bowen family of Lochmeyler. The root of title seems to stem from a grant made on 8 January 1539 when the then owner, Margaret Jenkin, conveyed lands in 'Treffnycholl and Treffnychol Isha', Rhosbreydeth, Llanvirn Eynon, and 'Trefveyer' (perhaps Treiva) in the lordship of Pebidiauk, to Elizabeth, daughter of Nicholas ab Owen, a younger son of Lochmeyler. From Elizabeth, the lands passed to her uncle, her father's eldest brother, Richard Bowen.

In 1545 Richard Bowen of Lochmeyler and his wife, Elizabeth (Wogan) brought an action in the Great Sessions against Henry ab Owen of 'Treffenicoll' concerning a messuage and sixteen acres at 'Clyn Mough', (now called Clyn Moch). Richard died on 1 August 1560, leaving by his 2nd wife, Margaret, an only child and heiress, Catherine Bowen. On 24 August following her father's death, the heiress assigned certain lands, which included part of Trenicol, to her mother who was to enjoy them as dower. On 20 December 1563 the widow married at Llandeloy church to Thomas Scourfield of the New Moat family, and on 20 May 1564 they leased lands at Trenichol, comprising ten acres, to James Peter of Portheiddy Fach, for the lives of grantors. Thomas Scourfield died on 20 July 1568, and Margaret then married a third husband, Jenkin Read. In 1596, William James Peter, (son and heir of the lessee of 1564), sued Jenkin Read(e) of Lochmeyler, gentleman, and his labourer Richard David, for £10 for forcible entry and depasturing at Trenicholl Ysha. On 18 August 1598, Margaret and Jenkin Read granted a lease for five years of a toft and twenty-four acres in Trenichol Ysha to Rice ab Ievan described as of Trenicholl Yssa, yeoman. Thus at this time holdings in Trenichol were held by two leaseholders – William James Peter and Rice ab Ievan, (also called Rees Ievan). The said Rice died about 2 January 1602/3 when he made his will, in which he mentions personal possessions including 'my goods and chattels at Trenicholl'.

In the meantime Catherine Bowen, heiress of the Lochmeyler estate, had married John Scourfield of Moat, by whom she had issue. Catherine died on 16 October 1608, her husband in 1610, and Lochmeyler passed to their son and heir William Scourfield. The thrice-married Margaret granted all her interest in the lands at Trenicholl Issa to her grandson, the said William Scourfield, on 12 September 1610. This transaction led to trouble. One John David, occupier of the ten acres at Trenichol Issa, alleged that they had been held in fee by James Peter, on whose decease, they passed to his son and heir, William James Peter. By a trust deed W. J. Peter settled the said acres on himself for life, then to his son and heir James William for ever. After W. J. Peter's death at Trenichol, John William demised the said acres to John David, whereupon William Scourfield of Lochmeyler ejected John David from the property. Accordingly, the aggrieved John instituted an action in the Great Sessions against Scourfield. Unfortunately the verdict is not recorded, but it seems clear that Scourfield was successful, for the list of his possessions compiled in 1622, following his death, includes 'a messuage and certain acres of lands in Trenicholl'.

From the foregoing it would appear that part of Trenicholl Issa was held by the Lochmeyler family, and the other part of that messuage as well as Trenicholl Ucha, the Porthiddy family. In September 1605 William James Peter's estate consisted of sixteen messuages, sixteen barns, sixteen gardens, eight orchards, and 1,720 acres in Trenicholl Isha and Ucha, Trevraneth, Llandeney, Llanreithan, Llandelwy, Porthiddy Vawr and Vach, Llanrhian, Trevatkoone, Trebredith, Treffynnon, Treyskaw, Trevoch-lloyd, Tregiwy and Llanhowell. After W. J. Peter's will had been proved in 1610 the estate devolved upon his eldest son, James Williams, gentleman, who had moved to St. Mary's parish, Haverfordwest. In September 1612, James Williams came to an arrangement with his younger brother, Thomas James, (it was not unusual in those days for brothers to bear different surnames), to break the entail on the estate which consisted of the properties described in 1605.

Thomas James signed the family pedigree recorded by Lewys Dwnn in 1613, and five years later served as Under-Sheriff of Pembrokeshire. By his wife, Ursula daughter of Hugh Garnons of Trefin, he had three sons and two daughters. However the paternal estate, or the bulk of it remained in the hands of his elder brother, James Williams of Haverfordwest, on whose death it passed to his only son, William Williams.

William died leaving an only child and heiress, Priscilla Williams. She married one John Hagley, and in September 1633 she and her husband were concerned with Edward Penford and Gilbert Hill in a transaction, probably to break the entail of the estate, then described as consisting of seventeen messuages, sixteen barns, seventeen gardens, eight orchards and 1,776 acres in those properties specified in the deeds of 1605 and 1612 already mentioned. In 1634 James Griffith, gent. was concerned with John and Priscilla Hagley, Thomas and Ursula James and their son, Richard Thomas James, gent. in making a conveyance of four messuages, four tofts, four gardens and 180 acres in Llandeloy parish – probably this represents Trenichol. The acreage may have been expressed in customary (Welsh) rather than statute measure, such being the custom in the Dewsland Hundred. Towards the middle of the 17th century the two messuages of Ucha and Issa were united to form one farm, known as Trenichol only.

About this time the tenant, John Charles had married Joan, daughter of Robert John of Cerbyd in neighbouring Llanhowel parish, and they were living at Trenichol in 1625. Their son, Thomas Charles married one Ursula Williams, but he had left Trenichol before 1670, and 13 years later was described as of Whitchurch parish, gent.

In 1640 Trenichol was the home of the vicar of Llandeloy, and in March of that year Henry Brett sued the Rev. John Phillipps of Trenickoll, clerk, for £200 due on a bond. By 1686 the property had passed to the ownership of the Allen family of Gelliswick, who granted the farm called 'Trenichol in Dewsland in the parishes of Llandeloy and Llanreithan', (then in tenure of Rees James and Stephen Harries), and two adjacent pieces of land comprising eight acres (formerly bought from Arthur Langharne, Esq.) to John Allen of Goodhook and William Skyrme of Llawhaden, on trust for the use of Daniel Poyer and his wife Priscilla, (daughter of the said William Allen) and their issue. The two adjacent pieces are described as bounded on the east by Llanreithan lands, on the west by Trenichol lands, and on the south by a stream. This clearly formed part of the marriage settlement on Priscilla.

From Daniel Poyer, it passed to his son John Poyer of Grove near Narberth. John married

Anne, daughter and heiress of Griffith Twyning of Parke in Henllan Argoed, and under the post-nuptial settlement made in 1724, Poyer settled the Grove estate and other lands including Trenichol, on his wife and his children. By will dated 20 May 1737 Poyer bequeathed Trenichol and £100 to his third son Richard Poyer when he attained the age of 21 years. The said Richard Poyer, a surgeon, lived in Pembroke where he died unmarried, leaving by will dated 25 September 1763, 'my estate called "Trenecole" to his sister Jane Poyer. Jane, who lived at Merrixton, also died unmarried, and by her will dated 10 May 1771 left Trenichol to her mother Mrs. Anne Poyer for life, with remainder to testatrix's sister Anne, wife of William Callen of Merrixton.

William and Anne Callen died in 1793 and 1808 respectively, and the property passed to their eldest son John Callen who died unmarried in 1822 and was succeeded by his next brother Charles Callen. From Charles Callen, (d. 1849), Trenichol passed to his son, Daniel Poyer Callen, (d. 1849) whose daughter Katherine married John Lennox Griffith Poyer Lewis of Henllan, Llanddewi Velfrey, and they died without issue in 1881 and 1886 respectively. The Henllan estate, which included Trenichol, then passed to J. L. G. P. Lewis's brother, the Rev. Richard Lewis, (later Bishop of Llandaff), from whom it descended in direct line to Mr. Richard Lewis, J.P., of Caermaenau Fawr who sold Trenichol.

Thus far we have considered the ownership of Trenichol, and in passing noted references to a few tenants who have not remained there for any appreciable length of time. However shortly after the middle of the 17th century we find there a family which became more stable even than the owners, holding the tenancy for nine generations, a period of some 270 years, one of the few farming families in Pembrokeshire to have sustained an unbroken tenancy for so long a period. It is this family that now engages our attention.

To trace the origin of a family surnamed Harries in Pembrokeshire is one of the most exacting, occasionally exasperating, of genealogical exercises. The name was widespread, particularly in Dewsland, and the general assumption that those bearing it derived from a common source, is demonstrably inaccurate. After the accession of Henry Tudor in 1485 the Christian name Henry or Harry became popular among Welsh folk, and when in course of the 16th and 17th centuries permanent surnames were adopted, large numbers became known as Harry which later developed into the standard form of Harries. Dewsland produced a flourishing crop of families so surnamed, for example, at Abercastle, Benchurn, Brimaston, Cruglas, Eweston, Felindre (Llanrhian), Hayscastle, Llanwngar, Llanunwas, Porthiddy, Priskilly, Treginnis, Trenichol and Tregwynt, many of whom traced to minor gentry stocks, yeomen and farmers.

The earliest known member of the family at Trenichol was John Harry(ies) who was assessed for one hearth in the taxation of 1670. John Harries and Lettice his wife had two children, namely Stephen who succeeded to Trenichol and Lettice who married William Griffith of Hendre, Llandeloy. Stephen served as High Constable of the Hundred of Dewsland three times in 1705, 1706 and 1707. Nothing is known of his wife except her name, Catherine, but she bore him two sons and three daughters, Stephen, William, Anne, Rebecca and Elizabeth. Stephen died in 1720 leaving his son, also Stephen to succeed. Stephen seems to have encountered difficulties, for at the Great Sessions of 1732 he described himself as 'a poor prisoner in Haverfordwest Gaol' having been imprisoned for a debt of £20 at the suit of Samuel Harries of Cruglas. Matters seems to have been resolved for two years later Stephen was Bailiff of Dewsland, subject to sureties in £200 for his faithful performance of duty put up by three gentlemen of his acquaintance. Further difficulties awaited him as while conducting one John Lewis to gaol the prisoner broke away and the sureties were liable to pay forfeiture for the bailiff's failure. His brother William took over the lease of Trenichol on 9 February 1733/4 which was then owned by John Poyer of Grove. The rent was £20 p.a., rendering 4 Winchester strikes of malt, 8 Winchester strikes of oats, 4 couple of hens and 2 fat geese at Christmas yearly, paying all taxes and rates on the property, not to cut any timber or to assign or transfer the lease without the landlord's permission. William Harries helped to promote the new chapel built at Trefgarn Owen in 1743 for Independants. He died in 1745 leaving a widow, Magdalen and five children, namely William, James, Dorothy, Martha and Elizabeth. James Harries of Trenichol made a will on 4 September 1823 and died in 1829, leaving a lease of Trenichol to his wife with remainder to his children Joseph, Thomas, George, Mary and John and £25 to his son, William.

By 1836 the five Harries brothers, sons of James Harries and known still as 'Y Pump Brawd' farmed the largest farms in the district, Trenichol, Lochmeyler, Castle Villa, Trewilym and Tredduog, all contiguous totalling some 1,400 acres. A letter in *The Welshman* of that year commented on the fact saying that 'they are men of good morals, real Reformers, and respected by all who know them'. The youngest son, John farmed Trenichol; he was baptised on 8 February 1811. By now the family had acquired several freeholds, and in 1832 having come of age he joined his four brothers and sister Mary, and the family trustee, in conveying their moiety of Cerbyd and Cerbyd Mill to William Meyler of Caerforiog, gentleman for £1,530. He married Elizabeth Owen and had by her three children, James, William and Mary Anne. His married life was brief for he died aged 27 and was buried at Llandeloy. James succeeded to the tenancy of Trenichol comprising of 232 acres. James Owen Harries was born 29 March 1833, married Martha Devonald of Welsh Hook and had five children, namely Arthur, John, Letitia, Jane and Hannah her twin. Arthur had a fine tenor voice, was a winner of several prizes at Eisfeddfodau and died unmarried in 1941. He was the last of the family in the direct male line to live at Trenichol.

The *Pembroke Telegraph* for 2 December 1943 records a funeral in St. Brynach's churchyard, Dinas, of John Harries, son of the Trenichol family and described as a 'sportsman and follower of hounds'.

Refs: Francis Jones unpublished essay 'Trenichol'.

TREPRISK, TRE-PRYSG, *Moylgrove*

George Owen wrote: '. . . the mansion house of Mr. John Bradshawe is by him newly built. It was in auncient tyme the inheritance of Phillip ap David whose son Griffith Philip had issue Owen ap Griffith who sold it and his other landes to John Bradshawe of St. Dogmaels Esq. who gave it to this John Bradshawe as a younger son's portion'. In the Pembrokeshire Plea Rolls of 1584 John Bradshawe, gent. is described as 'of Treprisk'.

There is no further information about the house or its owners until 1793 when Thomas James the elder is of Treprisk. He married Jane Pryse of Blaendyffryn, Cardiganshire. She was a widow when she died in 1793 and bequeathed Treprisk to her three sons, Thomas, William and Edward. Thomas appears to have died without issue and Treprisk had passed to William James by 1798. He married and had two sons, William and David and a daughter. William, the heir, was of Treprisk following his father's death. His will was dated 26 April 1830 and proved in the following year. Jane, his widow released her life interest to her son, William James in April 1835 for £50 and an annuity of £50. William James the son was alive in 1850. The Voter's List of 1894 tells us that John Havard was the tenant of Treprisk and by 1904 James Williams Williams of Cambray House, The Parade, Carmarthen, owned the freehold of the house and land of Treprisk.

Refs: George Owen, *2nd Book,* p. 268; VL 1894, 1904; Morgan-Richardson Deeds, ii, 517; ibid. 553 No. 2695; ibid. 470; ibid. 458, 477, 510; ibid. 506 No. 2158; BM Egerton 2586; Pembs. Plea Rolls No. 48; Francis Jones, *Historic Cardiganshire Homes and their Families.*

TREREES, TRERHYS, *St. Dogmaels**

Home of the Lloyd family descended from Rhys ap Robert ap Gwrwared. The first Lloyd at Trerees was Thomas, the second son of John Lloyd of Hendre and Jane of Pantyrhys, Cardiganshire. Thomas had one son John who married Jane, daughter of Thomas Warren of Trewern, and two daughters.

The earliest reference given was in 1362 in a grant of lands 'in the meadow near the well of Tref Reys, *(iuxta fonte tref Reys),* and a piece of land near Godyr gwefn in the fee of Cassia abbatsis Saneti Dogmaels in the fy of Kemmeys'. The free tenant of Trerees in 1586/7, Ieuan ap Rees, was presented for keeping 'unringed swine on land at Trekernew'. He was in trouble again in 1607 when he was summoned for trespassing on the land of Robert Morris, called Berth y Parrad, in the parish of 'Moilgrove' and taking away furze at a value of 40/-. A plan of Trerees farm dated November 1856 was drawn by Thomas Tamlyn, surveyor, showing it to comprise 111 acres 2 rods and 27 perches.

Refs: Pembs. RO DB/13/41; Rees CR; Bronwydd Deeds No. 1333; VL 1834; Protheroe IV fo. 101; Wagner MS 2; GGMS (Gwynfardd), p.10.

TRERHOS, *also called* PATRICKSFORD, *St. Lawrence*

Patricksford alias Trerhos was a lay manor in 1587. In the 16th century William Llewelin 'a blind man dwelled at Trerose in S. Lawrens . . .'.

On 26 December 1719 a prenuptial settlement of William Allen, the younger, and Martha, daughter of Martha Fowler, widow, of Haverfordwest, and mother of Hugh Fowler, described lands in 'St. Issells, Reynaldston, Hayscastle, three messuages and land in the townred of Trerose, messuage and land called Bonner, moiety of a water corn mill called Stone Hall Mill, in St. Lawrence, Goorid in St. Davids, messuage and land at Solva, and a messuage and land called Half Ploughland in Hubberston with a corn grist mill and brew house lately built on it, and a one third of a messuage and land called John Webb's Tenement in Llanstadwell'.

On 28 May 1748 John Allen of Gelliswick, Esq. and Mary his wife gave a lease to David Morse of Trerhos, of the messuage and land called Pen Issa yr Dref in Trerhos, for lives of lease and of Thomas and David Morse the two sons of Joseph Morse of Brimaston Hall, yeoman at £17 p.a. On 13 April 1757 John Allen granted a lease for three lives to David Morse of St. Lawrence parish of a moiety of a tenement in Trerhose townred, formerly leased to Thomas Morse, (grandfather of said David Morse), and he was still there in 1792.

In 1873 the Edwardes family of Sealyham (q.v.) owned Trerhos with James Harries, tenant farming 127 acres paying rent of £58 p.a. John Harries was the tenant in 1904.

Refs: VL 1834, 1894; Pembs. RO D/LP/ No. 5/28; ibid. DB/13. No. 108; ibid. D/EE/2; Landowners' Return 1873; BM Egerton MS 2586, fo. 323; Pembs. Plea Rolls 181; NLW, Morgan-Richardson Deeds No. 2042.

TRERICKERT (RICKARDSTON), TREICERT, *Nevern*

George Owen tells us in his *2nd Book* that 'Ricardston being of late the mansion house of the Bowens of that place was, as I finde in auncient wryttinges called Hoodes town of the Hoodes the first owner thereof, for this was the auncient inherytaunce of Lucas de Hoda . . . [who] having lost Bury and other landes were forced to take this Ricardston and Jordenson, being a village next adjoyninge, for his mansion place; which Lucas de Hoda had yssue ii sonnes Ricard and Jorden, who, partinge their father's patrimonie betweene them called each part after their owne names: Ricard de Hoda callinge his parte Ricardston and Jorden Jordenston, which names contynue to this day. Ricardston contynued in the name of Hoode untyl it descended unto one Perkyn Hoode, the particulare descendes I cannot lay downe, thie Perkyn had yssue Llewellyn, father to Griffith . . . (his) one daughter maried a gentleman of Cardigan sheere called David ap Owen ap Meredidd of Corrws in Iskoed whose daughter and coheire Dythgy maryed Matheas ap Bowen third brother to Sir James Bowen of Pentre Ievan, Knight, whose sonne Owen ap Mathias ap Owen was father to Morgan, father to Rees whose yssue being extinct the inheritance fell to his iii sisters: Agnes wieffe to John Owen Phillipes Esquier; Alison wieffe to William Owen; Margaret wieffe to John Phillips, younger . . . between which sisters and their heires at this instant there is no small trouble for the quartering of this house and demeisne, and great sommes of money allreadie spent.' Dwnn tells us that Lucas Hood 'a Frank by birth', was followed by his son Rickart ap Luwlas Hood who married Alice, daughter and heiress of Nicholas ap Sir William Martin. Their son Philip ap Rickart married Nest, daughter of Llewelyn ap Rhydderch ap Meredith of Henllys ap Owen ap Gruffydd ap Rhys ap Tewdur. Their son was Philip Fychan of Henllys.

About 1528 William Owen brought an action against William Bowen of Ricardston for stealing legal documents from Henllys, and that he oftentimes had enticed one of Owen's maid servants, called Christian 'with whom he was very familiar', to carry away evidence from her master's house.

By 1578 William Gwyn, a bitter enemy of George Owen was in possession of Ricardston and in 1579 there was a suit, regarding the wardship of Elizabeth, only daughter of Rees Morgan Bowen and an attempt was made by the Gwyns to abduct the ward. Rees Morgan had died in 1577 leaving Elizabeth his daughter and sole heiress '. . . after whose decease the whole inheritance of the above named Rees Morgan her father, was enjoyed by John ap Owen . . . uncle to the foresaid Rees by force of some fraudulent estate, which inheritance, after great expenses in law, was recovered by the sisters of the said Rees, being his next heirs whose issue enjoy most part of the said inheritance'. Elizabeth Owen died in 1587. 'Elizabeth sole child and heiress of said Rees (Bowen) was but a month old at her father's death, and died a virgin, (ye greatest fortune in her time in ye whole county of Pembrock being ye valued to be worth five thousand pounds), 15 December 1587, whereby her said Aunts, ye sisters of ye said Rees Bowen came to be heirs to her ample and large possessions, and the said John Owen in ye right of his mother was intitled to six tenements in Meliney parish, four in Nevarn, two in Bayvil, two in Eglosserow, two in Monachcloddy, five in Llanfyrnach, five in Penrith parish, three in Clydey, two tenements and a burgage in St. Dogmells, two in Llanychlloiddog, and one in Manclohogg, ye lordship of Monington, wich in all amounts to 36 tenements in Kemes over ye above 14 burgages and two closes in Cardigan, Tregibby and Haledare in Verwich and Penyralt in Langoedmore, being 19 more.'

In 1589 Henry Stedman is shown as of Richardstowne, near Newport, gent., in the Plea Rolls. In the 1786 Land Tax list, Mrs. Hay is owner with David Harry, tenant assessed at 1s. 2d.

In 1840 Anne Evans was owner, with John Evans the tenant farming 148 acres.

Refs: Protheroe IV, GWG fo. 105; Tith Map Nevern ph. 1840; BM, Egerton MS 2586 fo. 288; *Dwnn,* i, pp. 166, 175, 311; LT 1786; George Owen, *2nd Book,* p. 272.

TRESEISSYLLT, TRESISSLLT, *Granston*
Home of the Griffith and Harries (Vide Tregwynt) families. Its original name was Tresissyllt ap Cynrig and was a Knight's Fee in 1326. In the *Black Book of St. Davids* 1326 it is detailed: 'Ievan ap Moylmoroa, Orweyn ap Morice and their co-tenants hold two carucates at Trefseysilk in episicopal manor of Villa Grandi: note that the Lord bought at Trefseyssell a certain liberty called 'Hauancia' that is from 6½ bovates formerly of Mawr ap Ithel, from which was a customary rent to be paid to the Lord at Pentecost of a 1d. and one needle. Llewelin ap Kedivor and his co-tenants hold at Trefseysil one carucate, and pay yearly at Michaelmas 4½d. and 1lb. of wax and do services.'

In 1578 William Griffith of Tresissllt married Anne, daughter of John Scourfield of Moat and had issue: John, James and David. In the following century members of the Phillips, Lewis and Scourfield families had interests in the property. The IPM of William Scourfield of New Moat, taken 10 August 1622 shows that he owned a messuage and lands in Trecysillt and Penyrhiw Vach and Llanwnda parish, a messuage and lands at Goodigg in the same parish, held of John Owen, gent. in free socage as of his manor of Trecycillt.

John Harries was assessed for tax on Treseissyllt in 1786. The family still owned it in 1839 but it was let to Samuel Thomas who had inherited the lease from his father, farmer John Thomas who died in 1813. In his will, proved at Carmarthen 28 February 1814 and sworn under £1,000, he leaves: 'To my eldest son, James Thomas, my lease of Tregydd, and stock on it. To my eldest daughter, Pheby Thomas, now living with said James Thomas, £200, maintenance and choice of best bed at Tregydd, furniture, blankets, etc., and a horse. To my wife, Lettice and my son, Samuel Thomas, joint executors, all stock etc. at Tresissillt, lease of Tresissillt and mill under the late George Harries of Priskilly, Esq. dated 12 November 1803, being a lease for lives of John

Thomas, Samuel Thomas, and Mary Thomas: and another lease of tithes of Tresissillt from George Harries of Tregwynt, Esq. for three lives. To my son, James Thomas £400, choice of best horse, and maintenance at Tresissillt. To my eldest daughter Pheby Thomas £50 from Tresissillt. To my daughter. Mary Thomas £300, a horse, chest, blankets etc., and maintenance, a horse and saddle, while she is unmarried at Tresissillt, and also my part of the good sloop *Endeavour.*'

In 1862 the Rev. Henry Davies is described as 'of Tresissillt' He was married to Samuel's sister Mary, Samuel having died unmarried and intestate. In the will of Rev. Henry Davies, he left his personalty to his wife Mary Davies. 'To trustees of Harmony Baptist Chapel, Llanwnda, £400, the yearly interest to go to the ministry of that chapel of £300 and the interest of the remaining £100 towards carrying on a day school in connection with that chapel. To treasurers of Baptist college at Llangollen in North Wales, and to Treasurer of Baptist College, Delhi, India, £100 apiece. To trustees of Hill Park Baptist Chapel, Haverfordwest, £50.' In 1904 David Harries Bowen was in possession.

Refs: Francis Jones, 'Lay Manors of Dewsland'; Chaldecot Deeds & Docs; Tithe Map 1839 Granston ph; LT 1786; Pembs. Plea Rolls No. 149; Protheroe MS IV, fo. 103; *Black Book of St. Davids,* 1326; *Villa Grandi,* pp. 93, 95; Taylor's *Cussion,* 97a; WWHR IX, p. 153.

TRETIO FAWR, *St. Davids**

Arnold Jones, fourth son of William Jones of Brawdy and Mary Warren his wife, was of Tretio. He was High Sheriff of Dewsland in 1605 and still alive in 1616. He married a daughter of Morris Wogan of Stone Hall, and had a son, Henry Jones of Penbiri (Penberry).

Refs: Pembs. Plea Rolls, Nos. 92, 103, 141, 146; Protheroe MS IV, fo. 150.

TREVACCOON, *also* **TREFACCWN,** *Llanrhian*

Home of the Perkin, Harding, Propert and Harries families. In the second half of the 17th century the Perkin family lived at Trevaccoon. It was not then a large house, for David Perkin, gent. was assessed at only two hearths for taxation in 1670. His wife, Elizabeth, was the daughter of David Harries of Porthiddy Fawr by Grace Jones of Brawdy, by whom he had six children. His will was proved on 26 July 1694. The children were: 1. John Perkin who succeeded to Trevaccoon. (In 1695 he married Mary, eldest daughter of George Williams of Treyarched, by whom he had an only child, Dorothy Perkin. John Perkin's will was proved in 1708); 2. Grace Perkin; 3. Mary Perkin who was alive in 1694; 4. Elinor Perkin who married Thomas Rees of Mathry parish, by whom she had two sons, John and George Rees, both living in 1694; 5. A daughter who married Thomas Meyler of St. Nicholas parish; 6. A daughter who married William Harry of St. Nicholas parish, by whom she had a daughter, Elizabeth Harry living in 1694.

How Trevaccoon passed to the next owners, the Hardings, is not known. It is not unlikely that John Perkin's daughter Dorothy married Richard Harding who was living at Trevaccoon before 1728. The Hardings came from the Castleblythe/Puncheston/Little Newcastle area. Thomas Harding of Longhook, Castlebythe parish was assessed for two hearths in 1670; he died in 1697, the inventory of his goods taken on 6 October 1697. He left a son, Morris Harding. The Hardings owned Trevaccoon before 7 May 1728 when David Harding of Puncheston made his will. Among the relations he names is 'my niece Grace Harding, daughter of my brother Richard Harding of Trevackwn, gentleman'. Grace was the only child and on her father's death, inherited Trevaccoon. On 9 May 1730 she married the Rev. Propert son of David Propert of Trevigan, by whom she had two children, Richard, and Elizabeth Propert who married John Harries of Cryglas on 4 August 1756. When Richard died in his father's lifetime without issue in 1762, Trevaccoon passed to his sister, and remained in their descendants, the Harrieses until it was sold in the 20th century. The late Mr. Francis Green (whose mother was a Harries of Cryglas and Trevaccoon), once told me that there was a tradition that one of the Hardings ploughed up a 'rich treasure' in a field on Porthiddy land, afterwards known as 'Parc Harding'.

After it passed to the Properts and the Harrieses, the house was enlarged and improved, and according to a tradition that Francis Green had heard, one of the Properts, who was somewhat eccentric had a high scaffolding built in one of the rooms, on which he laid on his back for several weeks while painting a map of the world on the ceiling. Samuel Harries, (1759-1839) son of Elizabeth (Propert) and John Harries, built kennels and kept a pack of hounds. A choleric individual he was forced to resign from the Commissioners of the Peace in 1833. In 1835 his opponent, John Hill Harries of Priskilly wrote a letter decrying Samuel Harries and saying that it took three generations to make a gentleman. Samuel Harries married Mary, daughter of Thomas Williams of Popehill and their son and heir, John Harries, succeeded to Trevaccoon. He was High Sheriff in 1846. His wife Martha lived at Trevaccoon until her death in 1872 aged 76. After her death Trevaccoon was let to tenants. The estate was managed by agents until 1919 when it was sold. John and Martha's son George Harries, born 1818, bought Rickeston and Robeston Wathen and died in 1897.

A detailed list of repairs required at the house round about the year 1900 mentions the 'new building' and the 'old building' and the descriptions enable us to identify the parts in the present house which is an amalgam of the two. The Sale notice in 1905 mentions that there was a Drawing Room, two Sitting Rooms, Dining Room, Library, Entrance Hall and

staircase, 12 bedrooms and two dressing rooms and numerous kitchens, pantries and outbuildings. There was a walled garden and farming was carried out on a large scale. In 1921 'Trefaccwn' was advertised for sale. It then comprised nine bedrooms and five acres.

Refs: Unpublished notes for an essay from Francis Jones Archives; SC613 Carms. RO; ibid. SC 456; WWHR viii, p. 134; Pembs.Plea Rolls No. 11; ibid. Nos. 16, 37, 55, 62; VL 1834; Picton Castle Deeds; RO DB/13/111; LT 1786; Trant Deeds.

TREWALTER LWYD,
TREWALLTER LWYD, *Mathry*

In 1654 John Williams obtained a mortgage on this property of £25 which was not redeemed until 1675. In 1703 Lewis Mathias gent. leased Trewalter Lwyd to George Williams for 99 years at £5 p.a. and two couple of pullets at Shrovetide.

On 1 March 1727 James Williams of Treyarched, gent. granted a lease to Richard Reed of parish of Mathry, carpenter of Walterston, otherwise Trewallter, (now in possession of Samuel Williams, leaseholder), for 21 years at £10 p.a. and eight hens at Candlemas. On 3rd May, 1751 Francis Skyrme of Llawhaden, Esq. released to Bridget James of the parish of St. Edrins, spinster, for £125, Trewallter Llwyd in the parish of Mathry, (late in tenancy of James Williams, gent.), in as large a manner as the same was purchased from Lewis Mathias late of Llangwarren by James Skyrme deceased, father of the said Francis Skyrme. Bridget James married William Higgon of Spittle, and in 1759 they sold Bridget's share in Trewalter Llwyd.

In 1787 Lord Kensington leased a house and garden and ten pieces, (two acres, two stangs, 20 yards) of Trewallter Llwyd to Dorothy

Williams of Treyarched, widow for 21 years at 20/- p.a. rent. In the late 19th century this house was the home of Thomas Charles, father of Joseph John Charles who was the father of Ethel Charles, wife of Major Francis Jones.

Refs: W & W (H'west), Nos. 8484, 8485, 8486, 8487-8, 8490, 8491, 8493; LT 1786; Tithe Map Mathry ph. 1842; VL 1894.

TREWALLTERWEN, TREWALTERWEN, *St. Edrins*

Named after one of its early owners, Trewalter in St. Edrins parish acquired the addition of *wen* (white, fair), to distinguish it from Trewalter-lwyd (holy, grey) in the neighbouring parish of Mathry, and in some documents the name is given its English counterpart, Walterston. Of the eponymous Gwalter or Wallter, nothing is known. Standing on a wooded slope to the south of the parish church, the house as it is today presents no features that would elevate it above an ordinary farm house. The name of the earliest known owner, Thomas Meyler, appears in the Lay Subsidy of 1543. His son, John Meyler, married Anne, daughter of William Scourfield of Castle Villa, and by the prenuptial settlement made on 17 July 1573, the bridegroom settled his 'capital mansion' of Trewalter, a meadow in Tredduog, and Williamston, to the uses of the marriage. They had six children, Hugh, John the elder, John the younger, William, Margaret and Jane, all of whom were named in their father's will proved in 1611. Few references have been found to subsequent owners, but it seems possible that at some stage it formed part of the estate of the Wogans of Stone Hall. During the 17th century it became the home of Rees James, who also held Lochmeyler, and continued in his descendants until James James sold the estate to George Parry of Haverfordwest in 1815. It was subsequently the home of farmers like William Walters, living there in 1834 under a lease for life, and the Beynons who farmed Harglodd and Penbiri in St. Davids.

A tale is told of James James who had been ailing and infirm and hardly able to walk. However he insisted on going to see his reapers in the fields. On 15 September 1789 he set out as usual but was later found dead in a field. At the inquest the verdict was that he had 'died of his infirmities by visitation of God'. James had married Anna Louisa Maria, daughter of John Philipps Laugharne by whom he had an only child Anna Maria Cordelia, married to John Entwisle Peel of Haverfordwest. The estate was sold in 1831 and afterwards the Beynon family owned it. There is a local tradition that a cairn once stood in Park Cerrig Llwydion on Trewallterwen farm near to the Clunffwan stone. The old house was taken down. There was a wall where, it was said, treasure was concealed and at night some heard strange knocking sounds. Some tenants are supposed to have found money from time to time. When the estate was sold in 1831 the farm of 'Walterstone' comprised 294 acres worth £160 per annum.

Refs: Francis Jones essay 'A Tale of Three Homesteads', 1976; Trant Deeds; PRO AD iii, E210. D561; Tithe Map St. Edrins 1844; SC 1831; Pembs. Plea Rolls No. 63.

TREWARREN, *St. Ishmael's*

Home of the Warren-Davis family and built towards the middle of the 19th century. The Davis family formerly lived at Mullock. Gilbert Warren-Davis built the present house in the early 1840s. He was High Sheriff in 1839 and married Margaret Biddulph. They had two sons and six daughters, one of whom, Margaret Alice, kept diaries covering the years 1886-96. The eldest son, Henry Warren-Davis of Trewarren married Christabel Rolson and died in 1924. His widow died in 1940 and the estate was sold. In 1977 the owner-occupier is recorded as David Llewellin.

Refs: Tithe Map 1839; Landowners' Return 1873; Pembs. RO HDX/477, Nos. 1-7.

TREWELLWELL, *St. Davids*

Home of the yeoman family of Mortimer in the 18th and early 19th centuries, being then a farmhouse. Thomas Colby is listed as owner in 1786 with David Mortimer as tenant. Thomas Mortimer acquired the freehold in 1835. The last of the family, Thomas Mortimer, had an only daughter, Eleanor, who married the Rev. Thomas William Jones, Vicar of Llanybri and his son the Rev. Mortimer Lloyd Jones (b. 1828) was a graduate of Corpus

Christi, Cambridge. The estate was sold but Mortimer Lloyd Jones bought it back in 1875 and assumed the surname of Mortimer. Mortimer and Elizabeth had four sons, Reginald, Francis, George and Mansel. Their crest was: a li salient *argent* on a wreath *or* and *gules*. Motto: *Kowir i Dduw a dyn*.

The house was again sold at the end of the 19th century and bought by Colonel Howell who built the present mansion, incorporating the old farm into the rear of the premises. Trewellwell was advertised for sale in 1931 by Captain John Hamilton Howell. It had eight bedrooms on the first floor and farm outbuildings and comprised 108 acres. Capt. Howell was High Sheriff in 1927. In the early 1970s the remaining part of the original farm, built in 1776 and incorporated by Colonel Howell into his new house, was replaced by a modern extension.

Refs: SC 476 Carms. RO; Nicholas, *County Families,* 1875 edn., p. 949; VL 1834, 1904; Pembs. DX/57/35.

West Trewent

Hall

TREWENT HALL,
Stackpole Elidor

East Trewent, West Trewent, Trewent Mill and Trewent Point are marked on Colby's 1831 Map. It was the home of the Hall family in the 16th and 17th centuries. Their arms were: *argent* a fesse between three griffons' heads erased *or*. In 1551 John Hall, alias Howell of Trewent, gent. was summoned to answer Sir John Wogan. He was the son of Thomas Hall and Alice, daughter of Richard Cradoc. Richard and Alice had two sons, Robert the eldest of whom nothing is known and John who married twice, firstly to Margaret, daughter of Philip Herle of Scotsborough by whom he had three daughters and co-heiresses, Catherine who married Lewis Powell, Margaret who married Griffith Thomas of Penybenglog, parents of William Griffith; and Jenet who married John Thomas David Medd of Llandissilio. John Hall married secondly Jane, daughter of David Laugharne by whom he had a daughter, Grace who married Thomas Davies. Jenet's son, Owen John married Jane, daughter of Morgan David and their elder son, named John Owen succeeded. Their younger son was (Sir) William Owen a vicar. John Owen married a daughter of Harry Williams and they had a son, Harry Bowen of Egremont viv. 1685. Sir Hugh Owen was owner of the estate in 1786 when John Voyle was tenant of Trewent, with John Gwither and George Griffiths tenants of East Trewent. The Voter's List of 1894 shows that the Griffiths family was still farming East Trewent.

Refs: Dineley, *Progress,* p. 256; Pembs. Plea Rolls No. 9; GGMS; BM, Egerton MS 2586; VL 1834, 1894; PRO, Anc. Deeds D3506; LT 1786.

TREWERN, *Lampeter Velfrey*★

The house lies on the 100 foot contour line near the end of a slope in the Tâf valley, northwest of Whitland.

The first known owner was Owen Thomas (will proved 1661), whose great-granddaughter and heiress, Mary Thomas married in 1750 Thomas Beynon of Cethin who came to live at Trewern (iure uxoris), and it was the home of his descendants Protheroe-Beynon. It was sold about 1960 by J. Protheroe-Beynon and is the home of Major Tony Moon.

Originally, a house of marked size – John Thomas was assessed for three hearths in 1670. It was enlarged in the late 18th century. A photograph taken in 1871 shows a large house of three storeys with a concealed roof and two bowed wings. In 1873 John Thomas Beynon farmed 346 acres worth £497 p.a. The arms of Beynon: *or* a lion rampant *sable* between eight roses *gules*. Crest: a lion rampant. Motto: *Nihil utile quod non honestum* .

Mary Thomas was apparently the second wife of Thomas Beynon, and they had three children John, William and Anne. She was shown as 'widow, owner and occupier' in the Land Tax records of 1786 when she was assessed

at £1 4s. 0d. John, the heir, married and produced two children, John Thomas Beynon who married Catherine Sophia Philipps, and Rice Pryse Beynon, born about 1811 of Pentowyn, Meidrim who died 20 May 1889. The children of John and Catherine were: John, born 16 December 1829; Rhys, who married and had a son, Rhys Charles; Catherine who married Owen William George of Plascrwn and lived at Trewern and at Bath. She died 1898; and Ellen who married Edward S. G. Protheroe.

Refs: C. S. Allen, *Photographs in South Wales,* 1871; Landowners' Return 1873; Pembs. Plea Rolls.

TREWERN, *Nevern*

Situated in a small valley under the shadow of Carnedd Meibion Owen it stands at the foot of a steep declivity near the banks of a rill flowing westwards to the river Clydach, a situation that justifies the name by which it was known in early times, Trewern Waelod. In medieval times the district around Trewern was a fee.

Home of the Warren family descended from Dafydd Foel. 'Trewern, the mansion house of William Warren Esquier . . . called in auncient wrythynges Trewern-waylod. It is the auncient inheritaunce of the said William Warren for diverse hundred yeares past, how auncient it is not well knowne . . .' The first reference to Trewern is in 1344, Thomas son and heir of William Picton of Newburgh granted land within the precincts of the burgages of Fiscard, called 'Tyr Roys', for two years, to William Warin ap David Voil.

In 1430 Haverfordwest Corporation Deeds show 'Joan formerly wife of Lewis Wareyn of Traverne, widow'. In the mid-1550s William Jones of Brawdy married Mary Warren, daughter of William Warren, of Trewern who signed his pedigree for Dwnn in 1591. In 1614 Dafydd Emlyn wrote an Ode on the wedding of Thomas Warin of Trewern and Elizabeth daughter of Thomas Lloyd of Cwmgloyne; and Gwffydd Hafren also wrote an Ode in praise of Thomas Warin of Trewern. The following Warrens served as High Sheriffs: Thomas Warren 1639; William Warren 1674; John Warren 1712, and William Warren 1740. The south transept in Nevern Church is known as the Warren Chapel.

Fenton wrote: 'The line ended in four co-heiresses, the present Dowager Lady Kensington. This was Elizabeth, daughter of William Warren. She died in 1801 aged 90; Mrs. Williams of Popehill; the late Lady Keith who died in Switzerland, and Mrs. Jones of Llanina, Cardiganshire. Trewern fell to the share of the latter, and is now [1811] the property of Edward Warren Jones Esq.' Mrs. Jones was the last of the line to live there and in 1786 was assessed as owner occupier at £1 19s. 0d. land tax for Trewern.

After this Trewern was occupied by tenants, and used primarily as a farmhouse until the 20th century. Edward Warren Jones left the Llanina and Trewern estates to his friend Captain Longcroft, R.N., whose daughter, ward of E. W. Jones and an heiress brought them to her husband, Thomas Lloyd of Coedmore. The lands were willed to Peter Walter Warren Lloyd in his infancy, by Elizabeth Mary Lloyd on her death bed in 1947 aged 94. Peter Walter Warren Lloyd is an indirect descendant of the Warrens of Trewern, and he later sold the Trewern estate to his sister, Susan Watkins, (née Warren Lloyd), and her husband Stephen Watkins, J.P., now living at Trewern.

The present house dates from the Tudor period c. 1578, and for generations has been a farmhouse. It is E-plan having a hall and two wings and a central porch. The house is entered through a massive oak door with wrought-iron hinges and bar-holes. This leads to a large room once used as a kitchen, but from its size and panelled ceiling it was probably one of the principal apartments. This opens onto a hall from which a broad oak staircase leads to the oak-panelled bedrooms on the first floor.

In 1670 it was assessed for five hearths. A small building near the house is said to have been a cockpit and the late Mr. Francis Green told Major Jones that the tenant had told him that in this building 'the Warrens kept their vermin'.

In the Voter's List of 1834 it is recorded that the house was let to a parson, the Rev. David George who farmed Trewern then 200 acres, for 31 years (at £50 p.a. rent). He was an enthusiastic liberal and addressed numerous meetings to further that cause, and consequently his landlord gave him notice to leave. He moved to the nearby farm of Brithdir Mawr (q.v.), where he was living in 1872-74 when he served two years at Mayor of Newport. He was an eminent local figure who helped and counselled all folk in the locality. He died on 15 May, 1892, aged 82. One morning, during his tenancy, after a bad storm some damage was discovered to a chimney-stack. When a mason was sent to investigate and do repairs he had to climb up the kitchen chimney but lost his way and ended up in a secret chamber above the porch which was filled with treasure – silver plate and valuables probably hidden there at the time of the Reformation and forgotten. It is said that the parson and the workman made a pact and from time to time the parson would take a piece up to London, sell it and divide the proceeds with the mason. The story is told in more detail in Herbert M. Vaughan's *The South Wales Squires.* When Mr. Francis Green visited Trewern he copied an old inscription made with a diamond on one of the windows, which read:

Charming Miss Betty Warren
She intends drinking tea
With her brother Dick this evening 23 April 1723.
Oh loving Sapho return I thee request
Abound with flames of love embrace my waist
Rather suffer me to enjoy the pleasure
Your lips to kiss and behold your feature.

Mr. Green queries the word *waist* which was very faint, and suggested that it might have read *crest.*

Refs: Francis Jones 'Warren of Trewern', & *Historic Cardiganshire Homes and their Families*; PRO, Anc. Deeds, iii, E210, D1233; Fenton, *Tour Pembs.,* p. 306; George Owen, *2nd Book,* p. 275.

TREWILYM, *Eglwyswrw*

Home of the Cantington family variously spelt as Cantrington, Cantinton, Cainton and Canton. The house is on a slope on the east side of Nant Duad. There were originally two houses Trewilym Ucha and Issa.

The family descended from Sir William Cantrington, Lord of Eglwyswrw who died at Trewilym in 1227/8. The arms of the Cantringtons were: *gules* an eagle displayed *argent* armed *or*, a chief chequy *gules* and *vert*. His son, William, lived at Trewilym 'which by scite and ruines yet to be seene seemeth to have been inhabited with divers dwellings'. He married Gwladys, daughter of the Lord Rhys. His grandson called Griffith was alive in 1292 and his son, Griffith Cantington sold the Lordship of Eglwyswrw to Robert Martin but his line continued at Trewilym Issa and ended in an heiress, Elizabeth. She married Thomas Rees David Howell who died at his wife's home in 1538. They had a son, Griffith Thomas (d. 1569) of Penybenglog who was only three weeks old when his father died, and his wardship passed to William Owen, Lord of Kemes, who granted the wardship to Elizabeth Broughton, 'the wardes aunt then lyvinge at Trewilym, the grant dated the Xth of December H.8.30'. His grandson, William Griffith, father of G. W. Griffith the genealogist, sold Trewilym to George Owen of Henllys. The Wagner deeds tell us that 'This William Griffith sold Trewilym issa to Mr. George Owen, Lord of Kemeys, wch his auncestors held from Anno Domini 1228 until 1609 that he sold the same wch was about 379 yeeres or thereabouts and much other landes did he sell and doe away in the severall countyes of Pembroke and Cardigan to the value of Xl p Annum'. William Griffith died in 1618.

In 1579 George Owen leased Trewilym to Lewis ap Rowling. The Extent of Cemais tells us that in 1594 the rents of the free tenants at Trewilym were: land of William Griffith, gent. called Trewilym Issa 6d. per annum; land of James Bowen at Trewilym Ycha 3d. per annum and the land of Ieuan John Lewis there 4d. p.a.

In 1834 the estate was mentioned in the will of the then owner, the Rev. David Griffith who left everything for the benefit of his children.

Refs: Wagner MS XII (GWG); ibid. MS 12; Eglwyswrw Court Rolls 3 Oct. 1612 in Bronwydd Colln.; Llanst. MS 138, fo. 33; VL 1895; *Extent of Cemais,* 1594, p. 54; Bronwydd Deeds No. 1250 C/A Protheroe MS, XII, 11; Morgan-Richardson Deeds, ii, 509.

TREWILYM, *St. Lawrence*

First mentioned in the 14th century, Trewilym was home successively of the families of Dru, Scourfield, Skeel, Harries and latterly of Charles whose descendants were still in 1985, owner occupiers of the property. It is situated at the westernmost limit of St. Lawrence parish, on the lip of a short slope above a dingle through which a stream courses on its way to the sea at Newgale. Originally Trewilym consisted of two or three farms grouped together, but they are now a single unit consisting of over 600 acres. The name was variously known as Williamston and Trewilym until the end of the 18th century after which only the Welsh form was retained. The earliest known family at Trewilym was that of Dru or Drew. In 1248 Jordan de Armhull and Drew his son held lands at Wolfscastle and Newton, and it is not unlikely that the later dwellers at Trewilym were kinsmen of the foregoing. A number of ancient deeds in the Public Record Office, London, for the period 1370-82 contain useful information about Trewilym. In 1370 David Drew of Williamston demised a plot of land with two houses at Williamston Oger to Philip (?Henktot) and Mabel his wife, as security for a money loan. The deed was titled as Williamston Oger. The termination Oger defies explanation. Three years later, Margaret, widow of William Castel granted to John Howel of Wodestock a messuage, seven bovates in Williamston in the Lordship of 'Pebidiank', and a rent of one-halfpenny issuing from a messuage and one bovate held by John Wackly senior. In 1375 John Howel received a grant of messuage and lands in Wyllyamston. About this time the surname Dru reappears. On 19 August 1381 William Dru held lands 'in Williamston near Tankardstown in the Lordship of Pebidiog'.

No details have been found during the 15th century about the property, owners or tenants. In the latter half of the reign of Elizabeth I Trewilym surfaces again when it was owned partly by John Meyler, and partly by the Scourfields of Castle Villa. In 1573 the said John Meyler married Anne, daughter of William Scourfield of Castle Villa, and by their pre-nuptial settlement dated 17 July of that year the prospective bridegroom settled (*inter alia*) one tenement and land in Williamston to the uses of the marriage. Some years later, in 1583/4, by the prenuptial settlement of their son, also William Scourfield and Jane, daughter of Llewelyn Lloyd of Llanstinan, the prospective bridegroom settled properties in Williamston then held by five tenants, Thomas Jermyn, Richard Morrice, Richard Howel, Hugh Griffith, each paying an annual rent of 13s. 4d. and William Meyler paying an annual rent of 16s. 8d.

The last resident owner of Castle Villa, Thomas Scourfield, a younger son of New Moat, married Anne sole daughter and heiress of his second cousin, John Scourfield of Castle Villa. The union proved disastrous. Thomas plunged into a life of dissipation and in 1608/9 was obliged to borrow money through mortgages which he failed to redeem, and finally to break the entail on Castle Villa. A contemporary, landowner George Williams of Penybenglog in Meline, commented that '[Thomas], by his disordered lieffe wasted all his wife's estate and died very poor but a short space of time after his marriage'. The rake's progress – 'being given too much to comprise keepinge'. In 1611 Thomas mortgaged further properties including his home Trewilym, described as being 'in the former tenure of Lewis John Powell Goch but now of the said Thomas Scourfield'. His affairs continued to worsen and on 20 July 1615 Thomas and his wife sold the mortgaged estate to his elder brother William Scourfield of New Moat for £320. The spendthrift remained at Trewilym where he died not long after 1620. Shortly after 1624, Anne his widow sold the last remnants of the estate to her late husband's family and thereafter Trewilym formed part of the New Moat estate, and together with Castle Villa was let to farming tenants.

No reference has been found to Trewilym during the second part of the 17th century. It passed out of Scourfield hands, and in 1696 was owned by Owen of Nash and Great Nash. In 1786 'Williamston in St. Lawrence parish' was owned by Hugh Owen, and tenanted by David Williams. At this time Trehale, Newton and Trewalterwen also formed part of the Owen estates. Early in the 18th century a yeoman named Edward Skeel settled at Trewilym. His forebears originally came from Denmark where they were landowners, held important government offices, and bore the title of Count, their main residence being Gammel Estrop, an attractive county house now serving as a national museum. The branch that emigrated to Britain are first found in Laugharne and the vicinity, and it is from these that Edward came to Trewilym. He took part in local life, and in 1735 was a juror at the inquest on Thomas Lloyd of Trenewydd Fawr who had committed suicide. Edward Skeel died on 4 June 1746. His eldest son, James Skeel who succeeded as leaseholder to Trewilym served as High Constable of Dewsland in 1768. By Elinor his wife, James had three daughters, one of whom Phoebe Skeel, married James Lawrence of Rhoslanog near Mathry, and as we shall see, a descendant returned to Trewilym a century and a half later. Members of the family also settled at Hayscastle, and at Trenewydd, home of the Rev. Thomas Skeel, a celebrated minister who died in 1836 aged 78. After James Skeel's death, his widow Elinor married as her second husband, David Williams who settled at Trewilym, and by him had an only child, John who died in 1751 aged 25. David Williams died in 1805 aged 76 and was buried at Hayscastle, followed by Elinor on 19 April 1817 at the advanced age of 90. She was succeeded at Trewilym by her granddaughter, Mary who married Thomas Harries, a younger son of Trenichol.

The ownership of Trewilym changed hands several times. From the Owen family it passed to that of the James's of Trewalterwen and from them to John Hughes of Alltlwyd, Cardiganshire, described as owner in 1831, the occupiers being Miss Elizabeth Skeel and Thomas Harries. In that year the 'Walterston and Trewilliam Estates' were advertised to be sold on 28 July in six lots. Trewilym then comprised 329 acres 3 rods and 36 perches at an annual rent of £140. The property was bought by the sitting tenant, Thomas Harries. He married just before 1817, Mary Rees, niece of the Elizabeth Skeel who died at Trewilym in 1844, at the age of 82. After the marriage he settled at Trewilym where he spent the remainder of his life. A notable farmer and breeder of cattle, he won numerous prizes at agricultural shows and made several improvements to the farm. All the family were staunch Congregationalists and services were often held at the farmhouse. Thomas Harries died on 25 June 1885 aged 90 and his will was proved in the following year by his unmarried daughter Sarah. His wife had died in 1856 aged 68. None of his four sons remained at Trewilym; James settled at Cwmgloyne and Henllys in Nevern; John at Llanreithan and George at Trefgarn Owen. Trewilym was farmed by his competent daughter, Sarah. She died on 21 July 1890, and after her death the property was sold. Afterwards Trewilym passed through the hands of several owner occupiers. Thomas Williams was there from 1891-95 when another sale took place: after him came William Greenish Reynolds, still there in 1904, and some years later he sold the property to J. M. Griffiths. In 1919 he sold Trewilym to J. J. Charles of Henllys near Llanrhian and Phoebe Skeel his wife, who was descended from the Elizabethan Skeels of Trewilym. Francis Jones and his wife, Ethel née Charles, resided there briefly c. 1931 and their eldest son was born there.

Refs: Francis Jones unpublished essay, 'Trewilym in Dewsland', 1985.

TREWRACH, *Fishguard*
This is near the coast about half a mile north of the village of Dinas. Records go back to the 14th century when Griffith ap Ievan ap Llewellyn ap Eynon is described as being 'of Trefwrach'. In 1348/9 'Robert Harald granted to Walter Dyer of Dynas and Margaret uxor . . . lands in Trefwrach and Cylgenawan in Lordship of Fishgard in the barony of Kemys'. The Dyer family were still of Trewrach and Fishguard in 1558 when Walter Dyer granted to John ap Owen of Kynhaydre, land in Trefbover which had been granted to him in 1512 by William Dyer of Haverford.

A Mrs. James was owner in 1786 with tenants farming the land, and John Ritharch owned the freehold house and lands of Trewrach in 1834. James Rees James was owner in 1904.

Refs: Bronwydd Deeds 1323; ibid. 801; ibid. 822; ibid. 999; VL 1834, 1904; LT 1786; BM, Egerton 2586, 369a; *Extent of Cemais.*

TREWRDAN/TREFWRDAN, *Nevern**
Home of Jordan de Hoda, son of Lucas Hoda this farm is shown on Mudge's Map of 1819 as near to Trerickert. The earliest reference is dated 10 November 1490 in a condition of a grant 'from David Lloid ab Phillip ab Gr to Ieuan Lloid ab Gwillim, of a close called Jordanes Parke at the vill of Trefiordan, within the ploughland of Trefiordan. The condition being that said David pays 7 marks to said Ieuan, he may re-enter the lands'. By 1786 Thomas Keymer Esq. was owner, David James tenant, assessed at 6s. 8½d. in Land Tax. In 1840 Owen Evans was owner and Thomas James occupier farming 122 acres. The James family were still tenants in 1904. The Colby Map of 1831 shows Trewrdan Ucha, Issa and Rhoswrdan, three farms all adjoining.

Refs: Tithe Map Nevern 1840; LT 1786; VL 1904; Colby Map 1831; Bronwydd Deeds No. 1050.

TREYARCHED/TREARCHED, *Llanrhian*
A short distance from the hamlet of Croesgoch on the road to Mesur y Dorth there is a narrow lane turning off towards the north. On the roadside, and at the entrance of the turning is a cottage known as Lodge Treyarched and if we follow the lane we come to Treyarched itself, a farmstead set among a small grove. It remained in the hands of the same family for over three and a half centuries. The family started life at Treyarched as farmers and as such ended it. Although the family prospered, added considerably to its worldly possessions it never rose into the gentry class and rested content with the honourable status of farmers. The origin of the family still resists clarification but it is possible we can trace it to 1518 when a scribe recorded the conveyance of 'David ap Ieuan ap Meredith of Treffhucched for a term of 101 years to Hugh ap Gwallin ap Meredith of Treffhucched with remainder to Hugh's children by his wife Nesta, daughter of Rhys ap David Phillip'.

On 1 July 1592 John ap William ap Hugh ap Meredith bought the messuage and 33 acres in Treyarched for £6. John William Hugh Meredith married one Jenett, heiress of Trewalterlwyd, she was alive in 1625 and they had an only child, William ap John. William married Margaret Tudor, niece of the Rev. Harry Johnes of Torbant, vicar of Llanrhian. William died in his father's lifetime leaving an only son, George William who succeeded to Treyarched after his grandfather's death. Both the old gentleman and his wife were still living in 1623 when George took a wife. He married Barbara, youngest child of David ap Harry James of Portheiddy fawr, yeoman. Their prenuptial settlement was dated 20 April 1625. George William took his father's Christian name as his permanent surname and it was carried on by his descendants. Little is known of him. He died in 1650 leaving at least six children. John Williams the eldest son, inherited and mortgaged Walterston for £25 in 1653/4 and redeemed it in 1675. He was assessed at one hearth in 1670, married and had four children, one son and three daughters. George Williams his heir is first mentioned in a deed dated 30 March 1703 in a lease of Trewalter Lloyd (Llwyd). He married Elizabeth, daughter of

Rees James of Lochmeyler, prenuptial settlement dated 12 November 1675. He lived for 40 years after his marriage and died in 1717. In his will he bequeathed £40 to each of his daughters, Elinor, Constance and Joan: to his son, Arthur he left £60, a good pair of wheels, a tumbril, a longbody, a plough and a harrow and its teeth, to be delivered to him on his wedding day; to his sisters Anne, Lettice and Jenett, half a bushel of barley; the residue to his wife, Elizabeth and his son, John who were appointed executors. The total value came to £254 17s.

His heir John married Elizabeth, daughter of Francis Gough of Whitchurch. He had seven children, three sons, and four daughters and died in 1759 leaving Treyarched to his eldest son, George. When 51 years of age in 1770, George married Dorothy, daughter of Samuel Lloyd of Trenewyddfawr, a substantial yeoman and a leading Baptist. The date of George William's death is not known, but it occurred before 1784, for Samuel Lloyd of Trenewyddfawr by his will made in that year left £400 to 'my daughter, Dorothy, widow of George Williams lately deceased'. Dorothy died at Olmarch in 1800 and administration of her goods was granted to her only child, John Williams, born in 1770. He received his education at a local school, then at St. Davids, and finally at Haverfordwest. He settled at home and greatly improved Treyarched. He wrote a brief account of his early life which Francis Jones transcribed in his article, 'Treyarched'. He recounts how he came home in his 17th year to assist his mother in business. He tells us that the land she had in hand was Treyarched, Trewalter Lloyd, a house and garden at Trevine, the personal property, the stock and crop and £300. He details his improvements to the farm and recounts that he was married in 1793 to Margaret, daughter of William Davies of Pencoed. On his marriage he made an agreement with his mother. 'We had in cash £630, besides £124 that mother had after her Aunt. The agreement was, I had Treyarched farm, stock and crop and £194. Mother had Trewalter and £460. My wife's fortune was £500. Total cash I had to being £794.' He gives details of his farming improvements and progress and notes the birth

of his daughters, Dorothy in 1794, and Mary in 1788. He gives 'Certain Good Rules to follow, principally.

1. To live in fear of the Lord.
2. To speak fair words to all.
3. To make a good use of one's time, for what is not employed will be seen the want of.
4. To ponder and take second thoughts in action of importance or bargaining.'

On 25 March 1797 Peter Williams of Bristol conveyed in consideration of £1,150 the farms of Tresissillt and Trefelgar to his nephew John Williams of Treyarched and Thomas Lloyd of Trenewydd. The deed describes the boundaries and rights in detail. In 1807 John Williams reclaimed Trewalterlwyd from the tenants, and the Tithe Commutation Schedule compiled in 1842 showed that his property in Llanrhian parish consisted of Treyarched, 263 acres, Tresissllt 53 acres, and 28 other holdings ranging from 1 to 27 acres. John Williams died in 1847 and his widow in 1850 leaving nine children. George Williams inherited Treyarched but moved to Ffynnone in Little Newcastle parish and Treyarched was let to tenants. George married Mary Griffith of Llangolman. Both died in 1849 leaving seven children. Peter Maurice Griffith Williams, the eldest surviving son, inherited. He became a surgeon and settled at Newport. He married Mary Grace James. She died at Parrog House in 1873 and her husband in 1910. The Landowners' Return for 1873 lists P. M. G. Williams as owning 188 acres 3 rods, 38 perches in Llanrhian parish bringing in a estimated rental of £184 9s. 0d. Peter and Mary left four children, George Hugh Meredith

Williams who entered the Church and moved to Australia. John Daniel Evans Williams who became a doctor; Elgiva Alberta who married Walter John Vaughan of Fishguard, a solicitor, and had one daughter; Margaret Gwendoline who married a Captain Williams. The farm is now called Trearched, Francis Jones notes in his essay 'The local people pronounce the name as Trearched, but all early deeds and documents from 1569 down to this century, and there are many of them, consistently render it as Treyarched, with occasional variants such as Treierched. There can be no doubt whatsoever that the inclusion of the 'y' or 'i' represents the true form of the name.' The house was sold several times after 1910 and in now owned by Mrs. J. H. P. Jenkins.

Ref: Francis Jones unpublished essay 'Treyarched'.

TŶ GWYN, *Bridell*

One chronicler wrote of the area that '. . . the only gentlemen's seats are Ty gwyn and Plâs-y-Bridell. James Bowen was owner of Ty Gwyn in 1786 and it devolved to Thomas Bowen of Pantyderi whose son was William Bowen, J.P., D.L., barrister-at-law and Patron of the Living of Llanfairnantgwyn. He also succeeded to the estates, through his mother, of William Morgan Williams of Trefach. He was born 1875, and was J.P. and D.L, and married firstly, Charlotte Augusta Bearcroft and secondly, Jane Elizabeth Huntsman by whom he had a son and a daughter. Ty Gwyn was tenanted in 1844 by William Henry Davies and Mary his wife, one of the three natural daughters of Thomas James late of Place Lawrence, deceased. Her sisters were Frances and Margaret; there was also a natural son, Thomas James. The house was described in sale particulars in 1904 as '. . . large and commodious and of residential character' in its own grounds, planted with ornamental trees and surrounded 'by park-like fields'. It comprised 196 acres 1 rod and 3 perches.

Refs: Morgan-Richardson Deeds, ii, 416-7; Nicholas, *County Families,* 1875 edn., p. 896; VL 1834, 1894; SC 627 Carms. RO.

TŶGWYN (WHITEHOUSE),
Lampeter Velfrey

This was the home of the Willy family in the 18th century. Thomas Willy of Whitehouse had an estate worth £100 p.a. in 1743. The house then had a porch with room over, dining room, best room (bedroom), little room, hall, kitchen, dairy, cellar, garrets. His daughter, Mary, prenuptial settlement dated 21 June 1750 married John Evans, the second son of John Evans of Cardigan and Mary his wife. They had an only son, John Evans. By 1777 the Rev. Benjamin Twyning, clerk, was of Whitehouse which was owned in 1786 by a Mr. Bowen. The will of Benjamin Twyning was dated 13 September 1804, and he left his estate to his nephews Henry and William Twyning and another nephew Joseph Howell and their heirs. By 1834 John Morgan held a lease for lives of Whitehouse and it was still tenanted in 1904 jointly by William Davies and David Jenkins.

Refs: Morgan-Richardson Deeds, ii, 484; VL 1834, 1904; LT 1786.

UNDERDOWN, *Pembroke*

In the 16th century this was home of the Voyle family. Morgan Voyle of Haverfordwest, J.P. married Elvi, daughter of Francis Laugharne of St. Brides. Their second daughter Ethliw viv. 1591 married 'gwreig Henri o Uder Wod [Underwood] 1609'.

In 1788 Captain Charles Tyler, R.N., later Admiral Sir Charles Tyler of Cotterell, Glamorganshire, lived here, he died in 1835. He married Margaret, daughter of Abraham Leach

of Pembroke. She died 21 July 1835 leaving a large family. Underdown was owned by Lord Eyre Coote in 1820, but by 1840 was the home of Charles Poyer Callen. Colonel Owen Lowless was living here in 1977 but sold it in the following year to Mr. James Barrett who turned it into a private hotel. It is now a private house.

Refs: Dwnn, i, 177; Francis Jones Archives.

Bowen

UPTON CASTLE, *Upton*
Home of the Malefant and Bowen families. A small castle was built in the closing years of the 13th century. A description in 1810 said: 'The castellated mansion here, which is now in ruins, was the ancient residence of the Malyfants'. The mansion, to which the description 'castle' has been given in relatively modern times, was a fortified residence, somewhat similar in structure to that of Picton. Built during the latter part of the 13th century, it consists of three drum towers, incorporating a gateway at one end, which at one time must have opened onto a walled enclosure at the rear; behind the gateway, a small ranched building has been incorporated into later additions made to the structure, including the present residential portion which has been altered and modernised. Mr. Peter Smith concludes 'it may be regarded as a fortified first-floor hall, a large tower house or a small castle'. In the Hearth Tax list of 1670 we find that Hugh Bowen who then lived there was assessed for six hearths, and so comparable, so far as the part used as a residence is concerned, with nearby Carew Castle assessed for a similar number.

Sir Walter Malefant, mentioned in records of 1247 and 1255, was killed in a skirmish at Cardigan in 1258, leaving, by his wife, Avice, daughter of Sir Thomas de la Roche, a son who bore his father's Christian name. This Walter Malefant, who was living in 1268 married Joan, daughter of Henry fitzhenry, an illegitimate son of King Henry I by Nest, daughter of the prince Rhys ap Tewdwr. He, in turn was followed by a son, also named Walter who was living in the late 13th and early 14th century, and it is to him that the building of castellated Upton is credited. He witnessed a grant made by Alymer de Valence to the Hospitallers of Slebech in 1323, and held lands at Nash in the year following. Monuments in the adjoining church, including an effigy of a knight in 13th century armour, doubtless commemorate members of this family.

Through his wife, Elizabeth (or Isabel) de Londres, Walter Malefant became owner of the Carmarthenshire manor of Llandawke. His son and heir, William Malefant, is said to have married Margaret, daughter and co-heiress of John Fleming of St. George's Castle, Glamorgan, who brought properties in that county to her husband. William died in 1362, leaving two sons; William, who died without issue, and Henry. About 1401 Henry succeeded his elder brother, and had two sons, Sir Thomas who died in 1438, leaving issue, and Stephen who lived at Upton. Stephen Malefant was the last of the male line, and by his wife, Alice Perrot, left an only child, Alice Malefant, ultimate heiress of Upton.

Alice Malefant, heiress of Upton, married a member of one of the most illustrious families in south Wales, namely Owen ap Gruffydd, second son of Gruffydd ap Nicholas of Dynevor, son of Philip ap Sir Elidir Ddu knight of the Holy Sepulchre, who had lived at Crug near Llandeilo. Owen's elder brother, who succeeded to Dynevor (or Newton as it was then called), was Thomas ap Gruffydd father of the distinguished Sir Rhys ap Thomas, K.G. The family arms were based on an old family legend, which stated that an ancestor Urien Rheged had a retinue of ravens who accompanied him everywhere, this led to the coat of arms: an escutcheon *argent* a chevron *sable* between three ravens proper, and the motto *Dens pascit corvos.* These were also borne by the Upton branch.

Owen's residence, Cwrt Bryn y Beirdd near Carreg Cennen, was an ancient structure, and, happily, has retained much of its original character. By Alice Malefant he had a son Morris ab Owen usually described as of Bryn y Beirdd and Upton. Morris ab Owen, married Margaret, daughter of Henry Lewis of St. Pierre, Monmouthshire, by whom he had the following children: 1. John ap Morris ab Owen – inherited Bryn y Beirdd, and was living there in 1561, when he summonded Thomas Catharn alias Gaddern, gentleman, of Prendergast for a debt of £5 in the Great Sessions of Pembrokeshire. He married and had issue; 2. Rees ap Morris ab Owen – who established the line of Bowen of Llechdwnni, Carmarthenshire; 3. Thomas ap Morris ab Owen – inherited Upton; 4. Jane – married firstly, Hugh Vaughan from whom descend the Vaughans of Golden Grove; secondly, Jenkin Lloyd of Pibwr, Esquire of the Body to Henry VIII, High Sheriff of Carmarthenshire in 1541-42; 5. Elizabeth – married David Goch ap Rhydderch, and had a son, Rhydderch Gwyn of Glanbran, High Sheriff of Carmarthenshire in 1573.

Thomas ap Morris, the third son who received Upton as his portion, is often designated as Thomas ap Owen. His wife belonged to the powerful family of Herbert. According to the Golden Grove MSS she was Margaret daughter and co-heiress of John Herbert, but the herald Fellowes who recorded the pedigree, calls her an illegitimate daughter of Herbert, Earl of Pembroke. That her name was Margaret and that she survived her husband is abundantly clear, for on 8 April 1518 Philip Eynon, Chaplain, was admitted to the living of Nash on the presentation of Margaret ap Oweyn, widow and relict of Thomas ap Oweyn, 'true and undoubted patrons for this turn, by reason of the nonage of Rhys ap Oweyn son and heir of the said Thomas ap Oweyn, who is in her wardship by grant of King Henry VIII'.

In due course, Rhys ab Owen, the ward of 1518, inherited Upton. According to Fellowes, who wrote in 1530, he held an appointment in the Royal Household, being one of the Servers of the King's Chamber, and the same authority describes his wife as Isabel, daughter and co-heiress of Sir Edmond Tame, a Gloucestershire knight, by Elizabeth, daughter and heiress of John Grevill.

Rhys ab Owen predeceased his wife Isabel, she afterwards married Lewis ap Watkyn, Esquire, Serjeant-at-Arms to the King, by whom she had three sons and a daughter, William (a minor in 1547), James, Thomas and Katherine. After the marriage, Lewis came to live at his wife's home, and is described as of Upton when he made his will on 7 December 1547. He desired to be buried in the parish church of Nash, and mentioned his four children, his wife 'Isabel Tame', and also his stepson Rice ap Owen to whom he bequeathed his 'fallow horse' and all his other horses, the will was proved in PCC in 1548.

Later in 1553 or early in the following year, Isabel married her third husband, William Rees of Sandyhaven, a descendant of the Dynevor family, and so akin to her first husband. This is confirmed by the Episcopal Registers of St. Davids which state that on 24 October 1554 Phillipp Pyrry was presented to the rectory of Nash by William Pryse of Sandy Haven, Esquire, and his wife Elizabeth (recte Isabel) by reason of her dower from Rees Owen of Upton, esquire. By Isabel his wife, Rhys ab Owen had four children: 1. Rees; 2. Mary – married Gelly Barrett of Gelliswick (living 1578), and had four sons and three daughters; 3. Margaret ('Marred') – married William Parry son of Hugh Parry of Carmarthen and had two sons and a daughter; 4. Elizabeth – married William Reade.

Rees, only son of Rhys and Isabel, adopted the permanent surname of Bowen, although occasionally ap Owen is found. He married Elizabeth, daughter of Henry Wyrriott, (High Sheriff 1548 and 1559), of Orielton by Margaret, a base daughter of Sir Rhys ap Thomas. He was High Sheriff in 1564. On 12 December 1568, Rees ap Owen of Upton, esquire, granted a tenement in the fields of Cossesston (Cosheston) to Griffith White of Henllan, esquire, and the latter mortgaged two messuages in Cossesston to the former in the sum of £20, which were redeemed before 1573, (Lort of Stackpole Deeds). With some others he was responsible in 1570 for providing a light horseman with arms and furnishings, for the defence of Pembrokeshire against possible invasion. He died about 1572, in which year his IPM was held. By his wife, Elizabeth he had two children: 1. Henry; 2. Jane – married Rev. Henry Meyrick, described as 'parson of Kesston' by Dwnn.

Henry Bowen succeeded to Upton. He signed his name as Harry Bowen at the foot of the family tree that Lewis Dwnn recorded when he called at Upton on 5 March 1591, and handed the herald the sum of five shillings for his pains. He was described in 1594 as patron of the rectories of Upton and Nash 'appendant to the manor of Nash', and five years later as lord of that manor. Henry died at one of his farms, Christchurch, on 20 May 1621, and the I.P.M. taken at Haverfordwest Castle on 11 September following, returned that he had held the following properties – the manor of Upton, held of the barony of Carew; lands in Lower and Over Nash; two messuages in Christchurch, all in Carew parish; that his widow Elen was then living at Lower Nash; and that his son and heir, Hugh Bowen and his wife Elizabeth were living at Upton. He had 16 children in all, not all of whom are detailed here.

The eldest son, Hugh, born about 1578 succeeded to Upton. He married Elizabeth, daughter of James Lewes, of Abernantfychan, Cards. The prenuptial settlement was executed on 31 January 1599-1600, and the post-nuptial settlement on 1 March 1606/7. Like his father, Hugh Bowen, (still living in 1634), he was surrounded by a goodly brood: Rhys, the heir was followed by ten siblings. The eldest son Rhys Bowen, living 1608, succeeded to Upton. He married Sibyl, daughter of Morris Wogan of Boulston by Frances daughter of Sir Hugh Owen of Orielton. Very little is known about him, and he died before 1673. His heir was Hugh Bowen who succeeded to Upton. In 1662 he married Elizabeth daughter of Major-General Rowland Laugharne of St. Bride's. Blome's List of Gentry completed in 1673, lists the name of 'Hugh Bowen of Upton, esquire'. He had no issue, and administration of his goods were granted at Carmarthen to his next brother Morris Bowen on January 1692/93. The inventory of his goods at Upton amounted to £305 7s. 0d., and his goods at lodgings at Henry Morland's house in the parish of St. Giles, Middlesex, taken on 28 April 1693, worth £70 17s. 0d., included 'gold and silver' valued at £55 12s. 0d.;

Morris Bowen – succeeded his brother to Upton. He never married. His will made on 8 March 1698 provides a good example of what lawyers used to call the 'strict settlement'. The will was proved on 15 October 1706, and the inventory of his goods amounted to £411 1s. 11d. As will be noted, testator waived his next brother, William;

William – described as a 'Captain at Dunkirk', where he married and had several sons and a daughter. He was living in 1703, but nothing further has been found of him;

A daughter Ann, married John Jordan of Dumpledale (now called Ashdale);

The fourth child Frances married, as her first husband, Nicholas Adams of Holyland (d. 1680), and had issue. She died before 1665.

With this generation the main line of Bowen came to an end, and the estate passed under the terms of Morris Bowen's will, to his cousins in a junior branch.

The second son, John Bowen of Benton succeeded to Upton in 1706 under the terms of the will of his cousin, Morris Bowen. He was assessed at four hearths in 1670. Little is known of his career. He supported the Owen of Orielton interest in the Parliamentary election of 1714. His will, made on 17 November 1713, was proved at Carmarthen on 5 April 1715. He had been married twice. His first wife, a daughter of John Barlow of Cresswell, died without issue. His second was Martha, daughter of Owen Edwardes of Treffgarne by Damaris Perrott, by whom he had the following children:

1. William Bowen;

2. John Bowen – succeeded to Upton under the entail created in Morris Bowen's will. He died unmarried, and Upton passed to his elder brother William;

3. Francis Bowen;

4. Perrott Bowen – to whom his father bequeathed £10;

5. Rice Bowen – to whom his father bequeathed all his personalty. He married Mary

. . . and was alive in 1752 and died apparently without issue;

6. Damaris – to whom her father bequeathed one shilling;

7, 8, and 9. Margaret, Mary, Elizabeth, to each of whom her father bequeathed £10.

William Bowen, the eldest son matriculated at Jesus College, Oxford, on 13 February 1707/8, aged 18 years, was entered a student of the Middle Temple on 15 March 1709, and admitted a Fellow-Commoner at St. John's College, Cambridge, on 25 June 1712. He took Holy Orders, and in 1712 was presented to the rectory of Lawrenny. He was a Land Tax Commissioner in 1715, and in that year succeeded his younger brother, John, to the Upton estate, but did not live long to enjoy it, for he died before 16 January 1722 when administration of his goods was granted at Carmarthen to his widow. By his wife, Mary daughter of Hector Harries of Ireland he had the following children: 1. William Bowen – of whom little is known. He was a minor in 1726. He is said to have married, and to have died in France leaving issue; 2. Morris Bowen; 3. Martha – married the Rev. Mr. Mclaughlan of Ireland, clerk in Holy Orders. Both were living in 1774.

Morris Bowen, the second son, succeeded to Upton. He was a Justice of the Peace, and served as High Sheriff in 1746. Some time afterwards he left Upton and went to live in the town of Pembroke, and from 1753 he is usually described in deeds and documents as of the latter place. This residence may have been the capital messuage or dwelling house with court and garden, called Dr. Powell's house, in the east end of the parish of St. Nicholas, Pembroke, which Morris bought on 10 June 1745, for £500 from Mary, widow of John Powell, M.D.

Among Morris's other purchases was Newport Castle and its green, a water corn grist mill merets [sic] belonging, two messuages, and other properties, all in the village of Newport, Pembs., which he bought on 2 November 1753 from William Laugharne. About 1739 he had married Alicia daughter and heiress of Thomas and Lettice Knolles of Wenallt near Newport, the prenuptial settlement being dated 14 December 1739. She died 15 November 1753, aged 45, and was buried in Upton church. He died on 10 October 1758, in his 40th year, according to the memorial in Upton church. The will of Morris Bowen of the town of Pembroke, esquire, dated 14 October 1752, was proved on 12 January 1787. In his will he expressed a wish to be buried 'as private as possible consistent with decency and that my Corps may be deposited amongst my Ancestors in the Chappel at Upton'.

Morris Bowen left four daughters, co-heiresses, namely: 1. Mary – married before 1758 Thomas Skyrme of Pembroke, and had issue. She outlived her husband, and in 1787 was living at Shrewsbury; 2. Anne – married William McCormack of Truro. Their post-nuptial settlement was dated 13 July 1768. She died between 1776 and 1781, and had no issue; 3. Lettice – lived at Pembroke for some years, and by 1780 had moved to Todstone, in Herefordshire, and in 1787 was described as of Bromyard in that County. She died unmarried; 4. Martha – married when a minor, on 13 May 1771, to William Tayleur of Bunting's Dale, Salop., son of William and Mary Tayleur. Their prenuptial settlement was made on 21 March 1771. He is described as owner of Upton in 1786, with John Hooke as tenant. She died on 11 December 1775. They had issue.

A draft exemplification of a recovery of a fourth part of the Upton estate, clearly in respect of one of the above co-heirs, contained in the Papers of Great Sessions for 26 August 1764 describes the whole estate as consisting of the manor of Upton, 60 messuages, 20 cottages, 80 gardens, 20 orchards, 3 water corn grist mills, 1 tucking or fulling mill, and 6,050 acres in the parishes of Nash, Upton, Cocheston, Yerbston, St. Mary Pembroke, St. Michael Pembroke, Newport, Mynachlogddu, Manordivy, Eglwyswrw, Nevern, St. Dogmaels, and Meline, and the perpetual advowson of the rectory of Nash, with the chapelry of Upton, and the site of the castle of Newport.

These four sisters were the last of the Bowens to own Upton Castle and its estate. In 1774 they advertised the property for sale – the first time it had been placed on the market since medieval days. Also included was the Wenallt estate which had come to them through their mother. It is likely that the need for money prompted the sale, for some time prior to this the sisters had mortgaged three-quarters of both the Upton and Wenallt estates.

Upton Castle and the surrounding property was bought by Captain John Tasker who had returned from India where he had amassed a fortune. He served as High Sheriff of Pembrokeshire in 1798, and died without issue on 12 December 1800 at the age of 58, leaving the estate to his niece Maria Margaretta wife of the Rev. Thomas Woods, rector of Nash from 1796-1801. By him she had two daughters. In 1803 Margaretta married the Rev. William Evans, another clergyman, by whom she had three sons born at one birth at Upton Castle on 11 October 1803. Of these, John Tasker Evans became a doctor, and died on 21 May 1895, leaving by his wife Anne, a son Richard. Born on 23 May 1840, Richard Evans entered the Royal Navy where he rose to the rank of Vice-Admiral. He became a Justice of the Peace and a Deputy Lieutenant of Pembrokeshire. The Admiral, who died on 4 May 1927, was the last of the family to live at Upton Castle which he sold some time before his death to Mr. Stanley Neale of Cardiff whose widow lived there until her death in 1973.

Refs: Francis Jones unpublished essay 'Bowen of Upton Castle', 1976; Peter Smith, *Carmarthen Studies,* 1974, pp. 50-1; *Anc. Mon. Pembs.,* pp. 401 et seq.; Burke, *LG,* 1850, 1898; Dwnn, *Heraldic Visitations,* i, pp. 118-119; Owen, *Pembs.,* ii, p. 309; *Episcopal Registers of St. Davids,* ii, p. 837.

VAYNOR, *Llawhaden*★

There are two houses of similar name in the parish, Vaynor and Great Vaynor. Originally known as Faynor Fawr and Fach they are marked on Colby's Map of 1831. The records of these two houses have become involved and are difficult to interpret with certainty.

In early Wales the word maenor (faenor), included an area, not unlike the manor established by the Normans. The maenor also included a homestead within a stone-walled enclosure. Known thus as The Vaynor in the Barony of Llawhaden, which still includes a number of farms comprising a considerable area, it has over a thousand years of historical tradition.

According to the *Black Book of St. Davids,* 1326, the owners of Vaynor had to carry the holy relics of St. David before the Bishop when required and escort captured brigands to Llawhaden Castle and execute them.

Skyrme

The present mansion built at right angles to a gentle slope in the style of early gentry homes, has been the home of several land-owning families. In 1365 Philip Jan of Vainor bought lands from Roger ap David. In 1575 Henry Jones was of Vaynor, gent; by 1586 Evan Philip Gwrwared was of Vaynor, yeoman. The Gwrwared family was there until 1602. The Skyrme family achieved eminence and success as lawyers in Wales and the Marches while one achieved some notoriety as an monoglot English lawyer who, unaided wrote the will of a monoglot Welshman, an exercise in the impossible that drew on his head the wrath of the deceased's disappointed kinsfolk.

They settled in Pembrokeshire in the early part of the 17th century and owned that estate and Llawhaden for seven successive generation, until the death of William Skyrme in 1823. Two of them were High Sheriffs; John in 1716 and Thomas in 1769; William was coroner of the County in 1748, and several of them were Justices of the Peace. Their politics were suspect, for in 1726 Thomas Skyrme of Vaynor

and in 1760, William Skyrme of the same place were active members of West Wales Society of Sea Sergeants, notorious for its Jacobite sympathies. In the 19th and 20th centuries Vaynor was occupied by well-known yeoman families.

The house was owned by Mr. Pemberton when Francis Jones visited it in 1972. He describes it as a 'Long single pile house with a doorway with flushed stone Corinthian columns in the wall. In the centre of a broken pediment are the arms of Skyrme: a chevron between three escallop shells impaling a lion rampant – about 1650-1700. The crest missing'. Over the back door is a stone inscribed 'W.S. 1707', doubtless for William Skyrme.

After the death of William Skyrme in 1787 the mansion house and lands of Vaynor were put up for sale. The sale particulars state that the tenant was Mr. Thomas James, who 'had a lease for life of Thomas James, aged 39, his wife aged 35 and his daughter aged 13 years'; the freehold was offered of 'All that capital Messuage, or dwelling house and lands, with the barns, stables, outhouses, building, gardens, orchards, and water corn grist mill, thereunto adjoining and belonging, called and known by the names of Vaynor and Pontshane Mill. In the 'Remarks' it states.. 'The timber on this farm is worth £150. The Landlord covenants to keep the roof of the mansion house in repair, and to furnish the tenant with 60 barrels of Culm, yearly or 36s. in Lieu. The tenant allowed Timber growing on the premises for the use of the farm. About fifteen Bishop's acres of Church land lies intermixed with this land for which £4 10s. 0d. is paid to the Bishop of Saint Davids. A valuable Limestone quarry on this lot.' Francis Skyrme Esq. held a commission as Lieutenant of HMS *Iris* 28 October 1797. He was appointed Deputy Lieutenant of Co. Pembroke, 3 March 1800. He was appointed by George, Bishop of St. Davids, to be gamekeeper of the manor of Llawhaden, 28 August 1802. He died 12 February 1827 as Captain R.N. at Llawhaden House. He had two sisters, Anna and Hesther Skyrme of Haverfordwest, both spinsters in 1824.

Refs: Francis Jones, notes for an essay; Bronwydd Deeds Nos. 780, 801, 811, 1060, 1332, 1335, 7015; Pembs. Plea Rolls Nos. 54, 76, 91, 99, 121; BM, Egerton 2586; Spence Colby Deeds 1011; Map & Plan, 1821, Pembs. RO DB/13/37; D/RTP/SKY/ Nos. 238, 239, 248.

VAYNOR (GREAT), *Llawhaden*

In 1972 when Major Jones visited, the owner was Mr. D. Gibbon who retired from farming in 1987 and offered the farm for sale. Francis Jones described it as ' . . . a small agreeable residence, and seems to comprise two houses, the older one being in the rear. The newer part was built in the first half of the 19th century, and most of its reception rooms and bedrooms have shallow arched alcoves in them. There is a small hall. The house stands on a slope with a fine southerly view'.

The Land Tax for Llawhaden parish taken in 1786 shows Mr. Leach owner, with John Furlong, tenant, assessed at £2 4s. 0d. The house was also known as East Vaynor and Faynor Fawr. There was also a Little Vaynor owned by Lady Keith. The survey and valuation of the estate of Abraham Leach of Corston in the early 19th century includes Great Vainor. It then comprised 309 acres, 2 rods and 35 perches. Vainor Fawr house and gardens. In the Tithe Map of 1843 Abraham Leach is owner with Thomas George Gonne occupier. He married Mary Prust, illegitimate daughter of Robert Bateman, of Haverfordwest by Mary Lewis, the prenuptial settlement was dated 28 July 1841.

Refs: Picton Castle Deeds No. 128; Pembs. Plea Rolls No. 99; Pembs. GS; Pembs RO D/LLC/674 Tithe Map 1843.

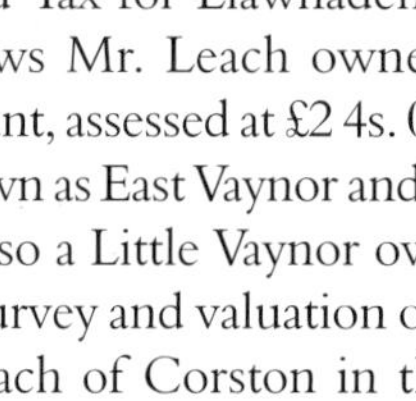

VAYNOR, *Manordeifi*
Marked as 'Fainor' on Mudge's Map of 1819. The Lloyds of the Bronwydd family, owned Vaynor in the 18th century. Marked on Bowen's Map of 1760 as 'Vaynor Vawr', it is now a farmhouse with no trace of its former status. Vaynor was part of the estate of Brigstocke of Blaenpant, Cards., in 1763.

Thomas Lloyd sold Bronwydd and settled at Vaynor, he died there in 1737; he was succeeded by his son, Robinson Lloyd, who married firstly Ursula Davies of Dyffyrn Wdig by whom he had a daughter, and heiress, Elizabeth who married firstly Thomas Owen second son of James Owen of Glôg, died 1768, and secondly, in 1778, John Ferrier. They had a son, also John viv. 1810. In 1785 John Ferrier and Elizabeth his wife, heiress of Robinson Lloyd, are of Cardigan town. Robinson Lloyd married secondly an unknown Margaret, viv. 1765. Robinson Lloyd died December 1742. She married secondly Thomas George of Molleston.

Land Tax records for 1786 show Mr. Brigstocke, owner, David Griffiths, tenant assessed at £1 10s. 0d. In 1787, Vaynor is shown in the prenuptial settlement of Mary Davies of Penhendrew, and Benjamin Griffiths of Vaynor, Manordeifi, settled on him in an Agreement of February 7-8 1787, by David Griffiths his father, of Vaynor, gent.; Rees Griffiths, son and heir of Benjamin Griffiths inherited the tenancy in 1848.

Refs: Francis Jones, *Historic Cardiganshire Homes and their Families*; Pembs. RO; James of Narberth, Solicitor papers; Griffith Owen Deeds No. 10213; Bronwydd Deeds No. 2838; LT 1786; VL 1834.

VORLAN, *Vorlan (now in Maenclochog parish)*
Home of the Vaughans descended from the Pontfaen family. Thomas Vaughan was assessed for three hearths in 1670. Thomas Vaughan, the first of the line at Vorlan, made his will in 1711. He left three daughters and co-heiresses; Mary, married to Roger Lewis; Elinor married to Richard Lewis, and Lettice married to John Thomas of Cilciffeth. They all had issue, nothing is known of them. In 1786 Vorlan belonged to Lord Milford. This was Lord Milford of the first creation. He was Sir Richard Phillips, 7th Baronet who was an M.P. and raised to the peerage in 1766. He died childless and the peerage became extinct. On Colby's Map of 1831 are Forlan Moat and Forlan fach; just east of Moat mansion, and Forlan and Castell Forlan, a promontory earthwork, south of Maenclochog hamlet. In the 1894 Voters List Elias Jenkins and Catherine Jenkins are listed as tenants of Vorlan Farm, and in 1904, G. Jenkins has the house and land.

Refs: LT 1786; Spence Colby Deeds; Pembs. RO D/CT/No. 5.

WALWYN'S CASTLE,
Walwyn's Castle
Home of the Holland and Laugharne families. The Holland family go back to Hugh Holland (d. 1584). He married in 1543 Jane, daughter of Hugh Conway. Their son Robert was Rector of Prendergast and author of *The Holy Historie.* His son Nicholas, living in 1635 was 'of Walwyn's Castle'. His son, another Nicholas Holland, was an attorney in Haverfordwest and died 'at a great age' in 1718 having married four times. He married firstly Dorothy Laugharne of Orlandon, secondly Elizabeth, daughter of Thomas Davis by whom he had four children; thirdly an unknown Martha and lastly Eleanor, sister of Lewis Mathias of Llangwarren, who desired to be buried with her husband in Walwyn's Castle church in 1720. Martha the third wife who died in 1704 presented a chalice to Robeston West church, inscribed 'The gift of Martha Holland to the Parish of Robeston West 1698'.

Nicholas and Elizabeth had four children, Rice, Warren, Nicholas and Frances who married firstly, Rowland Morgans of Pembrokeshire and secondly, John Morse of Haverfordwest. Warren died without issue, and Nicholas was of London and a silversmith, married and had a son, Charles Holland. Rice the eldest son married an unknown wife and had three children, Nicholas, Rice and Mary, viv. 1743. Nicholas, the eldest son married an unknown wife, Sarah . . . and had five sons; Nathaniel who was of Walwyn's Castle in 1734, Warren born 23 November 1709, William born 19 January 1711, Nicholas M.A. Merton College, Oxford, vicar of Mucking and rector of Stifford, Co. Essex, born 14 June 1713 and died 27 December 1771. He had married Jane, daughter of Edmund Clarke, counsellor-at-Law of Middlesex and Essex and had seven children all of whom left Pembrokeshire. The youngest son, Rice was born 24 March 1714.

John Laugharne was assessed for four hearths in 1670.

Refs: Francis Jones Archives.

WARPOOL COURT, *St. Davids**

Warpool Court has been variously named, Marble Hall, Warble Hall the Mitre Inn, Cwm or Gwm Warbol and the Mitre House. Also in the 19th century called after the rocky outcrop there, Bryn y Garn. In the 1880s-90s a Mr. and Mrs. Morgan lived there, they were followed by the Williams family who renamed the house Dewiscourt and they were responsible for the ornamental tiles around fireplaces and general improvements. Two entries both dated 1811 tell us of the frequent changes; '26 March Release of the messuage or dwelling house called Marble Hall otherwise Warble Hall and also five dwelling houses or cottages adjoining. Consideration £200'. Also 'Marble Hall otherwise Warble Hall afterwards known as Mitre Inn, and now called the Mitre House, situated in Warble Lane, St. Davids: also 4 dwelling houses or cottages adjoining'.

Refs: CRO Trant/Yelverton Papers, Vol. 1, Schedule. 17th cent. Papers of GS.

WATERWINCH, *Tenby*

This villa is sited in a deep dell near the coast just north of Tenby. In the mid-19th century the house belonged to the Norris family, C. Norris Esq. being in occupation in 1852. In 1921 Waterwinch was the country seat of Sir Edward Ridsdale, G.B.E. (b. 1864) who was M.P. for Brighton (1906-10) and Vice-Chairman of the Council of the British Red Cross Society. A Mr. Griffiths was in occupation in 1980 and he and his wife took in bed and breakfast visitors. They later sold the house. It was described as 'La

Waterwyche' in 1326 and 'le Water wynch mylle' in 1484.

Refs: F. P. Gwynne, *Sketches of Tenby,* 1852; Pembs. PR, iii, 122; B. G. Charles, *NCPN*, p. 106; M.I. St. Mary, Tenby churchyard.

WAUNBERRY, WAUNBERRI, *Mathry*

The John family tenanted Waunberry from the Scourfield estate from the 17th century to the end of the 19th century. In 1622 William Scourfield of New Moat owned 30 acres there. The earliest member of the family detailed is Thomas John, who with Richard and Owen James John were each assessed at one hearth. Thomas John had died by 1691 when his widow was granted administration of his estate. He left two known sons, John and Henry John. Another Henry John was tenant from 1765 until 1855. Ownership of Waunberry had transferred to the Rev. Joshua Rowley by 1842 when the Tithe Schedule showed Henry John as tenant farming 70 acres. He was succeeded by his son, James, (1894), and grandson, Abel and sister, Mary Anne who married David Morgan Francis of Clawddcam. Their son, Roderick Francis was of Waunberry, freeholder and in 1986 the owner was Mrs. Betty Francis, widow of Roderick Verdun Francis.

Refs: Poyston Deeds No. 72; NLW Slebech Deeds; Tithe Map Mathry ph. 1842; VL 1894.

WAUNGRON, *Lampeter Velfrey*

Home of the Philipps and Northey families. There are two houses, the mansion and Waungron Isaf which is a farm. Francis Philipps Esq. who died in 1682, was described as 'of both the Waungrons'. He was High Sheriff in 1679 and his will was proved in 1681; he was a descendant of the Pentypark family and had married an unknown Alice who predeceased him in 1674. They had two daughters, Elizabeth who married firstly, George Lewis of Henllan, and secondly in 1703, John Philipps of Colby who was her first cousin, by whom she had a daughter, Frances who married J. L. Hancorne. Francis and Alice's second daughter, Mary married Hugh Jones who died young in 1719 aged under 30, having been High Sheriff in 1716. He left a son, Thomas Jones of Carmarthen who married Bridget Price of Llanelli. Thomas died in 1740 predeceasing his mother whose will was dated 1757 and who lived at Upper Waungron. Francis and his sister Elizabeth raised a monument to their parents and grandparents in 1759. Mary's grandson, Thomas was of Waungron and married Anne Turner of Abergavenny by whom he had two children, Thomas who succeeded to Waungron, and William.

In 1876 Thomas Rees Oliver Powell died at Waungron. He was a barrister and Deputy Judge of the County Court but in the 1890s the property belonged to Major Augustus J. W. Northey of the 41st Regiment and of Eaton Square, S.W.1. He was D.L. and J.P. and married in 1853 Laura Sophia, daughter of Joseph Price, and had a daughter Elizabeth Amy Northey. He was son of Col. Lewis Augustus Northey, A.Q.M.G., and grandson of Sir William Paxton of Middleton Hall, Carmarthenshire. Lewis Augustus Northey was the son of Thomas Northey who died in 1780 and Margaret, daughter of J. L. Hancorne of Gower and Frances Philipps. The arms of Northey are: *or* on a fess *azure* between three panthers statant proper, semee of estoiles *argent* a pansy *or* between 2 lilies *argent*. Crest, a cockatrice, flames issuing from its mouth proper.

In a catalogue of 1918 when the estate was put up for sale the house is described as being within half a mile of the town of Whitland. There were eight bedrooms and dressing rooms, four reception rooms and numerous 'offices'. The farm was also included in the sale. The main house probably dates from 1840-50. Francis Jones visited both Waungrons in 1976 and wrote that 'today there is Waungron, the mansion which is 'modern' and south of it Waungron Isaf, (farm): and farther to the south is Waungron Uchaf (farm) the last two being the original mansions'. He visited the mansion which was a 19th century structure and Waungron Isaf which was early 19th century with a fine range of outbuildings.

Refs: Francis Jones, *Historic Carmarthenshire Homes and their Families* & Archives; Burke, *LG,* 1898, i, pp. 1108-9; LT 1786; C. S. Allen, *Photographs in South Wales*, 1871; GGMS (Gwynfardd), p. 8; Colby Map 1831.

WEDLOCK, *Gumfreston*

Wedlock

Home of the family of Wedlock, also spelt Widlock or Wedlake. In 1359 John Widelock was a juror at Tenby and in 1362 he held two messuages in Gumfreston and Widelock, worth 10 marks, held of John de Carew. He had taken the name of the property as his patronymic. The name was spelt variously as Woodlake, Woodlock and Widlock and they were described as 'Lords of Gumfreston'. The arms of Wedlock were: *sable* a chevron between three lions sejant *argent*. John Widlock had two daughters and coheiresses, one married David Roblin and the other, Christian, married David (Henry) Llewelyn 'with whome he had Gumfreston'. They had a son, John Llewelyn whose daughter, Jenet married Owen ab Owen and whose son was Sir James Bowen of Pentre Ifan, who 'had lands in Gumfreston and Widlock which William Williams of Talkrwth enjoys as heir to said Sir James Bowen'. The Williams family of Porthhowel, Carms., owned Wedlock in the 17th century, and the Meyricks in 1786. Thomas Williams owned it in 1904. Wedlock is now a farmhouse.

Refs: D. Pembs., ii, 328; GGMS; BM Egerton 2586.

WELSH HOOK, *St. Dogwells*

Home of the Wogan family originally, and now a farmhouse. Records go back to 1140 when it was owned by the de Kemeys family who were still owners in 1535. The next proprietor was William Jones of Brawdy who was there in 1575 and sold to the Cornock family. In 1619 it belonged to the Wogans of Stone Hall. On 23 May 1637 Howell Thomas of Nevern and Elinor his wife, mortgaged the farm of Yskyrne Eynon Nantgwyn, in that parish for the sum of

£25 to Grace Wogan alias Vaughan of Welsh Hook, widow, and Maurice (Morris) Wogan. During her later years she lived at nearby Welsh Hook, home of her grandson Morris Wogan, and was described as of that place as early as 1632. Morris Wogan, settled at Welsh Hook over the river just below Stone Hall, and married Catherine, daughter of John Owen of Priskilly in Mathry parish. On 10 December 1635 David Lloyd of Yr Ynyswen in Llanegwad, Carms., mortgaged two tenements in that parish to Morris Wogan, to secure £100. Morris died on 27 January 1640, and his IPM taken shortly afterwards showed that the Welsh Hook estate then consisted of 'a tenement and 20 acres in Dreenhill held by knight's service of the lordship of the Castle of Haverfordwest and worth 3s. p.a.; two tenements and 40 acres called Kilganawen Issa and Dyffryn Ffemant in the territory of the chapel of St. Michael in Fishguard and Dinas parishes, held by Knight's service of the Barony of Kemes, worth 10s. p.a.; four tenements and 40 acres in Ambleston held of the manor of Ambleston, worth 10s. p.a.; four tenements and 40 acres in Tretio Vaur and Trevoonus in St. Davids, held in free socage of the bishop's manor of 'Tutwall' (the tydwaldi, a class of tenants) worth 20s. p.a., a tenement, parcels, and six acres in Tretio Vaur, Tre lago, Ynys Vechan, and Trevoonus held in free socage as the preceding, worth 2s. 6d. p.a.; a tenement and 12 acres in Mabus Vach and Castle Rhedyn in Mathry parish held by knight's service of the manor of Castle Cenlas, worth 5s. p.a.; the unredeemed mortgaged tenement of Yskyrne Eynon Nantgwyn in Nevern, held by knight's service of the barony of Kemes, worth 6s. 9d. p.a.; and two unredeemed mortgaged tenements in Llanegwadfawr, Carms, held of the lord of "Lloge" as of the manor of "Dyrys Liogne" (Dryslwyn) worth 10s. p.a'.

The widow married secondly Hugh Laugharne of Eweston, Brawdy. Morris's only son, John Wogan aged six months and three weeks at the time of his father's death, succeeded in due course to Welsh Hook, and married Ursula daughter of Francis Laugharne by Lettice Vaughan of Pontfaen; after 1688 he went to live with his relations at Sealyham, where he made his will on 17 July 1706, proved on 1 August following, and left four children: 1. William, a minor in 1691, died at sea before 1706; 2. Grace died in 1740 aged 68 leaving issue by her husband John Tucker of Sealyham; 3. Mary, a minor in 1691, married the Rev. Atkins Williams, rector of Llanfyrnach; 4. Lettice who, according to the Tucker MS married Thomas Whitton of Ramsey Island off St. David's Head.

It was described as a manor in 1758 and again in 1770 when it was united with other manors and became the property of the Barlows. It changed hands again several times to *inter alia* the Tuckers and the Georges. In the early 1970s Welsh Hook was extensively modernised internally by the owner Mr. J. S. Roberts, of Newton West.

Refs: Francis Jones, *Historic Carmarthenshire Homes and their Families* & essay, 'Stone Hall' *NLWJ*; Pembs. Plea Rolls No. 157, ibid. No. 169; LT 1786; NLW Schedule of Sealyham Deeds 1938; Rees St. Johns, 1947, p. 106.

WELSTON, *Carew*

Home of the Cuny family. The present house stands on the site of an earlier house of the same name occupied by a member of the Cuny family in the middle of the 17th century. It was pulled down early in the 19th century. When Cromwell was besieging Pembroke he made Welston his headquarters. According to Fenton '. . . there is a quilted counterpane of white linen lined with crimson, that covered Cromwell's bed still in the possession of a lady, a descendant of that house, stained with ink spilled as he was writing one of his despatches during his confinement'. The 'confinement' refers to the attack of gout which obliged him to stay in bed for a few days. In the will of Richard Cuny of

Pembroke dated 24 October 1627, he mentioned four of his farms which he left to his son Walter Cuny including 'Welshtowne' (Welston). Walter was still in possession in 1638, and it was in Walter's time that Cromwell commandeered the house. Walter was Mayor of Pembroke when he died. His daughter married Francis Parry to whom there is a marble tablet in St. Mary's Church, Pembroke. John Powell Cuny was appointed Collector of Customs in the port of Milford in 1762, and William Edwardes, Lord Kensington and John Allen agreed to be his sureties. In 1767 he absconded and so John Lloyd and Eleanor *uxor* and Lord Kensington had to recover their losses from the receiver of rents of the Cuny estate. They were still in dispute regarding John Powell Cuny's affairs in 1786 when Counsel's opinion was sought on Abstract of Title of Mr. Powell Cuny, Esq. to an estate in Carew parish. By the 18th century the Cunys had moved to Golden near Pembroke.

The earliest reference to the family is to Walter Cuny who is thought to have been Gentleman Usher in the royal household of Henry VIII in 1526. His son, Richard Cuny lived first at St. Florence, moved to Lamphey Manor house c. 1618 then to Pembroke town, he also owned Golden (q.v.). He had married twice, firstly to Anne, daughter of Mathew Cradock by whom he had a daughter, Elizabeth, and secondly to Jane, daughter of Morgan Powell of Greenhill, viv. 1638, then a widow. By her he had one son, (Captain) Walter Cuny of Welston and six daughters. Walter was in the Parliamentarian army, was Mayor of Pembroke 1648 and 1661, and died after 1672. He married Lucy, daughter of Lewis Powell of Greenhill, and by her had six children. Richard the eldest son died without issue; Nicholas who married an unknown Sarah moved to Bristol and was a haberdasher, his will dated 15 September 1691. Nicholas and Sarah had four children, Richard Cuny who lived at Golden and died 1747, had an only son, Walter Cuny of Crossway, Glamorgan and was the father of John Powell Cuny who married Elvi, daughter of Rowland Philipps of Orlandon. They had five children; John Philipps Cuny who died an infant, John Powell Cuny born 1763, educated Jesus

College Oxford 1781 aged 18. B.A. 1786, Rector of St. Bride's 1786 until his death in 1824. He lived in Hill Street, Haverfordwest, where the Dragon Hotel stood. The other children were Elizabeth who married Samuel Chollett, Commissary General of the Island of Dominica; Richard Edmund Cuny viv. 1820 and Letitia who married Major Nathaniel Cameron, 79th Regiment.

In 1834 the property, described as 'a substantial modern house' was the seat of George Donne (or Dunn) Esq. The Dunns were still there in 1873, farming 173 acres worth £293 p.a. In 1900 John Evans was owner of the freehold of Welston Court and was High Sheriff in that year. By the 1930s Captain H. G. G. Ashton resided there; he was High Sheriff in 1944. His son, Col. Orme Ashton, Welsh Guards, succeeded and was still there in 1983. The house has since been sold.

Refs: Thomas Roscoe, *Wanderings and Excursions in South Wales,* 1836, p. 154; Poyston Deeds No. 92; WWHR XII, pp. 169, 173; Lewis, *TDW,* 1840; VL 1834; Landowners' Return 1873; Fenton, *Tour Pembs.,* 2nd edn., p. 205; Pembs. RO D/LP/792-4; ibid. D/LP/795 & 796, 797-8, 799.

WENALLT, *Nevern*

Home of the Warren, Jones and Knolles families. This property is southeast of Pont-y-Baldan in the valley of the Nyfer not far from the confluence with the Duad. Anthony Warren, third son of William Warren of Trewern by his wife Janet, daughter of Sir Rhys ap Thomas was of Wenallt and married Katherine Bowen of Trerickart by whom he had a son John Warren of Wenallt who 'fledd out of the countrey and died sans issue'. A George Rees was committed in Pembs. Great Sessions for burglary in 1663 at 'The house of Wenallt for stealing a gold ring, about £18 in money, a little leather bag and eleven lining bands from Mrs. Jones of Wenallt'.

Thomas Jones of Wenallt was High Sheriff in 1680. His daughter Lettice married Thomas Knolles who was a Land Tax Commissioner in 1705. Thomas Knowles paid tax on five hearths in 1670, and was of Wenallt *iure uxoris* in 1717. He was the son of John Knolles of Crugmor in Cardiganshire. Fenton wrote: '. . . I come to the ruined house of Wenallt, formerly of great respectability, in the possession of the several families of Johnes, Knowles and Bowen, though after it became the property of the last which resided at Upton Castle (q.v.) . . . was soon abandoned and the estate, falling among co-heiresses, was sold and suffered to go into decay'.

Refs: Fenton, *Tour Pembs.*, p. 309; Pembs. Plea Rolls Nos. 171 & 157; GWG MS; Wagner MS 12; VL 1834, 1894; Hampton Deeds; Papers of GS.

WERNDDOFN, *Llanfihangel Penbedw*

This large estate belonged to the Morgan family from the first half of the 17th century. Morris Morgan of Wernddofn (1656-1739) married Frances Lewis (1666-1719), and had a son, Morris born 1682. He married Elizabeth Howell and had a son, also Morris, born in 1720, (and four other children, two of whom married Howells', including Bridget who married Richard Howell). Morris succeeded his father in 1762 and married Rachel James who was a widow in 1758; Rachel and Morris had a son, Morris, baptised 1 October 1751 about four months after his parents' marriage and a second son, David, later Colonel David Morgan who married in 1793 Martha, widow of Rev. John Gwynne. She was a widow again in 1827 and her will dated 18 September 1829 mentions 'my sister's grandson William Price: my brother John Phillips'. Rachel Morgan, widow, of Wernddofn died in 1804 having been given Wernddofn by her son, Morris who had died in 1783.

The last in the male line was Colonel David Morgan who died without issue and intestate in 1825. Wernddofn passed to his next of kin, two brothers, John and Richard Howell of Ffynnonfelin, Llanwinio, Carmarthenshire, great-grandsons of Bridget Morgan of Wernddofn, (1689-1763), who had married Richard Howell. Shortly after inheriting, the brothers sold the estate to Thomas Brightwell, of Norwich (Vide Dolpwll). In 1837 John Colby is listed as owner and the estate consisted of 318 acres.

Refs: John Francis Deeds; LT 1786; Carms. RO, J. Francis Colln. Nos. 258-265, 268; GGMS II (Cadifor Fawr), p. 2; VL 1834, 1894.

WERNGOY, *Clydey**

Home to the James family who traced to Cadifor Fawr, and later by marriage to the Harries. The earliest record is of James Morris Griffith whose son, Abel James married Mary, daughter of Thomas Lloyd of Cilgwyn. Abel was born in 1610 and described in a deed dated 1690 as 'a weake sickly lame old man of 80 years, one side of his body being dead and useless'. His younger brother David James married and had a son, Morris James of Nantylladron, Clydey. Abel and Mary's son, Edward James married Diana, daughter of the Rev. Griffith Roberts, rector of Llanbettws by Cicely, daughter of Sir William Wogan of Wiston (d. 1625). Edward had a daughter and sole heiress who married Phillip Harries who came to Werngoy, viv. 1715. Their son, James Harries, the eldest son and heir, viv. 1729 married an unknown wife, Anne, by whom he had a daughter, also Anne, who married in 1763 Thomas Lewis (1723-1810), of Llwyngrawys. Anne died in 1798 leaving two daughters and co-heiresses: Anne who married Thomas Lewis of Clynfyw, who owned part of Werngoy *iure uxoris* in 1841 and Mary, who married William Summers of Moor and had issue.

Refs: Pembs. Plea Rolls Nos. 245, 246, 247; VL 1834, 1894; TM 1841; LT 1786; *Dwnn,* i, p. 108; WWHR VI, p. 207; GGMS (Cadifor Fawr); Carms. RO, J. Francis Colln. Nos. 188, 588.

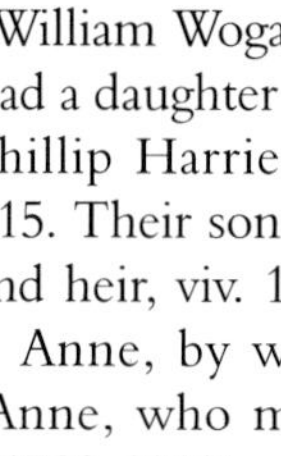

WESTERTON, *Ludchurch*
This was a residence of the family of Elliott, also seated at Narberth, Earwere and Crunwear. Westerton was built by John Elliott, (High Sheriff in 1586), who died on 31 October 1586. By his wife, Jane, daughter and co-heiress of John Vaughan of Narberth he had six sons and four daughters. It is from a transaction of the eldest son, Owen Elliott, that we learn about Westerton and its builder.

In 1600/1, Owen, then of Narberth, granted to his younger brother, Morgan, a lease of 'all that his great new house lately built by John Elliott, esquire, father of the said Owen and Morgan, in the parish of Lowechurch, called Westerton' and four decayed buildings adjoining, now forming a parcel 'of the said great house', and other nearby properties (specified), for the lives of the said Morgan Elliott, Anne his wife, and John their son. Thus Westerton was built before 1586 when the builder, the lessor's father died. Morgan Elliott's will was proved on 2 May 1678, his son John having predeceased him.

By 1786 the property belonged to Lord Kensington and in 1839 the Hon. William Edwardes was the owner. He later became the 4th Lord Kensington and was Lord Lieutenant of the county, M.P. for Haverfordwest and Comptroller to the Household of Queen Victoria.

In July 1974 Major Jones visited the house at the invitation of the then owner, Mr. Lawrence, who had put the estate on the market for £100,000.

Refs: Picton Castle Deeds; LT 1786; Tithe Map Ludchurch 1839; GGMS I (Adv. Carms.) fo. 211; Papers of GS.

WESTFIELD, *Rosemarket*
Home of the Davies and Bowen families. William Davies (the name is sometimes rendered as 'Davids') was assessed for three hearths in 1670. He was the descendant of Lewis Davies of Haverfordwest, a merchant, in 1530. In the Pembrokeshire Plea Rolls he is described as gent. William Davies made an inventory of his house in 1728 listing 14 rooms, all identifiable today. His goods, valued at £142 17s. 0d., included an old Norwegian boat. He made his will in the same year. He cut his elder sons off with the proverbial shilling '. . . to my eldest son John who had married a woman of ill fame and character – 1/-' and also 'to my idle and extravagant son William – 1/-'. He left the bulk of his estate to another son Charles and a lesser share to his next son Thomas who went into the Church. Mathew Bowen of 'Watchfield' was High Sheriff in 1741, and the house was tenanted and changed hands frequently after that date.

Refs: Pembs. Plea Rolls Nos. 7, 12, 227, 251; WWHR ii, p. 46; G. Nicolle, *Rosemarket,* 1982, pp. 11-13.

WHITCHURCH, *Whitchurch*
Fenton wrote: 'In a wood almost opposite to the church is a respectable mansion called by the name of the parish where, perhaps, the original founder may have resided, ancestor of the present proprietor, an offset of the prolific stock of Gwynfardd to whom all the gentry of this district, forming a perfect clan, trace their lineage. This parish has even had the reputation of being free from adders . . . '

This was probably the home of Nicholas Morgan, assessed for three hearths in 1670. James Bowen was the owner-occupier in 1786 when he was assessed at 13s. 9d. in Land Tax. In 1839 the Misses Margaret, Elizabeth, Frances and Joyce Bowen were the owner-occupiers with 219 acres. The last of them died in 1856. After that a clergyman, the Rev. Evan Thomas lived in the house. Francis Jones visited Whitchurch in 1974 and again in 1986. He describes it in his notes as ' . . . a large gentry residence with a walled garden and nicely laid-out grounds still well cared for. Now the home of a farmer, Mr. J. B. Vaughan Thomas'. He noted that 'the only woodland shown on Mudge's Map in 1819 is the wooded drive to the north of the church, and across the road where Whitchurch Farm (also called Plas Eglwyswen), stands. This is probably the house described by Fenton'. He gives a pedigree for the Griffith family of Whitchurch; Perkin ap Gwallter was succeeded by his third son, Griffith Perkyn who married Maud verch Gitto. They had three daughters, Anne, Margaret and Isabell. Margaret married John David Llewelyn ap Gwilym and had a son, Gitto ap John of Whitchurch who married Morfydd, daughter of Rees David ap Howel. Their son, John Griffith who married Jenet, daughter of George Bowen, died 25 June 1581, leaving a son, George Griffith who inherited Kilymaenllwyd *iure exoris.* He married 'Katherine, daughter of Eynon Morris of Kilymaenllwyd by Elizabeth, daughter of John Griffith by Elliw, base daughter of John Philipps, (reputed son of Sir Thomas Picton), by Agnes, daughter of John Voel of Lange Ridge, concubine'.

Refs: Fenton, *Tour Pembs.*, p. 289; LT 1786; VL 1894, 1904; Mudge Map 1819; Protheroe MS, IV, fo. 45; Tithe Map 1839.

WHITEWELL, *Penally*

A ruined house, described by Fenton as 'above the rank of such as farmers might have been supposed to inhabit'. These remains, according to an account written in 1922, must have been an important house at one time. 'They are situated within the bounds of Whitehall Farm, about 1½ miles west of Penally village. It was L-shaped, having a hall and a wing. The hall had a fireplace at the south end and it stood over a vaulted undercroft. The east wall has disappeared. The wing, apparently of two storeys, was also built over a vaulted cellar; it retains several ruined lancets and remains of fireplaces. The walls are heavily clothed with ivy and the interior is choked with undergrowth. The ruins of an outbuilding adjacent to the main structure comprise a gable pierced by a single lancet with a range of pigeon holes above.' Margaret, daughter of Philip Herle of Scots-borough, married John Hall of Trewent. They had three daughters, the eldest of whom, Margaret married Griffith Thomas of Peny-benglog who died in 1569. In 1786 Madam Barlow was owner with William Powell as her tenant.

Refs: Anc. Mon. Pembs. p. 291; LT 1786; VL 1894.

WILLIAMSTON, *Burton*

Home of the Bowen and Scourfield families. Fenton described it as an 'old baronial residence' and it was certainly at one time an Elizabethan manor house. He goes on 'Williamston, where for many years a family of the name of Bowen, an offset from the family tree at Upton, flourished, but which is now the residence of the Rev. Dr. John Philipps. This house I conceive to have sprung up in consequence of Benton Castle being abandoned as a habitation from the thorough change in the state of the country and the modes of life. The land at its back, between it and the haven, was in Queen Elizabeth's time noted as a park having deer, an addition it still retains, together with a very parkish appearance'. There are, in fact, two houses joined together. The oldest part of Williamston was built in the 13th century, and extensive additions and changes were made by succeeding generations. Its assessment at four hearths in 1670, shows it was of modest size at that period. From the Bowens it passed to the Phillips, and in 1786 the owner-occupier was the Rev. John Philipps, D.D., some of whose descendants adopted the surname Scourfield. In 1911 an interesting drawing of the house hung in the drawing room of Williamston. showing what it looked like prior to 1850. It showed a remarkable irregular building of considerable size, with as many as eight tall chimney stacks. Since 1850 many changes were effected, so that it became an L-shaped structure. During the first half of the 19th century, part of the house had been destroyed by fire, and that portion was rebuilt by Sir John Scourfield, first baronet. One of the latest, and most important, additions was made in 1896 when the old wing was taken down and rebuilt by Sir Owen Henry Phillips Scourfield, Bt. A photograph of the house as it was in Sir Owen's time is included in *Contemporary Biographies of South Wales and Monmouthshire,* 1907. Among the treasures then kept there was a handsome candelabra once owned by the Bonaparte family, an Eikon Basilik which had been presented to Catherine Scourfield of Moat in the 17th century, and a chair that had belonged to Lord Nelson.

Hugh Bowen of Upton, (q.v.), and his wife had a younger son, William Bowen. He married Margaret, daughter of John Laugharne of St. Bride's and settled at Williamston. In the floor in front of the altar in that parish church is a stone slab ornamented with a shield of arms showing three ravens, with a raven crest, and inscribed 'Here lys the Body of William Bowen of Williamston, gentilman, who lived an Honest Man and dyed as a Good Christian should the fifth day of November 1686'. He left five children. Hugh Bowen was the eldest son and heir. Few records have been found to him locally, for he became a collector of customs and settled at Mullingar, Co. Westmeath in Ireland. Williamston passed to his younger brother Thomas but the reason for such an arrangement is not clear. The second son, John Bowen inherited Upton (q.v). Thomas Bowen inherited Williamston, and is sometimes called 'the elder' to distinguish from a son of the same name. In 1708 Sir John Philipps of Picton Castle granted him a lease of small parcels of land in the Hundred of Howton, called Mabesgate, Burning Back, Watergate, Brooks Hedge, Bishops Wells, High Cross, Croft, the Yeeld house, Moor Meadow, and land near Oxland, amounting to 16 acres, for the lives of lessee, and of his sons William and Thomas aged 12 and 10 years, for 40 shillings rent and rendering £300 yearly. In 1726 he mortgaged property in Thurston and Howton, (which he had brought from Sir John Philipps), to his daughter Margaret Bowen. In 1715 and again in 1723 he was a land commissioner for the county. The last reference found to him is in December 1742 when, described as of Williamston, esquire, aged about 77 years, he gave evidence in a lawsuit between Wogan and Laugharne. He may be identical with the Thomas Bowen of Burton whose will was proved in 1746. By his wife Elizabeth daughter and co-heiress of Griffiths Davids of Mydrim, Carmarthenshire, he had the following children:

William Bowen, born about 1696, succeeded to Williamston, was High Sheriff in 1751, and died on 10 January in the following year, his will being proved on 12 May 1762; he had no issue by his wife Emma Owen of Orielton, whose will dated 22 April 1762 was proved in 1777;

Thomas Bowen, born 13 July 1721;

Hugh Bowen, twin with Thomas, one of the leases he granted remind us of the once flourishing oyster beds in the Cleddau – when on December 1763 he leased lands at Guildford in Burton for 99 years to Oliver Wilkin of Llangwm parish, yeoman, for a rent of £10 5s. and two barrels of pickled oysters, yearly. He died in 1766;

Morgan Bowen, matriculated at Jesus College, Oxford, on 26 August 1722, aged 19, graduate B.A. in 1728, and was buried at Burton on 3 March 1784; by his will made in 1776, he left a yearly rent-charge of £3 for the poor of the parish;

Jennett, baptised in 1690, married in 1728, Owen Phillips, M.A., rector of Walwyn's Castle, from whom descends the Lort-Phillips family;

Margaret.

Elizabeth, married in 1723, Richard Wright of Haverfordwest, surgeon, and had issue who lived at Popehill.

Dorothy – married Arthur Laugharne of Llanreithan, and had two sons and a daughter. Administration of his goods was granted to Dorothy in 1699.

Elizabeth – unmarried, named in the will of her brother Hugh in 1722.

Colonel Owen Philipps of Williamston (Pembrokeshire Militia) inherited Williamston through his wife Janet, daughter of Thomas Bowen. He married Anne Elizabeth, daughter of Henry Scourfield of Moat. Their son, John (b. 1808), assumed the name of Scourfield and inherited the property. He was created a baronet by Disraeli in 1876 and married Augusta Lort Philips of Lawrenny Park. A prominent Tory politician he in later life became a recluse who imagined himself to be a pauper. His son, Sir Owen, 2nd Baronet died without issue and the title became extinct. Sir Owen, by all accounts, was also something of an eccentric. He was over generous to the poor and whenever he visited Haverfordwest handed out coins galore to the populace. He had a passion for steam trains. A few years ago this handsome mansion was bought by Mr. Richard Fairclough. He converted the house into a nursing home. In 1989 the property, with its park now reduced to but four and a half acres was for sale as a going concern.

Refs: Francis Jones essay 'Bowen of Upton'.

WINTERTON, *Marloes*

In the early 18th century a family of the name of Roch was there, possibly descended from Mark Roch who held two hearths in Marloes parish in 1670. James Roch gent. a parliamentary voter, was there in 1760. He was a tenant of Hugh Meares who appears in the Land Tax records as owner. Hugh Meares had died by 1802 when his widow was shown as owner with Richard Llewhellin as tenant assessed at £2 2s. 10½d. Winterton changed occupiers in the 19th century being farmed by the Childs family and then into the early 20th century by the family of Richards.

Refs: LT 1760, 1786, 1802; VL 1894; Papers of GS.

WINTERTON, *Puncheston/Little Newcastle**

The whereabouts of this house is unknown but in the 16th century Jenet, daughter of John Symmons and Agnes, daughter and co-heiress of William ap Rees of Martel married Jenkin Cornock of Winterton. John Symmons was lord of the manor of Martel and died 17 March 1589. Jenet and Jenkin had a son, Richard alive in 1619 who in turn had two sons, Thomas who died without issue, and Lewis Cornock of Puncheston. The Cornock family were renowned for sheep rustling: in 1576 Richard Cornock of Wynterton sued Owen John ap Bowen of Trecoon gent. for saying 'Thou art a sheepe theiff and dost marke sheepe dayly, and my father and grandfather have many times sued thee'. Winterton formed part of the Martel estates. There was no house answering to that name in the 1786 Land Tax records.

Refs: Protheroe MS, V, 158, IV, 91; LT 1786; Bronwydd Deeds No. 763; *Extent of Cemais*; Pembs. Plea Rolls Nos. 18, 37; Poyston Deeds No. 31; Pembs. RO Deeds D/LP.

WISTON, *Wiston*

Originally known as Wyzo's Tun or castle and documented c. 1162-76 in connection with the church of Wiston, (Eastrewys), with Merryborough, the vicarage of St. Mary, granted by Walter, son of Wyzo and Walter, son of Walter to St. John of Slebech. (See Tregwynt q.v.)

The first proven Wogan at Wiston was Walter who owned a moiety of two fees there in 1324 but it is possible that others of his family preceded him there. Therefore 21 generations of the family owned the Wiston estate until it failed in the male line in 1793 and in the following year the estate was sold. It had been owned by the Wogans for some 570 years without a break and members of the family served as High Sheriffs for Pembrokeshire and Cardiganshire 11 times from 1543 to 1745. Poems of praise were written to Sir John Wogan of Wiston, (d. 1483) by Rhys Nanmor; a poem to Sir John Wogan (d. 1557) by Lewis Morgannwg; and other poems were written by Rhisiart Torwerth and Lewis Morgannwg amongst others.

A pedigree of the male line is given in the briefest form;

1. Walter Wogan held the moiety of 2 fees at Wiston in 1324.
2. Mathias Wogan, viv. 1348, also held moiety of Barony of Wiston.
3. Sir John Wogan, knight Senior. In 1392-99 held 3 parts of 2 knights' fees and moiety of a knight's fee in Wiston, held by knight's service of county of Pembroke, IPM 1419.
4. John Wogan, junior viv. 1425.
5. Sir Henry Wogan, Hir hen. Steward of Earldom of Pembroke in 1448, died 24 May 1475.
6. Sir John Wogan, Hir. Killed at Banbury 26 July 1469.
7. Sir John Wogan viv. 1484.
8. Sir John Wogan, gentleman Usher of King's Chamber, viv. 1521, HS Cards. 1541 & 1555. HS Pembs. 1543, 1550 & 1554. died 23 August 1557. Owned manor of Wiston and 3

parts of Barony of Dungleddau (Dungleddy) by knight's service of Earldom of Pembroke.

9. Richard Wogan, died pre-July 1557.

10. John Wogan lived at Wiston, HS Cards 1563. HS Pembs. 1567 & 1572, died 4 May 1580.

11. Sir William Wogan knighted before 1611, died 1625.

12. Sir William Wogan HS Pembs. 1636, died before 1654.

13. John Wogan died pre-Dec. 1642. He had two brothers; Col. Thomas Wogan, the Regicide, was one of the judges of Charles I, and Rowland (see No. 15).

14. Henry Wogan will proved 1662 left Wiston to Uncle Rowland Wogan.

15. Rowland Wogan died 31 July 1663.

16. Lewis Wogan, his son died 1694.

17. Lewis Wogan junior died 1714/15.

18. William Wogan HS Pembs. 1724 died 1730.

19. John Wogan HS Pembs. 1745 died 1759.

20. John Wogan mortgaged estate in 1767, died 1779. He left two sons; John Wogan died a minor, and

21. Thomas Wogan succeeded, died 1793 unmarried and the estate passed to his two sisters and was sold in 1794.

Fenton (1810) described the house as 'a large and awkward pile'. He mentions a sketch made of the old castle by the Buck brothers held in the Bodleian Library, Oxford. The castle in Fenton's time had been in ruins for about a century. The house and estate eventually were acquired by Lord Cawdor but even by 1900 little of the old house remained. In that year Francis Green paid a visit and wrote: 'Practically nothing is left of the old mansion of the Wogans at Wiston except for a portion of the old offices, which have been incorporated, into the modern farmhouse.' The tenant, Elizabeth Jones, who was possibly some 60 to 70 years of age, said that her family had occupied the place for three generations. The following information was given by Mrs. Jones who remembered the old mansion before it was pulled down. 'It had two sitting rooms and part of the kitchen (on the ground floor) of the present farmhouse was formerly the laundry of the old mansion and the wall between the sitting room and the stairs 2 ft. 6 ins. thick. In this room is an old cupboard, which belonged to the Wogans, and there is an old oak escritoire upstairs, which was used by that family. In an adjacent building were two parallel vaulted cellars. One of these is now used as a dairy. The arch of the other cellar had been pulled down and was used as an outhouse. To the west of the cellars is an outhouse, the floor of which is on about the same level as those of the cellars, which are a couple of feet or so below the level of the ground. This outhouse was the butler's pantry, housekeeper's room, and pantry of the old mansion. The butler's pantry formerly had a window on each side of his room, so as to enable the butler to see arrivals at the front as well as at the back door. The old mansion stood to the west of this building, the front door facing the outer fortification of the old castle. The doors of the rooms of the upper storey of the mansion were painted white with narrow blue lines round the panels. Some of the old tiles from the hall of the mansion are now in the pantry of the farmhouse. East of the old castle are the outbuildings of the farm, and also a fine walled garden, and in the southeast corner of the large field, (in front of the present farm house), which no doubt formed the demesne grounds of the old mansion are the fish ponds.'

The most notorious of the Wogans was Col. Thomas Wogan, the Regicide, son of John Wogan and Jane Colclough his wife. He was an active Roundhead, Member for Cardigan Borough in the Long Parliament in 1646. In 1647-68 he served in Pembrokeshire under Col. Horton, and the high spot of his career was the year 1649 when he sat as one of Charles I's judges and affixed his signature to the death warrant. He was summoned to trial on the restoration and imprisoned in the Tower of London but managed to escape and fled to the Continent and is thought to have died there.

There was a legal dispute in 1715 when Lewis Wogan tried to persuade Dame Mary Wogan, (of the Stone Hall branch), to leave her London home to come to Wiston to live with his family and to improve the ruinous house on the grounds that it was 'a meane house and hardly sufficient to contain ye family' and that she would like to see it in 'a flourishing condition'.

Refs: Francis Jones, *Treasury of Historic Pembrokeshire,* pp. 90-1; Lewis, *TDW*; *Dwnn,* i, 42, 90-1, 107-8, 165, 179-80, 220, ii, 45; WWHR VI, essay by F. Green, pp. 218-220, 229-231; Griffith Owen Deeds (iii); Fenton, *Tour Pembs.,* 322-3; Taylor's *Cussion,* p. 96a; Pembs. Plea Rolls; B. G. Charles, *NCPN,* p. 44; VL 1894.

WITHYBUSH, *Rudbaxton*

Home of the Martin, Phelps and Owen families. The Sparks family were tradesmen in Haverfordwest from the first half of the 17th century and had bought Withybush in the previous century. The Martin family had advanced themselves by successful participation in trade. The first to live there was Sparks Martin (b. 1713) who was High Sheriff in 1750 and a J.P. According to a story related to me, (says Francis Jones in his essay), by a descendant, one of the Sparks family won Withybush from the Pictons at a game of cards, whereupon an inflamed Miss Picton laid a curse on the winner, predicting that the day would come when his descendants would be without 'a thimbleful of earth to their name'. The Pictons certainly owned the property in Jacobean days, but it had been acquired by the Sparks family prior to 1667, for in his will made on 2 July of that year, William Sparks of Prendergast, corvisor, mentions 'my messuage called Withybush'. Sparks Martin married Martha Phillips of Trellewelyn (q.v.), and they had one child, a son who tragically died see *Treasury of Historic Pembrokeshire* pages 197-8. Sparks Martin left the estate to his sister Elizabeth who had married John Phelps who assumed the name and arms of Martin. The arms of Martin of Withybush were granted in 1788 as: *argent* a marten proper collared *gules*. Elizabeth the new owner of the Withybush and Trellewelyn estates was born on 18 May 1727, and married Samuel Phelps of Berwick St. John, Wiltshire, who died before 1786. Elizabeth died on 13 April 1809 at the age of 81 and was buried at Uzmaston. Her eldest son, John Phelps of Withybush served as High Sheriff in 1794, and after his mother's death took the name and arms of Martin. By his wife, Anne Scott he had 10 children the eldest of whom, Rev. Thomas Phelps J.P. succeeded and assumed the surname Martin. He died unmarried on 5 January 1865 having mortgaged the estate and alienated a number of farms and other properties. The second son, Sparks Martin Phelps married Mary Middleton of Frome. He lived for a time at Llangwarren, which he rented and died in 1855 and was buried at Rudbaxton. From him descended the Lloyds of Glangwili, Carmarthenshire. The third son, Samuel Phelps, Lieutenant, R.H.A. served in the Walcheren expedition, at Quatre Bras and Waterloo, and died on 13 December 1827, aged 37 leaving a widow and child. His portrait, in military uniform used to hang in Hermon's Hill House, Haverfordwest. John Phelps who died at Hastings on 1 January 1883 married Mary Anne Williams of Bideford and had among others, a daughter Florence Mary, who married in 1860 J. W. Phillips, solicitor of Haverfordwest. They had two sons, J. W. Phillips, junior, also a solicitor, of Portfield House, and Henry Game Martin Philips of Hermon's Hill House, Haverfordwest, both of whom, says Francis Jones, 'I knew well and had a great fondness for them'.

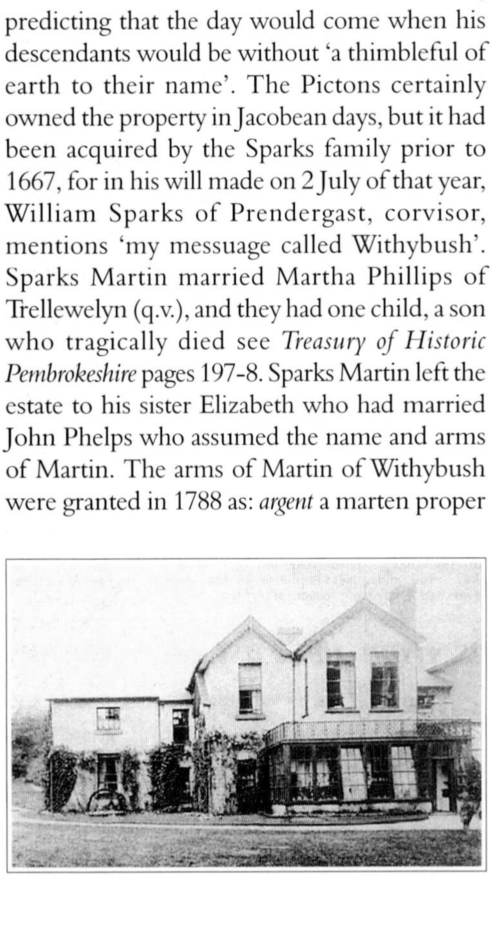

The last male member of the family was the Rev. C. M. Phelps (he did not adopt the name of Martin) who died in 1907. Well before his death the estate had been bought by William Owen, four times Mayor of Haverfordwest, who became High Sheriff in 1859. His sons, George Leader Owen of Withybush and Dr. Henry Owen of Poyston were also High Sheriffs (in 1894 and 1902 respectively). The Owens played a prominent part in Pembrokeshire affairs on the Bench and in civic realms. Dr. Henry Owen, mentioned above, was a considerable historian and the author of many works including *Old Pembrokeshire*

Families and *Gerald the Welshman*. He was the first Treasurer of the National Library of Wales and bequeathed his own library at Poyston to it.

During the last War the house was taken over by the R.A.F. and afterwards left empty and derelict. A photograph taken in 1947 shows Withybush in a parlous state and it was demolished not long afterwards, its site obliterated by a modern business estate.

Refs: Francis Jones essay 'Trellewelyn', *Pembs. Mag.*, 1985, No. 32; Fenton, *Tour Pembs.*, p. 180; BM Egerton 2586; Pembs. RO DX/152.

WOLFSCASTLE (CASBLAIDD),

*St. Dogwells**

On 15 June 1248 a commission of oyer and terminer to the King's Bailiff of Carmarthen, directed that 'whereas Anseim, sometime Bishop of St. Davids, proffered the King's Charter whereby it was granted that neither his men nor himself were bound to answer touching any free tenement, except before the King or his justices, on which account a plea in the county (court) of Carmarthen by the King's writ, between Agnes late the wife of Hugh le Poer, demandant, and William le Mareschal, Master Tankard de Rupe, Jordan de Armhull and Drew his son, tenants of a fee of the bishop's, of Wulvescastel and Newton,' has remained in that county (court) without a day, he is to try that plea and other pleas in the same county (court). In 1292/93 the Bishop owned 13 cattle, 350 sheep, and 41 acres of corn at Castrum Lupi, worth £13 0s. 4d.

In 1315 John de la Rupe obtained a grant for himself and his wife Elizabeth, from Nesta wife of Robert Corbet and one of the co-heiresses of Robert de Vale, of lands at Castell Loyth (Castell Blaidd) and Rinaston.

In 1326, where it is described as a manor, the only properties specified by name are fields which appear to be in the vicinity of Wolfscastle village, and the tenement of Broadmoor; buildings of wood and stone stood there, a fishery worth 12d. per annum, a water mill, and 6 acres of woodland.

In 1535/36 the value of the manor of Castrum Lupi was 10s. per annum.

In 1585-88, the bailiff of the manor was Thomas Wiks, and the average annual profits stood at 100s., and two fulling mills in the parish were then attached to this manor. It appears in the Taylor's *Cussion List of Manors* in 1587-8. The lordship or manor of Wolves Castle, with the tenement of Broadmoore, was leased on 8 March 1671/2 to Damaris Edwardes of Treffgarne, widow, for the lives of her three sons, John, Francis, and Owen, at an annual rent of £5.

On 2 November 1745 Richard, Bishop of St. Davids, leased to Rowland Edwardes of Treffgarne, the lordship of Wolves Castle alias Wolfscastle, the messuage called Broadmoor within the said lordship, in the parish of St. Dogwells, for the lives of lessee's wife Anne, William Tucker Esq. and Perrott Williams, gent. at a yearly rent of £5; and about 1750 the lordship or manor of Wolves Castle was still so held.

On 21 October 1781 the bishop granted a lease to William Ford of Stone Hall and John Harries of Priskilly, trustees for John Owen Edwardes, the lordship of Wolvescastle, and Broadmoor, for the lives of Anne (aged 58) wife of Rowland Edwardes, John Owen Edwardes of Hook (aged 37) and Anna Maria (aged 3) eldest daughter of the said J. O. Edwardes. At this time the main tenements in the manor were held by John Meyler (£25 p.a. rent), William Griffith (£25), John Harry (£4) and Elizabeth Hugh (£4), while the tenants at Broadmoor were Joseph Maddox (£20), William Phillip (£25), Elias Abraham (£7), Evan Bowen (7s. 6d.), William Richard (£3 10s. 0d.), and he also paid another £3 10s. 0d. for 'Gennet Humbarch', and William Abraham of Good Hope (£14).

In 1896 it was recorded that the manor of Wolves Castle was set on a lease for lives.

Refs: Report on Land in Wales, 1896, XXXIII, 444 ff; NLW, Church in Wales Recs., Nos. 170, 323; NLW, Eaton Evans and Williams Colln., No. 3861; NLW, Lucas Documents; ibid. MS 1390 D; Cal. Patent Rolls 1247-58, p. 30; BM, Harl. MS 6696, fo. 10a; Val Eccles, IV, p. 379; PRO, KR Inventories El 54.1.48, 21 Edw I; *Black Book of St Davids,* 1326, pp. 119-127; *Arch. Cam.*, Ser II, vol. V, p. 40.

WOLFSDALE/WOLFDALE, *Camrose*

Pencaer

Home of the families of Mortimer, Pencaer, Bowen, Reynish and Crowther. There are two houses of this name, Wolfsdale Hall and Wolfsdale House. It is impossible to be sure which family resided at which house as the name Wolfsdale or Wolfdale has been used throughout – *Ed.*

At one house were the Reynish family from the early 18th century until 1 February 1890 when the last of the line, Charles Crowther Reynish died. He was one of the three sons and four daughters of John Reynish, aged about 80 in 1851 and Anne Gaites his wife whom he had married in 1809. A John Bennett (1817-84) married Lettice; one of the four daughters of John Reynish of Wolfsdale, and their son, John Crowther Bennett (1842-82) was described as 'of Wolfsdale'. In 1873 he owned 685 acres.

John Reynish was the elder son of Thomas Reynish who had succeeded his elder brother, John Crowther Reynish whose will was proved 24 November 1809. Thomas and John were the sons of Thomas Reynish of Camrose, gent. and Catherine, daughter of John Crowther of Camrose, gent. Their prenuptial settlement was dated 27 March 1748, the same year as the death of his father, another Thomas Reynish.

In 1217 Llewellyn the Great, campaigning in South Wales, met Bishop Iowerth of St. Davids at Wolfsdale, with the result that Llewellyn agreed to retire, having first extracted hostages from the men of Roose as a pledge of their willingness to accept his rule.

The arms of Pencaer, lords of Wolfsdale in the time of Henry VII were: *Gules* on a fess engrailed between three bucks' heads caboshed, as many crescents.

Richard Pencaer was lord of the manor in about 1500 and his daughter Joan married John Warren of Trewern. In 1620 Morgan ap Owen (Bowen) of Wolfsdale was committed at Haverfordwest Sessions by Sir John Stepney, the Mayor and Thomas Cannon for making an assault and an affray on his own father, John ap Owen, gent. and William Jones with his 'sword drawn in a very outrageous manner'. John Bowen acquired Wolfdale from Owen Edwardes of Treffgarne in November 1661. He married Margaret, daughter and co-heiress of Philip Vaughan of Houndsbrook, Carms. Other members of this family also appear to have been in trouble one way or another over the years. In 1763 John Bowen born 1732, (son of George Bowen of Wolfsdale), and Sarah his mother sold the lordship of Wolfsdale and Camrose to William Cozens of Sandy Haven for £1,250. On 18 October 1832 William Cozens, grandson of the purchaser sold the manor to C. W. T. Webb-Bowen and Hugh Webb-Bowen, of Camrose. Wolfsdale Hall otherwise West Wolfsdale was put up for sale in 1913. The then owner, J. V. S. Bennett in 1937, advertised the Wolfsdale House estate for sale.

Refs: WWHR XI, 1926 pp. 14-15, 48, 49; Pembs. Plea Rolls No. 136; Landowners' Return 1873; *Annals Cambria*; SC 650 Carms. RO. Pembs. ROD/RM/11/32; GGMS III (Bleddyn ap Cynfyrn) fo. 43; Papers of GS (CF) 1620; ibid. 1651; BM Egerton 2586 fo. 348a; *Dwnn,* i, 87.

WOODSTOCK, *Ambleston*

Howell

Woodstock was the home of several important families. There were several houses called variously Upper Woodstock, Woodstock, Woodstock Mill, and Woodstock Slop.

The first known owner was Hywel Fychan, descended from Cadifor Fawr of Blaenerch. He was there circa 1300. He left two sons, John Howel of Woodstock and Philip Howell of Llys-y-fran. John Howell married Jane Joyce of Prendergast, and had two sons, John of Woodstock and Hick Howell who was knighted and whose son Richard was appointed Constable of Pembroke Castle on 16 February 1390. The said John Howell is named in several early records. On Monday after the Assumption 1381, David Drew of Wyllyamstoun granted a messuage 'in Wylliamystoun near Tankardystoun in the Lordship of Pebidyauk, (Trewilym in St. Lawrence parish) to John Howell of Wodystok'. His daughter and sole heiress married Stephen Perrott.

The arms of Howell of Woodstock were: *Azure* a dove volant *argent*. Woodstock was an extensive manor, we are told 'possessed in early times by Hako Hywel, a man of great property and power who is styled lord therof'. A survey of the estate on the attainder of Sir John Perrott, mentions that three hives of bees belonging to Sir John was in custody of John Hire in the manor of Woodstock, the hives valued at 3/-: also that there was ½ gallon of honey in John Hire's custody 'which cometh to Her Majesty for the half of her hives of bees lately killed there'.

The Perrotts were succeeded by a cadet branch of the Philipps family of Picton Castle. Richard Philipps settled at Woodstock and was living in 1615. Various other families were associated with Woodstock as tenants, principally the Williams's who tenanted Woodstock from the Perrotts from 1678 until the mid-1700s. Howell Williams was of Woodstock in 1678 having been given a lease in 1690/1. His son, Edward succeeded him and married Martha, daughter of John Higgon of Ambleston. Edward died in 1729 leaving two daughters and co-heiresses, Mary who married Thomas Meares of Haverfordwest, and Anne who married Watkin Lewes, Clerk of Penybenglog. They had two sons and three daughters.

The Land Tax List of 1786 shows 'Two tenements called Woodstock, both owned by John Tucker, Esq. one tenanted by John Williams, the other by Francis Llewelyn, assessed at 18s. and £1 4s. 0d. respectively, and a third called Woodstock, James Philipps, Esq. owner, James Morgan occupier assessed at £2 2s. 0d.' in the same list.

In 1904 LT, Benjamin David Thomas was shown as of Woodstock, Hugh F. Evans of Woodstock East, Thomas H. Philipps of Woodstock House and land joint, Thomas Price of Woodstock house and land. Fenton tells us: 'At Woodstock there was a chapel of ease to Ambleston parish, but has long been down, and even the cemetery has been ploughed over. Since then, a Methodist chapel has been raised there.'

Refs: Fenton, *Tour Pembs.*, 2nd edn. p. 196; PRO AD iii 400, & 478 & 479; ibid. D5932; Taylor's *Cussion,* fo. 96a; AD iii, D485; Lord Hampton Deeds No. 481049; ibid. 482682, 484049.

YNYS Y BARRY (BARRY ISLAND), *Llanrhian*

This literally means Barry Island and records go back to at least 1342 when it was mentioned in a transfer of lease from Philip Cadigan to John son of Philip Goch of Preskyli.

It was from this place 'where there always hath been and yet will be wild birds of the sea, gulls, mews and divers other birds', (part of the profits of Archdeaconry of Carmarthen), that the family of the celebrated Giraldus Cambrensis – Gerald of Wales, took their surname. It formed part of the manor of Llanrhian, and belonged to the Lloyds of Cilciffeth.

On 16 July 1550, Henry Hoper of Island, of the parish of Llanrhian gave Jennet verch James David Gove a bond for payment of £5, in default of which Jennet can enter on lands in Trevoughllwyd and Tyrevellwr gwynt in parish of Llanhowell.

In 1662 J. Barlow, widow of George Barlow Esq. seized of one third of certain lands in Llanrhian parish, which included 'the island called Ynnys y Barry'. In 1784 William Davies, gent. was the owner. His seal bore: a garb erect amongst stubble. In 1789 he subscribed ten guineas towards the repair of St. David's Cathedral.

In 1805 Richard Le Hunte of St. Botolphs gave a lease of 21 years of Ynys y Barry to Francis Fortune of Haverfordwest for £220 rent p.a. On Colby's Map of 1831, the whole area of the headland of Porthgain – Abereiddy is called Ynys y Barry and the farmhouse is called Barry Island; in 1848 the marriage settlement of William Reynolds of Barry Island, Minister of the Gospel, and Margaret Anne Thomas, settles Barry Island, otherwise Island y Barry (313 acres) upon the marriage. In 1882 they made over the property in favour of their son James William Reynolds.

In 1989 Ynys Barry became a country house hotel.

Refs: Slebech Deeds No. 405; Pembs. Plea Rolls No. 88; Pembs. RO D/Le Hunte No. 48, ibid. Nos. 56, 64, 65; Chancery Proc. 884/36 AD1533-38; W & W (H'west) No. 6183; LT 1786; NLW, Eaton Evans and Williams Deeds; Colby Map 1831.

FRANCIS JONES (1908-1994)

A BIOGRAPHICAL PROFILE

By H.C.-J.

In 1974 the late Sir Anthony Wagner, KCVO, KCB, D.Litt. (Oxon.), Garter King of Arms, wrote of my father in the Foreword of a book dedicated to him: 'To lead in a special field is a great but no in-ordinately great distinction, but to conquer for oneself from scratch a whole field is rarer. This is what Francis Jones has done for Welsh history and family genealogy. As an old friend may perhaps be permitted to say, how in himself no less than in his work Francis embodies and transmits that singular charm and excellency of the immortal Welsh bardic tradition he so worthily represents'.

Sadly my father did not live to see this, his last book, in print. He believed an historian's duty is to make his findings known to all. So it is now my duty to publish this volume.

Millions of words flowed from his pen but none gave him greater pleasure than these about his beloved home county where our family have lived for over eight hundred years.

This is his literary 'coming home' in a life cycle of unique achievements taking over 70 years of research.

To honour such a father is hard, but I feel this book is incomplete without a pen portrait of the man behind the words and the woman behind that man. I have tried to be dispassionate, but if I err on the side of admiration and affection I hope you will understand. My aim is to give an insight into the man whose words will take you down the ages to the homes and people of bygone Pembrokeshire.

The story began when the Norman Conquest was a nearer memory than the Battle of Waterloo is to us today. For 730 years our family held the Brawdy estate through seventeen generations before it was dispersed. Francis Jones's parents were steeped in family history and genealogy. It was only two generations since an ancestor was High Sheriff in 1773; of the House of Brawdy, only the old drive pillars remain, and sheep graze over the site of the old mansion where William Jones, standard bearer to Henry VIII lived.

Francis Jones was born in 1908 in the windswept village of Trevine perched high above the Celtic Sea on the St. Davids peninsula. The Wicklow hills in Ireland are seen on a clear day outlined by the setting sun. Inland are the sweeping curves of the Preseli hills which gave Stonehenge their bluestone pillars. Bishop Asser came from Trevine to go with his friend King Alfred the Great to found Oxford University.

As soon as he could walk and talk Francis Jones was immersed in family history, of coats of arms, and genealogies handed down orally in the old Welsh tradition. Such tales had also fired his own father, James's, imagination, and this adventurous teenager, my grandfather, emigrated to his uncle's ranch in the Welsh Patagonian colony in the 1880s to make his fortune. Maybe he hoped to return in triumph to reclaim the old Brawdy estate. He became ranch manager and horse breaker, and trekked herds of horses over the Andes to sell them to warring factions.

Riding the Patagonian Pampas

Tales of Chivalry

One night he was attacked by a mountain lion, in killing it with his knife he was badly mauled. He was found by Indians who nursed him back to health. On another expedition his companion died and James got lost trying to round up the horses on his own. He finally staggered home, a skeletal wreck having survived on wild berries and the snakes he caught and ate. Later an accident crippled him and his days of riding the pampas ended. He returned home for a long convalescence, married and scratched a living where he could. He was a natural linguist, and during his twelve year adventure he learned three more languages. During the two world wars he was often called on to act as an interpreter at Fishguard Harbour. His gun belt, a mummified paw of the lion he killed, a book of heraldry from his father, and his own essays and poems in Welsh are now heirlooms grouped round my desk as they were at my father's.

Francis Jones was the eldest of four children. He learned to speak Welsh and English when very young. An ability to remember long pedigrees showed a remarkable memory. He displayed intense curiosity at the hearths of the relations the family often visited to talk about the old days. He told me that his earliest memories were in his first year, and I believe him still. The family moved to the quaintly named Stop and Call hilltop area of Goodwick, where he went to primary school. When he was about six the family visited Haverfordwest market. The boy wandered away into St. Mary's church, and in that ancient empty place he was captivated by monuments with gaily painted coats of arms. As he stared up, sunlight streamed through stained glass windows to light up a knight's crested helmet high on the wall. That solitary moment decided his life. Inspiration, revelation, vocation or whatever, from then on he was dedicated to historical studies. It flowered in him till his death some eighty years later.

He started school before roads were tarmacadamed, cars were a rarity, when people read by candles at night, and golden guineas were in circulation; the sun never set on the British Empire, and the Boer War was a fading memory. The approaching holocaust of the Great War did not mute the laughter in school playgrounds then. He effortlessly won a scholarship to Fishguard County School. It was a long walk, with a glorious view over Cardigan Bay up to the hills of Snowdonia, and the unspoilt countryside provided a treasure trove of evidence of its continual occupation from the Stone Age. The next short years would decide many careers in this quiet backwater with its scanty opportunities. The schoolteachers were dedicated and well trained with a deserved status in the small community. They taught large classes of pupils whose families encouraged them to learn. All knew the key to opportunity was education.

Then, as always, one of Wales's biggest exports was its brightest and most adventurous youth. It seems the ABCDE of education was Ambition, Blackboard, Chalk, Discipline and Enthusiasm. Those teachers rarely complained of being under-resourced. Their resources were between their ears. Resourcefulness was their watch word. The prizes for neat handwriting and fastidious presentation inspired intense competition amongst pupils.

Francis kept a list of his fellow pupils' progress. Many strode out of the isolation of rural Pembrokeshire to become judges, professors, doctors, service officers, and captains of merchant ships. The class system was rigid then, but doors were open to all. The keys were talent and initiative, curiously two qualities that can be nurtured but never taught. These pupils learned long poems by heart, learned their multiplication tables by singing them, and excelled at mental arithmetic. They were always set holiday tasks.

I now have many of my father's holiday task notebooks; considering they were compiled by a boy barely in his teens their content range is astonishing. There are poems and essays for Eisteddfods in Welsh; also many maps of Pembrokeshire and the UK meticulously drawn, some even depicting the railway network. Masses of pencil and water-colour drawings of castles, historic houses of all types, churches and idyllic rural vignettes. There are cartoons of fellow pupils and masters, little articles and notes on Pembrokeshire families, legends and episodes from history. Snippets from the laws of Hywel Dda jostle with snatches of poetry from Blake, Keats and Shakespeare. There are carefully drawn copies of Egyptian hieroglyphics, the Morse code, maps of star constellations, the Braille alphabet, the Greek alphabet and drawings of the Zodiac signs. There are excerpts in old Greek and Latin, and even navigation tables copied from his seafaring grandfather's charts that he used when rounding the Horn in the days of sail. I was most touched to see the address of the College of Arms and a list of the boys' books on heraldry. There are over a hundred notebooks, and it is easy to see that they honed his natural gift for memory, which is a family trait.

Being a loner he didn't like team sports, though he was a good runner and swimmer and enjoyed fishing from the harbour. He longed to catch a giant conger eel, but left no record of doing so. It was a rare failure in his life. I often think of the lad pushing his way to school through the frequent Pembrokeshire gales. When the storms were spectacularly violent the school would arrange for a horse and cart to get the drenched pupils home.

Research notes when 14 years old.

Martha and James Jones, the parents of Francis Jones

I see from my father's reports that he was making steady progress at the top of his class. He won prizes in school debates, and recitations in chapel competitions. There was a rich and lively cultural life then, and talent emerged early. A chair he won at an Eisteddfod in 1922 is in my hall today. Other events were plentiful like fairs, open air boxing, pony racing on beaches, and agricultural shows.

Throughout his life my father needed little sleep. I came across a synopsis for a 38-chapter novel, and copies of letters to English publishers sending them his articles. So in addition to his examination work, he was already happily burning the midnight oil. Every day had purpose for him, even holidays. Whenever he could borrow a pony he would visit distant parishes to make further researches. More often than not, he walked great distances, spending nights with relations in cottages and farm houses. He would listen and fill his note books in English and Welsh as he sat on settles in front of open log and culm fires on the stone flagged floors as bards and poets have done round the 'Simne fawr' for centuries. He often left by way of a thank you, a poem usually written in Welsh, many of which are prized today. Evidently he managed his time with the precision of a computer. His fastidiousness showed in his personal neatness and he loved being well dressed, a trait that stayed with him all his life. I never once saw him unshaven.

His mother took him for his first trip to England. They stayed with a relation who had been a General in the Indian Army, and lived in some state in the Georgian spa town of Bath. It made a huge impression on the boy. So did the advice he was given; if he was to succeed in life outside Wales, he would be wise to flatten his vowels. He attended to this immediately, and with the naturally attractive timbre of his voice, his immaculate diction made him a compelling broadcaster, lecturer and raconteur for the rest of his life.

The short slim youth with the steady blue eyes became a familiar figure calling on local vicars to comb through parish records, to decipher names and dates from long fallen tomb-stones. He also consulted the Pembrokeshire parish pump pamphleteers who abounded then as they do now, to track down more information. They were generous in their help and encouragement, as were many of the gentry. Most were not the bucolic lechers as portrayed in 'Tom Jones', in fact they were capable managers, knowing better than most that a fool and his money are soon parted. Many had a tradition of culture, having libraries full of family and estate records. They opened their doors to the young scholar and soon my father was deep into ancient records and books, pioneering through archaic ledgers and copying old manuscripts and deciphering old seals. Lawyers and record offices gave him the same challenge, and dusty manuscripts would give him a clue to some historical jigsaw.

The tools of his profession were just pen and paper, but what a brilliant intellect directed them. He was uniquely self-sufficient in his lonely quest.

The early morning countryside was full of interest for him. His powers of acute observation picking out landmarks, houses, and wildlife as he walked or rode in the valleys along the coast. Patronage then did not have today's spiteful meaning. Francis Jones's charm, good manners, and his enthusiasm endeared him to the vicars, landowners and local historians of those far off days, and he had an instinctive feel of how the establishment worked.

Many of the family went to sea. One of my father's uncles owned a coastal trader plying its wares to Liverpool, Bristol and Cardiff. My father set sail in the summer holidays aboard the 'Ben Rhian' as unpaid cabin boy. He loved those voyages particularly the drama of heavy seas. His uncle's first mate (another relation), was a drunk soured by losing his Captain's ticket after being convicted of gunrunning in the Far East. My father wrote a particularly poignant story about one of his voyages. I long to find more notes about those days at sea when there were so many ships under sail, and when the bodies of poor sailors were often washed up on Pembrokeshire beaches. Many of my mother's family were seafarers, her brother brought home fine silks from Japan which were made into dresses for the girls to wear to chapel.

Francis easily passed his Higher School Certificate, cum laude. It was time for him to make a living. Not having the money to go to University, he made a wise decision. He became a student teacher acting as an apprentice to qualified schoolmasters. After years of practical experience and more examinations he in turn would qualify. He was posted to schools all over Pembrokeshire, St. Nicholas, Haverfordwest, Saundersfoot and Tenby. One of his brightest pupils was a boy who became the actor Kenneth Griffiths. More importantly, the school holidays gave him time for research and writing. Soon he was having so many articles published in local papers that he had to use a range of pen names. De Loy, Some One Else, Audax, Essex Harries, Dewisland, Ygrr and others. It was as well that he did not go to university as there is no substitute for experience, and that he was having in abundance. Many historians encouraged him, particularly Herbert Vaughan, author of *The South Wales Squires*, who became a lifelong friend.

My father wrote on a wide variety of subjects, avoiding narrow specialisation, and the petty jealousies that abound in academe. It was a lonely path, as all his published work had to stand public scrutiny by experts. He also knew failure. I found some of his articles with a terse comment, 'Rejected by' ... Evidently these spurred him on to turn obstacles into stepping stones. The deductive powers he applied to his output was such, that within a few years he built up a huge network of fellow scholars all over the UK and world-wide, and many consulted him. I have trunks filled with their letters in the archives.

In his early twenties he was already an authority on many subjects. He also found time for politics, becoming a speaker for the Primrose League. As a good traditional Tory he attacked a Mr. David Lloyd George ferociously, and his note books are full of anti-liberal barbs. His flashing ripostes put down many a heckler at the hustings so I have been told.

My father was twenty-three when he married my mother. She was the perfect match for this unusual man. She was tiny, vivacious, brown-eyed, brown-haired, the daughter of the Charles family of Llanrhian, well-to-do farmers. She was educated at the Hill House Lady's College in Haverfordwest, spoke Welsh, wrote well, painted in watercolours, played the piano, and she was an excellent horsewoman. Her parents having died young, she also had practical experience in running the farms they owned.

Ethel Charles was of old Pembrokeshire stock first recorded in 1242 and one of her ancestors, David Didwith, was Rector of Freystrop in 1390. She bought a small but useful dowry to their marriage. Her personality exuded warmth and kindness ' and she had a terrific sense of humour; we learned from her to find fun and laughter in the smallest unexpected things. They had four children in rapid succession, of whom I am the eldest. Mamma ran our home with meticulous thoroughness, and the house was charming and always welcoming. What warm unforgettable memories she left her family! She devoted her life to my father's work and yet gave us an idyllic childhood. My father sensibly, not having the slightest interest in money, left all those matters to her. They went on sketching expeditions, she helped read his proofs, he read his articles to her often acting on her suggestions. Yet she always had time for her children.

Ethel Charles of Henllys. Llanrhian

After marriage my father's interest in politics waned. Whether my mother being related to Mr. David Lloyd George had anything to do with it I do not know.

In the late 1920s my father discovered all Haverfordwest's old records, including medieval manuscripts rotting away in the Castle gaol cells. He volunteered to rescue and classify them. He started work wearing an old cassock to save his clothes from the dirt and dust. As he was forever rushing to and from his new treasure trove. he needed a key. So for official access he was made a Special Constable, and he founded the present Record Office. It was resolved at a council meeting that he would be paid a small sum for this work. At this, a historically challenged councillor banged off a newspaper letter saying what a waste of time and money this was. My father got his induction as an archivist, self taught and off his own bat. He was soon wearing another uniform when, in 1931, he was commissioned into the 4th Welch Regiment to start his third career.

He threw himself into soldiering with the same dynamism he gave to teaching and writing. Drill nights, lectures, weapon courses, week-end camps, summer camps, and more exams. Yet this did not stem his flow of articles which were now being more widely published in learned journals all over the UK as his reputation grew and his researches took him all over Wales and the borders. All my life I saw him writing late into the night. Even if we got up early, there he was, writing at his desk before going to work. Four or five hours sleep a night sufficed him, yet strangely I never saw him doze in the day. The older I get, the cleverer my father gets in my memory. The proverb that 'The hours before daybreak are sent from Paradise', was one my father believed, it comes to me now as in the early dawn I look out from my home high on the Preseli slopes and see across Fishguard Harbour up to Goodwick where my father's career began.

In 1936 he made a big career move, applying for a post in the National Library in Aberystwyth. Applicants needed a university degree, but this he blithely ignored. He travelled up for an interview with an old school friend Bertie Charles (later Dr. B. G. Charles), in an Austin Seven. They were both successful. My father then moved the family up to Cardiganshire. We lived at first in a delightful remote mansion, Plas Broginin, rented from the Pryse estates. A trout stream ran at the bottom of the drive. As we enjoyed breakfasts of freshly caught trout he landed, it seems the fishing was a factor in our going to live there. He loved the countryside all his life. He cycled to work some ten miles away, and his salary was £150 p.a. His fertile mind explored the new medium called 'The Wireless'. The BBC broadcast his scripts in 1938 and he mastered the microphone as easily as he had the pen. That is to say he would have an original

Bath time for officers of the 'Fighting Fourth' Welch Regiment by Fred May.

idea, write it, check, double check it, revise, polish, present it, then rehearsal, rehearsal, and more rehearsal. The thoroughness of his early education was paying off, and the advice he got during his visit to Bath. So fortune favours the prepared mind.

My father's teachers taught him that talent is useless without discipline and dedication. These ethics are neatly observed in one of his essays which I found. 'A man with strong discipline,' he wrote 'will impose a strong discipline on himself. If he is to realise his ambition he realises he will have to do certain things, things that will involve hard work which will often be unpalatable. Yet he will do them because it is essential if he is to advance. He will remain in his study on a fine day when all his instincts urge he should be enjoying himself with friends on a bowling green or in convivial company at a cocktail party. He will write not merely when the spirit moves him, but will buckle down to the task even when he is not in the mood to do so. He will not wait for inspiration, he will work for it. He who works in fits and starts is not likely to receive the laurels.' My father saw life as a race, in which the only thing that interested him was first place.

When I was small he used to take my brother and me out for long walks. I now realise these were mini route marches. Once I collapsed with fatigue. His words of advice echo in my memory. 'Remember,' he said, 'the weak fall out and die.' I got home under my own steam. However, I was grateful for my father's training when I was one of a small band to pass a mountain warfare course in Scotland. It lead my brother to be captain of rugby, boxing and cricket of the British Army teams in Berlin. My brother and I both did two years National Service on active service, and now it occurs to me that Mamma had a total of nine years in her life when her men were away and every telegram that came to her home could have been bad news.

My parents moved to Aberystwyth so that we could go to school. Our new home was a wonderful choice, its back garden led to the gorse covered hills of the open countryside and the sea was only a few hundred yards down the quiet road. They kept up their links with Pembrokeshire, my father having transferred to the Pembroke Yeomanry. Getting back for regimental duties (combined with researching) was easy then by GWR trains or by Crossville buses on uncrowded roads. The Yeomanry of those days continued the tradition of being rather like a county club where landowners and the professional classes filled the Officers' Mess. Many of their fathers had died in the Great War serving the same regiment, and sometimes there would be three generations of the same family during mess nights, all of whom had served or were in the regiment.

Family group

As the balmy days of the thirties unfolded so pleasantly, we went on family outings to picnic in the Cardiganshire hills, on river banks and on beaches. My father taught us to put up tents. He taught my brother and me to draw and to fish for trout, to box, and took us out to sea in a small boat. He and a friend sailed it up to Barmouth which gave my mother some anxiety as they had originally intended to go to Ireland but my mother vetoed that. Although my father's salary was small, he made it up with fees from articles, broadcasts and his army pay.

Hitler's savage blitzkrieg in Poland cut short our family unity. War was declared and a few days later we saw my uniformed father off at Aberystwyth station. The platform was crowded with families saying goodbye to their men. We waved to him through the clouds of steam from the engine as they all went out of sight into the darker fog of war. For the next five years my mother brought up four children on her own.

My father was posted to an experimental regiment of field artillery, every man of whom had a high IQ. After intensive training they took part in an army gunnery competition, winning the Silver Gun trophy by a huge margin. This elite regiment was then dispersed, the men promoted and posted to other regiments to pass on their expertise. My father was promoted to Major. There survives from this time, an article he wrote, 'The History of Cockfighting in Wales' subtitled, 'written on active service'. Even in the Battle of Britain he found time to write.

Orders for overseas arrived and his regiment boarded troop ships in the Clyde, and the convoy sailed for North Africa. I wonder if they sailed down the West coast to avoid the Channel U-Boats or whether as they rounded the Pembrokeshire peninsula, my father leaned on the ship's rail trying to catch a sight of his home county as they sailed for battle. The ships were crammed with ammunition, high explosive, and motor fuel. Knowing they might be torpedoed any minute cannot have made it a pleasure cruise. Memories of the Ben Rhian and mackerel fishing might have passed through his mind. Safely past Gibraltar they steamed for an amphibious landing in North Africa.

They were soon in action when a daring Panzer attack overran the infantry they supported. The regiment was then embroiled in a muzzle-to-muzzle engagement. It was the Battle of

Beja and they beat off the tanks in one of Rommel's last full scale attacks of the desert war. During the melee a shell exploded as he was standing between his signaller and a young officer. When he got up, both companions lay dead. My father told me that during a lull in a battle, a soldier was shouting for his officer, 'Mr. Smythe, where are you, where are you?' The Germans then attacked shouting, 'Meester Smythe vo bist du.' Mr. Smythe and his men then gave them a hot reception which broke up the assault. The scholar had been tried and tested in the carnage of war and had not been found wanting. He also knew the elation of victory in the desert in contrast to being drawn up on ceremonial parades on Tenby sands.

One of my father's keenest and best young officers was a Keith Joseph, later Lord Joseph. With the triumphant end of the Africa campaign, the regiment went to Palestine via Cairo for rest from the ferocity of modern battle to the calm of ancient pyramids and the Sphinx. My father visited historical sights whenever he could in Jerusalem, Damascus and the places familiar to him by name from his Sunday School days. Unfortunately his writings of that period were later lost in the destruction of war. The regiment then set sail for the Allied landings in Sicily.

My father wrote of his whereabouts despite censorship, in coded letters which he had arranged with my mother. After the Sicilian campaign his regiment was once again on Royal Navy ships for their third landing. This time on the Italian mainland at Salerno. This was viciously contested, with landing craft being blown out of the water. Those who managed to reach the beaches were immediately under close quarter attack. My father being second in command of his regiment, was a forward observation officer. He was in the first wave and made his way through the hurricane of exploding shells, mines and raking machine gun fire. The Division then laboriously fought the bitter campaign up Italy through tough terrain, foul weather and heavy casualties to Monte Casino.

25 pdr gun of F.J.'s regiment in action.
(I.W.M. official photograph. Ref. NA581)

Direct hit on German MK. 4 tank.
(I.W.M. official photograph. Ref. NA757)

Unloading guns onto Salerno Beachhead.
(I.W.M. official photograph. Ref. NA6632)

Aftermath of the Battle of Beja.
(I.W.M. official photograph. Ref. NA1042)

F.J. after Salerno

During a lull in 1944, he met Baron de Rutzen, a good friend who had often entertained my father at his home in Picton Castle. They had lunch together, no doubt talking of the far off Pembrokeshire days. The Baron went up to lead his Welsh Guardsmen in an attack. A short time later he was killed.

A happier story about my father is that he was sketching an old building, and the Brigadier, in passing, asked him to hurry up as he was holding up the attack. The battle went on and the building he had sketched was blown to smithereens.

My father was obviously being groomed to take over command of a fighting regiment of his own, when he was unexpectedly posted to the War Office in London as a staff officer. He was to join the Cabinet Office to write the official history of the Sicilian and Italian campaigns. He skipped off to Naples and cadged a lift home in an American plane.

Although he had his London job, he wanted to return to Pembrokeshire. So he leased Roch Castle, and we moved in and he used it as a base from doodle-bombed London, and while he went house hunting locally. None were suitable so we all moved up to London, where my mother went house hunting and found us a large flat in Queens Gate Place in South Kensington. It was ideal, quiet, but central, and Kensington Gardens were only a short walk away. He often walked to the War Office through what he called his four park walk through Kensington Gardens, Hyde Park, across to St. James's Park via The Green Park. My brother and I had previously been boarders at Haverfordwest Grammar School. He found us public schools in London and I never forget that our education was paid from his army salary, much of it earned on active service in the front line. My brother Dedwydd

Visiting ancient monuments between battles

Francis and Ethel Jones outside their South Kensington home

Post war. In the Surrey Yeomanry (QMR)

Lifelong friend from school days, F.J. and B. G. Charles

won a place at Oxford and was a star athlete. Of our sisters, Anne won an art scholarship, Elizabeth became a nurse. I had a nice side line: witnessing a brutal smash and grab raid in Hammersmith. I reported it to the *Daily Mail,* and got a fee. After that I would prowl London for news stories, and Hyde Park Corner was a good source for gang fights and violent battles among costermongers. I was uninterested in history being more concerned with up-to-date news. If this disappointed Daddy he never showed it.

My parents led a very busy social life, visits from Welsh relatives, scholars and professors, and I don't know how my mother coped with all the entertaining and us four children, but she seemed to thrive on it. My father was also back in the territorial army in the Surrey Yeomanry. Of course he immediately wrote the regimental history. He poured out a stream of articles, and planned several more books, of which this is one. He just put down his sword and picked up his pen and carried on where Mr. Hitler had interrupted him.

By far the most significant calls he made were at the College of Arms, where he found a treasure trove of ancient Welsh records concerning Welsh families and genealogy. They were as unclassified and muddled as those he had found in Haverfordwest. He made friends with a Herald, Anthony Wagner, a direct descendant of Owain Glyndwr, and an authority on Welsh history himself. They got permission for my father to classify the Welsh records. The volunteer archivist was back at work. Some of his articles appeared regularly in the Hon. Society of the Cymmrodorion. In all its long history only one man had more articles published by them. He was writing for *The Times, Burke's Peerage,* and many national magazines. In 1953, his book, *The Holy Wells of Wales,* was published to become a pioneering classic, still selling well today. It brought him a Honorary MA from the University of Wales. He was a military commentator of the Coronation route which gave him his first experience of a royal ceremony and involved him in its administration. He and my mother still spoke Welsh at home, and found it most useful in making quiet asides to each other at the many meetings and parties they attended.

He belonged to many London societies and clubs, and there is a story about him remarking to a bearded brown faced man next to him at a St. James's club, 'You look as if you've just come from the North Pole.' The reply was, 'Actually it was the South Pole.' My father drew himself up and said, 'Well I come from South Kensington.'

So passed fourteen years of family life, full of humour, excitement and interest. My parents often remarked on how happy those London days had been. He then finished his huge task at the War Office. He stayed on for over a year writing and researching particularly in the College of Arms. He then took the post of County Archivist at Carmarthen and the last of his gratuity paid for the move. It was a finely balanced act, not without worries for my mother. My parents were aged 52, when many look forward to retirement. For them the best was yet to come, and lots of it.

Then came momentous family news in 1963. The Royal appointment of my father to Wales Herald of Arms Extraordinary. The post was last occupied in the days of the Black Prince in the 14th century. In retrospect, I think it was a case of the job finding the man, and not the other way round. At his first official appearance he was clad in court dress and the fabulous tabard which had been eighteen months in the making by the Royal College of Needlework. His debut was processing with his colleagues of the Royal Household leading the royal party at the State Opening of Parliament. Afterwards he was presented to Her Majesty. When we asked him what his impressions were, he was very cool about it. But then after Salerno there was little left to overawe him. He kindly got me a seat in St. George's Chapel, Windsor for his first appearance in the Knights of the Garter service. After the ceremony the procession returned to Windsor Castle. Lord Cobham who had been installed that day approached my father. A snatch of a programme about Lord Cobham which I had made had just been repeated on 'Pick of the Week'. The new Knight of the Garter told the new herald that the BBC interviewer resembled him. He was tickled to hear it was indeed the herald's son. The Duke of Edinburgh then clapped Lord Cobham's shoulder and congratulated him on the programme. My brother, Dedwydd, had recently had two of his plays on at West End theatres so my mother had some reason to be proud of her three men.

Like many others in 1965, my father received a coded message that triggered off the greatest State Funeral since Queen Victoria was buried. Sir Winston Churchill had died. Plans for this of course, had been drawn up for some years, and officials proceeded with the meticulous organisation matched only by the sincerity of the nation's grief. Thousands of soldiers, sailors, airmen, court officials, the Royal Family, civil servants, politicians, the Foreign Office, the Home Office, the world press, and television all co-operated under the direction of the maestro of ceremonial Bernard, Duke of Norfolk.

The ensuing display astonished the world with its dignity and solemn grandeur. The candles round the coffin were those last used for the Duke of Wellington's funeral. It was the climax of nearly a thousand years of ceremonial experience. The heralds stood like statues flanking the catafalque at St. Paul's high altar, as pictures were flashed to every corner of the globe. I wonder if, as my father looked down the length of the cathedral at the gathering of royal families, presidents, prime ministers and heads of state he thought back to his Trevine childhood when his parents told him of the lives of great heroes? Did he think back to that instant when he gazed up at the knight's helmet in St. Mary's Church in far off Haverfordwest? Sadly, I will never know now.

It would not be honest of me to depict my father as a saintly figure, perfect in every way. He was human with shortcomings, but such was his iron self control they rarely surfaced in public. I don't think his intellect ever rested; he planned and analysed before he spoke or acted. He always kept his aims firmly in mind. To achieve them he learned to dissemble and to conceal his true thoughts. He despised failure, and had an unerring instinct for people's weaknesses. He kept in with those who could become useful to him, as they did with him too. He knew the old boy network at a high level and operated it with subtlety. His charm was a useful asset as his success mounted.

Farewell to Sir Winston Churchill from St. Paul's steps. F.J. on left of the picture.

One episode neatly illustrates this. He unwisely mentioned an outline of an idea for a book to another scholar. Later I saw him really angry for about the only time in my life. The man had coolly stolen my father's cherished idea. Now this person was a Power in the Land, so my father calmed down. Afterwards he went out of his way to help the man with the project which turned out to be a great success. That a tacit understanding then existed was proved by the enormous support this man gave my father in far more important undertakings from then on. I doubt though that Daddy ever dropped his guard again.

He kept his inner circle of friends for life, from school days, battlefield and court. They lived in cottages, farm houses, mansions, great castles and London flats. The obituaries to him in *The Times, Daily Telegraph* and *Observer* among others attest to his gift of friendship. He kept his mother's photograph by his bedside for as long as I can remember.

The only person with whom he ever shared his innermost thoughts was my mother. During the war years he was away, and it may have been a shock for him to find boisterous children instead of the tots he had left, but I don't think that affected him much in his attitude to us. The household kept silent when he was at his desk pretty much as before. Our mother dealt with the children's problems.

When I came out of the army, he put me into a job that he thought suitable. I left it after a short while, but he made no comment. After that he never offered to influence my career again. Neither did he ever praise my successes, nor condemn my failures. He left me to sink or swim on my own, as indeed he had done all his own life. The common ground we all had was humour. He revelled in amusing stories and jokes, though he was scathing if our wit was not up to scratch. He never gave quarter, and most certainly never asked for it. To be cut down by his sarcasm was a withering experience, and most certainly to be avoided at all costs as I remember it. It was cobra quick and stabbed like a rapier. We were always slightly afraid of him and anxious to please. I think he played on this sometimes. He would mildly shepherd our thoughts into an opinion which, wanting to please, we would gladly adopt. Too late, we would find ourselves between a rock and a hard place, with no way out. The hasty opinion would then be dissected with remorseless precision. Not nice at all. It is called mind games today I think; whatever it is – he was very good at it. For his sons he saw success in terms of a professional or a structured career, ignoring the fact that his own career was entirely self-motivated.

Bursting with pride I told him of a big freelance BBC contract I had landed 'Ah', he languidly remarked, 'the BBC is full of left-wing queers.' Once my brother disagreed with his opinion, and quoted chapter and verse proving his point. Father dismissed him with a sarcastic comment.

For many years I lived in a pretty Cotswold hamlet halfway between Carmarthen and Windsor. My parents in their pre car-owning days used to come up for they loved the area, to stay with us, and I would drive them up to Windsor for the Garter ceremonies. They took me to parties after the ceremony and great fun it was too. At one I overheard an interesting bit of conversation. It was addressed to a court official by a business tycoon. 'Listen, you get me that knighthood and I'll give you a yacht.' The courtier gave a wintry smile, and slid away. The last I heard was 'Now hang on, I mean what I say. She's forty-five feet long.' I told my father about this, he said, 'Ah, he's still at it then.' He quoted Napoleon to me: 'Men are easily won by ribbons and trinkets'. Daddy was frequently approached by worthies pressing to be included in the Honours List. He had a set drill, he would say he would do what he could, and usually do nothing. If they were included they were, he said, grateful for life. If not, he would advise them to keep on trying.

It is no surprise that history was deeply ingrained in my father's subconscious. Living in old dwellings with historical connections throughout his life, from ancient farmhouses, the little mansion Plas Broginin, to castles such as Roch and Carmarthen, and stately Queens Gate there were some curious episodes.

Once he was puzzled about the whereabouts of a particular gravestone he had wished to find. On going for a long walk he was approached by a figure who told him to look in a particular spot. Considering he had told nobody about the grave stone my father was puzzled, and thought it might have been a day dream. He visited the graveyard the following day. The head stone was exactly where the apparition had told him. He wrote up the experience and it was broadcast on BBC radio. Whilst living in the little house inside Carmarthen Castle, he had a series of strangely macabre dreams which he wrote down. One about a missing gold coin which he also wrote about and broadcast. I would be most intrigued if when we lived at Roch Castle he was ever visited by the royal mistress (who is a distant ancestress), Lucy Walter who once lived there. Maybe there are some things best left alone.

A herald's life appeared to me to consist of parading in gorgeous uniforms, solemn marching in ceremonies, and circulating at official parties such as the Buckingham Palace garden party exuding charm. I soon knew better as I saw the work behind the scenes. He was, I think responsible for all queries on Welsh genealogy that flowed into the College of Arms endlessly from all over the world. These included some bizarre and amusing letters from cranks. He advised and helped draw up coats of arms for ennobled Welshmen, for clubs, insignia for town corporations, regiments, High Sheriffs, Royal Mall stamps and commercial companies. He replied to thousands of people from all over the world wanting family and heraldic information about their Welsh ancestors. Photographs of coats of arms on pottery, silver, book plates, crests on fireplaces, old coach panels, paintings of gravestones and church plaques came even from China. He handled all these queries with meticulous thoroughness in addition to his duties as an archivist and historian. He was in constant demand to join committees, to become president of historical societies, to be a governor of many bodies, to lecture, to make presentations.

This as well as writing for radio, newspapers, TV, and advising on Post Office stamp designs. A steady stream of overseas visitors visiting Wales to trace their ancestry appeared at his house. He still wrote articles and researched his coming books. All this would have been impossible without my mother's help. She was not only his secretary, but still advised on his creative writings.

They started each day with a cup of tea at six o'clock. We often heard them laughing together as they prepared for their day. How lucky he was to have fallen in love with a woman who was equal to the big demands his work made on their partnership. Their research trips needed to be more time effective; having no car they relied on friends and public transport. My father claimed he couldn't drive. Actually he could, but his attention was easily distracted by fine views and houses in the country. He once took over the wheel of his army jeep from his driver in London. This man told me later it was the most frightening experience he'd had since being on active service in Italy. Although she could not drive my mother bought a small car, and passed her driving test at the first attempt. She was then over sixty. The instructor said she was the best pupil he ever saw. Afterwards my parents planned their excursions with the exactitude of military landings, clocking up many thousands of happy miles. My father referred to his chauffeuse as 'Boadica'; she never had a single accident.

Although public honours clustered to my father's name he never became pompous. I never saw him stand on his dignity, and he still delighted in collecting bizarre, outrageous stories and jokes. That he kept his sense of proportion is well expressed on a piece of paper I found on which he had written 'One of the most severe trials to which the head and heart of man can be put is great and rapid elevation. Some prove equal to their new dignity imposed on their conduct and attitudes. Others are unable to carry their corn. It is also a trial for one's friends and acquaintances, for few men are completely devoid of a measure of envy when they realise that they have been lapped in the race of life'. Well, hold his corn my father did, he was ever courteous and was kind to everybody. He still found time to help and encourage young students and fellow scholars, so carrying on the tradition of kindness shown to him when he started his career in Pembrokeshire.

He went out of his way to be kind to one eccentric who thought he was a peer and visited his imagined estates (which was most of industrial South Wales) to collect rents from his 'tenants'. He only got abuse. He asked my father to have a quiet word with the Queen about his treatment. My father arranged for a friendly eye to be kept out for this deluded man. Closer to home, a bumptious man with grandiose ambitions was arriving with fanciful ideas for ceremonials. We wondered why my father tolerated him. My exasperated mother suggested banning his visits; my father looked at her with enormous reproach 'Ethel, how could you be so cruel as to deprive me of my private jester,' he said. The visits continued, and the family joke ran and ran over many years.

My parents always loved racing. They had great excitement in seeing my jockey son, Gareth on TV winning at Cheltenham and Chepstow, and completing the Grand National. Maybe the youngster inherited some of his grandfather's winning ways. He once received an invitation to dinner by a man for whom he rode. The little gathering waited for the guest of honour, but no name was mentioned. Her Majesty the Queen Mother arrived and Gareth took her into dinner. Not even Wales Herald topped that.

My father got great amusement from the little ditty I composed to the tune of 'My old man's a dustman'. He often used to ask me to sing it to him. it went: 'My old man's an 'erald, 'e wears an 'erald's 'at. E's got an 'erald's baton . . . and 'ee knows what he can do with that'. He called it his Herald's Anthem.

Soon another great State Occasion was on him, this time he had a major role. It was the Investiture of the Prince of Wales in Caernarfon Castle in 1969. The Duke of Norfolk was Supremo, and the Earl of Snowdon and my father completed the trio organising the event.

Grandson Gareth Charles-Jones (No. 24) clears Beecher's Brook in the Grand National. (Photo: Bernard Parkin).

I was a green staff officer at the Investiture, leading the peers and gentlemen of the Prince's party in the procession. I was nervously standing at the start line when my father found time to wish me luck. So did Mamma, there's family for you.

Everything went without a hitch in the meticulous time table. The only discordant note being some nationalists who tried to throw eggs at the royal carriages. We inside the castle were puzzled to hear the ugly rumblings of the crowd bent on tearing the egg bombers apart. They were rescued by the police and normal cheering service was resumed. After the ceremonies Her Majesty presented the new Prince of Wales to the people from a balcony of the ancient ramparts to tumultuous cheering from the huge crowd. My father stood behind the Royal Family clutching his ivory wand of office. It was the peak of his career, and

The Investiture Procession. F.J. leading from left.

The Queen presents the new Prince of Wales. Directly above the Prince is Sir Anthony Wagner. F.J. to his right.

later he was made a Commander of the Royal Victorian Order, an honour bestowed by the Monarch's personal command. It really was the day from which dreams are made.

The most graphic example of my father's indifference to money came about during the Investiture. He got a letter from an agent offering a huge sum of money to do a lecture tour in America. He showed it to my mother, who said 'You had better answer it don't you think'. He carried on working at his desk. A week later it was still lying there. Again Mamma drew his attention to it. 'Ah yes,' he said, 'I'm too busy to answer it, will you just say no for me.' The sum offered would have bought a nice house.

Many hundreds of his articles appeared in newspapers, magazines and learned journals all over the world, and many books published. Yet in his huge archives I did not find a single author's contract. He would see his work in print never knowing what the fee was until it dropped through his letter box. Human nature being what it is he was sometimes not paid at all. This never ruffled him as he lived frugally, spending little on himself On one occasion an Editor of *The Times* had him paid in cash. The money never got home, but he arrived home in a taxi full of antiquarian books he had bought. My mother cut down his pocket money for a while after that.

My parents life settled down to an even tenor, and if anything his work output increased. Their little car clocked up thousands more miles, as they began the gigantic task of collating material for a series of books, county by county of historic homes and families in Wales. They started with Pembrokeshire, Carmarthenshire and Cardiganshire. By now my father

F.J. in his element – research visit to an historic Welsh house, 1971.

was a Fellow of the Society of Antiquaries, an Honorary MA, a Deputy Lieutenant of Carmarthenshire, a Director of the National Trust, a Governor of the National Library of Wales, a Freeman of Haverfordwest, and a Knight of the Order of St. John, and president of various historical associations; he was even made an honorary member of the Mark Twain Society in America.

My parents always enjoyed having people to stay at their home, and once entertained my BBC producer, David Glencross. David came down complaining of not feeling well and cast a gloom over our breakfast table. He apologised to my parents, 'Not at all,' said my father, 'you are a guest here, and you may cast as much gloom as you like.'

They seemed to get busier as they got older, my father's diary being full for months ahead, He found a pause to retire as County Archivist then aged sixty-five in 1974, then

Francis and Ethel Jones at Buckingham Palace after his being made Commander of the Royal Victorian Order.

charged on with his work enjoying every minute of it. I never in my life ever heard him say he was tired. He and my mother were now working in harness full time, and she was able to keep up with him too. What a couple. She also had her amusing episodes; once at a rehearsal for some royal event she became a stand in for the Monarch. From then on she was affectionately known as Mrs. Wales. For us children nobody could ever be a stand-in for Mamma.

One of the most pleasant official invitations my parents had was to the wedding of Prince Charles at St. Paul's Cathedral. My mother bought a new hat. I saw it on television, when a camera panned across five ex-prime Ministers in the congregation, Macmillan, Wilson, Callaghan, Home and Heath. It also picked out my parents sitting behind them. Although it was an ill starred marriage it was a spectacularly brilliant occasion, and neither of my parents lived to see the marriage break-up.

My father developed angina, but apart from a change of diet it made not the slightest difference to his work, and curtailed the official duties not one iota. He even worked on a new ceremonial order, a corps of Welsh gentlemen to attend the Prince of Wales, called the Teilo of the Order of St. David. Maybe another will now take up the cause.

Catastrophe hit our family in 1985. My mother died suddenly after fifty-four years of marriage to my father. Her memory lives with us all in every waking day. Shortly afterwards I returned to Pembrokeshire from the Cotswolds, and was able to see more of my father. In 1987 his Carmarthenshire book was published. It contained descriptions of no less than 600 properties, and over two thousand families that lived in them down the ages. It was a tour de force, ran into two quick editions and sold out.

Then, in his late seventies, he developed cancer of the stomach and half was removed. A few days later whilst I visited him, he insisted on getting out of bed and shaving himself. I doubt if I will ever see such will-power again. By way of convalescing he continued writing and researching this book. Many kind friends especially Thomas Lloyd and David Brunel White drove him about West Wales. With enormous determination he attended his last Garden Party at Buckingham Palace in a wheel chair. Is it any wonder that I feel compelled to publish his book? He suffered another misfortune when up in Aberystwyth for research work at the National Library, he fell and broke his hip. He had an immediate hip replacement in the nearby hospital, and later told my brother, 'I was lucky, they caught me while I was still warm.'

F.J. with guard dog Ben.

He, who had loved walking so much, adjusted to a new hip slowly. He courageously struggled on, in spite of the deterioration of his health. The desire to impart his knowledge of Pembrokeshire urged his frail fingers

F.J.'s last Knight of the Garter Parade at Windsor, 1988.

to work. After handling his pen and sword with such distinction he finally grew tired. My mother, the only person who had shared his innermost thoughts and supported him with her constancy and encouragement was gone. He was in his 86th year.

I wrote in the service sheet for his Memorial Service in St. David's Cathedral, 'Death came gently to my father. He died in his own home after years of loving care from my sister Anne. 'We children, Dedwydd, Elizabeth, Anne and I were around him as he slipped painlessly away as if one of the pages of his own books had been gently closed.' My father had never been physically demonstrative apart from the odd handshake or clap on the shoulder. I kissed him then for the first and last time in my adult life.

I organised our final tribute in St. David's Cathedral on the date of our Mamma's death. It is a place they loved, near to their birth places and Brawdy. There was a large and distinguished congregation. We all listened to the wonderful harp music of Susan Drake, and to the rich voice of our cousin, Arwyn Charles singing 'David of the White Rock'. For the first time three Garter Kings of Arms attended together. My father's richly coloured tabard was displayed near the High Altar for its only appearance in Pembrokeshire.

That is how we said goodbye to our parents.

HUGH CHARLES-JONES

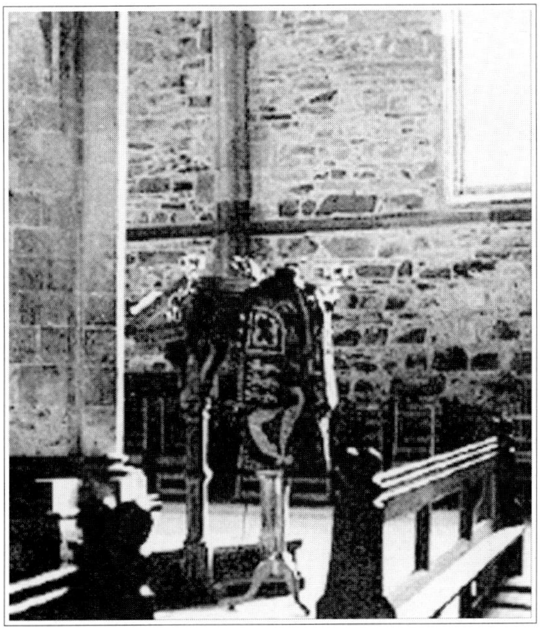

Francis Jones's tabard on display at his memorial service at St. David's Cathedral

STRANGE SEQUELS

Shortly after my mother died, I took my father to London for the State Opening of Parliament. Spectator tickets are eagerly sought, peers and heralds getting one each. My father always gave my mother his allotted ticket. I had never attended the ceremony.

Through a series of inexplicable coincidences totally unconnected with my father, I was given a ticket. Being late I only just got a place, but was able to see my father on parade, and he spotted me.

Some months later in my father's house I thumbed through a book called *Royal Ceremonies of State.* I spotted Mamma quite plainly in a photograph of the State Opening of Parliament. The strangest thing was that she was in the exact spot where I stood on the first time she was absent. It was where she could see my father. (Broadcast in full on BBC Radio 4, 1994.)

After my father's death, I was involved in some overseas business, and as a result was invited to the Opening of Parliament again and for lunch at the House of Lords afterwards.

This meant that for over 30 consecutive years a member of our family was present. I felt I was representing my parents in a closing chapter in the family history which began so long ago in a Pembrokeshire house. *H.C.-J.*

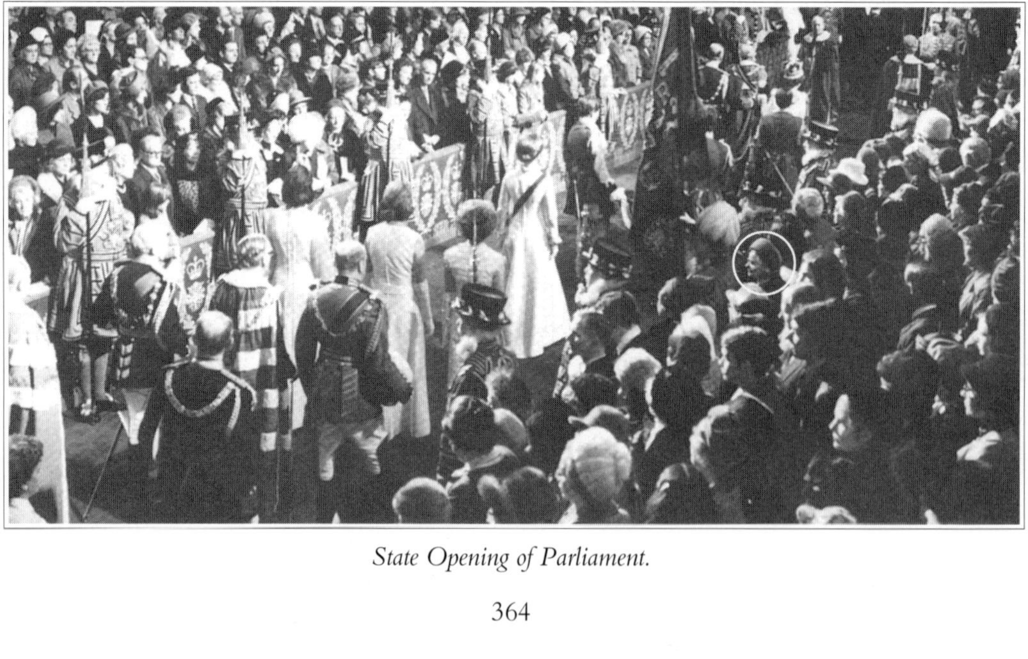

State Opening of Parliament.

BIBLIOGRAPHY

(with abbreviations)

Primary Sources

Carmarthen Record Office

Aberglasney Collection
Beckingale Collection
Castell Gorfod Collection
Cawdor Collection (II)
Cawdor Golden Grove Books I, II & III [G.G.B.]
Cawdor Mapbooks
Cawdor/Campbell Mapbooks
Cawdor/Lort
Cawdor/Vaughan
Charities Records
Cilycwm Parish Registers [p.r.]

Derwydd Collection
Dynevor Collection

Electoral Registers

Glasbrook Collection

John Francis Collection, Sale Catalogues
John Francis (Llanllawddog Deeds)

Landowners Return 1873

Plâs Llanstephan Collection
Protheroe-Beynon Collection

Quarter Sessions Order Books

St Ishmael Parish Registers

Tithe Maps [t.m.] and Schedules [t.s] for Pembrokeshire
Trant Collection
Trant/Yelverton Deeds
Trenewydd Deeds

National Library of Wales, Aberystwyth

Albany Chapel Records and Documents

Brigstocke Collection
Bronwydd Deeds and Documents

Calendar of Dynevor Documents
Church in Wales Records
Cilgwyn Deeds and Documents;
Cilymaenllwyd Deeds and Documents
Coleman Deeds
Crosswood Deeds
Croydon Deeds
Cwmgwili Manuscripts and Documents
Cwrtmawr Deeds

Dale Castle Pedigree Book
Derry Ormond Deeds and Documents
Derwydd Documents

Edwinsford Deeds and Collection

G. E. Owen Collection
George Eyre Evans Manuscripts and Deeds
Great Sessions Records

Lancych Deeds and Documents
Llangwarren Documents
Llidiardau Deeds
Llwyndyrus Deeds and Documents
Llwynwgwair Deeds and Documents
Llysnewydd Deeds and Documents
Lucas Manuscripts and Records

Maesgwynne Deeds
Manuscript Volumes
Morgan Richardson Deeds
Muddlescombe Deeds

Noyadd Trefawr Deeds

Ottley Papers
Owen and Colby Manuscripts, Deeds

Pembrokeshire Gaol Files
Pembrokeshire Plea Rolls
Picton Castle Collection
Pontfaen Documents
Poyston Documents
Probate Wills

Quaritch Deeds

Sealyham Deeds
Slebech Deeds
Spence-Colby Manuscripts

Thomas (Saundersfoot) Deeds
Trefgarn Owen Chapel Records
Trewern Deeds
Tucker Manuscript N.L.W. 10871B
Tynewydd Deeds
Tyllwyd Deeds

Vaerdre Book

Glamorgan Record Office
Cardiff Central Library Collection

Haverfordwest Public Library
Francis Green Manuscripts

Pembrokeshire Record Office
Cottesmore (Massey) Deeds
Court Papers

Episcopal Registers of St. Davids

Foley of Ridgeway Deeds
Francis Green Deeds

G. R. Barrett Deeds
Griffith Owen Deeds

Haverfordwest Corporation Deeds

James of Narberth, Solicitors, Papers

Land Tax Records
Lewis and James Papers [D/LJ]
Lloyd-Philipps Papers [D/LP]
Lochturffin Deeds.

Owen & Colby Estate Deeds

Newton Deeds & Documents

Pembrokeshire Plea Rolls
Penally Deeds
Price and Kelway Papers [D/PK]
Protheroe-Beynon Collection

Saunders-Davies Collection

Saunders-Davies Papers
Scourfield Deeds
St. Davids Episcopal Records

Trenewydd Collection

Williams & Williams Papers

College of Arms
Chetham Ms.
Crygbychan Ms.

Gilfach Ms.

Fellowes Visitations

Sir Anthony Wagner Collection

Public Record Office
Chancery Proceedings, Ser. 11 420/40
Chancery, Mitford, CO 603/25

Exchequer Accounts

British Museum
Egerton Manuscripts

Wood Manuscripts

Bodleian Library
Bodleian Manuscript Add. C177

Harleian Manuscript 6823

Printed Primary and Secondary Sources

Adams, J., *Ancient Description of Holyland,* 1836.
Allen, Col. F. S., *Family Records of the Allens of Cresselly,* 1905.
Allen, Charles Smith, *The History of South Wales and Monmouthshire* (illust.), Vols. I and II, Tenby, 1891. [Allen, S. *Wales and Mon.*]
Allen, C. S., *Photographs in S. Wales*, 1871.

Bacon, *Liber Regis.*
Baker-Jones, D.L., *Ffynnone.*
Barber, J. T., *A Tour through South Wales and Monmouthshire,* London, 1803.
Beazely, E. and Howell, P., *The Companion Guide to South Wales,* 1977.
Black Book of St. Davids.
Borrow, George, *Wild Wales, its People, Language and Scenery,* London, 1862.
Bridgeman, G. T. O., *History of the Princes of South Wales,* Wigan, 1876.
Brunker, John, *Llanegwad,* Carmarthen, 1937.

Buckley, James, *Genealogies of the Carmarthenshire Sheriffs from 1539 to 1759,* Carmarthen, 1910. [Buckley, *Sheriffs*].

Buckley, James, *Genealogies of the Carmarthenshire Sheriffs from 1760 to 1913,* Carmarthen, 1913.

Burke, *A Genealogical and Heraldic History of the Landed Gentry of Great Britain and Ireland* [Burke, *L. G.*].

Burke, *A Genealogical and Heraldic History of the Peerage and Baronetage,* 36th edn., 1874.

Burke, *A Visitation of Seats and Arms of the Noblemen and Gentlemen of Great Britain and Ireland.*

Burke, *General Armoury,* 1885.

Burke, John and Bernard, John, *A Genealogical and Heraldic History of the Extinct and Dormant Baronetcies of England,* 1st. edn., 1838.

Bushell, Rev. W., *An Island of the Saints,* 1931.

Busteed, H.E., *Echoes from Old Calentha,* 1908.

Carlisle, Nicholas, *A Topographical Dictionary of the Dominion of Wales,* London, 1811. [Carlisle, *T.D.W.*].

Carmarthenshire Studies: Essays presented to Major Francis Jones, ed. T. Barnes and N. Yates, Carmarthen, 1974. [*Carms. Studies*].

Charles, Prof. B. G., *Non-Celtic Place Names.*

Charles, Prof. B. G. Ed., *George Owen Second Book.*

Charles, Prof. B. G. Ed., *George Owen of Henllys,* 1973.

Clark, G. T., *Limbus Patrum Morganiae et Glamorganiae etc.,* London, 1886. [Clark, *Glamorgan Genealogies*].

Curtis, *Laugharne,* 1880.

Davies, Nola D., *The Story of Amroth, The Church and the Parish,* 1980.

Davies, E. M., *The Story of Llandyfeilog Parish,* Carmarthen, 1953.

Davies, Walter, *A General View, of the Agriculture and Domestic Economy of South Wales,* Vols. I and II, London, 1814.

Debrett, John, *Peerage of England, Scotland and Ireland,* 1st edn., London, 1802.

Dictionary of National Biography, 63 vols., London 1885-1900; reprinted Oxford, 1921-22. [*D.N.B.*].

Dictionary of Welsh Biography down to 1940, Cymmrodorion Society, London, 1959. [*D.W.B.*].

Dineley, Thomas, *The Account of the Official Progress of the First Duke of Beaufort through Wales, 1684,* ed. R. W. Banks, London, 1888.

Donovan, E, *Descriptive Excursion through Wales and Monmouthshire,* London, 1804.

Dwnn, *Heraldic Visitations,* see Meyrick, Samuel Rush.

Evans J. T., *Church Plate of Pembrokeshire.* 1905.

Evans, J., *Letters written during a tour through South Wales,* 1804.

Evans, S., *Hanes Pontyberem,* 1856.

Exchequer proceedings (equity) concerning Wales, Henry VIII, – Elizabeth, ed. Emyr Gwynne Jones, Cardiff, 1939.

Fenton, R., *An Historical Tour Through Pembrokeshire,* Brecknock, 1903.

Fenton, R., *Tours in Wales,* 1804-1813, ed. J. Fisher, Cambrian Archaeological Association, London, 1917.

Fishguard & Goodwick Silver Jubilee Tribute, 1977.

Green, Francis, *The Fortunes of Leweston.*

Green, Francis, *Wogan of Boulston,* 1902.

Griffiths, Ralph A., *The Principality of Wales in the Later Middle Ages, the Structure and Personnel of Government, I, South Wales 1277-1536,* Cardiff, 1972,

Gwilly Davies, S., *Wedi Croesu'r Pedwar Ugain, Atgafion,* 1967.

Gwynne, F. P., *Sketches of Tenby,* 1852.

Hall, S. C., *South Wales* 1861.

Hilling, J., *The Historic Architecture of Wales,* Cardiff, 1976.

HMSO, St. Dogmaels Abbey, 1962.

Howells, Roscoe, Caldey, 1984.

Howells, Roscoe, Old Saundersfoot, 1977.

Innes-Smith, R. W., *English Speaking Students of Medicine at the University of Leyden.*

James, D., *Sir John Perrot 1527-1591,* 1962.

James, *Haverfordwest and its Story,* 1957.

Jones & Freeman, *St. Davids,* 1856.

Jones, D., *Hanes* y *Bedyddwyr yn Neheubarth Cymru*, Caerfyrddin,1839.

Jones, Francis, *Historic Carmarthenshire Homes and their Families*, 1997.

Jones, Francis, *Holy Wells of Wales,* 1954.

Jones, Francis, *Historic Cardiganshire Homes and their Families,* 2000.

Jones, Francis, *Treasury of Historic Pembrokeshire*, 1998.
Jones, Francis, *God Bless the Prince of Wales,* Carmarthen, 1969.
Jones, T. Gwynn, *Welsh Folklore and Folk Custom,* London, 1930.
Jones, *Wales Illustrated*, 1830.
Jones, Theophilus, *History of the County of Brecknock,* Vol. I, 1805; Vol. II, 1809; rept., Brecon, 1908.

Kelly's Handbook 1887 & 1892.

Laws & Edwards, *St. Mary the Virgin, Tenby*, 1907.
Lewis, E. T., *Mynachlogddu, A Guide to its Antiquities*.
Lewis, E. T., *North of the Hills,* 1973.
Lewis, E. T., *Efailwen to Whitland,* Vol. I. Carmarthen, 1975; Vol. II, Carmarthen, 1976.
Lewis, *Early Chancery Proceedings concerning Wales,* 1937.
Lewis, Samuel, A *Topographical Dictionary of Wales*, Vols. I & II, London, 1833, 4th edn., 1849. [Lewis, T.D.W.].
Lipscomb, George, *Journey into South Wales,* London, 1802.
Lloyd, James J., *Hanes Eglwys Glandwr,* 1902.
Lloyd, K. H., *The Lords of Kemes 1087-1914*, 1930.
Lloyd, J. E., *A History of Wales from the earliest times to the Edwardian Conquest,* Vols. I & II, London, 1911, 3rd ed. 1939.
Lloyd, Thomas, *The Lost Houses of Wales,* SAVE, London, 1986.
Lluyd, E., *Parochialia,* Archaeologia Cambrensis supplement, 1909-11.
Lockley, R. M., *Pembrokeshire,* 1957.
Lockley, R. M., *The Golden Years*, 1948.

Malkin, Benjamin Heath, *The Scenery, Antiquities and Bibliography of South Wales,* Vol. II, 2nd ed., London, 1807.
Meyrick, Samuel Rush, (ed.), *Heraldic Visitations of Wales* (by Lewys Dwnn), Vols. I & II, Llandovery, 1846.
Miles D., *A Pembrokeshire Anthology,* 1983.
Miles D., *Pembrokeshire Sheriffs,* 1974.
Mirehouse, M. B., *South Pembrokeshire,* 1910.
Moll, *Desription of Wales*.
Morgan, Mary, *A Tour to Milford Haven in the Year* 1791, London, 1795.
Morris, John Edward, *The Welsh Wars of Edward I: a contribution to Mediaeval Military History,* Oxford, 1901.

Nicholas, Thomas, *Annals and Antiquities of the Counties and County Families of Wales*, Vols. I & II, London, 1872.
Nicolle, G., *Rosemarket*, 1982.

Oliver, G., *Medieval Buildings* 1987.
Owen, G., *Elizabethan Pembrokeshire*.
Owen, Dr. Henry, *Old Pembrokeshire Families,* 1902.
Owen, Dr. Henry, *Owen's Pembrokeshire.*

Parry, Thomas, (ed.), *The Oxford Book of Welsh Verse,* Oxford, 1962.
Penn, J. R. P., & Green, *Bowen of Roblinston & Camrose,* 1926.
Peters, Mrs. S., *History of Pembroke Dock,* 1905.
Phillips, G., *Llofruddiaeth Shadrach Lewis*, 1986.
Phillips, *History of Cilgerran,* 1867.
Phillips, *Memoirs of the Owen Family.*
Pike, W. T., (ed), *Contemporary Biographies of South Wales and Monmouthshire,* Brighton, 1907.
Pritchard, Rev., *History of St. Dogmaels Abbey*.

Rees, K., *South West Wales Guide,* 1976.
Rees, W., *History of St. John,* 1947.
Rees, Thomas, *The Beauties of England and Wales, South Wales*, Vol. XVIII, London, 1815.
Rees, Vyvian, *South West Wales, A Shell Guide,* new ed., 1976.
Roberts, B., *Baptist Historical Sketches in County Pembrokeshire,* 1907.
Roberts, Gomer Morgan, *Hanes Plwyf LIandybïe,* Caerdydd, 1939.
Roberts, Gomer Morgan, *Y pêr ganiedydd* (Pantycelyn), Cyf. I, Aberystwyth, 1958.
Roscoe, Thomas, *Wanderings & Excursions in S. Wales,* 1836.
Royal Commission on Ancient and Historical Monuments in Wales, *An Inventory of the Ancient Monuments in Wales and Monmouthshire, Vol. V, Carmarthenshire,* London, 1917. [R.C.A.M., (Carms)].

Sandby, Paul, *Views [in Wales] in Aquatinta from drawings taken on the spot,* London, 1775-77.

Skrine, Henry, *Two successive tours throughout the whole of Wales,* London, 1798.
Smith, Peter, *Land of Dyfed.*
Smith, Peter, *Houses of the Welsh Countryside,* London, 1975.
Smith, Lucy Toulmin, (ed.), *Leland's Itinerary in England and Wales*, Vols. 1-5, Centaur Press, London, 1964.
Spurrell, William, *A History of Carew.*
Spurrell, William, *A Guide to Carmarthen and its Neighbourhood,* Carmarthen, 1882.
Squibb, G. D., *The High Court of Chivalry,* Oxford, 1959.
Steegman, J., *A Survey of Portraits in Welsh Houses,* Vol. II: South Wales, Cardiff, 1962.
Summerson, J., *The Life and Work of John Nash, Architect,* London, 1980.

Thomas, W., *Original Designs in Architecture,* 1783.
Thorne, R. G., *History of the Leach Family.*
Timmins, Thornhill, *Nooks & Corners of Pembrokeshire,* 1895
Tivyside, The, Photographic Souvenir, 1871.

Vaughan, H. M., *The South Wales Squires,* London, 1926.

Wales, Historical, Biographical and Pictorial, Privately Published, London, 1908.
Walford, Edward, *County Families of the United Kingdom,* London, 1865.
Warlow, G. H., *History of the Warlow Family,* 1926.
Williams, B., *Hanes Casnewydd-Emlyn,* 1860.
Williams, Lloyd, *Crwydro Sir Benfro.*
Williams, Prof. D., *Aberystwyth*, 1976.
Willis, B., *Survey of St. Davids,* 1717.
Wood, J., *The Principal Rivers of Wales,* 1813.
Wynn, Sir John, *History of the Gwydir Family,* 1927.

Journals and Periodicals

An Index to the Transactions of The Carmarthenshire Antiquarian Society, 1905-1977, compiled by Andrew Green, Carmarthen, 1981. [C.A.S. *Index*].
Anglo-Welsh Review.
Annals Cambrai, Carms RO.
Archaeologica Cambrensis, London, 1846. [*Arch. Camb.*]
Black's Picturesque Guide 1853.
Cambrian Travellers Guide 1813 & *1840.*
Cambrian Journal.
Cambrian News (Newspaper)
Cambrian Register 1796.
Cambrian Tourist edn 1814.
Coastal Cottages of Pembrokeshire brochure 1987 etc.
Come to Pembrokeshire Guide 1936.
Country Life.
County Echo, The (Newspaper).
County Quest.
History Review.
Journal of the Historical Society of The Church in Wales.
Journal of the National Library of Wales.
Journal of the Royal Welsh Agricultural Society.
Neath Antiquarian Society Transactions.
Pembrokeshire Life.
South Wales Daily News (Newspaper).
The Carmarthen Journal (Newspaper).
The Carmarthen Times (Newspaper).
The Carmarthenshire Antiquary, Vol. 1, 1941. [*Carms. Antiq.*].
The Carmarthenshire Historian.
The European Magazine.
The Pembrokeshire Historical Society Magazine.
The Red Dragon.
The South Wales Daily News (Newspaper).
The Western Mail (Newspaper).
Trafnodion Cymdeithas Bedyddwyr Cymrui.
Transactions of the Carmarthenshire Antiquarians Society and Field Club, Vols. 1-29, 1905-39. [T.C.A.S.F.C.]
Transactions of the Honourable Society of Cymmrodorion. [*Trans. Cymmrodor*]
Transactions of' the Ceredigion Antiquarian Society.
Wales Magazine 1897.
Welshman, The.
West Wales Historical Records. [WWHR]
Western Telegraph, The (Newspaper).
Where to Stay in Wales 1976.

FAMILY INDEX

A

Ackland: Cleddau Lodge 44
Acland:
Amroth Castle/Earwere 2
Boulston 16
Philbeach/Filbetch 215
Adam: Hendre Riffith 109
Adams:
Buckspool 21
Holyland 115
Loveston 160
Morgans 171
Paterchurch 194
Adley: Cleddau Lodge 44
Aftecote: Popehill 224
Alexander: Arnoldshill 4
Allen:
Blackaldern 11
Butterhill 22
Cilrhiw 41
Cosheston (Hall) 52
Cresselly 56
Freestone Hall 82
Good Hook 94
Paskeston 193
Rickeston Hall 244
St. Brides 253
Trenichol 305
see also Hensleigh Allen
Allen of Dale Castle
Dale Castle 63
Hayscastle (Caslai) 105
Allen of Gelliswick:
Bicton 11
Broomhill 18
Fobston 80
Gelliswick 85-9
Sutton Lodge 268
Trenichol 305
Trerhos (Patricksford) 308
see also Allen of Dale Castle
Allen-Philipps: St. Brides 253
Andrew: Thornton House 272
Ankern: Carswell 30
ap Owen of Pentre Ifan
see Bowen of Pentre Ifan
ap Rhys *see* Rhys (Price, Rees, Rice) of Rickeston
Arden: Pontfaen 223
Arnold:
Porth Clais 225
Treginnis Issa/Lower 291
Ashton: Welston 331
Attwood: Cartlett (2) 31
Audley, Lord:
Newport Castle 182

B

Baine: Castle Morris 35
Ballinger: Clareston 44
Bamfield: Colby Lodge 50
Bamkin: Thornton House 273
Barett: Roch 248
Barham:
Barnards Well 8
Bwlch y Clawdd 23-4
Farthing's Hook (Clynffyrddin) 74
Trecwn 275, 277-8
see also Foster Barham
Barlow:
Denant 63
Grinston 97
Kilgetty 125
Rickeston 243
Robeston Wathen House 247
Rosemarket 249
Scotchwell 256
Talbenny Hall 269
Welsh Hook 330
Whitewell 334
Ynys y Barry (Barry Island) 341
Barlow of Lawrenny:
Lawrenny 137
Nash, Great 177
Nolton 184
Roch 249
Rosepool 250
Barlow of Rosepool:
Rosepool 250
Tancredston 271
Barlow of Slebech:
Arnoldshill 5
Blackaldern 11
Cefnhydre (Cynheidre) 36
Cilciffeth 39
Cilrhiw 41
Colby 50
Cresswell 56-7
East Jordanston 70
Kilgetty 127
Kilvelgy 131
Lawrenny 137
Lecha 138
Llanddinog 141-2
Llanunwas 150
Llether/Llethr 152
Martletwy House 165-6
Minwear/Minwere 167-8
Molleston 169
New House 180
Rosepool 250
Slebech 261
Sodston House 262
Summerhill 268
Trecadwgan 274
see also Barlow of Rosepool
Barrett:
Cosheston (Hall) 52
Cuffern 59
Dudwell 67
Gelliswick 84-5
Haythog 106
Philbeach/Filbetch 215
Underdown 321
Barry: Leweston 138
Bartlett: Cresselly 56
Barzey:
Arnoldshill 5
Lecha 138
Bassett:
Hermons Hill 113
Hilton 114
Bastin:
Portclew 225
Bateman:
Asheston (Trefasser) 6
Barret's Hill 8

Cronllwyn 57
Cuffern 59
Grinston 97
Haverfordwest 104
Hendre Riffith 109
Honey Hook 116
Rhoslanog Fawr
and Vach 233
Rickeston 242
Bateman of Honeyborough:
Garn, Y Garn 83
Honeyborough 116
Mynyddmelyn 174
Rosepool 250
Trellwyn 301
Trenewydd,
Llanllawer 302
Baten: Thornton House 272
Batine:
Denant 63
Llanwnwr 151
Battin(e): Barret's Hill 8
Beavans: Little Milford 139
Beddoe: Tregendeg 290
Beer: Sandyhaven 255
Bell:
Arnoldshill 5
Kilvelgy 131
Belton: Gelliswick 89
Benedictines:
Caldey Abbey 26
Beneger:
Bangeston, Angle 7
Bennet(t):
Llanion 145
Wolfsdale/Wolfdale 340
Berry:
Lochvane (Lochfaen) 158
Roch 249
Bevan(s): Marloes Court 164-5
Beynon:
Cilrhiwe Fach 42
Lochvane (Lochfaen) 158
Parc Cynhaethw(y) 192
Penberry/Penberi/
Penbury 199
Tregendeg 290
Trewal(l)terwen 312
Trewern,
Lampeter Velfrey 313-14
Bishop:
Portclew 225
Bland:
Merianog 166
Rhosmaen 234
Treleddyn 298
Bleddyn:
Treleddyn 298
Bleddyn ap Cynfyn,
Prince of Powys 42, 147, 157
Bleddyn ap Maenarch 207
Bolton: Bolton Hill 14
Bonsfield: Mullock 173
Borrodaile:
Hook, Ambleston 117
Bowen:
Bridell (Plâs) 17
Carswell 30
Castle Villa (Caswilia) 35
Castlebythe (Casfuwch) 36
Cuffern 59
Cwm Cerwyn 60
Drysgol Goch 65
Dudwell 67
Frongoch 83
Glanduad 91
Glanrhyd 91
Gwern Ffulbrook 100
Hendre, Meline 108
Honeyborough 116
Johnston (Hall) 121
Jordanston 124
Leweston 139
Manorowen 164
Merrion Court 166
Milton House 167
Musselwick/Muslick 174
Pantyderi 189
Penbedw 198
Pencelli Fychan/Fach,
Pencelly 199-200
Penybenglog 213
Pierston/Pearson 218
Roblinston 247
Simpson/Simpston 260
Stone Hall 267
Tarr 272
Treclyn 275
Trefach,
Llanfairnantgwyn 281
Trefach, Nevern 281
Treginnis Issa/Lower 290
Treglemais 292
Trellewelyn 300
Treseissyllt/Tresissllt 310
Trewilym, Eglwyswrw 316
Tŷ Gwyn 320
Tŷgwyn (Whitehouse) 320
Westfield 333
Whitchurch 333
Wolfsdale/Wolfdale 340
see also Webb-Bowen
Bowen of Llwyngwair:
Berry Hill/Bury 10
Brithdir 18
Cilgwyn 41
Coedllwyd 48
Henllan Owen 111
Holmus 115
Llwyngwair 154-5
Llwynihirion 155
Pistyll Meigan 219
Pontgynon 223
Rhosmaen 235
Rhosygilwen 234
Bowen of Lochmeyler:
Camrose House 26
Cerbyd 37
Llanreithan 147
Lochmeyler/Lochmeilir 157
Lochturffin 157-8
Trenichol 304
Bowen (ap Owen)
of Pentre Ifan:
Argoed 4
Cilrydd, Cilryth 42-3
Coedwynog 49
Cwmeog 60-1
Gumfreston 100
Hafod Tydfil 101
Henllys, Nevern 112
Llannerch (Y Bleiddie/
Bleiddiau) 146
Llwyngor(r)ras 153-4
Llystyn 156
Pentre Ifan 205-10
Trerickert (Rickardston),
Treicert 308-9
see also
Bowen of Llwyngwair;
Bowen of Trefloyne
Bowen of Trefloyne:
Carswell 30
Honey Hook 116
Trefloyne 287-8
Bowen of Upton Castle:
Gelliswick 85
Nash, Lower 178
Neeston 178
Pentre Ithel,
Pant Ithel 210
Popehill 224
Upton Castle 321-5
Wenallt 332
Williamston 334, 335
Bowen-Parry:
Cronllwyn 57
Manorowen 164

Bowlas:
Moor, Walwyn's Castle 170
Newton, Llanstadwell 183
Rosemoor 249
Bowling:
Bulliber 21
Fobston 80
Boya, Chieftain:
Clegyr Boia 45
Bradshaw(e):
Caldey Island 26
Cwm Cerwyn 60
St. Dogmaels 253
Treprisk/Tre-prysg 307
Brand:
Johnston (Hall) 121
Brightwell:
Dolpwll 65
Wernddofn 332
Brigstocke of Blaenpant (Cards.):
Vaynor, Manordeifi 327
Brock: Colby Lodge 50
Broughton:
Llangwarren 144
Brown:
Carnachen Wen 29
Ffynnon Gain 77
Honey Hook 116
Tregwynt 294
Trenewydd Manor 304
Browne:
Denant 63
Ramsey Island (Ynys Dewi and Ynys Tyfanog) 231
Brownlie: Rhydgarnwen 236
Brownrigg: Plâs Crwn 219-20
Brychan Brycheiniog 131
Bulkeley:
Bangeston, Angle 7
Bwlch y Clawdd 23
Bunker: Bunker's Hill 21
Burgh: Treffgarne Hall 286
Bushell: Caldey Island 26
Butcher: Gelliswick 84
Butler:
Arnoldshill 4
Barret's Hill 8
Coedcanlas 48
Denant 63
Felindre, Llanwnda 76
Hilton 114
Johnston (Hall) 120
Orlandon 188
Scovaston 259
Trecadwgan 274
Button: Sandyhaven 255
Byam:
Llanion 145-6
Sunny Hill 268
Byers: North Down 184

C

Cadarn (Catharne):
Prendergast 229
Cadefael, Lord of Cydywain in Powys 21
Cadell: Popehill 224
Cadifor ap Collwyn 217
Cadifor Fawr of Blaen Cych 33, 40, 42, 64, 77, 175, 191, 196, 216, 302, 332
Cadifor Fawr of Blaenerch 340
Cadigan:
Llanddinog 141
Llandeilo 140
Ynys y Barry (Barry Island) 341
Cadwgan:
Castle Cenlas 32
Trecadwgan 274
Cainton *see* Cantington
Cale: Philbeach/Filbetch 215
Callen (Callan):
Grove, Narberth 99
Lamphey Park 134
Merrixton 166-7
Mounton 172-3
Trenichol 306
Underdown 321
Camm: Pontfaen 223
Campbell (including Lord Cawdor):
Bangeston, Angle 7
Brownslade 19
Buckspool 21
Cartlett (2) 31
Henllan/Hentland 110
Linney 139
Merrion Court 166
Moor, Castlemartin 170
Mullock 173
Sandyhaven 255
Stackpole Court 264-5
Wiston 337
Campbell (Hook(e) Campbell):
Angle 3
Bangeston, Angle 7
East Jordanston 70
Flimston 80
Henllan/Hentland 110
Kingston 131
Canaston:
Canaston, Great 27
New House 180
Cannon: St. Elvis 254
Canon:
Cwmwdig 61
Gelliswick 85, 86
Haverfordwest 104
Kilgetty 125-30
Leweston 139
Popehill 224
Cantington (Cantrington, Cantrinton, Cainton, Canton) 58, 73, 96, 113, 189
Court (Cwrt), Eglwyswrw 53
Frochest 83
Hendre, Meline 108
Treddiog 279
Trewilym, Eglwyswrw 315
Caprich: Capeston 27
Caradoc Frei'chfras 268
Carew:
Alleston 1
Carew Castle 28
Coedcanlas 48
Wedlock 329
Carlyle: Caldey Island 26
Carpenter:
Martletwy House 166
Carrow: Johnston (Hall) 121
Castlemartin: Castleton 36
Catharne *see* Cadarn
Cawdor, Lord *see* Campbell
Chaldecot:
Treddiog 280
Trehal(e) 296
Chambers: Glyn-y-Mêl 94
Chance: Colby Lodge 51
Charles:
Asheston (Trefasser) 6
Grinston 97
Henllys, Llanrhian 111
Torbant 273
Trenichol 305
Trewal(l)ter Lwyd 312
Trewilym, St. Lawrence 316, 317
Charles, Prince of Wales (later Charles I):
Camrose North 27
Leweston 139
Chetham: Llandeilo 140
Child:
Begelly House 8-9
Bonville's Court 15

Newton, Llanstadwell 182-3
Childs:
Winterton, Marloes 336
Cistercians:
Treffgarn (Little) 284
see also Whitland Abbey
Clark: Robeston Wathen House 247
Cobb: Pembroke Castle 195
Cockburn:
Jordanston (Hall) – Trewrdan 123
Langton 135-6
Rhoslanog Fawr and Vach 233
Trefel(l)yn 283
Codd: Folkeston 81
Colborne: Thornton House 273
Colby:
Bangeston, St. Mary Pembroke 8
Bletherston 14
Clegyr(n) 45
Colby Lodge 50-1
Dyffryn Wdig 69
Ffynnon Coranau 77
Ffynnonau Bychan 77-8
Glanduad (Fawr) 91
Glôg (Glôg-y-Frân) 92
Grondre 97
Hafod Grove 101
Morgenau 171
Nantylladron 175
Pantyderi 189
Penarthur 197
Posty 227
Rhosygilwen 233, 234
Robeston Wathen House 247
Trewellwell 312
Wernddofn 332
Cole:
Eweston (Trewen) 73
Llwyngwair 154
Rinaston 246
Talbenny Hall 269
Thornton House 273
Tregam(m)an 289
Cooker: Hook, Marloes 117
Cope: Hook, Ambleston 117
Corbett:
Eweston (Trewen) 73
Hafod Grove 101
Nash, Great 177
Cornock:
Welsh Hook 329
Winterton, Puncheston/ Little Newcastle 336
Cosens: Merrixton 166
Cotton:
Boulston 16
Philbeach/Filbetch 215
Courtin:
Cilfowyr (Cilfowir) 40
Cowell-Stepney:
Prendergast 229
Cowie: Gelliswick 89
Cozens (Couzens):
Capeston 28
Denant 63
Robeston Hall 246
Rosepool 250
Sandyhaven 255
Treffgarne Hall 286
Wolfsdale/Wolfdale 340
Crabhole: Crabhole 55
Craddock:
Newton, Llanstadwell 182
Crosland: Colby Lodge 51
Crowe: Nolton 184
Crowther:
Fobston 80
Wolfsdale/Wolfdale 340
Crunn: Llanunwas 150
Crymes:
Thornton House 272-3
Cuny:
Golden 94
Lamphey Court 133
Welston 330-1
Cyhylyn ap Gwynfardd 43, 205, 212
Cilrydd/Cilryth 42
Cynfrig: Nantybugail 175

D

Dafydd Foel (Voel) of Trewern, Nevern 254, 314
Daniel: Ffynnonau Bychan 78
David:
Blaen Tâf 13
Brithdir 18
Brwynant 20
Cilast Ucha 38
Cilrhiw 41
Clegyr 45
Henllan Owen 111
Henllys, Llanrhian 111
Llanddinog 142
Nantybugail 175
Penyrallt, St. Dogmaels 214
Scleddau 255
Tredafydd 279
Trefayog 283
Trefel(l)yn 283
Treglemais 292
Trenichol 304-5
David ap David:
Penalltcych 196
David Ddu: Cilciffeth 39
Davids:
Clegyr(n) 45
Haverfordwest 104
Philbeach/Filbetch 215
Plâs Iwerill (Y Werill) 220
Treginnis Ucha 291
Westfield 333
Davies:
Alleston 1
Bwlch y Clawdd 24
Capeston 28
Carnachen Wen 29-30
Castle Malgwyn (Old) 33
Castle Villa (Caswilia) 35
Cilgelynen (Cilglynen) 40
Cilrhiwe 41
Clareston 44
Clyn Meredith 46
Clynfyw 46-7
Crabhole 55
Denant 63
Dudwell 67
Dyffryn Pibyll 69
Dyffryn Wdig 69
Gellifor, Gelli Fawr 84
Gilfachwrnell 90
Glanduad (Fawr) 91
Greenhill 96
Greenway 96
Grinston 97
Grove, near Pembroke Town 99
Harmeston 101-2
Hayston 106
Hendre Eynon 109
Honey Hook 116
Lancych 134
Llanddinog 142
Llanteg/Llanteague 149
Llwyngor(r)as 153-4
Martel 165
Martletwy House 166
Molleston 169
Mullock 173
Nash, Lower 178
Neeston 178

Newton, Llanstadwell 183
Park Court 192
Penalltcych 196
Penarthur 197-8
Penlan Cych 201
Penralltrheiny 202
Pentre Ithel, Pant Ithel 210
Penyrallt, St. Dogmaels 214
Plâsymeibion 221
Talybont 269
Torbant 273
Treddiog 280
Trefach, Nevern 282
Trefayog 283
Trenewydd, Llanllawer 302
Treseissyllt, Tresissllt 310
Tŷ Gwyn 320
Tŷgwyn (Whitehouse) 320
Westfield 333
Ynys y Barry
(Barry Island) 341
see also Saunders-Davies
Davies-Scourfield:
Castle Villa (Caswilia) 35
Moat/Mote/
The New Moat 168
Davis:
Coedwynog 49
Mullock 173
Sodston House 263
Dawes:
Bangeston, Angle 7
Carswell 30
Dawkins:
Biers Pool 11
Buckspool 21
Daykin: Llandigige Fach 141
Daysh: Thornton House 273
de Barri: Manorbier Castle 162
de Brian:
Kilbarth 125
Pierston/Pearson 218
de Brisau: Fletherhill 79
de Cantington see Cantington
de Carew *see* Carew
de Ffilbech *see* Ffilbech
de Hastings: Hean Castle 106
de Hilton: Hilton 113
de Hoda:
Trerickert (Rickardston),
Treicert 308
Trewrdan, Trefwrdan 318
de Hoton: Capeston 27
de Kemeys: Welsh Hook 329
de la Pole: Treffgarne Hall 286
de Martin *see* Martin
de Montgomery:
Pembroke Castle 195
de Prendergast:
Prendergast 229
de Rufe: Eweston
(Trewen) 73
de Rupe (de la Rupe):
Llandeilo 140
Pennar 201
Wolfscastle (Casblaidd) 339
de Rutzen:
Arnoldshill 5
Lampeter Velfrey 132
Minwear/Minwere 168
Slebech 261-2
de Stackpole:
Stackpole Court 264
de Staunton 216
de Vale:
Dale (Castle) 63
Philbeach/Filbetch 215
Treffgarne Hall 285
Wolfscastle (Casblaidd) 339
de Valence:
Dudwell 65
Leweston 138
Dean: Hasguard 104
Dedwith:
Clegyr(n) 45
Penrhiw/Pen-cw 203
Dedwydd (Dedwyth):
Bwlch y Clawdd 23
Cotty 53
Deedes: St. Dogmaels 254
Devandes: Cottesmore 53
Devereux: Lamphey Court 133
Devereux Jones:
Bolton Hill 14
Devonald:
Court (Cwrt),
Eglwyswrw 54
Fagwr Eynon Fawr 74
Graig 95
Helygnant 107
Pontygafel 224
Sodston House 262
Didwith: Llangloffan 143
Donne *see* Dunn
Douglas-Osborn: Cwmeog 61
Dru (Drew):
Trewilym, St. Lawrence
316
Dunn (Dwnn):
Caermaenau Fawr 25
Crickmarren 57
Penblewyn 199
Picton Castle 216
Tarr 272
Welston 331
Dunsany:
Kilgetty 131
Manorbier Castle 162
Slebech 262
Dyer:
Cefnydre (Cynheidre) 36
Fishguard 78-9
Trewrach 318

E

Eaton: Park Glas 192
Ednyfed Fychan of Gwynedd 12
Edward: Rhydydrissi 235
Edwardes:
Cartlett (2) 31
Coedllwyd 48
Coedwynog 49
Dyffryn Pibyll 69
Glanpwllafon 91
Glanrhyd 91
Grondre 97
Haylett 104-5
Hermons Hill 113
Hilton 114
Hook, Ambleston 117
Johnston (Hall) 120
Merrixton 167
Moor, Castlemartin 170
Newton, Rudbaxton 183
Treffgarn (Little) 284-5
Wolfscastle (Casblaidd) 339
Edwardes
(including Lord Kensington):
Barret's Hill 8
Blackaldern 11
Bolton Hill 14
Druidston 65
Fobston 80
Greenway 97
Haylett 105
Hayston 106
Hook, Marloes 118
Johnston (Hall) 120-1
Marloes Court 165
Pierston/Pearson 218
Popehill 224
Robeston Wathen House
247
St. Brides 253
Tregroes 293
Trewal(l)ter Lwyd 311
Westerton 333

Edwardes of Sealyham
see Tucker-Edwardes
Edwards:
Castell Gwyn 36
East Jordanston 70
Fagwr Goch 74
Ffynnonau Bychan 78
Forest 82
Scleddau 255
Summerhill 268
Edwyfed Fychan of Gwynedd
43, 48
Elizabeth I, Queen: Golden 94
Elliot(t):
Amroth Castle/Earwere 1, 2
Annikel (Annikell) 3
Farthing's Hook
(Clynffyrddin) 74
Greenway 96
Narberth-Plâs 175-6
St. Botolphs 251
Westerton 333
Ellis: Southfield 263
Ellys: Paskeston 193
Elson: Penybenglog 213
Estemond: Honey Hook 116
Estmond: Camrose North 27
Evan:
Asheston (Trefasser) 6
Caerau 24
Castlebythe (Casfuwch) 36
Narberth-Plâs 176
Pistyll Meigan 219
Evans:
Avellanau 6
Carn Huan 30
Castleton 36
Cerbyd 37
Cilau Wen 38
Cilgadfarch 40
Coedwynog 49
Colby Lodge 51
Cruglas 59
Dolemaen 64
Dyffryn Pibyll 69
Ffyn(n)one Gleision 78
Glastir (Glasdir) 92
Johnston (Hall) 121
Llandigige Fach 141
Llanmarlais 146
Longridge 160
Mabws Fawr 161
Mynyddmelyn 174
Parsele/Parselle 193
Penallt Cadwgan 196
Penally Court 197
Pencnwc 200
Pistyll Meigan 219
Pontygafel 224
Rhosygilwen 234
Rinaston 246
Sodston House 263
Studda 267
Tancredston 271-2
Tarr 272
Trefayog 283
Trefel(l)yn 283
Trefeugan 283
Treffgarne Hall 285-6
Trefin 287
Treginnis Issa/Lower 291
Trerickert (Rickardston),
Treicert 309
Trewrdan/Trefwrdan 318
Upton Castle 325
Welston 331
Woodstock 341
Evans of Peterwell (Cards):
Anastaslade (Slade) 2
Eynon:
Coed Rath 47
East Hook 69
Henllan/Hentland 110
Hook, Llangwm 117
Eynon ap Gwilym ap
Gwrwared (Eynon Fawr
o'r Coed):
Cilrydd, Cilryth 42
Pentre Ifan 206
Eyre Coote:
Underdown 321

F

Fairclough: Williamston 336
Farquhar: Castle Hall 32
Fawly: Ridgeway 245
Fenton: Glyn-y-Mêl 93-4
Ferrers: Bangeston, Angle 7
Ferrier (Ferrior):
Glôg (Glôg-y-Frân) 93
Pennar 201
Vaynor, Manordeifi 327
Ffilbech:
Philbeach/Filbetch 215
Fields: Milton 167
Fisher: Denant 63
Foley:
Canaston, Great 27
Dyffryn Ffilbro 68
Foley House 81
Hafod Tydfil 101
Ridgeway 245
Sodston House 262
Ford:
Berry Hill/Bury 10
Brimaston (Treowman) 17
Brithdir 18
Court (Cwrt),
Eglwyswrw 54
Eweston (Trewen) 73
Stone Hall 266-7
Wolfscastle (Casblaidd) 339
Fortune:
Anastaslade (Slade) 2
Leweston 139
Ynys y Barry
(Barry Island) 341
Foster:
Trecwn 277-8
Foster Barham:
Nantybugail 175
Trecwn 278
Fowler:
Capeston 27
Robeston Hall 246
Treffgarne Hall 286
Francis:
Glynhenllan 93
Pontfaen 223
Scleddau 255
Scolton Manor 256
Trebrithin 273
Waunberry, Waunberri 328
Fromand the Fleming
(Fermand or Fromand
Brown) 29
Tregwynt 294
Frost: Glandovan 90
Furlong:
Vaynor (Great) 326
Furmstone:
Bwlch y Clawdd 24

G

Gabb: Tregwynt 295
Gaddum: Orielton 188
Gale: Narberth-Plâs 176
Garnon:
Henllys, Llanrhian 111
Park Court 192
Garnons:
Cefnhydre (Cynheidre) 36
Glynhenllan 93
Longhouse 159
Penralltrheiny 202
Porth Clais 225

George:
Bridell (Plâs) 17
Brithdir 18
Cilast Ucha 38
Denant 63
Esgair 73
Ffynnon Coranau 77
Foley House 81
Llanreithan 148
Molleston 169
Mynyddmelyn 174
Nash, Great 177
Penysgwarn(e) 214
Plâs Crwn 219
Rhydgarnwen 236
Tregroes 293
Trellewelyn 300
Trewern 315
Welsh Hook 330
Gibbon:
Cartlett (2) 31
Rudbaxton, Great 250
Scovaston 259
Vaynor (Great) 326
Gibby:
Nash, Lower 178
Plâsymeibion 221
Gilbert: Glynhenllan 93
Gitto:
Pentre Ithel, Pant Ithel 210
Glyn: Trebrithin 273
Goddard: Fletherhill 79
Gonne: Vaynor (Great) 326
Goodere: Ivy Tower 119
Goodridge:
Anastaslade (Slade) 2
Gossawl 280
Gough: Honey Hook 116
Gould: Tredefaid 280
Gower:
Castle Malgwyn (New) 34
Castle Malgwyn (Old) 33
Glandovan 90
Glynhenllan 93
Lamphey Palace 132
Pontfaen 223
Grant:
Hilton 114
Kilgetty 130-1
Nolton 184
Greaves: Netherwood 179
Green:
Corston 52
Rhyd yr Harding 236
Greenish:
Gelliswick 89
Morfil 171
Gregson-Ellis:
Newport Castle 182
Greville:
Caldey Island 26
Castle Hall 32-3
Cilciffeth 39
Colby 50
Lecha 138
Paterchurch 194-5
Robeston Hall 246
Griffith:
Berllan 10
Blaen y Groes/Gors 12
Brwynant 20
Bunker's Hill 21
Bwlch y Clawdd 23
Carne Coch 30
Castle Cenlas 32
Cilau Wen 38
Coedwynog 49
Cronllwyn 57
Cwm Cerwyn 60
Dyffryn Ffilbro 68
Esgair Wilym 73
Glynhenllan 93
Gwern Ffulbrook 100
Helygnant 107
Llandeilo 140
Llangloffan 143
Llangolman 143
Llanwnwr 151
Manorowen 164
Nantylladron 175
Penybenglog 212-13
Plâsymeibion 221
Pontgynon 223
Rhosmoeled 235
Rickeston 243
Scleddau 255
Treclyn 275
Trefayog 282-3
Tregendeg 290
Trellewelyn 300
Trenichol 305
Treseissyllt, Tresisllt 309
Trewilym,
Eglwyswrw 315-16
Werngoy 332
Whitchurch 333-4
Wolfscastle (Casblaidd) 339
Griffith(s):
Berry Hill/Bury 10
Penally Court 197
Pointz Castle (Casbwnsh) 221-2
Griffiths:
Brithdir 18
Gilfachwrnell 90
Glanrhyd 91
Hook, Ambleston 117
Llanddinog 142
Llancych 134
Longhouse 159
Rhosdwarch 232
Rhosmoeled 235
Rhyd yr Harding 236
Trecadwgan 274
Trewent Hall 313
Trewilym, St. Lawrence 317
Vaynor, Manordeifi 327
Waterwinch 328
Gulston:
Cosheston (Hall) 53
Prendergast 229
Gwgan ap Bleddyn of Breconshire 15, 216
Gwilym (Gwillim):
Caerwen 25
Llystyn 156
Rhydydrissi 235
Trefawr 282
Gwilym ap Gwrwared 205-6
Gwither: Trewent Hall 313
Gwrwared (family):
Vaynor, Llawhaden 325
Gwrwared I and II 205
Gwyl(l)im (Gwillim):
Scollock 255
Gwyn:
Bwlch y Clawdd 23
Caerforiog 24
Court (Cwrt), Llanllawer 54
Cwm Cerwyn 60
Ffynnon Coranau 77
Trerickert (Rickardston), Treicert 309
Gwynfardd Dyfed 4, 7, 12, 13, 15, 38, 39, 58, 61, 62, 91, 107, 108, 110, 112, 146, 166, 171, 179, 189, 205, 212, 219, 222, 224, 266, 275, 333
Gwyn(n):
Felindre, Llanwnda 76
Glanpwllafon 91
Jordanston (Hall) – Trewrdan 121
Tredafydd 279
Trefel(l)yn 283
Gwynne:
Anastaslade (Slade) 2

Blackaldern 11
Brynaeron 20
Canaston, Great 27
Cilciffeth 39
Court (Cwrt), Llanllawer 54
Dyffryn Ffilbro 68
Fobston 80
Hayston 105-6
Paterchurch 194
Plâsymeibion 220-1
Tredafydd 279
Tregroes 293
Gwynne of Noyadd Trefawr:
Penlan Cych 201
Gwyther:
Brawdy-Breudeth 16
East Moor 71
Kilgetty 131
Tarr 272

H

Hagley: Trenichol 305
Hal Freda 20
Hall:
Llanmarlais 146
Trewent Hall 313
Halton: Torbant 273
Hamilton:
Cilciffeth 39
Colby 50
Cresswell 57
Hasguard 104
Jordanston (Hall) – Trewrdan 123
Kilvelgy 131
Langton 136
Lecha 138
St. Ken(n)ox 254
Thornton House 273
Hammett:
Castle Malgwyn (New) 34
Castle Malgwyn (Old) 33
Hand: Molleston 169
Harcourt: Trecadwgan 274
Harcourt Powell:
Hook, Llangwm 117
Harding:
Farthing's Hook (Clynffyrddin) 74
Longhook 159
Porthiddy (Portheiddy) 227
Trevaccoon (Trefaccwn) 310-11
Hargest: Clegyr 44
Harold: Haroldston 102
Harries:
Asheston (Trefasser) 6
Blaiddbwll 13
Brimaston (Treowman) 18
Broomhill 19
Bryndysil 21
Caerforiog 25
Castle Villa (Caswilia) 35
Castlebythe (Casfuwch) 36
Cefnhydre (Cynheidre) 37
Clegyr 44-5
Clyn Meredith 46
Cruglas 58-9
Cuffern 59
Cwmwdig 61
Dudwell 67
Glanduad (Fawr) 91
Goodwick (Wdig/Aber Goodick) 95
Graig 95
Grinston 97
Hayscastle (Caslai) 105
Heathfield (Lodge) 107
Hendre Eynon 109
Hendre Riffith 109
Henllys, Llanrhian 111
Hermons Hill 113
Hilton 114
Kilbarth 125
Llanddinog 142
Llandigige (Fawr) 141
Llaney 142
Llangloffan 143
Llanreithan 148
Llanunwas 150
Llwynygorras 155-6
Lochmeyler/Lochmeilir 157
Penarthur 198
Penberry/Penberi/Penbury 198-9
Penrhiw/Pen-cw 203
Porthiddy (Portheiddy) 226-7
Priskilly 230
Rickeston Hall 244
Roch 249
St. Brides 253
Trecadwgan 274
Trefach, Llanfairnantgwyn 281
Treffgarn (Little) 284
Treginnis Issa/Lower 290
Tregwynt 293-5
Trehowel 296-7
Trenichol 305, 306-7
Trerhos (Patricksford) 308
Treseissyllt, Tresissllt 309-10
Trevaccoon (Trefaccwn) 310-11
Trewilym, St. Lawrence 316, 317
Werngoy 332
Wolfscastle (Casblaidd) 339
Harries-Burrington:
Tregwynt 295
Harris:
Llaney 142
Treddiog 280
Trenewydd Fawr 303
Harry:
Clegyr 44-5
Cruglas 58
Cwmwdig 61
Hendre, Llandeloy 108
Llanunwas 150
Penbedw 198
Porthiddy (Portheiddy) 226
Trenichol 306
Trerickert (Rickardston), Treicert 309
Wolfscastle (Casblaidd) 339
Harry ap Philip of Blaen Cych 204
Harvey:
Sodston House 262
Hassall: Eastwood 72
Havard:
Crugiau 58
Newton, Rudbaxton 183
Treprisk, Tre-prysg 307
Haverfordwest Priory:
Butterhill 22
Hawkes: Milton House 167
Hawkesworth:
Berllan 10
Newport Castle 182
Hawkin: Mullock 173
Hawksley: Caldey Island 26
Hawkwell:
St. Ken(n)ox 254
Talybont 269
Hay:
Berllan 10
Pencelli Fawr/Pencelly 199
Treclyn 275
Trerickert (Rickardston), Treicert 309
Haye: Cilrhiwe Fach 42
Haylot: Haylett 104

Hayward:
Fletherhill 79-80
Rudbaxton, Great 250
Hensleigh:
Llanteg/Llanteague 149-50
Panteg (Panteague) 190
Hensleigh Allen:
Panteg (Panteague) 190
Henton: Castell Gwyn 36
Hergest:
Penarthur 198
Rhoslanog Fawr and Vach 233
Hicks:
East Hook 69
Hook, Llangwm 117
Tancredston 271
Higgon:
Folkeston 81
Haroldston 103
Newton, Rudbaxton 183
Scolton Manor 256
Tredafydd 279
Treffgarne Hall 286
Trefran, Trevrane 289
Trewal(l)ter Lwyd 311
Hilling: Scotsborough 258
Hitching: Grove, Narberth 97
Hitchings:
Buckspool 21
Clegyr 45
Hodges: Kilvelgy 131
Hoggetyn:
Trefran, Trevrane 289
Holcomb: Penarthur 197
Holcombe:
Brownslade 19
Cosheston (Hall) 52
Llanion 146
Llanreithan 148
Milton House 167
Nash, Lower 178
Holland:
Walwyn's Castle 327-8
Holt: Newport Castle 182
Holwell:
Castle Hall 32
Eastington 71
Hoode: Trerickert (Rickardston), Treicert 308
Hooke:
Bangeston, Angle 7
Upton Castle 324
Hook(e) Campbell
see Campbell (Hook(e) Campbell)
Hooper: Eweston (Trewen) 73
Hoper: Ynys y Barry (Barry Island) 341
Hore: Annikel (Annikell) 3
Horsey: Johnston (Hall) 120
Hospitallers of St John
see Knights Hospitallers
Houghston: St. Ken(n)ox 254
Houghton: Caerforiog 24
Howel:
Crugiau 58
Eweston (Trewen) 73
Trewilym, St. Lawrence 316
Howel ap Jenkin ap Robert:
Nevern 179-80
Howel ap Llywelin ap Griffith:
Cilgadfarch 40
Howel Dda 182
Howel Gawr 166, 232
Penybenglog 212
Howell:
Caerwen 25
Cotty 53
Eastlake 72
Glôg (Glôg-y-Frân) 92
Howelston 118
Lochvane (Lochfaen) 158
Penalltcych 196
Penarthur 197
Priskilly 230
Rhosdwarch 232
St. Botolphs 251
Talbenny Hall 269
Treddiog 280
Trenewydd, Crunwear 302
Trewellwell 313
Trewent Hall 313
Trewilym, Eglwyswrw 315
Tŷgwyn (Whitehouse) 320
Wernddofn 332
Woodstock 340-1
Howell ap Rhys ap Llewelyn:
Cilgwyn 41
Howells:
Caerwen 26
Penralltrheiny 203
Rushacre 250
Hu: Eweston (Trewen) 73
Hugh:
Cilgelynen (Cilglynen) 40
Court (Cwrt), Llanllawer) 54
Trebrithin 273
Wolfscastle (Casblaidd) 339
Hughes:
Felindre, Llanwnda 76
Glynhenllan 93
Harmeston 101
Llwynbedw 153
Milton 167
Penybenglog 213
Tredafydd 279
Trefel(l)yn 283
Trenewydd Manor 304
Trewilym, St. Lawrence 317
Humphrey: Penalltcych 196
Humphreys: Rhosygilwen 234
Hurd(e): Summerhill 268
Hurde: Cuffern 59
Husband: Arnoldshill 5
Hyatt: Gelliswick 86
Hyer: Summerton 268

I

Ieuan:
Newgale 181
Ieuan ap Llewellyn 232
Ieuan ap Owen:
Mabws Fawr 161
Ieuan ap Rees:
Henllys, Nevern 112
Ievan ap Gwilym ap Eynon:
Tredafydd 279
Instance:
Scollock 255
Istans:
Coed Rath 47

J

James:
Caerforiog 25
Caermaenau Fawr 25
Cilast Ucha 38
Cilgadfarch 40
Cilgwyn 41
Coedwynog 49
Crabhole 55
Gellifor, Gelli Fawr 84
Helygnant 107
Henllan Owen 111
Llanunwas 150
Llanwnwr 151
Llwyngor(r)as 153
Lochmeyler/Lochmeilir 157
Lochturffin 158
Lochvane (Lochfaen) 158

Marloes Court 165
Pantsaeson/Pantsaison 190-1
Penberry/Penberi/Penbury 198
Penblewyn 199
Penpedwast 202
Philbeach 215
Plâsymeibion 220-1
Pontygafel 224
Rhosmoeled 235
Rhydgarnwen 236
Robeston Wathen House 247
Sodston House 262
Southfield 263
Talybont 269
Torbant 273
Trefaes 282
Trehaidd 295
Trenewydd Manor 304
Trenichol 305
Treprisk, Tre-prysg 307
Trewal(l)ter Lwyd 311
Trewal(l)terwen 312
Trewilym, St. Lawrence 317
Trewrach 318
Trewrdan/Trefwrdan 318
Vaynor, Llawhaden 326
Werngoy 332
James ab Eynon:
Cilfowyr (Cilfowir) 39
James ap Griffith ap Howell:
Castle Malgwyn (Old) 33
Jameson:
Penally Abbey 197
Jan:
Vaynor, Llawhaden 325
Jenkin:
Blaen y Groes/Gors 12
Cefnhydre (Cynheidre) 36
Glanpwllafon 91
Roch 248
Trenichol 304
Jenkin ab Owen ap John:
Glynhenllan 93
Jenkin ap Howell of Nevern 111
Jenkins:
Brimaston (Treowman) 18
Castle Malgwyn (Old) 33
Coedllwyd 48
Ffynnon Coranau 77
Mullock 173
Newgale 181
Pantirion 190
Rhyd yr Harding 236
Rhydgarnwen 236
Trefigin 286
Treyarched/Trearched 320
Tŷgwyn (Whitehouse)
Vorlan 327
Jenner:
Park Glas 192
Jermin:
Paskeston 193
Joce (Joyce):
Prendergast 229
John:
Asheton (Trefasser) 6
Caerwen 26
Carn Huan 30
Cerbyd 37
Cilwendeg 43
Clegyr 44
Cruglas 58
Dolemaen 64
Felindre, Llanwnda 76
Glynhenllan 93
Hendre 108
Llanddinog 142
Llangolman 143
Llanreithan 148
Lochturffin 158
Parsele/Parselle 193
Penlan 200
Trecwn 275
Treddiog 280
Tregendeg 290
Trehal(e) 295
Trehenry 296
Trenewydd Manor 304
Waunberry, Waunberri 328
John ap Rees:
Cronllwyn 57
John ap Rees ap Owen:
Cefnydre (Cynheidre) 36
John ap Robert Goch of Preskilly:
Castle Cenlas 32
Priskilly 230
Ynys y Barry (Barry Island) 341
Johnes:
Caerwen 25
Cruglas 58
Penpedwast 202
Johns:
Brwynant 20
Carne Coch 30
Castle Morris 35
Court (Cwrt), Llanllawer 54
Manorowen 164
Nantybugail 175
Trecwn 275
Trellewelyn 300
Trenewydd Manor 304
Jones:
Argoed 4
Barnards Well 8
Blaen Mwrw 12
Bolton Hill 14
Bonville's Court 15
Caermaenau Fawr 25
Castle Malgwyn (Old) 33, 34
Castle Morris 34
Dolau Llanerch 64
Dudwell 67
Dyffryn Wdig 69
East Hook 69
Ffyn(n)one Gleision 78
Flimston 80
Forest 82
Gilfachwrnell 90
Harmeston 101
Haroldston 103
Heathfield (Lodge) 107
Hook, Llangwm 117
Hook, Marloes 117
Lancych 134
Linney 139
Llangloffan 143
Llwynbedw 153
Milton 167
Nantybugail 175
Nantylladron 175
Pantirion 190
Pantyderi 189
Park Glas 192
Penblewyn 199
Penlan 200
Penpedwast 202
Pentour (Pentower) 204
Pentre Ithel, Pant Ithel 210
Pentypark/Pentyparc 212
Pistyll Meigan 219
Rhosygilwen 233-4
Rhydgarnwen 236
Simpson/Simpston 260
Southfield 263
Sutton Lodge 268
Trecwn 275
Trefach, Llanfairnantgwyn 281
Trefawr 282
Treffgarne Hall 286

Trewellwell 312-13
Trewilym, St. Lawrence 317
Vaynor, Llawhaden 325
Wenallt 331-2
Wiston 337
see also Devereux Jones
Jones of Brawdy
and Llether
Brawdy-Breudeth 16-17
Crugiau 58
Cruglas 58
Cuffern 59
Esgair Wilym 73
Grinston 97
Lecha 138
Leweston 139
Llether/Lethr 152
Lochvane (Lochfaen) 158
Newgale 181
Penberry/Penberi/Penbury 198
Rickeston 243
Tancredston 271
Trefinert, Trevinert 287
Tretio Fawr 310
Welsh Hook 329
Jones of Brecon:
Treffgarne Hall 286
Jones of Brithdir:
Brithdir 18
Cilast Ucha 38
Plâs Iwerill (Y Werill) 220
Jones of Cilwendeg:
Cilforwyr (Cilforwir) 40
Cilwendeg 43
Llwynbedw 153
Plâs Iwerill (Y Werill) 220
Treffgarne Hall 286
Jones of Llanbadarn (Cards):
Cilwendeg 43
Jones of Llanina (Cards):
Cilrydd, Cilryth 43
Longridge 160
Pentre Ifan 210
Trewern 314
Jones Lloyd:
Dolau Llanerch 64
Lancych 134
Jordan:
Ashdale 5-6
Barret's Hill 8
Berllan 10
East Hook 69
Hayston 105
Hook, Llangwm 117
Jordanston 124
Neeston 178
Treleddyn 298
Trenewydd Fawr 303
Joyce:
Prendergast 229
Scollock 255
Jurdan:
Trefran, Trevrane 289

K

Kay: Colby Lodge 51
Keating: Keeston/Keyston (Tregethin) 125
Keith:
Longridge 160
Trehenry 296
Vaynor (Great) 326
Kelway: Cottesmore 53
Kemm: North Down 184
Kensington, Lord *see* Edwardes
Kethyn: Holmws 115
Keymer:
Glastir (Glasdir) 92
Haverfordwest 104
Robeston Hall 246
Scotchwell 256
Trewrdan/Trefwrdan 318
Keys: Carswell 30
Kinaston: Llanion 146
Kinner: Angle 3
Knethell:
Castleton 36
East Hook 70
Hook, Llangwm 117
Knights Hospitallers of St. John:
Berry Hill/Bury 10
Cuffern 59
Rosemarket 249
Summerhill 268
Knolles: Wenallt 331-2
Knox:
Cilrhiw 41
Colston 52
Llanstinan 149
Longhook 159
Martel 165
Martletwy House 166
Minwear/Minwere 168
Molleston 169
Slebech 261
Kylsant, Lord:
Amroth Castle/Earwere 2
Kymer:
Nolton 184
Panteg (Panteague) 190
Treffgarne Hall 286
Kynaston: Caldey Island 26

L

Ladd:
Penyrallt, St. Dogmaels 214
Lake:
Castle Hall 33
Lambton:
Brownslade 19
Laugharne:
Asheston (Trefasser) 6
Bangeston, St. Mary Pembroke 7-8
Castle Cenlas 32
Eweston (Trewen) 73
Hafod Tydfil 101
Hendre, Llandeloy 108
Llwynygorras 155
Pierston/Pearson 218
Pontfaen 222-3
Torbant 273
Laugharne of Llanreithan:
Hafod Grove 101
Henllys, Nevern 112
Llanreithan 147-8
Llanunwas 150
Laugharne of St. Brides, Orlandon and Pontfaen:
Brimaston (Treowman) 17
Caerforiog 25
Crabhole 55
Folkeston 81
Hasguard 104
Hayscastle (Caslai) 105
Haythog 106
Orlandon 188
St. Brides 252
Treindeg (Ryndaston, Rhyndaston) 297
Walwyn's Castle 327, 328
Lawrence:
Rhoslanog Fawr and Vach 233
Trefel(l)yn 283
Westerton 333
Le Hunt Wilson:
Jordanston 124
Le Hunte:
Penyrallt, Nevern 214
St. Botolphs 251
Ynys y Barry (Barry Island) 341

Le Moigne
(Le Mayne, Le Maen):
Rickeston 237, 238
Tancredston 270
Leach:
Begelly House 9
Brownslade 19
Bulliber 21
Castle Morris 35
Corston 52
Cosheston (Hall) 52
East Moor 71
Ivy Tower 119
Linney 139
Loveston 160
Nash, Lower 178
Pencnwc 200
Portclew 225
Sunny Hill 268
Vaynor (Great) 326
Leavesley:
Landshipping Ferry 134
Levett:
Brownslade 19
Lewes:
Coedllwyd 48
Penybenglog 213
Penyrallt, St. Dogmaels 214
Tredefaid 280
Lewis:
Berry Hill/Bury 10
Brithdir 18
Bwlch y Clawdd 23
Carn Huan 30
Carswell 30
Castell Gwyn 36
Castlebythe (Casfuwch) 36
Cilrhiw 41
Cilrhiwe Fach 42
Clyn Meredith 45-6
Clynfyw 47
Coedllwyd 48
Cronllwyn 57
Dolau Llwyd(ion) 64
Dolpwll 65
Dyffryn Pibyll 69
Felindre, Llanwnda 76
Ffynnon Coranau 77
Fron 83
Glanrhyd 91
Good Hook 94
Grondre 97
Grove, Narberth 99
Hafod Tydfil 101
Hean Castle 106, 107
Helygnant 108
Hendre, Meline 108
Hendre, St. Dogmaels 109
Henllan Owen 111
Llangolman 143
Manorowen 163-4
Merianog 166
Minwear/Minwere 167
Molleston 169
Morfil 171
Nantybugail 175
Narberth-Plâs 176
Pantirion 190
Penarthur 198
Penlan 200
Penpedwast 201
Penrhiw/Pen-cw 203
Penybenglog 213
Plâs Crwn 219
Popehill 224
Posty 227
Rhosmaen 234
Rudbaxton, Great 250
Trefach, Nevern 281-2
Treginnis Issa/Lower 291
Trehenry 296
Treseissyllt, Tresisllt 309
Trewilym, Eglwyswrw 316
Werngoy 332
Lewis of Henllan:
Caerau 24
Caermaenau Fawr 25
Henllan 109-10
Trenichol 306
Lewis ap Watkyn:
Upton Castle 322
Lewis-Bowen:
Clynfyw 47
Coedllwyd 48
Lindley: Golden 94
Ling: Llether/Llethr 152
Llewelin:
Bwlch y Clawdd 23
Clynfyw 46
Cronllwyn 57
Crugiau 58
Esgair 73
Nash, Lower 178
Trerhos (Patricksford) 308
Llewellin:
Boulston 16
Carswell 30
Martel 165
Pentre Ithel, Pant Ithel 210
Rudbaxton, Great 250
Trewarren 312
see also Purcell-Llewellin
Llewellyn:
Esgair 73
Scollock 255
Scotchwell 257
Llewelyn:
Cilwendeg 43
Esgair 73
Gumfreston 100
Penalltcych 196
Trellewelyn 298
Wedlock 329
Woodstock 341
Llewelyn (Llewellyn) o'r Coed
ap Owen 146
Llystyn 156
Pentre Ifan 207
Llewhellin:
Cornish Down 52
Treginnis Issa 290
Winterton, Marloes 336
Lloyd:
Brimaston (Treowman) 18
Coedwynog 49
Colston 51
Fagwr Goch 74
Ffynnon Coranau 77
Ffyn(n)one Gleision 78
Freestone Hall 82-3
Gilfachwrnell 89
Glanduad (Fawr) 91
Glynhenllan 93
Hafod Tydfil 101
Haroldston 102
Hayscastle (Caslai) 105
Hermons Hill 113
Kilgetty 129
Lancych 134
Llandigige (Fawr) 141
Llangloffan 143
Newport Castle 181-2
Pantsaeson/Pantsaison 191
Penbedw 198
Pentre Ifan 209, 210
Pistyll Meigan 219
Priskilly 230
Rhosmaen 234
Rhosygilwen 233
Sandyhaven 255
Stone Hall 267
Tredafydd 279
Trefach,
Llanfairnantgwyn 281
Trefach, Nevern 281
Trefaes 282
Trefawr 282
Trefel(l)yn 283

Trefigin 286
Tregam(m)an 290
Trehenry 296
Trehowel 296
Trenewydd Fawr 303
Trerees, Trerhys 307
Lloyd (Llwyd) of Blaen Cych:
Bachendre 7
Cilgadfarch 40
Dolau Llanerch 64
Dolau Llwyd(ion) 64
Penrallt Llyn/Penralltyllyn 196-7
Lloyd of Bronwydd 49
Berllan 10
Berry Hill/Bury 10
Blaen Tâf 13
Cilrhiwe 41-2
Cwmeog 60, 61
Esgair Wilym 73
Hafod Grove 101
Henllys Nevern 112
Llwyngor(r)as 153
Pencelli Fawr, Pencelly 199
Pencelli Forest, Pencelly Forest 199
Penpedwast 202
Vaynor, Manordeifi 327
Lloyd (Llwyd) of Cemaes and Blaiddbwll 7, 124, 212, 224
Blaiddbwll 13
Clynfyw 46
Drysgol Goch 65
Gilfachwrnell 89
Rhosygilwen 233
Trehenry 296
Lloyd of Coedmore:
Forest 82
Trewern 314
Lloyd of Cwmgloyn:
Argoed 4
Cwmgloyn 62
Hendre, St. Dogmaels 108
Llwyngor(r)as 153
Pontgynon 223
see also Lloyd of Trefigin
Lloyd of Ffosybleiddiaid:
Pentypark/Pentyparc 212
Gelliswick 87
Lloyd of Llanstinan:
Llangwarren 144
Llanstinan 148
Lloyd (Llwyd) of Morfil and Cilciffeth:
Bicton 11
Castlebythe 36
Cefnhydre (Cynheidre) 36
Cilciffeth 39
Cilgelynen (Cilglynen) 40
Grove, near Pembroke Town 99
Llandigige (Fawr) 141
Morfil 171
Rickeston Hall 244
Trellwyn 301
Ynys y Barry (Barry Island) 341
Lloyd of Trefigin:
Esgair 73
Trefigin 286
Lloyd George:
Ffynnonau Bychan 78
Lloyd-Philipps:
Dale (Castle) 63
Hayscastle (Caslai) 105
Llangwarren 145
Pentypark/Pentyparc 212
Llwyd:
Lancych 134
Penbedw 198
Llywelyn (Llewelin):
Crugiau 58
Llywelyn ap Owen 63
Treffgarne Hall 285-6
Locke: East Jordanston 70
Lockley:
Cwmgloyn 62
Hafod Tydfil 101
Long: Glynhenllan 93
Longcroft:
Pentre Ifan 210
Trewern 314
Longueville:
Eweston (Trewen) 73
Looney (Lynny, Lang):
Norchard 184
Lord: Orielton 187
Lort:
East Moor 70-1
Linney 139
Roch 249
Lort of Stackpole Court:
Brownslade 19
Bulliber 21
Merrion Court 166
Stackpole Court 264-5
Lort-Phillips:
Ashdale 5, 6
Lawrenny 137-8
Llanddinog 142
Porthiddy (Portheiddy) 227
Loughor: Crabhole 55
Loveling: Clegyr 44-5
Lowless: Underdown 321
Lucas: Hook, Ambleston 117
Lucy:
Trecwn 276
Trehal(e) 295
Ludsopp: Lydstep Palace 160
Luke: Summerton 268

M

Mabe: Hayston 105
MacNaghten:
Sodston House 263
Maelgwn, Prince:
Castle Malgwyn (Old) 33
Malefant:
Denant 63
Marloes Court 164
Upton Castle 321
Mannix: Eastwood 72
Mansel: Arnoldshill 4
Marchant (Merchant):
Penybenglog 213
Marcroft:
Anastaslade (Slade) 2
Marloe: Marloes Court 164
Martel: Martel 165
Martin:
Court (Cwrt), Eglwyswrw 54
Cronllwyn 57
Hasguard 104
Henllan/.Hentland 110
Lecha 138
Lochmeyler/Lochmeilir 157
Merrixton 166
Nevern Castle 180
Newport Castle 181-2
Pointz Castle (Cae Bwnsh) 221
Summerton 268
Trewilym, Eglwyswrw 315
Martin (Lord Audley):
Newport Castle 182
Martin of Rickeston:
Rickeston 237
Tancredston 270
Martin of Withybush:
Carne Coch 30
Penrhiw/Pen-cw 203
Rhoslanog Fawr and Vach 233
Trefel(l)yn 283
Trellewelyn 300
Withybush 338

Marychurch:
Norchard 184
Mason:
Colby Lodge 51
Massy:
Cottesmore 53
Ferny Glen 76
Newgale 181
Mathews: Stone Hall 267
Mathias:
Bryn 20
Castle Cenlas 32
Castle Morris 34-5
Castlebythe (Casfuwch) 36
Dyffryn 68
Fern Hill 76
Frongoch 83
Glastir (Glasdir) 92
Hayston 106
Lamphey Court 133
Little Milford 139-40
Llangwarren 144-5
Lochmeyler/Lochmeilir 157
Lochturffin 158
Nantylladron 175
Pencnwc 200
Penlan Cych 201
Priskilly 230
Ramsey Island (Ynys Dewi and Ynys Tyfanog) 231
Rhos y Bayvil 232
Roch 249
Summerton 268
Trebrithin 273
Tredrissi 280
Trefayog 282-3
Trefeugan 283
Trewal(l)ter Lwyd 311
McCormack:
Upton Castle 324
McGeoch: Stone Hall 267
Meares:
Corston 52
Eastington 71
Haroldston (Hall) 103
Henllan/Hentland 110
Kingston 131
Llanion 145
Martletwy House 165-6
Narberth-Plâs 176
Pennar 201
Pierston/Pearson 218
Talybont 269
Winterton, Marloes 336
Meilir:
Lochmeyler/Lochmeilir 157
Melchior:
Clyn Meredith 46
Llandeilo 140
Mabws Fawr 161
Southfield 263
Mendes:
Bonville's Court 15
Merchant:
Penybenglog 213
Meredith:
Hook, Ambleston 116
Meredydd:
Berry Hill/Bury 10
Merriman:
Coedcanlas 48
Merydith: Carswell 30
Meyler:
Bwlch y Clawdd 24
Caerforiog 25
Cerbyd 37
Cilciffeth 39
Howelston 118
Penysgwarn(e) 214
Trewal(l)terwen 312
Trewilym, St. Lawrence 316
Wolfscastle (Casblaidd) 339
Meylett:
Studda 267
Meyrick:
Castleton 36
Denant 63
Fleet 79
Hasguard 104
Llanion 146
Paterchurch 194
Simpson/Simpston 260
Treglemais 292
Wedlock 329
Meyrick of Bush:
Bangeston, St Mary Pembroke 8
Bush 21-2
Gumfreston 100
Norchard 184
Michalski:
Llangolman 143
Middleton:
Scotsborough 258
Miles:
Carn Huan 30
Helygnant 107
Hendre, Meline 108
Longhook 159
Milford, Lord
see Philipps of Picton Castle
Mille: Trellwyn 301
Miller: Denant 63
Mirehouse:
Angle 3
Bangeston, Angle 7
Brownslade 19
Eastington 71
Henllan/Hentland 110
Moody:
Thorne 272
Moon: Trewern, Lampeter Velfrey 313
Moore:
Glanduad/Glanduad Fawr 91
Musselwick/Muslick 173-4
Penrhiw/Pen-cw 203
Mordaunt:
Hilton 114
Scovaston 259
Moreiddig Warwyn 175, 222, 276
Morgan:
Anastaslade (Slade) 2
Blaenbylan 12
Brynaeron 20
Carnachen Wen 30
Cartlett (1) 31
Cilfowyr (Cilfowir) 39-40
Cilgadfarch 40
Cilwendeg 43
Coedllwyd 48
Dolpwll 64-5
Ffynnonau Bychan 77
Gilfachwrnell 89
Grondre 97
Haythog 106
Hoaten 114
Johnston (Hall) 121
Little Milford 140
Llwynbedw 153
Penbedw 198
Pencelli Fawr, Pencelly 199
Ramsey Island (Ynys Dewi and Ynys Tyfanog) 231
Rhydgarnwen 236
Tregam(m)an 289
Tregroes 293
Trenewydd, Crunwear 302
Trenewydd Fawr 303
Tŷgwyn (Whitehouse) 320
Warpool Court 328
Wernddofn 332
Whitchurch 333
Woodstock 341

Morgan-Richardson:
Morgenau 171
Rhosygilwen 233, 234
Morgans: Bicton 11
Morris:
Anastaslade (Slade) 2
Bachendre 7
Blaiddbwll 13
Brimaston (Treowman) 17
Castle Villa (Caswilia) 35
Cerbyd 37
Clynsaithman 47
Cwm Cerwyn 60
Ffynnonau Bychan 77
Gilfachwrnell 89
Hafod Tydfil 101
Hayscastle (Caslai) 105
Howelston 118
Llanreithan 147
Llanteg/Llanteague 149
Llether/Llethr 152
Llwynbedw 153
Merianog 166
Nantylladron 175
Pentre Ithel, Pant Ithel 210
Pistyll Meigan 219
Plâs Iwerill (Y Werill) 220
Rhosmoeled 235
St. Elvis 254
Tancredston 270
Trebrithin 273
Trefigin 287
Tregam(m)an 290
Trellyffa(i)nt 302
Morrison: Portclew 225
Morse:
Boulston 16
Brimaston (Treowman) 17
Dudwell 67
Graig 95
Hayscastle (Caslai) 105
Hilton 113
Musselwick/Muslick 174
Parsele/Parselle 193
Penalltcych 196
Priskilly 230
Rinaston 246
Trerhos (Patricksford) 308
Mortimer:
Castle Malgwyn (Old) 33
Cilfowyr (Cilfowir) 39
Court (Cwrt), Llanllawer 54-5
Garn 83
Hendre Eynon 109
Llanwnwr 151
Penysgwarn(e) 214
Trefinert, Trevinert 287
Treginnis Ucha 291
Trehowel 296-7
Trewellwell 312-13
Wolfsdale/Wolfdale 340
Morton:
Heathfield (Lodge) 107
Mossylwyke:
Folkeston 81
Munster, Count:
Castle Malgwyn (Old) 33
Myles:
Carn Huan 30
Longhook 159

N

Nash:
Jeffreston House 120
Landshipping House 135
Llandigigie Fach 141
Nash, Great 177
Penarthur 198
Nash, John (architect) 23, 50, 77-8, 260
National Trust:
Colby Lodge 51
Stackpole Court 265
Tregwynt 295
Neale: Upton Castle 325
Newport:
Treffgarne Hall 286
Newton:
Newton, Llanstadwell 182
Trefran, Trevrane 289
Nichol: Carswell 30
Nicholas:
Blaiddbwll 13
Brithdir 18
Graig 95
Hayscastle (Caslai) 105
Mynyddmelyn 174
Pencraig 200
Trefigin 286
Treindeg (Ryndaston, Rhyndaston) 297
Noot: Sodston House 262
Noote: Capeston 27
Norris: Waterwinch 328
Northey:
Sodston House 262-3
Waungron 328-9
Norton:
Amroth Castle/Earwere 2

O

O'Grady:
Thornton House 273
Ormond: Talybont 269
Osbwn Wyddel 90
Owen:
Amroth Castle/Earwere 2
Camrose House 26
Castle Villa (Caswilia) 35
Coedwynog 49
Colby 50
Crickmarren 57
Cronllwyn 57
Cwm Cerwyn 60
Cwmgloyn 62
Dyffryn Ffilbro 68
East Moor 71
Glôg (Glôg-y-Frân) 92-3
Hermons Hill 113
Hill, Ludchurch 113
Landshipping Ferry 134
Llandre 142
Llangloffan 143
Llwynihirion 155
Lochturffin 158
Mabws Fawr 161
Manorowen 163
Portclew 225
Poyston Hall 228
Priskilly 230
Rhosmaen 234
Rhosygilwen 234
Rosemarket 249
Scleddau 255
Summerhill 268
Torbant 273
Tregam(m)an 290
Treindeg (Ryndaston, Rhyndaston) 297
Trellyffa(i)nt 301-2
Trerickert (Rickardston), Treicert 308-9
Treseissyllt, Tresissllt 309
Trewent Hall 313
Vaynor, Manordeifi 327
Owen of Cwmgloyn:
Cwmgloyn 62
Pentre Ithel, Pant Ithel 210
Tregam(m)an 290
Owen of Great Nash:
Nash, Great 177
Treginnis Issa/Lower 290
Treginnis Ucha 291
Trewilym, St. Lawrence 317

Owen of Henllys:
Berllan 10
Berry Hill/Bury 10
Bwlch y Clawdd 23
Cilrydd, Cilryth 42
Clyn Meredith 45-6
Coedwynog 49
Court (Cwrt), Eglwyswrw 53-4
Crugiau 58
Cwmeog 60-1
Esgair Wilym 73
Frochest 83
Hafod Grove 101
Haverfordwest 104
Henllys, Nevern 111-12
Llwyngor(r)as 154
Merianog 166
Nevern 179
Newport Castle 181-2
Pencelli Fawr, Pencelly 199
Penpedwast 201-2
Pistyll Meigan 218
St. Ken(n)ox 254
Tredafydd 279
Trefaes 282
Trewilym, Eglwyswrw 315
Owen of Orielton:
Bangeston, St Mary Pembroke 8
Castle Cenlas 32
Cilgelynen (Cilglynen) 40-1
Coedcanlas 48
Greenhill 96
Grove, near Pembroke Town 99
Henllan/Hentland 110
Howelston 118
Johnston (Hall) 120
Lamphey Court 133
Landshipping Ferry 134
Landshipping House 135
Llanstinan 149
Lochturffin 158
Longhook 159
Martel 165
Monkton Old Hall 170
Morfil 171
Newgale 181
Orielton 185-8
Paterchurch 194
Roch 249
Rosemarket 249
Scotchwell 256
Scotsborough 258
Trecwn 276
Trehal(e) 295
see also Owen of Great Nash; Owen of Trecwn
Owen of Pentre Ifan *see* Bowen (ap Owen) of Pentre Ifan
Owen of Trecwn:
Barnards Well 8
Court (Cwrt), Llanllawer 54
Nantybugail 175
Trecwn 275-6, 278
Owen of Withybush:
Alleston 1
Poyston Hall 228
Withybush 338-9
Owen ab Einion Fawr:
Pentre Ifan 206
Owen ap Gwilym Ddu:
Bryanog 20
Merianog 166
Owen Fychan: Helygnant 107
Owens:
Castell Gwyn 36
Denant 63

P

Packington of Westwood (Worcs.): Denant 63
Pakington:
Haroldston 102
Haylett 104
Hook, Ambleston 116
Palmer:
Gelliswick 89
Johnston (Hall) 121
Parkes-Gibbon: Pentre 204
Parr: Blaiddbwll 13
Parry:
Castell Gwyn 36
Colby 50
Cronllwyn 57
Ffynnon Coranau 77
Fobston 80
Lecha 138
Llandigige Fach 141
Manorowen 164
Pentre 204
Penybenglog 213
Philbeach/Filbetch 215
Portclew 225
St. Dogmaels 254
Scleddau 255
Scotsborough 258
Trecadwgan 273
Tredefaid 280
Trewal(l)terwen 312
Parry of Noyadd Trefawr (Cards.):
Castle Malgwyn (Old) 33
Forest 82
Penlan Cych 201
Parry-Bowen *see* Bowen-Parry
Parsell: Barret's Hill 8
Pawlett: Rosemarket 249
Paynter:
Broomhill 18-19
Dale (Castle) 63
Hook 118
Peacock: Stone Hall 267
Pecke: Holmws 115
Peel:
Cottesmore 53
Denant 63
Stone Hall 266-7
Pegge (hermit):
Benton Castle 9-10
Pemberton:
Vaynor, Llawhaden 326
Pencaer:
Wolfsdale/Wolfdale 340
Penn:
Camrose House 26
Thornton House 273
Penry 268
Penygored Company:
Castle Malgwyn (New) 34
Perceval: Coedcanlas 48
Perkin:
Caerwen 25
Carnachen Wen 29
Cuffern 59
Rhoslanog Fawr and Vach 233
Trevaccoon (Trefaccwn) 310
Perkins:
Asheston (Trefasser) 6
Longhouse 159
Penrhiw/Pen-cw 203
Penysgwarn(e) 214
Trefayog 283
Perrot (Perrott):
Angle 3
Bicton 11
Canaston, Great 27
Carew Castle 28
Clegyr Boia 45
Cornish Down 52

Denant 63
Eastington 71-2
Farthing's Hook (Clynffyrddin) 74
Folkeston 81
Honeyborough 116
Scotsborough 257
Woodstock 340-1
Perrot (Perot, Perrott) of Haroldston:
Caerforiog 24
Fletherhill 79
Haroldston 102-3
Haroldston (Hall) 103
Haylett 104
Little Milford 139
Longhook 159
Peter:
Tregam(m)an 289
Trenichol 304-5
Pettijohn:
Castle Villa (Caswilia) 35
Peveril (Peverill):
Pantsaeson /Pantsaison 191
Rhos y Bayvil 232
Tregam(m)an 289
Phaer (Pher): Forest 81-2
Phelps:
Boulston 16
Linney 139
Llangwarren 144
Milton House 167
Sodston House 262
Studda 267
Trellewelyn 300
Withybush 338
Philip:
Fagwr Eynon Fawr 74
Philip ap David: Cwmwdig 61
Philip ap Gwylim:
Stone Hall 266-7
Philip ap Ieuan ap Meredydd:
Cilfowyr (Cilfowir) 39
Parc Cynhaethw(y) 191
Philipps:
Blaiddbwll 13
Dyffryn 68
Folkeston 81
Gelliswick 89
Hayston 105
Hook, Marloes 118
Lydstep Palace 160
Merrixton 166
Neeston 178
Pembroke Castle 195
Pentre Ifan 209-10
Rhosmaen 234
Robeston Wathen House 247
Slebech 262
Southfield 263
Williamston 334-6
Woodstock 341
see also Lloyd-Philipps
Philipps (Lord Kylsant):
Amroth Castle/Earwere 2
Philipps of Cilsant:
Blaen Tâf 13
see also Philipps of Picton Castle
Philipps of Orlandon:
Musselwick 174
Orlandon 188-9
Pontfaen 222-3
Philipps of Pentypark:
Bonville's Court 15
Felindre, Llysyfran 76
Ffynnon Gain 77
Pentypark/Pentyparc 211-12
Waungron 328-9
Philipps of Picton Castle (including Lord Milford):
Anastaslade (Slade) 2
Annikel (Annikell) 3
Caerau 24
Carew Castle 28
Cartlett (2) 31
Castlebythe (Casfuwch) 36
Cosheston (Hall) 53
Cotty 53
Eastington 71
Fletherhill 79
Ford 81
Gelliswick 85, 89
Good Hook 94
Haroldston 102
Haythog 106
Jeffreston House 120
Kilgetty 130-1
Kilvelgy 131
Lampeter Velfrey 132
Llanteg/Llanteague 149
Martletwy House 165
Molleston 169
Nash, Great 177
Parc Cynhaethw(y) 191-2
Penally Court 197
Pentypark/Pentyparc 211
Picton Castle 217
St. Brides 252-3
Sandyhaven 255
Slebech 262
Tarr 272
Trefloyne 288
Vorlan 327
Woodstock 341
see also Philipps of Orlandon; Philipps of Pentypark
Philipps Laugharne of Orlandon *see* Philipps of Orlandon
Philips:
Plâsymeibion 221
Portclew 225
Phillip:
Cilrhiwe 42
Treddiog 280
Phillipps:
Treglemais 292
Trenichol 305
Phillips:
Blaen Tâf 13
Cilgadfach 40
Cwmbettws 60
Eweston (Trewen) 73
Fagwr Eynon Fawr 74
Ffynnonau Bychan 78
Haroldston (Hall) 103
Hayston 106
Kilbarth 125
Llanddinog 142
Manorowen 163
Moat/Mote/The New Moat 168
Penpedwast 202
Penralltrheiny 202
Penysgwarn(e) 214
Porthiddy (Portheiddy) 227
Ramsey Island (Ynys Dewi and Ynys Tyfanog) 231
Rhosdwarch 232
Rinaston 246
Robeston Wathen House 247
Roch 249
Slebech 261
Trebrithin 273
Trecadwgan 274
Tredafydd 279
Trefach, Llanfairnantgwyn 281
Trefin 287
Treglemais 292
Tregroes 293
Trellwyn 301
Trenewydd, Crunwear 302

Trerickert (Rickardston), Treicert 308
Treseissyllt, Tresissllt 309
Phillips of Bolahaul (Carms.):
Llanreithan 148
Phillips (Philips) of Trellewelyn:
Carne Coch 30
Dudwell 67
Penysgwarn(e) 214
Rhoslanog Fawr and Vach 233
Trellewelyn 298-300
Philpin:
Asheston (Trefasser) 6
Caldey Island 26
Tregam(m)an 289
Picton:
Bicton 11
Cartlett (2) 31
Poyston Hall 227-8
Scollock 255
Trellyffa(i)nt 301-2
Trewern 314
Withybush 338
Pill Priory:
Butterhill 22
Studda 267
Plowden:
Panteg (Panteague) 190
Pointz: Pointz Castle (Cas Bwnsh) 221
Popkin: Llanreithan 147-8
Popton: Honey Hook 116
Powell:
Bangeston, St. Mary Pembroke 7
Blaen y Groes/Gors 12
Clareston 44
Greenhill 96
Hill, Ludchurch 113
Hook, Llangwm 117
Musselwick/Muslick 174
Rhosmoeled 235
Rinaston 246
Waungron 329
Whitewell 334
Poyer:
Alleston 1
Canaston, Great 27
Grove, Narberth 97-9
Portclew 225
Trenichol 305-6
Poytyn: Poyston Hall 227
Price:
Anastaslade (Slade) 2
Berllan 10
Caerforiog 24
Castleton 36
Clareston 44
Dyffryn Ffilbro 68
Glenover 92
Hermons Hill 113
Lochturffin 158
Penarthur 197
Pencelli Fawr, Pencelly 199
Simpson/Simpston 260
Treclyn 275
Woodstock 341
Pritchard: St. Ken(n)ox 254
Probin: Eastlake 72
Propert:
Crugiau 58
Hendre Eynon 109
Llandigige Fach 141
Llaney 142
Trefeugan 283
Trevaccoon (Trefaccwn) 310-11
Protheroe:
Castle Villa (Caswilia) 35
Colby Lodge 50
Crugiau 58
Penbedw 198
Pencraig 200
Stone Hall 267
Treddiog 280
Trefel(l)yn 283
Protheroe-Beynon:
Trewern, Lampeter Velfrey 313-14
Prout:
Corston 52
Moor, Castlemartin 170
Prust: Cinnamon Grove 44
Pryce: Bwlch y Clawdd 24
Pugh: Good Hook 94
Purcell-Llewellin:
Tregwynt 295
Purser:
Castell Gwyn 36
Ffynnon Gain 77

R

Ramsden:
Cosheston (Hall) 53
Pembroke Castle 195-6
Rawling:
Lamphey Palace 132
Raymond:
Asheston (Trefasser) 6
Cilgelynen (Cilglynen) 41
Jordanston (Hall) – Trewrdan 123
Pointz Castle (Cas Bwnsh) 222
Trecadwgan 274
Read: Trenichol 304
Reed:
Trenewydd Manor 304
Trewal(l)ter Lwyd 311
Rees:
Ashdale 6
Asheston (Trefasser) 6
Berry Hill/Bury 10
Brithdir 18
Bwlch y Clawdd 24
Castle Cenlas 32
Cerbyd 37
Cilast Ucha 38
Cilfowyr (Cilfowir) 40
Clegyr 45
Cuffern 59
Gilfachwrnell 90
Hafod Grove 101
Hermons Hill 113
Llwyngor(r)as 153
Merianog 166
Pentre Ifan 210
Pontfaen 222, 223
Pontgynon 223
Ramsey Island (Ynys Dewi and Ynys Tyfanog) 231
Rhosmaen 235
Roch 249
Scovaston 259
Thornton House 273
Treclyn 275
Trefaes 282
Trefinert, Trevinert 287
Trellewelyn 298
Rees ap Howel:
Cilast Ucha 38
Rees ap John: Cilgadfarch 40
Rees (Rhys) of Dyffryn Tâf:
Penybenglog 212-13
Reignold *see* Reynolds
Revell:
Cefnydre (Cynheidre) 36
Forest 82
Reynbot:
Folkeston 81
Hilton 113
Reyner:
Rinaston 246
Treindeg/Ryndaston, Rhyndaston 297

Reynish:
Camrose North 27
Wolfsdale/Wolfdale 340
Reynolds (Reignold):
Blaiddbwll 13
Hendre, Llandeloy 108
Hendre, Meline 108
Treglemais 292
Trewilym, St. Lawrence 317
Ynys y Barry
(Barry Island) 341
Rhys:
Sandyhaven 255
see also Rees; Rice Rhys
(Price, Rees, Rice)
of Rickeston:
Caerwen 25
Grinston 97
Pointz Castle
(Cas Bwnsh) 221
Rickeston 237-42, 243
Scotsborough 257-8
Tancredston 270-1
Rhys ap Griffith,
Lord of Deheubarth
33, 101, 286, 315
Rhys ap Rhydderch:
Crugiau 58
Cwmgloyn 62
Rhys ap Robert ap Gwrwared
307
Rhys ap Tewdwr,
Prince of Deheubarth
274, 298, 321
Rhys ap Thomas 25, 237
Carew Castle 28
Carew Rectory 29
Rhys Chwith 40, 41, 149, 178
Rice:
Caerwen 25
Moor, Rosemarket 170
Mullock 173
Pistyll Meigan 219
Robeston Wathen House
247
Rich: Haylett 105
Richard:
Rhydgarnwen 236
Trefin 287
Richards:
Croft House 57
Llanwnwr 151
Pierston/Pearson 218
Rickeston 242, 243
Scotsborough 258
Sealyham 260
Thornton House 273
Trenewydd Fawr 303
Winterton, Marloes 336
Richardson: Cilau Wen 38
Rickert: Posty 227
Rickson:
Caerwen 25-6
Grinston 97
Rickeston 242-3
Scotsborough 258
Tancredston 271
Ridsdale: Waterwinch 328
Rind:
Allenbrook 1
Crabhole 55
Ritharch: Trewrach 318
Robert: Henllan Owen 111
Robert son of Lodomar:
Minwear/Minwere 167
Roberts:
Colby 50
Gelliswick 89
Hean Castle 107
Hook, Ambleston 117
Lacerry 132
Little Milford 140
Llangloffan 143
Narberth-Plâs 176
Rhoslanog Fawr and Vach
233
St. Botolphs 252
Treginnis Issa/Lower 290
Treginnis Ucha 291
Trehal(e) 295
Welsh Hook 330
Robertson: Castle Hall 32
Robin:
Frongoch 83
Treginnis Ucha 291
Robins: Trecwn 278
Roblin:
Cuffern 59
Keeston/Keyston
(Tregethin) 125
Roblinston 247
Robyn:Hendre Riffith 109
Roch:
Bicton 11
Bridell (Plâs) 17
Butterhill 22-3
Capeston 27-8
Cinnamon Grove 44
Clareston 44
Druidston 65
Eweston (Trewen) 73
Fobston 80
Grinston 97
Henllys, Llanrhian 111
Linney 139
Llether/Llethr 152
Lochvane (Lochfaen) 158
Nash, Lower 178
Norchard 184
Orlandon 188
Paskeston 193
Pierston/Pearson 218
Rhoslanog Fawr and Vach
233
Rickeston Hall 244
Rosepool 250
Sodston House 262
Tancredston 271
Thornton House 273
Winterton, Marloes 336
Rodger: Helygnant 108
Rogers:
Arnoldshill 4
Carnachen Wen 29, 30
Cilrhiw 41
Eastlake 72
Goodwick (Wdig/Aber
Goodick) 95
Penrhiw/Pen-cw 203
Pentypark/Pentyparc 211
Rooke:
Treindeg/Ryndaston,
Rhyndaston 297-8
Rossant:
Cosheston (Hall) 52
Hayston 105
Paskeston 193
Rotch: Castle Hall 32
Routh:
Good Hook 94
Sion House 260
Row:
Linney 139
Rosepool 250
Rowe:
North Down 184-5
Penally Court 197
Rowland(s):
Dyffryn Ffilbro 68
Esgair 73
Glenover 92
Pantsaeson/Pantsaison 191
Rhos y Bayvil 232
Rhosmoeled 235
Rowley:
Waunberry, Waunberri 328
Rudebac:
Rudbaxton, Great 250

Runwa (Runwae, Runway):
Crabhole 55
Hook, Marloes 117-18
Russell:
Brimaston (Treowman) 17
Hayscastle (Caslai) 105
St. Brides 252

S

St. Bride:
St. Brides 252
St. Davids,
Lord: Roch 248
St. Dogmaels Abbey:
Cwm Cerwyn 60
Llandeilo 140
Tregroes 293
St. John of Slebech:
Minwear/Minwere 167
Wiston 336
Sampson: Scotchwell 256-7
Sandbrook: Dolpwll 65
Saunders:
Pentre 204
Treffgarn (Little) 285
Saunders-Davies:
Cilast Ucha 38
Moat/Mote/The New Moat 168
Pentre 204-5
Saurin: Orielton 187-8
Savage: Roch 249
Sayer: Tregwynt 295
Scale:
Capeston 28
Musselwick/Muslick 174
Scarfe: Lamphey Court 133
Scone: Thornton House 272
Scourfield:
Honeyborough 116
Llether Wogan 153
Lochmeyler/Lochmeilir 157
Priskilly 230
Robeston Hall 246
Treglemais 291
Treseissyllt, Tresissllt 309
Williamston 334-5
Scourfield of New Moat and Castle Villa:
Castle Villa (Caswilia) 35
Cerbyd 37
Farthing's Hook (Clynffyrddin) 74
Ffynnon Gain 77
Hayscastle (Caslai) 105
Howelston 118
Llanwnwr 151
Lochturffin 158
Moat/Mote/The New Moat 168-9
Tancredston 270-2
Treddiog 279-80
Trehal(e) 295
Trenichol 304-5
Trewilym, St. Lawrence 316-17
Waunberry, Waunberri 328
Scourfield-Lewis:
Colby Lodge 51
Scowcroft:
Hendre, Llandeloy 108
Scurlock: Paskeston 193
See of St. Davids:
Bishops Palaces 11
Brawdy-Breudeth 17
Brimaston (Treowman) 17
Castle Morris 34
Clegyr Boia 45
Court (Cwrt), Eglwyswrw 53-4
Cruglas 58-9
Felindre, Llanwnda 76
Henllys, Llanrhian 111
Jordanston (Hall) – Trewrdan 121
Kilbarth 125
Lamphey Palace 132
Llanddinog 141
Llandigige (Fawr) 141
Llangwarren 144
Llwynygorras 155
Lochvane (Lochfaen) 158
Longhouse 159
Longridge 159-60
Mabws Fawr 161
Park Court 192
Pencnwc 200
Pointz Castle (Cas Bwnsh) 221
Priskilly 230
Ramsey Island (Ynys Dewi and Ynys Tyfanog) 231
Rhyd yr Harding 236
Tancredston 270
Trecadwgan 274
Treddiog 279
Treffgarn (Little) 284
Treglemais 291-2
Vaynor, Llawhaden 325
Wolfscastle (Casblaidd) 339
Seton: Stone Hall 267
Shield: Park Glas 192
Shuttleworth:
Llwynygorras 156
Simleat: Studda 267
Skeel:
Hayscastle (Caslai) 105
Trewilym, St. Lawrence 316, 317
Skyrme:
Cilforwyr (Cilfowir) 40
Cilwendeg 43
Colby Lodge 50
Greenway 96
Hafod Tydfil 101
Hoaten 114
Llawhaden 151
Longridge 159-60
Merrixton 166
Torbant 273
Tregendeg 290
Trenichol 305
Trewal(l)ter Lwyd 311
Upton Castle 324
Vaynor, Llawhaden 325-6
Smith:
Ford 81
Glynhenllan 93
Jeffreston House 120
Scotsborough 258
Smith-Cuninghame:
Caldey Island 26
Sparkes: Treglemais 292
Sparks: Withybush 338
Spence-Jones:
Ffynnonau Bychan 78
Spranger: Cilrhiw 41
Stancomb: Folkeston 81
Stanley:
Newton, Rudbaxton 183
Stedman: Trerickert (Rickardston), Treicert 309
Stedman of Strata Florida (Cards.): Glandovan 90
Stephen(s):
Arnoldshill 4
Cuffern 59
Glanduad (Fawr) 91
Trenewydd Fawr 303
Stepney:
Panteg (Panteague) 190
Prendergast 229-30
Sandyhaven 255
Stepney-Gulston:
Prendergast 229

Steward:
Little Milford 139
Stewart: Fobston 80
Stokes:
Annikel (Annikell) 3
Bangeston,
St Mary Pembroke 8
Cornish Down 52
Cuffern 59
Folkeston 81
Hean Castle 107
Netherwood 179
Pontgynon 223
Roch 248-9
St. Botolphs 251-2
Scotchwell 256
Scotsborough 258
Sunny Hill 268
Thornton House 272
Sulivan: Benton Castle 10
Summers:
Milton House 167
Moor, Walwyn's Castle 170
Penybenglog 213
Ramsey Island
(Ynys Dewi and Ynys
Tyfanog) 231
Rosemoor 249
Sutton Lodge 268
Surman:
Rosepool 250
Scotchwell 256-7
Sutton:
Haverfordwest 104
Haythog 106
Newgale 181
Swan:
Hill, Ludchurch 113
Swann: Merrixton 166-7
Symmonds:
Treffgarn (Little) 284
Symmons (Symins, Symyns):
Castle Malgwyn (Old) 33
Cilau Wen 38
Clyn Meredith 46
Colston 51
Ffynnone 78
Forest 82
Llanstinan 149
Llanunwas 150
Longhook 159
Martel 165
Nantybugail 175
Slebech 261
Symon:
Henllan/Hentland 110
Symond:
Druidston 65
Kilbarth 125

T

Talbenny:
Talbenny Hall 269
Tancred:
Cuffern 59
Dudwell 65-7
Harmeston 101
Johnston (Hall) 120
Leweston 139
Tankard:
Cuffern 59
Tasker:
Fletherhill 79-80
Haylett 104
Hayston 105
Honeyborough 116
Moor, Rosemarket 170
Rosepool 250
Upton Castle 325
Tayleur:
Upton Castle 324
Teale:
Fobston 80
Tew:
Trefran, Trevrane 289
Thomas:
Angle 3
Argoed 4
Barret's Hill 8
Bryanog 20
Brynaeron 20
Caerwen 26
Cartlett (1) 31
Castell Gwyn 36
Castle Hall 33
Cilas Ucha 38
Cilciffeth 39
Cilfowyr (Cilfowir) 40
Cilrhiwe Fach 42
Cilrydd, Cilryth 43
Clyn Meredith 46
Coedllwyd 48
Colby Lodge 50, 51
Cornish Down 52
Court (Cwrt),
Llanllawer 55
Crugiau 58
Cruglas 58
Cwm Cerwyn 60
Cwmgloyn 62
Dolpwll 65
Dyffryn 68
Eweston (Trewen) 73
Felindre, Llanwnda 76
Ffyn(n)one Gleision 78
Frongoch 83
Gilfachwrnell 90
Glanduad (Fawr) 91
Glastir (Glasdir) 92
Henllan/Hentland 110
Henllan Owen 111
Kilvelgy 131
Lampeter Velfrey 132
Lamphey Park 134
Lancych 134
Landshipping Quay 135
Lecha 138
Llaney 142
Lochturffin 158
Longhook 159
Longhouse 159
Merianog 166
Nantybugail 175
Narberth-Plâs 176
Parc Cynhaethw(y) 191
Park Court 192
Penbedw 198
Penpedwast 201-2
Penrhiw/Pen-cw 203
Pentre Ithel, Pant Ithel 210
Plâs Crwn 219
Posty 227
Rhyd yr Harding 236
Scotsborough 258
Scovaston 259
Thornton House 273
Treclyn 275
Treddiog 280
Trefaes 282
Trefel(l)yn 283
Trefloyne 288
Trefran, Trevrane 289
Tregendeg 290
Treginnis Issa/Lower 291
Trehal(e) 295-6
Trenewydd Manor 304
Treseissyllt,
Tresissllt 309-10
Trewern,
Lampeter Velfrey 313
Whitchurch 333
Woodstock 341
see also Vaughan Thomas
Thomas ap David ap Howel:
Drysgol Goch 65
Thomas ap Lewis ap William:
Cilgelynen (Cilglynen) 40

Thomas ap Owain:
Treffgarn (Little) 284
Thomas ap Rees:
Esgair Wilym 73
Thornborough:
Arnoldshill 5
Tibbetts: Castle Cenlas 32
Tocker *see* Tucker
Tooley: Arnoldshill 5
Trevannion:
Sodston House 262
Tucker:
Cleddau Lodge 44
Treleddyn 298
Welsh Hook 330
Wolfscastle (Casblaidd) 339
Woodstock 341
Tucker (Tocker) of Sealyham:
Carnachen Wen 29, 30
Felindre, Llanwnda 76
Hook, Ambleston 116-17
Llangloffan 143
Llanwnwr 151
Mabws Fawr 161
Sealyham 259
Tucker-Edwardes:
Carnachen Wen 29
Henllys, Llanrhian 111
Hook, Ambleston 117
Mabws Fawr 161
Sealyham 259-60
Treffgarn (Little) 284
Trerhos (Patricksford) 308
Tuckett:
Berry Hill/Bury 10
Tudor, House of 237
Pembroke Castle 195
Tudor Trevor 224, 268
Turberville:
Lochturffin 158
Twdwr,
Prince of Deheubarth 161
Twyning:
Bryn 20
Llandre 142
Longridge 159
Penybenglog 213
Tŷgwyn (Whitehouse) 320
Tyler: Underdown 320

U

University of Wales:
Pointz Castle
(Cas Bwnsh) 222
Uphill:
Portclew 225
Urien Rheged 237, 321

V

Vaughan:
Barnards Well 8
Cefnhydre
(Cynheidre) 36-7
Cilgwyn 41
Farthing's Hook
(Clynffyrddin) 74
Glandovan 90
Hean Castle 106
Hendre, Meline 108
Jordanston (Hall) –
Trewrdan 121-3
Lamphey Palace 132
Llandigige (Fawr) 141
Llaney 142
Llangloffan 143
Llanmarlais 146
Llannerch (Y Bleiddie/
Bleiddiau) 146
Llanwnwr 151
Nantybugail 175
Narberth-Plâs 175
Pentre Ifan 208
Penyrallt, Nevern 214
Pistyll Meigan 219
Pontfaen 222-3
Posty 227
Priskilly 230
Rhoslanog Fawr and Vach
233
Thorne 272
Trecwn 275, 276-8
Trefel(l)yn 283
Vorlan 327
Vaughan Thomas:
Pentour (Pentower) 204
Vernon:
Stackpole Court 264
Vickerman:
Hean Castle 107
Netherwood 179
Vongler:
Colby 50
Voyle (Voel):
Colston 51
Cwmwdig 61
East Moor 71
Haverfordwest 104
Newgale 181
Philbeach/Filbetch 215
St. Elvis 254
Trewent Hall 313
Underdown 320
Vychan: Caerwen 25

W

Wade:
Anastaslade (Slade) 2
Ferny Glen 76
Wake:
Pierston/Pearson 218
Wakes:
Penally Court 197
Walker:
Cinnamon Grove 44
Walmsley:
Bwlch y Clawdd 24
Walter:
Broomhill 18
Dale (Castle) 63
Haverfordwest 104
Llandigige (Fawr) 141
Roch 248-9
Rosemarket 249
Trefran, Trevrane 289
Treglemais 291
Walters:
Haroldston (Hall) 103
Llandigige (Fawr) 141
Penbedw 198
Trewal(l)terwen 312
Ward:
Sodston House 262-3
Thornton House 273
Warlow:
Barnards Well 8
Castle Hall 32
Dudwell 67
Llandigige Fach 141
Llether/Llethr 152
Lochturffin 158
Newgale 181
Warren:
Barret's Hill 8
Llystyn 156
Longridge 160
Merianog 166
Penally Abbey 197
Warren of Trewern:
Bowood 16
Brithdir 18
Cilgwyn 41
Cilrydd, Cilryth 43
Court (Cwrt),
Llanllawer 54

Helygnant 108
Pentre Ifan 210
Pontgynon 223
Trewern 314-15
Wenallt 331
Warren-Davis:
Trewarren 312
Warrington: Carew Castle 28
Waters: Penally Court 197
Wathen:
Marloes Court 165
Talbenny Hall 269
Watkin: Loveston 160
Watkins:
Rhosdwarch 232
Trewern 314
Watson: Stone Hall 267
Watts:
Brimaston (Treowman) 18
Hayscastle (Caslai) 105
Webb:
Alleston 1
Carew Castle 28
Greenhill 96
Hasguard 104
Llwyngor(r)as 154
Webb-Bowen:
Camrose House 26-7
Sodston House 263
Wolfsdale/Wolfdale 340
Wedlock (Widlock, Wedlake, Wydelock):
Gumfreston 99-100
Wedlock 329
Welch: Kilvelgy 131
Wetherhead:
Glandovan 90
Wettar: Portclew 225
Wheatley: Bunker's Hill 21
White:
Bangeston, Angle 7
Cuffern 59
Henllan/Hentland 110
Lacerry 132
Loveston 160
Parc Cynhaethw(y) 192
Whitland Abbey (Carms.):
Hill, Ludchurch 113
Trefawr 282
Whitlock: Carew Rectory 29
Whitton: Ramsey Island (Ynys Dewi and Ynys Tyfanog) 231
Whyte: Carswell 30
Widlock (Wydelock) *see* Wedlock
Wilcox: Grinston 97
Wilkins:
Rhoslanog Fawr and Vach 233
William:
Bwlch y Clawdd 23
Cilast Ucha 38
Coedwynog 49
Cwmeog 61
Hill, Steynton 113
Llanwnwr 151
Rhosmoeled 235
Treyarched/Trearched 318
William ap David: Martel 165
Williams:
Bonville's Court 14-15
Caerforiog 24
Caldey Island 26
Carswell 30
Cefnhydre (Cynheidre) 37
Clegyr Boia 45
Clegyr(n) 45
Cottesmore 53
Court (Cwrt), Llanllawer 54
Cronllwyn 57
Cwmwdig 61
Ffynnone 78
Fobston 80
Glanpwllafon 91
Glynhenllan 93
Gumfreston 100
Heathfield (Lodge) 107
Hermons Hill 112-13
Hill, Ludchurch 113
Ivy Tower 118-19
Llandigige (Fawr) 141
Llaney 142
Mabws Fawr 161
Manorowen 162-3
Merianog 166
Merrixton 166
Morfil 171
Morgans 171
Narberth-Plâs 176
Norchard 184
Pantsaeson/Pantsaison 191
Penalltcych 196
Penarthur 198
Penberry/Penberi/Penbury 199
Pencelli Fawr, Pencelly 199
Pennar 201
Penralltrheiny 202-3
Pentre Ifan 208
Penybenglog 213
Pistyll Meigan 219
Plâs y Berllan 220
Pontgynon 223
Popehill 224
Porth Clais 225
Ramsey Island (Ynys Dewi and Ynys Tyfanog) 231
Rhoslanog Fawr and Vach 233
Rhosmaen 234
Rickeston 243
Rudbaxton, Great 250
St. Elvis 254
Sodston House 263
Thornton House 273
Treyarched/Trearched 318-20
Trebrithin 273
Trefach, Llanfairnantgwyn 281
Tregroes 293
Trehal(e) 295
Trehowel 296-7
Treleddyn 298
Trenichol 305
Treprisk, Tre-prysg 307
Trewal(l)ter Lwyd 311-12
Trewilym, St. Lawrence 317
Treyarched/Trearched 318-20
Warpool Court 328
Wedlock 329
Wolfscastle (Casblaidd) 339
Woodstock 341
Williams of Cwmgloyn:
Cwmbettws 60
Cwmgloyn 62
Pontgynon 223
Trelyffa(i)nt 302
Willy:
Treffgarne, Lampeter Velfrey 285
Tŷgwyn (Whitehouse) 320
Wilson:
Hean Castle 107
Jordanston 124
Neeston 178
Penybenglog 213
Winstanley: St. Dogmaels 254
Winterhay:
Hill, Ludchurch 113
Wizo (Wyzo) the Fleming 216, 293

Wogan:
Arnoldshill 4, 5
Caerforiog 24
Cerbyd 37
Denant 63
Dudwell 67
Llangloffan 143
Merrion Court 166
Milton 167
Parsele/Parselle 193
Prendergast 229
Rinaston 246
Southfield 263
Treddiog 279-80
Wogan of Boulston:
Boulston 15-16
Cefnhydre (Cynheidre) 36
Crabhole 55
Jordanston (Hall) – Trewrdan 121
Llanstinan 148-9
Philbeach/Filbetch 215
Rhoslanog Fawr and Vach 233
Treglemais 291
Trenewydd Fawr 303
Wogan of Stone Hall:
Eweston (Trewen) 73
Stone Hall 266-7
Trewal(l)terwen 312
Welsh Hook 329-30
Wogan of Wiston:
Arnoldshill 5
Cilrhiwe 42
Colby 50
East Jordanston 70
Eweston (Trewen) 73
Fobston 80
Good Hook 94
Hean Castle 106-7
Lawrenny 137
Penallt Cadwgan 196
Picton Castle 216
Wiston 336-8
see also Wogan of Stone Hall
Wolfe: Butterhill 22
Woodhead: Tredefaid 280
Woods: Upton Castle 325
Woolcock:
Cruglas 58
Rhosmoeled 235
Woolley: Plâs Crwn 219
Worral: Glynhenllan 93
Worthington:
Glyn-y-Mêl 94
Wright: Popehill 224
Wyrriot:
Castle Cenlas 32
Landshipping House 135
Orielton 185, 188
Wythyn:
Pointz Castle (Cas Bwnsh) 221

Y

Yeates:
Hendre, Llandeloy 108
Yelverton: Blaiddbwll 13
Yonge: Cuffern 59
Yorke: Langton 136
Young(e) 92
Argoed 4
Crugiau 58
Cuffern 59
Glastir (Glasdir) 92
Pencelli Fychan/Fach, Pencelly 200
Penyrallt, St. Dogmaels 214
Tredrissi 280
Tregam(m)an 289-90
Yryss:
Farthing's Hook (Clynffyrddin) 74

THE FRANCIS JONES ARCHIVE
and Websites

The Francis Jones Archive was compiled in seventy years of research and comprises over 52 archive boxes of material. The files on thousands of west Wales families have pedigrees, heraldic information, genealogical information, extracts from deeds, notes on burials, court cases and land acquisitions. There is unpublished material on houses of historical importance including original notes for this book and others. The Archives are a vast reservoir of information on many other subjects relating to Wales and its people. Francis Jones listed over 8,000 historical Welsh homes throughout Wales.

The archives are catalogued at

www.brawdybooks.com and *www.westwalesgenealogy.co.uk.*

We undertake research for those unable to visit us, or you may call, by appointment, to undertake research in person. We charge a small fee for these services.

The Pembrokeshire Family Archive Index

BOX 1

A

File 1 – Absolam
Ackland
Adams
Andrew
Amblot of St. David' s
Arnold
Atho
Ayleway
Aubrey

File 2 – Allen + article 'A Pembs. County Family in 18th Century' - EIJ

File 3 – Ap Rice of Rickeston & Scotsborough

B

File 1 – Barham of Trecwn
Barlow
Barlow of Cresswell & Lawrenny
Rosepool
Slebech
Barrett of Roch & Pentypark
Gelliswick
Pendine & Tenby + notes of Barretts in Co. Carms.
Barron
Barlett
Barzey Bateman
Batine

File 2 – Misc. Notes on various families
Beddoe
Bell
Bennett
Berry
Beynon
Bolton
Bowlas
Bowling
Browne
Bushell
Butler + article 'The Butler's of Pembrokeshire' – FJ extracted

File 3 – Bowen of Argoed & Treicert (Rickeston)
Glanduad
Gwern Fulbrook
Llwyngorras
Llystyn & Llanerch y Bleddie
Pentre Ifan – *see also* Llwyngwair
Pontgynon
Troed-y-awr
Trefloyne

File 4 – Bowen of
- Brestgaen
- Lewiston
- Lochmeyler & Camrose
- Manian
- Prendergast

Misc.

File 5 – Bowen of Upton Castle

File 6 – Bowen of Llwyngwair & Pentre Ifan

File 7 – Bowen of Llwyngwair – article

C

File 1 – Cadogan
Canon + article on Kilgetty
Cantington & Canton
Carrow
Catharne
Child of Begelly
Clement

File 2 – Codd
Cole
Colby
Corbet
Cornock
Councill
Crabhole
Crowther
Craddock of Newton
Crunn
Misc.

File 3 – Callan + article, extracted – unpublished & hand-written

File 4 – Campbell 1700 – 1777

File 5 – Campbell 1755 – June 1796

File 6 – Carnach Wen (house)

File 7 – Cilceffeth – Court (list of papers of Court Estate)

File 8 – Cwmwdig (house)

BOX P2

D

File 1 – Davies of Duffryn Wdig

File 2 – Davies of
- Barry Island, Byhold & Llandeloy
- Brawdy
- Castle Villa + article ' Davies of Castle Villa' ?
- Cilygelynen
- Crinow
- Fishguard
- Haverfordwest & Wistfield, Rosemarket
- Hayscastle Parish
- Llanddinog
- Llwyngorras
- Mathry
- Mullock & Trewarren
- Park y Pratt, St. Dogmaels
- St. Davids
- Trevine

Misc. – Davies

File 3 – Dawes of Bangeston + article

File 4 – Devonald of
- Cemaes
- Llanfyrnach
- Llandawke + article – typed copy from Mrs. H. R. Charles

Misc. – Devonald
Dunn
Dyer
Misc. 'D'

E

File 1 – Eaton
Edwardes
Edwards
Ellis
Evans
Eynon + Misc.

File 2 – Elliott of Earewere + article

File 3 – Evans of
- Llandeloy
- Llwyngorras
- Mabus
- Trevaylog

Misc.

F

File 1 – Ferrior
Fenton
Filkin
Fisher of Penrhiw
Fiztharry
Foley of Ridgeway
Folk
Fowler
Foy
Furlong
Misc. including – Farrell

File 2 – Ford of Stone Hall & related families + article ' Stone Hall & its families'

G

File 1 – Garnons
Gibbin
Gibbon
Gobogh
Gough

Gower
Grant
Green
Gwillam of Pembroke
Gwrda
Gwrwared
Gwyther
Misc.

File 2 – George

File 3 – Griffith

File 4 – Griffith of Pen-y-benlog

File 5 – Griffith of Pointz Castle + an account of the trial of Thomas John & Samuel Griffiths P.C. after the French Landing in 1797

File 6 – Gwynne

File 7 – Gwyther & Harries of Llanrhian

H

File 1 – Harries + article ' Harries of Eweston' unpublished?

File 1a – Harries of
Llanrethian
Llanrhian
Lochmeyler
Newgale
N. Pembs.
Penrhiw & Dinas Island
S. Pembs.
Treginnis
Trehowell
Trevine
Misc.

File 1b – Harries of Tregwynt

File 2 – Hall
Hamilton
Hammett
Harding
Havard of Newport
Hassell
Haward of Fletherhill
Hawkwell
Hensleigh
Herbert
HI' s etc. including article ' Hicks of Tancredston'
Higgon of Scolton
Higgon of Tredafydd in Parish of Nevern & Llanychllwydog
Higgon – Misc.

File 3 – Holcombe + draft 'Holcombe of Brownslade' hand-written
HO' s Misc.
Howell of Lochvane
Hughes
Hunt
Llanhowell
Rushacre
Trewellwell & Treddiog
Woodstock
Misc.

BOX P3

J

File 1 – J's Misc.
Jones of
Bonvilles Court
Castle Morris
Lancych
Linney
Llanfairnantgwyn
Pentower
Vaynor
Waungron & unplaced
N. Pembs – Misc.
S. Pembs – Misc.

File 2 – Jenkin Lloyd of Blaidbwll, Cemais

File 3 – James of Brawdy + article 'A Tale of Three Homesteads'
Lochmeyler
Misc.
Pantyphilip
Pontsaeson + article
Trehaidd & Treprisk
Trehowell
Trenewydd
Walterston

File 4 – Jennings + article 'Diary of a Young Lady of Fashion' extracted

File 5 – John of Caerwen + Article ' Annals of a Yeoman Family' extracted

File 6 – Jenkins, James & Jones
Jenkins of Solva
Kingheriot
Joce
Jordan

K

File 1 – K's Misc.
Knethell
Keymer
Kynner

L

File 1 – L's Misc.
La – Lu

File 2 – Laugharne

File 3 – Lewis of Henllan – Sched. of Docs.

File 3a – Lewis-Bowen

File 4 – Lloyd of Hendre & Cwmgloyne
+ typed & scanned article
Cwmgloyne etc. Notes
N. Pembs. – Misc.
S. Pembs. – Misc.
Cilgetty
Cilrue
Dale Castle
Dewsland – Misc.
Fishguard
Ffoshelyg, Dre Llanerch, Lancych
Henllys & related houses
Longhouse & related houses
Treneydd Fawr
Trefach & Llanfairnantgwyn

File 5 – Lloyd of Cilciffeth & Morvil + article

File 5a – Lloyd of Cilciffeth etc. Family notes

File 6 – Lort of
Eastmoor
Prickerston
Stackpole
Roger Lort – d. 1613
Henry Lort – d. 1640
Sir Roger Lort – d. 1662/3
Sir John Lort – d. 1672/3
Lort – general notes
& Correspondence x 2 files
Lort, Barlow etc. – printed booklets

File 7 – Llanrhian History

BOX P4

M

File 1 – Manorowen + article

File 1a – Martin of Rickeston
(ap Rice & Griffiths)

File 2 – Marychurch

File 3 – Mathias of Llangwarren
& related houses

File 4 – Mathias of
Hook
Dewsland
Cile

File 5 – Malefant
Martin
Maurice
Melchior
Meyler
Miles
Misc.

Files 6 & 7 – Meares

File 8 – Mendus

File 9 – Meyrick of Bush

File 10 – Morgan of
Blaenbylan + article
N. Pembs.
S. Pembs.
Dewsland
Dolpwll,
Wernddofn
Morris

File 11 – Morse

File 12 – Mortimer of Trewellwell & Trehowell

N

File 1 – Nash
Nicholas
Misc.

O

File 1 – Ormond
Owen of
Berllan
Colby
Cwmeog
Henllys
St. Kennox
Trecwn & Priskilly
Wenallt

File 2 – Owen of Orielton

P

File 1a – Palmer/Palmour + envelope
Paynter, Pavin & Pavin Phillips
Perkins – Misc.
Perkins of St. David's
Perkyn
Perrott

BOX 5 Covers the remainder of P, R, S

BOX 6 Covers S, T, V, W, Y

WELSH HISTORICAL SOCIETIES

Notice to all researchers of Welsh history

The National Library of Wales is a vast treasure house of Welsh records.

We highly recommend their efficient and supremely helpful staff and up-to-date facilities for any imaginable facet of past Welsh historical records.

The National Library of Wales

Aberystwyth, Ceredigion, Wales SY23 3BU

Telephone: 01970 632800 Fax: 01970 615709

www.llgc.org.uk e-mail: holi@llgc.org.uk

Carmarthenshire Antiquarian Society

Membership Secretary: Mrs E. Dale Jones

Telephone: 01267 232085

The London Pembrokeshire Society

Hon. Secretary: David Morris

Telephone: 0208 6731767

Ceredigion Antiquarian Society

Membership Secretary: Gwyn Davies

Telephone: 01970 625818

Pembrokeshire Historical Society

Hon. Secretary: Mrs A. Eastham

Telephone: 01348 873316

THE WELSH HISTORIC GARDENS TRUST

This charitable trust was formed ten years ago to raise the profile of the historic parks and gardens of Wales and to play a role in their preservation and restoration. At that time the future for gardens in Wales looked all too bleak. Many had fallen victim to insensitive planning, lack of money or sheer indifference. Things are rather different today. There is a great deal of interest in visiting gardens of all descriptions and learning about their history. But the dangers have not gone away. If the gardens that people love to visit are to be preserved for their children and their children's children, an organisation dedicated to fostering knowledge and an informed understanding of this great national heritage is still essential.

If you would like to join the Welsh Historic Gardens Trust, please contact:

The Membership Secretary,
Peter Williams,
Llangunnor House, Crickadarn,
Builth Wells,
Powys LD8 3PJ
Telephone / Fax: 01982 560 288

PENBROKE
S. Annes Chapel
The Grene
Monton Priory
St. Maryes
S. Michaels
The Scale of Pases
40 80 120 160
THE
Dynas heade
Strumble heade
Llanglas heade
The Cowe and ye Calfe rockes
Dynas
Llanunda
Capel Llanyhangle
Llanllawyn
Manernowen
Fiscard
St. Nicholas
Llanachaier
St. Katterns
Llonuaier
Merther
DEWYSLAVE
Treuenyth
Letterstowne
Castle Male
Llanryan
Llanrithon
Llanedryn
IRYSHE
St. Lawrance
St. Dugwels
Llanhowel
Llandeloy
Hayes Castle
Revelston
S. Davids heade
Gorid Chapell
Whitchurch
HUND
Trauegare
Whitsand Bay
St. Davides
Riston
Brodye
Spittle
St. Nones
St. Steuans
St. Aylue
Plumston Rocke
Camrose
R. Castle
Roche
Rodbaxton
St. Leonard Chapell
The Bishop and his Clarkes
Portclais
The Horse
Ramsey Island
Rihye Rocke
Knowleton
Lamston
SEA
The lyttle Haven
ROWSE
Haverford West
Harreston
West Walton
Goltop Rode
St. Margrets chap.
Bolton Hill
HUND.
Walwin cast.
Hascard
Robertston
Johnston
St. Brides Island
Nesseton
Sandy
Stanton
The priorye
S. Brides
Marlas
Yardlanstone
Hubberston
St. Ismels
Pylles
Newton
Scaline Island
Midlan Island
Gatcholme Island
Sandy Haven
Dale
Dale Rock
The Stack Rocke
The Block-house
Rat Island
West Popton
Stokeholme Island
Milford Haven
Hentland
Kilpaston
Uggarston mill
Freshwater
Gupton
Shepe Island
WEST
Performed by Iohn Speede. And are to be solde in Popes head alley by Iohn Sudbury and George Humbell, at London. 1610. Cum Privilegio.
R. C. Strongbow E.1
Wil. Marshall E.2
Will Valence E. 3
Lawrence Hastings. 4
Iohn D. of Bedford E.5.
Wil. de la Poole Marque. 6
Iasper Hatfeild E. 7
Will. Herbert E. 8
Ed. Prince of Wales 9
Anne Bolleyne Marchionesse
Wil. Herbert Erl. 11